OCCULTIST FREEMASONRY
in the 18th century
and the
ORDER OF ÉLUS COËNS

OCCULTIST FREEMASONRY
in the 18th century
and the
ORDER OF ÉLUS COËNS

With 4 reconstituted schemas of the primitive
Table of the World and the
Invocational Tracings

by
RENÉ LE FORESTIER

Translated and Introduced by

Sâr Phosphoros
Sovereign Grand Commander
Christian Knights of Saint-Martin

TriadPress
Fox Lake, IL

Occultist Freemasonry in the 18th century and the Order of Élus Coëns
by René Le Forestier

Translated by Sâr Phosphoros

First English Edition
Published 2023

ISBN: 978-0-9973101-5-3

Triad Press, LLC
123 S. US Highway 12 #33
Fox Lake, IL 60020

Translator's Introduction

The name of Élus Coëns, or Élus Cohen as it is more commonly known since the 1940s revival by Robert Ambelain, Georges Lagrèze, and others, evokes an air of mystery nearly unparalleled in the worlds of occultism and Freemasonry. This is all the more true in the English-speaking countries, where the average seeker after the arcane mysteries does not even have access to what little material exists. In order to learn anything more than the barest outline of the doctrines and works of this theurgical fraternity, one often must be a high-grade initiate of one of the Martinist Orders; and even then, the accounts typically consist of as much legend as history, with a good portion of it being transmitted by word of mouth. Now, there will be, without doubt, some who will not be happy about the translation of this work into English, fearing that it will give away secrets of the Order, or that it will shatter the illusion of some precious legends; and in some respects, they will be right. It is impossible to read this well-researched and meticulously documented work without having some of your preconceived notions challenged. But it must be remembered that this seminal work has been available to the French-speaking world for nearly a century. It is only right that English-speaking students and researchers should be afforded the same opportunities as our Francophone counterparts. And the Lodge Masters, Grand Masters, Free Initiators, and all other conservators of this venerable tradition may rest assured that the most secret and well-guarded rites and practices are not divulged herein in any detail.

This leads us to the question, then, of who, precisely, a work such as this is intended to reach, and to what end. A glance at the title of this tome gives us a pretty clear idea. There are three overlapping and progressively narrowed categories addressed in the words of the title: Occultism, Freemasonry, and the Order of Élus Coëns; there is also the era of the 18th century which could perhaps be seen as a fourth category, but one that is much too broad to address in this introduction, except as it relates specifically to the other three groups.

Occultism: Occult researchers and practitioners of the modern era, and especially in the English-speaking lands, may have little or no knowledge of this seemingly obscure group. It is well understood that the French occultists of the 19th century - Eliphas Levi, Papus, et al. - have greatly influenced the shape of the Western Mysteries as we have them today. But it is the occultism of the Élus Coëns that paved the way for the occult boom of later years. The Élus Coëns represented in many ways a refinement of the occult doctrine. They were not at all interested in the fortune-tellers or the puffers (so-called alchemists who wasted their hours puffing away at the bellows in a vain attempt at generating wealth). They were, in fact, quite purely mystical at their core, their works and operations seeking only to manifest the reality of that deep spiritual conviction. In this way, their work, although employing the means of high ceremonial magic, was better represented in later years by the thaumaturges such as Abbé Julio than by other high ceremonial groups such as the Hermetic Order of the Golden Dawn. Even modern iterations of the Élus Coëns have added or removed practices, and otherwise altered the doctrine that makes it, for better or worse, fundamentally different from the vision of Martinès de Pasqually. The Élus Coëns was also one of the very first orders to not only admit, but to place a central attention on the inherent esotericism of Freemasonry, which leads us to our next brief consideration.

Freemasonry: The general history of Freemasonry, its establishment in England and Scotland, its real and legendary connections to the medieval guild system, its fantastic legends connecting it to the old Knights Templar, the Rosicrucians, and a host of other groups and personages of remote antiquity, are well known and explored at length in many volumes on this subject. Most of these researches, though, concern themselves principally with the Blue Lodge, that is to say the first three degrees of Freemasonry: Entered Apprentice, Fellowcraft, and Master Mason, or as they are known in French Masonry: Apprentice, Companion, and Master. But much less has been written concerning what are considered by many to be the most mysterious and intriguing of the family of Masonic degrees, the so-called Scottish degrees, or High-Grade Freemasonry. Now, when we mention Scottish degrees, one is immediately led to think of the Ancient and Accepted Scottish Rite, brought into being on May 31, 1801, in Charleston, South Carolina, USA. But every amateur Masonic historian knows, of course, that this Rite did not simply manifest suddenly out of thin air, nor is it even an American invention, contrary to the uninformed claims of many American Masons and to the chagrin of those loathe to admit that they are practicing a French rite; but that is precisely what it is. In any case, long before the Scottish Rite of 33° were the various Scottish Rites, Régimes, and Systems of France from which the AASR would eventually emerge. Regardless of whatever history the Scottish rites may have had at one time in Scotland, the vast majority of degrees called "Scottish" are of French invention. And it is within this milieu of Scottish degrees and lodges that we find the system of the Élus Coëns competing, on the one hand, for a prominent positioning within the French Masonic world, and on the other, operating something entirely spiritual with its theurgical rites, for which the Masonic degrees are merely a convenient framework. But this marriage of Freemasonry and high magic would pave the way for the Egyptian Rite of Cagliostro, the Rites of Misraim and Memphis, and the occult bodies that would follow after them.

Élus Coëns: The third aspect of the title of this work concerns the subject matter proper. Not much needs to be said here, for the exposition of the Rite is the very purpose of this volume. A few introductory comments, however, may be made. Let us look first at the name of this Order. The French word Élus is the plural of Élu, meaning Elect or Elected. The words Élu and Élus have been left untranslated here when they refer to the name of the Order or when referring to the names of certain degrees; otherwise, the word has been rendered as "elect." The second term, Coëns, is in the modern reimagining of the Order rendered as Cohen or occasionally even Kohen. This word comes from a Hebrew word referring to the ancient Jewish priesthood. So, the meaning of the name of this order amounts to something like Elect Priests. As to the spelling of Coëns, we have left it as it originally appeared at the time of its founder, Martinès de Pasqually. The use of this spelling also helps to distinguish it from the later reconstructions.

The Order of Élus Coëns is probably best known today as the school from which emerged one of its most prominent members, Louis-Claude de Saint-Martin. The writings of Saint-Martin bear the unmistakable mark of the Élus Coëns. Some of the most recognizable terms and concepts employed by Saint-Martin, such as "Reintegration" and "Man of Desire" are directly attributable to the teachings of the Élus Coëns, as well as the basis of his mystical numerology. When the teachings of Saint-Martin were codified into a proper school of instruction and initiation by Papus, Augustin Chaboseau and others towards the end of the 19th century, under the name of Ordre Martiniste, even more elements of the old Élus Coëns were introduced, or re-introduced. The Ordre Martiniste re-adopted a pseudo-Masonic degree structure and incorporated certain ritual and symbolic elements originally used by the Élus Coëns. This work will therefore be most enriching for the modern Martinist who wishes to learn more about the history, ritual, and doctrine that helped shape this cherished tradition.

There are a number of comments that need to be made concerning certain words used in this work and their particular meaning in this context, as well as some other general notes. Some of these notes could perhaps be relegated to footnotes or endnotes within the text, but with over 1,500 notes by the author, it seemed unwise to clutter them any further with notes from the translator. Having already addressed the name of Élus Coëns, let us look at the spelling of the name of its founder. One would not think there to be much uncertainty about the spelling of a person's name, but everything surrounding the Order of Élus Coëns seems to be cloaked in mystery, even down to the founder's name. Different authors have given his name variously as Pasqually, Pasquallys, Pasqualis, Pasquallis, Pascualis, etc. Even his first name has been rendered alternately as Martinez, Martinès, Dom Martinès, Martinets, etc. The spelling used by the author of this book, as well as by Papus in his work, and which has been retained in the translation is Martinès de Pasqually, which seems by most accounts to be the most historically accurate.

Pasqually's great literary contribution was a work written for his initiates, whom he called "Emulators," concerning the underlying doctrine of the Order. This work, whose abbreviated title is *Treatise on the Reintegration of Beings*, is referred to throughout this work simply as the Reintegration. Therefore, whenever this word, Reintegration, appears capitalized, it is referring to this treatise. The content of the treatise amounts more or less to an esoteric exegesis of certain biblical texts. It was never intended to be published to the world at large and was only distributed to certain high adepts of the Order. This unfinished manuscript was eventually published in France some 125 years after Pasqually's death. This enigmatic treatise has been a source of mystification not only because of the sometimes bizarre doctrines and interpretations it contains, but also because of Pasqually's peculiar terminology and a grammatical deficiency that would suggest that French is not his first language. The Reintegration is cited copiously in the present volume, and its grammatical irregularities have made it especially difficult to translate at times. Often times his meaning is relatively clear in spite of the poor grammar. In many of these instances the grammar has been automatically corrected through the process of translation. This may be good in the sense that his meaning - often obscure in its own right - comes through clearer in the English than it did in the French; but on the contrary, the reader is not able to appreciate some of the many linguistic peculiarities of the original. In short, some of Pasqually's bad grammar has been "cleaned up" through the process of translation. Therefore, some of Le Forestier's comments attempting to make the passage more intelligible may seem redundant or unnecessary. But for the most part the author's clarifications are most welcome, for even setting the grammatical aspects aside, the specific terminology used by Pasqually constitutes an esoteric jargon particular to his doctrine and Rite.

When commenting on passages by Pasqually and other authors, Le Forestier utilizes parentheses ( ) to set off his in-text commentary. Therefore, we have decided to use brackets [ ] to insert our own occasional translation note.

There are a number of terms used by the present author, by Pasqually, and by French Freemasonry in general that should be addressed briefly. First, the term "type" is used in this work in the sense of an archetype or pertaining to a typology, though in a different way than how it is used, say, in Patristic Theology. Pasqually's types are unique to his system. Because of this very specific use of the word "type," every attempt has been made to not use the word to mean: kind, sort, genre, etc. Here are some other terms to keep in mind while reading this work:

Bible: When Le Forestier refers to the Bible, he is referring specifically to the Jewish Bible, or as Christian would refer to it, the Old Testament. The New Testament is referred to as the Gospels or New Testament.

Chevaliers Bienfaisants de la Cité Sainte: The history of the founding of the Knights Beneficent of the Holy City is addressed in this work. When the name Chevaliers Bienfaisants is mentioned in the work, it is for the most part left untranslated.

Cult: When we see this term, images may come to mind of some fringe fanatical brainwashing group. But these unfavorable connotations do not exist in the French usage of the term, which reflects a meaning much closer to the Latin term from which it is derived: cultus. The Latin word *cultus* means, depending on its context, cultivation, culture, civilization, refinement, or worship. In the French it is used to mean a rite, sect, or form of worship. In the Élus Coëns it refers to certain rites and operations. Since we consider it to be a technical term of the Order, we have retained it as "cult."

Écossais / Écossaise: This word simply means "Scottish"; and Écossisme refers to the widespread phenomenon in 18th century France to establish and affiliate with one of the "Scottish" Rites.

La Chose: This means in French, literally, "the Thing." This term was used by Pasqually and his followers to refer to the Order, the Operations of the Order, and to certain entities manifested within the context of those Operations. Although the term seems to be used somewhat indiscriminately to refer to these multiple things, it should nevertheless be seen as a technical term of the Order, and for this reason has been left untranslated in the text.

Louveteau: This term (literally: young wolf) was used in the French Lodges to refer to the son of a Mason who was able to be initiated into the Lodge before the age of 21, which is the standard minimum age of acceptance within Freemasonry. In the American Lodges this is known as a "lewis."

T.P.M.: In some of the old letters and documents of the Order these initials are utilized to indicate one's Masonic title. Le Forestier has rendered the meaning to be Très Puissant Maître, which we translate here as Very Powerful Master. We would note, however, that Thory, in some of his writings on the Élus Coëns, has taken this to mean Tout Puissant Maître, or All-Powerful Master. This minor inconsistency does not affect the present work in any way, but it may be of interest to the students of the older works.

Venerable: The Venerable, or Venerable Master, is the Master of a Lodge, equivalent to the Worshipful Master of American Blue Lodges. The other two principal officers in the French Lodges are the First and Second Surveillants, equivalent to the Sr. and Jr. Wardens.

Any other technical terminology should be understood well enough within the context of the work. One last usage to note, though, is that the word "Spirit" when capitalized in French works designates some astral, spiritual, or disincarnate entity. When it appears in lower-case it is typically referring to a spiritual or spiritous substance, or one's "spirit" as in their personal energy or state of mind, or any of the other common uses of the word. This convention has been retained in this translation.

The author is not always kind to Pasqually, and much less so to some of those who would come after him such as Cagliostro and St. Germain, but this work is by no means a diatribe against Pasqually or the Élus Coëns. Over-all it is an extremely thorough and well-written account of the doctrine, practices, and history of the Order. The author remains ever erudite without slipping into pedantry. It is not a perfect work. For example, when comparing Pasqually's doctrine with Gnosticism he seems to confuse certain Gnostic schools together indiscriminately and to apply a radical dualism across the board that is probably better suited to Manichaeism and certain select other schools; but we may perhaps forgive him in part, seeing as how the discovery of the Nag Hammadi texts was still decades away, and the level of available scholarly research was nowhere near to what it is today. He also seems to occasionally confuse certain theological terms, such as referring to the Transfiguration as Jesus' post-resurrection state, as opposed to the display on Mt. Tabor, which is the actual reference; or referring to Jesus' "Ascension three days after the crucifixion," which of course would mark the Resurrection, not the Ascension. He also seems to be unaware or to ignore the valuing of the Hebrew letters, for in note 1133 he refers to the letter Shin as having the value of 21, and Samekh having that of 14, which, of course, is merely their order of placement within the Hebrew alphabet, not their ascribed values, which would be 300 and 60 respectively. But aside from a few minor errors, which could in all likelihood be chalked up to simple oversight, this work constitutes without question the most thorough and well researched study of the topic.

Sâr Phosphoros
Sovereign Grand Commander
Christian Knights of Saint-Martin

TABLE OF CONTENTS

Outline of a religious history. – Identity of the Operations and of the true divine cult. – Revelation and tradition of the true cult through Abel, Seth, Enoch, the second posterity of Noah, Jacob, Moses, Solomon. – Ceremonial of the Elus Coens observed by the Patriarchs and the Prophets. – Mystical meaning of the prostrations and burnt offerings. – Traces in the Bible of sympathetic cooperations and "traction." – "Mysterious year" and "Spiritual days." – Calculation of time taught to the different peoples by the "spiritual professors." – Incertitude of the secret calculations of the Elus Coens. – Astrological doctrines: hierarchy of the planetary circles; central axis and solar body; comets; favorable or inauspicious influence of the planets according to the conjunctions; good and evil planetary Spirits; importance of the equinoxes and the phases of the moon.

BOOK II
THE ELUS COENS AND THE OCCULTIST TRADTION

"Great Kabbalist" Pasqually. – Commentaries on the Bible justified by a secret tradition and by illumination. – Tanaim and Amoraim. – The two Talmuds, Halacha and Haggadah. – Chaldean and Persian influences. – The Jewish Gnosis and its mediators. – Work of the Chariot and Work of Creation. – Gematria, Notarikon, Temurah, Zeruph. – Philo and the symbolic interpretation. – The Sepher Yetzirah. – The Kabbalah and its principal themes. – The Zohar.

Significance of the title of Coens. – Fundamental distinction between the Hebrews and the Jews. – Pasqually and Hebrew. – Motifs borrowed from the Bible: the "el"; régime of the adepts; prophetic inspirations; "the man of desire"; the "glorious form"; the "traction"; the sacred computation; biblical formulas; ritual of the Operations; costume of the Operant; the burnt offerings; the new moons; prohibition of the lame; significance of the number 40; blood energy of organic life; "baptism of the blood"; millenialism. – Talmudic themes: oral and secret tradition; mystical interpretation of the proper and geographical names; allegorical exegesis of the biblical narratives; Haggadic elements of the Reintegration; eminent role of Seth, Enoch, and Elijah; good and evil principle; supremacy of man over the angels; candles of representation.

Kabbalistic themes: Denary and Sephiroth; Dominion and Malkuth; Adam Kadmon; Anima Mundi; ternary composition of the beings; Major Spirit and Metatron; the Reconciler of the Kabbalists; quaternary powers becoming octonary; spiritual posterity of Adam; role of the moon and Balance; mysticism of the numbers 3, 4, and 6. – Chaldean astrology &

demonology. – Ionian physics: Heraclitus; creative and destructive central
fire; Sibylline Books. – Mazdan cosmology, anthropology, and
eschatology. – Concordances with Manicheaism, Sabeanism, and
Mithraism. – Secondary importance of these agreements. – Pythagorean
arithmatic. – The Neopythagoreans of the 1st to the 3rd centuries. – The
arithmosophy of the Middle Ages. – The Humanists: Nicolas de Cusa,
Reuchlin, Georgio de Venise, C. Agrippa, G. Bruno, Van Helmont. –
Arithmosophy become secret science in the 17th century. – Its influence
over the Masonic symbols. – Relative originality of the arithmosophy of
the Reintegration: theosophical concept of the One, of the Ten, and of
the Four. – The Platonic Dyad. – The Kabbalistic Senary and Septenary.
– The Jewish Quinary. – The Egyptian Octonary. – Original concept of
the Ternary and Nonary. – Arithmetic combinations of the Pythagoreans
and their disciples. – Indigence of the mystical geometry of Pasqually
compared to that of the Pythagoreans and Neopythagoreans. – The circle
and the triangle.

Arguments in favor of the free will of the Spirits and the Minor. – Traces of docetism, montanism, and Manichaeism. – God-Man of the religion and of magic. – Reason for the attraction exercised by the Order on mystical Christians: "vision of Christ"; identity of the Spiritual Minor and Minor and of the Reconciler; mystico-rationalist conception of the miracle. – Need of proofs shown by the mystics of the 18th century. – What the thaumaturges take part in. – Lavater and Pasqually. – The Elus Coens and the spirit of the times.

BOOK III
ORGANIZATION AND HISTORY OF THE ORDER

Table of Contents

ILLUSTRATIONS

FOREWORD

"There are," said Maeterlinck in his *Trésors des Humble*, "perfect ages where intelligence and beauty reign most purely, but where the soul does not show itself. That is very far from the 18th century, at least on the surface, for its profundities with Claude de Saint-Martin, Cagliostro, who is more serious than one may think, Pasqualis and so many others, still hide many mysteries from us." Without any prejudice to the "gravity" of the Grand Copht, which remains strongly subject to caution, even after the recent defense of Dr. Marc Haven, one may not but approve the citation which places unrivalled the philosophy of Amboise and the Master of the Élus Coëns; his sole error would be perhaps to give precedence to the first over the second. Saint-Martin and Pasqually are indeed the most typical representatives of the mystical tendencies of their time, the most ardent chiefs of the resistance opposed by spiritualism to the progress of rationalist materialism, but to consider the influence exercised by each of these two men, it would seem to do wrong to Pasqually to place him in the second rank. The works of the Unknown Philosopher, it is true, are read in all of Europe, but obscure in form as well as in essence, they were intelligible only to rare, privileged individuals, and the author of the treatise *Des Erreurs et de la Vérité* was always less the head of a school than a mystical man-about-town and an ecstatic solitary. Pasqually, who was the first and for a rather long time the only guide of Saint-Martin upon the paths of occultism, has been on the contrary a leader of men who knew how to give a body to his doctrines, to find the means to apply them practically, and to enroll faithful disciples into a very organized secret society. The historical importance of Pasqually is therefore quite superior to that of Saint-Martin, and to give the history of the Order of Élus Coëns is, to take the terms used by Maeterlinck, to elucidate one of the mysteries that hide the profundities of the 18th century.

This study is all the more justified seeing as the society founded around 1760 by Pasqually is, as much by its doctrines as by its objectives, the most interesting of the occultist groups which, in this era, have taken shelter under the Masonic acacia.

Disdaining the material and immediate advantages that numerous adepts would seek through the study of the secret sciences, "by stopping," as says Mr. Dermenghem in an apt formula, "at the ambiguous astral plane, instead of rising to the divine plane," the disciples of Pasqually have not asked of alchemy treasures or the panacea, of astrology the prescience of the future, of Kabbalah the phylacteries against the dangers or diseases that threaten human life. They have practiced theurgy, not in order to put the Spirits at their service and, by their intermediary, command nature or acquire transcendent knowledge, but because they were tormented by the need to know they belonged to the class of privileged mortals to whom the divinity grants the favor of supernatural manifestations, portent of their future beatitude. The rites that they have borrowed from ceremonial magic have less of the means of compulsion than the more efficacious modes of adoration and supplication. The Élus Coëns were, as indicated by the second term of their double name, the "priests" of an esoteric religion whose mystical aspirations would lift them by a great beat of the wing far from the material world. The perfect impartiality of these "men of desire" with regard to terrestrial goods, their profound contempt for the positive and practical results that so many occultists would await from their dealings with the beyond, the fervor and tenacity of their efforts to obtain a response to the question which troubled their disquieted soul fills with respect, any opinion that one may have moreover upon the very basis of their credo and upon the cult which was its expression.

On the other hand, Martinès de Pasqually has built an extremely curious mystical and metaphysical system. Composed of materials borrowed from the secret tradition, it presents an echo, weakened by still very clear, of the diverse esoteric doctrines which have taken form in the Orient in the first centuries of our era, after having received the heritage of the most distant past, and which have then penetrated into the Occident by the intermediary of the Jewish Kabbalah.

Thus, the Order of Élus Coëns constitutes, under the cover of Freemasonry, one of the last links of the long chain of mysterious and jealously closed associations whose members would claim, by magical processes, to communicate with the divine in order to participate in the privilege of a blessed immortality. The disciples of Martinès are, in the 18th century, the successors of the mysteries of Asia, Egypt, Greece, and Italy, of the Valentinians, the Orphics, and the faithful of Mithra; they profess, in the era of "Light," the mystical doctrines of the Neoplatonists, the Gnostics, and the Kabbalists, and cultivate, in the time of the Encyclopedia, the "secret wisdom of the Ancients."

∴

The plan adopted for this study was prescribed by the double aspect under which is presented the association with which it deals. The Order of Élus Coëns is, by its form, a Masonic rite practicing the three symbolic degrees and designating its superior degrees by denominations familiar to all the Brothers; but it is, at its foundation, an occultist group which pursues, by means which are its own, a mystical aim kept carefully hidden, and the latter takes precedence over the former. The Élu Coën is much less interesting as Mason than he is as theurgist. It was therefore necessary first of all, and it is to what the first two books are attached, to bring to light the esoteric doctrines of the association, to make known the nature and the aim of the-magical processes by which it tries to enter into relations with the supernatural world and to seek in the older mystical systems the origin of its theories and practices. The original traits and characteristics once traced, nothing remained but to summarize in the third book the history of the society, that is to say to expose its organization and to show what role it has played in the Masonic world and in the mystical milieu.

∴

The contributing sources are of two types: 1. General works and monographs; 2. Documents recently published or incompletely utilized by previous studies. In the first category figures, following chronological order:
(Guillemin de Saint-Victor): Recueil précieux de la Maçonnerie adonhiramite, 1785.
Pernéty: Dictionnaire mytho-hermétiques, 1787.
Barruel: Mémoires pour servir à l'histoire du Jacobinism, 1796.
J.-J. Meunier: De l'influence attribuée aux Philosophes, aux Francs-maçons et aux
      Illuminés sur la Révolution de France, 1801.
Thory: Annales originis Magni Galliarum Orientis, 1812.
A. Lenoir: La Franche Maçonnerie rendue à sa véritable origine, 1814.
Thory: Acta Latamorum, 1815.

J. de Maistre: Soirées de Saint-Pétersbourg, 1821.
Molitor: Philosophie der Geschichte, 1824.
Franck: Kabbale, 1843.
Gérard de Nerval: Notice sur Cazotte (placed at the head of a reprint of le Diable
    Amoureux), 1845.
Kloss: Geschichte der Freimaurerei in Frankreich, 1852.
Caro: Essai sur les doctrines et sur la vie de Saint-Martin, 1852.
Ragon: Orthodoxie maçonnique, suivie de la Maçonnerie Occulte, 1853.
Matter: Saint-Martin, le Philosophe Inconnu, sa vie, ses écrits, son maître Martinez et
    leur groupe, 1862.
Saint-Martin: Correspondance inédit avec Kirchberger, 1862.
Allgemeins Handbuch der Freimaurerei, 1863-1867.
Frank: Saint-Martin et son maître Martinez de Pasqualis, 1866.
F. Fabre: Documents maçonniques, 1866.
de Gleichen: Souvenirs, 1868.
Chaignet: Pythagore et la philosophie pythagoricienne, 1874.
Daruty: Recherches sur le Rite Écossais, 1879.
Nettelbladt: Geschichte freimaurerischer System in England, Frankreich und
    Deutschland, 1879.
A. Prost: Corneille Agrippa, 1881-1882.
Gould: History of Freemasonry, 1884.
Cornelius Agrippa: De la Philosophie Occulte (translation by Jules Bois: Haute
    Science, 1893-1894).
Allgemeins Handbuch der Freimaurerei, 1900-1901.[1]
Bischoff: Thalmud-Katechismus, 1904.
Bischoff: Im Reiche der Gnosis, 1906.
Begeman: Vorgeschichte und Anfaenge der Freimaurerei in England, 1909.
Wolfstieg: Bibliographie der Freimaurerischen Literatur, 1911.
de Faye: Gnostiques et Gnosticisme, 1913.
Bischoff: Kabbalah, 1917.
Alfaric: Ecritures manichéennes, 1918.
Saintyves: Essais de Folklore biblique, 1923.
Vulliaud: La Kabbale juive, 1923.
Frazer: Le Rameau d'Or, 1924.
Frazer: Le Folklore dans l'Ancen Testament, 1924.
Zielinski: La Sibylle, 1924.
A. Lantoine: La Franc-Maçonnerie chez elle, 1925.
Wittemans: Histoire des Rose-Croix, 1925.
Kreglinger: Religion d'Israel, 1926.

    The second category comprises texts taken either from dogmatic treatises or
the confidential correspondence of adepts, and which have been very widely used.
They are found in the following publications:
Martinès de Pasqually: Traité de la Réintegration des êtres.
        This capital work, work of the founder and chief of the Society, was
        published for the first time in 1899; a manuscript copy, found among the
        papers of Saint-Martin, had been communicated by its possessor, the
        historian Mr. Matter, to Franck who has reproduced the first 26 pages in his
        Saint-Martin. The two texts present only insignificant differences.

Papus: Martinès de Pasqually, 1895,
Papus: Louis-Claude de Saint-Martin, 1902.

The documents reproduced by these two works come from the Lodge of the Élus Coëns in Lyon. These fragments of archives consist, according to their editor, of 28 letters from Pasqually to Willermoz (1767-1774), 48 letters from Saint-Martin to Willermoz (1771-1790), 10 letters from other members of the Order (1778-1787), catechisms, communications, and reports. In his first book Papus extracted from the correspondence of Pasqually with Willermoz various information and dates; he analyzed moreover 20 letters from the same to the same, a letter from the second to the first, and printed the catechisms of several degrees. In the second book he has published in full 45 letters from Saint-Martin to Willermoz. The works of Papus are only of interest for the original texts that they make known, for the commentaries with which the editor accompanies them are extremely tendentious. Dr. Encausse, who, under the name of Papus, tried to revive the ancient society by calling it: Ordre Martiniste, does not seem to have understood very well what those whom he claimed to be the successor were or sought; he has judged it no longer necessary to study, even superficially, the history of Freemasonry or that of occultism, upon which he utters with imperturbable assurance the most monumental blunders.

G. Bord: La Franc-Maçonnerie en France des origines à 1815, 1908.

The author has drawn from a depot, of which place he does not indicate, some documents of the first order: letters from adepts and biographical notes on certain ones among them.

Nouvelle Notice Historique sur le Martinésisme et le Martinisme.

(Introduction to a reprint of *Enseignements Secrets de Martinez de Pasqually*, by Franz von Baader), 1900. This pseudonymous note which was attached above all to refute the fantasies of Papus, makes numerous citations from letters of adepts preserved in private archives.

J.B. Willermoz: Les Sommeils, 1926.

Contains an important correspondence between Willermoz and the baron de Turkheim.

.·.

The most often cited works appear in this list below, where they are preceded by Roman numerals representing them in the references given in the endnotes:
I. Traité de la Réintégration.
II. Papus: M. de Pasqually.
III. Papus: Saint-Martin.
IV. Nouvelle Notice Historique.
V. Bord: Franc-Maçonnerie.
VI. Willermoz: Sommeils.
VII. Gleichen: Souvenirs.
VIII. Matter: Saint-Martin.
IX: Franck: Saint-Martin.
X. Thory: Acta Latomorum.
XI. Thory: Annales originis.

BOOK I
Doctrines and Practices of the Élus Coëns

FIRST CHAPTER
The "Reintegration": Cosmology and Anthropology

The "Traité de la réintégration des êtres dans leur premières propriétés, vertus et puissances spirituelles et divines" [Treatise on the reintegration of beings into their first estates, virtues and powers, spiritual and divine - trans.], dogmatic work and compendium of the secret doctrine taught by Pasqually, has the form of a course professed ex-cathedra. The author addresses himself to the reader in the tone of a master who talks with his disciples; he foresees their objections and refutes them in advance, anticipates the questions that they may pose to him, strives to dissipate their eventual doubts by certifying his good faith and the exactitude of his information. This treatise, written only for the members of the Order, was the Gospel of the Élus Coëns. Copies were delivered to all the subscribers of the society, by the same right as the degree papers and instructions.[2] Begun in February 1771, the work, to which Pasqually devoted himself entirely at the start of 1772[3], remains unfinished.[4] But, incomplete though it may be, the treatise presents in its 388 pages of print in-octavo, a development important enough to give a sufficient idea of the mystical system of the society.

Moreover, what consoles the reader who finds himself at the last page in the presence of a text brusquely interrupted, is that the doctrines that constitute the material of the treatise are only able to be extracted at the price of a rather painful labor. The work betrays at times the haste with which it has been drawn up, the inexperience of the author, and the lack of proper French writing. Pasqually ignores completely the rules and most elementary aspects of composition. Unable to follow, or even conceive, a clear and logical plan, he loses himself in digressions, or repeats himself and tries in vain to resume, time and again, the interrupted thread of his discourse.

The fatigue of the reader wandering without guidance in this labyrinth is increased again by the barbary of style and the obscurity of terms. The treatise has been thought out in a foreign language, as well as calling to attention turns of phrase and expressions such as: "for a time immemorial" and "bring might of law upon," and faults of language and syntax of which one will find in the citations too numerous examples, and which render certain passages nearly unintelligible. Cluttered, obscure, and incorrect over the course of the whole work, the style becomes frankly unbearable when the author tries to heighten the tone. Two invocations, chosen at random, may give an idea of what Pasqually is capable of writing when he aims at the sublime. Moses, while offering a sacrifice to the Lord between the Madian desert and mount Horeb, addresses to him the following prayer: "O Eternal, creator of all powers! Receive the sacrifice that I make to you in all holiness and in the purity of the divine power that you have deigned to give me in your mercy and for your great glory! I submit myself to your infinite greatness! Dispose of me according to your will; receive the sacrifice that I make to you from my soul, from my heart, from my body, and from all that belongs to me, spiritually and temporally; receive it for the expiation of the sin of the father of men and that of all his posterity. Just as all comes from you, all returns to you."[5] Adam, making an act of contrition after his first fault, expresses himself in these terms: "Father of charity, of mercy; Father living and of eternal life; Father God of the Gods of heaven and earth; God strong and most strong; God of justice, of suffering, of reward; God of peace and clemency, of charitable compassion…God of peace and satisfaction…Magnificent God of every contemplation of created beings and unalterable rewards; God father of mercy without limit on behalf of his feeble creature; hear the one who laments before you of the abomination of his crime."[6]

∴

The treatise on the Reintegration presents itself as a sort of summary and secret version of the first books of the Pentateuch, particularly of Genesis and Exodus. It exposes in its manner the creation of Adam and Eve, treats on the original sin, relates the history of the posterity of the first couple and of the descendants of Cain and Seth, describes the deluge, then passes to Noah, to Abraham and his descendants, to the posterity of Isaac, narrates the exodus from Egypt, extends obligingly over the role played by Moses, says some words on the Judges and interrupts itself abruptly after the interview of Saul and the Prophetess.

The account manifestly loses every interest for Pasqually as soon as Moses leaves the scene. The legislator of the Hebrews is for our author the central personage. Under the pretext of exposing the teachings that Moses, interpreter of Jehovah, gave to the people of Israel, Pasqually attributes to the prophet, "who speaks with truth according to the Eternal,"[7] and then presents as revealed by God himself, the metaphysical theories that he makes known to his disciples. This tendency, so clearly shown in the second half of the treatise, comes through already in the first, for the alleged history of the Patriarchs, from Adam to Jacob, serves only to illustrate allegorically the mystical doctrines exposed by the Reintegration.

These doctrines constitute an esoteric cosmogony and anthropology, attempting to give the key of the past, present, and future destiny of man and are justified by a biblical exegesis that borrows its methods from symbolism, arithmosophy, and mystical geometry.

∴

The cosmology of the Reintegration is essentially a pneumatology. "Before time, God emanated spiritual beings."[8] "These emanated Spirits, originating in the quadruple divine essence, were distinguished among themselves by their virtues, their powers, and their names; they formed four classes, much more powerful than those of the Cherubim, Seraphim, Archangels and Angels that God created later on, for they had within themselves a portion of the divine power."[9] Alone, these "divine spiritual beings" emanated directly from God and who were innate in the divinity as "the seminal of the reproduction of forms" innate in the different organisms which compose the material universe, are "real and imperishable," that is to say have a personal existence, absolute and eternal; they will exist always "in the circle of divinity."[10]

Now, it happened that certain of "these divine spiritual chiefs prevaricated" in abusing the liberty that God had granted them. God had indeed allowed the free emanated beings to act "in accordance with their thoughts and their particular will, for it is not within him to read into the second causes nor to impede therein the action, without deviating from his own existence of Necessary Being and his divine power."[11] "God may only read into the thought when it is conceived and may not destroy the will of the spiritual beings."[12]

The revolted Spirits wanted to play a role superior to that which had been attributed to them. "Secondary agents," they could only act as instruments of the divinity. Driven by pride, they wanted to emanate in their turn spiritual beings which would depend only upon them. They thus encroached upon the divine omnipotence by attempting to give birth by their own power "to third and fourth causes."[13]

The error of the first Spirits, the "simple criminal will," which is the "principle of spiritual evil," had three important consequences.

First, God created the material world "in order to be the fixed place where these perverse Spirits would have to act, to exercise in privation (that is to say deprived of all communication with God) their malice" and in order to be "the boundary of their evil operations."[14] In this prison the fallen Spirits, no longer being part of divinity, who had broken all relations with them, were "emancipated," that is to say free, no longer only to will, but also to act in all independence in the domain which was assigned to them.[15]

In the second place, the divinity, in order to give to this prison a sort of guardian, proceeded a second emanation, that of the "Spiritual Minor," that they commonly call Adam or "First Temporal Father," but that the initiates name "Réau" or "Roux" [red, reddish - trans.], terms signifying "Man-God, very strong in wisdom, virtue, and power." This spiritual being, provided with three gifts "which in him are the thought, image, and resemblance of the Creator,"[16] was destined to be ceaselessly opposed "by the evil demon in order to contain and combat it." In order to be at the height of his task, he received the same power with which had been endowed all the first Spirits at the moment of their emanation and, "although emanated after them, he became their superior and their senior by his state of glory and the strength of the commandment that he received from the Creator."[17] All the Spirits were subject to him: the perverse Spirits, because they had lost their first power in punishment of their prevarication, the good Spirits, because the Minor had received, at the time of his emanation, the primitive power distributed to the first emanated Spirits."[18] "As the prevarication of the Spirits happened before the Minors were emanated, they were not able to receive therein any stain nor any communication (contagion); it also happened that there was no change in their class, and for this reason they were the trustees of the great power of the divinity. The redoubtable quaternary power (authority over the Spirits) was confided to them, these Minors being "pure and spotless Spirits, emanated from the bosom of justice and holiness itself in order to manifest the strength and glory of the Creator."[19] The first Adam, eponymous type and representative in biblical history of the class of Spiritual Minors, came therefore in the celestial hierarchy immediately after the Creator. He had not in his being any grain of matter. He was, it is true, clothed in a form, but of a "glorious form,"[20] "in order to operate all his will upon the active and passive forms."[21] This "God-emanated," to which the angels were submissive[22], was the true "Emulator" (disciple) of the Creator. His power was extended over the whole universe, or "universal creation," and over all its parts, that is to say upon the earth, or "general creation," "general part from which emanates all the elements necessary to give substance to the particular," and over the "particular creation," or assembly of existing beings "whether in the celestial body or in the terrestrial body," the "particular" including "every active and passive being inhabiting from the terrestrial surface and its center to the celestial center called mysteriously (that is to say by the initiates) heaven of Saturn."[23] In a word, to the First Adam was submitted the universe, the earth, and all the inhabitants of the celestial circles.[24]

Finally, as a result of the rebellion of the first spiritual beings, "all the Spirits, even those remaining faithful, are subjected to the Minors and the inhabitants of the divine world feel the effects of the first prevarication and will continue to feel them until the end of time. They expiate the crime of the first Spirits, as the present Minors expiate the crime of the first man."[25] "Scarcely had the perverse Spirits been banished from the presence of the Creator, that the inferior Spirits and ternary minors received the power to operate the laws innate within them to produce spiritual essences for the formation of the temporal world in order to contain the prevaricators within the dark boundaries of the divine privation. In receiving this power, they were at once emancipated; their action, which was pure, spiritual, divine, was changed as soon as the Spirit had prevaricated; they were no longer temporal spiritual beings destined to operate the different laws that the Creator prescribed to them for the entire accomplishment of his will. It is then that the quaternary spiritual Minors were emanated from the midst of the divinity and occupied in the divine immensity the place from which the ternary minor Spirits would come to be emancipated in order to operate temporally."[26] "Without the prevarication of the first Spirits, the divine Spirits would not have been subjected to the temporal. Without this prevarication no change would have occurred to the spiritual creation; there would not have been any creation of the divine boundary, be it supercelestial, celestial, or terrestrial, nor Spirits sent in order to operate in the different parts of creation, since the ternary minor Spirits would have never left the place that they occupied in the divine immensity in order to operate the formation of a material universe."[27]

The universe being henceforth composed of four worlds: the divine, the supercelestial, the celestial, and the terrestrial,[28] God formed four classes of Spirits: superior, major, inferior, and minor.[29] The superior and major Spirits, acting in a milieu where all is spirit and nothing is matter, have never possessed the ability to produce "spiritous essences."[30] The inferior and minor Spirits had the faculty to produce the "temporal spiritual essences,"[31] but they had used it only at the moment when they were emanated, in order to form "the temporal world which must serve to molest the prevaricating Spirits."[32]

The role assigned to the Spirits of the supercelestial was "to assure the correspondence of man with the Creator and to serve as double boundary to the creatures who govern the celestial and material worlds in which the prevaricating Spirits are enclosed."[33] Auxiliaries to Adam, they kept watch over the inviolability of the frontiers separating the prisons of the evil Spirits from the supercelestial. Agents of the laws of the universe, they were appointed particularly to the conservation of time, that is to say to the maintenance of the vital energy in the material universe.[34] The inferior Spirits, inhabitants of the celestial world, were specially charged to assure the existence of matter.[35] The Man-God, who resided in the same domain, acted there as "pure divine Spirit."[36]

It is indeed that the order established by the Creator did not have the sole aim of assuring the solidity of the prison enclosing the rebel Spirits. It had above all for its goal to place the Man-God in a state to fulfill in the best possible conditions the task which had devolved upon him. Placed in the celestial world, which is very similar to the supercelestial and divine worlds, and is likewise the abode of the divinity[37], Adam was assured the direct aid of the latter with which he was, on the other hand, in contact through the intermediary of the Spirits of the supercelestial, agents of Providence. One may therefore say that "it was uniquely for man that all these things were thus disposed" and that, "as they had to serve as boundary to the perverse Spirits, they were subjected to the Minor so that he is able to exercise upon them his power and his commandment according to his will and according to the laws of order."[38]

∴

Such was the sublime state of the Man-God, or Adam, or Roux, or Réau; but, to his misfortune, he enjoyed, as the first emanated Spirits, his free will and, like them, he abused this dangerous privilege. His pride caused him to consider the power that God had granted him over the universal creation as nearly as great as that belonging to the Creator. This sin of pride was immediately known by the "evil demons," that is to say by the fallen Spirits. One of the principals of these Spirits presents itself before Adam "under the apparent form of a body of glory" and persuaded him "to operate the demonic science in preference to the divine science that the Creator had given to him in order to subjugate every inferior being."[39] The tempter said to Adam: "Adam, you have innate within you the word of creation of every kind...operate (create) creatures since you are creator. Operate before those who are outside of you; they will give all justice (homage) to the glory which you are due."[40]

The assertion of the "evil demon" was in part founded, but it willfully allowed to pass under silence an important detail. Adam indeed had within him "an act (power) of creation of posterity of spiritual form, that is to say of glorious form," he possessed "a word of spiritual and glorious reproduction,"[41] but he would only be able to use it with the cooperation of the Creator. "The will of the First Man having been (if the will had been) that of the Creator, scarcely would the thought of man have carried it out that the divine spiritual thought would have likewise acted in immediately fulfilling the fruit of the operation of the Minor by a being as perfect as him. Adam would have been truly the creator of a posterity of God."[42] "From his impassive form (not subject to suffering) would emanate forms glorious as his own in order to serve as dwelling for the Spiritual Minors that the Creator would have sent there"[43]; from "the Man-God of the universal earth" would have issued a divine posterity and not a carnal posterity.[44]

Yielding to the perfidious suggestions of the tempter, Adam undertook to create "spiritual beings" without divine cooperation[45], in the presence of "those who were outside of him" and in order to earn their admiration. This fault was more serious than that to which the universe owes its origin. It is true that the crime of Adam "although arising from his will, did not come immediately from his thought," since the idea had been inspired by the perverse Spirits. But the prevarication of Adam has been more considerable than that of the first Spirits in that Adam has put in use all his virtue and divine power against the Creator, by "operating at the wish (under the desire) of the demons and by his own will an act of creation, which the perverse Spirits would not have had the time to do, the Creator having prevented their evil will from manifesting."[46]

The punishment did not keep him waiting and was doubly severe: first by the result of the criminal act, then by the change of state of the guilty. God "enclosed in the form of matter created by Adam a minor being that the unfortunate Adam has subjected in a frightful prison of darkness."[47] Instead of a glorious form similar to his own, Adam produced indeed only a "dark form" (material)[48] which he called, when he saw the result of his dark undertaking, "Houwa" or "Woman," that is to say, mystically, "flesh of my flesh, bone of my bone, work of my operation conceived and exercised by the work of my soiled hands."[49] "The Creator allowed to exist the impure work of the Minor so that he be molested from generation to generation for a time immemorial, having always before his eyes the image of his crime…so that his posterity could not claim ignorance (to be unaware of) his prevarication and so that it learn by this that the pains and miseries that it endures and will endure unto the end of the ages does not come from the Creator, but from our father, creator of impure and passive matter" (subject to suffering).[50]

Furthermore, Adam was banished from the celestial world and plunged "into the depths of the earth from where had arisen the fruit of his prevarication."[51] The Creator transformed at the same time the glorious form of Adam in a form "material, passive, and subject to corruption."[52] "This second body of terrestrial matter had the same apparent figure as the body of glory into which Adam had been emaneted"[53] this corporeal form, similar to that which Adam had involuntarily given to Houwa, is a coarse copy, a dull reproduction of the glorious form, pure and unalterable with which the Man-God had been primitively clothed.[54]

Prisoner of this material form, Adam had to inhabit this same earth "over which, before his crime, he reigned as Man-God and without being mixed up with it or its inhabitants."[55] He was there "compelled to operate (act) as a purely temporal spiritual being (composed of a soul and a body), subject to time and to the sorrow of time (death) to which he was not previously subjected.[56] The form of matter that he had created in his criminal pride, Houwa, served him to perpetuate the race of the fallen Minors, for, "condemned to reproduce materially, he is only able to make use of material spiritous essences for his reproduction"; he used a "Word which acted, emanated, and emancipated outside of him spiritous essences following the law of temporal spiritual nature" and thus there was only able to come from him "material corporeal forms."[57]

Finally, and this was the most terrible consequence of his fault, Adam found himself henceforth separated from God and exposed to the snares of the perverse Spirits. When he was in his "state of glory," he knew directly the thought of the Creator and that of the demons; he read the one and the other like an open book because "the privilege of the pure and simple spirit (not imprisoned in matter) is the ability to read the Spirit by one's natural spiritual correspondence."[58] As a result of this immediate communication with the divine thought, he was "thinking." But, if "nothing is able to escape the knowledge of the Spirit, it is quite the contrary among the Minors incorporated into a form of apparent matter,"[59] for "the body is only a chaos (prison) for the soul, that is to say for the minor Spirit which finds itself enclosed therein."[60] Just as "the form is become passive, from impassive which it would have been if Adam had united his will with that of the Creator," so "the soul is become subject to the suffering of privation"[61]; so that after his fall, Adam, 'thinker' that he was previously, at a time when "as pure Spirit he read with discovery the divine thoughts and operations," is become "pensive,"[62] that is to say that from now on he no longer had but a passing and fragmentary knowledge of the divine thought by way of effluvium that the initiates call "good intellect." Furthermore, he was, to his misfortune, much more accessible to the suggestions of the demon, because the demonic thought communicated directly and constantly to him by the "evil intellect," whereas the divine thought is only able to penetrate into the spirit after the path has been cleared by the good intellect "which prepares and arranges the particular minor soul to receive impressions from the major good Spirit," so that "the Minor is only by time (by moments) thinking in conjunction with the good Spirit."[63] In other words, the Minor, at first in constant communication with divine thought, when he remained under a luminous form in the celestial world, is found, after having been exiled in the terrestrial world and clothed with a body of matter, under the dominion of the perverse Spirits, with which he inhabits the prison, and he is only able to resist their seductions by the effect of the grace that God grants him from time to time in order to help him triumph "over the intellectual notions that he receives on the part of the evil Spirits."[64]

Nevertheless, the role that God had assigned to Adam, in emanating him, had imprinted upon him an indelible character. The power conferred to the Man-God was "so considerable that, despite his very prevarication, he was still superior to every other spiritual Spirit, be it emanated or emancipated."[65] Also, "the Minor did not lose, like the prevaricating Spirits, the direct communication with the Creator and his intelligences. He retained the faculty and the first power that he had received at the time of his emanation into the universal body."[66] Moreover, the severe punishment with which he was stricken led him to come to his senses. Adam repented for his crime and God had mercy on him. He did not leave Adam at the rank of "Minor of demonic Minors to which he had become the subject." He reconciled spiritually with him and reestablished him "in the same virtues and powers that he had beforehand against the infidels of divine law. It is through this reconciliation that he (Adam) has obtained for a second time powers for and against every living being."[67] But the terrestrial Adam, degraded and plunged into matter, was no longer able to lay claim to complete possession of the privileges of which the Man-God had enjoyed in his state of innocence; thus, "the Creator only gave him a power inferior to that which he possessed before his crime."[68]

The fall of Adam had, as that of the first Spirits, universal consequences. The emanated Spirits, which had already suffered following the revolt of their brothers, were doubly affected by the prevarication of Adam and by the pardon that he was granted. "The prevarication of Adam was infinitely greater than that of the demons; the Spirits inhabiting the immensity (divine) felt then an attraction even greater than the first time, and this accursed operation of man operated upon them a new change in their laws of action, that is to say that at the instant of Adam's crime the Creator brought the might of law upon the spiritual beings from his immensity, and their laws of action and operation were no longer the same as they were, not only before the prevarication of the first Spirits, but at the time of the emanation of the First Man."[69] "Just as the inhabitants of the divine world paid tribute to the justice of the Creator for the expiration of the crime of the first Spirits, so did the spiritual inhabitants of the general terrestrial world pay tribute to the Eternal for the prevarication of the first Minor committed at the center of the temporal universe."[70] The guardian appointed to the prison enclosing the perverse Spirits having had to quit his post for unworthiness, the good Spirits alone remain to assure the supervision exercised over the two inferior worlds to prevent the perverse Spirits from coming out of their place of exile[71]; they were, moreover, compelled to serve as intermediaries between God and the Minor. "Without the prevarication of man, the divine Spirits would never have only been subjected in one manner alone to the temporal (to contribute to the upkeep and fixed duration of the universe); through the prevarication of man, the inhabitants of the different classes of the immensity were compelled to contribute to the reconciliation and purification of the Minors."[72]

Adam, fallen but forgiven, shows himself unworthy of the divine mercy, for he commits a new sin. When Adam and Houwa "were to come out of their first operant place,"[73] they received the order to reproduce forms similar to themselves, but they obeyed "with so furious a passion of their material senses" that the divinity refused to cooperate with their work. Therefore, their first-born Cain, that is to say "son of my suffering" fell under the influence of the demonic powers, to the great despair of Adam.[74]

This new punishment led only to the passing repentance of the guilty, and he soon fell again into the same error. He abandoned himself again with Houwa to the delirium of the senses in order to procreate two daughters: Cainan and Aba I, then, after an interval of six years, four other children, two males and two females.[75] Nevertheless, the first-born of this second series was engendered and conceived conforming to the intentions of the Creator. "Adam and Houwa cooperated in the form of their son Abel by a very succinct operation of matter, that is to say without excess of their material senses." Therefore, "the Creator could not refuse to correspond with their operation by establishing with the form that they had effected a minor being endowed with every virtue and spiritual divine wisdom."[76] Adam called this child Aba IV, that is to say "child of peace," or Aba X, that is to say "being elevated above every spiritual sense,"[77] and he was "like the God-Man just upon the earth."[78] Cain, furious to have had to cede his birthright to Abel, and encouraged in his revolt by his two sisters, Cainan and Aba I, "conceived to operate a cult to the false gods and to the prince of the demons, so that they would give him a power superior to what the Creator had given to his brother Abel,"[79] and, carried away by his hatred, he killed Abel by feigning to embrace him.[80] The expiatory blood of the Just that the Lord had endowed with his own wisdom sealed the second reconciliation of Adam with God and, in announcing to Houwa the tragic end of his beloved son, Adam was able to assert to her "that his crimes had had been expiated by the victim Abel, his son."[81] But the murder of Abel deprived men of a light illuminating their dark path. God bestowed these gifts of the Just, which were reversible, upon another Minor. "Adam conceived then at the wish (with the agreement) of the Creator a third posterity which he named Seth, which means: admitted to the posterity of God"[82] and "the Creator himself instructed by means of his spiritual envoy Heli the blessed man Seth in the secret divine spiritual motives, which contained and directed all nature, whether spiritual or material."[83]

∴

Beginning from the third posterity of Adam the fate of humanity is fixed forever; the design and the personages of the drama that will play out until our day upon the earth are laid out for the "duration of time." The human race is comprised of two classes: descendants of Cain and posterity of Seth. The first are the damned, the prisoners of matter. Skillful in the crudely useful arts, they discovered the means to build towns, to smelt metals, to exploit the mines, to hunt wild animals[84], but the Lord let them err in spiritual darkness. When the deluge will have annihilated the first perverted humanity, the accursed race reappeared with the descendants of Ham. The second ones have learned from Seth to practice the cult agreeable to God[85], but these favorites of the Lord are as weak as was the First Man. The posterity of Seth unites, despite the divine prohibition, with the "children of men, that is to say the concubine daughters of the posterity of Cain" and it "fell from all the divine spiritual knowledge that Seth had communicated to it."[86] The history of the Jewish people will only be the detailed account of these relapses followed by a repentance and an ephemeral reconciliation. The Hebrews, although illuminated with different renewals by a divine envoy, soon forget the sublime truths which were revealed to them; they then lose all communication with God and entire generations fall again into darkness, until a new prophet appears whose teachings will not have any more lasting success.

The Bible, suitably interpreted, instructs us therefore on the destiny of the Minor who belongs to the posterity of Seth. Spirit fallen from heaven; his downfall never definitive. "Every corporeal form is always a chaos for the divine spiritual soul, because this form of matter is not able to receive the communication of the divine spiritual intellect, being itself only an apparent being; the Minor, on the contrary, by his emancipation is susceptible to receiving this communication at each instant, because it is an eternal being."[87] He may be "reintegrated," as in this world, into the state where God had returned Adam after his second reconciliation with him and enjoy the privileges that had then been accorded to the father of the sacrificed Abel. This sacrifice ought to be the supreme goal of all the efforts of the Minor and he must commit himself to the path of salvation. He is essentially a free will. The thoughts, good or evil, come to him, it is true, from beings distinct from him: the "holy" thought is suggested to him by a divine Spirit, the criminal thought by an "evil demon,"[88] but he preserves his free will, for these suggestions are not "operant wills and the Minor is the master to accept them or reject them."[89] On the other hand, the divine prescience did not know how to bind the human will, since God could not foresee the decisions that the Minor would make and the actions following consequently; if he has established upon immutable laws all that exists in the universe, he has left to his creature a full liberty, seeing "that he does not have within himself his prescience and does not take any part in the secondary causes of the universe."[90] Finally, if man, plunged into the demonic atmosphere of this material world where he breathes at each instant, the "evil intellect," seems to be in a bad position to resist it, the Creator has re-established the equilibrium by detaching "from his divine spiritual circle a major Spirit in order to be the guide, support, counsel, and companion of the Minor, which emanates and descends from the immensity in order to be incorporated at the center of elementary matter (material world) and to operate according to its free will in the terrestrial circle,"[91] Thus the Minor is able, in his fight against the perverse Spirits, to oppose two weak evil influences: demonic Spirit and evil intellect, by three very strong spiritual powers: his soul, endowed with the innate knowledge of the good, the suggestions of the detached major Spirit close to him, and the good intellect.[92]

But, if this victorious struggle against the demonic temptations and the bonds of matter is a prerequisite and necessary condition to reconciliation, it does not suffice to assure it. It is necessary that the Minor, in order to achieve this goal, receives the aid of an Elect Minor. The help that this "reconciler" brings to him is double: he transmits to him the instructions received directly from the Creator on the worship that ought to be given to the divinity by a "spiritual operation"[93] and communicates it to the "men of desire" to whom he has sent the gifts that he has received[94] by marking them with a mystical "character" or "seal," without which no Minor is able to be reconciled, since, for want of having received this mysterious ordination, he remains, whatever else be his personal merits, a Minor "in privation" (without communication with God).[95]

These supernatural beings, the Elect Minors "appointed by order of the Creator to mark the minor spiritual beings who must accompany the triumph of the manifestation of divine justice[96], receive temporal birth and life by the divine will and inspiration alone, and although their form be emanated from the posterity of Adam, the Minor who inhabits this form is truly thinking without ever being pensive, because the Eternal manifests to him his own will through the vision of one of his deputies who announces to him without any mystery what he must do in order to carry out exactly the divine will."[97]

The Elect Minors live on the margin of human society in order not to sully itself by its contact. "The Eternal withdraws them from among the profane (has them live separate from the profane) and the permanent impure ones of the earth and shelters them from every intellectual communication with the ordinary Minors."[98] They appear as luminous meteors over the course of the ages; the Eternal recalls them to him by unknown paths and the following generations do not know that they have existed, for the "Creator allows ordinary mortals to forget, by the succession of time, the memory of these blessed beings and, ignoring their fixed abode and the route that they have taken in order to get there, they ignore also their works, their actions, and their temporal spiritual operations (operations by which the divine Spirit manifests itself in the material world)."[99] Therefore the men of whom the Eternal wished to make "children of God" soon lose the memory of the formulas and ceremonies of the divine cult, that had been taught to them by the last Elect Minor to have appeared among them; they transgress the protection given to them to contract unions with the "children of men," that is to say the Minors "in privation," such that their posterity "falls away from all the divine spiritual knowledge" and that the sending of another emissary becomes necessary.[100]

CHAPTER II
The "Reintegration": Typology, Arithmosophy, mystical Geometry

The cosmological, pneumatological, and anthropological doctrines exposed in the preceding chapter form the substance of the treatise on Reintegration and we would be able to keep it at this brief analysis if we wished simply to render an account of the ideas it contains. But in this shimmering and confused work, the form offers as much interest as the foundation. Similar to the Oriental rugs where some very simple motifs repeat themselves to infinity with different colors and following the most varied arrangements, the treatise has recourse, in order to take up the same themes, to modes of demonstration curious by their strangeness and which, sometimes, look deeper into the principles already known.

First of all, the esoteric exegesis of the Bible, which is, just as we have already stated, the very basis upon which rests the dogmatic outline of Pasqually, is applied systematically, so well that the biblical accounts present themselves as a vast allegorical fresco. For the initiate who knows how to understand the secret meaning of the Scriptures, all there is symbolic unto the least details: events, locations, buildings and furnishings are only figures, most of the personages are so many reproductions of fundamental types: Minor in privation, reconciled Minor, regenerated Minor, Elect Minor, Spirits of different ranks, and up to the Creator. God manifests himself by his emanations, the worlds of the Spirits, the world of matter, the destiny of man reflected in full and on nearly every page of the sacred texts. The abundance of scriptural apocalypses is such that it is necessary to limit it to some examples.

The Terrestrial Paradise is the image of "the first glorious (luminous) stratum where is found the first Adam."[101] Noah's Ark "represents the chaotic envelope which contained every principle of creation of corporeal forms"[102] and the Minors who are found shut up there in a deep darkness, while it floated upon the waters, represents "the retreat of the reconciled Minors and the Righteous under the shadow of the great light (plunged into Limbo) where they will effectively remain a space of time in waiting."[103]

The dove which came out of the ark, fluttered around for the first time and landed above is "the true figure of the angelic spirit which directed the ark and informed Noah of the will of the Creator."[104]

The "great sign of the fire of different colors and forming a semi-circle, of which one extremity led to the summit of Mount Ararat and the other extremity led to the ark" was a vision of the "seven principal universal spirits."[105]

Sinai, ascended by Moses whilst the people remained at the foot of the mountain, "symbolizes the distance which separates the Creator Being from the general creature or the earth."[106] The struggle of Moses against the Mages of Egypt proves that "all operates in the universe by action and by contraction (reaction), without which nothing would have movement or life, and without life there would be no corporeal forms. Likewise, without demonic reaction, nothing would have spiritual life outside of the divine circumference."[107] The transformation into the serpent of the rod of Moses and that of the Mage, his adversary, is "the real explanation of the changing of the glorious forms of the superior demonic Spirits and of the divine Spiritual Minors into the form of vile terrestrial matter which holds them in privation." The return of the rods to their first state shows "that every species of forms which acts in this universe does not really exist in nature, nor of itself, but only by the being who animates them, and that all that appears to exist will disperse as promptly as the two serpents were dispersed." It announces therefore "the destruction of the earth and of its inhabitants."[108]

The passage of the Red Sea is a vast symbol: the first division which crosses the sea represents the men leaving the earth when the Creator delivers them from darkness. The Israelite warriors who marched following the first division and were likewise illuminated by the column of fire, "figure by their election what the Creator had done with a number of major Spirits in order to be the guides and defenders, while Israel waged spiritual war against its enemies, and these Elect are none other than the shadow and the instruments of the major Spirits that the Creator had joined to Israel."[109] "The different marches, that Pharaoh made in pursuing the Israelites, represent to us the ruses and the detours that the demonic Spirit employs in order to attach his intellect of abomination and to destroy by it, the power of man...But, as the divine Spirit, protector and defender of man, uses the same means to molest the demonic Spirit, it serves Israel as well to carry out the destruction of Egypt."[110]

Mount Moriah is called "mysteriously (mystically) by the friends of the wise (the initiates) Earth elevated above all senses," because the construction of the Temple, which served as its base, "actually represents the emanation of the first man." The justification of this interpretation is found in the fact that the Temple of Solomon was constructed without the help of tools composed of metal, to show that the Creator had formed the first man "without the help of any physical material operation."[111]

The Tabernacle is a symbol: 1st, of the supercelestial world; 2nd, of the celestial world; 3rd, of the body of man; 4th, of the world or universal circle.[112] Indeed, it is in the Tabernacle that Moses "carried out a part of the action of the spiritual inhabitants of the supercelestial, without the mixture of action with any other Spirit." He entered there each time that he had to request something on behalf of Israel, and he was in "direct communication with the Eternal and with the pure Spirits of the supercelestial." On the other hand, the Tabernacle represents the celestial part by its four directional gates[113], "which are the true figures of the four spiritual powers that the Creator has given to his Minor and by which he is able to make use of those of the four regionary chiefs (Spirits commanding the regions of the North, East, West, and South) and of all that is at their dependence."[114] In the third place, the Tabernacle, in which Moses had enclosed the divine Law, is the image of the "particular world or small world, which is none other than the body of man" or of the "corporeal form of apparent (sensible) matter in which is enclosed the Minor or divine spiritual soul."[115] Just as the inhabitants of the supercelestial and of the universal circle operate each in their particular in the redoubtable Tabernacle, so too all these different spiritual beings work and operate in the body of man with the Minor who is enclosed there."[116] The eastern gate of the Tabernacle represents the heart of man[117]; it is by it that penetrate into man "the most sublime Spirits as many good as evil."[118] The western gate represents the eye of man, the southern gate represents his ear.[119] Finally, "the Tabernacle truly made allusion to the universal circle in which every spiritual being, inferior, major, and minor, makes in the Tabernacle the same actions of operations as in the universal immensity."[120]

∴

The signification of the "types" is much more instructive than that of the symbols, for "a type says more than a symbol, a type is an actual representation of a past event, as well as an event that must occur in a short while"[121]; "a type foretells an infallible event which is under the immutable decree of the Creator."[122] It shows that "all the epochs and the first elections repeat themselves among men and make known to us that they will repeat until the end of the ages.[123]

The types are, in the sensible world, the simultaneous or repeated reflections of the transcendent entities: Creator, superior and major Spirits. They manifest, in the different periods of the history of humanity, the eminent dignity of man, his past and his future. They reappear in series and often in triads. The principal biblical personages are able therein to represent several, according to the acts that the Scripture attributes to them.

The type of the Creator is reproduced by Adam engendering a temporal posterity[124], by Moses giving, according to divine instructions, the plan of the Ark of the Covenant.[125] The type of the Spirit of the Creator "which floats upon the radical fluid for the disentangling of the chaos,"[126] is "truly made" by Moses floating in his cradle upon the Nile, by Noah carried by the Ark during the Flood.[127]

The type of the Major Spirit and that of the Inferior Spirit, "which has in its power the construction of forms," is discovered in Moses and Bethzaleel. Just as "Moses has communicated to Bethzaleel the orders of the Creator for the construction of the Tabernacle, so has the Creator communicated directly to the Inferior Spirits the law of the creation of the spiritous essences. Just as Moses gave to Bethzaleel the plan of his work, so did the Inferior Spirits receive by a superior deputy the image of the apparent form of the universe. Just as Bethzaleel found without trouble all the necessary materials, so did the inferior Spirits produce from themselves the three fundamental essences of all the bodies with which they adorn the universal temple."[128] The type of the emanated Spirits is found in the posterity of Adam.[129] One of the seven principal Superior Divine Spirits and one of the seven principal Major Spiritual Beings "which operates for the conservation and the support of this universe" is repeated by the second posterity of Noah.[130]

"Cain, elder son of Adam, is the type of the first Spirits emanated by the Creator, and his crime is the type of what these first Spirits have committed against the Eternal. Abel, second born of Adam, makes by his innocence and his holiness the type of Adam emanated after these first Spirits in his first state of justice and divine glory. The destruction of the body of Abel carried out by Cain, his elder brother, is the type of the operation that the first Spirits made to destroy the form of glory by which the first man was clothed and to render him by this means susceptible to being as those in divine privation."[131] The type of the first prince of the demons is repeated by Pharaoh "who hardened the heart of his people against Israel."[132]

Abraham and Ishmael revive the types of Adam and Cain "in their material operations."[133] Indeed, "Ishmael makes the type of the physical operation of Adam for the reproduction of his carnal posterity, operation that Abraham repeats together with his concubine. Their son Ishmael, arising from the cupidity of their material senses, was excluded from the paternal house, because he had been conceived without the participation of the divine will, but only by the concupiscence of the senses of matter. The bread and water that Ishmael and Agar received from Abraham and with which they went where their fate would lead them (into the desert), represented the last spiritual and temporal food that they received from this Patriarch; this type repeated again the last spiritual food that Cain received since he had conceived (planned) to commit the murder of his brother Abel."[134]

"Agar makes the type of the sister of Cain, his accomplice and the more guilty; the lack of material nourishment when Agar was with her son and which engaged them to implore the Creator, represents the suffering and consternation that Cain and his sister were in when the murder of their brother Abel was made known and when they turned away from there excluded from any participation in the sciences and in the divine spiritual nourishment. The angel who appeared to Agar and Ishmael, who satisfied their hunger and their thirst and indicated to them the place where the Eternal had fixed their dwelling, recalls to us the grace that the Eternal granted to Cain and to his sister in marking their forehead by his angel with an invincible seal of the divinity, which announced to one another that they had obtained mercy from the Creator and that they again enjoy a time of divine spiritual nourishment which had been withdrawn from them in relation to their crime."[135]

On the other hand, Abraham repeats the type of Adam, father of Abel, for, "after having been reconciled in part with the Creator, he had, by divine authority, a son by his wife Sara, though her advanced age had placed her outside a state to conceive. This child, conceived without the passion of the material senses, was called Isaac, which repeats rather perfectly the birth of the second posterity of Adam in his son Abel...Isaac...being perfectly instructed in the divine spiritual sciences, testified to his father the desire that he had to operate the great divine cult for the glory of the Creator. He told him, according to the inner instruction that he had received from the divine spiritual intellect, that it was time that he made use of all the divine sciences in which he was instructed, and that he offered a sacrifice to the Eternal."[136]

Jacob and Esau are replicas of the Prevaricating Spirit and of the Minor at first innocent, then fallen. Indeed, Jacob was "the elder by conception and Esau was the second," just as the Spirits have been emanated before Adam. But Esau, having come into the world first, was in possession of the birthright, just as the Minor first had that right and the power to command the Prevaricating Spirits. He had been stripped of his privilege by the maneuvers of Jacob, "to whom the Scripture has given the name of supplanter," as Adam was deprived of it for allowing himself to be tempted by the demon; and he deserved this punishment, for, like Adam, "he preferred the terrestrial cult to that of the Creator; he occupied himself entirely with the hunt instead of attaching himself to the combat of the demonic intellect which had seized his brother Jacob."[137]

The Patriarchs represent, moreover, all the personages of the eternal drama. They are that of the Divine Major Spirit "which serves as particular Spirit to every Minor being and will conduct him before the Creator." They had received "the double divine power and furthermore the power to render the character reversible upon the Minors in privation and this by their own spiritual operation (action) upon these Minors."[138] This is why Abraham, Isaac, and Jacob are "the types of the divine action operated by the divine Spirit with the Minors past, present, and to come."[139] These three Patriarchs have therefore, "repeated the type of the First Man, Réau or Roux"; the double divine spiritual power, which had been granted to man in order to triumph over the Prevaricating Spirits and which man had lost following his crime, being thus reduced in his power to simple Minor, is manifested to the Jews under the names of Abraham, Isaac, and Jacob."[140]

It is likewise by triads that is reproduced the type of the Minor who sees the glory of the Creator: first come Adam, Abel, and Seth, then Noah, Shem, and Japhet, finally Abraham, Isaac, and Jacob.[141]

One of the types most frequently represented is that of the Elect Minor[142], already manifested by the Patriarchs. Its representatives have been successive: Abel, Enoch, Noah, Melchizedek, Joseph, Moses, David, Solomon, Zorobabel.[143] Abel, who represents furthermore the type of Adam emanated after the prevarication of the first Spirits[144] is the "type of the Minors endowed with divine grace, that the Creator would give rise to in man"[145] and it has reconciled Adam with the Creator.[146] Enoch "reconciled the second posterity of the children of Seth, as much the living as the deceased, upon whom he caused to pass the authentic character or seal of his operation."[147] Noah reconciled the earth with God; Melchizedek "confirmed these first three reconciliations by blessing the works of Abraham and of his three hundred servants."[148]

All the events related by the Bible are types, simple or multiples. The typological exegesis furnishes such a mass of significant comparisons that Pasqually himself gives up on exhausting this vein. It will suffice to cite three examples borrowed from Exodus. The type of the error of Adam has been reproduced by the people of Israel when they make the Golden Calf, for "they expected to produce by this means a figure similar to that of man in order to then establish it as a god; their pride has been humiliated when they have received only a crude and inanimate form, without any substance of action."[149] Moses, in having Joshua, designated to succeed him, ascend Sinai with him and then bringing him back to the foot of the mountain, "represented the Major Spirit that the Creator detached from his divine spiritual circle in order to be the guide, the support, the conductor, and the companion of the Minor who emanates and descends from the immensity in order to be incorporated in the elementary circle" Joshua, in descending with Moses from the mountain, "made perfectly the type of the Spiritual Minor that the Eternal emancipates from his immensity in order to go operate, according to its free will, in the terrestrial circle."[150]

The organization of the divine cult by Moses presents a cluster of the most diverse types. The Creator has ordained for Moses to take his brother Aaron in order to interpret and to become assistant to Ur, in order to execute his spiritual operations; the name of Aaron signifies: "man elevated into divine grace or divine prophet," and the name of Ur: "fire of the Lord or Spirit of the divinity."[151] "Moses was then the type of the Creator, Aaron that of the liberator, Ur that of the conductor, Joshua that of the defender. These four men each made one of the types of the quadruple divine essence."[152]

∴

The lights that bring us the intelligence of the symbols and types are completed by those given by the secret science of numbers. This science has nothing to do with ordinary arithmetic. Expression of exterior and superficial relationships to the profane, the number is, for the initiate, at once a symbol and a type; it has an absolute and transcendent value, a substantial reality; it is the essence and the raison d'être of things. "Every law of temporal creation and every divine action is founded upon different numbers..., every number is co-eternal with the Creator, and it is by these different numbers that the Creator forms every figure, all his agreements with creation, and all his agreements with his creature."

The numbers are "the secret divine spiritual relationships which contain and direct the whole of nature"[153]; "It is this virtue of numbers that has caused the sages of all times to say that no man may be learned, be it in the divine spiritual, or in the celestial, terrestrial, and particular (heaven of the stars, earth, and living beings) without the knowledge of numbers. The knowledge of the laws of the spiritual nature is one thing, the knowledge of the laws of order and agreement of material men is something else. The laws of men vary like the shadow; those of the spiritual nature are immutable, all being innate within them from their first emanation."[154]

Arithmosophy has been known to man only through divine revelation: "the Creator himself instructed, by way of his spiritual envoy Heli, the blessed man Seth" in the science of numbers[155] and Pasqually, after having lengthily set forth the mystical value of the numbers 10, 7, 6, and 4, asserts that he has reproduced exactly "the sublime spiritual instructions that Seth received from the Creator by means of his deputy Heli."[156]

It is therefore in the arithmosophy that Pasqually finds the justification and the development of his mystical cosmology and anthropology.

"The *Unity* is the first principle of every being, as much of spiritual as of temporal," and belongs to the Creator.[157]

Two is "the number of confusion," that which "directs the association of the will of man with the demonic suggestion."[158] It is this junction which was the first error of Adam, and which had for its effect "the operation of confusion" from which arose Houwa. Therefore, "the number of confusion belongs to the woman."[159]

Three or the *Ternary* is the type of matter. It represents three fundamental substances: sulphur, salt, and mercury, "emanated from the imagination and the intention of the Creator" and from which the various combinations have produced the constitutive elements of the terrestrial and celestial bodies and the living organisms. Whatever be the infinite multitude of "spiritous principles" and their manifestations, it always comes down, in the final analysis, to the three first substances. Therefore, "the ternary number taught the knowledge of the ternary unity of the spiritous essences of which the Creator has used for the creation of the different apparent (visible) material forms."[160] It is thus that Bethzaleel and two aides in the construction of the Ark "alludes truly to the ternary number, which constitutes the powerful faculty of the inferior Spirits, producers of the three spiritous essences, from where have come all the corporeal forms."[161] The tripartite composition is found in the body of man and in that which constitutes the existence of the Minor. Indeed "the entire frame of a human form" is divided into three parts: the head, the trunk, and "the bones of the Isles" (iliac bones). Each of these parts has its own properties and faculties, and "these different faculties make a perfect allusion to the three kingdoms that we know in nature: the animal, vegetable, and mineral."[162] Likewise, the body of man has three different kinds of life: the life of matter, instinct or passive life, which animates as much the animal deprived of reason as the rational animal, the "demonic spiritual" life, which may be incorporated into the passive life, and the "divine spiritual" life which presides over the first two.[163] The role of the Ternary is not only to make known to us the composition of matter. But it "indicates yet by the origin of the three spiritous essences which constitute all the forms, the direct action of the inferior Spirits, since they have emanated from themselves mercury, sulphur, and salt for the structure of the universe,"[164] and it is thus the specific sign of the class of these Spirits which are called "ternaries,"[165] but it is also the Word, since it is the reason of "the creation of every form whatever through the junction of the intention, the will, and the word, which give birth to divine action."[166]

Four or Quaternary is "the divine spiritual number of which the Creator has made use for the spiritual emanation of every living being."[167] "Quadruple divine power," it is the number of the classes of the superior, major, inferior, and minor Spirits, which are the modes of manifestation of divinity.[168] Number of the creative energy, it is what the Eternal has used in order to emanate and emancipate the Spiritual Minor.[169]

"Man finds within himself the repetition of this quaternary number which makes him correspond with his Creator: body 1, (which is) the organ of the soul 2, the soul organ of the major Spirit (Spirit of the celestial) 3, and the major Spirit organ of the divinity 4."[170]

"All the emanated and emancipated beings (contained in the 4 classes of Spirits: superiors, majors, inferiors, and minors) as well as their laws and powers, arise from this same quaternary number or from the quadruple essence of the Divinity which encloses all."[171]

"The Eternal had invested man with every divine spiritual power, as being the act (the manifestation, the product) of the quadruple essence of the divinity."[172] "The Minor, being emanated from the quadruple essence, carried necessarily the number of his emanation which distinguished him from all the emanations made before him and put him above ('below' is an obvious error in the text) every emanated spiritual being."[173]

"From the quaternary, all temporal things and all spiritual action are derived."[174]

It is the number of "the central axis fire" which has condensed, modeled, and combined "the spiritous principles, produced in a state of indifference" (inert by nature) in order to give birth to "all the corporeal forms, just as by its action it maintains them during the course of their temporal duration fixed by the will of the Creator." For "no body may exist without having with it a vehicle for the central fire, upon which vehicle the inhabitants of this axis act continually as having arisen from themselves."[175] "The central fire continually directs its action upon all the corporeal forms whatever the apparent matter, consolidated by this same operation, in order to communicate movement to them, the faculty to act and react."

"This central axis is the general, particular, and universal agent (that is to say which acts upon the earth, upon the living beings, and upon the whole universe) adhering to the supercelestial circles and organ of the inferior Spirits which inhabit it, and which operate in it upon the principle of apparent corporeal matter." The body of man contains "a vehicle of this fire, which is the principle of material life." It "bears the quaternary number to know: 1st, the central axis; 2nd, the organ of the inferior Spirits; 3rd, the organ of the major Spirits (that is to say that the inferior Spirits are the organs of the major Spirits); 4th, the major Spirits organs of the Divinity."[176]

The number *Four* being the number of the central axis fire "contributes to the perfection of the forms taken by undifferentiated matter, because it gives movement and action to the form and because it presides with every created being, as being the principal; number from which all is derived."[177] The Quaternary is moreover the sign of the spiritual correspondence of the human soul with the quadruple divine essence by the intermediary of the major good Spirit. This relationship includes in effect four terms: minor soul, divine intellect, major good Spirit, Divinity.[178] Furthermore, the body of man is the organ of the soul, the latter is the organ of the good intellect, which is the organ of the major Spirit, this last being the organ of the divine Creator: gradation which also gives the number Four.[179] Finally, the Quaternary is the number which indicates to the Minor from where he comes and what was originally his power. Adam originally possessed the Quaternary; his fall has stripped him of it. He will be able to rediscover it by adding up the four characters which compose it, and which designates the different faculties that he had received from the Creator; he will be capable then of understanding "all the numbers of spiritual power that are innate within him."[180]

Five or *Quinary* is the number of the demonic Spirit.[181] The Quinary has been formed by the demons when they had wanted to add to the Quaternary, number of their emanation, an arbitrary unity, that is to say when the will to create without the consent and cooperation of the Divinity had tried to join itself with the divine creative energy. This prevarication of the perverse Spirits "adulterated their spiritual power and transformed it into a limited and purely material power under the direction of an authority taken by themselves."[182]

Six or *Senary*, that the initiates call "number of the daily operations,"[183] is the number of creation, for "it is by the Senary that the Creator caused to come from his thought all the species of images of apparent corporeal forms which exist in the universal circle." The is the explanation of the six days of creation according to Genesis; the symbolic image employed by the Bible signifies the Creator, "pure Spirit, superior to time and to the successive duration."[184] "Each of these days or these thousand years ought only to consider itself (to be considered) as the duration of the operation of the six divine thoughts."[185] These six days indicate the duration and the limits of the existence of matter "which will last six thousand years in all its perfection."[186]

Seven or *Septenary* is the number "more than perfect that the Creator used for the emanation of every Spirit outside of his divine immensity."[187] Its evident value is manifested by the impossibility of dividing it into two equal parts "without destroying it or adulterating it." Its indivisibility by two, number of confusion, is the mark of perfection.[188] It is the sign of the superior Spirits "who had to serve as first agents and certain cause in order to contribute to carrying out every sort of movement in the created forms in the universal circle." For, "the particle of uncreated excentral fire[189] would never produce anything in the corporeal forms if it had not reacted by a principal and superior cause, which is none other than the divine septenary agents, which preside as chiefs over the different actions and the different movements of all bodies, in which they have to carry out their thoughts and their will according to what they have conceived." Just as the soul of the Minor has for organ the body, the corporeal human form, so do the septenary Spirits have for organ corporeal beings."[190] The Eternal, after having "carried out six divine thoughts for the universal creation," gave the seventh day "seven spiritual gifts" and "he attached seven principal Spirits to all his creation for support in all his temporal operations according to the septenary duration that he had fixed for them. The cooperation of the seven principal Spirits is indicated in the physical world by the action of the seven planets which influence the temperature, the seasons, and maintain the universe."[191]

"The septenary number is calculated philosophically (mystically) by seven thousand years in regards to the temporal and the duration; but when Scripture says that on the seventh day God himself dedicated his own work by blessing the universal creation, it is necessary to understand by this blessing, the junction of the seven principal Spirits that the Creator unites to every creature included or contained in all his universal creation."[192] The "correspondence" of the seven major Spirits that the Creator has "attached in his universe in order to instruct the inferior and minor creature of his will, and to the number of which is the Holy Spirit, is taught to us by Scripture, which mentions the seven Angels, the seven Archangels, the seven

Seraphim, the seven Cherubim, the seven Dominions, the seven Powers, the seven Judges of Israel, the seven principal chiefs which were under Moses and Aaron, the seventy years of the Captivity, the seven weeks of Daniel, the seven days of the week, the candelabra with seven branches which was placed in the Temple of Solomon and which is still represented in the Saint Peter church of Rome."[193]

But the Septenary, "which has given perfection to every created being, is the same that will destroy and abolish everything." When the Senary will have exhausted its power, that is to say when the effect of each of the six divine thoughts will be accomplished, "will come the seventh period, the seventh millennium, during which matter will fall into a terrible decline where it will remain until its entire dissolution."[194] "The central axis fire will dissipate the apparent forms as promptly as it has formed them."[195] For "just as the elementary fire has the characteristic of reducing to ashes all that it embraces, so does the central axis have the faculty of devouring and dissipating entirely all that is reintegrated into it, without which remains therein not any appearance nor any substance suitable and proper to be inhabited by a Spirit."[196] At this moment, "the Creator will withdraw matter to himself with as much promptness and ease as he had conceived it for the creation of his work. Thus, just as all will have existed in a succession of degrees within degrees by divine order, so will all be brought together in the end by gradations and will return to its first principle."[197] "The universe, having been conceived in its entire perfection by the number seven, will likewise be reintegrated by this same number into the imagination of that which has conceived it."[198] "There will not remain of the creation any vestige when it will be reintegrated into its principle of emanation."[199]

Eight is the number of the "double divine power which had been confided to the first Minor (Adam) in order to triumph over the prevaricating Spirits." The Creator has attributed it to the Spiritual Elect or Elect Minors "whom he favors and appoints to the manifestation of his glory." The Octonary belongs also to the Spirits of the supercelestial who "act not only upon the celestial world and the material world, but also upon the circle of the universal axis." They fulfill, therefore, a double office; furthermore, "by their rank and their mission, they have the act of a double power," since "they serve as double rampart to the atrocity of the demonic operations."[200]

Nine is demonic, for it is the number of matter multiplied by itself.[201] The Scripture (esoteric) furnishes several proofs of this diabolical character of the Nine; here is an example: "Cain and his nine sisters, permeated by the demonic intelligence, were no more than a sole thought, a sole intention, and a sole action. Their three spiritous principles and first essences, their three virtues (faculties), and their three powers added up to form Nine."[202] The proof that the number Nine is radically evil is that the sum of the numbers figuring any multiple of 9 always gives the number 9. Thus, when Cain joined with his two sisters in order to engage in a demonic operation, the accursed operants formed the number 27 by the addition of their three demonic numbers, 9; the same total is obtained by adding successively eight more times the number 3 to itself; or 27=2+7, that is to say 9; likewise, 27x9=243, but this last number= 2+4+3 or 9. [203]

Ten or *Denary* is the "divine number."[204] The initiates represent it by the numeral 1 inscribed in a circle. The Denary is "the origin of every spiritual being, major, inferior, and minor, and of every law of action, whether spiritual or spiritous," since it "contains the first nine numbers which signify them."[205] "No minor being may be learned without perfect understanding of this great denary number of the

Eternal and of all its contents of emancipation and creation."[206] The Spirits of the first class are called superiors or denaries.[207] There have been ten Patriarchs and ten Elect Minors.[208] These groups of privilege beings "form the complete denary divine spiritual number."[209]

Eleven "is affixed[210] to every kind of corporeal form, complete, analogous to the terrestrial body and to all that arises from it."[211]

Twelve "has been the principle of the division of time."[212]

The arithmosophy teaches not only the mystical value of the first twelve numbers, it indicates to us moreover the manner in which they engender one another, and attribute to the numbers by which they express themselves a value and an absolute reality. By analyzing the numbers, by making their sum or their product, by adding their signs to obtain new numbers, one finds the confirmation of the principles that we have set forth.

The proof that the manifestation of divine power is identical to this very power follows from the fact that the Quaternary contains the divine Denary[213], since the addition of the four numbers which are in power in the Quaternary (1+ 2+3+4) gives 10. "Add these numbers from 1 to 4 and you will see clearly that all is proven and that all exists by the famous divine number, which is the denary number"[214] Furthermore, the first four numbers are the elements of which are composed the four numbers of divine power, that is to say: 10, "great and first divine power"; 7 (=3+4), "second power of the Creator"; 6 (1+2+3), "third power of the Creator"; 4, "quaternary number which ends and concludes the four divine powers of the Creator contained in his co-eternal denary number."[215]

One may again group as follows the first four numbers:

1+2=3, number of matter.

1+2+3=6, number of creation.

1+2+3+4=10, number of divine power.[216]

The Quaternary is, on the other hand, formed from 1 (number of the divine unity) and 3 (number of matter).[217] It is therefore the number of the Minor, which has for its origin an emanation from the divine Unity contained in matter as punishment for the first error of Adam. The property of the Quaternary, demonstrated above, in particular that it constitutes the Denary by the addition of the numbers that it contains, shows that the Minor is superior to the two major and inferior worlds, since, in order to form the perfect denary number of the Creator, they are obliged to be added 7+3.[218]

The Quinary, "number of which serves the demons in order to operate the contraction (reaction) against the divine spiritual action," is composed of 2 (number of confusion or carnal generation) + 3 (number of matter).[219]

The Senary, "number of the divine thoughts which have operated the universal temporal creation," may be analyzed in three different manners: by 1+2+3, by 2+4, and by 3+3 (number of matter added with itself).[220] That is to say that the creation of the universe has for its formula: Divine Unity + material generation + matter; or rather material generation + emanation; or even : matter combining itself with matter.

The Septenary is the sum of 4 and 3, so that 7 is "the number which constitutes the power of action of the major Spirit, which is double, that is to say that by the number 3 it acts upon the forms and by the number 4 upon the spirit of the Minor."[221]

The passive (vegetative) soul is in possession of the Ternary, and the impassive (spiritual) soul is in possession of the Quaternary.[222] But these two lives, inferior and minor, passive and impassive, originate in a pure Spirit and are intimately bound, which shows the addition of the Ternary and the Quaternary, of which the sum is the Septenary, number of the major Spirit from which they emanate.[223]

The Octonary, "number of the double divine power," is formed from 1+3+4 and the "Unity only joins with the Ternary in order to form with the Quaternary the number of the double power."[224]

The Nonary, formed by the "junction of the Quinary, imperfect and corruptible number, and the Quaternary, perfect and incorruptible number, is the number of the subdivision of the spiritous essences of matter and that of the spiritual divine essences." "In making this junction, man degrades his divine spiritual power by rendering it demonic spiritual."[225]

Finally, if we consider separately the figures expressing certain numbers, then, taking them for their proper value, we multiply them or add them, we thus obtain other numbers represented by figures which are another revelation.

For example, by multiplying the Ternary by the Quaternary, "which is found exactly in the terrestrial, celestial, and supercelestial worlds," one has for a product 12, whose figures added (1+2) give 3," which shows that the corporeal form of all the beings existing in these worlds arises from the three principles: sulphur, salt, and mercury.[226]

If one multiplies the number of the seven stars composing each of the innumerable constellations spread among the seven planetary circles by the number of the seven virtues inherent to each of these little stars or "ordinary planetary signs," the product is 49, whose figures added (4+9) give 13; now this number is expressed by a 1 and a 3, whose sum is 4 or the Quaternary.[227]

The addition of the figures representing the various proportions of the Ark of Noah, which is 300 cubits in length, 50 in breadth, 30 in height, produces 380, that is to say 3+8=11, "number of every kind of corporeal form, complete, analogous to the terrestrial body," from where it follows that the Ark was the image of the earth.[228]

In joining the Quaternary to the number 12, product of the "quaternary of 3," one finds the number 16, that is to say 1+6=7, "spiritual product which shows you that nothing exists or is able to exist but by the Spirit, and which shows at the same time that your emanation is spiritual."[229]

Finally, by joining to the Denary the series of numbers that it contains, that is to say 10+2+3+4+5+6+7+8+9+1, we obtain the number 55, which one may read as 5 and 5, "which indicates the division of the Denary into two quinary and demonic numbers. Indeed, the prevarication of the first Spirits is to have wished to divide and subdivide the quadruple divine essence and this by their own spiritual faculty…they discovered neither Quaternary Unity nor pure and simple Denary Unity, but only two quinary numbers instead of the divine Denary that they wanted to place in their possession and into their power."[230]

The numbers are not the only hypostases of the transcendent realities that the treatise of Reintegration reveals to us. These realities are also made known to the initiate under the form of geometric figures, which must not be considered as simple schemas destined to represent graphically purely intelligible truths, but as one of the aspects under which are manifested the divine intelligence and will.

The state of the universe before the fall of the First Man is indicated by "the universal figure in which every spiritual nature, major, minor, and inferior, operates."[231] It is composed of four circumferences opposed two by two, and whose centers are united by straight lines; in the middle of the figure is an equilateral triangle whose summit is pointed towards the bottom and whose base blends with the horizontal line uniting the centers of the two circumferences on the right and left.

The superior circle, which bears the Denary, is the "divine spiritual circle whose center is the type of the Divinity." This circle "marks the superior supercelestial chief and the immensity of the superior denary Spirits." its center is the summit of a great isosceles triangle, whose two other angles coincide with the centers of the two circles on the left and right. The circle on the right, where is inscribed the Septenary," marks the immensity of the major septenary Spirits which are under the denary Spirits." The circle on the left, which bears the Ternary, "marks the immensity of the inferior Spirits which are under the denary and the septenary Spirits." To the great isosceles triangle is opposed at the base another triangle whose summit is inscribed in the inferior circle, which bears the Quaternary. This last circle "marks the immensity of the divine spiritual Minors."

"The four circles are the type of the quadruple divine essence." The circle of the Denary represents "the absolute unity of the Divinity." The circle of the Septenary is "the first spiritual emanation that the Creator has emancipated from the circle of the Divinity." The circle of the Quaternary is "the third emanation emancipated from the circle of the Divinity."[232]

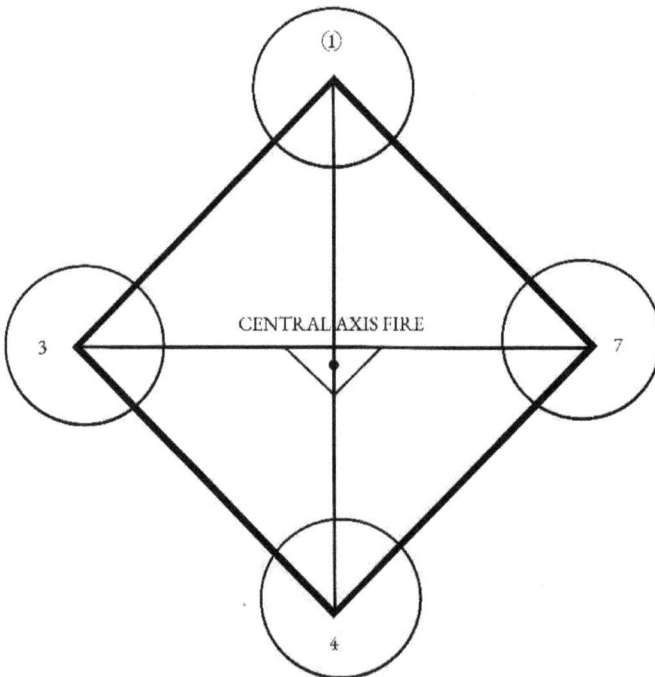

The reconstruction above is hypothetical, the information given by the treatise presenting contradictions.

The superiority of the divine spiritual Minor (animated by the spirit of God) is marked by the position of his domain. Indeed, the quaternary circle is "in aspect" of the denary circle, whereas the ternary, or inferior, and septenary or major circles are, "outside the line of the perpendicular, which belongs only to the minor circle of the Man-God," and are only in aspect between themselves" in order to communicate directly the orders that they receive and will receive from the Creator until the end of time concerning their temporal spiritual actions." Thus, the Spirits of the major and inferior classes "appointed to the conservation of time and matter, are only able to operate in universal latitude (in the material universe)." The Minor, on the contrary, "who operates in the supercelestial immensity or in the universal creation," commands the major and inferior Spirits, and his power extends into the immensity of the longitude" (toward the superior worlds).

The indications given by the respective position of the circles are confirmed and specified by the lines that unite their centers. These lines do not only show that "all has been ordained to exist and to act in an intimate correspondence"; each of them still has its particular signification. The horizontal line, which joins the center of the septenary circle to that of the ternary circle is the central axis fire, "fire which is the principle of the life of every being of created body," and the small triangle to which it serves as the base is the "general terrestrial body" (the earth).[233] The vertical line, which, departing from the center of the denary circle crosses the general terrestrial body, cuts through the middle of the central axis fire and ends at the center of the quaternary circle, establishes the superiority of the Minor over all the Spirits, since it shows that "no spiritual being has preserved as distinctly as the minor Spirit the direct and principal correspondence with the Creator." The Spirits of the supercelestial themselves are not exempt from obeying the Minor. It is necessary to remark indeed that the perpendicular departing from the very center of the denary circle crosses this last, abode of the Spirits of the supercelestial, which shows that "if they act not only upon the celestial world and the material world, but even upon the circle of the universal axis (central axis fire vivifying the universe," and if "the union between man and God is carried out by their mediation," they are none the less "subjugated to one another."

The sides of the two great triangles are no less instructive. Those of the superior triangle show the action of the First Cause exercising itself directly and simultaneously upon the major and inferior circles. The sides of the inferior triangle, which, coming out of the quaternary circle, end at the extremities of the base of the superior triangle, at the very place where are found the centers of the septenary and ternary circles, showing at the same time the superiority of the Minor over the Spirits of these circles, and the "perfect correspondence of all the spiritual beings (major, inferior, and minor) with the Creator from which they are emanated."[234]

The figure by which is manifested the economy of the universe where lived the Man-God has been destroyed by the error of Adam. Since the fall "man is no longer in aspect of the Divinity, as indicated at first by the position of the quaternary circle." The two triangles are kept divided "in order to express the privation of the Minor subjected to the troubles of the body and spirit."[235] But this figure has for present man only a retrospective interest; it not only reveals the past, but it also foretells the future. The "reintegration" will consist, for "the minor spiritual posterity of Adam," of re-entry into the quaternary circle, "first chief residence that the Minor has inhabited since his divine emancipation," and from where the error of Adam has excluded his descendants only "for the whole duration of time."[236]

The domain in which the spiritual Minor is condemned to live "for the whole duration of time" is represented by three circles, that the profane knows, but of which he is unaware of the true nature and destination. Humans have, in all eras and up to our day, studied carefully the "sensible circle" (the earth), the "visual circle" (the heaven of the planets), and the "rational circle" (the heaven of the fixed stars); but they have only ever sought by this study to "extend their knowledge of space and the limits of the universal, general, and particular creation," to "procure with more certitude the different means to traverse the surface of the earth." Their spirits plunged into darkness only consider these circles materially and as "being proper to satisfy their covetous passion of matter."[237] The initiate conceives these circles "spiritually." He knows that they must be his abode until the end of time because they are "the three different circles where the minor Spirits accomplish their pure and simple spiritual operations, according to the immutable order that they have received from the Crematory in order to succeed in their reconciliation and their reintegration into the supercelestial."[238] He identifies the sensible circle with the "minor circle" (abode of the fallen man), the visual circle with the "intellect circle" (abode of the Spirits who cause to penetrate into the spirit of the Minor the good or evil intellect), and the rational circle with the "major circle" (abode of the septenary Spirits). The initiate knows besides that in reality the different planetary and elementary bodies reside in the intervals of these three circles "which are none other than a distinct expanse in which the equitable Minors (the Just) will finish carrying out their temporal action (the progress in the path of reconciliation) invisible to corporeal men (hidden from the profanes enslaved by matter). This operation (reconciliation) begins at the sensible circle; the Minors pass from there into the visual circle, where is accomplished the force of their spiritual operation that we name reaction of operation (stronger and more prolonged operation)[239], then they are going to enjoy rest in the shade of their reconciliation in the rational circle, place where the Just rest while waiting for the First Man and his posterity to be reintegrated into the divine circle."[240]

The universe is composed then, since the fall of Adam, of four circles: "the sensible circle, of which the body of man is the type because he is immediately attached to it, which is attached to the visual circle, which is attached to the rational circle, and the rational to the supercelestial."[241]

The equilateral triangle completes the series of mystical figures. The triangle is, in the final analysis, but a graphic transcription of the Ternary, for it "represents none other than the three spiritous essences that have cooperated with the general terrestrial forms"; one of the angles represents sulphur, another salt, and the third mercury.[242] Consequently, the number 3 being "the principle of all corporeal life,"[243] "the exact figure of the general terrestrial temple is an equilateral triangle.[244] This triangular figure indicates therefore, not the apparent form, but the nature and composition of the bodies of matter. Yet the transcendent reality is always reflected in the material world and if, to our eyes of flesh, the earth is round, it is none-the-less, in the mystical sense, of triangular form. Thus, when Adam portioned, according to the order of the Eternal, the earth between his sons and himself, he was unable to make more than three parts, "the earth having no more and being perfectly triangular." Adam had the West, Cain the South, and Seth the North.[245] "Just as there are only three spherical circles: the sensible, the visual, and the rational, so are there only three terrestrial angles, so too is the universal creation divided into three parts." For the same reason there are only able to exist upon the earth three principal nations, represented at first by the posterities of Cain and of Seth and the female posterity of

Adam, then by the three children of Noah: Ham, who had the South, Shem, who received the West, and Japhet, to whom was attributed the North.[246]

The triangle is also the figure of the fallen man, who, "by the three spiritous principles which compose his form of apparent (visible) matter and by the proportions which rule there, is the exact figure of the general terrestrial temple."[247]

But, just as the three spherical circles of the material world are dominated by the supercelestial circle, so does the triangle, or ternary figure, contain the Quaternary; this is what is shown by the triangle bearing a point in its center, figure known to the initiates alone.[248] "This figure clearly designates the quaternary number by the three bases placed in junction and by the point which is at the center."[249] It indicates that "It is only the junction of the spiritual principle, or of the quaternary number, with these three essences (sulphur, salt, and mercury) which has given them an intimate relationship and has caused them to take a sole figure and a sole form, which represents truly the general terrestrial body divided into three parts: West, North, and East."[250] The point inscribed in the triangle is the figure of Sinai, where God spoke to Moses face to face and dictated his laws to him. "This spiritual mountain, bearing the denary number, occupies the center of the general receptacle (universe) and, since the earth is triangular, this mountain ought to be to the earth what the point, or the center, is to the triangle." This makes known that "this earth contains within itself a living being, emanated from the Creator and similar to that which is enclosed in the apparent form of all the Minors."[251]

The punctuated triangle was figured at the summit of Mount Moriah, upon which Jacob marked "by three stones placed triangularly" the place where he had his vision. "The placement represented the corporeal form of the earth. Jacob remained at the center in order to show that the Creator had placed the Man-God at the center of the universe to command and govern all the emanated and created beings."[252]

The symbolic, the typology, the arithmosophy, and the mystical geometry are, as one has been able to convince oneself by reading the present chapter, only variations executed on the principal themes set forth in the preceding chapter. But these themes themselves reproduce a fundamental motif which is the preoccupation to establish the sublime origin of man, the eminent dignity of the Minor, the greatness of his role, past and future. It is to this central point that converge the cosmological and penumatological doctrines, and all the apparatus of proofs borrowed from the most unusual modes of demonstrations.

The First Man, Adam or Roux, or Réau, Spiritual Minor "emanated and emancipated" by virtue of the Quaternary[253], was "the Man-God of the universal earth,"[254] a "God-emanated" and "the true emulator (disciple) of the Creator."[255] Superior in power to the first emanated Spirits "which operate in the spiritual worlds and in the material worlds."[256]

By his fall he has lost this privileged situation; nevertheless, certain of his descendants will be able to rediscover it: "Man will not always crawl upon the earth, but one day he will be reinvested with his first power and then he will walk upright against those who have caused him to fall."[257] By the "reintegration," that is to say by the return to the former state of things, "the minor spiritual posterity of Adam re-enters into the quaternary circle, first seat of power that the Minor has inhabited since his divine emancipation," and of which the error of Adam has only excluded his descendants "for the duration of time" (duration of the material world).[258]

But the thesis of the treatise on the Reintegration upon human destiny presents lacunas or at least obscure places. If it strongly marks the point of departure and clearly enough the point of arrival, it gives only a very vague idea of the intermediary period, that is to say the duties and powers of the "temporal spiritual Minor" during his terrestrial life and the means which are offered to him in order to work in this world toward his future reintegration. In what exactly consists of the "reconciliation" and the "regeneration," what are the modes and the effects of the aid brought to the spiritual Minor by the Elect Minor or Reconciler, what is the Nature of the cult required by the Divinity? On all these important points the treatise gives only confused indications or proceeds by allusions of which he does not furnish the key.

This silence, moreover, appears natural if one considers that the treatise is a dogmatic work and not a ritual. It explains and justifies the latter, it does not replace it. It is therefore to the ritual of the Élus Coëns that it is necessary to appeal in order to clarify the points that the treatise leaves in the shadow. We will only have a full comprehension of the doctrines taught by Pasqually after having seen what practices his disciples engaged in and what results they believed to be able to look forward to.

CHAPTER III
The "Operations"

None of the known documents give a clear and complete idea of the character and the ceremonial of the Operations of the Élus Coëns. The plans, tables, and sketches of figures, to which Saint-Martin, then secretary of Pasqually, referred in transmitting to the adepts of Lyon the instructions of the master, and which were, indeed, as indispensible as would be a map for a traveler adventuring in an unknown region, have not reached us.

It is, moreover, very doubtful that the Élus Coëns had ever been in possession of complete and definitive instructions. The correspondence shows that the papers of the Operations were scarcely rough drafts at the moment when Pasqually began to have his disciples "work"[259] and that, in striving to focus this first outline, he went, urged on by the impatience of his pupils, a little randomly and without plan drawn up, promising much, having little, forgetting sometimes what he had prescribed some months earlier and falling into contradictions that he was obliged to recognize.[260] In April 1770, that is to say three years after the organization of the Order, Pasqually announces that he is going to work on the Invocations assigned to the seven operative days of the week, and of which each would speak to one of the good geniuses of the planets, as well as to their supreme chief. He then promised to draw up the Invocations for all the Operations of each month, of each equinox, with the exception of the two solstices.[261] It seems that this breviary remained in the planning stage, for we no longer find mention of it again. In any case, the ritual of the principal Operation, that of the Equinox, had not yet the following year received its definitive form. The Equinox Working, which Willermoz would engage in for the first time in September 1771, was presented to him in July as a provisional plan which would be developed the following year. Pasqually saw to tell him, it is true, that the complete ritual would be sent to him when he was more advanced in his initiation and that he would reserve the instruction already received "for a time when he will have made more progress." But it follows from the letter, when one takes the trouble to read between the lines, that the insufficient preparation of the adept was only a convenient excuse to mask the embarrassment of the master incapable of furnishing for the set date a completed ritual. Pasqually had, four years prior, promised Willermoz a "grand invocation of midnight" for his Equinox Working; the grand invocation not being ready, Pasqually suddenly discovered that "this matter was not pressing" and he ordered Willermoz to content himself for the time with "lesser particular invocations" that were sent to him.[262] Six months later Willermoz indeed received for the working of the spring equinox, a new "lesser invocation," but it still lacked a complete plan of the three circles, which were necessary for him to put an end to his "uncertainty on the kind of layout that must be used."[263]

The slowness with which Pasqually constructed his edifice did not keep him from making mistakes. He was obliged to draw back to more modest proportions his original plan, which, in the course of its execution, proved to be too ambitious. After having promised to Willermoz, in April 1770, that he would have him work in the "four circles,"[264] and having announced, at the end of 1771, the dispatch of this plan, he had sent to him, in January 1772, under the pretext of not "overburdening him too much," a plan bearing only three circles.[265] In fact, the ritual of the Operations was not definitively completed when Pasqually left France in May of the same year. It is only in October 1773, that is to say at the moment when to Order dissolved, that he dispatched from Port-au-Prince "the different tables of operation and the different invocations which ought to follow the tables."[266]

Nothing proves, moreover, that these papers, in which the adepts would discover little new detials[267], had been the crowning of the edifice.

The account which follows is the hypothetical reconstruction of a ritual left in an outlined state, but it gives a sufficient idea of the nature, the general economy, and the essential aim of the theurgical ceremonies to which the disciples of Pasqually devoted themselves.

∴

The simplest of the ceremonies was the "Daily Invocation" which was called at last "Daily working of the Réau-Croix." Pasqually had at first prescribed two Invocations per day, then had reduced them to one alone. This one had even ceased to be obligatory daily, but was able to be done at any time, without having regard to the months, nor the days of the moon, nor even the hours of the night.

The adept traced a circle, at the center of which he placed a candle inscribed with "the W." He was allowed to trace there also some "convention" (hieroglyph). He placed himself in the circle while holding in his hand a light which he lit up in order to read his Invocation, which began by these words: "O Kadoz (Holy), O Kadoz, O Kadoz, who will grant me to be as I have been in my first principle of divine creation? Who will grant me further to be restored in eternal virtue and spiritual power?"[268]

A more important ceremony was "the Invocation of the Three Days."[269] These three consecutive days would fall in the period comprised between the "renewal of the moon" (new moon) and the end of its first quarter. Under this reservation the Élu Coën was able, at his Will, to proceed with a series of invocations from the first to the fourteenth day of the new moon.

The operant traced upon the floor of his chamber a circle of three feet in diameter, at the center of which he inscribed the W. He was able as well to draw in the circle "arbitrary signs of convention, provided that all his drawings only tended towards the good." He perfumed his circle by carrying around a little handled dish, earthen and brand new, containing burning coals, upon which he had thrown some pinches of the following balsamic mixture: "four sols of saffron, male incense, flowers of sulphur, black and white poppy seeds, clove, Canella in rods, teardrop mastic, sandarac, nutmeg, and mushroom spores." His dish in hand, he goes around the circle by departing from the West and making his way toward the North. Having then placed a "star" (candle) upon the W and standing upright in the circle, a second candle in the left hand to illuminate his paper, he read a "prayer in invocation" and "conjurations." This ceremony, renewed each of the three days, was able to be, at each session, repeated three times in a row.[270]

Papus distinguished two categories of Operations properly called, and sees there two degrees of initiation, the Operations described in 1770 corresponding, according to him, to an initiatic grade more elevated than those elaborated in 1768. One will be, it seems, much closer to the truth by giving to this classification a purely chronological value. As Pasqually has, in the course of these two years, often modified his instructions on essential points, it is permitted to admit that the ritual drawn up in 1770 is only a development of the ritual communicated in 1768 and that the former was destined, not to be superimposed upon the latter, but rather to replace it. Papus, moreover, has not remarked that the correspondence alludes, not to two, but to three successive rituals, since the instructions given in 1772 prescribed a layout and ceremonies different from that of those indicated in 1770. On the other hand, if the second and third rituals claim some superiority over the first from the liturgical point of view, the general disposition, character, and aim of the three kinds of Operations are identical.

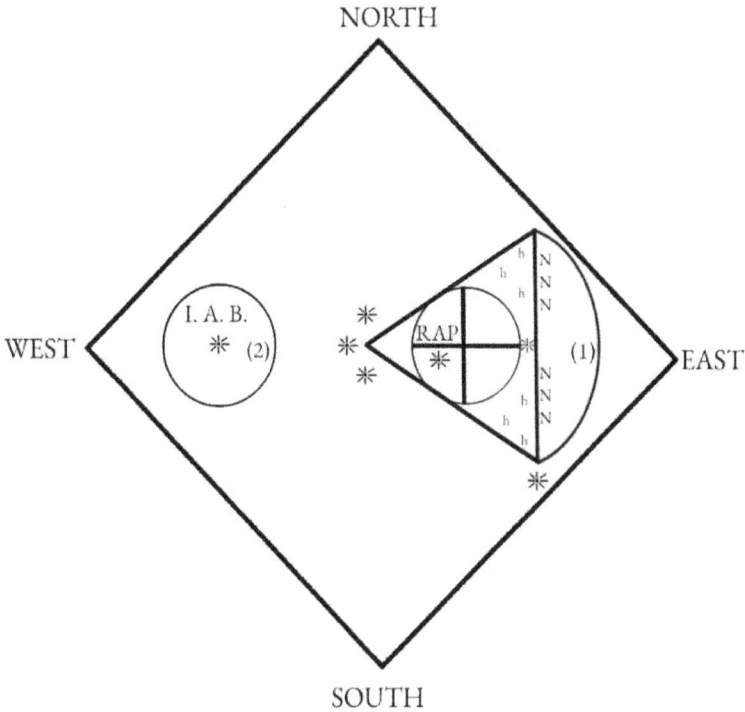

Legend: (1): Quarter Circle.
(2): Circle of Retreat.
N: Name of prophets and apostles.
h: Hieroglyphs of prophets, apostles and angels.
The asterisks indicate the place of the "Stars" (candles).

The sketch above has been reconstituted in the absence of any physical documentation, by bringing together different passages from the letters of Pasqually to Willermoz; that of September 11, 1768, notably, furnishes on the subject numerous pieces of information (II, 80-82). The *L.C. de Saint-Martin*, published in 1902 by Papus should give, in an appendix, at least four figures reproducing the layouts of the Chamber of Operation, but, although a note on page 95 refers to the 4th figure concerning the "simple ordination of the Grand Architect," no example contains the promised figures.

∴

The operant is clothed in a special costume. He was dressed completely in black: jacket, breeches, and stockings. When he wants to be perfectly in order with the instructions, he would have himself made up in a hat and shoes soled with a sheet of cork, "in order to have nothing unclean or impure in the place or upon him." The shoes would, in every case, be of the sort called "pope slippers," that is to say without pieces, of a style to be worn "in a slip-shod manner" and easily removed. He passed, over his black clothing, a long white robe, bordered at the bottom by fire-colored cloth about a foot wide; the sleeves "tailored in the style of an alb," would be garnished the same, but only about a half foot in height; the neck bore the same border, about three fingers wide. He then passed over his robe: first a blue cord in saltire around the neck, then a black cord hanging from the right shoulder to the left hip, then a red sash "from right to left, around as a belt below under the abdomen," finally an aqua-green sash "from left to right over the chest."[271]

The Operation prescribed in 1768 was repeated for three consecutive nights. Each morning the operant read the office of the Holy Spirit; the evening come, he entered alone for six hours into a chamber which would be sheltered from any indiscrete glance, he recited there the seven Psalms and the Litany of the Saints, which he read in a book of the mass. He then drew upon the ground with the chalk the prescribed figures. He traced first in the East angle of the room a quarter circle whose segment was turned towards the Orient. Having drawn the line of the segment, he inscribed in the isosceles triangle thus formed a small circle intersected by a cross. He then drew in the West angle of the chamber an entire circle called the "Circle of Retreat." The two figures were separated by a space of two feet. In the Circle of Retreat and in the Quarter Circle were finally drawn letters and hieroglyphs: notably the capital letters R A P, upon the West branch of the cross inscribed in the small circle, and the letters I A B, in the Circle of Retreat.

Setting aside, then, his chalk, the operant arranged the eight candles which he had brought. He placed three at the angle of the Quarter Circle, one beside the letters RAP, two at each end of the arc of the circle, one in the middle of the line, and the last at the center of the Circle of Retreat. All this preparatory work, for which two hours were planned, being finished, the adept was ready for the Operation which had to begin precisely at midnight.

When the twelve strikes sounded, the operant took off his slippers, removed from the Circle of Retreat the lit candle and placed it with his right hand, outside of the circle, in which he stretched himself out, abdomen to the ground, and the forehead rested upon his two closed fists. After having remained six minutes in this position, he raised himself, lit the candles of the Quarter Circle with "new" fire, arranged at the ends of the Quarter Circle, the candle beside the letters R A P, and the one placed in the middle of the segment line, and prostrated himself in the Quarter Circle. He then replaced his slippers and placed himself in the Circle of Retreat, the right knee to the ground and his two hands squared, flat upon the ground. Thus stationed, he "raised" the names inscribed in the two circles and in the Quarter Circle, that is to say he repeated them three times by inserting them into the following formula: "In quali die X, X, X, invocavero te, velociter exaudi me." He asked God to grant him, by virtue of the power that he has given to his servants, the grace that he

36

desired "of a sincere heart, truly contrite and submissive." He beseeched him to have him "repeat"[272], as a sign of his mercy, one of the hieroglyphs that he had traced with the chalk in the middle of the chamber, between the Quarter Circle and the Circle of Retreat. Taking then the small earthen dish, with a handle and new, containing a coal lit with the "new fire," he throws a good pinch of the aromatic mixture whose composition has been indicated previously, and he takes it around the Quarter Circle. After having thrown three more pinches on it, he senses four times the West angle. The censing ended, the operant extinguishes the candles, save that which burns in the middle of the Quarter Circle. He carries it into the Circle of Retreat, where he places himself, and, after having recited the Invocations, he puts himself on duty to observe the "Passes."

The operant should not, on the first night, come out of the Circle of Retreat except between one-thirty and two o'clock in the morning. At that moment, he erased all the figures traced upon the ground while repeating the invocations for the signs representing the good Spirits and the "exconjuration" for those of the evil ones.[273] Every trace of his work being dispersed, he withdraws from the Chamber of Operation to go put himself to bed.

All the ceremonies described above would be repeated on the two following nights, with this sole difference that the operant oriented differently each time, by returning it from one point to the other, the small triangular talisman that served him as "shield" against the evil Spirits.[274]

∴

The Operations of which the correspondence makes almost exclusive mention starting from 1770, are called by the adepts, "Equinox Workings." Their gestation was rather long, for they were only put into practice after two years.[275] The Equinox Working lasted three days. The Operation of the first day began with "the exconjuration of the South" (that is to say of the infernal powers).[276] As it is one of the rare prayers made known to us by the authentic documents, here is the text:

"I conjure you Satan, Beelzebuth, Baran, Leviathan[277]; to all you, formidable beings, iniquitous beings, of confusion and abomination, to you all alert, terror, and shuddering, prompt to my voice and command, to all you Great and Powerful Demons of the Four Universal Regions, and to all you, demonic legions, subtle Spirits of confusion, horror (error?) and persecution, hear my voice, tremble when it will be heard among you all in general, without destination, and in particular in each of your accursed operations; I command you by the one who has pronounced pain of eternal death against you all, chiefs of the regionary Demons, as well as your adherents, seducers of the Divine Spiritual Minors. To you directly, Satan, I excommunicate you, bind you, and limit you in your formidable region by the name of the Most High, Eternal God, Avenger and Rewarder, Vaur, tenth name that the Creator has returned to the power of his minor being, in order to have power and authority over you and over all those who are in your Diabolical Dominion, that by this same thrice holy name (I) stop you and annihilate you in your abyss of darkness and spiritual privation, superior 10, major 7, inferior 3, and divine spiritual minor 4[278], may my thought work (act) against you, Satan, by my omnipotence and by that of those who surround me, that the Creator has subjugated spiritually in order to be my support, my guide, and my invincible shield[279], by you and by any of your adherents against which I protest for a time immemorial. I command you, Satan, by the four Divine Powers, Vabaham

10, Vakiel 10, Diamel 10, Arai 10, and by that of the four Divine Spiritual Regionary Chiefs, Diaphas 8, Diamaim 7, Memaiai 3, Heli 4, may you be by the Eternal contained within the limits that I fix you, may you forever be devoid of every power and correspondence with me, may every action of operation on your part be unable to reach me, having been confounded and annihilated by me according to my power over you and yours, your fellows and equals like you in demonic virtue and power, that I limit and bind in the southern region for your greatest shame and for that of all your impious court; let it be done thus as I have conceived it, and as the power of the Man-God of the earth has pronounced it. Amen."

The same exconjuration was repeated for Beelzebuth, for Baran, and for Leviathan, whose name replaced successively that of Satan, and each time, the exorcist presented in the South corner the talisman that he held in his hand.[280] He had thus his "shield," with which he would be able "to be in surety if, on the first day or one the second, he was presented with something (an evil spirit)."[281]

The operant then pronounced a Special Invocation, then that of the first day of the Working of the Three Days. The second day he repeated the Ex conjuration of the South, the Special Invocation, then he pronounced the second Invocation of the "Great Work."[282] on the third day the program comprised, after the Ex conjuration and the Special Invocation, the "Grand Ex conjuration of the Serpent," with the exclusion of the two Invocations of the Great Work.

These various defensive or propitiatory ceremonies formed the prelude to the Operation proper, for which the correspondence indicates two rather different rituals, the one dating from 1770, the other from 1772.

The first, upon which a letter from Pasqually to Willermoz from March 13, 1770, gives rather detailed information[283], consisted of a layout comprising a Quarter Circle, drawn in the East corner, bearing the letters R A P and containing a large circle called the Circle of Communication[284], the Circle of Retreat, situated in the West corner, with the inscription I A B, and seven small circles. The placement of the latter was marked upon the draft by letters which were not simple reference marks but had a mystical significance and likely represented the initials of the names of the Septenary Spirits invoked. Two of the small circles flanked the extremity of the circle segment pointing South, to the sides of the letters MR; two others made their counterpart at the extremity pointing to the North, near the letters WG; two others filled the angles formed by the extremities of the segment and origin of the rays, near the letters OZ and IA[285]; the seventh and last was inscribed in the projecting angle near the letters IW.

The "stars," or candles, figured "by the number eight" on the East side of the schema: they illuminated the Circle of Communication and the seven small circles. A ninth candle was placed in the West, at the center of the Circle of Retreat.

In each of the two large circles was inscribed a "word," that is to say the secret name of a Sprit. Other words were drawn exteriorly; there were four there, facing the four cardinal points, around the Circle of Communication, and an indeterminate number around the Circle of Retreat.

The operant, after having lit the candles, recited the "seven Psalms of David," then prostrated seven times: first in IAB, then in MR, in WG, in R A P, in OZ, in IA, finally in IW. He then perfumed three times the Circle of Retreat; three times each the two small circles by MR and the two by WG; three times the Circle of Communication; three times each the two small circles by OZ and IA; four times the small circle by IW: "which made in all 28 strikes of censing, which produced the mysterious number of 10."[286]

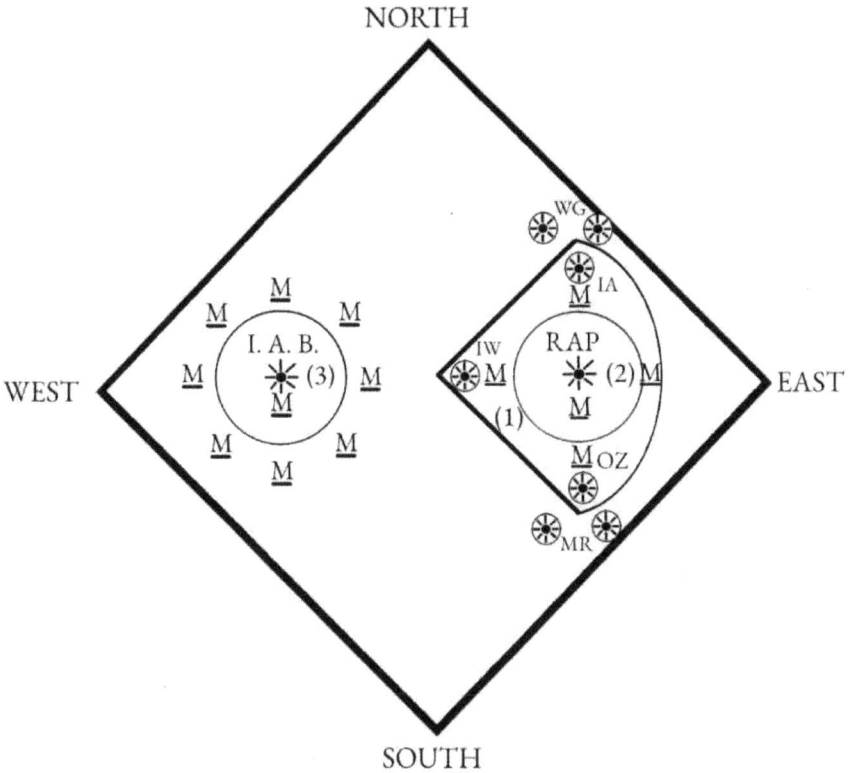

Legend: (1): Quarter Circle.
(2): Circle of Communication.
M: "Mots" [Words] that is to say, secret names or hieroglyphs representing the tutelary Spirits. The other initials not underlined represent the names of the Septenary Spirits.
The asterisks represent the "Stars" (candles) placed in the middle of the circles.

After the censing's, the operant extinguished the candles of the small circles after having each time pronounced the word inscribed beside each of them and then having erased it with his hand. he began with MR, continued with WG, passed to OZ and IA, to end at IW.

He then placed himself in the Circle of Communication, "kneeling on the right knee and the left knee high" and "raised," that is to say pronounced in a loud voice, then erased, the four words inscribed around the circle in starting from the West, to continue by the South, the North, and the East." These four raised words signify the four celestial regions and those which direct them spiritually."

Taking into hand, then, for illumination, the burning candle at the center of the Circle of Communication, he read the Invocations while holding himself straddled over the "word marked by the letter RAP." His reading finished, he erased this word, went to place himself standing upright in the Circle of Retreat, face turned toward the East, having between his legs the word marked by the letters IAB, after having "hidden" the candle from this circle, the only remaining lit; it is thus that he "made his observations."

At the moment he withdraws from the Chamber of Operation, he replaced the candle in the Circle of Retreat, "raised" the words written at the center and around the circle "with the same usages and ceremonies" as previously and lit a light with the candle of the Circle of Retreat which, "having there consecrated a word (because a word had been consecrated by him), had to be extinguished like the others, in order to perform the dismissal of the Spirit which is attached to it.

∴

The indications given by the correspondence on the ritual dating from 1772 are more clear, having been written by the pen of Saint-Martin, which did not stumble at each phrase like that of Pasqually.[287]

The layout is completely modified. It is composed, essentially, of three concentric circles, bearing the W at their common center and called respectively: Center Circle, Middle Circle, and Exterior Circle. Two rays, marked by punctuated lines, directed toward the South and stopping at the circumference of the Exterior Circle, delimit the "Southern part" and he had recommended to the operant "to trace faithfully this Southern part, without adding or taking away anything found between these two lines." The sides of the exterior circumference facing East, North, and West are bordered by four small circles called Circles of Correspondence. The three eastern, northern, and western quarters of each of the large circles bear four names of Spirits, accompanied respectively by the Denary, Octonary, Septenary, and Ternary and surmounted by hieroglyphs, or characters, of Patriarchs, Prophets and Apostles, "joined to the work in order to increase its (theurgic) strength and especially to contain the Evil." Above these signs the layout presents dotted lines indicating the place where the operant would inscribe in his drawing twelve names of Spirits, chosen freely by him either from the list of names of the Special Invocation, or from the alphabetical index of 2,400 mystical names which had been communicated to him[288], but with the reservation that each of these names had to be marked in the index by one of the sacred numbers (10, 8, 7, or 3) corresponding to that which accompanied the fundamental name, above which it had to be placed. The operant drew likewise from the index the four names that he inscribed in each of the Circles of Correspondence, while observing that all the names composing one of these four groups would begin with the letter and bear, in the index, the number inscribed, upon the layout, in the corresponding circle.

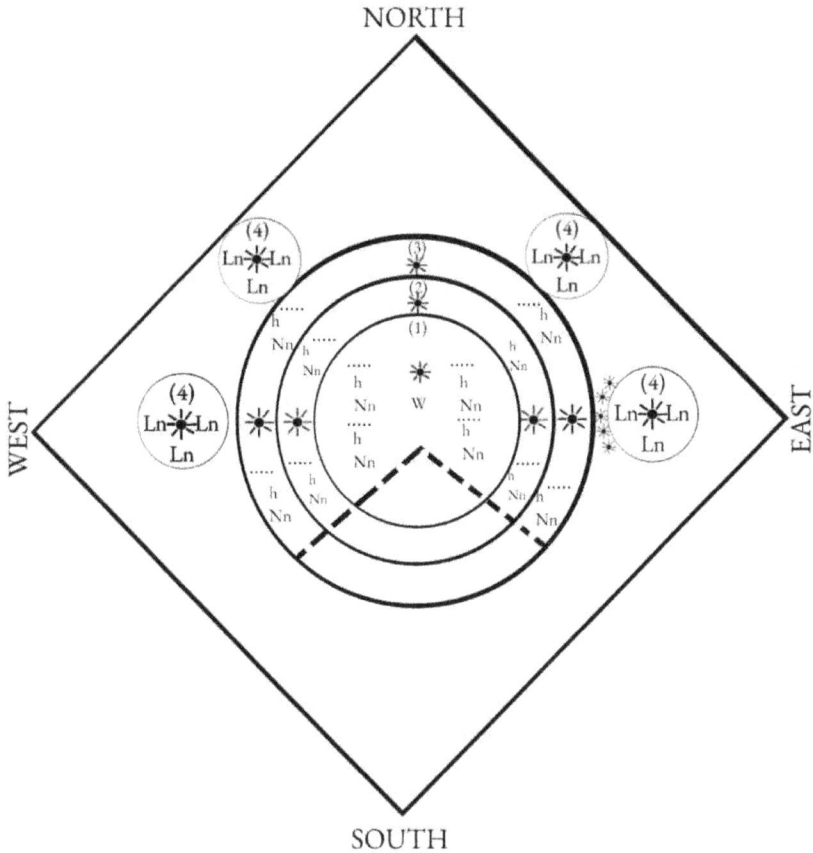

Legend: (1): Center Circle.
   (2): Middle Circle.
   (3): Exterior Circle
   h: Hieroglyphs or "characters" of
   the Patriarchs, Prophets, and Apostles.
   The points surrounded by rays
   represent the candles illuminating the circles.
   (4): Circle of Correspondence.
   Nn: Names of the Spirits accompanied
   by a Denary, Octonary, Septenary, or Ternary.
   Ln: Letter accompanied
   by a number by which had to begin the four
   names chosen from the index.
   The candles placed upon the Circle
   of Correspondence of the East are
   "the candles of the absent ones."

The illumination is composed of seventeen candles: seven in the Center Circle, one of which is over the W; three in the Middle Circle, three in the Exterior

Circle; one in each of the Circles of Correspondence. Furthermore, the "candle of the absent," placed on the side of the Eastern Circle of Correspondence facing the large circles, represents the Élus Coëns who, in their respective residences, engage in the Equinox Working at the same moment. There were as many candles as sympathetic operators.[289]

The operant made four prostrations in the following order: one toward the West, one toward the East, one toward the North, one toward the South. He "consecrated" (by censing) the four Circles of Correspondence following the ritual of the Work of the Four Circles[290], then, standing upright in the Center Circle, he invoked the twelve fundamental names, while having each of them followed by the name that he had joined to it on the tracing. He then pronounced a Particular Invocation, containing seven names that he drew at will from the Special Invocations and among "those of the Work"; among these names he chose "for chief" the one that he thought would be the most powerful, all while reserving the right to take, but only among the six other names already elected, another "chief," if the first "was no longer suitable" to him (that is to say, if the Operation of the preceding day had not led to "Passes").

These ceremonies finished, the operant placed himself in the Western vicinity of the Exterior Circle "for the contemplation of the passes."

∴

As important as were the ceremonies of the Operations: prostrations, censing, invocations by prayers and figures, they would nevertheless not be absolutely efficacious; they were indispensible but not sufficient. Three factors were indispensible to corroborate their action: the mystical virtue of the operant, a favorable astral influence, finally the assistance of divine grace.

The mystical virtue of the adept depended in its turn on three conditions: his state of grace, a supernatural faculty which was conferred on him by the ordination, and the sympathetic cooperation at a distance by his equals in initiation. "The precision of the ceremony does not suffice alone," wrote Pasqually in 1768 to Bacon de la Chevalerie, "it is still necessary to have an exactitude and a holiness of life by the authority who leads the intellectual circles of adoption (by the adept who wishes to enter into relations with the Spirits) there must be a spiritual preparation made by prayer, retreat, and 'moration'" (expectation).[291] The Élus Coëns had to observe a "rule of life" of a very evident ascetic character. It was forbidden him, "for his entire life," to consume the blood, fat, or kidneys from any animal at all and to eat the meat of domestic pigeons.[292] He was only able to indulge with an extreme moderation in the pleasures of the senses, for, in order to reach the supreme degree, he had to keep himself far from all impure matter, and above all from that of "fornication (sexual relations) which leads to dissention in the soul."[293] He observed a long period of fasting each equinox; he had imposed abstinence from food for eleven hours before every Operation, that is to say that after having dined precisely at noon, and getting up from the table at exactly one o'clock, he was no longer able to take food until after the Operation, which began at midnight. He had, nevertheless, permitted him to drink, if he felt the need, but only of water, coffee and liquor being severely prohibited.[294]

He had prescribed him to carry out certain acts of special devotion. On Thursday he had to sit in the office of the Holy Spirit, at any hour of the day. If he wished to gain the help particular to the Apostles, he was able in addition to recite on that day the Miserere Mei and the De Profundis, in the evening before going to bed. He recited the Miserere standing in the middle of his room, "face turned toward the corner facing the rising sun," then, in order to say the De Profundis, he "kneeled with his face prostrated to the ground." If he had the custom to recite another prayer currently in use, he was permitted to do it, but the devotions prescribed for Thursday were "of an indispensible order, just as the regulations of life."[295] He prepared himself for the Operations by a retreat, or "quarantine," which imposed upon him a type of life difficult to reconcile with the professional or mundane obligations of a man occupied with business or well known in society.[296]

The state of grace was the best defense against the attacks of demons. In order to avoid the danger, which the simple Invocations[297] did not present, of being "molested by the evil Spirits," the operant had at his disposal, it is true, powerful arms: the exconjurations and the triangular talisman that he called his shield. But these arms were without virtue if the Élu Coën decided to operate without being "perfectly pure." One of the principal disciples of Pasqually, Bacon de la Chevalerie, has left us evidence of the perils, which exposed also a grave imprudence. He had felt suddenly overwhelmed by an adversary of a strength superior to his own; "suffocated by an icy cold which rose from his feet to his heart, he saw himself close to annihilation, when luckily being rushed into the Circle of Retreat, it seemed to immerse him, by entering there, into a warm and delightful bath which returned his spirits and restored his strength."[298]

To the physical and mental preparation at the time had to be joined obligatorily, the virtue of ordination. It was necessary that the operant had been ordained Réau-Croix by three "Very Powerful Masters," that is to say by three Élus Coëns already furnished with this sacred character.

The ordination was conferred by three identical ceremonies, celebrated for three consecutive nights, and of which each had for officiant a different Very Powerful Master. The officiant traced the circles and made, "as many in prayers as in perfumes," the same liturgical acts as for an ordinary Operation, then he offered a "burnt offering of expiation." The victim was a goat's head, or, in its absence, that of a male lamb, clothed in its skin and hair. It was absolutely necessary that the head was black, "otherwise the burnt offering would be a thanksgiving and not expiation." The officiant prepared this head "just as one prepares the roebuck before slaughtering it," He set up three "new fires" in burners "conforming to the ancient usage where they brought grilled chests (whose base was in the form of a grill) to make the burnt offerings in the open countryside." Upon the fire placed at the North of the Chamber of Operation he put the head with the eyes, but without tongue or brain; he then placed the brain upon the fire of the South, and the tongue upon that of the West.[299]

When the flesh began to be consumed, the candidate kneeled on his right knee, threw three rather large grains of salt into each fire, and passed his hands three times over the flames of each one, as a sign of purification. He then recited a prayer, pronounced the "ineffable word" and "raised" (pronounced in a loud voice before erasing them) the characters, numbers, and hieroglyphs which had been, in the beginning of the ceremony, traced in front of the burners.[300]

After the burnt offering, which preceded all the other ceremonies, the candidate recited, in addition to the ordinary conjurations and invocations, special conjurations and invocations, then the officiant had him drink "the chalice in ceremony" and gave him to eat "the mystical or cementing bread," Finally the officiant carefully collected the ashes from the three fires and joined them to those provided by the preceding ordinations and of which a part had beforehand been given to him.

Once ordained, the new Réau-Croix left behind the title of Respectable Master in order to take that of Very Powerful Master[301]; he received a scapular and a talisman similar to those worn by his colleagues, and his name was inscribed "in the secret circumferences and the universal index of the Grand Sovereign."[302]

The mystical virtue of the Réau-Croix was reinforced by the sympathetic cooperation of his chief and his colleagues. The conjurations and invocations by which he repelled the evil Spirits and called the good ones only had all their efficacy if they were corroborated by the simultaneous conjurations and invocations of the other Réau-Croix. The collaboration of the head of the Order naturally constituted the most powerful aid. He was mystically represented by the candle which burned in the middle of the Quarter Circle and "that sole light was the symbol of his sympathetic presence at the Operations."[303] The ceremony of ordination could not be done without his assistance at a distance[304], and he renewed this formal ordination at every important Operation by sending to each Réau-Croix the mysterious influx capable of giving to the rites an irresistible force "against the evil demons and on the good beings."

But, as indispensible as was the assistance of the Master of the Élus Coëns, the support given by the other Réau-Croix to the Operations of each among them was no less necessary. The "candles of representation" placed, on the sketch of 1768, between the segment of the circle and the line of the arc, the "candles of the absent" figuring on the plan of 1772, realized mystically the presence of the other Réau-Croix who "operated" at the same moment, in communion of desire and intention with the officiant. The Réau-Croix were also regularly notified fifteen days in advance of an ordination, in order to be able to collaborate there across space.[305] Likewise, the success of the Operations depending in large part on their synchronism, Pasqually took care to give, at least eight hours in advance, all the necessary instructions, so that his disciples were able to "put themselves in order."[306] This previous agreement did not allow the first date indicated to be changed, whatever be the legitimacy of the scruples that incited one of the participants to solicit a postponement. Willermoz, having asked Pasqually on February 5, 1772, to delay for four days the Equinox Working prescribed for the following March 5, so that the preparatory retreat that he had to observe would not attract the attention of the profanes by obliging him to keep himself separate from the enjoyment of the Carnival, the Master had his secretary tell him that this postponement was impossible: "all the arrangements and all the orders were given for the 5th," the change caused a considerable trouble and "would perhaps put the remote Réau-Croix in jeopardy of missing the period set for the works which ought to be done in concert."[307]

Moreover, the date of the Operation was not able to be changed for another reason, and far more pressing, namely that it was determined by astrological circumstances. The moment when the Operation takes place is of primary importance because, calculated exactly, it brings to the officiant the assistance of a favorable astral influx. This is one of the points of doctrine upon which he expresses himself most clearly: "All these things (Invocations, Conjurations, Operations)," he said, "are given with precision of hour, days, week, moon, months and years"; so that "an Operation of principle (in principle an Operation) outside of its time is without fruit," also "it is only in following scrupulously what is prescribed to us by God that one may even hope for success in his works.[308]

To the astral influence is added, to determine irrevocably the date of the Operations, that of the numbers. Pasqually took notice that, if he had chosen May 11, 12, and 13 for the ordination of Willermoz, it is not only in order "to meet with (agree with) the days relative to the seasonable lapse," but above all because the mystical addition of 11, that is to say 1+1, gives 2, "number of confusion" (evil influences that the exconjurations must remove), that of 12 gives 3, "terrestrial and corporeal number" (material elements of the Operation), and that of 13 gives 4, "number of power" (over the Spirits).[309]

∴

Nevertheless, if the success of the Operations depends at the time on the scrupulous observation of the ritual, on the ordination, on the physical and mental purity of the officiant, three elements by which "the effect is increased without doubt (certainly) in the course of time, by the instructions and thanks to what each may bring there,"[310] if it depends also on the assistance of the Master and of the adepts, as well as the influence of the stars and numbers, the Élu Coën must not forget that the divinity remains ever free to refuse a favor of which it is, in the final analysis, the supreme dispensator. Pasqually has need to recall often, whether directly or by the pen of his secretary, this essential principle to his disciples disappointed by the negative result of their Operations. He points out to them "that it is not in man's power to satisfy entirely on this subject, and that to God alone belongs this sublime operation,"[311] that "even when we believe ourselves in the best state, when all the ceremonies are employed with the greatest regularity, la Chose [the Thing] may still keep its veil for us as much as it pleases it, it is so little to the disposition of man that he may never, despite his efforts, be certain to obtain it."[312]

∴

As strange as the practices of the Élus Coëns may have seemed to us up to here, we do not yet know their most remarkable character. What indeed classifies them apart among the traditional magical ceremonies, with which one may be tempted to confuse them, are the ends in sight for which they have been conceived and ordained. Ritual, rule of life, ordination, sympathetic cooperation, and astral influence are the means converging towards a precise goal: the "work" aims to obtain a result in which the adepts see the supreme reward of their asceticism, their devotions, and their vigils. An Operation is less an act of faith, adoration, or even propitiation, as an experiment in the scientific sense of the term. The object of this experiment is the production of a phenomenon, that we have already seen indicated under the mysterious name of "Pass" and that the most intimate confidant of Pasqually comes to present to us as the supernatural revelation of a "Thing" ordinarily hidden under a veil that the divinity consents from time to time to let raise by the initiates. To know the method and the implications of this revelation, is to have the key of the theosophical system of the Élus Coëns.

CHAPTER IV
Nature and significance of the "Passes"

The adepts have never spoken but in covered words on the aim and nature of their "Operations," of the results that they expected or believed to obtain, or the supernatural powers to which they addressed themselves. For love of secrecy, and perhaps also restrained by a sort of religious fear which dares not express the object of its worship, they designate under the conventional and vague name of "la Chose" [the Thing] the workings as well as the manifestations of the mysterious being that they invoke, and those beings themselves. Nevertheless, in reading attentively the correspondence of the initiates, in noting the secrets escaped from some among them, one succeeds at raising, in part, the curtain that hides the sanctuary.

An Operation had as its final goal to bring about a manifestation of a supernatural order. This essentially momentary and fleeting moment, called for this reason a "Pass" in the language of the adepts, affected in different fashions the senses of the operant. He felt "goosebumps all over his body,"[313] "which announces the principle of the traction that la Chose exercised over the one working,"[314] or he heard sounds, or better yet he saw sparks and flashes.[315] Saint-Martin insists particularly, in his instructions given to the adept of Lyon, Willermoz, on behalf of the Master, on the auditory and visual phenomena. He recommends to him to never let slip "what strikes your senses of sight and hearing."[316] The operant, therefore, had to take care, so as not to be surprised by "the promptness of the pass,"[317] to watch for all that came to strike, even in the most vague and brief fashion, his ear or his eyes and to repeat itself, so as to stretch unto its extreme limit the scope of attention, that "we are often only as deaf and blind as we believe to be"[318]; the visual phenomena were nevertheless the most frequent and, in general, "the manifestation operated itself sensibly by the vision."[319] It seems even that the goosebumps and the mysterious sounds were only indicated as consolation vouchers for the adepts who never saw anything.[320] The abbé Fournié, who was one of the more favored operants, teaches us on the faith of his own experience that Pasqually had the gift to "confirm" his teachings by "exterior" visions, at first vague and as rapid as a lightning flash, then more and more distinct and prolonged.[321] According to the Master himself, these flashes could be colored variously: "white, blue, clear white-red, of mixed color or all white, color of a white candle."[322] It is in order to allow them to be seen that, at the end of the Operation, the candle placed in the West, outside the Quarter Circle, was withdrawn and even a little obscured. The semi-darkness allowed "their liberty to the things which must appear free from all elementary (material) light, seeing that the things bear within themselves their brightness, be it white, red or otherwise.[323]

What adepts have perceived, or at least had believed they perceived, like luminous manifestations, is what affirmed, outside the declarations of Pasqually himself, "certificates signed by some among them: the Marquis d'Hauterive, the captain of artillery Defore, the Baron Calvimont, the stockholder from Bordeaux Defournier, the "venerable Brothers" Tabory, Schild, and Marcadi. These "emulators" (disciples), particularly favored by "la Chose," had, before even arriving at the supreme degree of initiation, but, it is true, "set in order," some similar visions "day and night, without light nor candle, nor any other fire."[324]

These fleeting flashes were considered the manifestation of a Spirit who responded to the call of the operant. The form that they were fond of was compared to that of the hieroglyphs traced on the floor of the Chamber of Operation.[325] If concordance was established, or supposed, the operant assessed that "la Chose," yielding to his supplications and allowing itself to be compelled by the ceremonies and formulas of the Operation, had, just as he demanded of it in the Invocation, "repeated" one of the mystical signs representing the prophets and the apostles from whom he had particularly solicited the intercession, that is to say that one of the mediators had appeared to him, in the space of a lightning flash, under its "glorious" form.

The interpretation of the Passes was the most important and the most delicate part of the work of the Élus Coëns.[326] He had taught them indeed that the evocation could attract evil Spirits, always ready to torment or dupe the Spiritual Minors. The "Demonic Chief, whose whole task is to submit the Minors to his dark laws and to have them appear to them as clean and clear as those that the Creator has put in his creation,"[327] employed against them "his general demonic intellect" (exerting himself over physical nature). "By his word of commandment, he insinuated this evil spirit along with its adherent Spirits (subordinates), who then communicated it to the Minors that the Prince of the demons seeks ceaselessly to seduce and to submit to his laws."[328] Moses himself had not been sheltered from his snares: the three Mages of Egypt, "who only gave themselves to the demonic operations," "fought continually the spiritual power of Moses, and they did not cease to oppose his spiritual works unto the ninth operation, which he performed for the glory of the Creator. This repetition of operation on the part of the Mages (this obstinance to thwart the efforts of the Spiritual Elect) did not leave Moses alarmed nor even shake his great faith that he had in the Creator," and it was only in the course of the tenth operation that he succeeded in triumphing over his demonic adversaries.[329]

The demon held without respite to win to his cult the Minors, as he had done with Jacob, with Nimrod who "delivered himself to Babylon for iniquitous operations."[330] His hellhounds strove "to lead the operant into great error," by "amazing him with illusory things or sophisticated remarks."[331] Using the stratagem which had already served the rebel Spirits in order to dupe Adam by presenting themselves to him "under the apparent form of a body of glory"[332]and by the example of the four Sages (magicians) of Egypt who, by the confession of Moses, "had done the same things as him in his first four Operations,"[333] they could produce a false Pass, a luminous phenomenon that the operant, for want of suitable interpretation of what he had seen, took it for a manifestation of a "good Spirit."

Even when the divine Spirits were the authors of the manifestations, it is important, in order to estimate the proper value of the reward granted to the works of the operant, to distinguish whether the luminous phenomenon had been produced by Spirits of the supercelestial or celestial themselves, or simply by the Spirits inferior to their orders, that is to say, to use the language of the initiates, whether the "glorious form" glimpsed had been assumed by a Spirit of the superior spheres or by an inhabitant of the elementary sphere.

The Élu Coën had to know indeed that there existed two types of "glorious form." The first, "apparent form of figure that the Spirit conceived and gave birth to according to its needs and according to the orders that it received from the Creator, a form as promptly reintegrated (dispersed) as it was begotten by the Spirit," was not "subject to any elementary influence whatever, it was not susceptible to any nutriment and no particle of the central fire acted upon it."[334] "The glorious form does not control the Minor Spirit or other Spirit in divine privation, since it is, like the Minor and like every other Spirit, delegated by the Eternal to manifest among men, and sometimes when it pleases the Creator, the glory of this divine being,"[335] Such was the nature of the cloud that had served as bulwark and guide to the errant Israelites in the desert: it "was an apparent body produced by the action of an infinite multitude of pure and simple Spirits, which were an aspect of the divine creative Spirit come out (sent) by the Eternal (out of) the denary circle. This divine Spirit marched before Israel as a column of fire, and the column of cloud followed its trail with precision and exactitude, according to the laws of order, that the divine Spirit operated upon all these Spirits conforming to the will of the Creator on behalf of Israel and to the detriment of the demons. This cloud, being formed by the power of the Spirits without the help of any matter, was a true body of glory."[336]

This immaterial fire, which owed nothing to the terrestrial elements since the Spirits of the supercelestial and celestial drew it from their own divine fire,[337] had been before the fall of Adam the "corporeal glorious form of the First Man that he had the faculty to construct, to dissipate, to change at will according to the actions that he had to carry out conforming to the orders that he received from the Creator." It was the garment with which were covered the spiritual inhabitants of the supercelestial and celestial in order to manifest itself to the Minor because "without this envelope, they could never operate on the other temporal beings without consuming them by the innate faculty of the pure Spirit to dissolve all that approaches it."[338] The supernatural light had a purifying virtue: "However righteous be the Minor before the Creator, it must always be purified by the spiritual fire of the filth that it contracted through its stay in a form of matter, even if it had rejected all the attacks that the evil intellect had wished to bring upon it."[339]

The second "glorious form" was, on the contrary, the garment of the Spirits of the central axis which could draw from their fire the three fundamental essences, constitutive of matter, and to thus produce a luminous form. These apparitions had much less value than those of the first category, for the Spirits of the central axis, "simple subjects" of the superior Spirits, manifested themselves on the order of the latter, when the Spirits of the two more elevated circles did not deign to appear in person; but, on the other hand, they were easier to identify because the Spirits of the central axis "could only operate a single form," whereas the spiritual beings inhabiting the three superior worlds could "produce new forms at each instant and vary to infinity."[340]

∴

By what processes the Élus Coëns succeeded, in principle, in determining whether the Spirit of which they determined to have constituted a manifestation was a demon, an elementary Spirit, "a distinct and spiritual being or a particular septenary Spirit that the Creator has subjected to the powerful virtue of the minor quaternary Spirit,"[341] or better yet one of the Spiritual Elect, prophets, or apostles, whose hieroglyphs and characters were traced in the Quarter Circle and could be "rendered," that is to say reproduced by the Passes[342], the known documents do not reveal to us. They are likewise silent on the usual results of the interpretation, but, in confronting what we know of the aim and anticipated results of the Operations with the esoteric doctrines and interpretations of the biblical texts contained in the Reintegration, we are able at least to succeed in giving a likely solution to the problems that the treatise poses, to complete the information furnished by the correspondence of the adepts on the Operations themselves, and to thus give us an idea, as far as we are allowed to conceive, of the occultist system of the Élus Coëns.

The "reconciliation" is the preparatory stage, and obligatory, to the "regeneration." This latter is, properly speaking, the return of the Minor into the supercelestial[343], where he will see himself "reintegrated into the first properties, virtues, and spiritual powers" granted to Adam at the moment of his emanation[344]; it will only be the share of those among the Spiritual Minors who will have been previously "reconciled," that is to say restored into communication with the divinity and come out of the state of "privation" where the fall of the First Man has plunged all his posterity.

The reconciliation begins "at the sensible circle" or "minor circle," abode of the fallen man (the earth). It draws itself, after the terrestrial death of the Minor, into the "visual circle" or "intellect circle," dwelling of the Spirits who communicated to him during his life here below "the good intellect" or "the evil intellect." Indeed, "it does not suffice for the reintegration of the beings reconciled from time that they act and operate in the sensible terrestrial circle. They must by all necessity act spiritually in all the spaces of the universal circle, until they have finished the course that the Creator has fixed for the Minors in emanating them from him and in emancipating them from his divine immensity."[345] Finally the Minor arrives in the "rational circle" or "major circle," where reside the septenary Spirits; here he "rests in the shade (under the protection) of his reconciliation," having recovered the state of innocent Adam. This is what is indicated by the symbol of Noah's Ark: "the rational Minors (endowed with reason, that is to say men) who were enclosed in the ark and the time that they remained in privation of the elementary light represents to us the withdrawal of the reconciled Minors and of the Just under the shadows of the great light where they effectively rest for a space of time in waiting, no longer having in them to operate any temporal action."[346] Thus re-established in his original dignity, after having "payed tribute to divine justice by his different courses of operation in the three sensible, visual, and rational circles," the Minor awaited "the end of time," that is to say the final annihilation of the worlds returning to the source from which they were emanated, revolution in the course of which "the First Man and his posterity would be reintegrated into the divine circle."[347]

This definitive reintegration, which is equivalent to the disappearance of every objective and individual existence, presents for the Minor much less interest than that which has restored him first into the major circle, since this latter constitutes the sum of bliss that may be promised to the Spiritual Minor.[348] It is therefore the logical aim of his activity here below[349] and, as it has reconciliation as its necessary condition and guarantee, it is to that that it must devote all its attention and cares.

The first stage of reconciliation, that which has for its theater the sensible circle and is thus accomplished during the terrestrial life, has for its sign the manifestation of a spiritual being which reveals its presence by sensations such as goosebumps, noises, and above all flashes variously colored and assuming forms more or less distinct. The supernatural being who announces thus to the Spiritual Minor that he is come out of his "state of privation," is called the "Reconciler." The role of reconciler may be played by beings of different essence. It was at first a Spiritual Major Being that the Eternal sent after the Patriarchs and "whose nature they were only able to ascertain by the different spiritual operations that this Spirit operated himself among these Minors reconciled and not yet regenerated."[350] The Patriarchs, after their reintegration, have become in their turn Reconcilers, particularly those who, like Abraham, Isaac, and Jacob, had been during their terrestrial life in communication with the divinity by the intermediary of a celestial envoy[351] and to whom the Eternal had given the double power accorded originally to Adam in order to triumph over the prevaricating Spirits.[352] The Reconciler may be finally one of the Hebrew prophets that God inspired directly or one of the ten Elect Minors who, at different epochs, have reconciled the people of Israel with Jehovah. Patriarchs, Prophets, and Elect Minors fulfill presently, with the Spiritual Minors, the function they performed in relation to the Hebrews in biblical times: by inscribing their names or their hieroglyphs in the Quarter Circle of the Chamber of Operation, the Élus Coëns call on their intercession.

It is evident, although Pasqually never seems to have realized it, that these ancient Minors were only deputy Reconcilers, as were, as we have just seen, the Spirits of the central axis, the true Reconciler being a Major Spirit or "Being of double power, which will have eternally to operate its powerful faculties in the different classes where will be placed the first and the last sanctified and reconciled."[353] The task assigned to the Reconciling Spirit was so important that instead of being, as the other superior Spirits, "returned to his state of stability in the divine immensity, as he was before the creation," when the material world would come to disappear, "this being will be eternally occupied with operating his double power towards the classes of Spirits which will be distinguished in all eternity (which will remain distinct until the final reintegration), namely: the first just sanctified Spirits and the Spirits who will only be sanctified and reconciled last" (in the visual circle).[354] But, if the Major Spirit alone had to remain to carry out the reconciliation in the visual circle after the dissolution of the sensible circle, it seems that he had been authorized to make himself often represented in this last circle by the elementary Spirits and regenerated Minors. In any case, although the distinction made between the two glorious forms establishes degrees in the favor granted by "la Chose" to the operant, the mystical value of the reconciliation does not appear to have depended absolutely on the nature of the being that manifested itself.

By their "pass" the Reconcilers, whatever they be, make known to the operant that he is indeed a Spiritual Minor, and they transmit to him at the same time the gifts that they have received from the Eternal, or to use the mystical term, they imprint upon him a "seal" which, "invisible to corporeal man," is nevertheless "the temporal action of reconciliation"[355] and lacking which, no Minor may be reconciled. "This seal was sent to them (to the Just and Spiritual Elect) visibly and without any mystery on the use that they would have to make of it on behalf of those who had to receive it."[356] In appearing to Cain and his sister after the murder of Abel, the angel "marked them (symbolically) on the forehead with the invincible seal of the divinity, which announced to one another that they had obtained the mercy of the Creator and that they enjoyed again a time of divine spiritual nourishment (communication with the divine) which had been withdrawn from them in relation to (because of) their crime."[357]

This seal is the Octonary, the mystical Eight, number of the double divine power, number that the Creator "has destined to the Spiritual Elect that he wishes to favor and to appoint by the manifestation of his glory"[358] and by which the Reconcilers themselves are marked, for it is by this number that have been all the successive reconciliations.[359]

We see now what importance the Passes must have had to the eyes of the Élu Coën, since supernatural phenomenon obtained by an Operation is the seal, obligatory mark of salvation, and what the Spiritual Minors alone could receive, contained as the other men "in the form of matter created by Adam" and like them "subjugated in a frightful prison of darkness," but condemned only to a "limited privation"[360] of which the sign of reconciliation announced the end. Thus, the door of salvation opened itself before the operant, witness to an authentic Pass; the flash that he had seen was the announcement and the promise of the form of glory that he would don one day. He knew henceforth that, "reconciled" here below, he was able after his terrestrial death to achieve in the "intellect circle" his reconciliation "by the force of a more prolonged spiritual operation called by the initiates reaction of operation (redoubling of operation)[361] and to be finally reintegrated into the glorious state where the First Man found himself before his downfall. The legitimate hopes that give rise in him to the success of an Operation would only incite him to renew an experiment whose favorable results would confirm the indications given by the first manifestation.[362]

∴

There is no doubt that the Operations had been for the disciples of Pasqually the grand affair and raison d'être of their secret association. The treatise on the Reintegration has for its principal object to give them a theoretical base; its cosmogony and anthropology aim before all at justifying them in principle. When one re-reads it in the light of what the correspondence of the adepts on their works teaches us, many obscure passages are illuminated, and the allusions, until then veiled by the emphatic style and barbarous language of the hierophant, are specified with every desirable clarity.

The most prominent trait of the mysticism of the Élus Coëns is, if one considers the means employed by them in order to obtain a response to the question that they posed to the divinity, its specifically theurgical character. Every mystic seeks, by definition, to enter into rapport with the transcendent world, but, just as there are in the relations that man maintains with the divine a cult of latria and a cult of dulia, there exists an ecstatic mysticism, which shoots all right towards God, and a theurgical mysticism, which addresses him by the intermediary of secondary powers, Spirits subordinate to the First Cause. Ecstatic mysticism, more ambitious in appearance in proportion to its aim than it suggests, is in fact less demanding, because it does not encroach upon the indefeasible rights of divine omnipotence and expects simply a grace, humbly solicited and that he strives to merit by the fervor of his faith and the ardor of his love, the direct communication to which he aspires. Theurgical mysticism, on the contrary, all while proclaiming most strongly its unreserved submission to the divine will, claims no less, by means of compulsion, which are magical processes, to force the Spirits, agents, and emissaries of the divinity, to obey the human creature, which would only be in order to show itself to him. It is this genre of mysticism that the Élus Coëns cultivate.

The treatise on the Reintegration refuses to the Minor, even to the Spiritual Minor, the faculty of communicating directly with God, It professes that, since the fall of Adam, "man is no longer in sight of the divinity"[363] and it specifies that the Denary, number of the divine omnipotence, "is able to be operated only by the Creator," so that "no Sage (initiate) has made use of this number, reserving it always with respect to the Divinity."[364] Pasqually places, it is true, the intuitive knowledge, or "inner way" of the pure mystics, above what one obtains with the help of the sense, or "external way," and which is the anticipated result of the Operations. He ranks ecstasy among "the divine spiritual operations": "separation and suspension which comes to the soul when it contemplates the Spirit, because the body of matter may not have any part in what is operated between the Minor and the Divine Spirit."[365] When Moses is prostrated upon Sinai, his soul is "suspended from his body and is become true thinking being. In this state his spiritual being received the orders that the Creator gave him face to face."[366] Pasqually even goes on to rank in the category of ecstatic visions certain communications of a superior order which, although only putting in play intermediary Spirits, amounts to the inner way, for they do not consist of sensible manifestations, do not require ceremonies, and do not depend in any way upon human will. Indeed, if "Spirits susceptible to divine operations with the Minor are all those which reside from the supercelestial world unto the ends of all the temporal worlds,"[367] those of the supercelestial "operating and acting upon all that exists spiritually, are not held back by the boundaries of the universe and, not having by them any limit of matter, one may not subjugate them or assign them to any elementary region."[368] To enter into relations with the "pure Spirits of the supercelestial," that is to say with those who are nearer to God, is "to take up direct communication with the Eternal." To say that Moses penetrated into the Tabernacle by the door of the East when "he operated a part of the action of the inhabitants of the supercelestial without the mixture of action with any other Spirit," signifies, since the door of the East is none other than the heart of the Minor, that the Spirits of the supercelestial communicate with him by the inner way. Now, "it is through the heart that the Minor receives the greatest satisfaction as well as the greatest favors that the Creator sends him directly by the inhabitants of the supercelestial." The heart, or door of the East, is superior to the ear, "organ of conception" (intelligence of the divine laws by oral tradition) and the door of the West, that is to say the eye, "organ of conviction" (as witness to the Passes).[369]

But Pasqually considers the "ecstasies of divine contemplation" as well as the communications with the Spirits of the supercelestial, as the privilege of those who "have confirmed to us their reality," the prerogative of the "sages and strong elect of the Creator," that is to say of a very rare elite.[370] The inner way has been practiced by Abel "who strove ceaselessly to address to the Creator spiritual cults which amazed his whole family" and which were "the actual type of that which the Creator would await from his First Minor"[371]; by the four elders of the second posterity of Noah, who practiced "a spiritual cult"[372] or "great divine cult which was reserved to them,"[373] by the seven principal disciples of the spiritual professors of the second generation after Noah, "who were always reserved for the great cult"[374]; by Enoch, by the ten Spiritual Elect, particularly by Moses, "whose fear and labor were infinitely more considerable for this kind of operation," who nevertheless, as it is indicated for the spiritual operation of Abel, lasted "only an hour of time," for it did not include all the apparatus and ceremonial of the temporal spiritual operations.[375]

The Spiritual Minor, whatever be his zeal and the virtue of his ordination of Réau-Croix, cannot aspire to similar privileges. All that he has the right to expect from the pure Spirits of the supercelestial, is that they deign to enter into his tabernacle by the East door, in order to "dispose him to receive and support the effects of all the divine spiritual operations which are made there conjointly with the Minor." Thus fortified by divine grace, he addressed himself to the Spirits of the celestial as did Moses in his second genre of operations "in leaving open the door facing the celestial region of the chief to whom he had need to address himself," that is to say in utilizing, in order to "assign" the Spirits and to oblige them to manifest themselves, the astral influence represented in the symbol of the Tabernacle by the four doors, which are "the true figures of the four spiritual powers that the Creator has given to his Minor and by which he may make use of those of the four regionary chiefs (Spirits residing at the four sections of the horizon) and of all that is at their dependence." For "the key of the doors of the Tabernacle is the Spirit which keeps watch at each of them and who alone is able to open it for or against the advantage of the Minor. But, if the Minor is not able to open these doors himself, he can have them opened and closed when it pleases him."[376]

The success of a temporal spiritual operation, characterized by a phenomenon falling under the control of the senses, depends therefore on three factors: the consent of the Creator, the intervention of a Major Spirit, and finally the action exercised by the will of the operant over the being that he invokes. It is this that proves the reconciliation of the First Minor who has operated by the help of the intention of the Father, of the will of the intermediary Spirit, and of the word of Adam.[377]

The liberty of the Father and of the inhabitants of the denary circle being thus safeguarded, the treatise on the Reintegration accords to the Minor an effective authority over the Spirits of the other circles since the Creator, although restoring to Adam only a power inferior to that which he possessed before his crime, has nevertheless granted him "powers for or against every created being"[378] and that "there is no distinction to be made there in between the subjection in which the Minor holds the good Spirits and that in which he holds the evil Spirits."[379] It was not only to encourage the disciples who despaired to see arrive "their time and their success" that Pasqually told them, in alluding to the Spirits that they invoked without success: "For finally man is their master!"[380] His treatise asserts expressly that "man may sometimes come out, were it not for the lack of time, from the privation of the quaternary power (authority over the Spirits) of which he has been deprived by the prevarication of Adam for the duration of his temporal course,"[381] which amounts to saying that the Operations of the Élus Coëns are able to return to them, at least temporarily, the faculty to command the Spirits, which is essentially the aim of theurgical magic.

CHAPTER V
The Operations and the Divine Cult

In his treatise on the Reintegration, Pasqually does not only teach an economy of salvation for the use of the "men of desire," he also attempts to do the work of an historian by presenting the secret cult practiced by the Élus Coëns as the sole positive religion having existed in spirit and in truth from the origins of humanity, and whose traces are found in the most ancient and venerable documents. This *disciplina arcani* is concerned yet with two other points of view on the history of civilization: it is the common source from where the first peoples have drawn the laws organizing social life, and it unites, in a bold synthesis, the adoration of an all-spiritual God with respect to the astrological tradition of ancient Asia.

The Operations in which the Élus Coëns engage are the authentic form, but known by the initiates alone, of the true divine cult, whose final aim is to produce "the spiritual fruits provided by the temporal spiritual operations,"[382] that is to say to make appear "the Spirit that the Sage (initiate) subjugates by the force of his operation."[383] The ten "cults" (ceremonial rituals) of which is comprised the divine service contribute to the three principal aims which are essentially those pursued by the Operations. The "cults of expiation" and "of particular general grace" must appease the Creator and attract his benevolence upon the humans, of which the operant take's part, and upon the earth where he presently resides. The "cults against the demons," "of preservation,"[384] "against war," "to oppose the enemies of divine law," remove the perverse Spirits. The cults "to cause the descent of the divine Spirit," "of faith and perseverance in the divine spiritual virtue," "to fix the divine conciliating Spirit with oneself," "annual or of dedication of all the operations to the Creator" have for their aim to obtain the manifestations.[385] The struggle of Moses, endowed with "spiritual power," against the three Mages of Egypt, who, in the presence of the Pharaoh (type of the prince of the demons), are ceaselessly opposed to the "spiritual works" of the Reconciler of the Hebrews "unto the ninth operation that he made for the glory of the Creator," teaches us that "the true cult of the Creator, as well as the ceremonial, has always remained among the men of the earth and that it will remain there until the end of the ages. But the weakness and iniquity of men has often made them abandon this divine knowledge, so as to engage only in that of matter, and this is what the three Mages of Egypt, who give themselves only to the demonic operations, represent to us."[386]

The true cult is essentially the putting of human beings in touch with the divine Spirits, for "the Creator has established the immensity of the supercelestial to fix the order and the ceremonial laws that the emancipated Spirits have to carry out in the whole expanse of the three temporal worlds in correspondence with the Spirits emanated from the divine immensity."[387] But this cult is not able to be entirely spiritual, because the fallen Minor is forced to resort to matter in order to communicate with the Spirits: "the cult that man would have had to fulfill in his state of glory being established only to one sole end (being uniquely an intellectual communion with God) would have been all spiritual, whereas the one that the Creator demands today from his temporal creature is to two ends (has two characters): the one temporal, the other spiritual."[388] The Operations are therefore in part spiritual by their aim, which is to put one in touch with a Spirit, and also by the fervor with which the man of desire is animated, they are, from this point of view the "actually type of the cult that the Creator would expect from his first Minor"[389]; but they are in part temporal (material), seeing that the Minor is only able to know the divine Spirit through the intermediary of sensible manifestations and following ritual ceremonies where the elements and the bodies: fire, lustral water, air agitated by the voice of the operant or charged with perfumes, chalk serving to trace the geometric figures and hieroglyphs, gestures of defense or propitiation, prostrations, and burnt offerings play an obligatory role.[390]

The Bible, interpreted and completed by the Master of the Élus Coëns, teaches us how the true divine cult has been revealed and transmitted by secret tradition. The ceremonial of the Operations has been taught to the Spiritual Minors by the Elect, who have received divine inspiration or to whom God has sent his instructions by the channel of a celestial emissary and who have proved the reality of their mission by the supernatural manifestations that they were capable of bringing about. For example, when Abel celebrated the divine cult at the same time as his brothers, the "signs" came only to him; Abel has, consequently, instructed his father Adam.[391] Seth has transmitted to his son Enos "every ceremony of divine spiritual and terrestrial operation."[392] Enoch, from the seventh generation after Seth and which must not be confused with Henoch, son of Cain and founder of the town that bore his name, was "the grand type of the ceremonial and of the divine cult among men past," Son of Jared or Ared, whose name signifies: "Man illuminated by God," he was "none other than a holy Spirit under a form of apparent matter." He constituted a body of initiates that he chose among the descendants of Seth and of Enos and with which he forbade any alliance with the "children of men," that is to say the descendants of Cain. He prescribed to his disciples "a ceremonial and a rule of life in order to be able to invoke the Eternal in holiness."[393] The seven Elect Minors of the second posterity of Noah, which "was truly a posterity of God in which it was conceived, just as had been Abel, without the excess of the senses of matter," so that the descendants of Noah who made up part of it were called by him "Man-Gods of the earth," "were only occupied with the divine operations which aimed at the greater glory of the Creator" (manifestations) and received "all the immutable laws of order that they would have to observe later on in their different operations."[394] Charged to re-establish the divine cult upon the earth after the deluge, they formed an elite among the reborn humanity. Not having had "any part or portion of the earth," "true thinkers with the divinity alone" (in direct communication with God himself), they only operated spiritual works and, although enclosed within a corporeal form, they enjoyed the same virtues and the same powers (power of commandment over the Spirits, good or evil) that Adam enjoyed in his state of glory."

The four born first among the seven brothers, whose complete number represents the Septenary Spirits, formed the group of the privileged Elect submitted to a rigorous asceticism. Entirely devoted to the cult of the Creator, they did not take wives. The divine cult that they practiced "was governed in a fashion different and superior to the cult established by their predecessors, which was a mixed cult of the spiritual and of terrestrial matter," therefore "their conduct in all the spiritual operations is a mystery for the temporal terrestrial men who are occupied only with the cult of the earth."[395] The three final brothers were the doctors of a cult adapted to the coarser nature of the Minors. They did not participate in "the operation of the great divine cult" (intellectual communication with the divinity or with the Spirits of the divine circle) which was reserved to their four elder brothers. There were "two cults to operate: the one temporal terrestrial and the other spiritual simple."[396] After having received the necessary instructions and "being assured of the will of the Creator by their divine spiritual operations" (after having obtained manifestations), they went to evangelize the three terrestrial regions: West, South, and North, inhabited by the descendants of Shem, Ham, and Japhet.[397] These ignorant Minors knew only "that there existed an all-powerful being above every created thing" and they called him "Abavin 8," which meant in their language: "doubly strong Spirit by which the Creator has operated everything" (the Demiurge).[398] The three missionaries "perpetuated among their brothers the ceremonial of the divine cult"[399] and they "operated such great marvels among these peoples (manifestations obtained by the Operations) that they had no difficulty in instructing them," but they began by preaching to them "a purely temporal doctrine" (historical religion, namely the cult of Jehovah), in order to put it within their reach and to elevate them then from the temporal cult to the spiritual cult.[400] Finally "they have them observe the meditations, the prayers, and the ceremonial suitable to prepare themselves for the different operations that they had to perform."[401]

When the posterity of Noah and that of the three missionaries had become too numerous, each of these latter gave to one of his sons, "by order of the Creator," "the divine spiritual instruction on the different cults, the final (supreme) ordination, and the spiritual benediction"[402] and "made clearly recognized (by a successful Operation) the virtues and powers which they were granted by the Eternal." The three new Sages chose the seven most zealous subjects and set them to work on the operations of the divine cult, as the duty and the right of these chiefs was to make a spiritual election,"[403]

After this era were presented other "successors, spiritual professors," who were aroused by God like the former ones. Their posterity increasing more and more in the three parts of the earth, the three new chiefs each chose twenty-one subjects, for a total of sixty-three. "The seven principal operants were always reserved for the great cult on both sides (in each region) and the fourteen subjects who remained were destined for the spiritual instruction of the people,"[404]

The tradition of the true divine cult was nearly interrupted by the prevarication of Jacob and his children who allowed themselves to be led astray by their material prosperity. The Prince of Demons persuaded Jacob to render to him a cult. The Patriarch studied "the natural demonic sciences"; he resolved to "reduce them in practice and to operate them."[405] He invoked the Demon at the setting of the sun upon Mount Moriah or Mahanaim, whose first name is composed of "Mor," that is to say: "destruction of corporeal apparent forms" (sensible), and "iah," which signifies: "vision of the Creator," and whose second is equivalent to: "the two camps," that of the demons and that of God. Scarcely had Jacob made his invocation that the Lord caused to appear to him an angel under the form of a man. Irritated by the reproaches with which the angel overwhelmed him, Jacob threw himself upon the divine messenger and began a fight that lasted all night and from which he came out lame. He then repented for his prevarication. To respond to his supplications and "in view of a perfect reconciliation," the Lord sent him a "natural vision (that Jacob perceived with his eyes) which offered itself to him under a human form." This Spirit taught Jacob "the means to obtain from the Creator what he requested, blessed him truly, and ordained him anew."[406] The Patriarch was "restored in divine spiritual power to operate after his ordination the different divine cults." He nevertheless had imposed upon him a penitence of forty years. At the expiation of this period of "privation" he returned to Mount Moriah at the sixth hour and, "having prepared everything for his operation, (traced the circles and the figures), he remade his prayer from the sixth hour unto around half the night. Then he made the necessary invocations to definitively stop the effects of the justice that the Creator had had him threatened with by his angel (exconjuration of the demons). He succeeded according to his desire and four angels came to instruct him on what he still had to operate to obtain from the Creator his entire reconciliation," The eighth day after his final operation, Jacob set himself on the path again to return to the summit of the mountain and, having arrived there at the end of the ninth day, at sunset, "he prepared himself as usual in order accomplish his final reconciliation." He received in the middle of the night, "the certitude of his perfect reconciliation," for he saw seven Spirits who "rose and descended upon him." Among them he recognized the one who had blessed him and the four angels who had come to instruct him. He also saw "the glory of the Creator" at the place where the angels came out and returned. Following this vision, Jacob "committed himself to operating exactly the divine cult in the future."[407]

Moses, who re-established the divine cult after the exodus from Egypt, invoked the Creator in order to know whether the sacrifice that he had made had been agreeable to him. The Creator sent him an angel who taught the chief of the Hebrews that to which he was destined. When Moses made a second Operation between the desert and Mount Horeb, the divine Spirit called him by his name and instructed him in the manner by which he would enter into "the center of the splendor of the divine fire" which surrounded Mount Horeb, "mountain called mysteriously Burning Bush" (that the initiates considered as the place where was produced a glorious manifestation). There he received from the Lord the four divine powers "necessary in order to go operate against the four demonic regions," that is to say the same powers with which Adam had been invested in his state of Glory.[408] "This shows us that every man of desire may very perfectly obtain from the Creator this quadruple power, though clothed by a material body."[409] Moses gave a remarkable proof of this quadruple power in the course of his struggle against the magicians of Egypt. When, on the tenth day which would put an end to the divine spiritual operations of the Elect over the land of Egypt, one of these magicians, slaves to the demons, dared to approach him and enter into the circle that he had traced upon the ground, Moses then repelled him by pressing upon the chest two fingers of the right hand and pronouncing a conjuration. Scarcely had he achieved it "that he made upon the body of the Mage a change that astonished (struck with terror) all the spectators."[410]

After crossing the Red Sea, "Moses began to establish the divine cult among Israel" and he "regenerated" in the space of 49 days all the different cults.[411] The divine cult was also practiced by Solomon in the temple of Jerusalem "where the different woods and the different perfumes consecrated to the sacrifice (cult) have been put into use."[412]

The treatise goes on in detail about the assimilation of the divine cult made mention of in the Bible with the Operations of the Élus Coëns.

The ceremonial of religious acts accomplished by the Patriarchs and the Prophets is represented as identical to the ritual observed by the Réau-Croix. The gift granted to Adam, Seth, Enoch and Noah to "construct spiritual edifices (where matter only plays a secondary role) for the glory of the cult of the Creator"[413] alludes very clearly to the layout of the Chamber of Operation. Abel executes "the first divine operation by tracing the circles suitable to the center from which he offers the first perfumes" and "he dedicates to the Creator his own corporeal form by prostrating himself humbly."[414] Seth teaches his son Enos "every ceremony of divine operation, spiritual and terrestrial, celestial, aquatic and fiery," that is to say consults the course of the stars and causes the lustral waters, the flames of the luminary, and the new fire to intervene in liturgical acts. Enoch, "grand type of the ceremonial and of the divine cult," is the first who erected among the descendants of Seth "an altar of white stone different from what we call marble" (circle traced with the chalk); "it is upon the center of this altar that Enoch offered himself in sacrifice (prostrations) and received the fruit of his cult" (luminous manifestations); he admits his disciples to "the knowledge of his list of catholic works" (general index of the hieroglyphs representing the Spirits invoked by the operant) and he makes them raise "an edifice which had only a sole apartment" (Chamber of Operations).[415] The first born of the second posterity of Noah fixes "the interval of time necessary for the operations." He, the first of the seven brothers, puts his hand to the censer and makes the burnt offering to the Creator; he pronounces, the first, in a low voice, "the grand invocation for the descent of the Spirit in consummation of the burnt offering of expiation and reconciliation."[416] His three younger brothers, "the three spiritual masters," place their disciples in "their mysterious circle of operation" and keeps them there "for the space of time necessary to accomplish without too much haste, the spiritual work that was indicated to them."[417]

The magician of Endor becomes "a man of the Eternal, a Spiritual Elect, though woman." "Understand, she said to Saul, the words that I tell you according to the Spirit that vivifies me and of the one that animates it." She promised to Saul, if he frees himself from the suggestions of the demon, the "fruit of the operations and of the workings that she is going to undertake at his entreaty," In order to properly mark that the ceremony of evocation had begun an "Operation," Pasqually takes care to note that the magician "appeals to the Eternal" before "bringing her steps to the operation," The apparition of Samuel, who, in the Bible remains invisible, for Saul, but that the Prophetess saw under the form of an "Elohim, old and covered with a sacerdotal tunic (méhil)," becomes in the treatise of Pasqually "the spirit of Samuel clothed with a body of apparent glory," that the magician shows to Saul while telling him: "Here is the one who knows more than I."[418]

The mystical reason of certain acts prescribed by the ritual is brought to light by the commentary on the Bible. In prostrating oneself in the circle that he has traced, the operant offers, by the example of Moses, his body and his soul for the deliverance of his brothers: before climbing Horeb, the chief of the Hebrews had, by his prostration, offered this second time his sacrifice of himself in three distinct divisions: his soul, because nothing more perfect may be offered to the Creator than the Minor Spirit who has his resemblance with the Divine Spirit; his heart, or the spiritual power that the soul receives at the moment of its emanation; his body, to express the three spiritous essences from where arises all the forms contained in the universe."[419] After having entered into the Burning Bush, divested of all metals and all impure matter, he made his prostration there "face to ground, body extended its whole length, representing the resting place of matter brought low by the presence of the Spirit of the Creator, or again the necessary reintegration of all the corporeal particular forms into the general form."[420]

The burnt offering preceding the ordination of the Réau-Croix is a replica of the "grand operation that Moses made before the exodus from Egypt" and of which the treatise gives the mystical meaning. "Moses had them take a white lamb of one year, without exterior or interior stain. The lamb represented the purity of the soul and body of the children of Israel…Moses had ordered the Israelites to slaughter and skin the lamb that they had chosen. He would then have it cooked, eating the meat from the head down to half the body and the rest consumed by fire. By the cooking of the lamb, Moses represented to the Israelites the purification of their corporeal form in order to dispose themselves to the communication of the divine spiritual intellect, and, in ordering to burn what remained of the lamb, he wanted to represent to them the reintegration of the spiritous essences into the central axis from where they had arisen."[421]

The sympathetic cooperation of the Réau-Croix with the works of each between themselves is clearly indicated in the apocryphal biblical accounts. Adam has joined his two sons for his "cult of divine operations."[422] Enoch reunites his disciples so "that they assist him in his holy operations."[423] When the first-born of the second posterity of Noah "was alone at the altar of sacrifice" (in the circle), "his three brothers found themselves immediately after him in a straight line as principal assistants to the great operation of the divine cult" (candles of representation). "This has been repeated by Moses assisted in his operations by Aaron, Ur, and Betsaleel. Aaron has repeated the same thing in taking his children to assist (cooperate) with his work. The same order has been followed in the service of the temple of Solomon."[424] When Moses undertook his tenth and final operation before the Pharaoh, he had to support himself for this supreme proof through the collaboration of Aaron, Ur, and the four Hebrew Sages.[425]

Finally, the Reintegration also finds in the Scripture traces of "the traction operated by la Chose," on which Pasqually speaks in his correspondence. At the moment of the murder of Abel, Adam and his two daughters, who were witnesses to it, "fell backwards," "this downfall arose from the vision that they had on the effective nature of the spiritual Minor and Major of Adam and that they were unable to sustain without falling in failure."[426]

After the murder of Abel "a divine spiritual voice" having asked Cain what he had done to his brother, the assassin responded insolently: "Have you given him to my keep?"; then "the Spirit caused him so considerable a pull, that he was at once thrown down."[427] When the two sons of Tubalcain, on the verge of piercing Booz with their arrows, who had killed by mistake his father Cain, hear a supernatural voice which prevents them from drawing, they fall backwards and lose their bearings for a moment.[428] At the moment when Abraham lifted the blade over Isaac the divine Spirit, invisible but present, "caused such a strong pull on Abraham that he was thrown down and put him outside a state to continue his sacrifice."[429] When Jacob wanted to sacrifice to the demon, "the presence of the divine Spirit made such a strong impression or electrification over his corporeal senses and over the animal spiritual ones of Jacob that he was therein thrown down." Then, when the dawn brought an end to the struggle that the Patriarch had kept up all night against the angel, "the Spirit made so strong a pull upon the person of Jacob that he withered his Achille's tendon." When Jacob finally proceeded with the final operation of reconciliation, "he was so strongly worked by the fruit (result) of his operation that he was no longer able to stand upright"; he had to lie down on his left side, his head rested upon a stone, in order "to consider all that came to him from his divine spiritual work."[430] As soon as Saul saw the Prophetess "in the act of her work, he began to tremble and shake like a leaf of a tree. The Prophetess, seeing him battled (tested) by the force of the operation, said to him: You are in fear before the Spirit of the Lord."[431]

We have seen in the chapter treating the Operations that their date was fixed by virtue of calculations whose elements and results were unknown to profane science. At the basis of this mystical chronology was what Pasqually called "the mysterious year" and he asserted on the other hand that the art of measuring the duration had been taught to men by the Spiritual Elect and that all the divisions of time, in use in the course of the ages by the different nations, were of the borrowings made from sacred chronology. He produced in support of this last thesis a sole example, but ingeniously presented. To believe him, the descendants of Shem, Ham, and Japhet, "who lived nearly as the brutes, did not have fixed among them the hours, the days, the months, the years, and the seasons, and all their temporal and spiritual science is limited to distinguishing the day and the night." The three Sages who went to evangelize them "began to establish among them a measure of time that they modeled on the spiritual division, for that law was indispensible to establish the divine cult among these nations."[432] They made them understand notably "that the night was not made (did not exist, was not an obstacle) for the divine Spiritual Minor, considering that this being could not remain without action relative to its spiritual nature,[433] that it does not take into account the night which is imposed on the posterity of Adam[434] and that the work days of the Spirit, that the Sage subjugates by the strength of his operation, are not calculated like the days of material work."[435]

The three missionaries taught to their disciples the cult established by their four elder brothers who followed one another from six o'clock to six o'clock in the "mysterious circle" at the rising of the sun, "so that the four operations of these disciples began at sunrise and finished at the next sunrise." It is from this first given that starts the first calculation of the children of Noah.[436] The notion of the circadian day, that Pasqually calls: "temporal ordinary day of the universal nature," has therefore been given to men by the sum of these four successive operations. These latter were, "following the mysterious, spiritual, temporal convention" of the initiates, so many "spiritual days," since, "each operation being accomplished in an interval of six hours (during six hours) formed effectively one day relative to the divine spiritual cult,"[437] and that the "First Sage," the elder of the second posterity of Noah, had fixed the interval (duration) of time necessary for the operations at a quarter of the ordinary days,[438] so that "the operation made by the four disciples was the principle of their daily calculation,"[439] that is to say their "spiritual day." But as, on the other hand, there had to be "four consecutive days of spiritual operations" (four successive ceremonies of which each last six hours) "in order to fix a complete time to the Spirit" (at the end of which the Spirit would manifest itself) "on behalf of the one who operated and invoked it,"[440] the twenty-four hours of the "temporal ordinary day of the universal nature" also represented the time that the initiates had to devote to their operations in order to obtain Passes, and it had thus united there a common measure to the two chronologies, "civic" (profane) and sacred.

One would expect, therefore given this, that Pasqually would establish the different divisions and duration of a "spiritual" year whose "civic" year would have reflected it. But the indications that his treatise gives on the mysterious year are confused and contradictory, and it is in vain that one seeks to discover therein its elements and nature in the passages where he prophecies on the subject. Although he asserts that "the times suitable to the operations have been, from the beginning, regulated and fixed among men" and that "all these things have been transmitted by the divine Spirit and do not arise from human conventions,"[441] he does not present the spiritual year as a measure of immutable time, independent of arbitrary humanity. He shows it to us, on the contrary, stretching out and as diluting in the course of the ages, so that the religious ceremonies, at first amassed in a short space of time that they filled entirely, space themselves out more and more as we draw nearer to the contemporary era.

At first composed, in the era of the second posterity of Noah, of 28 "temporal days" during which the seven disciples of the three "spiritual professors" took turns four times in order to operate in turn their four successive operations,[442] the spiritual year becomes, starting from the following generation and for 150 years, equal to seven ordinary weeks during which the seven disciples charged with the cult no longer make but one operation in twenty-four hours.[443] Then "three spiritual professors, raised up by God like the former ones," reduce the number of operations made by their seven principal disciples to two per 28 temporal days and fix the duration of the spiritual year to around three ordinary months comprising seven operations.[444] This computation remains in force for a century and a half. Finally, the spiritual year takes on a different value among each of the three nations instructed by the Elect. The peoples descended from the three sons of Noah adopt, "having to be separated shamefully from the divine cult and dispersed among all the people," three kinds of "spiritual calculation" or mystical computation. The descendants of Ham preserve the sacred year of 3 months, those of Shem make it 6 months, those of Japhet give it 12 months like the calendar year.[445]

Among the Hebrews we no longer find, at the time of the Patriarchs, any trace of the sacred year other than the four operations of six hours or "spiritual days," "division of time of the ceremonial of the prayer and of the cult which has been practiced by Abraham, Isaac, and Jacob,"[446] but without it being told to us how many times these operations took place in the course of an ordinary year. We learn only that "Jacob made in an ordinary year four divine operations by four intervals from six o'clock to six o'clock. He then made, for six consecutive days, an operation of divine spiritual vigil,[447] which makes in all ten operations in seven days' time. The total of these operations contains the denary number sacred to the divinity and the septenary number consecrated to the Spirit."[448] The treatise is not much more explicit in that which concerns Moses. It simply says that, in restoring the divine cult, the legislator of the Hebrews institutes anew the four "daily" (per 24 hours) vigils, or four prayers of six hours, and re-established the four annual operations, of which the last represents "the grand operation of Moses in giving thanks for the blessings that he had received."[449]

It would be difficult to guess, according to indications so vague, the principles by virtue of which Pasqually calculated the dates of his year that he had every reason to call "mysterious." In this fog, where the author likely loses himself as much as his readers, two benchmarks remain visible: the mystical value of the number of the successive operations, placed under the invocation of the Denary, the Septenary, and above all the Quaternary, and an astrological doctrine of which one has been able to have a presentiment of the influence in seeing what importance Pasqually attached to the phases of the moon and to the equinoxes to set the date of the Operations in which the Réau-Croix would engage.

∴

This doctrine is exposed in the treatise on the Reintegration with a great clarity. The "body of the inhabitants of the celestial world (the stars) formed a sphere which is supported and substantiated directly by the fire of the Spirits of the axis from where these bodies are emanated. Therefore, their duration is as an eternity in comparison with the duration of the body of the inhabitants of the material world."[450] The celestial bodies are the "vehicles" of the fire of the central axis which has "set in motion the three spiritous essences: mercury, sulphur, and salt, in order to cooperate with the formation of all the bodies" and "it is upon this vehicle that the Spirits of the axis continually operate for the equilibrium and maintenance of all the forms." It is thus that began and is maintained "the passive (vegetative) life to which every being is submitted, as much celestial as terrestrial."[451]

The stars are distributed in planetary circles. Each of these circles is composed of six principal stars, equal in magnitude, in virtue, and in power, "which receive the order of action, of movement, and of operation by the superior star which is at the center of the six composing the planetary circle."[452] "The star at the center is the superior planetary being, it is this star which governs these major and minor planetary bodies and is called superior, because it is upon it that the solar influence is going to be shed immediately. This superior star communicates what it has received to the major planetary stars which occupy its circle. The majors communicate to an infinity of lesser stars, which are in junction with them and that we call inferior planetary signs or bodies, and these inferior planetary signs, after having received the influential action of the superiors and the majors, sheds it with exact precision upon the coarse terrestrial bodies."[453] Thus the seven planetary circles, or seven heavens, receive from the supercelestial all their virtues and all their powers and then communicate them to the general terrestrial body[454], so that the seven planets "operate for the modification of the temperature and the support of the action of the universe,"[455] and that the seven planetary circles "contain the seven principal agents of the universal nature."[456]

These seven planetary circles are distributed in three groups corresponding to the three different circles in which, just as we have seen previously, "the minor Spirits accomplish their pure and simple spiritual operations in order to succeed in their reconciliation and their reintegration into the supercelestial."[457] The Rational Circle is identical to the circle of Saturn, or "Saturnary I" which is the most elevated of all the celestial circles. This superior circle separates from the four supercelestial circles all the other planetary circles of the same order. The other planetary circles, those of the Sun, Mercury, Mars, Jupiter, Venus, and the Moon, are "all included in the immensity of the sensible circle."[458] On the other hand there is correspondence and intimate connection between the circles of Saturnary I, the Sun, Mercury, and Mars, which "repeat the true figure of the supercelestial"[459] because "the division of the divine immensity into four domains (superior, major, inferior, and minor) is found repeated in the celestial (major domain) by these four circles which mark distinctly the four celestial horizons."[460] Therefore, these four circles are called "major celestial circles." "They are stronger in action and reaction than the three planetary circles placed below them, because they are in the immediate vicinity of the supercelestial." Their four planets govern the three inferior planets: the Moon, Venus, and Jupiter, "attached to the three angles of the last celestial triangle" also called "simple sensible triangle."[461] It is by these three last planets that "the general terrestrial is substantiated and that it is maintained in the movement proper to the vegetation (life) that is natural to it. Venus presides over conception (fertility, generation), Jupiter over putrefaction (dissolution of the bodies), the Moon, sensible circle or humid envelope, cooperated by its fluid to modify and mitigate (moderate) the action and reaction of the two principal chiefs of the temporal corporeal vivification (organic life), which are the central axis and the solar body."[462]

The first "uncreated fire, gives life and movement to every kind of body"; the second "acts, reacts, and vivifies the vegetation of all the particular bodies and of the general terrestrial body."[463] It is superior to all the other stars because it is "the star most fitting to be the aspect of the uncreated fire-axis."[464] It is, after that, "the principal agent of the universe."[465] It marks half the distance which separates the Denary Circle from the most inferior planet, the Moon. It is immediately below all the spiritual supercelestial circles and the Saturnary Circle. It occupies the sixth rank, whether one descends from the supercelestial (Denary, Septenary, Ternary, Quaternary, Saturnary Circles), or one rises from the Lunary Circle (Moon, Venus, Jupiter, Mars, Mercury). This place "assimilates it to the six thoughts which have been employed by the Eternal for his universal creation."[466] Thus directed is the course of all the stars in concert with Saturn and the central axis fire.[467]

Finally certain stars "that the vulgar call comets" and which present themselves "extra linear from the planetary circles," so that they descend sometimes closer to the earth than usual, while shining then a more brilliant light, have a particular role: they announce the birth of an Elect Minor. Such was the star that the men call in their ignorance Latham, that is to say: "sign of confusion and terrestrial suffering," and which appeared at the moment of the birth of Enoch.[468] The narrow and reciprocal dependence of the material and the spiritual in a cosmology where the stars are at the same time the agents of the physical laws and individual beings, endowed with thought and will, imposes on the Spiritual Minor an exact knowledge of the celestial revolutions. Man, who since the fall of Adam is become "the subject of the planetary bodies formerly inferior to him,"[469] must, when he renders to the divinity a spiritual cult, take into account the influence of the stars, and not only because he received by the intermediary of the celestial bodies the vital energy, of which the material part of his being is tributary, but moreover because, in the two spaces occupied by the inhabitants of the celestial and terrestrial worlds, are also found "simple spiritual beings which operate on behalf of the spiritual inhabitants of the celestial world and the material inhabitants of the terrestrial world."[470]

He must forget no longer that "the planetary circles are still susceptible to being inhabited by malign spiritual beings who are opposed to the powers and combat the faculties and influential good actions that the good planetary spiritual beings are charged to shed in the entire world."[471] There is, therefore, besides the divine astral influence, a demonic astral influence of which the history of humanity gives numerous examples. More than once the Minors, deceived by the perverse Spirits, have believed that the Creator was one of these prevaricating Spirits and that the Minors had been emanated from the "Great Prince of the South, principal chief of all material being," and they have imagined that they had to obey blindly all that the Prince of the South had inspired in them by his inferior agents. They have believed in the purpose of the "regionary prince of the western part, or major prince of the terrestrial demons," when he told them that "the sun was the eye of this great universal prince (prince of the universe) and the house of the one who directs all that the sight and imagination of men may perceive and comprehend," or in the teachings of the "northern terrestrial regionary prince," who assured them that the moon was the house of all the major, inferior, and minor Spirits and persuaded them to have recourse to it "in order to obtain from the great prince all the means and all the faculties which are necessary for you to make your power equal to ours." The perverse chiefs taught the Minors that they had seduced the manner to communicate with the inhabitants of these two houses "by recommending to them to do no work nor operations upon these houses except when they would be in conjunction and in perfect opposition, which forms the eclipses of the sun and the moon, because then they would obtain from the principal chiefs inhabiting these houses all that of which they would have need."[472]

The Spiritual Minor does not devote himself to astrolatry, he gives worship neither to the sun nor to the moon, but he must take into account the influence of the stars in order to set the moment when he will make his temporal spiritual operations, in order to avoid the periods predominated by the malign Spirits who are able to profit from their ascendency in order to provoke deceptive manifestations. It is necessary for him to use "the knowledge of astronomy and the faculties of power of the planetary stars over the general (universe) and particular (living organisms) creation, that the children of Shem, Ham, and Japhet have received from their instructors and that they have transmitted to all the peoples of the world."[473] The stars which enter before all the others in line of value are the sun and the moon, whose eminent role in the universe we have come to see. The sun sends at the beginning of spring, at the moment when the vegetation renews under its rays, vivifying effluvia which supports the operant in his workings. This is why one of the successors of the spiritual professors of the second posterity of Noah no longer "operates in the Western part (Europe?) the grand cult but once in the four seasons, namely at the equinox of March each year."[474] The descendants of Japhet have imitated it in beginning the spiritual year at the equinox of March and having it last until the equinox of the following March.[475] The Élus Coëns follow the example given by these distant ancestors. But all the important dates of the annual course of the sun may be favorable to the Operations. Thus, the descendants of Shem have counted two spiritual years in one ordinary year; those of Ham have taken for limits to their sacred years the two solstices and the two equinoxes.[476]

The influence of the moon, nearest star to the earth, mediator and moderator of the astral influx, is no less decisive for the success of the Operations. Thus, the "lunary calculation is the first which was given to man by the Creator"[477] and "it is essential to the man of desire, be it spiritual or temporal, to be instructed in the four different manners to calculate the different days that the moon operates (during which it exercises its influence) in the whole elementary (physical) universe by its renewal, its first quarter, full, and its last quarter."[478] It was by the Sages of the second posterity of Noah that the lunary calculation, "which elevates man to the highest knowledge of the natural universe and of its revolutions," has first been known.[479] Indeed when their seven disciples had made in turn their four successive operations, "they found them at the number of 28 intervals, and, reflecting that the moon appeared over the earth for the same number of 28, the equality that they saw between the number of lunary operations and that of their operations made them adopt the number of 28 operations in 28 spiritual days for one spiritual month,"[480] which was, therefore, a quarter of an ordinary temporal month, as the spiritual day was itself a quarter of a temporal day. Then, "having reflected seriously on the different courses of operation that the star made over the earth and upon them, and having found there a perfect relationship with their spiritual operations, they thought fit to take the number of 28 operations of the moon, or the 28 ordinary temporal days of the moon, to fix their spiritual year."[481] The Spiritual Elect of the second posterity of Noah made their two monthly operations "at the beginning and at the end of the crescent of the moon, that is to say at the renewal and a little before the end of the full moon"[482] and "the times of the cults of Moses and Solomon were at each renewal of the moon, and since men have existed this cult has operated among them."[483]

But, whether the date of the Operation is determined by the height of the sun over the horizon at noon or by the phases of the moon, it is always tied to the periodic return of the celestial phenomena, and the divine cult may be from this point of view assimilated "with the simple culture of the earth for which it is necessary to observe the intervals of time of the days, weeks, months of the moon."[484] One has then the right to say "that the Creator, who prescribed to man this indispensible temporal law when he condemned him to the culture of the earth," has "likewise subjected the temporal spiritual cult not only to an exact ceremonial, but again to a faithful observation of the times and the seasons,"[485]

The importance of the "conjunctures," already marked by the fact that the important operations take place at the equinoxes, stands out again in the detail of the instructions given to the disciples. If the Élu Coën must engage specially on Thursday in exercises of devotion, it is because this day is marked by the sign of Jupiter "which David used for his reconciliation."[486] But it is the moon which commands as sovereign all the calculations in which the master engages. "I am obliged," writes Pasqually to Willermoz on November 16, 1771, "to govern myself by the lunary course for my work here below, because it is the star that principally directs the inferior part."[487] The invocation of the Three Days had to be placed between the renewal of the moon and the end of the first quarter, because "then the superior good agents which govern it operate it for two times seven days conforming to their laws and orders." The period going from the full moon to the new moon cannot be suitable to this triduum "because then, this planet going into decline, its good virtue declines likewise, so that its good power, as well as its good superior agents, leave it to the direction of the inferior ternary Spirits, among which it is found more often with evil elementary Spirits."[488] For the same reason, when the Réau-Croix engaged in the two annual Equinox Workings, "they worked from the first quarter until the moment when the moon was full, that is to say by beginning their Operations four or five days before its fullness."[489] Pasqually's secretary, in sending to Lyon new instructions for the Equinox Working of 1771, remarked that he hastened to transmit the final decisions of the Master, lest, "the moon soon becoming new," Willermoz make improper use of the preceding instructions.[490] When Pasqually, upon the pressing prayer of Willermoz, finally consents to have the adept of Lyon "ordained," he doubts that the ceremony had its full effect because the time is not favorable. For want of anything better he orders his Substitute General, Bacon de la Chevalerie, to work at the ordination from the 11th to the 13th of May in order to, at least, "encounter the days relative to the passing of the season," but he recommends to him "to attack (to begin the censings by) the West corner as his chief angle" and he expressly forbids him "to attack the East directly, this time being passed."[491]

BOOK II
The Élus Coëns and the occultist tradition

FIRST CHAPTER
Jewish esotericism, on its origins in the 18th century

Pasqually has always been of an extreme discretion upon his sources. If he asserts that he has received the order to teach man what he knows "depending upon whether he has it from those who have been charged to show it to him,"[492] never does he furnish indications on the personalities of these masters; sometimes he employs vague formulas as: "that is what has been said to me,"[493] sometimes he refers to "one of his faithful friends, beloved by Truth, protégé of Wisdom,"[494] whose name he does not give, or to friends of Wisdom"[495] on which he is all too stingy with information.

But if the head of the Élus Coëns is silent on this point, his treatise speaks for him. All the doctrines exposed in the Reintegration or in the correspondence of Pasqually with his disciple's bear, by the principles that they suppose and the tendencies that they reveal, trademarks so indelible that it is easy to discover their origin. It is more than a hundred years since the mystic Molitor has awarded to Pasqually the title of "grand Kabbalist,"[496] and Molitor had reason. The author of the Reintegration is one of the last doctors of the secret school which, after having in the Middle Ages codified the Jewish mystic, heir of the most ancient esoteric and magical traditions, still had in the 18th century enthusiasts in the Jewish communities of Holland, Germany, Italy, and Poland. Certain contemporary occultists would have been stricken by this particular character of his teaching. "They had wished, at the time, to persuade me," wrote the baron de Turkheim in 1821 to the old Élu Coën Willermoz, "that Pascualis (*sic*) had got his manuscript from an Arab named Raschid, that the original had been composed in Chaldean and then translated into Arabic and Spanish. A Jew named Hirchfield, died two years ago...claimed to possess a part of these manuscripts."[497] Whether the assertion of Hirchfield, or rather Hirschfield, was founded or not, it no less remains that the Reintegration belongs to the long series of works where were deposited the mystical ideas that Jewish esotericism had received in Anterior Asia and imported into Europe by passing especially through Spain. The treatise of Pasqually is a belated and stunted branch come out of the Kabbalistic tree which had taken root in the 13th century in the rich humus accumulated by the ages and in which the two Talmud's, that of Jerusalem and that of Babylon, and the Midraschim had already drawn an abundant sap. It is in the secret Jewish tradition and not elsewhere that the quarry must be sought from where Pasqually has drawn the materials of his edifice.[498]

∴

Jewish esotericism has developed on the fringe of the Bible and under the influence of the religions of Mesopotamia and Iran.

The Bible was not only a sacred book where the faithful found, with the elements and reasoning of his faith, religious prescriptions and moral regulations; it was also a criminal and civil code from which they claimed to extract the maxims and laws ruling the relationships between the member of the profane community. Now, from the religious point of view as from the social point of view, the precepts of Scripture applied only to some particular cases and responded only to the needs of a rudimentary society. After the Law of the Old Testament had been fixed in the time of Ezra (around 450 B.C.), the development of social life and the evolution of religious concepts made necessary new or more precise regulations, while the current of ideas which, since the Exile, pushed the people of Israel to isolate themselves fiercely among neighboring peoples and related races, and to repel every foreign influence, rejected it to the exclusive study of the Mosaic Law. The same state of mind existed three centuries later at the time of the Maccabees when the biblical canon was definitively decided.

The "doctors of the Law," who held a plurality of functions of the theologian, casuist, and legist, had therefore to perform strongly, all the more as the Jewish spirit, subtle and contentious, was punctilious without measure on the questions of ritual and on the texts invoked to decide conflicts of interests or to judge misdemeanors and crimes. But they had at their disposal two precious auxiliaries in order to give their decisions an authority to which an individual opinion could not claim, even supported by logic and equity. These two means, which were furnished to them by profound concepts rooted in the minds of the Jews, were the faith in the existence of an oral tradition preserving the commentary given by God himself on the written and public text of the Law, and the belief in an inspiration of supernatural origin coming to enlighten the elect of the Lord when the human intelligence had exhausted its resources. The more celebrated Hebrew doctors agree to declare that Moses received not only the Law, which was deposited in the Pentateuch, but that the more secret and more exact interpretation of this law was communicated to him on Sinai; and that he was commanded to make known to the Jewish people the text of the Law, but to neither write nor divulge its interpretation. So, Moses revealed it only to Jesus Navé (others say to Aaron) and the latter to the first pontiffs who succeeded him, under promise of silence.[499] On the other hand it was logical that a people among whom the prophets have played so great a role in all eras admit without difficulty that divine inspiration came to the relief of the perplexed jurist. The new prescriptions were therefore presented as borrowings made from this secret commentary of the written Law or as inspired by an illumination which had revealed to the doctors the latent meaning of the sacred text.

Thus gave rise first to a complementary interpretation of the Scripture pursued unto the slightest details, following step by step the words of the Bible, and whose results were summarized under the form of precepts in the Mischna, or teachings given by the Tanaim (Masters, Doctors), who for around four centuries (from 150 BC to 220 AD) commented with an indefatigable zeal upon the Torah and particularly the Pentateuch. The Mischna was fragmentarily drawn up starting from the 3rd century to our era, when the mass of decisions pronounced or transmitted unto it orally by the Tanaim to their disciples became so considerable that the most vast memory was not able to contain it. The rabbi Jehudah, surnamed Ha-Nasi (the patriarch) or Ha-Kadosch (the holy), grandson of Gamaliel I, compiled in a sort of manual the elements of these first collections. The Mischna of Jehudah was considered as a canon to which they soon attributed a greater value than to the Bible itself. "The Torah is like water," says the Sopherim treatise, "and the Mischna like wine." It was studied and commented upon in its turn like the Bible had been by the Tanaim. Their successors, the Amoraim (Commentators), rabbis of the synagogues of Jabne, Sephoris, and Lydda in Palestine, of Syra, Nahardea, Pumbeditha, and Uscha in Babylonia, took it for three centuries for the text of their impassioned controversies whose conclusions constituted the Gemara (Complement). A more vast compilation, collecting the decisions of the Amoraim and the Tanaim, gave birth to the Talmud.

There exist two Talmudic collections: the one from Jerusalem finished in the middle of the 5th century of our era, and the one from Babylon, completed at the beginning of the 6th century. Both reproduce the same Mischna, but the first gives the Palestinian Gemara and the second the Babylonian one. The latter is the much more considerable work; it fills twelve thick folios, whereas the one from Jerusalem is contained in one rather thin folio. The Talmud of Babylon was, from its origin and unto the modern times, the true representative of the Talmudic tradition.

The Talmudic academies remained flourishing in Babylonia at the era when the social and intellectual life had completely disappeared in Palestine; from their works came the Midraschim (Interpretations), which, following the path traced by the Tanaim and the Amoraim, prove how enduring there remained among the Jews the taste for judicial controversies and theological disputes. We find these academies at the end of the 10th century in Spain. In the 11th century, Samuel Ibn Nagdila published at Grenada an Introduction to the Talmud; Gerschom Ben Jehudah made to appear at Metz and Mayence commentaries on fourteen treatises of the Talmud, and Salomon Jizchaki, called Raschi, wrote in Aramaic, commentaries on nearly all the treatises accompanied by the Gemara. In the 12th century Maimonide composed in Arabic a commentary on the Mischna which has remained celebrated; in the same era and in the following centuries, French and German rabbis, writing in Aramaic, enriched the commentary of Raschi. The Talmud preserved until the end of the 18th century an authority superior to that of the Bible itself, and most of the Jews only understood the latter by the citations made thereof in the Talmud.

$$\therefore$$

Inexhaustible mine from where a race obstinately faithful to its national traditions has not ceased for twelve centuries to draw all that is necessary to its intellectual and moral life, the Talmud was not only for the Jews a code of religious and civic legislation. Its character to interpret the Mosaic Law explains the prestige it enjoyed in their eyes but does not give the whole measure of influence that it exercised on its readers: they sought there rules of conduct, but they found there in addition what satisfies their imagination and their sensibilities. The oriental spirit does not care to classify ideas following the rigorous logical method practiced by the peoples having passed through the school of Greek dialectic and Roman law; even when it has a set aim, it only gets there making long detours and stopping at all the crossroads and all the points of view it encounters along its route.

The discussions of scholastic spirit and inspired by a narrow and formal devotion furnishes the substance of the treatises of the Talmud, but do not exclusively comprise the text, which includes two distinct but intimately mingled elements: through the Halacha (conduct, morals) winds capriciously the Haggadah (narrative) which relates anecdotes or legends, of an edifying character in general, but which often have only very vague connections with the subject of controversy and where the marvelous is the principal element of interest. These arabesques sometimes overwhelm the main lines of the design to such a degree that they make one forget the original theme. In the Talmudic Haggadah are preserved vestiges of magical cults, remains of ancient folklore, traditions surviving in the popular memory or imported from neighboring lands, fragments of foreign theogonies and mythologies, and finally mystical and metaphysical concepts come from Iran and Chaldea. It seems that Jewish thought, constantly brought back by a jealous religion to the sole study of the Law, seeks every occasion to venture into the forbidden regions upon which the Bible, in spite of its touchy exclusivism, cannot help but to throw a furtive glance. For example, the power to make rain fall, attributed by the Book of Kings to Elijah, is frequently accorded by the Talmud to particularly well known rabbis; one of these treatises, Thaanith, contains numerous legends on this subject. Three other treatises say of the celebrated rabbi Simeon Ben Jockai, who lived in the 2nd century AD, that he knew astrology, understood the words of angels, demons, and palms, and had the custom of performing miracles. One treatise mentions the faculty had by the rabbi Chanina Ben Dosa to heal illnesses by prayer.

With this legacy of a remote past are associated more recent influences. Just as the Fathers of the Church, in combatting the Greek philosophy, have developed and deepened their doctrine while at the same time adopting the technical language and methods of this philosophy, so does the Jewish religious spirit, which, during the Exile, had to struggle against the fascination exercised over them by the Babylonian pantheon and the Persian mythology, change for the worse, although it had therein its rigid monotheism while appropriating in large measure the vocabulary and images with which the ancient Orient had clothed its astrological conceptions. The visions of Isaiah and Ezekiel, that one may read in the Bible, bear witness to these borrowings. The theophany of Ezekiel, conceived in the vicinity of the ziggurats, temples with seven declining levels consecrated to the planets, shows the divine course descending from the north of heaven in the form of a pyramid. The four monstrous animals: the bull, lion, eagle, and man, correspond to the symbolic figures representing the four cardinal points; the wheels seen by the Seer recall the colures, of which one passes through the equinox's points and the other through the solstitial points and which were known by the Chaldean astrologers.[500] The Babylonian and Persian demonologies and angelologies likewise show through in the post-exile interpolations. The practices of anti-demonic Chaldean magic are indicated in the Book of Tobit, and the name of the demon Aschmodai (Asmodeus), over whom triumph the young Jewish heroes, is one of the well-known Persian demons: Aeschmo-Deva. The Jewish religion adopted the inferior spirits of the oriental mythologies: Kerobim are similar to the sphinxes of Egypt and serve as framing to the Lord or protect by their wings the Ark of the Covenant in the Holy of Holies, Chaioth with feet sparkling like polished bronze, with hands moving under vast deployed wings, with a face recalling at the same time that of a man and lion. The angel Michael of the Jews (Mikael: Who is like God) is the Babylonian Marduk, warrior god, divine messenger, beneficent intercessor. The Book of Esther is a Jewish adaptation of the myth of Ishtar and Marduk. The Bible is aware of an angelic hierarchy: at the head, the angel "who has within itself the name of God," (Exodus XXIII, 21), then the six archangels (Tobit XII, 15), and finally the "Overseers," the "Grand Council of Saints," (Psalm 89) who decide with God the destiny of the peoples (Daniel, IV, 14). Under the influence of the Persian theology the Aebaoth, the "celestial cohorts," who seem to have originally been the personification of the host of stars turning below the north pole, abode of the Chaldean Anou and "fixed point of the flight of phenomena," become intermediary beings between the supreme God and the material world.[501]

On the other hand, the knowledge that Judaism had at Babylon of Mazdan dualism led to the increase of the importance of Satan; at first simple "Informer" of the errors of man in Ezekiel, he strikes, in the Book of Job, the righteous with unmerited misfortunes in order to make them doubt the justice of the Eternal; finally, his power becomes scarcely inferior to that of God, with whom he quarrels over the direction of the universe and the empire over men.

If the Bible had not been able to barricade completely against this invasion of foreign concept, the apocryphal and apocalyptic works of the era of the Asmoneans, recanted or completed in the first centuries of the Christian era[502] and the Talmudic treatises were left to be invaded without resistance. The Book of Enoch testifies with what restless vigilance certain Jews observed the map of the heavens and the movement of the stars. In the Apocalypse of Abraham, the patriarch traverses seven superimposed heavens, all peopled with angels, before losing himself in the bosom of God. The Testament of the Twelve Patriarchs and the Similitudes of Enoch represent the world as the theater of a gigantic struggle between God and Satan, called Belial, and who commands the innumerable legion of the angels of evil; but the Testament of Levi, the one of Simeon and the one of Zabulon announce that, when the time will be accomplished, Satan will fall and the evil Spirits will be hurled into the darkness and into the inextinguishable fire.[503] The Haggadah of the Talmud expressly recognizes, as well as the Midraschim, that the Jews have brought back from Babylon the names of the months and the idea of the angels. The six principal angels that are related in the Talmudic legends have a Persian origin easily recognizable; the angel Mittron (called by the Hellenizing Jews Metatron, Divine Assessor) who occupies the most elevated rank, is a replica of Mithra; the name of the angel Sandalfon is composed of a Persian root and a Pelvi root whose association signifies: the Master of the Expanse, the Elevated.[504] Conversely, it is likely from the two bisexual gods of Chaldea that the Talmud and Midraschim have borrowed the idea current with them that all that God had first created was male and female, so that the First Adam united within himself the two sexes.[505]

The intellectual fermentation formented by the foreign contributions gave scope to the speculation. The elements of a Jewish gnosis are found very distinctly in the Haggadah of the Talmud. This gnosis rests on an esoteric commentary of biblical narratives, this commentary relying upon the idea indicated above of a secret tradition or a particular illumination that gives the mystical meaning of the texts that the vulgar understand literally. The Jewish gnosis seeks before all to make disappear the fundamental antinomy of a perfect and infinite God creating an imperfect and finite world by establishing between these two irreconcilable terms transcendent intermediaries: the Divine Wisdom, the Breath or Spirit of God, the Word of God, the Angel of God.

The first two words of Genesis: be-reschit (in the beginning) were interpreted mystically. In the Proverbs (VIII, 22), Wisdom (chochmah) proclaims: "The Lord possessed me before the beginning of his work, as the beginning of his path," and she adds: "I was near to him (outside of creation) as the conductor of the labors." She says again in Ecclesiasticus: "I alone have traced the circle of heaven, I have traversed the depths of the abyss; I had to operate in the waves of the sea and upon the whole earth." Finally, the Book of Job (XXVIII, 25) says of her: "When He portioned the waters according to measure, when He gave a law to the rain and traced his path with lightning, He looked at her." The Targum of Okelos[506] giving to "be" (which signifies: to, with, in) the meaning of "with" and identifying "reschit" with "chochmah," translates the beginning of Genesis in this way: With Wisdom (be-chuchma, in Hebrew be-chochmah) God created, etc. The expression is not abstract; Wisdom is considered as a sort of demiurge who collaborated with the creation. The personality that the commentators attributed to it seemed justified by the verse of

Genesis (I, 26) where God says: "We want to make a man in our image." This plural could not, to their eyes, have any reason to be unless creation had had more than one author.

The Spirit or Breath (rouach) of God that Genesis showed resting over the waters before the creation of the world (I, 2), was considered as the manifestation and the instrument of the creative intelligence. It was blended with the chochmah that the Book of Wisdom represented as "a breath of the strength of God, a pure effluvia of the splendor of the Almighty, a reflection of the eternal light and a spotless mirror of the divine energy," (VII, 25-26) and even as "the one seated near to the throne of God," (IX, 4).

Starting from the third verse of Genesis the successive stages of creation are preceded by the words: "Wajomer" (and He said). This divine word, already represented as a manifestation of the Lord in Genesis[507], is considered in the Psalms as a creative force exercising itself by the voice (XXIII, 6&9; CXIX, 8-9). The Targum of Jerusalem employs, in all the passages where the Bible has God intervene in person, the expression: the Word (memra), in place of the name of the Lord.

The Angel of God had likewise become a divine hypostasis[508] sometimes it replaced God (Genesis XIV, 10; XXI, 17; XXII, 11; XXI, 13; Exodus III, 6, in the Burning Bush); sometimes it is the interpreter of the Lord and then it speaks in the first person (Judges II, 1&4; Malachi III, 1). In the Talmud a leading role is attributed to the angel Mittron or Metatron who often acts in place of the Lord.

∴

The mystical speculation in which numerous doctors engaged is called by the Talmud "Pardes" (Paradise). The word, coming from Persia, signified: "Park of the Animals" and likely recalled the mysterious animals, the Keroubim, that Ezekiel described in his vision, where they draw or carry the divine chariot. The Haggadah of the Talmud and of the Midrasch contain two secret doctrines called "the Work of the Chariot" (Maaseh Merkabah)[509] and "the Work of the Creation or of the Beginning" (Maaseh Bereschit); the first treated on "divine things": essence of the divinity, heaven, hell, angels, demons; the second occupies itself with cosmogony, cosmology, and mystical anthropology. These doctrines are not set forth systematically but fragmentarily, with the occasional discussion on the correct interpretation of biblical verses, and as, according to the Talmud of Babylon, the doctrine of the Chariot was held so secret that its study was only permitted to an elite, the results of this speculation only appeared by flashes and isolated treatises. Moreover, if the Talmud reports that the rabbis Ben Asi, Ben Soma, Elischa Ben Abuya, and Akiba Ben Joseph (2nd century AD) have "penetrated into Paradise" in order to say that they are engaged in mystical studies, it does not give to the expression the lauditory sense that we would suppose. The general spirit of the collection is hostile to these perilous excursions into a forbidden domain, lest they have the effect of "destroying the plantation," that is to say to undermine the monotheistic faith, and it does not hide from us that Elischa is become "asher" (apostate) and has allowed himself to be seduced by a heresy, probably dualist, for being too occupied with Metatron.[510]

For as strict as was this reprobation of mystical tendencies, it seems that it was above all an obligatory homage to the traditional orthodoxy, for the Talmud bears witness involuntarily to the attraction that they exercised upon a number of doctors. One striking proof of this flavor is the ingenuity that the rabbis had displayed in order to invent the four kinds of "keys" that allowed them to discover the secret meaning of the terms used by the sacred book. "Gematria" (from the Greek geometria) replaced one particularly important word or difficult interpretation with another word whose letters added together represented an equal sum.[511] "Notaricon" (from notarikon, abbreviator) considered the letters comprising a word as the initials of words forming an expression or even an entire phrase. "Temurah" formed new words by anagram. "Zeruph" employed several types of metagrams; it replaced, for example, the first letter of the alphabet with the 22nd and last, the 2nd with the 21st, etc.[512], or else the first with the 12th, the 2nd with the 13th and so on.[513] The Talmud also associated Gematria with the different kinds of Zeruph, so that the processes used to extract an esoteric meaning from the biblical text and serving to mystical ends lent itself to infinite combinations.

The Jewish mystic, of which the Talmud reveals the existence and vitality, developed above all in the midst of the communities of the Diaspora, more accessible than the Palestinian synagogues to be influence by the religious and philosophical doctrines of the foreign peoples. The most important contribution was that of the Hellenizing Jews of Alexandria who attempted to reconcile their national monotheism with Greek philosophy and with the popular, animist and polydemonist beliefs of Syria and Babylonia. The Greek translation of the Bible, called the Septuagint, which was made in Egypt in the 3rd century BC, was already preoccupied with suppressing every anthropomorphism in the holy text; it had translated Jehovah Zebaoth of the Hebrew as the Master of Powers and thus established intermediary beings between the One and the world. In the treatises of the neoplatonist Philo the Jew is found applied systematically the method of allegorical exegesis which permitted, without knocking heads with Mosaic law, to discreetly enrich the Jewish theodicy with ideas for which the orthodox Judaism had, at least officially, so strong a repugnance. This method has not been created by him[514]; it was already familiar to the Talmudist rabbis who relied on Psalm LXXVII: "I will speak to you in parables, I will show you in figures the things hidden since the beginning"[515]; but he does not apply it with a rigor and an ingenuity which have made of his commentaries models of the genre. Concerned with establishing a fundamental concordance between the Bible and Greek philosophy, particularly the Platonic, he saw in the Pentateuch, and especially in Genesis, a collection of myths expressing in a figurative fashion the ideas set forth by the Greeks. Philo considered in "de Mundi Opifico" that, in order to be better understood, the Scripture had accommodated itself to the feebleness of the popular intelligence; that it was therefore impossible to take it in a literal sense and that it was necessary to seek there, above all in the passages which appear most revolting to reason or morals, a more elevated and more profound meaning, which was allegorical. He discovered tropological meanings in the simplest words, the most clear precepts, and even in narratives. In the "Creation of the world according to Moses" he explained allegorically the titles of the holy books, the Cherubim, the flaming sword, the personages of Cain and of the Giants, and gave a mystical interpretation of the passage: "Noah being awakened learned..." In his treatise "On the septenary and the feasts" he translated Chaldea as false knowledge, Adam as pure human reason, Eve as sensual perception, and he attaches a secret meaning to the numbers, for example to those which express the dimensions of the Tabernacle. In the "Book of Dreams" he gives a mystical interpretation of the passage where the Bible, relating the voyage of Jacob, says that he came out of Beer-Scheba (Well of the Oath) in order to return to Harran: the well symbolizes knowledge which is an inexhaustible source; Harran is the metropolis of the senses; Laban, who dwells there, represents the men incapable of grasping the pure ideas and to whom the senses offer a refuge; also Jacob, who represents the men eager for transcendent truths, only goes to Harran in passing, as a stranger who ceaselessly longs to return.

Although Philo is counted among the representatives of a philosophical school, he is less a philosopher teaching his doctrine publicly, as had done Socrates and Plato, his master, than a doctor of a "disciplina arcani" and a Talmudist who only wrote for rare disciples. Like the Talmudists, he believed in the secret tradition of an oral revelation and in the light given by divine illumination. He professes in his Book III of his "de Mose" that the Pentateuch has been revealed in three fashions: 1st, direct and personal revelation: God pronouncing the ten Words (Decalogue) and then writing them himself upon the two Tablets of the Law; 2nd, dialog between Moses and God; 3rd, words or scripture inspired by God or by his representatives. On the other hand, he repeats that what he writes is meant only for the initiates and men of mature spirit and pious hearts and may not be confided, so to speak, but in the Holy of Holies; he insists on this point that the holy and mysterious revelation on God and his Powers ought to remain carefully hidden, because not all men are capable of preserving the deposit of divine wisdom.

One of the themes that he treated thus for the initiates and that the Jewish mystics developed later with predilection is that according to which man, or Microcosm, is the image of the world, or Macrocosm, just as inversely the cosmos is a greater and more perfect man, created on the model of the suprasensible man, or First Adam (Adam Kadmon), and having two kinds of souls: one vegetative, arising from the divine vital power which gives to the beings existence and movement, and a spiritual soul emanated from the divine spirit.[516]

The metaphysical concepts of Philo were echoed throughout the Talmud of Babylon and that of Jerusalem, at least in their haggadic parts, and later in the Midraschim.

∴

From the 4th to 6th centuries of our era, the Jewish gnosis fell into languor, but under Arab rule, that is to say starting from the 7th century, is produced a new mystical flowering which persisted until the 12th century with alternations of decline and rebirth. The most notable works of this period are the "Sepher Yetzirah" (Book of Creation), written in Syria or Palestine under the direct influence of the Christian gnosis and which shows God creating the world through the intermediary of the 10 Sephiroth (Numbers or celestial Spheres), divine attributes hypostasized, in association with the twenty-two letters of the Hebrew alphabet in a manner to form the "32 marvelous paths of wisdom" from where are come all the sensible bodies; the treatise "Hechaloth" (the Tents) describing the dwellings from on high and the celestial legions; the "Alphabet of Akiba" which gives a symbolic interpretation of the Hebraic letters, of the names of the Lord, and of the angels; the "Apocalypse of Enoch," that of Noah, that of Moses, the "Prike (Chapters) of Rabbi Eliezer" which contains systems of mystical astronomy, a very developed angelology and demonology, and a myth very much in favor in this period, that of the fall of the angels.

The Kabbalah came out of this long mystical incubation in the 13th century. The word, which henceforth designated the secret Jewish doctrine condensed within a theosophical and theurgical system, signifies "tradition," but indirect, tradition, in contrast to the Torah. The Talmud calls all biblical writings Kabbalah, with the exception of the Pentateuch which it names "written Torah." According to it the Law of Moses had alone been revealed directly by God to the legislator, the other books figuring in the biblical canon had been dictated by the divine "ruach" or Holy Spirit. Likewise, the secret Jewish doctrine called Kabbalah did not rely on a direct teaching, but it is considered to have been inspired by the "holy lights," that is to say by the celebrated rabbis of the 1st and 2nd centuries AD, such as Simeon, Ben Jochai, Akiba, Nechunjah, Ismael Ben Elija.

The Kabbalistic school has not to its credit any original creation. It is rare that one finds in the numerous works that it has produced a theme of which one cannot discover the model in the earlier mystical treatises, and it is not without reason that they are placed under the patronage of reputed Talmudists of the great rabbinical period: their true authors avowed thus to be only the trustees of concepts bequeathed by their predecessors. In fact, the Jewish gnosis, whose elements were found in the Haggadah of the two Talmud's and the Midraschim, in the works of Philo, and in the writings dating from the 8th and 9th century, is at the basis of the Kabbalah which is contented to draw from it a homogenous and harmonious system.

The principal structure has been furnished by the Sepher Yetzirah, with its Sephiroth and its mysticism of the letters. The doctrines of Philo, which have been known by the Kabbalists since the Middle Ages by the intermediary of the Christian, Jewish, and Arab religious or mystical philosophies, have been frequently made use of. For example, with Philo the passage from the absolute Unity to the individual existence, from the immanent God to the visible world is made in three stages: division of the One into a trinity formed by Reason, Wisdom, and Intelligence; birth of the world of ideas, which is the model of the sensible world; formation of the material world which is the imperfect image of the intelligible world. The Kabbalah, for its part, placed below the Azilah world, domain of the En Soph (absolute One), three worlds: that of Creation (Beriah), that of Formation (Yestzirah), and that of Accomplishment (Asiah). Likewise, while the angels, personification of the forces which sustain and renew continually, are set out by Philo in three classes: that of Goodness, that of Power, and that of Mediation, the Sephiroth of the Kabbalah form three "columns": column of Grace, the column of Law, and the column of the Middle. Finally, the Kabbalists have embellished the theme of Adam Kadmon by brilliant and ingenious variations.

The Kabbalah employs the processes familiar to the Talmudists: allegorical exegesis, mysticism of the letters and numbers. "The literal sense of the Scripture, it says, is the envelope, and woe to the one who takes this envelope for the Scripture itself! Such a man will not have his part in the future world… The Scripture has a body, which are the commandments; it has clothing, which are the Haggadah; and it has a soul which has been revealed to those who were found close to Mount Sinai." "Each word of the Scripture hides a mystery."[517] The processes employed for the spiritualization of the letter are the same in the Talmud and in the Kabbalah. Here is, as a sample, the Kabbalistic interpretation of the biblical narrative concerning the circumstances of the death of Sarah: Sarah dying represents the human body; she dies in the city of the Four Keriath-arba, that is to say that this body is composed of four elements constituting all material existence; she died at Hebron, whose name comes from the root "habar," to bind, that is to say the dissolution of the union existing up to then between the four elements; Abraham, who comes to mourn for Sarah, represents the soul lamenting over the dissolution of the body and restoring the calm only at the moment when it is judged worthy to return to its author; only then does it dare to say to the sons of Heth, that is to say to the Just and Blessed: Compared to you I am at once unworthy and stranger; stranger by the body, unworthy by my soul. The Just respond: Take your place among us. Ephron, that the Bible calls the chief of the Beni Heth, is a psychopomp angel and his true name is Douma (Master of Silence). The symbol is continued until the arrival of Rebecca, who is the daughter of Bethuel (daughter of God: Bath El), himself son of Milka (king of the universe: Melek), and wife of Nahor (companion of intelligence), the brother of Abraham (living fraternally with the soul).[518]

The Kabbalah originated in the South of France and in northern Spain. We see in general the rabbi Isaac the Blind of Nimes, who lived at the beginning of the 13th century, as having given the first development to the metaphysical concept of the Sephiroth, at the same time divine attributes, manifestations of En-Soph, and constitutive elements of Adam Kadmon, prototype of the material world. This idea, which formed the center of the Kabbalistic doctrine, served, in the second half of the same century, as text to the speculations of the Spanish rabbis Abraham Alubafia, Joseph Gikatilla, and Todros Abulafia who was treasurer to King Sanche II de Castille, and to whom the Kabbalah owes the notion of the 10 Kelippoth (husks), material forms of the world of phenomena corresponding to the 10 Sephiroth, ideal forms of the intelligible world. The mysticism of the divine names and the esoteric interpretation of letters of the Hebrew alphabet were specially cultivated by Nachmanides, rabbi and physician at Gerone in Catalogne, by Abraham Abulafia, and by Joseph Gikatilla. But the most eminent Kabbalist of this period was Moses de Leon, born at Avila; he is considered the author of the "Sepher Zohar" (Book of Splendor), although he had claimed only to be the editor.

The Zohar, central book of the Kabbalah, is, in form and foundation, wedded to the Midraschim of the preceding centuries. The seven treatises of which it is composed[519] offers a prolix and confused commentary on the Pentateuch with innumerable digressions. The Kabbalistic doctrines have only known systematic exposé starting from the redaction of the "Pardes Rimmonim" (Park of the Pomegranates), work of the Spanish rabbi Moses Cordorero (16th century).

If the Zohar does not neglect to study the Law, it nevertheless places first importance on the mystical speculations, and there is certainly the reason for the attraction that it exerts, not only upon the Jews, but too upon the scholars of the Renaissance period such as Pico de Mirandola and Jean Reuchlin. Moreover, we have only up to the present considered one of the aspects under which the Kabbalah was presented to curious minds. Treating, under the name of the Theoretical Kabbalah, on the nature of God and on the origin of the world, it was concerned, in its quality of Practical Kabbalah, with dynamic and theurgical magic, and taught the art of commanding the Spirits, foretelling the future, seeing at a distance, and fabricating amulets. At once hierophants and magicians, the Kabbalists have been, from the 8th to the 18th century, diligent collectors and faithful conservators of the secret sciences bequeathed by the ancient Orient.

The Zoahr was passionately studied in the synagogues, not only in Spain but also in Italy, at the beginning of the 14th century. The Jews expelled from Spain, Portugal, and Navarre brought the Zohar into all of Europe. In the 16th century the Kabbalistic theories were set forth, from the speculative point of view, by the works of Cordovero and his disciple Samuel Gallico, and developed, from the theurgical point of view, by Isaac Luria and pupil Chazzim Vidal. In the 17th century, all the Jews having some culture devoted themselves to the study of the Kabbalah. Opposed in the 18th century by the progress of rationalism, these studies nevertheless still counted admirers among the Jews attached to the national traditions, notably in the sect of Sebastian's whose adherents were numerous in Amsterdam, Hamburg, Venice, and Leghorn, and in that of the Frankists, very spread in Poland, whereas the Spanish Jews, by residence or by language, preserved an unacknowledged predilection for the secret science which had formerly found in their lands its greatest doctors.

CHAPTER II
The Sources of the Reintegration: Bible and Talmud

The mass of works, manuscripts, or printed matter, in which are found disclosed the Jewish mystical doctrines is so considerable, and we are so badly informed on the career of Pasqually before he appeared as the founder of the Order of Élus Coëns, that to seek to identify exactly his sources would be a vain task. On the other hand, it is easy to establish at what point his inspiration was specifically Jewish and to point out characteristic concordances between the fundamental ideas of the Reintegration and the concepts familiar to the Bible, the Talmud, and the Kabbalah.

First of all, the name of Coëns that Pasqually gives to the members of his Society is most significant. The word is an adaptation of the Hebrew term Cohanim, which designates the most elevated priestly caste, constituted at Jerusalem under the reign of Solomon to assure the divine service in the Temple. The Cohanim who had the Levites under their orders, was thought to be passed down in direct line from Aaron, and it was natural to believe them in possession, by familial tradition, of secret truths revealed verbally by the Eternal to Moses, and that the latter had confided to his brother. The Reintegration, which had the Coëns enter into their function well before the reign of Solomon, and even before the apostolate of Moses, saw in them the ministers of the true religion whose knowledge and practice were reserved to the initiates alone.

The Élus Coëns are given therefore, by the very title they held, as the inheritors and trustees of the secret Jewish tradition. Jewish but not Hebraic, for Pasqually made between the two words a distinction that was curious and full of implications. Whether this be by attachment to the race of which his parents abjured the religious faith, if he was truly of Jewish origin as tradition claims, or in order to explain the fact that the Jews were at the same time despised by the crowds as greedy and unscrupulous merchants and revered by the occultists as the holders of secret knowledge, he does not wish one to confuse the true Jews and the Hebrews, the intellectual aristocracy and the mercantile commoners.

The Hebrews "no longer possess the divine laws and are content with the ceremonial of a law that has been taken from them ignominiously"[520] following the prophet Moses who has said to Israel: "You will see the worship of the Lod pass to the other nations to your detriment and your shame…it will only be by virtue of this same worship that the different nations will keep you in subjugation."[521]

This downfall had already been announced symbolically in the era of the Patriarchs. When Abraham ascended Mount Moriah, where he wanted to sacrifice Isaac, but upon which the angel of the Lord would appear to him, the two servants that he left at the foot of the mountain "represented the estrangement that these two nations, that of Ishmael and that of Israel, would have in the future from the divine cult from where they fell into divine spiritual privation."[522] Likewise Esau, in losing his birthright, "showed the true figure of what eventually happened to Israel which, spiritual first-born in the world and first inheritor of divine law, would be supplanted by those who would only have (would have only had) to come after it."[523] Israel has experienced the disgrace that struck the nations of Shem, Ham, and Japhet when they "have been shamefully separated from the divine cult and dispersed among all the peoples."[524] "The cult that they (the Hebrews) exercise makes known that they are only led by false principles and by the prince of darkness. They are slaves of the figure (form) of the ceremonial of the law."[525] Having lost all contact with the divinity, no longer knowing the spiritual blessings, these unfortunates "are only subdued by the cupidity of material goods"[526] and "nothing is more rapinous than the heart of the Hebrew."[527]

But, as many Hebrews, whose name signifies "confusion,"[528] are worthy of contempt, just as many Jews or Israelites[529] deserve respect, for Jew signifies "just" and "nothing is stronger and more acceptable to the Creator than the prayer and invocation of the Jews."[530] Nor does Pasqually admit that the least suspicion, even the most founded in appearance, comes to tarnish the reputation of the elect people who remain faithful to their mission. He protests against "the ignorance of the so-called scholars" who have styled "the children of Israel treacherous and thieves," because, according to the Bible, they have, in coming out of Egypt, brought vases of gold and silver, different utensils of precious metals, and perfumes that they had borrowed from the Egyptians in order to celebrate the divine cult." Pasqually saw to remark first of all that the Jews have acted by order of the one who came to deliver them from servitude and that "the carrying off of things that was done at the hand of Israel was a true punishment that divine justice exercised upon the Egyptians in depriving them of the most precious objects of idolatry." It is necessary to consider then that these objects were equal to about a million, which could not suffice to enrich twelve hundred thousand men, to sustain them for forty years in the desert, and to provide for the expenses of the wars that they conducted. "They have not made in the desert, nor in arriving in the Promised Land, any sort of trade nor commerce of material goods with the riches that they had carried off from Egypt," for "all these implements of gold or silver have not served to any other use with Israel than to the decoration of the Temple and of the Ark of the Covenant that Moses erected to the glory of the Creator in order to operate there the different divine cults." Thus, in carrying off the precious objects belonging to the Egyptians and consecrating to divine service that which originated with the demon, the Jews have "one of the spiritual types which operate in the universe"; they have shown "the inevitable fate of all those who engage entirely in matter." The reproaches made against them on this subject "can only be dictated by ignorance and pride" and the benevolent advocate estimates that this pious pilfering is all to the honor of his clients.[531]

These true Jews, disdainful of the goods of this world and devoted only to the divine sciences, Pasqually does not tell us under what name they are known in the Occident, but it is easy to guess. Has he read their treatises in the original text? It seems doubtful, though he seems to have had some notion of Hebrew. The name of Houwa that he gives to Eve is cribbed from her Hebrew name: Hava (Living) and when he calls her "Hommesse," he transports into the French vocabulary the Hebraic grammatical process which formed the term ischa designating the woman by adding a feminine ending to the word isch, which signifies man.[532] The interpretation that he gives of the two successive names of the father of the Hebrews conforms to the generally accepted etymology, although he had made some inspired additions through his mystical theories.[533] The disdain that he professes for the vowel-points, unknown to the Talmud, Midraschim, and Zohar, and which he rejects because "the Judaic language is quite simple and without the punctuation of human convention which has been introduced into the language of the Hebrews,"[533] shows, at the same time as the veneration in which he holds the mystical works, a certain knowledge of the Hebraic writing. Drawing from the Masoretic reform an argument in favor of the distinction established by him between the Hebrews and the Jews, he declares that the "Hebraic tongue," which is used by the posterity of Heber and which is asserted to be the true Jewish language, is only an alteration of the primitive tongue.[535] "The Hebrews use indeed the same characters as the Jews, but the different punctuations, accents, and chevrons that they add to these characters make them pronounce them in a manner opposite to what they are in their pure nature of simplicity."[536] On the other hand, the "Judaic tongue," which alone has preserved the original purity of the language in which the Bible was written, is "the language of the holiness of the Divine Spirit who directs the operation of the righteous men or Jews."[537] "The true Jews recognize that the original alphabet of their language comes from the celestial part and not from the conventions of men. They find all the characters of this language clearly written in the arrangement of the stars, and it is from there that they are drawn."[538] "Adam and his posterity have spoken first the Judaic language which is what the divine spiritual had from all time reserved for its minor creature."[539]

But, if Pasqually knew some touch of Hebrew, nothing shows that he had been capable of attacking the original texts whose reading presented such difficulties that they were only able to be surmounted at the price of long studies[540]; it is therefore likely that he has known them by the partial translations which had been published starting from the 16th century[541] and especially by the numerous versions and commentaries in Spanish which seems to have been his mother tongue.

Be that as it may, the Reintegration is completely permeated by the spirit that animated the Jewish Talmudists and Kabbalists; its author has the same respect for the Mosaic law, he develops like them the themes borrowed from the biblical texts and he is shown to be as attached as them to the popular Jewish beliefs.

∴

The impersonal concept of the divine characterized by the name "la Chose" that the Élus Coëns give it, corresponds exactly to one of the fundamental ideas of the primitive religion of Israel. The ancient Jews gave the name "Elohim" to anonymous forces which presided over the life of nature, but which was also able to reveal itself subjectively to man by a violent and paralyzing emotion, a physical trouble whose "traction" mentioned by Pasqually is but one mitigated form.[542]

The diet prescribed to the Élus Coëns resembles the one that the Torah imposed on the priests, in which Leviticus (III, 17) forbade, like Pasqually did with his disciples, consuming the blood and fat of animals, and Saint-Martin, then secretary and zealous disciple of Pasqually, reminded Willermoz that he could eat nothing, at Easter time, except unleavened bread, by referring to what was ordained by "the Law of Moses."[543] It is likewise with the Jewish Passover that Pasqually has taken the high significance of 14 Nisan, obligatory date of the paschal supper beginning from the 7th century.

Certain themes and certain favorite expressions of the treatise are borrowed directly from the Bible. The concept of the Spiritual Elect or Elect Minor, of the man inspired by God, be it directly or by the intermediary of a divine emissary, and its interpreter with the Spiritual Minors, manifestly shows prophetism, a particularly frequent phenomenon in the history of Israel. The power of the Judges rested on the prestige of the Seers, spokesmen of the divinity, and to whom individuals consented freely to submit their disputes. If the prophets posterior to the Exile: Abdias, Aggea, Zachariah, the third Isaiah, Malachi, Joel, Jonas, are on the whole priests and theologians, those before the Exile: Amos, Hosea, the first Isaiah, Michah, Nahum,

Jeremiah, Sophonia, Habakuk, Ezekiel, the second Isaiah, are "men of God," seers and inspired[544]; they are the prototypes of the Spiritual Elect of Pasqually. The Elect Minors receive from the supercelestial, manifesting itself under the sensible form of a reconciler, such as the "Deputy Heli" who appeared to Seth, the necessary information on the worship to give to God or "sublime spiritual instructions," on the Septenary, Denary, and Quaternary[545], just as Nabi, confused with Ro'eh or Hozeh (Seer) from the ancient period, was for the Jews before the Exile an intermediary between the Spirit of God and Israel, and that the Hebrew prophets, inspired by the divine Ruach or, like Ezekiel, Isaiah, and Daniel, instructed by an angel, came periodically to remind the forgetful people of the cult of the true God. The comparison is made by Pasqually himself when, establishing a relation between the historic role of the prophets and the intervention that is attributed to them in the Operations, where they are invoked at the same time as the Patriarchs[546], he declares that the Creator "has judged necessary for the advancement of man to elect spiritually from the minor beings and to endow them with the prophetic spirit, not only in order to hold man in the laws, precepts, and commandments that he has given them, but also for the greater molestation of the malign Spirits and for the manifestation of the great divine glory.[547]

The term by which the Reintegration generally uses to designate the Spiritual Minor, that is to say the man whose ardent aspiration toward the divine makes him apt to understand the secret teaching dispensed by Pasqually, is employed by the Book of Daniel where the angel Gabriel says to the Seer: "I have come to tell you that you are the man of desire; meditate, therefore, on these words and understand the vision," (IX, 23). "Daniel, man of desire, hear the words that I say to you," (X, 11). "Fear not, man of desire, peace is with you," (X, 19).

The "glory" or luminous apparition by which the divine envoy is manifested to the mortals in the course of the Operations is an essentially biblical theme. When the Lord made the covenant with Abraham, "a furnace of fire and a flaming torch pass between the pieces of the victims," (Genesis, XV, 17). It is from the midst of a burning bush "where the Lord appeared in a flame of fire" that the Eternal spoke to Moses (Exodus III, 2) and the "Glory of God" or luminous cloud which had guided the Jews in the desert rested upon the Propitiatory in the Tabernacle. The Bible, it is true, sometimes represented this glory as a material fire capable of devouring flesh and oblations when God accepted the sacrifice. When Moses and Aaron sacrificed the first victims before the Tabernacle "the fire came out from before the Eternal and devoured the burnt offerings and the fats," (Leviticus VI, 13; VII, 24). Likewise, "the flame rose from the stone and consumed the meat and bread "offered by Gideon, announced to him thus his impending victory (Judges VI, 21)." The fire of the Lord fell and devoured the burnt offering, the wood, and the stones, the very dust and also the water which was in the canal encircling the altar" when Elijah brought it upon the prophets of Baal (III Kings XVIII, 38). When Solomon had ended his prayer in the Temple, "the fire descended from the heavens and consumed the burnt offerings and the other sacrifices, and the glory of Jehovah filled the house," (II Chronicles VII, 1-2). Pasqually was not unaware, moreover, of the devouring force that this divine fire may possess, and he remarked that the spiritual inhabitants of the supercelestial were unable to enter directly into communication with the other temporal beings "without consuming them by the innate faculty of the pure Spirit to dissolve all that it approaches."[548] But the Bible was also aware of an immaterial fire that is above all supernatural light and splendor. The light that God made resplendent at the beginning of Creation (Genesis I, 3) is not the light of the sun, which is only created on the fourth day, but rather "the light of the eternal light of God," light "with which the Lord is enveloped as a cloak," (Psalm CIV, 2) which surrounds him with its blinding radiance when he appeared to Ezekiel: "swirling fire, surrounded by a nimbus and glowing like amber, sparkling like polished silver...illuminating the earth by its glory," (Ezekiel I, 4; VIII, 2), that Daniel (VII, 9) saw under the appearance of a torrent of fire gushing and spreading before God, and which formed the chariot and the flashing horses which took up Elijah from the earth (IV Kings II, 11). The glimmer of the Passes is evidently less brilliant, but there is between it and the supernatural light of which the Bible speaks a difference of intensity and not of nature.

Just as the weak flash expected by the Élus Coëns was but a pale reflection of the dazzling theophanies depicted by the Bible, so did the sensation of pressure that, according to the Bible, the human creatures experienced in the vicinity of the divine become in the Operations the "traction operated by la Chose," less prominent phenomenon, but analogous. At the moment when the Lord went to appear before Abraham, the latter "was enveloped by darkness and a holy terror," (Genesis XV, 12). Before appearing to Elijah on Horeb as a fire, the Eternal announced his approach first by a violent wind, then by a trembling of the ground, and lastly by a weak breath (III Kings XIX, 11-12).

The method according to which Pasqually had derived the divisions of time by sacred computation corresponds to a characteristic of the Sacerdotal Code [549]: in the passages of the Pentateuch emerging from this ancient document, the Hebrew word from Genesis (I, 14) that one ordinarily translated as "time" or "season" is never used to designate the seasons of the climacteric year but is applied to the sacred seasons of the ecclesiastical year which was determined by the moon.[550] The Reintegration itself uses the biblical term to designate the duration of the stay that the Minors must make in the three circles "where they will be obliged to act for a time, two times, and half a time. The first is in the sensible, the closest to terrestrial matter; the second time is in the visual, the closest to rarefied matter, and the half a time is in the rational, which is closest to the supercelestial."[551]

Among the multiple qualifications that Adam gives to the Eternal in his act of contrition[552] figure those of "God of the Sabbath" and "God of the celestial and terrestrial hosts of this universe" (Jehovah Zebaoth), which are the ritual expressions in use in the Bible.[553] The invocation of the Three Days likewise employs a sacred term in giving to the Lord the qualitative of Kadosh (Holy).

It is not until the ritual of the Operations that one finds it outlined in the Bible. Manoah, father of Samson, wishing to know whether the unknown being who had told him to come on behalf of the Lord was truly a divine emissary, "took a goat and libations and put them upon a stone, and he offers them to the Lord who operates marvels, and he and his wife were attentive. When the fire rose toward heaven, the angel of the Lord rose there also in the midst of the flames...and the angels of the Lord disappeared before their eyes and Manoah recognized that this was the angel of the Lord," (Judges XIII, 19-21).

The costume of the operant recalls the priestly vestment particular to the Kohanim of the family of Aaron who alone had the right to penetrate into the Mischkan, the reserved partition of the Tent of Convocation containing the Holy Place and the Most Holy Place: linen underpants, unpleated tunic, multicolored linen cincture: white, hyacinth, purple, crimson. A belt of various colors was also worn by the Coën-Hagadol or High Priest.[554]

The burnt offering for the ordination of Réau-Croix is inspired overtly by the sacrifice offered by every Jew stricken with a legal impurity and in the course of which the officiant burned upon the altar an animal stripped first of its skin. Moreover, Pasqually was perfectly informed on the question of the sacrifices current among the Jews. In a letter addressed to his Substitute General he distinguished very precisely between the expiatory sacrifice, which had for its aim to obtain the forgiveness of a violation of one of the prescriptions of the Law, and the "pacific" sacrifice, spontaneous act of piety or token of recognition and which he calls "thanksgiving," therefore recommending that the hide of the lamb be black, "otherwise the burnt offering would be of thanksgiving and not of expiation."[555]

Finally, the leading role played by the phases of the moon in the determination of the date of the Operations is a remembrance of the new moons consecrated among the Jews, as with the Egyptians, by a special sacrifice.[556]

The spirit and imagination of Pasqually were on this point obsessed with the specifically Jewish ideas and traditions, so that he has introduced into his account concepts that did not play an integral part of his mystical system, and that he ties to it arbitrarily.

The prohibition from receiving the lame into the Order of Élus Coëns, which recalls the prescription of Leviticus (XXI, 18-21), and the verse from Judges (II, V, 8): "The blind and the lame will not enter into the Temple," is justified artificially in the Reintegration by the wound that Jacob received in the course of his struggle with the divine Spirit: "It is since this time that it has been forbidden on behalf of the Eternal, whether in the temple of Moses, or in that of Solomon, that any person marked by the letter B from birth should be admitted into the divine cult under any pretext whatever."[557]

The number 40, so often cited in the Bible where it probably signified an indefinite period, reappears under the form of a stock phrase in the Reintegration: "The 40 days that the rain fell during the deluge represented the 40 years of suffering by Adam after his prevarication."[558] Just as "the fruit of the corporeal reproduction of man can only have passive, active, spiritual life after 40 days," the animals have been closed up 40 days in the Ark, and it is again the same space of time that Noah passed with them upon Ararat during which the flood waters receded.[559] After the deluge the earth remained sterile for 40 years.[560] Jacob, restored in divine spiritual power, could only operate the various divine cults 40 years after his ordination.[561] Moses remained 40 years outside of Egypt after the murder of the Egyptian[562] and he dwelled 40 days in the cloud of Sinai before descending therefrom bearing the Tablets of the Law.[563]

When Pasqually made of the blood the means of organic life, "the trunk and seat from where the soul presides and acts upon all the general (matter) of the particular form that it inhabits,"[564] he paraphrases the verses of the Bible: "You will not eat the blood of animals which is their life," (Genesis IX, 4); "The vital principle of all the creatures resides in the blood," (Leviticus XVII, 14). The mystical development of this notion, that is to say the idea that, man being guilty by this vital principle of material origin, the anathema provoked by the error of Adam falls upon the blood, that consequently the bloody sacrifice, represented by the circumcision, is a form of obligatory purification, already expressed by Leviticus,[565] is found again in the Reintegration which develops the theme again and again, in making the effusion of blood the prerequisite condition of the reconciliation. "This blood of Abel shed upon the earth is the true type and the reaction (strongest action) of the action of divine grace which has made peace and mercy with the earth and its inhabitants. This was likewise the type of the covenant that the Creator had to make with his creature after his reconciliation, just as we have seen the First Man return to grace after the sacrifice of Abel. Has this not been clearly repeated by the circumcision of Abraham, by which this Father of the Multitude obtained his perfect reconciliation with the Creator, and it was by the effusion of his blood that this patriarch knew the covenant that the Eternal made with him."[566] "Abraham, coming out from being prey to demons, testified to the Creator the joy of his divine reconciliation (after the sacrificial ram replacing Isaac), and, in order to mark his faith and his perseverance in his reconciliation, he asked the Creator to make a covenant with him. It was then that he was told by the divine Spirit: Abraham, circumcise your flesh and the blood that you shed upon the earth before the Lord will be a certain proof of the covenant that the Creator made with you. This is what they call vulgarly (among the profane): "Baptism of the blood."[567] "The circumcision of the effusion of the blood of Abraham was a true type of the purification of corporeal matter. This effusion served again to purify that passive life and to dispose it to retain impressions of the different divine spiritual operations that the Creator had ordered anew to his servant Abraham, in order to turn away from the false cult that he operated in preference to that of the divinity. It is not doubtful that, by this wholly spiritual operation, the passive life or the animal soul was not entirely tied with the impassive life or active spiritual soul."[568]

Jewish millennialism is reflected neatly in the passage of the treatise where it says that the Minors reintegrated into the virtues and powers of the First Man await the end of time in the rational circle "in the shade of their reconciliation,"[569] an image which clearly alludes to the Reign of a Thousand Years during which, following the belief current in Israel, the Just would enjoy a perfect bliss while awaiting the end of the world.

The Reintegration is not wedded to the works of the mystical rabbis only by the claim to be a secret commentary on the Pentateuch, it is also by the postulates upon which it is supported and by the processes that it borrows from them.

Pasqually appeals to the faith in an esoteric tradition and personal revelations. He gives himself, be it as the depository of sublime secrets revealed "to the blessed Seth,"[570] or as the interpreter of a "truth of Wisdom" who has "dictated" to him what he wrote.[571]

The fundamental theme of his treatise, that is to say the oral Torah or substance of revelations made by God to Moses on Sinai and communicated by the Prophet to some initiates, is the common source of all Jewish esotericism.

The discourses that Pasqually places in the mouth of the principal personages of Genesis and Exodus are, as remarked Ad. Franck[572], a replica of those that we find in the Midraschim.

But the three most characteristic traits of resemblance are: 1st, the mystical interpretation of the names of personages or localities cited by the Bible; 2nd, the allegorical exegesis of passages of the sacred text; 3rd, the intervention of the Haggadah in the dogmatic account.

Although Pasqually seems to have had some knowledge of the Hebraic letters, for he teaches in one place that the first, Aleph, expresses the divine thought, and the second, Beth, its action[573] we must abandon our search of whether his interpretations rest upon a method seriously conceived and faithfully followed. Only a Hebraist specially trained and endowed with a never-failing patience could attempt to discover whether the master of the Élus Coëns has had recourse to the Gematria, Notarikon, Temurah, or to the various genres of Zeruph in order to find mystical equivalents to the biblical names. It does not, perhaps, do him wrong to suppose that he has simply imagined the interpretations confirming his theories, being quite assured that his readers believed him and therefore, his words. Whatever be the case, he makes frequent use of the Talmudic process. "The spiritual interpretation of the name of Benjamin means: Son or Child of my sorrow."[574] "The true spiritual name of Bethzaleel, constructor of the Tabernacle, is Beth, that is to say carrying out the action of the divine thought."[575] Cain signifies: "son of my suffering"[576]; Seth: "admitted to the posterity of God"[577] Jared: "man illuminated by God."[578]

The name of Egypt means: "place of divine privation or land of malediction"[579]; that of the Nile: "principle of action and temporal spiritual operation"[580]; that of Sinai: "height and elevation of divine glory"[581]; that of the desert of Jeraniaz: "listen to the Lord"[582]. The name of the desert of Phializath, situated between Madgal and the Red Sea, signifies: "regeneration of action," while Madgal is equivalent to: "aspect of abomination" and the Red Sea to: "abyss of bitterness."[583] Lathan, name of the comet appearing at the birth of Enoch, ought to be interpreted: "sign of confusion and terrestrial suffering."[584]

Some of the names of which Pasqually indicates the mystical meaning have been either forged by him or borrowed from Talmudic legends; such are Deliacim, first name given by Jared to the son whom he later called Enoch and which signifies: "resurrection of the Lord into the posterity of Seth"[587] Cainan, younger sister of Cain: "child of confusion"[586]; Aba I, third child of Adam and Eve: "child of matter or of divine privation"[587]; Booz, tenth son of Cain and murderer of his father: "son of slaying"[588] Aba 4, surname given by Adam to Abel: "child of peace"[589]; Aba 10, another surname of Abel: "being elevated above every spiritual sense."[590]

Pasqually applies systematically the method of allegorical interpretation of which Philo the Jew had made so brilliant a use and set the rules of use for Jewish mystics. We have been able to see that he employs it for long pages when he treats on the "types" and on the symbols, particularly those that provide to his speculation the Tabernacle and Mount Moriah.[591] he writes again concerning the "privation" that Adam had earned by his prevarication: "It is for this that the angel of the Lord said, according to what is related in the Scripture: We drive out from here the man who had knowledge of good and evil, for he was able to trouble us in our wholly spiritual functions, and we keep guard that he not touch the tree of life and so that by this means he does not live forever. The tree of life is none other than the Spirit of the Creator that the Minor attacks unjustly with his allies. That he does not live forever signifies that he does not live eternally like the first demonic Spirits in an accursed virtue and power."[592] He teaches that "the essence" (the true meaning) of the threats that the Creator makes to Adam in driving him out of the Terrestrial Paradise, according to what the Scripture relates: "Go cultivate the earth, it will give you nothing but thorns," is that, in procreating carnally, Adam had placed in the world imperfect beings, "for there are not sharper thorns than those that may be borne in the heart of a good father, a criminal posterity."[593] He asserts that "the darkness, by which the Scripture threatens to damn them, does not signify a privation of brightness and light, but only a privation of divine spiritual action in the immense celestial circumference where the true reconciled Spirits (truly reconciled) will go to make their successful reintegration."[594] Alluding to a tradition according to which Moses had communicated the divine law to the Hebrews while having his face covered by a veil which hid likewise the Tablets of the Law, he adds this commentary: "This red veil, which hid from the people the face of Moses and the tablets upon which were written the intention and the will of the Creator, represented very perfectly the perverse Spirits who serve as scandalous veil to all the Minors who make a connection with them.[595] The red color of this veil represents the insinuation of the demonic intellect into the principal senses of the form of the Minor, which deprives him of all communication with the divine spiritual impression, be it by type or by mystery, or even in pure and simple spiritual nature. The face of Moses veiled announced the state of privation of divine knowledge when Israel was going to be subjugated by the covenants that Moses saw that the people had made with the prince of demons and the ignorance when these people were going to fall from the spiritual type that Moses operated before them."[596]

The Haggadic elements are abundantly represented in the Reintegration which is, nearly as much as an esoteric commentary, a complement to the Bible, from Genesis to the First Book of Kings.

It is true that it happens from time to time that Pasqually simply refers his readers to known texts. For example, he judges it useless "to enter into the detail of the temporal conduct" of Abraham, Isaac, and Jacob, because "the Scripture says enough on this subject."[597] He recognizes that "the Scripture speaks amply enough on the different gifts that the Creator has placed in certain men emanated by him for the manifestation of his glory"[598] and that, in which concerns the seven plagues with which Egypt was stricken by Moses, "one may be satisfied with all that the Scripture reports to (on) this point."[599] He does not stop to detail all the particular facts which passed among the Israelites since their exodus from Egypt, because the Scripture "speaks amply enough on their different marches and encampments."[600] He excuses, on occasion, the concision of the sacred text; speaking on the second posterity of Noah, of which the Bible has not made mention, he remarks: "The Scripture does not speak on this second posterity: the silence of the Scripture on this subject ought not astonish us; it has left behind subjects most interesting for the man of desire; perhaps in this it has had some very legitimate reasons, perhaps also the translators have not found these details very necessary to the man incapable of satisfying his curiosity (whose vain curiosity is never satisfied)."[601]

But, when he undertakes to complete the biblical text, without which his additions always come to the support of his particular theories, he shows an imperturbable assurance, and, to judge by the abundance and precision of the details, one would believe to hear the account of an ocular witness. Sometimes he fills out a passage too concise in his eyes. Genesis was content to say that Adam had named the animals, that is to say, just as the Talmudist rabbis understood it, had exercised his right to command them. Pasqually has it said by the Creator: "Command all the active and passive animals and they will obey,"[602] then he adds: "After this operation the Creator said to his creature: 'Command the general or the earth; it will obey you.' Which Adam did. He saw by this that his power was great, and he knew with certainty that very second all comprising the universe. After these two operations the Creator said to his creature: 'Command all the created universe and all its inhabitants will obey you.' Adam again carried out the words of the Eternal; and it was by this third operation that he learned to understand the universal creation."[603]

Sometimes, as in the episode of the Prophetess, the Reintegration modifies on a number of points the biblical account. According to the Bible, Saul, wanting to know the outcome of the battle that he was going to take to the Philistines, and having consulted in vain the Urim and dreams, went during the night under a disguise to the magician of Endor who practiced necromancy (rigorously forbidden by Saul himself) and he orders her to "make to show" (from Sheol) the shade of Samuel; the latter appeared and announces to the king that the next day he will meet the Judge in Sheol. The Reintegration relates that Saul, intending to attack and pillage the Gabaonites, previously reconciled with God by Joshua, and who had implored and obtained the aid of the Philistines, but doubting the value of his preferred tribe, that of Benjamin, orders the Prophetess to come find him. The diviner, knowing that the chiefs of Benjamin have the intention of making her perish for fear that she does not bring the king to justice, refuses to come and takes refuge in a place situated a league from Galboa. Saul has her sought with orders to bring her back by force; they end up discovering her and, upon the promise given "faith of king" that there would not be any harm done to her, she invites the king to go to her and evokes a Spirit in his presence.[604]

Most often the additions that the treatise brings to the biblical accounts are of anecdotal character in the manner of the Talmudic accounts. Pasqually knew the nature of the provisions brought into the Ark: "These provisions were not sought-after things and delicacies as would be the pure flour and other things chosen and susceptible to flatter the taste. They consisted only in simple ordinary fruits of the earth." He even knew that: "more than two thirds remained in the Ark when everyone had come out of it."[605] He knew the entire history of the posterity of Cain: "Cain having withdrawn after his crime into the region of the South with his two sisters had a posterity of ten males and eleven females, and constructed there the town of Henoch for the edification of which he imagined to dig into the entrails of the earth with his first-born named Henoch." "He left his secret, whether for the smelting of metals, or the discovery of mines, to his son Tubalcain. It is from there that it is come to us that Tubalcain was the one who had first discovered the smelting of metals."[606] He is particularly well informed on the circumstances of the death of Cain: "Great man of the hunt," he engaged with passion in this exercise in the company of Booz, his tenth son. "It is this last one who gave death to his father Cain, which happened in this manner: Cain having resolved to go hunting ferocious beasts accompanied by two children of Henoch, his grandsons, did not prevent his son Booz from taking part in the hunt that he had planned to do the day after the morrow. Booz for his part planned with two of his nephews, sons of Tubalcain, to go on the hunt the same day as his father, but likewise without having anticipated his plan. Booz, not having children, had placed all his affection in his two nephews. Booz, without knowledge took the same route as his father Cain and, both being in a forest that they were accustomed to scouring, Booz saw the shadow of a figure across this forest named Onam, which means Suffering, let fly an arrow that was going to pierce the heart of his father, having taken him for a ferocious beast." Booz, desperate, begged his nephews to kill him; yielding to his prayers, they aimed their arrows at him when "a voice was heard and said: Whoever will strike dead the one who killed Cain will be punished to die seventy-seven times." Booz, object of "the general enmity of the whole first posterity of Cain, was forced to leave the town of Henoch and withdraw into the desert of Jeranias where he finished his life in contrition and penitence."[607]

Pasqually knew again that the posterity of Abraham, Isaac, and Jacob, "has dwelled 430 years in Egypt"[608] and he knew the reason for which the army of the Pharaoh had engaged itself imprudently in the bed of the Red Sea: "As the Pharaoh had, in the obscurity of the cloud sent by God, lost sight of the fugitive Israelites, he ordered his army to light torches in order to follow the enemies and to seek a trace of their footsteps, but this resource was more fatal than advantageous to the Egyptians, for the army of the Pharaoh, being occupied with following the trace of the enemy's footprints, did not notice that it had left the shore of the sea and that it walked into the middle of the waters which were suspended on each side."[609]

But it is on the childhood of Moses that the author of the Reintegration possesses the most unpublished information. He teaches us that the father of Moses was called Tupz, that is to say: "full of divine goodness," and not Amram, and his mother Maha, that is to say: "divine spiritual fertility," that they had three children: "Merian at 66 years and 3 months for the father and 48 years and 3 months for the mother, Aron at 79 years 7 months and 61 years 7 months, finally Moses at 82 years 10 months and 64 years 10 months."[610] Three pages of the treatise are dedicated to an episode in the flavor of oriental tales. They relate that the daughter of the Pharaoh, proud of the beauty of her adopted child, had seen one day to present him to the sovereign; as she crossed a public room the attention of the child, which she carried in her arms, had been attracted by "a large square where the crown and the scepter of the king were placed" and above all by a carbuncle "which threw a considerable fire among the precious stones which adorned the crown of the king." "The princess...adhering to the desire that the child showed to take all these jewels, examined the chamber to see whether she was observed and, seeing no one, she leaned Moses over the crown and the scepter. This child takes them with eagerness, but not being able to remove (lift) them, the princess helps him and puts the crown on his head. In this interval (at this moment) the child lets the scepter fall at the feet of the princess and wanted then to take off the crown from atop his head. He let it fall on the table and put his foot on it." A "chamberlain" had been present at the scene without being seen by the princess; he was going to report to the king and counsel him to have killed this child from an exiled race and whose act was a deadly omen. Informed by her father of the condemnation to death charged against her protégé and of the name of the informer, the princess, in order to prove that the child had not acted "by contempt nor by wickedness," saw to bring "a great dish of fire." "They placed this dish on the table with the scepter and the crown of the king. As soon as the young Moses had noticed the fire, he rushed over without looking at either the scepter or the crown; he took in his right hand a lit coal and brought it to his mouth where it extinguished itself after having burned him on part of his tongue." The Pharaoh, convinced by this experiment that Moses had not acted "by the impulsion of the God of Israel that he held with him in captivity," banished his chamberlain and spared Moses who was left stuttering following this ordeal.[611]

To these general traits which the Reintegration gives a properly Talmudic physiognomy, come to be added secondary but significant resemblances.

The personages of Seth, Enoch, and Elijah, who play so great a role in the Reintegration in the quality of Elect Minors, are also given primary importance by the Talmudists. They unanimously represent Seth as very knowledgeable in the divine things. The treatise Hechaloth (Dwellings or celestial regions) attributed to the High Priest Ishmael, and which relates his ascension, shows Enoch becoming after his death Metatron or second person from the divinity. God reveals to him all the secrets of creation, conferring on him the right to command all the angels and makes him "a splendid vestment in which are woven all the lights."[612] The Talmudists, supporting themselves on a popular tradition which announced the coming of Elijah as hierophant charged with explaining all that human reason is powerless to understand, had the custom to conclude their controversies on an unsolvable question by citing the proverb: "Elijah alone could explain this." The same prophet is often shown by the Talmud visiting the most celebrated rabbis, coming to their aid when they are in danger, intervening on their behalf in their private affairs.

The good intellect and the evil intellect of the Reintegration are, under another name, the "good and evil desire" (perhaps a good and evil Spirit) of which speak the Talmudists. They know likewise a protector being of each man, similar to "the companion Spirit of the Minors which surrounds them with its spiritual circle in order to defend them from demonic shock that the perverse Spirits operated at each instant against them"[613]

They already asserted the supremacy of man over the Spirits or Angels. Certain ones related that the Creator had at first made Adam so great that his head touched the firmament; the angels prostrated and complained that the Lord had given them two sovereigns: one in heaven and another on earth. In order to calm their dissatisfaction, the Lord leaned on Adam's head and reduced his height which, even after this operation, still reached fifteen hundred feet. The rabbi Ben Esra relates on his part that, as the angels reproached the Lord for having granted Adam too great a power, he asked them if they knew the names of his creatures.[614] The Talmud declares that the righteous are greater than the angels.

The candles of representation that the Élus Coëns lit for the Operations proceed from the idea expressed by the Talmudic treatise Ketuboth which asserts that the spirits of the dead return willingly to the places where a light burns for them. Pasqually has simply utilized for the sympathetic cooperation of the Réau-Croix a postulate which is applied to the dead.

CHAPTER III
Sources of the Reintegration: Kabbalah and Oriental Traditions

The images and concepts proper to the Kabbalah are very recognizable in the Reintegration.

The theory set forth by Pasqually of the existence of the Spirits before their emanation is, as has been remarked Ad. Franck[615], "strictly conforming to the Kabbalah." Just as, for the Kabbalists, the En-Soph is the sum of the potentials and as the Sephiroth are the divine attributes, at first immanent, then exteriorized, so does Pasqually state that the Spirits "existed in the bosom of the divinity, but without distinction of action, thought, or particular understanding; they are unable to act or feel but by the sole will of the superior being which contains them and by which all were propelled...This existence in God is an absolute necessity; it is that which constitutes the immensity of divine power. God would not be the Father and the master of everything if he had not innate within himself an inexhaustible source of beings that he emanates by his pure will and when it pleases him."[616]

The Denary Spirits are a replica of the six Sephiroth, or individualized attributes, by which is manifested, following Kabbalistic metaphysics, immanent God or En-Soph, and all that Pasqually says on them and on the number ten is applied exactly with the latter. Like the Sephiroth, "the first emanated Spirits were innate in the divinity, they are real and imperishable, they have a personal, absolute and eternal existence, they will exist always in the divine circle."[617] These Spirits of the first class are called "Superiors or Denaries"[618] because "ten is the divine number, origin of every major, inferior, and minor spiritual being, and of every law of action, whether spiritual or spiritous,"[619] The initiate understands the "great denary number of the Eternal and all its contents from emancipation and creation."[620] The Denary "is the number of the immense divine circumference which the first emanated Spirits occupied."[621] The ten Patriarchs of whom the Bible speaks are only terrestrial images of the transcendent Sephiroth. "No Patriarch has borne the name of his material origin (his true name is not the one under which he is known by the vulgar), and they are all (their secret names) different from one another. There are ten Patriarchs, there are ten spiritual names which operate the cult of the divinity by its proper denary number."[622]

The Kabbalistic theme of the Sephiroth has been so despotically imposed on the imagination of Pasqually that he has, for a time, departed from the prudence with which be ordinarily conceals his borrowings. He remarks indeed that the divine circumference bearing the Denary is "called vulgarly Dominion."[623] Now, Dominion, or Royalty, is precisely the name of the tenth Sephirah, Malkuth, which represented in the system of the Kabbalah the sum of the intelligible World (first triad of the Sephiroth), of the mental World (second triad), of the physical World (third triad), and which was the harmony of the universe. Moreover, certain details of the passage that we have cited reveals plagiarism, and clumsy plagiarism. It is thus that Pasqually, forgetting that he sometimes elsewhere attributes to the major Spirits the number 7, to the inferior Spirits the number 3, and that before the revolt of the perverse Spirits the Minor did not yet exist, declares that, at the time of the first emanation, the divine circumference was the abode of "every Spirit, superior 10, major 8, inferior and minor 4"; now the sum of these three numbers, that is to say 22, is the number of letters of the Hebrew alphabet that the Kabbalists considered as the principles which, added with the first 10 numbers or Sephiroth, formed the "thirty-two marvelous paths of Wisdom," that is to say the types of all the material objects, of all physical phenomena, and all bodies.

The gigantic form of the Adam Kadmon of the Kabbalah, of the First Man, anthropomorphic schema of the universe (macrocosm), of which the Sephiroth are the constitutive parts, and which finds its reduced copy in the human being (microcosm), projects its great shadow over many passages of the treatise. The Tabernacle in which Moses has contained the divine law is the image "of the particular world or the lesser world, and the tabernacle of the Minor is the genuine type of the world, because it contains within its small expanse all that the greater world contains in its immense space."[624] "The form of man is the image of the general repetition of the great work of the Creator."[625] "The particular terrestrial corporeal form" (human body) which the Minors inhabit "is similar to that of the earth and has been likewise produced conforming to the image of the divine thought."[626] "Just as the inhabitants of the supercelestial, the celestial, and the universal circle each operate in their particularity in the redoubtable Tabernacle (symbol of the universe), so too all these different spiritual beings work and operate in the body of man with the Minor (minor Spirit) which is contained there."[627] "Man bears by his form the true figure of the apparent (sensible) form which appeared in the imagination of the Creator and which was then operated (realized) by the divine spiritual workers and unites in substance with apparent solid passive matter (submitted to suffering) for the formation of the universal temple (universe), general temple (earth), and particular temple (organized beings)."[628]

The human body being at the same time an organism and a representation of creation, both spiritual and material, the numerical superiority of the divine influences over the diabolical influences is indicated by the digits of the hand of which the medius represents the human soul (or rather the consciousness), the thumb the good Spirit, the index the good intellect, while the annular and articular represent respectively the demonic Spirit and intellect.[629]

On the concept of Adam Kadmon, the Kabbalah had deduced the idea that every material body, whatever be its nature, its stature, or its place in the universe, possesses a soul, a Spirit which drives it[630], so that the phenomenal world is a collection of organisms of identical composition. This idea, as well as that of the ternary composition of living beings, having become an article of faith for the occultists beginning in the 16th century, is expressed very clearly in the Reintegration. "This earth contains within itself a living being, emanated from the Creator and similar to that which is enclosed in the apparent form of all the Minors."[631] "All the catholic (universal) bodies have been formed by the descent of the general Minor (anima mundi) into the general terrestrial form (corpus mundi) and by the junction of the major divine Spirit (spiritus mundi) with the general Minor."[632] "The laws which rule our world and the beings which live there are the same for all the other worlds and all the spiritual beings who inhabit them,"[633] so that "the inhabitants of the terrestrial and celestial worlds are only particular beings" (having an individual existence) at once material and spiritual.[634]

The major Spirit which, according to the Reintegration, fixed, at the moment of creation, "by order of the Creator, the limits of the reach of the general body (universe) and the particular bodies, as much the celestial (stars) as the terrestrial (living organisms), as well as the different faculties and properties that he gave to all the bodies,"[635] is a replica of the Metatron, adopted by the Kabbalah, chief of the celestial phalanx composing the third World, that of Formation, and which, after having given to him alone the existence of the material world, is charged with maintaining the movement and harmony of all the spheres, and under his orders are myriads of angels, each of which is in charge of a natural phenomenon: phases of the moon, revolutions of the celestial bodies, succession of the seasons, vegetation, etc.

The type of the Reconciler, reproduced successively by the Elect Minors, is found in seed form in the Zohar where the name of Moses "may very well not designate the historic personage but a type."[636] This Bible of the Kabbalah says indeed that Moses, who has delivered Israel a first time, will return to deliver it at the end of time, and, noting that Shiloh, of which it is a question in Genesis (XLIX, 10), has the same numerical value as Moses, it sees here the manifestation of the spirit of Elohim.[637] Moreover, the Zohar admits, like the Talmud, the coming of at least two Messiahs or Redeemers (Goels).[638]

The quaternary power of the First Minor becoming the octonary power of the Elect Minor recalls the thesis of the eminent Kabbalist, the rabbi Meir, who asserts that with the advent of the Messiah, each Israelite will doubly recover the privileges granted to man before his sin.[639]

The compensating role assigned by Pasqually to the moon, "which cooperates by its fluid to modify and to mitigate the action and reaction of the two principal chiefs of the corporeal vivification, which are the central axis and the solar body,"[641] recalls the celebrated "balance" of the Kabbalists who conceive all existence as the result of the antagonism of two contrary forces held in equilibrium by a middle term. This theme is found to be reprised several times in the Reintegration where "action and reaction" are presented as the necessary condition of the existence of all its forms.

The graphic representation of the universe such as it was constituted before the prevarication of Adam, described by the Reintegration, is a reduced copy of "the Kabbalistic Tree" or "Tree of Life," figured in the manuscripts of the Zohar. It is composed of ten circumferences, bearing the name of the Sephiroth, arranged in three parallel columns and united by straight lines which represented the "channels" allowing them to communicate between themselves.[742]

Finally, certain details of the arithmosophy of the treatise are directly inspired by the Kabbalah. The number 3, that Pasqually attributes to the material world, corresponds to the triad of letters of the Hebrew alphabet which, in the Kabbalah, symbolizes the three Sephiroth representing air, water, and fire, and which, thus comprising the three fundamental elements, is the image of the earth. Pasqually has simply replaced the three elements known to the ancient Greek philosophers with the three elements of alchemical theory.

The four circles: Superior, inferior, major, and minor, have an air of kinship with the four Worlds of the Kabbalah: that of the Sephiroth or emanations of En-Soph, that of the Angels or ideas, that of the Types of the individuals and objects, and that of the Phenomena of the Material world.

The six circles of creation, whose number may, moreover, be calculated on that of the six days of Genesis, corresponds also to the "Diadem of Diadems," circularly formed envelopes formed by the six inferior Sephiroth and destined to mitigate the too bright light emanating from the En-Soph, light which destroyed the first created worlds. These six envelopes allow in the Zohar the comparison of the universe to a nut whose kernel is surrounded by several husks.[643] Likewise, the duration of six thousand years assigned to the universe by the Reintegration is a concept often expressed in the Kabbalistic texts.

∴

The mystical current, the eddies of which one sees in the Talmud, which is inflated in the Midrashim and the esoteric treatises from the 7th to the 10th centuries and ends up flowing to the very brim in the Kabbalah, carried on its troubled waters materials lifted in the oriental regions where they had originated. The most dense among them: Chaldean astrology and demonology, Ionian physics, Mazdan, Manichaean, Sabian, and Mithraic concepts, Pythagorean arithmetic and geometry, were deposited in the Reintegration in more or less dense sedimentary layers.

Pasqually believed, like the ancient Chaldeans, in the double influence, beneficent or malefic, of the stars, in the predominant action of the stars upon cosmic life, in the prophetic role of comets. But, by virtue of the principle which gives to all bodies a soul endowed with intelligence and will, he also carries over to the mental plane the astral influences that the Chaldeans conceived overall from the material point of view. "The superior, major, and inferior planetary bodies are really constituted in divine spiritual life and in passive corporeal life."[644] "Just as the soul of the Minor has the body as its organ, so do the septenary Spirits have the corporeal beings for their organs" (the planets).[645] "The seven principal Spirits that the Creator has attached in its universe in order to instruct the inferior and minor creature of its will, and to lift it up by these means and by that of the spiritual intelligence to the perfect knowledge of divine works[646], are also attached to all creation in order to support it in all its operations according to the septenary duration (7,000 years) that God has fixed"[647]; "they preside as heads in the different actions and different movements in all the bodies"[648] and "operating on behalf of the material inhabitants of the terrestrial world."[649] In summary, the action of the septenary Spirits is double: by the number 3 (matter) they act on the forms (action of planets upon organic life), by the number 4 they act on the spirit of the Minor[650]; from them emanate at once "the passive soul" (vegetative) marked by the Ternary, and "the impassive soul" (divine spark) bearing the Quaternary.[651]

On the other hand, "the celestial and terrestrial worlds are the prison of the prevaricating Spirits"[652]; consequently, the influences coming from on high may be ill-fated. Now, after his fall, Adam is become "subject to the inconsistency of the temporal events and to that of the planetary bodies, formerly inferior to him"[653] the Minor has therefore as much to fear from the stars as to hope from them: "it is passed in proverb among men that there are evil planetary influences and this is quite so," because "the planetary circles are susceptible to being inhabited by malignant spiritual beings who are opposed to the powers and combat the faculties of the good influential actions that the good spiritual planetary beings are charged to shed upon the whole world."[654]

Finally, "the planetary sign" which marked the birth of Enoch "astonished (frightened) the posterity of Seth and yet more that of Cain…because…it understood that it was the prognostication of the scourge that the Creator had hurled upon it. This sign was none other than a star extra-linear to its planetary circle and it is what the vulgar call a comet."[655]

When Pasqually speaks[656] "on the seven stars comprising each of the constellations distributed among the seven planetary circles" he republishes a Chaldean astronomical doctrine, collected by the Talmud, and according to which each of the seven heavens had a "fortress" and each fortress contained seven stars.[657] When he says that the place where the Just, while awaiting their definitive reintegration, remain under the shadow of a great light, called "philosophically" (for the initiates) "Saturnary circle,"[658] he follows the Chaldean classification which placed Saturn in the heaven furthest from the earth, and which led the Talmud to put the seventh heaven, Arabath, heaven of Saturn, immediately below the throne of God and to lodge there the Guph, domain where is found the reservoir of souls and where return those of the Just after having victoriously traversed their terrestrial career.[659]

The cardinal points, known from the beginning of astrology, become in the Reintegration "the four celestial regions from where Moses had come out, by the four divine powers, the four exterminating angels who would molest the Egyptians and at the same time see to the defense of the people of Israel" at the time of the exodus from Egypt.[660] The four spiritual powers that the Creator has given to his Minors are those by which "he can make use of those of the four regionary chiefs and of all that is at their dependence."[661]

The moon, whose influence is decisive for the success of the Operations, is the god Sin, the most powerful of the gods of Chaldea, that the Jews had known at Babylon, and of whom their women wore the crescent on their amulets. The Talmud notes that "Israel calculates according to the moon" and "the peoples" according to the sun.[662]

The circadian day, that the Chaldean astronomers knew and that they seem to have received from the Sumerians or the Kushites, is observed by the four elders of the second posterity of Noah; "when they re-establish the divine cult, they each exercised their spiritual operation for six hours, it is from there that the present day of twenty-four hours has been restored in its first state of diurnal and nocturnal nature,"[663]

The demons that Pasqually fears attack, like those against which the Chaldean magic sought to defend, the bodies as well as the spirit of men. They destroy just as much as they tempt and bribe. "They are occupied without respite with the degradation of forms and the corruption of spiritual beings."[664] "The demons have power over the corporeal forms of apparent matter…they are even able to destroy that particular form,"[665] "The demons have sworn to dissolve and destroy every species of creation."[666] "The prince of the demons sees to attack through his intellect Spirits the corporeal form of man, because this form contains a minor being more powerful than them."[667]

Lilith, killer of children, who attacks boys until the eighth day and girls until the twentieth after their birth, and that the Kethuboth treatises of the Talmud of Palestine and the Sanhedrin treatises of the Talmud of Babylon recommend to keep at a distance by never leaving a new-born sleeping without light during the critical period, this female demon, sister of the Babylonian Lalu, haunts the imagination of Pasqually when he speaks of the "demons who persecute the minors in the moment that they begin to enter into this lower world and even when they are unable to make use of their corporeal senses; which one may easily perceive by the different movements, cries, and agitations of the new-born," so that "we cannot doubt that the demons are around the corporeal form from the time that the Minor is incorporated there."[668]

The Reintegration has faithfully preserved a characteristic detail of the mystical topography in use in Chaldea, namely that the region of the South is the habitat of the demon. "Cain, after his prevarication, was obliged to go live with his two sisters in the South part where he was relegated to dwell set by order of the Creator and by the authority of Adam. This is the type of the place where the demons have been banished."[669] "This southern part has been cursed by the Creator, being marked by the Scripture to be the asylum of the Majors (demons) and the Minors (damned) who will have prevaricated."[670] "The crow coming out of the Ark took his direction toward the South in order to show us where Cain had withdrawn and where Ham withdrew and all his posterity."[671] Egypt, land where Israel was enslaved, is situated "in the South part."[672] Agar and Ishmael, in leaving Abraham (type of the divine Spirit), went to live in the South.[673]

∴

The theory of which Pasqually calls the central fire or "central axis fire" seems to have come to him from the physicists of Ionia by the mediation of the esoteric Jewish literature.

In the Pythagorean philosophy, the central fire, first monad, harmony of the contraries, has created the world, governs it, confers it unity and eternity. It is the vital node of the universe, being situated at the innermost center of the sphere of the All. It is the source of heat, being, and life, the directive and sovereign force of the world. The stars are moved around the igneous hub which serves as the pivot of universal movement. The Pythagoreans gave to the central fire quite varied divine names, but it was above all for them the soul of the world, an igneous principle, an ether, a quintessence. It represented at once the most subtle form of matter and its activity considered as vital energy.[674]

Heraclitus repeated this idea and gave it its definitive development. His "divine fire," living and intelligent element, whose invisible heat gives life to everything, which contains the universal and divine reason, this fire of which our soul is but a spark, is the central fire of Pythagoras, spiritualized and divinized. But Heraclitus presents the action of the central fire under a double aspect. It is the generative element by the effect of a principle of alteration; from the transformations that it has undergone by condensation or rarefaction are born the elementary bodies: air, water, and earth. But it will also be the destructive element when the disappearance of the principle of alteration leads to the annihilation of the different degradations of the igneous principle and returns it from the multiple to the unity.

This theory had a corollary which divided cosmic life into cycles constituted by the periodical return of creations and successive destructions. The idea of the end of the sensible world through a general burning found place in a number of philosophical or religious systems of Asia Minor and ancient Greece. It figures prominently in the teachings of the Stoic School, in the cult of Apollo, and above all in the Jewish apocrypha known under the name of the Sibylline Books.[675] It is probably in the Jewish traditions relating to these works that Pasqually has found it. If he has not retained the accessory idea of periodical destructions, he very clearly expresses the principal theme when he speaks of the "fire which must put an end to the universal creation"[676] and of the conflagration by which the earth will be destroyed with all its inhabitants.[677] "The central axis fire will dissipate the apparent forms as promptly as it formed them."[678] "Just as the fire has the property of reducing to ashes all that it embraces, so does the central axis have the faculty of dissipating entirely all that reintegrates into it without there remaining any afference or any substance suitable and proper to being inhabited by a Spirit."[679] "There will not remain of universal creation any vestige when it is reintegrated into its principle of emanation" (into the source from where it has come out).[680]

It is possible, furthermore, that the idea of the central axis fire which figures in the diagram of the universe before the fall of Adam[681] had been inspired by Plato, or by a concept of oriental origin reproduced by the Greek philosopher. In the treatise of the Republic, Er, the man who has passed twelve days in Hades and reports his revelations therefrom on cosmology, speaks of a column of light that crosses the heavens and the earth, in uniting the poles and forms the axis of the world.[682]

∴

Mazdaism, which the Jews had known during their captivity in Babylon when they were passed under the dominion of the Persians, has left traces in their secret traditions, not only in angelology, as we have already established, but also in other points of view, as shows the Reintegration. It is indeed impossible to attribute to a fortuitous encounter the fundamental analogy existing between the doctrine of Pasqually on the causes which have led to the creation of the material world and that of man, and the account of the Avesta, according to which the Evil Principle, Anra Mainyu, having attempted to invade the spiritual world created by the Good Principle, Ahura Mazda, the latter has formed the sensible world, which is like a boulevard at the limit of the two domains and is guarded by the double men of the Fravashis, or Ferouers, divine sparks which reside in every human being and have descended here below voluntarily in order to fight with the demons.

The echo of the Mazdan eschatological theories is yet more striking because it is heard completely unexpectedly. Regarding the Ark of Noah and the reasonable Minors (endowed with reason, that is to say men) who were found enclosed there, the Reintegration alludes in passing to the "oath that the Creator has made that neither the First Man nor any of his posterity be (will be) reintegrated into the circle before the great battle which must be engaged in by the true Adam or Réau between the earth and the heavens for the greater advantage of the Minors."[683] The theme of a superterrestrial combat that would lead to the triumph of the Good over the Evil is likely a transposition of the religious plan of the old myth of the sun-god vanquishing the celestial dragon and all the powers of darkness and cold that are opposed to him. This motif, which one discovers in the struggle of Marduk against Tiamat, related by the Babylonian poem of the Creation and in the seasonal myths of the New Year, of the revival of the sun and the rebirth of the springtime vegetation, had become in the Jewish apocalypses the final triumph of the Messiah over Gog and Magog, but the transformation of the periodical and provisionary victory of the sun in a decisive battle was due to the Avesta, which showed Azhi vanquished by the seventh of the Ameshas Spentas (Immortal Saints), Straosha, protector of the faithful of Mazda, psychopomp and indefatigable adversary of the demons. The sacred book of the Persians also announced the resurrection of Gayomert, the primitive man, and of all humanity at the moment of the final judgment which would follow this great battle, so that "the reintegration of the First Man and of his posterity into the circle," foretold by Pasqually, corresponds trait for trait to the end of time described by the Avesta.

It seems also, to properly read the Reintegration, that the treatise contains another remembrance of the Iranian traditions. Mazdaism was only provisionally dualist, since it did not conceive of the struggle of Good and Evil as having to endure eternally. It proclaimed that the opposition of the two principles would cease at the end of time, and that consequently nothing is absolutely evil nor cursed forever. After the triumph of Sraosha over Anra Mainyu and the disappearance of the latter, the Evil Thought ceased to exist. The bath of molten metal where the wicked were plunged was a particularly energetic rite of purification from where they came out washed and worthy of the blessing, whatever had been their crimes.[684] The Zohar had collected this idea expressly in the most ancient parts of the religious code of the Persians and unknown to other theologies. It professed that the archangel of Evil himself would one day rediscover his name and his nature as an angel of light; then from his mystical name, Samael (angel of poison or of death), would be cut off the first part with the ominous meaning and he would preserve only the second: El, name common to all the angels.[685] The Reintegration appears to subscribe implicitly to the Mazdan thesis; at least that is what one may infer from a passage which indirectly alludes to the forgiveness finally granted to the perverse Spirits. Treating on the third reconciliation of the posterity of Adam "at the end of time," the treatise remarks: "It will be then that the perverse Spirits will recognize their errors and their abominations in remaining for a time immemorial with the shadow of death, in divine privation, and in the most terrible lamentations. It is then that they will perform a work more painful and more considerable than they had done for the duration of the temporal ages."[686] Pasqually did not say what would be the nature and the aim of this "chastisement," promising "to enter later into the detail of the kind of work that must be done by these perverse Spirits." He has not kept his promise, at least in his treatise, but if we consider that he gives to the word "work" the sense of painful efforts leading to the reconciliation with God, that "time immemorial" signifies, in his language, a duration exceeding what the human intelligence may imagine but not eternal, and that finally he connects with this work of the demons the number 49, which he has interpreted several page above[687] as equivalent, by mystical addition, to the Quaternary[688], number of the being reintegrated into its first spiritual and divine properties, virtues, and powers, one is led to conclude that he foresaw the moment when the perverse Spirits would obtain their definitive reconciliation.[689]

Mazdaism is not the only religious system of which certain dogmas seem to have tinted the mystical ideas set forth in the Reintegration. It is easy to find there characteristics with resemblance to Manichaeism, Sabianism, and the cult of Mithra.

Mani divided humanity into two groups of which one, the Elect, followed the teaching of Adam and Seth, and the other, that of the Damned, recognized for heads Eve and Cain. He showed Seth setting Adam on guard against the perfidious coquetries and preventing him from succumbing. The Manichaeans invoked as authorities the writings of Adam, Seth, Enoch, and Noah.

The name of Seth returns often in the sacred books of the Sabians or Mandaeans, beside those of Abel and Enoch. These books related that, when the Utras (Emanations), wishing to create in their turn, had formed the Cheschucha (World of Darkness), the superior powers had sent, in order to combat them, the Manda of Hajje or Gabra Kadmaya (First Man) who, armed with four divine attributes, had vanquished them.

Among the Mithraics the equinoxes were holy days, and the initiations took place preferably in March or April, that is to say at the spring equinox.

These connections are, moreover, more curious than probative. The first centuries of our era, during which have flourished these three religions which made for a harsh rivalry to the nascent Christianity, have been, to use the expression of

Renan, an era of "unbridled syncretism." The mythic sap exhausted was no longer capable of creating original symbols, also the religious systems were made of reciprocal borrowings and executed infinite variations on oft-repeated themes. All the dogmas at this period have an air of family, and the mystical treatises drew with full hands from these granaries where all the grains were intermingled. It is furthermore by these points of contact with bodies of doctrines so different in appearance that the Reintegration proves to be a faithful heir of the apocalypses which had seen the light of day some fifteen hundred years before it.[690]

.˙.

The arithmetic and geometry secrets contained in the Reintegration are the legacy of the distant past. The idea to attribute to the numbers a mystical value goes back to the most ancient times of which civilization has kept the memory. Formulated philosophically, it comes down to saying that the being is identical to the number, and that the number is, at the same time as the being itself, the material element and the formal element, the cause and the principle, so that, if all things are numbers, the science of numbers is the science of things.[691] Practically, it attributes to each of the first ten (sometimes twelve) numbers a transcendent significance which gives the key to the enigma of the intelligible world and the sensible world.

This doctrine is commonly called Pythagorean arithmetic because it has been systematically formulated by Pythagoras, or at least transmitted by the Pythagorean Philolaus, but the denomination having become traditional does not take into account the question of origins, for the elements of which this esoteric arithmetic makes use certainly existed before the Pythagoreans, and the nationality of their master is uncertain.[692]

The Neopythagoreans of the first century of our era were dedicated with fervor to arithmosophy and attributed to the ten numbers often contradictory characteristics or having double or triple use. Moreover, at the example of the first Pythagoreans who had attempted to express the numerical relations by figurative constructions, they derived from the mystical arithmetic a likewise mystical geometry, by establishing a relationship between the numbers and the figures. The generation of the numbers appeared to them as the generation of things, the properties common to the figures and to the numbers manifested to their eyes the properties of the actual objects. In the same period Nicomachus of Gerasa composed an "Arithmatic Theology" where he undertook to demonstrate the divine nature of each of the first ten numbers with the help of the most subtle symbolic and mystical interpretations.

The Neoplatonists of the 3rd century cultivated arithmosophy with predilection. Iamblicus has still more of a taste than Plotinus for the mysticism of numbers of which he celebrates the marvelous powers and upon which he founds the principles of his theodicy. The whole doctrine of Proclus comes down to three triads: psychic, intellectual, and divine. In the following century Saint Augustine speculates on the mystical value of numbers.

The Middle Ages had notions of arithmosophy even before the Arabo-Latin versions of the works Aristotle had been able to make it known to them.[693] It is necessary, therefore, to admit the existence of a secret tradition and, as the mystical science of numbers found favor again from the beginning of the 13th century, the mode of transmission of the Pythagorean doctrines which escape their historian, Mr. Chaignet[694], appears quite clear: it is by the Jewish mystics that they are passed into the Occident and by the Kabbalists that the Christians knew them.

In the 15th century, Nicolas de Cusa, whose philosophical system is a mixture of Pythagorean and Alexandrian ideas, professes that the forms of things are intelligible numbers which constitute therein the essence, but that, these numbers being in our intelligence, the knowledge is none other than the operation by which the numbers of the soul are correlated to the numbers of things.

In the 16th century, arithmosophy knew a new popularity when the humanists, who, under the name of Platonic philosophy, amalgamate neo-Alexandrian theories, axioms attributed to Pythagoras, and Kabbalistic themes, take it upon themselves to seek in the Hebrew texts the Pythagorean doctrine, and in the Kabbalah the true philosophical doctrine of the Scripture. Reuchlin claimed to be the restorer in Germany of Pythagoreanism by making known the "Hebraic Kabbalah," because "the philosophy of Pythagoras has been tied to the maxims of Chaldean knowledge," and in his works on the Kabbalah: *de Verbo Mirifico, de Arte Cabbalistica*, he set forth a profoundly altered Pythagorean arithmosophy.[695] In his book entitled: *De Harmonia totius mundi*, Georgio de Venise professes that the numbers, which are intimately united with the divine essence, first emanated in order to rule the harmonies of heaven, then to descend therefrom into the sensible things. He asserts that "this doctrine revealed by God to the Hebrews has been communicated likewise to some gentiles such as Plato and Pythagoras."[696] For Cornelius Agrippa of Nettesheim the numbers give the key of the occult philosophy and of the secrets of magic; each number has its proper virtue and its particular function; essential elements of all that is in time and space, numbers enjoy the principal role in the formation of bodies, and the laws which govern the numbers are revealed above all in the shape of the objects.[697] Giordano Bruno, the greatest of the Pythagoreans of the Renaissance, plays with the geometric figures that he considers as intimately tied to the numbers and as giving to things their properties and their essence. He exalts the mystical mathematics in which he sees the means to discover the secrets of nature and to rise up finally to the contemplation of God.[698] The alchemist and theosopher Van Helmont seeks in the mysticism of the numbers the key of the Great Work and of the transcendent truths.

At the end of the 16th century, Pythagorean arithmetic ceased to be cultivated openly. The division which, in the following century, was made more and more exclusive between the mystical tendencies and the scientific postulates, relegated it among the occult sciences, but it continued to figure in the secret doctrines of the cenacles which preserved vividly the esoteric tradition and, beginning from the 18th century, it manifested its vitality in furnishing to speculative Freemasonry some of its symbols and "sacred numbers."

Pasqually does not seem to have borrowed uniquely from the Jewish occultists the elements of his arithmosophy, for it includes developments that the Kabbalah had not known, but it is most difficult to identify his other sources because he deviates in addition to an extent from theories accepted by the majority of mystical mathematicians. His system, without being profoundly original, has a much more personal character than all the other speculations of the Reintegration.

For the numbers One, Ten, and Four, he follows in the main the Pythagoreans, who had for these numbers a particular veneration, but he quarters himself resolutely on the mystical terrain and abstains from purely intellectual speculation.

He insists less upon the Monad than the Pythagoreans. These latter, who were above all philosophers, saw in the One the father of numbers, and consequently of beings the demiurge of the world, the root of existence, the principle of knowledge and individuation. They held by the concept of the One three sorts of unity: the absolute unity or God, form separated from things; the unity-element, considered as form inseparable from things; finally, the unity of the actual being. Pasqually, theosopher before all, considered only the divine unity and does not linger to contemplate, for it is for the Jewish mystic the Incomprehensible and the Unknowable, the En-Soph of the Kabbalah, which the latter, despairing of grasping it by intelligence, sometimes calls it Non-being. He has not even retained a Pythagorean idea that had stricken the Jewish mystics of the Middle Ages, that is to wit that the One added to the Even makes it Odd, which could not be done if it did not partake of the two, so that it may be called Even-Odd. The Kabbalists, in identifying the Odd with the male principle and the Even with the female principle, made of the Monad the prototype of the androgynous Adam Kadmon.[699]

On the other hand, he agrees with all his predecessors in attributing to the Decad an importance of the first order. With it shine forth, according to the Pythagoreans, the superior force and the sublime power of the One; it is the divine and uncreated force which produces the eternal permanence of the things of this world. Ten is the perfect and universal number; its envelopes within itself the essence and true power of the numbers, since the first ten numbers, of which the Decad is the limit, suffice to explain the infinite variety of objects, their attributes, modes, and properties. Proclus qualifies the Decad as "holy," because it produces all the perfections and all the numbers. For Iamblicus it is the collection of all the emanations of the One, an idea developed most particularly by the Kabbalah which symbolizes the Cause of Causes by the point of the Yod, whose value is ten, and which founds its whole construction of the intelligible world on the ten Sephiroth, unfolding of the En-Soph. Pasqually inscribed likewise the numeral 1 in a circle in order to symbolize the intimate union of the Unity and the Decad, of the immanent God that the first typifes, and of the emanating God that the second represents.

The Quaternary, with which Pasqually made to play so eminent a role in his system, is likewise a replica of the "mysterious and holy" Tetrad of the Pythagoreans, "number of numbers and God which contains the source and root of the eternal nature." It was, for the first as for the last disciples of Pythagoras, the "life in oneself" (Autozoon), but, as the similar can only be known by the similar, and as the life within oneself understands the intelligible life, the sensible life, and the physical life, the soul, which knows all these beings, must be, like them, the number 4. This number is found in the animal species, in the parts comprising the human being (head, seat of reason; heart, seat of life; navel, seat of the faculty to carry roots and germs; sexual parts, seat of the faculty to conceive and engender). It is the number of justice because it is the product of absolutely equal factors. Proclus speaks of the "Sacred Quaternary"; Iamblicus sees here the principle of universal harmony. For Nicolas de Cusa the soul is the number 4.[700] The Quaternary appears frequently in the arithmetical speculations of the Kabbalah; it is, as a specifically Jewish symbol, the Tetragrammaton, secret writing of the ineffable name of the Lord. Pasqually is shown faithful to his inspirers by giving it a purely mystical value.

The ill-omened significance of the number Two, so accused by Pasqually, is encountered among the Neopythagoreans, whose arithmosophy was submitted to the influence of the Platonic doctrines. The primitive Pythagoreanism which deified the numbers could not attribute to any of them an absolute imperfection.[701] For the successors of Plato, on the contrary, for Speusippeus and Xenocrates, the Dyad, contrary to the Monad which is beauty, good, and spirit, is the expression of matter and of evil. The Neopythagoreans adopted this point of view and, seeing in the Monad the eternal and efficient cause or God, considered the Dyad as the passive and material cause of the sensible world. The undefined Dyad is the inferior element, the plurality, the movement, the feminine sex, the darkness and the evil, because it is the principle of division which is opposed to the unity and makes effort to destroy it. The Manichaeans saw in the Two the sign of the Second Principle, cause of evil and adversary to the One, which was at once the absolute existence and the Good. For C. Agrippa, 2 is the number of evil, of the demon, of the material plurality.

The significance of the number of creation attached by Pasqually to the six comes directly from the Kabbalah. In the cosmogony of the Zohar the six inferior Sephiroth or "operatives," which are ranked in tiers below the supreme triad constituted by Kether (Crown), Hochmah (theoretical Reason), and Binah (practical Reason), form the creative Senary: "The six days of creation are lights emanating from the Word for the illumination of the world." These six instrumental causes of creation have revealed in six days the plan hidden in the thought of the three supreme architects. Likewise, the world will endure for six millennial periods, number whose total is reduced to ten, for, a "great year" being composed of six centuries, the six thousand years of the existence of the world form ten great years. It was at the end of the sixth "day" or sixth millennium that the community of Israel would find its place at the end of time, when the Messiah arrived.[702] This idea is reproduced textually by Pasqually: "The name of days that I give to the six operations of the creation cannot belong to the Eternal who is an infinite being, without time, without limit, and without expanse; but these six days foretell the duration and limits of this matter, that is to say this matter will last six thousand years in all its perfection...each of these days or these thousand years, ought only be considered as the duration of the six divine thoughts."[703]

The considerable importance that Pasqually attached to the Septenary and to the Spirits which are marked thereof is explained by the vitality of a Chaldean tradition of astrological origin which made the universal life to depend on the action of the seven planets. This thesis was anchored so profoundly in the imagination of all the civilized peoples of ancient Asia that one finds therein from time to time indelible traces in the divisions of time and in the dogmas of all oriental religions. It is superfluous to recall the persistence of this tradition among the Jews: seven-branched candlestick, weeks of the year, etc. But the Septenary had received from the Kabbalists a particular significance of which Pasqually has made the faithful echo. The secret of the number Seven was for the Kabbalah that God has completed by it the six phases of time.[704] Pasqually says in his turn: "On the seventh day (or seventh millennium) matter will fall into a terrible deterioration, where it will continue until its entire dissolution... the septenary number, which has given perfection to every created being, is the same which destroys and abolishes everything."[705]

It is probably to the Jewish traditions that one must attribute the origin of the ill-omened meaning attached by Pasqually to the number Five. For the Pythagoreans it expressed the natural bodies, for it gave to things, in addition to volume, the quality and color, the exterior and visible form; thus, the physical bodies had for them five elements: fire, earth, water, air, and quintessence which incorporates the first four. Furthermore, it signified justice; this was therefore a morally good number. Among the Jewish mystics, Five was, on the contrary, demonic because it was the number of destructive angels that, according to an account deposited in the paraphrase of Deuteronomy by Ben Ouziel, Jehovah had sent to punish the Israelites who adored the Golden Calf.

The mystical value granted by Pasqually to the Octonary, "doubly strong number," is perhaps a remembrance of an Egyptian concept which, in dividing the four elements into male and female, obtained the Ogdoad, symbol of the vivifying force, carried over by Pasqually to the mystical plane. For the first Pythagoreans it was, it is true, the number of all the superior faculties: love, friendship, prudence, reflection; but it had become with the Neopythagoreans, notably with Iamblicus, the cause of th outflow of things and the dispersion of beings, that is to say exactly the contrary to the return to the divine that it essentially represents in the Reintegration.

It is in his commentary on the Three that Pasqually shows the greatest independence with respect to the Chaldean, Jewish, and Kabbalistic traditions, all while following in part the Pythagorean school. The Ternary is among the Semites a sacred and divine number of the first order; it seems to be from Chaldean origin as a spiritual manifestation of the First Cause. Iamblicus makes of it the soul of the world or the demiurge. The triads, which play a principal role in all oriental theogonies, are staged with predilection by the Kabbalah. It is remarkable then that, on a point where the Jewish mystic had taken so distinct a position, the author of the Reintegration had so resolutely turned his back to his habitual inspirers. On the other hand, if he makes, at the example of the Pythagoreans, Three the number of matter, he parts with them on the intrinsic quality of the Ternary. For the disciples of Pythagoras, Three is not only the number of everything, since everything has three dimensions, the "plane number," the number of the physical things which have an expanse, it is also the first perfect number because it is the first number that has a middle, a beginning, and end. For Pasqually, it is a fundamentally evil number since it represents matter.

Finally, on the Nine, "demonic" number, according to the Reintegration, Pasqually agrees neither with the Pythagoreans, who see in the Ennead justice, nor with Iamblicus who finds there the principle of all identity and all perfection, nor with the Kabbalah, which sometimes associates the triads by three in order to express a more complete development of the being. Unless Pasqually has borrowed his interpretation from an unknown source, he seems to have wished to fly by his own wings and to have drawn his condemnation of the Nonary, multiple of the Ternary, from the evil renown that he gave to the latter.

He has manifestly accorded to Eleven and Twelve too little attention for as much as we have lingered on these two numbers.

The combinations of numbers and ciphers, in which Pasqually displayed such ingenuity, were known to the Pythagoreans and have been practiced by their imitators.

For the disciples of Pythagoras, 5 is justice because it is the middle of 10, which is the All, and that, dividing it into two equal parts, it gives to each part what belongs to it. It is also marriage, being the symbol of the cohabitation of the male and female, since 5 = 3 (first odd number, male) + 2 (first even number, female). 6 is the number of the living body, because 5, the number of the organisms, adds to it an element: the soul, which produces the functions of life. It also represents Aphrodite or generation, because it is the first number of the Decad formed by the multiplication of 2 by 3, that is to say of the first even number by the first odd. 9 is justice, being the first squared product by the first odd number (3) multiplied by itself. 8 is the number of the highest moral and intellectual qualities, for it is the first cubic number (2 multiplied by 2 = 4, 4 multiplied by 2 = 8).

Four is the sacred number, because it is the arithmetical middle term between 1 and 7, for it exceeds the first term by the same sum which it is exceeded by the last, but above all because by it is stopped the progression of the first numbers whose addition comprises the perfect Decad (1+2+3+4=10), therefore 4 is the root of 10, which is itself the manifestation of the absolute power of the One; consequently, if every being, by which it alone may exist, is decadic, it is also tetradic, since the Tetrad contains within it the germ of the Decad. Furthermore, every tetradic and decadic is at the same time, considered as number, a unity: thus, each number is at once, 1, 4, and 10.

The Great Tetractys, upon which the Pythagoreans took their solemn oath of fidelity, owed its prestige to the fact that it was formed of 8 numbers by addition of the sum of the first four odd number (1+3+5+7=16) to that of the first four even numbers (2+4+6+8=20) which gives 36; now this number is equal to the sum of the cubes of 1, 2, and 3 (1+8+27=36).

Seven being the sum of 3 and 4 and forming with this last number an arithmetical mean between the two extremes of the Decad (1, 4, 7, 10) expresses health, light, reason, and Minerva. It is the number conceived without mother, since none of the numbers contained in the Decad engender it by multiplication of a number by another number or by itself, and also the virgin number, since it does not engender any of these same numbers. 7 is the law of human existence. Man comes into the world after 7 months of gestation and his life unfolds by periods of 7 years: early childhood from 1 to 7 years, childhood from 7 to 14 years, youth from 14 to 21 years, adolescence from 21 to 28, manhood from 29 to 35; then he declines, and the phases of this decline are also submissive to the number 7. The sun, productive cause of all the fruits of the earth, only possesses this power because it is the function of the number 7; it has the 7th place in the universe, for its sphere comes after that of the 5 planets and of the fixed heavens; the moon, after 7 days, is in quadrangular conjunction with it and that is why the 7th day is critical.[706]

All the mystical philosophies which have cultivated the Pythagorean arithmetic have delivered more or less the same speculations. For Proclus, the Holy Decad is the sum of the three triads, psychic, intellectual, and divine, and of the One, and each of these triad's forms with the One the Sacred Quaternary. Saint Augustine attributes to the soul the number 3, image of the divine Trinity, and to the body the number 4, since every organism is composed of the four elements. Therefore man, consisting of a soul and a body, has the number 7 which is found everywhere: there are, for example, in the life of the individual, 6 ages crowned by a 7th term, death.[707] Giordano Bruno considers the Tetrad as the perfect number, since it is at once itself (as number), the unity (as sign), and the Decad (the sum of the numbers from 1 to 4 that it contains being equal to 10). C. Agrippa calculates that 3 added to the unity forms the number 4 which, multiplied by 3, gives 12, sacred number among them, and that 3, added twice to 4, arrives, in passing by the number 7, at the great Unity 10, which is perfection. Georgio de Venise believes that the true reason to believe that the world has been made in six days is that 6 is the first perfect number resulting from the combination of the first three numbers, since 6 equals 6 multiplied by 1, or 3 multiplied by 2, or 2 multiplied by 3, or finally 1+2+3.

The mystical geometry of Pasqually appears quite rudimentary when one compares it to that of the Pythagoreans and above all of the Neopythagoreans. The first established extremely ingenious connections between the unity and the point, the dyad and the line, the triad and the triangle. Their dialectic displayed its resources particularly in the correlation of the tetrad with the pyramid, which they identified with the 4, whether because it is formed from four planes, or because it surmounts a triangular base (=3) with a summit (=1). They related it also to the Decad, since it presents 4 planes and 6 lines, that is to say 10 elements, so that the relationship of the Denary and the Quaternary, already demonstrated by the arithmetic, was again proven by the geometric figures. The Neopythagoreans relied upon the figure called "gnomon," upon a number of "eteromech" figures, upon the curvilinear figures, and upon the "diaule" in order to establish that the Dyad, or Even, summarizes in itself the characteristics of the changing and unformed multiplicity, always in movement, generation, and becoming.[708]

The sole connection that one may find between their theories and the mystical figure outlined by the Reintegration, or the ideas expressed by its author, is that the Pythagoreans held the circle to be the perfect, completed, entire figure, since it has a beginning, a middle, and an end, and since they saw in the triangle the principle of generation and form of everything, because all bodies whatever be their form, may be resolved into triangles. These analogies are too vague to allow us to conclude a direct borrowing. Furthermore, the symbolic significance that Pasqually gives to the circle and to the triangle had become traditional since the most remote times. The circle, graphic representation of the horizon which limits the range of human vision, appears to have, as far as one goes back in history, served to represent space, and the emanationist doctrines have found in it the most exact expression of their cosmogony. As regards the triangle, the Egyptians, on the testimony of Eusebius, was used to represent the earth. Plato had declared in Timeus that the physical raisons d'être and the operation of the elements are triangular, and the Neoplatonists had revived and carefully preserved this idea; one of their last representatives, Geogio de Venise, stated that the world is formed of triangular elements in remarking that 3 is the image of the form which, by means of 2, expression of the angle, reduces matter to the unity. If the definition of the shape of the earth given by the Reintegration has at first seemed strange, the treatise of Pasqually has only reproduced a theme very ancient and very well known among the occultists.

CHAPTER IV
The Magic of the Élus Coëns

The Operations, with their tracings, lustrations, censings, prostrations, invocations, and conjurations, pertain too manifestly to ceremonial magic for it to be necessary to lay stress on the nature of the practices in which the disciples of Pasqually engaged; but it is interesting to seek out its origins and precise character.

Heir of the mystical sects of antiquity and of the Neo-Alexandrian epoch, the Order of Élus Coëns had found in their inheritance the magical elements that they had themselves received from a distant past and that it put to use in its turn.[709] Here again it was inspired by the mystical doctrines of the Theoretical Kabbalah, but, in order to compose its ritual, it still had to appeal to other masters: the occultists of the Middle Ages and the Renaissance.

What they call Practical Kabbalah was well anterior to the Theoretical Kabbalah. It was a residue of the primitive cults founded on the fluidic or penumatological, natural, or antidemonic magics. Despite the anathemas that the Bible hurled against the magicians, it contained legends testifying to ancient bonds which fastened the Jewish people in Chaldea, classical land of magic: Adam, driven from the Terrestrial paradise, and also his first descendants were made to live in Mesopotamia, the "land of the ancient secret wisdom"; it was from Ur in Chaldea that Abraham set out for the West; it was from Chaldea that Isaac and Jacob brought their wives. The curses of the prophets was intended above all for the magical practices in which the Jews engaged, and particularly the Jewish women. In Babylon, the Israelites were for 70 years in contact with the magical cults persisting in the Babylonian and Persian religions. Talmudists and Midrashim practiced astrology, oneiromancy, believed in the virtue of the formulas and amulets against the evil eye, the attacks of ferocious animals, illnesses, or accidents. The Kabbalah attributes to Abraham knowledge in astrology and the art of making amulets for magical aims. One Kabbalistic sect, which had formed in the second half of the 16th century, possessed a truly magical ritual which imposed upon the officiants a special costume composed of four white vestments superimposed, prescribed particular ceremonies for the celebration of the Sabbath and gave the text of prayers addressed to the Sephiroth and the Angels. The founder of the sect, the rabbi Loria or Luria, thaumaturge as much as theologian, was thought to have exorcized publicly an epileptic that tormented the soul of a Jew drowning without having made the prayer to Schem.

The belief in the knowledge of the Jews in magic and especially in the supernatural powers of the Kabbalists was widespread among the Christian occultists. In the 17th century J.B. van Helmont wrote in his "Hortus Medicinae" (Leyde, 1667): "A magical force, asleep through sin, is latent in man. It may be revealed by the grace of God or by the art of the Kabbalah." The theurgical rites appealing to the Practical Kabbalah appear to have existed until the 18th century in the bosom of the Jewish sects connected to the Frankists, so widespread in central Europe.

It is possible that Pasqually had had knowledge of these ceremonials, but it is doubtful that he has borrowed from them, for the magic practiced by these sects was coarsely utilitarian: discovery of treasure, assured gains in negotiations, foreknowledge of circumstances favorable to an undertaking, preservation of health, such were the aims that it ordinarily offered, when it did not aim to satisfy a vain curiosity through vision at a distance or the faculty to see the Spirits. The preoccupations of the Élus

Coëns aimed higher than these vulgar objects. As for the Practical Kabbalah, which is known to us by the classic works like the Zohar, it formed indeed a sort of encyclopedia of the proper means to combat witchcraft and processes such as suggestion and hypnosis aiming at obtaining altered states, but it did not indicate ritual magic proper. Therefore, Pasqually has not, in matters of magic, taken from the Kabbalah except the principle upon which rests the tracing of the hieroglyphs in the Chamber of Operation.

The theurgical process particularly advocated by the Practical Kabbalah was founded upon the marvelous power of the divine names. The origin of this concept is lost to the night of time; it is derived from one of the fundamental postulates of every kind of magic, that is to say the essential identity of the sign and the thing signified. The name of a god was, among the Chaldeans, a hypostasis of the god itself. The gnosis or knowledge of the divine names in their vulgar sense and their esoteric sense was the great religious mystery and the object of initiation among the Egyptians.[710] For the Gnostics, the psychic himself could not be saved unless he knew the secret name of the Archons which, pronounced exactly, forced the evil powers to allow the soul to cross the barriers separating it from the Pleroma. Among the Jews, the magical power attributed to the name of God rendered it taboo. The prohibition against pronouncing the true name of the Lord was observed with such exactitude that its pronunciation fell into a complete forgetfulness. The Masoretic text itself, where special signs, points, or marks written between or under the consonants, indicate the vowels in all the other words, does not ever vocalize it and has continued to mark only the consonants thereof: Yod, He, Vav, He, that is to say to note it under the form called the Tetragrammaton. According to the Talmud of Babylon, the secret of its pronunciation was lost to the priests themselves since the beginning of the 3rd century BC[711], and it is likely that it is to this mysterious name, whose pronunciation transmitted by oral tradition was known only to initiates alone, that the Talmud alludes when it decrees that the secrets of the Torah must not be revealed except to a man acquainted with "magical practice" and "magical formulas"; it uses, moreover, the expression: "transmission of the name," as a synonym of esoteric science.[712]

The Kabbalah had been meticulous on this principle in associating with the speculations on the letters of the Hebrew alphabet the faith in the infinite power of the Schem-ha-mephorasch, or secret name of the divinity, whose irresistible action over the Spirits, as much the celestial as the elementary, the Talmudic Haggadah already mentioned. Considering that each of the letters composing this sacred name is a part of the divine energy, it is grouped by 4, 12, 42, or even 72 in order to form four magical formulas of which each had a determined power. The names of the angels were, according to it, nearly as powerful as those of the Lord, since each of them represents one of the emanations of the divinity, and that they contain for the most part the syllable "el" which signifies the Most High.[713]

The putting into practice of this concept is quite marked in the Reintegration. The Schem-ha-mephorasch is found implicitly mentioned in the passage where Pasqually speaks of the "all-powerful name of the divinity, the same as the one that the Jews uttered long ago, that they understood most perfectly having come from their language, and that Adam and his posterity had also pronounced."[714] "The Hebrews also knew this word formerly and know it still today, because there has always been someone among them (a true Jew) who has possessed a part of the knowledge of this first language."[715] And so the Reintegration, which claims to represent the pure "Judaic" tradition, executes numerous variations on this theme, that the name is the expression of the power of the being who bears it, and that speech is the instrument of the faculty of creation and commandment. "When the forms (ceremonies) operate some virtue (have some efficacy) it is not by themselves, but by the characteristic power of the spiritual being that inhabits them, that is to say by its divine spiritual animal name" (name by which a Spirit emanated from God is known on earth).[716] "All the minor Spirits and all the spiritual souls have truly one name which distinguishes them in their powers and virtues in relation to their temporal work."[717] "There are ten spiritual names which operate the cult of the divinity by its characteristic Denary."[718]

"Enoch, grand type of the ceremonial and of the divine cult, gave to each of his six disciples an initial letter of the names of God. He held these assemblies of divine operations with his ten Elect by ten in ten months, and at each assembly he revealed a new initial of the holy name of God, so that after seven meetings each of them possessed two powerful names with which he commanded every created thing from the terrestrial surface unto the celestial surface. The two words consisted in seven letters, four of which formed the redoubtable, powerful and invisible name of the Eternal (Tetragrammaton) which governed and subdued every created being in the celestial body[719], and the three others formed a holy name which compelled every created being on the terrestrial body." Moreover, these ten Elect were "restored in their divine spiritual virtues and powers and performed great marvels by their operations."[720]

The name, being a sign of power, and a determined power, is different or changed when this power is itself modified. Thus, the names (not revealed by the treatise) of the four primitive classes of the emanated Spirits "were stronger than those that we gave commonly to the Cherubim, Seraphim, Archangels, and Angels, which had only been emanated since."[721] Adam, "Man-God in his state of Glory, had his own name attached directly to his spiritual being. It is by the virtue of this name that he manifested in the universe every temporal divine operation."[722] After his prevarication he lost the memory of his "spiritual name" which was "Aba 4" (number of the Quaternary); at the time of his reconciliation with the Lord, he was given the new name of "Bian 6" (number of material creation) "called Adam" (with the nickname of Adam). This second name, though still "very powerful," is quite "inferior to the first name of his emanation, because the reconciliation was not purely spiritual, but temporally spiritual."[723] Inversely, when the third son of Adam had to be the intermediary of the reconciliation between the Creator and his father, Adam changed "by divine inspiration" the name that he had first given him to that of Seth.[724]

It is remarkable to see the Reintegration subscribe without reserve to an opinion of primitive magic which considered the god or Spirit invoked as obliged to obey from the moment that its true name was correctly pronounced. When Jacob seeks to be restored in communication with the Lord, he obtains his reconciliation by invoking him by his three "ineffable names" before giving him the name of "God of Abraham, of Isaac, and of Jacob" under which the prayers of the official Jewish religion know him.[725] When Adam wished to create by his authority, "the Eternal, having promised Adam with an oath that he would act with him in all the operations that he would make in his name (by his name), could not stop himself from accomplishing the immutable promise that he had made him to support him in all the circumstances where he would have need...He (Adam) commanded him by his divine immutability to keep to his word on behalf of the material creation of Adam...God, according to his promise, joined his spiritual operation to the temporal operation of

Adam, however contrary to his will...and granted him the crowning of his work."[726]

Pasqually also underscores this idea, familiar to the Kabbalists, that the name manifests its power above all when it is pronounced aloud, that is to say under the form of Word or Speech. It is by his "speech" that God has emanated the spiritual Minors.[727] The mouth is "the organ of the powerful speech of man."[728] "Adam had in him a powerful Word, since it had to give birth by his words of commandment, impassive glorious forms, similar to that which appeared in the imagination of the Creator."[729] "The Word that the Eternal had put into Adam in order to produce a posterity of God was only the intention and will which would operate by the powerful speech of this First Man."[730] When Adam, seduced by the demon, undertook to create in his turn, "he used all the powerful words that the Creator had transmitted to him."[731] "Although man only traverses the different immensities in thought, whereas the spirits are able to traverse actually and in nature the infinite expanse of the divine immensity..., the speech of man gives him superiority over all the inhabitants of the divine world; it is stronger and more powerful than theirs, and the reach that it may have surpasses yet that which the divine beings may traverse."[732] The materialization of the quaternary triangle in the circles of the major spirits and inferior Spirits shows "the power of the words of commandment which is given to the Minor over the inhabitants of these two circles."[733]

The mystical name, written or represented by the conventional signs known to the initiates alone, is a mute order, less efficacious than the pronounced name, but which acts as adjuvant to the word. That is why the Élu Coën traces in the Chamber of Operation the hieroglyphs or "characters" of the mediators that they invoke. The letters inscribed in the Quarter Circle fulfills the same office. The hieroglyph IAB, that the printed text gives, is probably a transcription error and ought to be read IAH or IAO, names of God used often among the Gnostics, who had borrowed them from the Jewish mystics and inscribed them upon their "seals" and the "apologies." What authorizes this reading is the name of the "Great Circle of Supreme Power" given to the Circle of Retreat, by Bacon de la Chevalerie, Substitute General of Pasqually.[734] The hieroglyph RAP likely represents Raphael, "the one who leads in the name of the Lord," that is to say, mystically, who drives out the demonic Spirits, name of the angel who, in the Book of Tobit, teaches the heroes of the narrative the magical recipes, fumigations, and unctions, which set the demons to flight and that the Élu Coën invokes as a particularly powerful defender. There is every reason to believe that protective names were likewise inscribed upon the talismans whose points the Operant turned successively towards the demons, and that he called his "shield," a word recalling the hexagram, bearing an inscription of the Tetragrammaton, that the Kabbalists called the "shield of David."[735]

∴

Apart from these concordances of detail with the doctrines and practices of the Jewish occultists, the ritual of the Operations had nothing which distinguished it from the traditional forms of ceremonial magic. It would therefore appear useless to research by what models Pasqually was inspired, if two works, that he had likely known, do not seem to accuse him overtly of plagiarism.

One Jewish occultist work of the 8th century, known under the name of the "Book of the angel Raziel" or the "Book of Adam," indicates a magical ceremony, which, although holding to a different aim from the one pursued by the Élus Coëns, displays curious analogies with the Invocation of the Three Days and with the ceremony of the Ordination. "When," says the mystical book, "someone wishes to execute an undertaking, he must beforehand do what follows: he will count three days starting from the new moon, will abstain from all food which may display the slightest suspicion of impurity (ritual), particularly form all food containing blood, will not drink wine, will avoid every conjugal relation during these days, will bathe each day before sunrise in running water. He will take two white turtledoves and sacrifice them with a double-edged copper blade, using the one side to sacrifice the first turtledove, and the other for the second. He will then gut the animals and wash their entrails with water. He will take three measures of old wine, pure frankincense, and a little thin honey, mingle them with the entrails and fill the whole body of the turtledoves. He will then cut each body into nine pieces and place them upon coals before the rise of the day. He must for this wear a white vestment and be barefoot. He will then invoke the names of the angels who perform the service that month, and each day will burn three pieces of each turtledove. The third day he will gather the ashes, spread them over the ground of the dwelling in order to sleep over them during the night. Before going to sleep, he will invoke the names of the powerful and holy angels and will lie down without having spoken to any man. Then the angels will appear to him during the night without any veil and will reveal to him all that upon which he will ask them without fear."[736]

The second model that Pasqually seems to have followed was less ancient. When a contemporary historian declares: "At the foundation, neither Martinès de Pasqualis nor his disciple Saint-Martin, nor Cagliostro, nor Eteilla innovate; they continue the tradition and, when one compares their magical conjurations with those attributed to C. Agrippa, one realizes that the adepts of the 18th century have only introduced arbitrary variants,"[737] he is mistaken as regards Saint-Martin, who has never elaborated a magical system, but he indicates exactly the source where have drawn the thaumaturges of the era of the "Enlightenment," when he says in another place: "The translation in 1927 of the Occult Philosophy of Agrippa by Levasseur remained, despite its weakness and its inaccuracies, the fundamental manual of all the doctors and seekers in magic."[738] It is nevertheless necessary to bring a correction to this opinion: if it is true that the Magical Works of Agrippa, put into French by Pierre d'Adan, appearing in 1744, and that the Occult Philosophy translated by Levasseur have been abundantly plundered, the 4th Book of this last work, which did not figure in the translations that we have cited, and whose paternity, attributed to Agrippa, is not certain[739], seems to have been particularly made use of by the master of the Élus Coëns.

The 4th Book of Occult Philosophy, entitled "On magical ceremonies," is a treatise on demonology founded on astrological calculations supposing knowledge much more extensive than shown by Pasqually. The work furnishes the elements of a "calculation confided in the Egyptian letters (hieroglyphs) by the important author Trismegistus"[740] and which permitted, by means of "letters collected from the figure of the world, from the rising of the body of the planet, according to the succession of signs, across each degree and of each degree seen of the planet, the projection being made of the degree of the ascendant," to form the secret name of the Intelligences presiding over each planet. The treatise describes moreover the forms that the Spirits prefer of Saturn, Jupiter, Mars, Venus, Mercury, the Moon, and the Sun.

The aim that is proposed by the author and the means that he advocates are, in principle, very different from what the disciples of Pasqually research and practice.

It teaches the art of obtaining from the Spirits, by magical constraint, revelations on the future. The mechanical process that it recommends is to rapidly traverse the consecrated circle from East to West until the vertigo brought about by this circular movement produces an ecstasy in the course of which the adept receives the revelations of the Spirit evoked. Finally, it does not shrink back from the "citations" of the evil Spirits: if it hints that this operation in dangerous and imposes great privations, it considers it nevertheless licit and indicates it in the ritual. But the instructions given to those who wish, by magical ceremonies, to compel the Spirits to obey them recall to such a degree those that Pasqually prescribed to his disciples, that it is difficult to see in a parallel meeting the work of chance.

The adept is prepared religiously for his work for a number of days corresponding to the entire lunation; another number of days of preparation, recommended by the "Cabalists," is forty. During his retreat he observes an absolute chastity, was separated as much as possible from his profane affairs and from all business, follows a diet from which are excluded all foods having had sensible life and drinks only pure spring water. He makes a daily prayer in the very place where the evocation will take place and spreads perfumes after every prayer.

The preparatory period ended, the adept fasts for an entire day and, at the new moon, enters on a completely empty stomach, covered by a long, plain linen vestment, after having made the prescribed oblations, barefoot, into the "holy place." He consecrates "the site with the sprinkling of the blessed water and the fumigation in order to exorcize it." He draws the circle with the blessed coal[741], after having prayed, gives thanks to God and makes a fumigation; he writes on the periphery of the circle the names of the angels and, in the interior, the "elevated names of God," and he marks there the four corners of the world. This circle, bearing divine names and those of good Spirits "which lend us defense," must protect him against the evil Spirits; in order to "fortify it more he adds characters and pentacles." "The pentacles are sacred signs helping us to bind and exterminate the evil demons, and to attract the good Spirits in order to reconcile them to us. They are comprised of characters (hieroglyphs) and names of good Spirits of the superior order, of geometric figures and of the holy names of God."[742] Beside the circle is a triangle where is placed the Book of the Spirits.

Once entered into the circle, the disciple of Agrippa sees to the sprinkling of the water, spreads the sacred perfumes, and worships kneeling. He is then set to prayer facing the Orient and while kneeling recites the Psalm: Beati immaculati in via. He senses everything while praying and finally beseeches the angels, by invoking them by their divine names, to design to illuminate him. In the case where he believed to have to fear particularly the attacks of the demons, he may see to precede his invocation with the reading of some supplementary prayers and some Psalms "in order to defend."

"After the working, one erases the circle and dismisses the Spirits according to the rite."

∴

However exact may be the concordances between the rituals outlined by the Book of the angel Raziel and the 4th Book of Occult Philosophy, these presumed models do not indicate two details, extremely interesting by the primitive concepts from which they proceed.

The obligation imposed on the Operant to line his soles with cork is a remembrance of the dynamist or fluidic magic. The prescription takes on all its significance if one compares what Frazer says on the magical virtue: "The primitive philosophy conceived holiness, magical virtue, the taboo as a physical or fluid substance with which the sacred man is charged, just as a Leyden bottle is charged with accumulated electricity, and, like one may discharge the electricity by contact with a good conductor, the holiness or magical virtue may be discharged and disappear by contact with the ground, which, according to this theory, serves as excellent conductor to the magical fluid. Therefore, in order to prevent the charge from dissipating, it is necessary to prevent the sacred person from touching the earth, he must be isolated."[743] This primitive concept had, moreover, left traces in the notions of "el" and of "qodech" that the Bible makes known to us. That of the "el" or divine energy, impersonal and spread out everywhere, but condensed in certain objects, stones, trees, springs, or in certain beings, animals, or men, "is the foundation of the whole religion of Israel."[744] The vehicles of this supernatural and mysterious force are "Qodech" or, according to the word used in the 18th century, "Kadosch"[745]; the organisms that it visits are endowed by it, as long as its presence lasts, with an abnormal vigor which allows them to exercise around them an irresistible action. But the management of this divine force demands many precautions, because its intensity renders it dangerous by the sudden discharges that it may produce. It is "checked"(taboo) for the profane. "No profane object could ever be found in the proximity of the sacred places, and each infraction of this rule immediately released a violent discharge of divine forces, the rupture of equilibrium provoked a shock to be manifested by the effects of lightning strikes."[746] Leviticus (X, 1-2) shows us the sons of Aaron devoured by a flame shooting from the Ark because they had approached it with a censer that they had neglected to light according to the liturgical rules, and which was therefore profane. Even for the man consecrated by the ordination, this invisible and sovereign force remains redoubtable. In wearing soles of cork, the Élu Coën took precautions, certainly without suspecting it, against the violent shock that could be produced by the meeting of his body charged by the "el" with a spot of ground that had not been consecrated by his lustrations and fumigations.

On the other hand, the rule which ordered the Operant to light th candles and the burners with a "new fire," did not only apply, as believed Saint-Martin, the principle that "among us all must be new"[747]; it continued a very ancient tradition, of which one finds traces throughout the entire world, and which only permitted for use in worship the fire obtained on the spot by invariable processes and used by vanished civilizations. The fire destined for the sacrifice was lit in India by the pramantha, that is to say by the heating of a piece of wood turned rapidly in the opening of a bored log. This is the same manner that the Mexican priests lit the new fire after the cycle of 52 years.[748] The grammarian Festus (2nd or 3rd century AD) notes that this process originally used was replaced by the custom of drawing the new fire from the solar rays reflected by a concave mirror or refracted by their passage through a transparent body.[749] Prudence wrote at the end of the 4th century, in his Cathemerinon, in appealing to Christ: "You teach us to seek by the shock of a pebble the light that the flint contains in some kind of seed."[750]

The Church had preserved these ancient customs in the paschal ceremonies. "On the Saturday preceding the Sunday of Easter it was usual in the Catholic lands to extinguish all the lights in the churches then to light a new fire, sometimes by means of flint and steel, sometimes by means of a burning lens. It is with this fire that one lights the great paschal candle which then serves to relight all the lights extinguished in the church."[751] In Rome the new fire was obtained at Easter with a metal striker, at Paris with a flint and they sang: "God, who by your son has brought to the faithful the fire of your light drawn from a pebble in order to serve for our use, sanctify this new fire"(Office of Holy Week, Paris, 1756). At Mayence one lights the paschal candle with a prism or a mirror. At Florence, on the morning of Holy Saturday, the prayer of the Basilica of the Holy Apostles set the fire of a new candle by striking a tinderbox on three stones originating from the tomb of Christ and with this candle lit the paschal candle.[752]

In certain parts of Swabia, one could not light the fires of Easter by means of iron, steel, or even flint, but only by rubbing pieces of wood. In the Highlands of Scotland, one lit on the first of May the "tein-eigin" (forced fire or fire of misery) by having a wooden shaft turn in the hold of a plank. This custom existed also in Wales, in Hungary, in Ruthenia, in Masuria, in Albania. The prohibition on using steel was so rigorous that in Scotland those who lit the "fire of misery" had to rid themselves beforehand of every metal object that they might have on them. In Sweden the fires of joy are still lit with two pieces of flint.[753]

.·.

The faithfulness to the magical tradition to which the ritual of the Élus Coëns testifies is asserted again by the knowledge and supernatural faculties attributed to the head of the Order. It does not suffice, indeed, following the orthodox magical doctrine, that the doctor in magic, the "Sage," has learned from his unknown masters, from these "friends of Wisdom" of whom speaks the Reintegration, the secret formulas and efficacious ceremonies, it is still necessary for him to be provided with exceptional gifts of clairvoyance and power which makes of him a privileged being and entitles him to choose among his disciples those who will be worthy to receive and capable to transmit the depository which had been committed to him. "God gives to his Elect without any corporeal distinction the knowledge of his spiritual gifts for the advantage of the men of the earth, just as he commands to the same Elect to transmit their gifts and their spiritual virtues only to those who are worthy of a similar inheritance.[754]

Pasqually claims, therefore, to be more than a hierophant teaching transcendent truths to his disciples. He is above all a Coën to the extent that he was an heir of the ancient magicians[755], and he possesses the supernatural powers of the spiritual Elect. The Jewish priest enjoyed superior faculties, he communicated directly with the divine world only because he was himself more than an ordinary man. He was endowed with holy virtues that the rites of consecration had precisely as their object to give him. He exercised his functions only after a complex initiation by which he was communicated the sacred substances which, on the one hand, rendered him worthy to penetrate into the transcendent world and, on the other hand, immunized him against the danger presented by the contact with the objects that were condensers of the "el."[756] According to the Bible, Elijah, of whom Pasqually repeats the type of Spiritual Elect, had healed the Syrian general Namaan of leprosy, rendered drinkable the unhealthy waters, and magically transformed venomous plants into edible vegetation (IV Kings II, 19-20; IV, 38; V, 1).

At the example of the Coëns and the Prophets, Pasqually, being directly in contact with divinity, knows through intuition or intimate illumination, the physical laws of which the profane science strives in vain to pierce the mystery; trustee of a part of the divine intelligence and energy, he is able to interpret the manifestations obtained by the Operations, to foresee the future, to know what has happened in the most distant places, to heal the sick without recourse to human remedies. He is, by the power that he affirms to possess, one of these Sages "who have learned how to know the strength of the Denary number by their perseverance in their divine spiritual operations, through the means by which they have obtained the same gifts which had been given to Seth."[757] He plays, among his disciples, the same role that the three missionaries of the second posterity of Noah have fulfilled with the Spiritual Minors of whom they have made the ministers of the true divine cult. Like them, in consecrating the Réau-Croix, he exercises the right to make "a spiritual election" and he confers "the supreme ordination and the spiritual benediction."[758]

He may even confer at a distance this "supreme ordination." Willermoz, who had already been ordained Réau-Croix in 1768, at Paris, by the Universal Substitute of Pasqually, attributing the negative result of his workings to "the invalidity" of his reception, Pasqually undertook, two years later, to validly ordain the adept of Lyon himself, without leaving Bordeaux. It sufficed that the new ceremony took place at the spring equinox and that an absolute synchronization was established between the acts of the officiant and those of the recipient. Willermoz had to make a special tracing in the Chamber of Operation: in moving back the Circle of Retreat and in rendering the two rays of the Quarter Circle more oblique, there would be preserved between the two figures a space sufficient for tracing there a circumference of about six feet in diameter, that is to say large enough to contain the extended body of the recipient, whose height was five feet eight inches. He would trace furthermore in the West a Circle of Correspondence in the middle of which would burn a candle representing Pasqually. On the day agreed upon, Willermoz would, at precisely 10 o'clock at night, prostrate himself "entire face (stretched face to ground) in the circle," the head turned toward the east corner, that is to say in the direction of the Quarter Circle, and remain a half hour in this position. For his part, Pasqually, having entered "into his corner" at precisely 9 o'clock at Bordeaux, "labored" there until one hour after midnight. His prostration ended, Willermoz extinguished the lights of the Quarter Circle, erased all his tracings and retired from the Chamber of Operation. The same working, in parallel, would be repeated in five days, but would begin an hour later and would start with the invocations, after which Willermoz would extinguish the candle representing Pasqually, while saying: "Blessed be the one who assists me and hears me; O Bagniakim, amen." He would proceed then to the "ordinary work" by merely seeing to it that the hieroglyph traced previously in the Circle of Reception was found exactly between his legs.[759]

While the Réau-Croix exercise, and only passingly, the quaternary power, their master claims for himself, if not explicitly, at least very clearly, when one takes the trouble to read between the lines of his correspondence, the double divine spiritual power of the number Eight "that the Creator has destined to the Spiritual Elect that he wishes to favor and to appoint to the manifestation of his glory" and that "man may not attain to the Creator without infinite labors and without suffering the pain of the body, the soul, and the spirit."[760] He may indeed, by his personal Operations, promote magically the "undertakings, whether spiritual or temporal," of his "emulators." When the Réau-Croix Willermoz and de Grainville had to go to Paris in April 1770 "to handle definitive arrangements for the good of the Order," their master wrote to them: "May the Eternal bless your undertaking entirely for this subject. I would contribute there no less by my impending works so that he deigns to favor you, whether spiritually or temporally, and keeps you for a time immemorial in his retinue. Amen. Amen. Amen."[761] Also, in order to be always in a position to project at the desired moment this beneficent fluid, Pasqually was engaged "by oath," in his quality of "sovereign spiritual head of the divine spiritual circles of operation" to keep "as is usual, and even ordained and prescribed, his circles open all year in order to be in a position to never be surprised and fall into error, be it for his own particular purpose, for the Order, for the particular and general instructions, and for the propagation of the Order."[762]

Pasqually has the gift of second sight which permits him to be witness to the workings of the adepts at more than two hundred leagues of distance, and he may suggest to them across space the guidance that they ought to hold to in grave circumstances. The day when Bacon de la Chevalerie felt overwhelmed by the superior force of one of the demons that he conjured in the course of an Operation, he escaped the peril by rushing from the Quarter Circle into the Circle of Retreat "pressed by an obscure and irresistible determination"; he learned later on that it had been inspired to him by Pasqually who worked for his part at Bordeaux and who had "seen him in his failure."[763]

The Master of the Élus Coëns unites in his person all the gifts which would have been distributed by the Divinity among the seven Spiritual Elect of the second posterity of Noah. The Reintegration has already shown to us that he was initiated into the secret sciences communicated to the last three brothers: which is to be able, for the sixth brother, "to understand from the literal and hieroglyphic character, the divine celestial, terrestrial, spiritual, superior, major, inferior, and minor,"[764] that is to say cosmological, penumatological, and anthropological doctrines exposed in the treatise, and, for the seventh, "the perfect knowledge of all the hieroglyphic characters of every demonic spiritual being" or the science of exorcisms, and "the gift to construct spiritual edifices for the glory of the cult of the Creator,"[765] or, in other words, the art of tracing the circles, the angles, and the characters in the Chamber of Operation. If he does not seem to have made use of the gift of "terrestrial plantation and cultivation" (magical fertilizing of plants and herds) granted to the fifth brother, the Reintegration shows that its author had particular knowledge in biology and that his omniscience extended unto phenomena more repugnant than organic life. In spite of, or rather because of its strangeness, the theory that it sets forth with an imperturbable assurance on the generation of worms within a body in putrefaction deserves to be reproduced in whole. "In addition to the Power," the Reintegration teaches doctorally, "that the body of man has to reproduce itself corporeally, it has also that of vegetating passive animals which are truly innate in the substance of this material form. When the material agent being has left its form, this form goes into putrefaction." There comes from that "reptiles which exist until the three spiritous principles which have cooperated in the corporeal form of man be reintegrated" (dissolved). This putrefaction comes neither from itself, nor directly from the corporeal form, but because "the seminal of all things subject to vegetation is innate in the envelope, whether terrestrial or aquatic." "The body of man having arisen from the general earth and having innate within his form of matter the three principles that have cooperated with him to form his envelope, whether terrestrial or aquatic...there still resides in this particular form a seminal of animals susceptible to vegetation. It is by this seminal that putrefaction occurs in the bodies after what they commonly call death. The three principles that we call sulphur, salt, and mercury, operating by their reintegration (set at liberty), collide by their reaction with the seminal ovaries which are in all the expanse of the body. These ovaries again receive by it a new elementary heat, which strips the reptile animal species from its envelope, and this envelope, thus dissolved, is tied intimately with the coarse humidity of the cadaver. It is the junction of this envelope of the reptiles with the coarse humidity of the cadaver which carries out the general corruption of the body of man and which then puts a final end to its apparent form. The life and action that the animals have in the radical humidity arise only from the operation of the central axis fire which strips, as its final operation, all the impurities which surround the three spiritous essences that are still contained in the form of the cadaver. Their elementary fire conjointly with the central fire maintains the form of the apparent figure of these reptile animals by the operation of refraction of their rays of spiritous fires which, later on, coil up upon themselves when they no longer find fluid to operate, that is to say when all has been entirely consumed by them."[766]

But the faculties of which Pasqually made the greatest use are those which had been distributed to the four elder brothers and which give him all the powers of a true magician. More favored than Adam, who had only been able to communicate to Seth "the laborious ceremonial and not ever the spiritual fruits arising from his temporal spiritual operations" (interpretation of the Passes)[767], he was able, like the elder, "to interpret to his brothers the fruits arising from their operations,"[768] that is to say to understand the meaning and the exact significance of the supernatural phenomena observed by the adepts, and this knowledge is one of his prerogatives. He disclosed, it is true, to his disciples the moment when, by the effect of their practice of "la Chose," they would succeed "in being instructed and trained as well in the interpretation as in the work,"[769] but, so long as he was with them, he did not give up his monopoly.[770] The adepts communicated to him the journals in which they preserved their sketches and they were invited to observe with the greatest attention whether some of the figures traced upon the board, or "any others at all," were "rendered" to them and to send their notes to the Master who reserved the right to make use of it "as he judged fit for their advantage and their instruction,"[771] He wrote on March 13, 1770, to Willermoz: "Their journals have been very well successful to me (have been very useful to me) in the research I have made and that I have very well interpreted on the present and future events which have been most perfectly carried out by me with success by the grace of the Great Architect of the Universe.[772]

The manifestations to which he was himself witness gave him information on the value of the results obtained by the Operations of his disciples. He wrote on May 9, 1772, to Willermoz, disheartened by his repeated failure: "I was informed by my working that, if you had in your own any satisfaction, it was not considerable."[773]

Pasqually was able, like the second brother, to prophecy the manifestation of divine justice,[774] that is to say to announce by what manner the world will end and which of the Just will be reintegrated into the divine circle. But he is also capable of foreseeing future events, the most important as well as the most insignificant, through the interpretation of the Passes observed by the Réau-Croix.[775]

Like the third brother he has received the "gift of universal, general, and particular astronomy"[776] which puts him alone, of all the members of the Order, in a position to calculate the planetary junctures on which depend in great part the success of the Operations.[777] He does not proceed with these important calculations according to what is given by the vulgar science, for the computation that he observes is "the mysterious equinoxes year going from one equinox to the other and beginning with that of September,"[778] and the date of these equinoxes is fixed according to the first quarter of the moon of March and that of September "without worrying about days that the profane science declares equinoxes."[779] If the Réau-Croix have the right to choose for their Equinox Working a series of three days in a period of eight days, this period is determined by Pasqually according to his occult calculations[780] and they must await the results of these calculations in order to know in what mystical time the moon of the following month will fall.[781]

Like the fourth brother, Pasqually "is endowed with the knowledge of the Powerful Word that the Creator used for all his temporal creation." He is able, consequently, to operate on behalf of human bodies for their preservation over the course of their duration" and to radically heal the sick.[782] He also speaks his mind on empirical medicine which is occupied only with matter "in being attached only to that animal instinct which is innate in every passive being." "If some natural event gives rise, upon the form of men who are attached to temporal life, to some contraction (contrary action) which disturbs in it the laws of order, they cry out to the phenomenon, they are all terrified, and, through ignorance, they confide in the care and the instinct of one of their fellows who, most often, are as ignorant as them and who will be in greater pain than the afflicted if a similar accident happened to them. This conduct is not at all surprising from them, who, in similar cases, have no recourse to their first divine spiritual principle, the only medicine that is able to radically heal."[783] By virtue of this principle, Pasqually undertook "to operate against illnesses and for the preservation of the faithful members of the Order."[784] He gave them consultations by correspondence and indicated the cures that he had already operated. The one of which he had performed having the greatest merit had had for its beneficiary his own wife. He had, it is true, experienced a semi-failure in March 1770, after having "labored" for "the general re-establishment of the health" of Mrs. Pasqually. One Operation, prolonged for more than twelve days, had obtained only a "very weak glimmer of her health."[785] But five months later a new Operation had been crowned with a brilliant success, and Pasqually was able to inform Willermoz "of the grace that he had obtained from God by the force of his workings corroborated by the sincere legitimate prayers of his true disciples and emulators of the Order." The pride that his victory inspired in the therapeutic was all the greater considering that the illness had been quite serious and that the physicians, losing hope for a healing, had abandoned the patient. "My wife," wrote Pasqually, "suffered from the most dreadful ailments which are susceptible of reducing the individual of the human nature to its reintegration by force against the prescriptions of the duration of its course (death before the normal term): 1st, dissolution of the blood; 2nd, blood loss for fifty-four days; 3rd, obstruction of the uterus; 4th, looseness of all the intestinal parts; 5th, nephritic colic; 6th, engorgement of the glands of the groin on the right side; 7th, rheumatism sciatica pain." A consultation of "all the celebrated physicians and surgeons of Bordeaux" in the presence of all of Mrs. Pasqually's family and some "emulators," had given up on the sickness for lost. The physicians, recognizing the impotence of human science in the present case, had "ordered" Mrs. Pasqually to "submit to the prescriptions of her husband." This latter had set himself to work without delay, and "on the third day of his work he saw a sign," whose interpretation announced to him the healing of his wife and revealed to him at the same time the danger that had pursued her." An efficacious proof of the grace that I have received," said the happy spouse in ending his long statement, "was that on the fourth day of my work I had my wife rise and roused her a little, which caused to split an abscess that she had in the lower abdomen, which yielded a quantity of dreadful matter."[786]

Pasqually assured that this miraculous healing had caused much noise in the town and throughout the whole province, which they believed without trouble. In any case, the magical powers of the head of the Élus Coëns were so greatly held as invariable by the occultists that, thirty years later, the baron de Turkheim wrote to Willermoz: "I have always had the idea, and reliable friends have confirmed it to me, that the author of the Reintegration had been in communication with various beings and those who inhabit the earth, just as he had magical knowledge and has put it into practice."[787]

∴

Whoever Pasqually's masters were, Kabbalists of the Middle Ages or Occultists of the Renaissance, the magic of the Élus Coëns is distinguished by a very personal characteristic: it is pure of all sorcery and singularly indifferent to material goods. The praise is not slight, for the majority of the magicians of all times and all lands are not extremely scrupulous on the nature of the Spirits that they wish to subdue, and even those who repel all commerce with demonic or simply suspect beings, such as the elementary Spirits, concealed poorly under the pomp of mystical formulas, the ardors of a declamatory devotion, and the rigors of an asceticism for show, the very selfish aims that they pursue: riches, honors, perfect health, knowledge refused to the vulgar, prescience and divination, such are the ends to which the magicians generally put the world of the Spirits into movement.

The Élus Coëns are horrified by the impure Spirits. They believe well, like all occultists, that the magical ceremonies have by themselves, and whatever be the supernatural power invoked, a real efficacy and the Reintegration makes sure to point out that Adam obtained a result from the operations that he had undertaken by rejecting entirely the ceremonial that the Creator had prescribed to him, and by observing the one that the demon had taught him. But the treatise adds that the results obtained constituted a severe punishment for the crime committed by the First Man and the implicit lesson that he draws from this experience is clear: every Operation is only truly able to succeed with the consent and direct or indirect collaboration of God. There, in the final analysis, is the profound reason for the predominant role played in the Operations of the Élus Coëns by the Divine Name and the "Spiritual Names" of the intermediaries between man and the Creator. As regards the aim of the Operations, the attention of the adepts is turned too exclusively towards heaven and the future life to be distracted by immediate and passing advantages. Pasqually asserts indeed to have healed his wife by supernatural means which he offers to employ on occasion on behalf of his disciples, but they must only consider this miraculous cure as a rare and brilliant proof of the particular graces distributed to their master in order to aid in the "triumph and manifestation of the glory of the Lord."

The astrological calculations of Pasqually aim only to set the date of the Operations and are never put to the service of judicial astrology.

What they call foreknowledge of the future, and which has such attraction for the weak human, is not, according to the treatise, from a rational point of view, but a calculation of probabilities; from the mystical point of view, it does not exist outside supernatural revelations that God dispenses to the rare elect when they have observed scrupulously, in spirit and in action, the ceremonial of the Operations. It is not necessary to believe as "the crude people in these so-called sooth-sayers, fortune tellers, magicians, wizards, sorcerers or sorceresses; no one may read into the past but by the present[788] and thus, having a perfect knowledge of the one and the other, it is not difficult to read more or less into the future…" "When it is necessary for the success of any work to read into all the operations, actions, contractions (reactions), vegetations, revolutions, and other temporal spiritual things which are executed in this universe by the Spirit or by man, the one who is able to succeed in this may not call upon a soothsayer or fortune teller for this, since he may obtain this knowledge only after painful spiritual and corporeal efforts which make the one who labors on the marvels of the mover of the universe to feel the pain of the soul, body, and spirit. Man may not be instructed in any knowledge of the operations of the universe except by submitting to painful and formidable labors," such as "the works of Moses and the seven Sages of Israel" who "have battled, conquered, and exterminated the enemies of the true divine cult." Moreover, what matters the knowledge of the future? The only one that counts is the one which awaits us after death and "the spiritual science of the Eternal is not the art of a soothsayer."[789]

Pasqually admits, like many occultists, the possibility of artificial generation, of that "homofactio" that Paracelsus operated in the abdomen of a horse, for which the Italians extracted the mandrakes pushed under a gibbet and who had given to the Count de Kuefstein mysterious beings that he preserved in a jar. But he rejected it as an abominable art. After having established, by the voice of Moses speaking to Israel, that the procreation of the human body arises only "from the spiritous essences innate in man," he adds, taking always Moses as exponent: "If you wish, by your authority, to employ principles opposed to the substance of action and divine and temporal spiritual operation, reproduction would not arise therefrom, or, if one originated therefrom, it would remain without participation of divine operation, it would be placed in the ranks of the brute animals, even there it would be regarded as a supernatural (abnormal) being, and it would be repugnant (would be an object of horror) to all the inhabitants of temporal nature."[790]

Alchemy, still so cultivated in the 18th century, and which a number of occultists had more or less practiced since the Renaissance, is expressly condemned by the Reintegration. Pasqually himself had, it is true, made some borrowings, perhaps moreover without really taking it into account. He had found in the numerous Hermetic treatises that appeared in the 17th century under the name, probably apocryphal, of Basil Valentine, the theory according to which the bodies are composed of three fundamental elements: sulphur, salt, and mercury.[791] When he speaks of the sister of Moses, called Merian (Virgin Earth), "daughter wise in divine knowledge and who made a sacrifice of her virginity in order to operate the true cult permitted to her sex,"[792] he was inspired manifestly by the alchemical works which made of Mary the Jew, sister of Moses, herself said to be a master in the art of transmutation, one of the luminaries of the spagyric art. But the Reintegration nevertheless disapproves of the search for the chrysopea by transparent allusions. It recalls that the First Man had committed an error in wishing to act upon matter, "by tracing six circumferences similar to those of the Creator"[793]; it insists upon this idea that "the first (original) matter had only been engendered to be at the sole disposal of the demons"[794]; it demonstrates that in forming the number Nine, "number of the division of the spiritous essences of matter and of that of the divine spiritual essences," by junction of the Quinary, "imperfect and corruptible number," and the Quaternary, "perfect and incorruptible number," that is to say in seeking to dissociate the bodies in order to form gold with their elements otherwise combined, and dedicating to this job the power granted by the divinity to Adam in order to dominate matter, "man degrades his divine spiritual power by rendering it demonic spiritual."[795] The Spiritual Minor must carefully refrain from any work being applied to the elements of matter so long as, not having been returned into direct communication with God, he is not enlightened on the dangers that these practices present. It is necessary for him to remember that he is the descendant of fallen Adam who, even after his reconciliation, has remained "susceptible to being a man of error in all his spiritual and temporal human operations, which happens to man every time he operates only by virtue of these three ternary powers, which are: aerial, terrestrial, and fiery power (air, earth, fire). It is therefore dangerous to the man of desire to use these three powers in whatever operation it be without having previously obtained from the Creator the quaternary power which is withdrawn from us by the prevarication of Adam."[796] Therefore, the Élu Coën is not worthy to exercise his empire over the elementary Spirits, mixed beings, indifferent to good and evil, presiding over the transformations of matter and that the alchemists strive to arrange with their laws. If it does not put in doubt the reality of the Great Work, it considers that the riches procured through the spagyric art, demonic science, are deadly gifts which deter man from what ought to be the goal of his life in this world, that is to say the cult of the divine: "The prince of this matter favors for a moment his proselytes in order to remove from them, whether in thought or in action, their divine spiritual principle, but, when he has set them at the summit of their satisfaction, he leaves them in the midst of traps that he has laid for them and hurls them into the abyss."[797]

The magic of the Élus Coëns is, by its aspirations and its principles, profoundly religious. In practicing it, they obey a divine law, "the Creator, who is immutable, having said expressly to his reconciled man (Adam) that no knowledge of the divine sciences would be given to him until he will have gained it through his works."[798] Their theurgy, respectful of the unlimited power of the divinity, is addressed onto its emissaries[799] and claims only to compel them to manifest themselves with the agreement of the infinite power on which they depend, and as proof of the graces that the future life reserves to the elect.

There is evidently a contradiction between an absolute submission to the decrees from on high and the claim of the adepts to command the divine Spirits. But the same antinomy is found in all the acts by which man undertakes to enter into communication with the divine. All the positive religions, and unto the spiritists, have preserved in their rites the indelible traces of the primitive magic which believed the human will capable of inciting or thwarting natural phenomena by acting, with the help of appropriate gestures and words, upon the fluids which produce them or the Spirits from which they proceed. Faith in the magical power of the man particularly endowed, by symbolic act or consecrated formula, has been strongly disparaged by a more rational notion of physical laws and above all by the concept of a supreme God, a Creator with whom his creatures have no common measure. But the transposition on the transcendent plane of the will of power innate with man has never entirely abdicated its rights. The faithful, in whatever religion to which he belongs, seeks always, more or less consciously, to take away by great struggle the favor that he implores. The ritual prayers have kept something of the incantation, and the mystical value of the sacraments resides essentially in their magical virtue. Every cult is a compromise between two opposed principles, and its proper value consists rather less in the measure that it has eliminated the magical elements than in the object that those who practice it have in sight: material and immediate advantages or blessings that are spiritual and situated in the beyond. The moral dispositions of the believers are therefore more important than the dogmas that they profess or the rites that they observe. By virtue of this, the secret cult of the Élus Coëns yields nothing to the mystical systems most worthy of respect.

CHAPTER V
Esoteric Christianity

The mystical system of which the preceding chapters have traced the great lines and summarily indicated the origins, has nothing which connects it to the period and to the land where it had found disciples. The treatise on the Reintegration would have been able, if one was satisfied with the citations made up to the present, to have been written at the end of the Middle Ages by a rabbi versed in the Talmud, the Midraschim, and the Kabbalah, and familiar with the philosophico-religious doctrines of the occultist sects flourishing in the Near East and in Egypt in the first centuries of our era.

Nevertheless, this strange plant having sprouted up again in French soil, in the States of the Most Christian King, for the faithful of the Catholic, Apostolic, and Roman Church, had submitted to the influence of the environment. Pasqually, who made, and very loudly at the occasion, a profession of "Catholicity," had to accommodate his doctrines to the very sincere Catholic faith of his adepts, so that his treatise cites Christ beside Moses and leans expressly on the New Testament. The rabbi that we have discovered in him was, in short, a converted rabbi. Only he was less profoundly so than he wished to have it believed, or, perhaps, believed himself. His façade of Christianity is a thin rough cast rejuvenating an ancient edifice, but which flakes and crumbles as soon as a hand is laid on it.

That the doctrine professed by Pasqually was, in the historical sense of the term, only Christian in name, is a fact that every reader of the Reintegration may ascertain, but, before bringing it more completely to light, it is necessary to prevent a prejudicial objection which would serve nothing less than rendering the demonstration impossible. We have seen that the treatise is, at least under the form that we know it, remaining incomplete, the paraphrase of the Bible which serves as its foundation, stopping at the 1st Book of Kings. Now, one of the principal disciples of Pasqually, J.B. Willermoz, head of the Élus Coëns of Lyon, asserted in a confidential letter that the treatise "would go until the Ascension of Our Lord," and, at the bottom of one of the two manuscripts that Mr. Matter has had under his eyes, was found the following note: "The author has not been very lengthy in this treatise, which ought to be much longer. It is especially at the coming of Christ that it ought to be more considerable, according to what he himself has said to his friends."[800] Have we the right to bring judgment upon so important a point of the doctrine of Pasqually in absence of any direct documentation, when we lack precisely the part of his work where the question would be specially treated, where the Gospel would logically be commented upon with as much abundance as had first been the Bible?

It is permitted to respond affirmatively, and for several reasons. If we do not possess a complete and systematic account of the concepts of Pasqually on the nature and mission of Christ, the author made there numerous enough allusions in what we possess of his work so that we are able to deduce therefrom with a sufficient surety what he thought on this question. On the other hand, it is very doubtful, supposing that Pasqually had ever decided to write it, that this second part would have thrown more clarity on the object of our interest. This hypothesis rests on the following two considerations: first, among the various questions on which Pasqually promises to return "elsewhere," "later on," "in another place," or "in its place,"[801] there never figures anything concerning Christ himself. Pasqually is engaged in further explaining why the Lord had said that the one who killed Cain would be punished seven times and the one who killed the murderer of Cain seventy-seven times by death,[802] in giving revelations on "the final revolutions which will happen to the creature (creation?) at the end of all duration,"[803] on "the fire which must put an end to the universal creation,"[804] on the manner by which "all at the end will return as in the beginning."[805] He promises a report on matter, on the anatomical constitution of the heart of man,[806] on "the particular properties of his four members,"[807] on the "details on the principles of the different celestial and terrestrial bodies," "a positive knowledge of all the virtues and powers of Saturn, of the Sun, and of the other planetary circles,"[808] "an account of the epochs,"[809] a mystical commentary on the number twelve.[810] Biblical exegesis, eschatology, cosmology, anthropology, astrology, and arithmosophy, such are the matters upon which Pasqually had proposed to give supplementary indications; in no part does he speak of developments touching on Christology.

The motives of this reservation are easily guessed when one notes, and this is the second argument in favor of our thesis, with what care Pasqually avoided explaining himself straightforwardly on a theological question with which a heterodox could only touch upon with the greatest prudence if he did not wish to scandalize the faithful of the official and national religion. Each time that it happens that the author of the Reintegration speaks on Christ, he intermingles with such perseverance the most varied ideas, he falls, over the course of the same sentence, into so many contradictions of terms and images that the obscurity with which it is enveloped cannot simply be the involuntary effect of his imperfect mastery of the language and the confusion of his thought. One must see there rather the confession of the difficulty in which he finds himself in having to smuggle a prohibited merchandise. His uneasiness would have been greater still if he would have been obliged to directly tackle a commentary of the New Testament and, if it would be perhaps excessive to advance that this was the obstacle which prevented the completion of his treatise, one has at least the right to suppose that he would not have, in the second part of his work, explained more clearly or more completely this delicate point than he has done in the text that has reached us.[811]

∴

The Christian decor behind which is concealed the true doctrines of the Reintegration is assembled and painted with care.

Pasqually returns again and again to this idea that the Jewish people, through their repeated apostasies, lost the title and dignity of people elected by God, and no longer possess therefore a monopoly on communication with the divine, so that the true religion has ceased to be exclusively Jewish in order to become universal. By their criminal covenants with the prince of the demons, the Hebrews are then called: "children of darkness and children of the blood of matter, and they have been replaced by those called: children of the divine grace."[812] In saving Moses, in giving him her own mother as wet nurse, and in ordering the latter to present him each day, the daughter of the Pharaoh "announced the covenant that the idolaters would make in the future with the divine laws."[813] In prescribing to the Jewish families who did not have lambs among them to join together for the Passover with those who had them, Moses "announced by this the covenant that the rest of the idolaters of Egypt (symbolic designation of the non-Jewish world) would make in the future with the divine law, which has effectively arrived,"[814] for "the rest of the Egyptians, after the destruction of the Pharaoh and his army, joined themselves to the law of Moses."[815]

Christianity, universalist religion to which were converted the men belonging to all the races of the earth, is expressly represented as the heir of the divine law proclaimed by Moses. The prophet had promised in the name of the Eternal that "the operation of election, or spiritual name given to the soul or to the Minor, is perpetuated among the idolatrous people more ('who would no longer be' or 'who were then the most') in privation of the knowledge of the true cult of the divinity, which is clearly manifested today in the Christian church by the sacrament of baptism where the newborn receives a spiritual name completely different from the one that it bears by its temporal material origin."[816]

The Reintegration speaks on the foundation of the Church, on its existence and its mission in terms that would have been approved by the doctors in the Sorbonne. It calls Christ: "living God,"[817] "Word of God,"[818] "Son of the Creator,"[819] "Man-God"[820]; it recalls that he went, after his death, "to render an account to his father"[821]; it puts him, with the Trinity, outside of its cosmogonic and penumatological theories by noting that "the action of the Eternal, which is Christ, and his operation, which is the Holy Spirit, are not included, neither the one nor the other, in any sort of emanation or emancipation," so that "their actions and their operations will always be divine spiritual ones, without any subjection to time or to the temporal."[822] The treatise professes that "Christ is come in order to reconcile the living and the dead with the Creator. God the Son, by his passion and by the effusion of his blood, has opened the gates of heaven to all those who were dead in divine privation."[823]

Pasqually, using a process familiar to the Christian apologetic, discovers in the accounts of the Bible symbolic allusions to the teachings of the Gospel, to the dogmas of the Church, and a prefiguration of the advent of the Savior.[824] Esau, supplanted by Jacob, "confirms this prediction of the Scripture that the first will be the last."[825] In invoking the Creator by the triple cry: Be with me, the God of Abraham, of Isaac, and of Jacob, Jacob professes the dogma of the Trinity, for the first name evokes the type of the Creator "by the multitude of spiritual powers which were given" to the patriarchal father of the Hebrews; the second name evokes "the divine Son or the divine action in the great posterity of God which arises from Isaac, in which the election and the manifestation of the divine glory was operated"; the third name "recognizes the true type of the Spirit by the great marvels that the Creator had done for him in openly demonstrating to him the divine glory."[826]

This symbolic exegesis is applied especially to the character and mission of Christ and to the events which have marked his passage upon the earth. "Abel was a rather striking type of the manifestation of the divine glory that was operated one day by Christ for the perfect reconciliation of the past, present, and future posterity of the First Man."[827] "Having come only by order of the Creator and for a simple (for only one) divine spiritual manifestation, he would have been able to say as the Christ: My kingdom is not of this world, for he would not enjoy any part of matter, nor participate in anything to do with the division of the earth, which would only be distributed to the posterity of the men arising from the senses of matter. He was also promptly withdrawn from the number of this material posterity after having fulfilled his mission according to the will of the Creator."[828] "The form of Abel conceived without excess of the material senses was spiritual rather than material, and it is by this spiritual conception that we consider the form of Abel as a true figure and the form of Christ originating spiritually from an ordinary form without assistance from material physical operations and without the participation of the senses of matter."[829] Eve, who was "inundated with a joy and an inexpressible satisfaction" when she bore Abel in her womb, and Adam, who "became again just as satisfied and joyous," are the type of the Virgin, of Elizabeth, and of the two "temporal fathers" "by the thrill that Elizabeth felt in her soul when she greeted her cousin Mary who came to visit her" and "by the satisfaction that the two temporal fathers felt."[830] Abel immolated by Cain "made the true type of the Messiah and the true figure of the Operations of Christ"[831]; "Abel has been truly immolated in order to accomplish the entire reconciliation of his father Adam."[832] The murder committed on him by Cain in the presence of his two sisters "had represented the defeat of the corporeal individual of Christ (the crucifixion) carried out by men in the presence of two women, Mary of Zebedee and Mary Magdalene."[833] "The blood that has flowed from Abel the Just is the type and the certain resemblance of that which Christ would shed."[834] Also, after the murder of Abel a "spiritual interpreter" appeared to Adam and Eve and declared to them: "The Creator tells you through my words that you have, the one and the other, produced this posterity of Abel that in order to be (so that he be) the true type of the one who will come in a time in order to be the unique and true reconciler of all your posterity."[635] Adam, in announcing to Eve the death of the Just, had already made known to her "that his crimes would come to be expiated by the victim Abel" and, serving as the formula that would come out of the lips of the tortured expiring on Golgotha, he had told her: "All is consummated."[836]

"The birth of Enoch was marked in the heavens by a planetary sign"[837]; "his coming into the world foretold the advent of a universal reconciliation (of the universe with the Creator), the sign which appeared at his birth foretold the one that appeared at the birth of Christ, and his type is that of the three distinct operations that Christ had to make among men for the manifestation of the divine glory, for the salvation of men and for the molestation of demons."[838] "The patriarch Minors would be during their temporal life a real type of the advent of the Messiah and of his omnipotence for the manifestation of divine justice which must be carried out by him upon all the emanated beings."[839]

The divine cult that Noah operated by coming out of the Ark "was the true figure of that operated by the divine Man for the reconciliation of the first Minor."[840] Addressing himself to the surviving men, he announced to them: "someone greater than I, who will be born among your posterities, will instruct you more particularly on the justice and reward that he reserves to the creature at the end of time, according to the confidence that it will have had in its Creator."[841]

Isaac was, at the moment when Abraham prepared for the sacrifice, "the true type of the one that the Creator would send upon the earth in order to carry out the true sacrifice,"[842] The ram sacrificed in his place was "shadow and figure of the victim who would be offered in turn by effective nature, just as the oblation of Isaac by his father had predicted it."[843] The ram that Jacob gave to Esau when he had conceived the project to supplant his brother "announced the betrayal that the Man-God would experience on the part of one of his brothers and disciples named Judas Iscariot,"[844] Moses saved from the waters by the Egyptian princess is "the type of the advent of Christ into this world," for the princess "represented the mother of Christ."[845] The lamb that he sacrificed as an offering of expiation is "a symbol of the victim who would be immolated eventually for the salvation of the human race,"[846] and the reconciliation that he has carried out between Israel and the Lord represents "the operation of the divine Man or Son of the Creator."[847]

Finally, Pasqually expressly dates from the coming of Christ the foundation of the true divine cult and represents the appearance of Christ as the last stage of a progressive revelation: "Moses has surpassed Abraham and the Sages of Egypt by his operations; the cult exercised in the Temple of Solomon was above what preceded it, Christ has operated a cult infinitely greater than the others. This last shows us clearly that all the past cults were only figures of what he has done."[848]

∴

The Christian color that such passages give to the Reintegration could only deceive superficial readers.

We note first of all that Pasqually never refers to the evangelical texts. The Epistles of Saint Paul and the Acts of the Apostles, nevertheless, offer him arguments to support his most cherished theories. The conversion of Paul on the road to Damascus, produced by a manifestation accompanied by "traction," the vision in the course of which Christ declared to him: "I have chosen you to bear witness to the things that you have seen and of those that I will show you," his dialectic that one has defined exactly by saying: "All that the apostle will be will be able to preach to the Jews and to the Gentiles will come from this undeniable experience: Christ is resurrected, for I have seen him as I see you,"[849] all which confirmed expressly the axiom set forth in the Reintegration and according to which the eye is the organ of conviction.

The apostolic writings also furnished completed models of the Spiritual Elect, proving the reality of their mission by the supernatural gifts that the divinity had granted them: whether Saint Paul himself who declared to have gripped the soul of his first catechumens of Corinth, "not by persuasive discourses of wisdom, but in the manifestation of the Spirit and power," or the deacon Stephen who, "filled with grace and power," carried out in the midst of the people "extraordinary miracles and signs." That Pasqually has neglected comparisons which were so favorable to his thesis is a significant fact; it may have only one explanation: the concern of invoking as authoritative Scripture only the Bible, nothing but the Bible, to the exclusion of every other source of revelation.

Upon another point, the silence of Pasqually had a different reason, but just as symptomatic. The downfall of Israel as trustee of the true religion was the subject of evangelical parables: the vineyard rented to other workers when the winegrowers had killed the son of the master sent to them; man invited to weddings and hurled, hands and fists bound, into the exterior darkness while the beggars from the street took their place in the banquet hall. But, while agreeing on the principle, the New Testament and the Reintegration differed profoundly on the opinion of its consequences. For the first, Christianity is the universal heir of Judaism; for the second, the knowledge of the true divine cult, withdrawn from the Hebrew people, has remained the monopoly of some sages, elected by the Lord to preserve it and transmit it by secret tradition. Therefore, Pasqually guards himself carefully to draw the attention of the readers to the abyss that separates the Christian religion, public and open to all, from his own esoteric credo.

The orthodoxy of the Reintegration therefore manifests itself uniquely through the mention it makes of Christ, but the caution is not narrow-minded. It would be necessary, in order to be content thereof, to be unaware, or to have forgotten, the very precise and special meaning that Pasqually gives to the word "type." For a reader less familiar with the terminology of the Reintegration, the term signifies: prophetic phenomenon, prefigurative manifestation, and that is quite the meaning that more than one of the passages cited above seem to attach to it. But when one is reminded that, for Pasqually, a type "is the figure not only of an event to come but also of a past event,"[850] one sees that the author of the Reintegration has only borrowed from the orthodox apologetic one of its methods in order to throw one off his intentions, and that the conclusions to which he holds are very different from the principles upon which the Christian theologians founded their demonstration. For the latter, the life and passion of Jesus were the denouement prepared and announced by the scenes of the long drama which began with the error of Adam, and this outcome had for its consequence the end of the reign of the Law and the advent of the reign of Grace. For Pasqually, on the contrary, Jesus, "regenerative being,"[851] is one of numerous manifestations of the type of the "Reconciler," that is to say of the Spirit emanated from the circle of the divinity in order to return into communication with God the Minors fallen into privation and which, in order to fulfill this mission, animates each time a "body of apparent matter." The advent of the being that the Christians call the Christ is therefore no longer a conclusion nor a unique and extraordinary phenomenon; it must be placed with a number of episodes of which the Bible furnishes so many examples, and which will be able to be renewed until the end of time, since the weakness of the Minors renders so brief the periods of reconciliation that divine mercy has granted them in the course of the ages. Considered under this aspect, the Christ of Pasqually is no longer at all the Savior of the Christians. He is in reality a new incarnation, after so many others, of "the doubly strong Spirit" of the Octonary Spirit, of which Moses said, speaking to Israel: "It is with you when you deserve it and is removed from you when you render yourselves unworthy of its doubly powerful action."[852]

Consequently, the personality of the Jesus of the Gospel is diluted to the point of disappearing almost completely, his figure grows blurred and becomes a pale and lifeless shadow. Jesus of Nazareth, who has lived under Tiberius and who was crucified by Pontius Pilate, is confused with all the biblical personages of which the Octonary Spirit has used to catechize the Minors and bring them back to God.[853] This is what the Reintegration recalls time and again, and in a particularly formal fashion when it declares: "All the reconciliations operated by Heli, Enoch, Noah, Melchizedek have been done directly by Christ, for, although they have been carried out by the assistance (means) of Minors emanated for this end, these Minors have nevertheless only been apparent figures of which Christ has used in order to manifest the glory and mercy of the Creator on behalf of the reconciled. We know with certitude that the number eight is innate (essentially endowed) of double power given by the Creator to Christ, and it is he who teaches us what the Messiah has operated on behalf of the temporal men of the first and second posterity of Adam."[854]

This transcendent Christ or Messiah is a pure Spirit acting "by his own doubly powerful operation and granted immediately from his head,"[855] for he possesses Eight, "number of the double power given by the Creator to Christ"[856] or "sign of the doubly strong Spirit belonging to Christ."[857] He is the true Reconciler since "the name of Christ signifies: receptacle of divine operation"[858] and Messiah: "divine spiritual regenerator."[859] It is thanks to him that the Patriarchs, "who operate the will of Christ conjointly with the doubly powerful spiritual being, have reconciled their posterity with the Creator."[860] The Minor Elect are only instruments. Pasqually counts therein ten, probably by respect for the mystical value of the Denary or in remembrance of the ten Patriarchs that Genesis enumerates from the creation of the world until the Flood, and this list, which begins with Abel and continues with Enoch, Noah, Melchizedek, Joseph, Moses, David, Solomon, and Zorobabel, is closed by the Messiah, that is to say Jesus Christ.[861] Thus the Savior of the Christians is no longer a God who is made flesh in order to redeem humanity by an unprecedented sacrifice and whose effect ought to be definitive. He is the tenth proof of a type; he is found reduced to the rank of a Minor inspired by a Spirit emanated over and over from the divine circle, and he is placed on the same plane as personages of whom some were presented by the Bible as simple men, kings, or heads of armies. He is only one of the "apparent forms" under which is manifested the reconciler Spirit, and he does not even constitute the last of the series, for the treatise specifies that he is "one of the types of the divine action operated by the divine Spirit not only among the Minors past and present, but again among the Minors to come."[862]

Pasqually returns several times to this idea in making a connection between the historical Christ and the other avatars of the Reconciler. He insists on the fact that "Noah has repeated the same type as Melchizedek, Zorobabel, and Christ. Here are those who have been appointed by order of the Creator to mark the minor spiritual beings who come into being to accompany the triumph of the manifestation of the divine justice carried out by the power of the Man-God and divine according to his immediate correspondence with the Creator."[863] He assimilates the "works of Moses and Christ with the work of Seth, and to that which the Sages have operated after him."[864] He teaches that "Adam, Enoch, Noah, Moses, Solomon, and Christ have made great use of the triangle in their workings."[865]

Jesus, last appearance of the Elect Minors, interests him moreover less than those who preceded him. "In the first times of the posterity of the First Man, Heli, that we call Christ, and that we recognize with certitude as a thinking being (in direct intellectual communication with God) has reconciled Adam with the creation."[866]" Heli reconciled the First Man with the Creator by the intermediary of his spirit which made a connection with the First Minor emanated. Enoch, by his justice, operated on behalf of the posterity of the children of Seth, as many living as deceased,"[867] and "reconciled thus the first posterity of Adam."[868] "Noah reconciled the second posterity of Adam, in reconciling his own with the Creator, and then reconciled the earth with God. Melchizedek confirmed these first reconciliations by blessing the works of Abraham and his three hundred servants."[869] "Abel was a type of the Minors endowed with the divine grace that the Creator would make to be born among men in order to be spiritual instruments of the manifestation of his justice. Among the minors destined to these sorts of spiritual operations we consider firstly Enoch, the seventh of the posterity of the one that replaced Abel, that is to say of Seth. Enoch made, through his mission, his works, and his operations, and by the cult that he professed, the true type of the direct action of the doubly strong Spirit of the Creator. It is nothing other than a holy Spirit under a form of apparent matter."[870] There "had to be eventually a new type of the will of the Creator, just as we have seen that there have been several successors from the past types down to this day. The first principle of the divine spiritual religion that had been established among the posterity of Seth was preserved and restored to vigor by the power of Noah, who himself is again a type of spiritual election for the general and particular reconciliation (of the earth and of men) with God."[871]

The Christ of the Christians has seen, it is true, the "glory of the Creator," but he shares this favor with all the personages that the Bible places in direct relation with the God of Israel: Noah, Abraham, Isaac, Jacob, Moses, and Elijah, and, the type of these elect beings having been repeated by triads, Jesus forms an element of the third beside Moses and Elijah, for "in their operations on Mount Tabor they have seen altogether the glory of the Creator."[872] Or better yet he completes with Enoch, Melchizedek and Elijah the number of the four Just "two of whom have been risen from the center of the earth by the spiritual fire and the other two have been in their own body of spiritual glory just as Christ proves by his resurrection of divine man."[873]

.·.

This polymorphous Christ, belated offspring of the docetist heresy, disturbed the beautiful equilibrium that the Fathers of the Church, the theologians, and the councils had striven to maintain between the two natures of the Savior. If the Jesus Christ of the Christians commanded them in his capacity of Son of God and as the second person of the Trinity, he also interested their sensibility by his human nature which, having made him to endure the sufferings of the flesh and of the spirit, connected him to their condition. The Gospels, in recounting the episodes of his terrestrial existence and his death, had so vigorously outlined his figure that, for centuries, he continued to live, real and present, in the imagination of the believers. With the metaphysical Christ of the Reintegration, the divine essence of the Octonary Spirit emanated from the Supercelestial absorbed the human element to the point that the sensible form of the Reconciler became a phantom with multiple aspects, devoid of all individual and plastic personality, having nothing more in common with the Minor of flesh and blood that he came to save than an empty appearance.

Although, if the balance, where we have seen Pasqually weigh the two terms constituting the mystical entity of Christ, tipped manifestly in favor of the divine, he made it oscillate brusquely in the contrary sense in presenting in other passages of his treatise the Man-God of Christian theology as a repetition of the type of the First Adam and Man restored to a hundred-fold what he had first lost.

The point of contact between these two different aspects of the esoteric Christ is established by means of the number Eight and by a predicate added surreptitiously with the name of Man-God currently employed by the theologians to designate the Savior.

The Octonary, assigned by the Creator to the Spirit of the Supercelestial in order to render him capable of reconciling the fallen Minors, had also been attributed to the First Minor who possessed before his fall "the double power belonging to Christ," for the First Adam was, in his state of innocence, equal to the Spirits of the Supercelestial. He was, like them, "thinking," that is to say in intellectual communication with the divinity. One therefore has the right to say that the First Man was "the true Adam or the Christ"[874] and to call him "Minor Christ"[875] and "God emanated."[876]

On the other hand, the First Adam having been appointed to the material prison where the perverse Spirits were enclosed, "the Minor was in his first principle the Man-God of the earth and of all creation, and was not able to be subjected to the suffering of time or temporal suffering (death)"[877] and that is why "he had been named by the Eternal Man-God and commander of every spiritual and temporal being."[878] Therefore Noah called his second posterity "Man-Gods of the earth," since he had, in repopulating the earth with the beings saved in his ark, "made himself the type of the Creator."[879]

Jesus Christ, "Man-God and divine of this universe,"[880] has recalled the type of the First Adam, "being as pure and as perfect as is the action of the Eternal which is the Christ."[881] "The advent and the resurrection (with transfiguration) of Christ, just as the descent of the divine Spirit into the Temple of Solomon (Shekinah) have made us see in nature (by sensible fashion) the glorious form that primitive Adam possessed." Furthermore, Jesus is an exact replica of fallen Adam, as proves "the appearance that the chief of the demons makes in the presence of Christ, Man-God of the earth. This perverse being would not have appeared to him under a human form and would not have attacked him if the Man-God had not been clothed in a body of matter and if he had used the glorious form which is innate in him, for then the spiritual and demonic contraction (contrary action) would not have been able to take place, since the pure Spirit has the privilege to bind and to stop every operation of the impure Spirits. In appearing to the divine man, the chief of the demons wished to corrupt the form of corporeal matter of this divine being and above all to seduce the spiritual being who resides in this body."[882]

The Reconciler Spirit, in being joined to fallen Adam, causes the rebirth, at least partially, of the First Adam. "It was by this cult of the Divine Man or Christ that the Creator re-blessed the universal creation by re-blessing Adam whom he had damned as principal chief of every created being and as divine man of the earth."[883] "At the time of the reconciliation of Adam with the Creator the three personages of this act were Adam, Christ, and the Creator, Christ being the will who realized the intention of the Father."[884]

∴

The double aspect under which the Reintegration presents the Christ of the New Testament informs us on the nature of the Christianity of Pasqually. The Christian Kabbalists, such as Reuchlin composing his *Verbum Mirificum* with the monogram of Christ joined to the Tetragrammaton, had sought to have the mystical theories of the Kabbalah held in the framework of the Christian doctrine by presenting the Talmudic esotericism as an echo of the revelations made by the Savior to his disciples. They thus absorbed the secret Jewish tradition into Christianity. Pasqually follows an opposite course: he tends to integrate historical and traditional Christianity into his mystical system by giving to the fundamental themes and to the consecrated theological expressions an appropriated meaning and by using the methods of orthodox exegesis in order to succeed in his particular ends.

The second and the third person of the Trinity, that is to say the Son and the Holy Spirit, become "the action of the Eternal which is Christ, and his operation which is the Holy Spirit."[885] If "it has been taught to us that God was in three persons," it is "because the Creator has operated three divine actions distinct from one another on behalf of the three Minors, Abraham, Isaac, and Jacob" (each of whom had been witness to a theophany).[886]

"What one commonly calls original sin is what we call spiritually a decree pronounced by the Eternal against the posterity of Adam until the end of the ages" and which rendered the soul "subject to the suffering of privation" and the "material and passive" form.[887]

"What one commonly calls Purgatory signifies the spiritual asylum (reservoir of the constitutive elements of matter from which is formed the sensible world) where the Minors deceased (come out) from this lower world will go to accomplish in divine privation the rest of their simple spiritual operations (without mixture of material elements) according to the decree of the Creator."[888]

Pasqually is not content to transpose more or less overtly the Christian motifs. To the list of orthodox citations that one has read above, it is necessary to contrast a much more considerable retinue of passages where, taking the opposite view of the Christian apologetic, the author of the treatise reverses the terms of the demonstration by finding in the mission, life, and passion of Jesus, a new illustration of his fundamental doctrines, of which he had already discovered the confirmation in his esoteric commentary on the Bible.

If Jesus is mounted upon an ass in order to enter into Jerusalem, it was in order "to effectively represent" the forgetfulness into which fell periodically the true religion "in the midst of Ishmael and Israel," just as, when Abraham and Isaac ascended Moriah, they kept 'the ass with them in order to show us the ignorance where these two nations would one day be, and that to their prejudice the light would be transferred to the midst of the darkness and the gentile peoples."[889]

The birth of Christ represents the material incorporation of the First Man. "The entry of this Spiritual Major, or Word of the Creator, into the body of a virgin girl recalls clearly to us the entry of the First Minor into the abyss of the earth in order to be clothed in a body of matter. The different sorrows and the revolutions which try the body of this virgin girl in pregnancy and childbirth are the figure of the subjection and demonic spiritual revolutions that the general terrestrial body endured and is obliged to endure relatively to the prevarication of Adam."[890] Furthermore, "this corporeal formation of Christ recalls to us the material incorporation of the First Man who, after his prevarication, was stripped of his body of glory and took upon himself one of coarse matter while being hurled into the entrails of the earth. For, before this divine Spirit, doubly powerful and superior to every emanated being, carried out the divine justice among men, it inhabited the pure and glorious circle of the divine immensity. But, when it was delegated by the Creator, it left this spiritual dwelling in order to come to be confined in the womb of a virgin girl. Now, concerning the absence that this Minor Christ made from his true abode, does this does not recall to us the expulsion of the First Man from his body of glory?"[891] Likewise, by his "glorious resurrection" (Transfiguration) Christ has proved "physically" that the descendants of Adam had originally inhabited "a body of incorruptible glory."[892]

Jesus, that the evangelical accounts show to us fighting victoriously against the demons, acts as one of the Octonary Spirits who, "acting not only on the terrestrial world and the material world, but again on the circle of the universal axis," fulfills a double office and "have by their rank and their mission the action of the double power, since they serve as double rampart to the atrocities of the demonic operations."[893]

The eclipse of the sun which accompanied the death of Christ "is the real type of the scourge that happened to the demonic Spirits that Christ, by his operation, reduced lower than they were in their privation against the general and particular creation.[894] This eclipse recalled, moreover, the darkness of ignorance where the Hebrews were found plunged when they had eclipsed from their memory the holy divine names. This eclipse made at last the true type of the general matter (material world) which will be eclipsed entirely at the end of time."[895]

"The rupture of the veil of the Temple is the true type of the deliverance of the Minor deprived (until then) of the presence of the Creator. It explains the reintegration of the apparent matter which veils and separates every minor being from the perfect knowledge. It explains the tearing and the descent of the seven planetary heavens which veil by their body of matter from the Spiritual Minors the great divine light that reigns in the celestial circle."[896]

The words that Christ addressed to his apostles "at the end of his last temporal operation at the Mount of Olives," when, having come to rejoin them, he found them asleep and told them while rousing them: "Do not sleep, for the flesh is weak and the Spirit is prompt," are "a proof of the intimate connection of the malign Spirits with the body of man."[897] The power that the demons have to destroy the human bodies is also demonstrated by "the defeat (destruction) of the body of Christ destroyed by the hand of men."[898]

Jesus has not taught men a new cult. He has only "confirmed" the law forbidding the divine service to the lame[899] and the religious exercises that he has prescribed are those very ones which had originally served, just as we have seen, to set the divisions of time: "Christ has left to his disciples, through his divine spiritual institution, the daily prayer and invocation of six hours which completes (forms) the ordinary day of twenty-four hours.[900] Secondly (posteriorly) Christ has set for his disciples the time when they would exercise the four great divine cults."[901]

The esoteric interpretation that Pasqually gives of the descent of Christ into Hell is a transposition of a theme that Christianity had moreover, while adopting it, left in an outline state. It tends to illustrate the theories of the Reintegration on the annunciating seal of salvation and on the manner by which the Elect Minors confer it to the Spiritual Minors by the manifestations that the Élus Coëns expect from their works. Recalling the "three days that Christ is remained unknown to the world and its inhabitants," the treatise enumerates the three operations that he made during this time. "The first day he descended into the places of the greatest divine privation, commonly called the Underworld, in order to deliver from horrible servitude, the Minors marked with the seal of reconciliation." His second operation "was made on behalf of the Just that they call the Holy Patriarchs, who still pay tribute to the justice of the Creator, not for having led a criminal life, nor for evil spiritual conduct, but in order to purge the stain that they have contracted by their stay in a form of matter. The character that the Regenerator placed upon these Holy Patriarchs was a major spiritual being, more powerful than the glorious Minors, and which they (the Spiritual Minors) were only able to distinguish by the different spiritual operations that this being operated itself at the center of these Minors reconciled and not yet regenerated. It gives them the power to render the doubly strong character of its operation reversible upon the Minors in privation and this by their own spiritual operation upon the Minors on behalf of whom they would operate for the greater glory of the Creator and the greater shame of the demons." What this amounts to in ordinary language is that the transcendent Christ, or Reconciler, imprints on the Spiritual Minors the seal of redemption by delegating a Major Spirit who clothes the Patriarchs with a body of glory, permitting them to manifest themselves to the eyes of the operant.

"The third operation of Christ alludes to the third day of his burial, and it was made upon two kinds of Minors who were more or less closed up in divine privation. Thus, this third operation was divided into two substances (was comprised of two actions, had two effects) one of which was visible to ordinary mortals and the other invisible to these same mortals." The object of the first "substance" is "to shorten the course and the operations of the Minors in the three circles, so that these Minors can then rest in the shadow of their reconciliation." The second consists in "the plan that he has drawn up for them himself by his resurrection (under a glorious form), and by his own instruction that he left to his faithful elect by his divine spiritual words; and this second substance is visible to corporeal men."[902] So, in summary, Jesus, by his descent and his appearance in the Underworld, has demonstrated the truth of what Pasqually teaches to his disciples on the nature and the consequences of the results of their Operations.

The inversion of the symbolic interpretation, which tended to represent as a simple repetition the phenomena that the Christian apologetic considered as a prefiguration, leads Pasqually to insist on features which make of the birth, of the terrestrial career, of the passion, and of the ascension of Jesus a replica of the details related on the life and death of Abel, of Elijah, and of Enoch by the Bible or by a secret tradition of which the master of the Élus Coëns is claimed to be the trustee.

Abel "being only three years old was always growing in goodness and wisdom, in virtue and in good example all the time that he remained among men as righteous Man-God upon the earth."[903] If "the blood which has flowed from the Just Abel is the type and the certain resemblance of that which Christ would shed," that is not to say that the death of the first Just had not been of any other value than to announce the crucifixion, it had already operated a reconciliation: "this has been repeated clearly by the circumcision of Abraham," also "it is sensible that the effusion of the blood of Christ is the confirmation of all the preceding types,"[904] just as "in his quality of Man-God and of divine man he has certified to us, by his circumcision that he has suffered, the covenant of the Creator with Adam, Noah, Abraham, and all his creation."[905]

The birth of Enoch, "which is the great type of the ceremonial and of the divine cult among the men of the past, the type of reconciliation of the human race," was announced by "a star or comet which appeared regularly at the moment when a Minor makes his entrance into this world."[906] He was "emanated" by his father Jared "by the Spirit." Jared knew by the divine Spirit, "from which he received the knowledge daily," "the marvelous type that his son Enoch would make of the divine Spirit and the very action of the divinity for the conduct and defense of the Minors against the attacks of their enemies."[907] Enoch made among the posterity of Seth and Enos "an election of ten subjects to whom he declared the will of the Creator." One of his disciples "admitted by Enoch to the divine reconciliation" having had "an atrocious conduct which stirred up dissension among the disciples," Enoch "made with the nine Just an assembly in which he communicated to them entirely his secret.[908] The heart of these nine Just was so strongly seized that they remained in a space of dejection or drowsiness which lasted for about an hour. During this time Enoch made his invocation to the Creator on behalf of these nine disciples which then turned into the situation where there were found all the scourges with which the Creator would use to strike the earth and the remainder of its inhabitants...Scarcely had Enoch finished speaking and blessing the nine disciples that a flaming cloud descended from heaven and took him up rapidly to bear this holy Spirit to its destination. His disciples who lost sight of him lamented and said: What are we going to become, O Eternal, without the assistance of our master Enoch? Without entering into the detail of the particular conduct of Enoch towards his disciples and his secret election, it suffices to observe what was just said in order to see clearly that the true Messiah has always been with the children of God, but nevertheless unknown."[909]

If the human bodies are subject to putrefaction, "it has not been the same for Christ, Abel, Elijah, and Enoch, as much for their spiritual being as for their material form," because "these spiritual beings are not susceptible to putrefaction, also their reintegration, both spiritual and temporal, has been very succinct (rapid)."[910]

These different features, of which certain ones are borrowed directly from the Bible, [911] are a more or less shrewd paganization of what the Gospels relate on the subject of the childhood of Jesus of Nazareth, of the Annunciation, of the star of the Magi, of the betrayal of Judas, of the Last Supper, of the sleep of the Apostles and of the vigil of Christ in the Garden of Olives, finally of the Transfiguration and the Ascension. It is particularly necessary to underscore the passage where Pasqually says expressly that the Messiah has appeared upon the earth quite a long time before Jesus, and without men having had knowledge of his presence, at least those who were not initiates of the true doctrine.

It is by the same spirit that the treatise is inspired when it happens to refer to the Christian feasts and to the ritual of the mass: it seeks therein only a new confirmation of its secret doctrines. In order to show that Jesus Christ has only reminded men of the rules of the divine cult which had already been revealed to them after the Flood, it points out that "these same disciples who comprise the Christian church make yet today their prayer and their invocation four times per day"[912] and that there are "four intervals of prayer utilized in our churches"[913] and it concludes: "Here is what is recalled by the first order of the divine spiritual cult established among the first Noahchite (issued from Noah) nations by the wise children of Noah, and the Christian Church observes faithfully this institution by its four great annual feasts, two of which must be made at the two solstices (Christmas and Corpus Christi), and the other two at the two equinoxes (Easter and All Saints). This is what is recalled by the second spiritual order of the divine cult established among these first nations."[914] Likewise, the mystical principle of sympathetic cooperation, of which the Élus Coëns make use in the course of their Operations, and that the treatise assures to have been put into practice by Adam, Enoch, Moses, Aaron, and in the Temple of Solomon, is consecrated, to which Pasqually assures, by the Catholic cult, since "the Church of Christ still represents to us today in the sacrifice that it offers upon the altar of purification (consecration of the host) by the hand, the intention, and the words of the celebrant assisted by the first, second, and third deacons."[915]

CHAPTER VI
Gnosticism and Rationalist Mysticism

The point of view where the Reintegration is positioned in the presence of the God of the Christians in assimilating it with one of the divine Spirits of the Supercelestial, recalls invincibly the process of the Gnostic doctors such as Valentinus, Ptolemy, Heracleon, Marcion, Appelle, who had made the person of Jesus to enter into the world of ideas which were familiar to them by identifying him with one of their Aeons.[916] The treatise of Pasqually presents, furthermore, analogies so striking with the Gnostic works: revelations on the invisible, on the hierarchy of the divine entities, on the revolutions of the transcendent world, on the connections of this world with humanity[917] that the Élus Coëns seem apparently very close to the Gnostic theosophy.

The common feature most striking is the doctrine of emanation to which Pasqually adheres expressly in professing that "every spiritual being comes directly from the eternal emanation" of the First Principle,[918] so that "these spiritual beings are certainly innate in the divinity"[919] and "that a spiritous (material) essence has never been able to exist and will never exist in the divine immensity, which is the residence of the pure Spirits where is operated every divine emanation and from where arises every kind of emanation."[920]

One may object, it is true, that this doctrine, which goes back to the Chaldean theology, was born well before the school of Basilides and Valentinus, but what is specifically Gnostic, is the thesis according to which the formation of matter is due to a revolution provoked in the transcendent world by a sin committed against the Father and that the events from on high have a repercussion on the constitution of the cosmos and on the destiny of humanity. In the myth of Sophia, born from the creative imagination of Valentinus, the materials of the sensible world, which is the Evil, are born from the sin of the thirtieth Aeon who had wished to contemplate the Father, just as in the Reintegration the capital sin of Adam has been "the thought that he had to read into the divine Power."[921] For the whole Gnostic school, the Creation is the consequence of the fall of some of the first Spirits, and Pasqually expresses himself like one of the doctors of this school when he writes: "Without the prevarication of the demons there would not have been temporal material creation, either terrestrial or celestial"[922] "the change operated by the prevarication of the perverse Spirits was so strong that the Creator made force of law (made his power felt, imposed his law) not only against the prevaricators, but in the different classes of the divine immensity. You must think of it (this is Moses who speaks to Israel) by the life of confusion that leads you here below, by the creation of time, and by the different actions which are operated in the supercelestial, the celestial, and the terrestrial, where all teaches you the universal change produced by this prevarication."[923]

Another principle admitted by the Gnostics, and which is moreover at the base of all the religions and all the philosophical systems resting on dualism, is that life or existence results from the active antagonism of the Good Principle (divine spirit) and the Evil Principle (matter) or rather from the obstacle that the second opposes to the first and that the latter wishes to surmount. Pasqually expresses this idea, in passing, but very distinctly: "All is operated in the universe by action and contraction (reaction); without this nothing would have either movement or life, and without life, there would be no corporeal forms."[924] This law of the material world is also for him that of the intelligible world: "Without the demonic reaction, nothing would have spiritual life outside of the divine circumference."[925]

Pasqually teaches, as do the Gnostics, that the human soul is an emanation of the divine substance, that following a downfall it finds itself here below imprisoned in the bosom of matter, that it would be incapable of coming out of by itself unless a divine being came to its aid in order to make it remember its noble origin and to promise him salvation.

The division into three classes that the Gnostics made of humanity: Pneumatics, who possessed the Gnosis and reveal it to other men; Psychics, who are able to be saved, if they listen to the teachings of the Pneumatics; Hylics, incapable of extricating themselves from the bonds of matter and fatally damned, corresponds exactly to the distinction that Pasqually established between the Spiritual Elect, or Elect Minors, who communicate with the Spirits inhabiting the divine circle, receive their instructions, and transmit them to the ordinary Minors; Spiritual Minors, whose type is the first posterity of Noah "who practiced a cult mixed of the spiritual and terrestrial matter"; and finally the Minor children of Cain "terrestrial temporal men," for whom "the conduct of all the spiritual operations is a mystery, because they are only occupied with the cult of the earth."[926] The determinism, common to the two systems, is put strongly into relief by the treatise of Pasqually. Alone, he said, "the spiritual minor posterity of Adam" will re-enter into the quaternary circle from where he is excluded only "for the whole duration of time."[927] "The name of Seth signifies: being admitted to the divine cult or perfect executer of the manifestation of the glory of divine justice. Therefore, the posterity of Seth was called: Children of God and not Children of Men. This title of Children of Men was reserved to the female posterity of Cain which was engendered by the operation of the demons, because its corporeal origin first arises from the sole faculty (from the sole effect) of its prevarication."[928] Consequently, Seth forbade his son Enos "any relation with the profanes or the Children of Men, that is to say the concubine girls of the posterity of Cain and that this race was never united with the Children of God who were the posterity of Seth."[929] "The incredulous will remain until the end of the ages in privation of the divine light,"[930] this is what was announced by the raven released by Noah after the end of the Flood: having taken its route towards the South, abode of the damned, "it did not return to join the ark in order to show the separation that the Creator made of the posterity of Cain with the children of Seth."[931]

Predestination, consequence of the divine arbiter, is manifested, in the Reintegration as with the Gnostics, by an identical figure: a "seal" or "character," sign and condition of salvation. "Enoch made to pass upon the posterity of the children of Seth the authentic character or seal of his operation. It is with this seal that he marked those who were worthy to accompany the Christ (the Reconciler) when he rendered an account to his father."[932] At the time of his descent into the Underworld, Christ has "delivered from horrible servitude the Minors marked by the seal of reconciliation,"[933] for "there had likewise (even) been placed upon the slaves of the demons (the Minors in privation) similar character, and it is by this means (the appearance of Christ) that the slaves of the demons received the seal of the divine reconciliation."[934] But Christ has not been able, even by his sacrifice, to save the posterity of Cain, because he has "only reconciled with God those that the spiritual operation of the Just (manifestations in the course of the Operations) had marked by the seal."[935]

The idea of the successive reincarnations of the transcendent Christ is familiar to the Gnostics. A theory common to their various schools is that the Gnosis, or knowledge of the means to return one day to the primitive order, that is to say to the separation of the domains of the Good and the Evil, has been revealed in different epochs by a divine mediator.[936] This concept, which may be the effect of a Hindu influence, sometimes takes a form recalling the Christology of the Reintegration: an important Gnostic work, the Book of Elchasai, showed Christ taking the figure of Adam, then that of Enoch and other Patriarchs.[937]

To these principal concordances are added resemblances, secondary, but rather striking.

The name of klesis (call, convocation) given by Heracleon, disciple of Valentinus, to the class of the Psychics "who wish to go to the Lord" makes one think of the "men of desire" for whom Pasqually rites, and it is the image of the Gnostic Demiurge, creator of the material world, who seems to have been presented in his spirit when he says in his treatise: "In the spiritual picture (conceived by the imagination of the supreme God) was included every corporeal being; but however without substance of matter. This picture contained principally the Spiritual Minor who would contribute to the formation of the bodies."[938]

In the system of Marcion, the first emanated Spirits had wished to create without the knowledge of the First Cause. The First Man has committed the same error and engendered first the woman, material being whose number is Three, then a posterity of beings of matter thoroughly evil, and it is again the Adam of the Reintegration, creator of Houwa and punished for this crime, that recalls the God of Israel, presented by Appelle, disciple of Marcion, as a Spirit who was the author of evil in clothing the souls by a sinful flesh, and the Archons, who, according to the 4th Book of the Pistis Sophia, were bound by Jeu to the sphere of the Zodiac in expiation of the sin that they had committed in procreating, despite his prohibition, Archangels, Angels, Liturgies, and Decans.

The Barbelo-Gnostics, or disciples of the Mother, relate that, when Adam and Eve, expelled from Paradise, had entered into the sensible world, their bodies were dense and had ceased to be luminous.

The majority of biblical personages of whom Pasqually made interpreters of the divine Spirit were particularly revered by the Gnostics in their capacity of doctors of the Knowledge. They invoked the apocalypses of Adam and his testament written by Seth. The Sethians and the Archontites presented Seth, who, born of a pure seed, had replaced Abel, killed by Cain, as the guide in the path of salvation. They possessed from him seven books where he had deposited the revelations that an angel had made to him and they assured that, when after the Deluge the accursed race of Ham had spread upon the earth, the Mother has resurrected Seth under the form of Christ.[939] The cycle of the Christian Gnosis, which had been formed among the Sabeans and included the Testament of Adam and the Books of Seth, had also revelations of Enoch under the name of whom have been published by the Gnostic Christians works which described the celestial spheres and announced the advent of Christ. The Pistis Sophia attributed to him the two Books of Jeu, which describe the fall of the soul and its raising.[940] According to a legend, related by a Gnostic treatise, Melchizedek had been constituted, by Noah dying, guardian of the tomb of Adam and priest of the Most High. An abundant literature appears to have circulated under his name in the first century of our era and the Pistis Sophia has received therefrom numerous fragments. In one of the legendary accounts, attributed to Athanas,

Melchizedek received a visit from Abraham to whom God had presented him as an image of his beloved son. This theme has long been developed by several Gnostic authors, and the Manichaean Hierakas regarded Melchizedek as the divine Spirit here below.[941] Among the Archontites, the Ophites, and the Valentinians circulated an Apocalypse of Elijah and an Ascension of Isaiah which had rather narrow connections. They showed the Seer rising in spirit across the seven heavens unto the throne of the Most High and descending again therefrom with Christ who assumed successively the forms of the intermediary heavens in order to finally take on, upon the earth, a human figure.[942]

On three points: astrology, allegorical exegesis, and arithmosophy, the analogies are particularly marked. The majority, not to say the totality, of the Gnostic systems are obsessed by the idea of astral fatality and make the seven planets to play a preponderant role in their speculations. The principal doctors of the sect professed that the Gnosis was contained in the Bible and in the apostolic accounts and are to be extricated therefrom by allegorical interpretation of which a secret tradition indicated the laws. Basilides gave to the initiates an esoteric teaching; Ptolemy made allusion to instructions kept hidden that the school claimed to hold from Jesus himself and which it had received by oral tradition. Many Gnostics, like the Marcosians among others, were dedicated to the mystical interpretation of Genesis and Exodus. Those of Rome, whose doctrines Hippolytus relates in his *Philosophumena*, sought the secret meaning of the Pentateuch and the New Testament. Heracleon has interpreted allegorically the 4th gospel, and his extremely ingenious commentaries on the parables of the Samaritan, the sick son of the centurion, and the descent of Jesus into Capernaum, are masterpieces of mystical exegesis. Ptolemy has written a symbolic commentary of the Prologue of Saint John.

The secret science of numbers has been practiced by nearly all the Gnostics, but principally by the members of the Roman group, who, in the 2nd century AD, were quite versed in Pythagorean arithmetic, returned to fashion by the Neopythagoreans. Since the previous century a disciple of Valentinus, Marcus, had applied the mystical arithmetic to the theology of his master, who had perhaps given him the example of this genre of speculation. With Valentinus, the first two couples of the Pleroma form the powerful Tetractos; the first four couples form the supreme Ogdoad; the 5th and 6th Aeons, Word and Life, emanate five syzygies from whom are born the Decad. Marcus, in his turn, composed numerical glosses on the Pleroma, its two Tetrads, its Ogdoad, its Decad, its Dodecad, its thirty Aeons, and also, in reducing the letters to the numbers that they express in Greek, on the names of the Aeons, of Christos, and of Jesus. Among the Barbelo-Gnostics the incorruptible Aeon, or Church, is formed by four hypostases. In the system of the Archontites the Mother, source of light, resides with the angels in the Ogdoad, which is the abode of the Good Principle, whereas the Hebdomad, composed of the seven heavens guarded by the Archons, is the abode of necessity, that is to say of the physical laws. Basilides had composed his Abraxas by the numero-literal method. Heracleon forms the Tetrad with the first four Aeons, makes of Six the number of matter, places the Pneumatics in the Ogdoad and the Psychics in the Hebdomad.[943]

However numerous, and sometimes striking, may be the coincidences indicated, they do not authorize us to see in Pasqually a belated disciple of the Gnostics. These latter have built their system in a period when philosophical and religious syncretism were a watchword followed by all the cultivated minds. They have taken from all hands the materials of their composite edifice and, like the number of themes constituting the common foundation of the mystical and rather limited doctrines, the different secret disciplines born in the first centuries of our era all have an air of family. The allegorical method, for example, was employed then by all the writers: pagans like Plutarch, Christians like Origin, or Jews like Philo; it is nothing specifically Gnostic. One may say as much of astrology, pneumatology, and even arithmosophy.[944] If, therefore, one is able to admit with Mr. Matter that the secret science of Pasqually is a mixture of Gnosticism and Judaized Christianity, both nourished by the Kabbalah, it is necessary to hasten to add with him: "The Gnostics having professed or consulted all the systems of Greece and the Orient, included therein the Jewish and Christian texts, there are naturally among Gnosticism, in all the theosophical speculations, a few scholars, and there is no Jewish scholar, however Christian he may become by his studies, who does not have some remnant of familiarity with the ideas of the Kabbalah,"[945] It is indeed in the Jewish mystical works, which have undergone profoundly the influence of the Gnostic concepts and symbols[946] and of which the Kabbalah was constituted the inheritor, that Pasqually has truly received the echoes of the Gnosis, sometimes resonating so clearly in his treatise. The Work of the Chariot and the Work of Creation, of which we have already had the occasion to speak, are born in the 2nd century AD in the era when lived Saturninus and Basilides and when the Gnostic systems of the Pagans and Christians of Syria were formed. The last work seems to have been founded on emanation, whose principle was then admitted by the Kabbalah. The idea of the universal role of thesis and antithesis in the production of cosmic life has long been commented upon by the Jewish doctors whose Kabbalah has received the teaching. The Zohar sets forth the thesis of the repercussion produced in the organization of the world by the fall of the angels, then by that of man, and of the downfall by which have been waiting in punishment for the first defiance, not only the descendants of Adam, but also the beings who populate the very heavens which approach the divinity.[947]

But, if Pasqually has known indirectly some of the themes rejuvenated and rehabilitated by the Gnostics, he has ignored the more characteristic ones,[948] and he has over all neither penetrated the profound meaning of their doctrines, nor grasped the exact significance of the terms that he unconsciously borrowed from them.

First of all, he does not admit, like them, a descending series of emanations, since, in his treatise, all the successive emanations arise directly from God, and he does not know the syzygies. But, above all, he rejected the latent dualism which, among the disciples of Basilides and Valentinus, opposed the inert matter to the divine spirit. Faithful to the Jewish tradition, he believes in the formation of the world ex-nihilo and professes that God has "created all from nothing."[949]

As there is a fundamental incompatibility between the concept according to which a personal God is the unique source of the being, and the Gnostic theory which has the universe and life result from the intermingling of the two principles existing by themselves for all eternity, Pasqually has attempted to reconcile the two antagonistic ideas by attributing to the "creation" the formation of matter, and to "the emanation" the origin of the spiritual beings. "Creation belongs only to (only concerns) the apparent matter; but the emanation belongs to the spiritual beings."[950] "The first matter has been conceived and begotten by the Spirit and not emanated by him."[951] It goes without saying that the emanation thus understood is no longer at all that of the Gnostics, since it designates, by a special and arbitrarily chosen term, only a particular kind of creation, that of the Spirits. Pasqually recognizes it overtly in saying that "it is by (for reason of) this infinite multitude of emanations of spiritual beings that God bears the name of Creator."[952] As for the material world, it is for Pasqually, as for the Gnostics, an evil work. This is not because it arises from the contamination of the Good Principle by the Evil Principle, but because it has been formed to be the prison of the rebellious Spirits, since "no pure Spirit can be enclosed in a body of matter, except those that have prevaricated,"[953] and "the first matter was only conceived by the good Spirit in order to contain and subjugate the evil Spirit in a state of privation."[954] Thus matter, far from having always existed, has been created for a clearly definite and temporary end. Chaos, of which the Bible speaks and which, according to it, existed "from the beginning," was only the first stage of creation. Matter has been created under the form of "chaos" in which was enclosed the three fundamental essences of all bodies which would serve for the formation of the universe. These essences were in an indifference (inert) which rendered them susceptible to receiving the impression of the exterior agents in order to then operate according to the intention of the Creator."[955] The Ark "in which were contained the different animal beings, actually explains the chaotic envelope which contained every principle of the creation of corporeal forms."[956]

Furthermore, matter has no reality: it is "arisen from the divine imagination."[957] When Genesis teaches that God has created all in six days, it means that the Creator, "pure superior Spirit in time and with successive duration," has "operated six divine thoughts for the universal creation,"[958] "He is called Creator because all his creation arises from his imagination, and it is because his creation arises from his divine thinking imagination which has produced all that is called image."[959] Therefore matter will vanish when God ceases to think it: "the same divine faculty which has produced all will recall all to its principle and, just as every species of form has taken principle (has begun), so will it dissipate,"[960] and "there will remain no vestige of the universal creation,"[961] since "apparent matter has arisen from nothing, except from the divine imagination, it must return into the nothingness."[962] "The reintegration of the corporeal form of the Minor will only be operated by means of a putrefaction inconceivable to mortals" (complete disappearance of which nothing gives the example here below).[963] The bodies, formed from this matter without substantial reality, only exist by the Spirits who inhabit them and give them movement and life." "All kinds of forms which act in this universe do not really exist in nature (through the effect of natural forces) nor by themselves, but only by the being that animates them."[964] The body of man is "a necessary organ of his spiritual soul," but, "it is not necessary to consider this corporeal form as a real body of existing matter. It arises only from the first spiritous essences destined by the first Word of Creation to retain the different impressions suitable to the forms which must be employed in the universal creation. It is not possible to consider the present (sensible) corporeal forms as real without admitting a matter innate in the divine Creator, which is repugnant to his spirituality."[965]

On the other hand, Pasqually does not believe, as do the Gnostics, that a period of expansion of the divinity will be succeeded by a period of re-absorption during which the emanated Spirits will return to be lost within the bosom of the Pleroma. Emanation, such as he conceives it, is a definitive creation whose effects will be eternal. The spiritual beings, asserts the Reintegration, are "real and imperishable," they "will exist eternally in a personality of distinction (personal and distinct) in the circle of the divinity"[966]; also "when time will have passed (at the end of the world) the Spirits operating in the supercelestial, the celestial, and the terrestrial will not pass."[967]

But it is by his anthropology that, as has remarked Mr. Matter[968], Pasqually is separated more resolutely from Gnosticism. While for the latter man is the creature of the rebellious Spirits, who have formed him without participation of the First Cause and is therefore subordinated to them by his very origin, he was, according to the Reintegration, originally superior to the astral region, to the Spirits that govern it, as well as to the perverse Spirits, and it is as a result of the error of Adam that we are fallen under the dominion of the latter. Consequently, the goal to which we ought to aim is, in the eyes of the Gnostics, redemption, that is to say the release of the divine spark that entered, without the knowledge of the Spirit creators of man, into the Corruption of the material body and which must return to its source. It is, according to Pasqually, to the contrary: "the reintegration of beings into their first properties, virtues and spiritual and divine powers,"[969] that is to say the restoration of man upon the throne from where he first commanded all the Spirits, good or evil.

Finally, on a point which he ought to take particularly to heart because of his Judaizing tendencies, Pasqually took on, probably at the example of the Talmudic or Kabbalistic works by which he was inspired, the anti-biblical Gnostics. Their chief, Marcion, in his Antitheses, where he made to stand out the contrast existing between the Mosaic tradition and the Christian doctrine, opposed the supreme God, having goodness for its essence, creator of the invisible world, remaining unknown to humanity until Christ had come to reveal his existence, and that of the inferior God, creator of the material world, God of the Bible, cruel and bellicose judge, of whom Moses had been the interpreter. It is to this blasphemous doctrine on Jehovah demiurge that Pasqually makes allusion when he relates that "the perverse Spirits persuaded the Minors that the creator of the universe was one of them"[970] and when he asserts energetically that "every creation arises directly from the Eternal and that it is impossible to create another universe."[971] It is rather to the Marcionites, who, drawing their final consequences from the premises posed by their master, had ended up identifying the God of the Bible with the Devil, that the Reintegration responds when it adds: "These perverse Spirits went forth to persuade these Minors that the universal creation was falsely attributed to the divinity, that this God that they had previously heard[972] was none other than one of them who directs all creation and even man since his advent upon the earth, and consequently, the emanation of the Minors comes from the great prince of the South (the demon), principal chief of every material and sub-material being, which means vehicle of the central axis fire incorporated into a form,[973] they had to recognized him and obey him blindly in all that he would do to inspire by his inferior agents."[974]

∴

On questions of importance: character of the emanation, origin and nature of matter and of man, theory of involution, Pasqually is therefore clearly separated from the Gnostics, but it is upon the terrain of morals that is dug between the two doctrines an impassible gulf. Gnosticism, whose entire speculation is dominated by the Chaldean astrological tradition, accords to the astral fatality an influence as sovereign in ethics as in physics. The tyranny of the sidereal Archons, who seek ever to retain the divine spark in the matter where it is enclosed, weighs insuperably upon the will of man. It condemns the Hylics to eternal damnation. The Psychics are unable to free themselves by their own strength; for them, in order to resist the evil instincts and the temptation of matter, the aid of the Gnosis and the relief of grace are necessary. To this fatalist doctrine Pasqually opposes with insistence the thesis of liberty and human responsibility, proposition founded on the principle of distributive justice which is at the basis of biblical ethics, to which the Talmud and the Kabbalah were remained invariably attached[975] and that the treatise proclaims with a remarkable vigor: "The Minors who at the end of time remain to be reconciled will be called the last by the Eternal, and the justice that he will exercise against them will be stronger than that which he has exercised and will exercise against the demons, because the Minor had been filled by the Eternal with an authority and a power superior to that of the perverse Spirits, and because the more the Minor has received, the more will be asked of him."[976]

The principle of human free will is so important in the eyes of Pasqually that, when he discourses thereon, he forgets completely that at other moments he divides humanity into the Just and the Damned, into descendants of Seth and sons of Cain. Of these two juxtaposed and contradictory concepts, that of the liberty of the human will is held most visibly to his heart.

In the first place, all the Spirits are morally free once they have emanated and "emancipated." Just as Jehovah made, in the Bible, a covenant with Israel under certain conditions, that is to say concluded with the Hebrew people a pact which implies the responsibilities of the counteractants, just as the Creator, in emanating the Spirits, has passed with them a "convention" setting "the borders where they are to exercise their power following eternal laws, precepts, and commandments," but they were, within these limits, "free and distant from the Creator," and to refuse them the free will, "with which they have been emanated by immutable laws," would be to destroy in them "the spiritual and personal virtue (strength) which was necessary for them to operate" (act).[977]

By virtue of their liberty, the Spirits became, under the First Cause, Second Causes over whom God no longer had action, for "God is an immutable being in his decrees and his spiritual gifts."[978] This fact explains how the error of the perverse Spirits was possible: "God could not in any fashion contain and stop the criminal thoughts of the prevaricating Spirits without depriving them of the particular action innate within them, having been emanated in order to act according to their will and as second spiritual cause according to the plan that the Creator had traced for them. The Creator does not take any part in the good and evil second spiritual causes, having himself supported and founded every spiritual being upon immutably laws. By these means every spiritual being is free to act according to its will and its particular determination."[979] "The divine spiritual chiefs have preserved their state of virtue (strength) and divine power after their prevarication by the immutability of the decrees of the Eternal."[980] "The demons enjoy fully and entirely their actions according to their thinking will. It is therefore in this demonic court as regards law and order, of horror and abomination, as it is, without comparison, in the divine spiritual court."[981]

As regards the Minor, God left him entirely at liberty, and for three reasons: first because his body is moved by a Spirit, and every Spirit, as we have just seen, is free by definition, then because "it is not in God to read into the second temporal causes, nor to prevent the action thereof, without deviating from his own existence of spiritual being and his divine power," and finally because, "if the Creator took any part in the second causes, he would of all necessity have to communicate himself not only the thought but also the will, good or evil, to his creature or he would have to have it communicated by his spiritual agents, who would emanate immediately from him, which would return to him."[982] This is why "the Creator abandoned Adam to his free will, having emancipated him by a distinct manner from his divine immensity with this liberty so that his creature had the particular and personal enjoyment, present and future, for an impassive eternity, provided, however, that it was conducted according to the will of the Creator."[983]

It is true that the heart of fallen man is a battlefield where clash adverse forces: "The thought arises in man from a being distinct from him. If the thought is holy, it arises from a divine Spirit. If it is evil, it arises from an evil demon."[984] But "it is to man to reject the ones and receive the others according to his free will."[985] "Nothing may prevail against the tabernacle (heart) of the Minor if the Minor does not give his consent."[986] "The Minor is joined to the most sublime (powerful) Spirits, whether good or evil, in order to operate his will, good or evil, conforming to his liberty."[987] "Liberty gives birth to the will and the will adopts the thought, good or evil, that the spirit has conceived; and, as soon as it has obtained the fruit thereof, the Minor returns upon himself and, meditating on the product of his operation, he himself becomes the judge of the good and evil that he has committed."[988]

The moral liberty of the Minor is so complete that the sin by intention is as grave as the sin by action, for the fault consists less in the act than in the will which held it. The crime of the prevaricating Spirits was an intention not connected with effect[989], that of Adam has been less of creation without the cooperation of God than of claiming "to probe deeply and perfectly" the divine omnipotence and that which had been granted to him over the universe.[990] This thought of pride, similar to the hubris in which the Greeks saw the tragic fault of their heroes, and the justification of the terrible chastisements which struck them, has allowed the demons to tempt Adam. Pride has been the breach by which the evil intellect has been able to penetrate into the heart of the First Man and it is by a fault of intention that his descendants are rendered, still today, accessible to the suggestions of the demons.

Pasqually does not admit the excuse so often invoked to the acquittal of the sinners: the weakness of the flesh incapable of resisting temptation. "It is not the corporeal form of matter that makes man succumb to temptation. This form is not charged to lead itself; it is only the organ of the Minor. It only makes the good or evil wills (suggestions), which the Minor receives from the good or evil Spirit, to operate. Therefore, when man succumbs to it, he must not blame his fall on his corporeal form of matter, but he must attribute it only to his will alone."[991] The only "innate faculty" that one may "call weakness" is rather a quality than a defect, and "cannot displease the Creator: it arises only from a true spiritual humanity which teaches to do good for the evil that the demons operate against us by our thrown-down (damned) fellow men." A similar weakness "earned on the whole the name of mercy."[992]

The Reintegration combats with no less vigor the thesis which denies human liberty and responsibility by claiming them to be incompatible with divine prescience and in thus placing in the charge of the omniscient and all-powerful God the evil that he must necessarily foresee and that he has not prevented. The Prophetess, interpreter of the Eternal, said to Saul: "If it was in the power of God to be diviner, he would be the mover of the good and the evil; he would be so cruel a tyrant to permit and allow the evil to be done by his creature in order to then punish him for what he would have been able to prevent himself. I dare before all his divine spiritual heart and before all his temporal heart to defy this omnipotent God to penetrate and to conceive the action and operation, as any event whatsoever, that is to occur to every spiritual minor being, if this being has not first conceived it himself in his thoughts. If this thing was truly in his power he would truly be unjust not to stop the deadly events that he knew must occur to his creature. It is necessary for the temporal Spirit (clothed in a body of matter) to have formed some thought in order for the good or evil action arising from this thought to be known by the Eternal. If it is good, he receives it; if it is evil, he rejects it; but he does not oppose himself to the will of his creature."[993] Pasqually addressing himself directly to his disciples, said for his part: "If it had been within the possibility of the Creator to stop the action of temporal spirituals (Minor formed by a Spirit and a body), he would not have permitted his Minor to succumb to the insinuation of the demons, having emanated him (since he emanated him) expressly in order to be the particular instrument of his glory against these same demons." Man was a "second" sent by his general in order to combat his enemies. If this lieutenant, having disobeyed the received orders, succumbs, he will be punished, "because he had the strength in his hands," But the general himself is not vanquished. If this "deputy," instead of attacking the enemies, joined with them, in order to deliver the battle to the general, he is a traitor: such was the prevarication of the First Man towards the Creator.[994]

∴

Pasqually is less a Gnostic by the ideas contained in his treatise than for having, like the Gnostics, a systematic syncretism. Just as in mineral water an analysis reveals, besides salts which give it its particular character, "traces" of varied bodies figuring therein in infinitesimal quantities, one finds in the Christology of the Reintegration, in addition to some fundamental concepts tinged with Gnosticism and Kabbalah, vestiges of heretical doctrines with which the first centuries of our era abounded.

Pasqually rallies in passing to Docetism when he asserts that the "body of Christ suffered no pain in the torments that they exercised upon him."[995]

He draws closer, in assimilating man with Christ, to Montanism whose sectarians, numerous in the 2nd century, believed that Christ was incarnated within every fully initiated Christian, and, coming to the logical conclusion of their principle, worshipped one another. Tertullian relates that such was the custom of the Christians of Carthage in the 2nd century. In the 8th century, Elipand of Toledo called Christ a God among gods, because all the believers were gods like Jesus himself. In the 13th century, the sect of the Brothers and Sisters of the Free Spirit professed that man is able to unite himself with divinity and to make but one with the productive source of all things, and that the one who had thus elevated unto God formed veritably part of the divinity and was the Son of God in the same sense and of the same fashion as Christ himself.[996]

Mani taught that the knowledge of salvation had been revealed in various epochs by Christ, apparent in the First Man and who has incarnated under the names of Buddha, Zoroaster, Jesus, and Mani himself.

Finally, the esoteric Christianity of the Reintegration is connected, like the Operations in which the readers of his treatise engaged, to the magical tradition. One of the most competent historians of this secret science established that primitive humanity had conceived two types of human gods: the god-man of magic, being similar to the other men by his spiritual and physical nature, but superlatively endowed with extraordinary powers over natural phenomena and over the transcendent forces which they produce, and the god-man of religion, being different from man and superior to him, who is incarnate for a more or less long time in a human body and manifests his exceptional power through his miracles and prophecies.[997] In making of the Christ of the Gospels at once the type of the Spiritual Elect and that of which the Élu Coën is a reduced copy, Pasqually tends to confuse the man-god of religion and the man-god of magic. What he, manifestly, retains above all from the apostolic narratives are the miracles, the appearances, and the Transfiguration, "testimonies" by which Jesus proved his divine nature and his supernatural power, just as had done the Spiritual Elect that the Bible named Abraham, Isaac, Jacob, Elijah, Moses. But the success of an operation proves that the Réau-Croix possesses, at least in part, the same powers, and the quaternary power that he exercises is an announcement and a promise of the Octonary power that he will possess one day. Thus, the whole system, Christian in name, mystical in form, built by Pasqually, aims in the final analysis to restore religion to magic.

∴

When one sees upon what paths, dangerous to their orthodoxy, Pasqually, under the color of esoteric Christianity, led his disciples, it is permitted to question how these latter, whose Christian faith was most sincere, have never distanced themselves from it. They took part, it is true, in his Operations where magic ceremonial played a manifest role, but it was a white magic, a divine magic whose spiritual aim could render it licit in their eyes. In the Reintegration, on the contrary, the fundamental dogmas of their religion were strongly shaken. If they are not informed thereof, it is, it seems, firstly because the mystics, more inclined towards enthusiasm than taken to analyzing the ideas, do not have in general a very developed critical sense, then because the barbarous language of Pasqually, the strangeness of his mystical vocabulary, the obscurity, involuntary or calculated, of his dialectic, and finally, above all, the skill with which he sidestepped on the nature of Christ[998] covered his intentions with a veil so dense that it would have been necessary, in order to pierce it, to have a clairvoyance and a liberty of spirit incompatible with the profound respect that the Grand Sovereign inspired in the Élus Coëns.

They found, moreover, in the teaching of their master a well-formed affirmation to flatter their imagination and to attach them to his Order, which is namely that the Spiritual Minor, otherwise called the adept who had been witness to manifestations, was restored to the state of the First Adam, himself assimilated to the Reconciler or Christ, so that the disciples of Pasqually who united in their Operations were elevated above the ordinary human condition and became true Children of God, akin to his divine Son. This promise was contained implicitly in the title of the most elevated grade of initiation, in the name to which the ordination gave all its mystical value and which conferred to the adept the quality of "Very Powerful Master": Réau-Croix being composed of the secret name of the First Adam (Réau) and of the term designating the Christian symbol par excellence.

It even seems that for the disciples of Pasqually the final goal of the Operations was to put them in communication with the one that their faith called Our Lord, and that certain Passes have been considered by them as "sensible manifestations of Christ."[1] Mr. Matter, who supports this hypothesis, calls attention to the testimony of a person worthy of confidence according to whom an initiate of the supreme grade, the comte d'Hauterive, affirmed to have attained, following several Operations crowned with success, to the "physical knowledge of the active and intelligent cause." The historian notes that by this formula the school of Pasqually designated the Word, the Son of God of Christian theology and he concluded that the Élus Coëns claimed to succeed "in the intuition or appearance of Christ."[999] This opinion is quite defendable, but with the corrective that by "appearance of Christ" it must be understood as the luminous apparition of the hieroglyph representing him. This adjustment is justified by a passage from a letter of Saint-Martin to Kirchberger in which the old Élu Coën declares that, in the school through which he had passed twenty-five years prior, communications of every kind were numerous and frequent, that he had had his part therein, like the others, and that in this part "all the signs indicative of the Repairer were included." Now, the personality of the Repairer is not in doubt, Saint-Martin having taken care to add that "this Repairer and the active Cause are the same thing." On the other hand, the expression: indicative signs, appear rather to indicate a symbolic and partial epiphany. That this fragmentary vision had been the goal pursued by the mystics who look to the school of Pasqually, is what stands out in a remark by the same Saint-Martin. Responding to Kirchberger, who talked to him about the visions of d'Hauterive, the theosopher, with whom the teachings received by Pasqually had left profound traces, concluded: "If the facts of Mr. d'Hauterive are of the secondary order (caused indirectly by Christ), they are only figurative relative to the great inner work of which we speak (intuitive knowledge of the active and intelligent cause) and, if they are of the superior class (representatives of Christ in person), they are the great work itself."[1000] Finally, Pasqually seems to have encouraged this way of seeing whether the design that he sent to Willermoz, in order to make him understand the appearance of a luminous manifestation to which he asserted to have been witness in the course of an Operation, actually represented, as it appears, the Shin (Hebrew S) that the *de Verbo Mirifico* of Reuchlin said to be the hieroglyph representing Christ.

As, following the ancient axiom adopted by the occultists, "like can only be known by like," the Élus Coëns had therefore the right to believe that, on the day when was operated "the manifestation of the divine glory by the perfect reconciliation of the past, present, and future posterity of that First Man,"[1001] there would no longer be any difference between the reconciled Minors and Christ. Thus, every Spiritual Minor was a Christ in power and, if the Reintegration never expressed this doctrine clearly, it is at least the conclusion to which lead the deductions of certain Élus Coëns, such as Bacon de la Chevalerie, Substitute General of the Grand Sovereign, who was considered similar to Christ,[1002] and the Abbé Fournié who wrote: "Since this Man, Jesus Christ, is born of God Man-God, we must conclude that if we also do the will of God, we will be born (mystically) ourselves of God Man-Gods and will enter into eternal union with God."[1003] These disciples were further along than their master feigned to want to lead them,[1004] but their error shows us fully what ideas the secret teaching of Pasqually gave rise to among the simplistic spirits little familiar with the subtle distinctions of theology.

The Order had yet another attractiveness for its members: it gave to their faith the material proof for which, perhaps without acknowledging it, they felt the imperious need. It is necessary to insist upon this fact, for it alone explains why the disciples of Pasqually have followed their master blindly. He was aware of this disposition of spirit, and he knew how to use it. He spoke in a rather peremptory tone in the name of an uncontrollable revelation and professes for the Bible and for the Gospel an unreserved respect. He rails against "the pretended scholars who do not conceive the possibility of the deluge, being unaware of why the Creator has sent this scourge upon the earth, not hesitating to deny this fact." He reproaches them "for holding up to ridicule those who add faith therein" and for "regarding as imaginary persons those very ones with whom the Creator has made part of this event before he arrives, and the decree that he had made in his immensity," and he refuses to yield to "their feeble arguments."[1005] But this faith, unshakable in appearance, has need of a support. It is, one could say, a faith that wants proofs founded on the witness of the senses. What was, in fact, an Operation, if not the obstinate search for a material proof establishing the reality of the doctrines taught by the founder of the Order? Pasqually recognizes it expressly in his correspondence and, foreseeing the doubt that his disciples would have on his theory of spiritual reconciliation and that they would ask of him a "physical proof," he said to them in the Reintegration: "When you will have had the good fortune to know the kind of work of Seth and that which the Sages have operated after him (Operations leading to manifestations), you will no longer pose such questions to me."[1006] Just as it could be done in our day by a professor of chemistry or physics demonstrating a natural law by the result predicted from an experiment done in determined conditions, he presents the manifestations, whether he makes them flash to the eyes of his disciples discouraged by unfruitful attempts, or that he cites the names of the adepts who have been witness thereof, like the touchstone with which is recognized the value of his teaching.

The Reintegration proceeds from the same state of mind in setting forth what one may call the mystico-raitonalist concept of the oracle, that is to say of the supernatural deed considered as the necessary confirmation of a dogma, and as tangible demonstration, alone capable of establishing a solid conviction. It does not believe that the period of miracles may be closed, if the faith is to remain as living as it was in their era. It does not admit that the faithful may be content with indirect proofs furnished by the Scriptures. It speaks derisively of the simple faith which passes for manifest and actual proofs. "The men of this century have moved away from all divine knowledge under the pretext of a pretended blind faith which has made them totally lose the idea of the true faith. Faith without works (sensible proofs)[1007] cannot be regarded as true faith. The works that man is able to produce through weak faith (inner illumination, intimate experience) which is innate among all men, cannot be considered as truly belonging to the faith."[1008] Therefore the disappearance of miracles since the death of Jesus has shaken the religious fervor: "Men arisen (born) since the last epoch of Christ, no longer having before their eyes the divine manifestations which were operated under the first centuries, have lost sight of the great divine cult" and, "as they no longer see to perpetuate the marvels of the justice of the Creator, one no longer finds a Just (sincere believer) in this cnetury."[1009] The spectacle of nature, where is manifested the action of Providence, may suffice to convince a Savoyard Vicar of the existence of God and to feed a tepid and vague deism, but the true believer, that is to say the man of desire, has the duty to be more exacting: "How will the men of this century be reconciled (brought back to God) who have never seen any physical, spiritual, or divine manifestation be operated before them, except those which are operated by the immutable laws which must set in motion and maintain the universal creation for the duration that the Creator has prescribed to it?"[1010]

The sole efficacious means of returning to the sense of the divine the vigor that it has lost, is to recall that the eye is the organ of conviction,[1011] that "the faith of man cannot be living and perfect, if it is not set into motion by a superior agent" (manifestation of a Spirit), when "man produces works which are no longer sensibly belonging to him (since the success of the Operations depends on the collaboration of transcendent beings) and which manifests all the strength of the faith that acts in him."[1012] In short, it is necessary to go and seek the miracle where it is currently hidden, that is to say in the Chamber of Operation. It is there that the men of desire, who have not, like the men of the age "abandoned the spiritual sciences in order to engage in the negotiation (in the business) and cupidity of material goods, which has placed a thick veil over their eyes,"[1013] will be marked with the seal "which, by the spiritual operation of the Just, the men who are to be reconciled have received," seal which was "sent to them visibly and without any mystery" and which would be to "dispose them to be strengthened more and more in the faith and confidence in the mercy of the Creator and to sustain with an invincible firmness every powerful manifestation of the divine justice which may be operated spiritually (by the manifestation of a Spirit) before them by Christ (by the intervention of the Reconciler) among the inhabitants of the earth living in divine privation,"[1014] He will experience the "incomprehensible (marvelous) change" which was produced among the patriarch Minors when, Christ having appeared to them in the Underworld, "they were by these means (this manifestation) more strongly convinced than they had been during their passing life of the inviolable tenderness that the Creator had and would have eternally for his creature."[1015] In the image of Esau which Isaac blessed, when his elder son complained of being dispossessed of his mystical heritage (communication with the divine), while telling him: "The blessing that I shed upon you comes from the Eternal, like the dew which is shed over the plants to substantiate them, comes from on high," the Élu Coën coming out of the Chamber of Operation "will withdraw much more satisfied with his Father than he was beforehand,"[1016] after having established that, in order to employ the word consecrated by his school,[1017] the teaching of his master had to be found "confirmed" by a manifestation.[1018]

It is quite true that Pasqually was forbidden from furnishing to his "emulators" grossly material proofs, since the "glorious form" glimpsed in the Passes borrowed, according to him, its light from a supercelestial fire which had nothing in common with that of the central axis, which allowed him to say to the Réau-Croix: "The truth speaks to the man of desire a language that he may not ignore because it borrows nothing from matter. It is wholly spiritual, having emanated directly from the Creator."[1019] But this supernatural phenomenon nevertheless drew all its value from what had been perceived by the eye of the Operant. It constituted, whatever was its origin, a fact of experience like those upon which is founded every reasoned conviction.

This need of tangible facts coming to justify a mystical postulate was not peculiar to the Order of Élus Coëns. It is the characteristic trait of the mysticism of the 18th century. The rationalism dominant then admitted only the axioms demonstrated by the witness of the senses and practiced only the empirical method. Contemporary mystics, all while remaining attached to the objects in which its rival is disinterested, is pulled along despite himself by the current that he claims to rise above and involuntarily makes concessions to the spirit of the times. The mystic may, by definition, do without the evidence of the external senses in order to assure his beliefs; the authority of the sacred books and the intimate understanding is sufficient for him. He considers as closed the period when miraculous deeds were necessary to make the truth triumph in the eyes of the skeptics and is content with inner revelations which give to his faith the clarity and strength of evidence. But in the 18th century the scientific spirit, which, in order to be convinced, wanted to see and touch, believed only in the reality of a priori constructions after having submitted them to the control of the experiment, and admits as proof only principles set forth from the phenomena whose manifestation man can instigate or modify at will. This spirit was essential to all intelligence and permeated into the minds which, by their structure, would remain seemingly inaccessible to it. The mystical contemporaries of Pasqually have all, to various degrees, from the convulsionary Jansensists to the spiritualist Mesmerians, come under its influence. The same need of proofs torments the pietists of all kinds. They refer, more or less openly, to what the Gospel of Saint John says: "If I do not do the works of my Father, do not believe me. But, if I do them, when you do not want to believe, believe in the works so that you will know and believe that the Father is in me and I in him," (X, 37-38).

The imposters use this disposition of the minds in order to exploit their dupes. Gassner carried out in Bavaria marvelous cures by exorcizing the sick; the School of the North expects at Stockholm an appearance of Saint John; Schroepfer plots manifestations in the back room of his cafe in Leipsig; Gugomos promises to his subscribers, whose contributions will allow him to raise in Iena his Adytum Sacrum, to make fire descend from the sky to consume the innocent victim upon the altar; the disciples of Cagliostro were persuaded to have seen at Lyon the prophet Elijah soar above their assembly in an azure cloud.

Under whatever form is manifested this desperate call to the evidence of the senses, it is the indication of the mental disarray into which the constant progress of rationalism plunges the spirits most faithful to the traditional beliefs. Faith in the revealed dogmas, disparaged by a critique more and more aggressive, maintained only imperfectly the hereditary religion which had to seek other support. It was able to be propped up on an ethical argument; the "natural religion," preached among others by Rousseau, presented, in making appeal to the sentiment, some of the essential doctrines of Christianity: Providence, divine justice, absolute decrees of the ethical conscience, future life with its rewards and punishments, sublimity of the evangelical moral. But this religion stripped Christianity of the mystical elements which had given it such dominion over the souls. It no longer remained but to return to it its specific virtue: to re-establish the supernatural into its rights, by establishing, in order to strengthen the faith of the believers and to confound the incredulous, by manifest deeds violating the natural laws and inexplicable to the reason, that the transcendent world existed in reality and in action. This idea would come naturally to the readers of the Bible and the Gospel when they felt the surrounding skepticism creep deceitfully into their heart: Had not Moses, Elijah, and Jesus been obliged to rely on miracles in order to convince the blind crowds? Why refuse to the divine goodness and omnipotence the right to use a mode of demonstration so efficacious in an era when the triumphant incredulity rendered it as necessary as in the times of which the Scripture has preserved the memory? Lavater, always in search of facts of supernatural origin coming to confirm what a religion of which he was the minister taught him, is the most known representative of these mystical rationalists. Pasqually, long remaining in the shadows, is the only among them who has imagined a practical manner, and theoretically founded, to satisfy their thirst for certitude and their hunger for the marvelous, and the Élus Coëns, so amenable to his instructions, are indeed the children of an era to which they seem at first strangers as much by their aspirations as by their magical operations.

BOOK III
Organization and History of the Order

FIRST CHAPTER
The Masonic Rite: The Class of the Porch

At the example of all the contemporary occultist groups, the secret and mystical society founded by Pasqually has taken since its constitution the form of a Masonic rite.

Freemasonry, quite flourishing in this period, included two distinct but intimately bound sections: Symbolic Masonry and Scottish Masonry.[1020] The first, imported from England around 1730, is comprised of three grades: Apprentice, Companion, and Master, that the color of their ribbon caused to be commonly called Blue Dgrees, and named its assemblies Lodges. The French Lodges faithfully observed the usages of their English sister-Lodges, professed like them a sentimental humanitarianism, and had as its official program to see to the social education of Masons by teaching them to practice between them equality and fraternity. Scottish Masonry, born in France, some fifteen years later, cultivated what they called High Grades, whose holders sat in Chapters or Councils, displayed ambitious titles, and claimed to constitute an aristocracy called to govern the Blue Lodges and possessing knowledge of which ordinary Masons were unaware. The Scottish degrees, which abounded beginning from 1750 but which were in general only variants of some fundamental types, were distinguished by an extremely developed ritual, dramatic initiations, and complicated ceremonies occurring in picturesque or ostentatious settings.

The wealth of form veiled poorly the poverty of the foundation, and the magnificence of the ceremonial was equal only to the intellectual indigence of instructions and catechisms. The staging aimed above all to feed the base curiosity or to flatter the vanity of wealthy Brothers. Scottish Masonry would have been, therefore, only a source of puerile diversions if the mystery with which the entire society was surrounded had not attracted into its bosom candidates who aspired to satisfactions of a more elevated order. A metaphysical anguish tormented at the time a number of spirits that the weakening of the traditional faith left without support and without guidance, and who, on the other hand, were unable to be content with the simplistic solution given by the utilitarian materialism to problems exceeding the range of human intelligence. These restless spirits believed that Freemasonry knew the response that they sought in vain in the dogmas of positive religions and in the theories of rationalist philosophers. They were persuaded that the Lost Word, of which the Masons held in high regard, was quite a different matter than the primitive equality and fraternity, and that the Masonic secret concerned either the elements of the occult sciences cultivated in ancient times and preserved in the course of the ages by initiates ignored by the masses, or a definitive and complete revelation which gave the key of the enigma of the world.

The fabricators of the High Grades had taken into account that unacknowledged hope and, in order to give some spice to their productions, they had slipped into the symbols and into the instructions coming from their inventive mind very clear allusions to alchemy, theurgy, and theosophy. But the mystical ingredients drawn at random and without discernment from ancient works, incorporated arbitrarily into inspired homilies or into ceremonies without significance, excited again the thirst that they claimed to quench. Always hoping to find in a degree superior to the one that they had attained the supreme revelation that they were promised, and each time deceived, the pilgrims of the ideal pursued degree after degree a ceaselessly fleeting goal. They had counted on discovering in the Lodges the "True Light" and they found themselves in the presence of a new mystery: after so many vain searches, deceiving initiations, and money spent for the rights of reception and diplomas, they were still to wonder what the Lost Word signified and what the Masonic secret hid.

Nevertheless, the majority did not lose courage. They persisted to believe that the Masonic symbols were a secret language whose exact interpretation would reveal first truths, and that the "true" Masonry gave an esoteric teaching of an inestimable value. This state of mind, widespread among the members of the Lodges and Chapters, reveals how the most celebrated impostors of the 18th century have found under the acacia the great number of their dupes. But it also explains why the founders of occultist sects have, in the same period, copied the vocabulary, the allegories, and the ceremonies of a secret society where they knew how to easily raise troops. Picking up the theme already exploited by the authors of the Scottish degrees, they put themselves forth as the representatives of the pure Masonic tradition, adulterated by ignorance or deceit, and promised to explain in satisfying and convincing fashion, the profound meaning of the symbols. They therefore carefully preserved the characteristic lines of the setting in order to neither mislead the Masons of the Blue Lodges desirous of hearing their knowledge, nor the Scottish Masons that their high grades has not satisfied.

This is the path that Pasqually followed. He gave to his society the Order-name that the Freemasons bore. The Order of Élus Coëns presented itself as a system of Scottish Freemasonry, trustee of the true secret tradition. It borrowed from the Masonic Order its symbols and a good part of its ritual, but under this veil rendered voluntarily transparent is sketched, in the first degrees, in order to put to the test, the disposition of the recruits,[1021] the doctrines set forth in the Reintegration from which their papers borrowed its mystical vocabulary, whereas the superior degrees have as their principal object the Operations and serve as novitiate to the chosen adepts who will be admitted to the supreme and secret degree, the grade of Réau-Croix.

∴

The imitation of the formulas, themes, and usages familiar to Masonry is flagrant in the correspondence of the Élus Coëns, in the Reintegration, and in the ritual of the operations.

The adepts are adorned with ostentatious titles made popular by the Scottish degrees: Chevaliers Maçons, Élus, Commandeurs [Knight Masons, Elect, Commanders]. They named their groups Orient and their directing committee, Grand Orient or Sovereign Tribunal. The Réau-Croix are called: Very High, Very Respectable, and Very Powerful Master [Très Haut, Très Respectable, Très Puissant Maître]. Pasqually is entitled: Grand Sovereign.

But, even here where the borrowings are most manifest, the imitation is more formal than substantial, and Pasqually adapts themes and formulas to the mystical doctrines which give to his society its original character. The Élus Coëns invoke in the Lodge the Great Architect of the Universe and place his name at the head of their letters, but having it followed by the word that ends the Christian prayers. Saint-Martin employs at the end of a letter addressed to Willermoz the traditional Masonic formula, but he alters it in a significant fashion: "Hail, P.M. (Powerful Master) by all the numbers which are known to you."[1022] The modifications are yet more profound and more characteristic in the initial formulas. An official letter from Pasqually beings as follows:

> *From the Grand Orient of Orients of Bordeaux to the Grand Orient of Lyon.*
>
> *In the name of the Great Architect of the universe, amen+ amen+ amen+.*
>
> *Joy, peace, and prosperity.*
>
> *From the Grand Orient of Orients of the Chevaliers Macons Élus Coëns de l'Univers [Knights Masons Élus Coëns of the Universe], the Masonic year 3.3.3.3.5.7.9.4.4.6.601, of the rebirth of the virtues 2448, of the world 4.5, of the Hebraic era 5727, of Christ 1767, from the last to the first quarter of the fifth and sixth moon of the aforesaid year, the 19th of June.*
>
> *To our Very Respectable and Very High Master, our Inspector General, Knight, Conductor and Commander at the head of the columns of the Orient and the Occident and of our Sublime Orders, salutations, Very Respectable Master, be blessed forever (here a circle surrounded by four crosses), Amen.*[1023]

Saint-Martin, in his capacity as secretary, is less prolix, but he imitates his master in the measure permitted to him by his inferior rank. He begins in these terms the first letter that he writes, by order of the Grand Sovereign, to Willermoz:

> *In the Name O.T.G.A.O.T.U, Amen.*
>
> *Peace, joy, salvation and benediction to the one who hears me. Amen.*
>
> *From the Grand Orient of Orients of Bordeaux, the M. year 3.3.3.3.5.7.5.7.9 of the world 4.5., of the rebirth of the virtues 2448, of the Hebraic era 5731, of Ch. commonly styled 1771. The 4th of March.*
>
> *V.P.M. (Very Powerful Master)*[1024]

"The heading," rigorously imposed on all the Brothers who write to the "Very High, Very Respectable, and Very Powerful Sovereign Grand Tribunal," is addressed: "To the Grand Orient of Orients of the S.T. of the Chevaliers Maçons Élus Coëns de l'Univers, raised to the glory of the Eternal in the northern region under the very high and very powerful Constitutions of our Very Respectable, Very High, and Very Powerful Grand Sovereign, sitting presently at the Grand Orient of Orients. Paris," and ending the request in "saluting him by all the mysterious numbers known only to us" and in "praying the Eternal that he holds the Sovereign Tribunal in his holy keep, just as all the heads in particular who comprise it for a time immemorial. Amen, amen, amen."[1025]

The Reintegration strives to give a mystical basis to two of the oldest Scottish degrees, well known and practiced under the name of Élu of the Nine and Élu of the Fifteen. It relates that, when one of the ten Spiritual Minors "elected" by Enoch[1026] had fallen away and pushed into revolt a part of his own disciples, "there remained only the number of nine Just upon the earth to whom he communicated entirely his secret."[1027] Later, when Moses, at his descent from Sinai, found the Jews worshipping the Golden Calf, he made "his invocation to the Creator in order to obtain from him the spiritual election of the number of the Elect Avengers[1028] of the insults done to the Eternal. He was ordered by him to take fifteen men from the tribe of Levi. He portioned them into three bands of five men each and then said: Let those who love the Creator take in hand the flat blade which rests on their left thigh. The fifteen Elect aimed over the field the knife in their right hand.[1029] Moses performed the blessing thereof, then he said: Let the first band, where are Simeon and Levi, walk from the rising sun towards the setting, the second from the rising sun towards the south, and the third from the rising sun to the north wind. The three bands will go thus and return three times across the camp of Israel...and they will then return to me being accompanied by Aaron."[1030] Under the pretext of completing one of the narratives of Exodus[1031], Pasqually incorporated into his esoteric version of the Bible the essential traits of the two principle degrees of the Élu [Elect]. The least Scottish Mason could not fail to grasp the allusions made to the fateful numbers, to the password, to the daggers, to the "travels" that the candidate made across the Lodge in three successive directions and at the end of which he was brought back to the Venerable by the Brother Introducer who had guided his steps since his entrance into the Lodge.

The three deadly blows that the three rebel companions had dealt to Hiram according to the legend of the Degree of Master, the weapon of the Elect Mason, and the signs of recognition of several Scottish degrees were likewise recalled by the version that the treatise gave of the murder of Abel. It related that Adam and Abel having come to pay a visit to Cain and his two sisters, Cain embraced his brother and "in this embrace dealt upon Abel three blows of a wooden instrument made in the form of a dagger. The first blow pierced the throat, the second pierced the heart, and the third pierced the entrails."[1032]

There is nothing up to the ritual of the Operations that has not made borrowings from Masonry, but in giving also to the great secret society a mystical significance or a theurgical meaning. The Élu Coën would, when he entered into the Chamber of Operation, not have upon him any object of metal, "not even a pin," and would wear his shoes "slipshod,"[1033] all like the Masonic candidate at the time of his reception. The only reason for these prescriptions was that, according to one of the fundamentals of magic, all metal repels the Spirits and that, on the other hand, the shoes had to be able to be removed rapidly at the moment of the invocations. The ribbons by which the Operant was adorned were "the celestial blue cord around the neck" (ribbon of the blue degrees), the cord "passed from right to left" (cord of the degrees of Vengeance), the red sash and the green sash (color of the Scottish degrees). But the red sash, which girded the body below the abdomen, and the green sash, which surrounded the chest, made "by their placement allusion to the material animal and spiritual separations."[1034]

∴

The care that Pasqually took to not miss any occasion that allowed him to have Masonic themes returned into the framework of his theosophical system has inspired one of the most bizarre ideas of his treatise, that is to say the assimilation established by the Reintegration between the descendants of Noah, or Noachites, and the Chinese "because the nation of the Chinese and the Japanese came directly out of the posterity of the children of Noah, namely from the first posterity of Shem, Ham, and Japhet who each inhabited a corner from that region of China from where all the peoples have arisen, and the last three of the seven males who, with the three females, formed the second posterity of Noah."[1035]

The name of the Noachites and their identification with the Masons had been popularized in the Lodges by the Book of Constitutions, bible of English Freemasonry. In its second edition, dated 1738 (the first had appeared in 1723), it relates that Mathuselah had, with his son Lamech and his grandson Noah, withdrawn from the corrupted world and that these three Just ones had preserved in all its purity the ancient religion, as well as the Royal Art (of Masonry) until the deluge. After the flood the sons of Noah, who had been instructed by Methuselah, had in their turn become trustees of the true religious and Masonic tradition, so that, when they were established in the plain of Sennaar, they lived there as "true Noachites," name which the Masons had first borne, according to certain traditions."[1036] In another place of the work an obligation was made to the Masons to faithfully observe "the three articles of Noah," a formula left unexplained, but which likely alluded to the three virtues whose practice the rules of the stonecutters agreed to recommend: fraternal love, mutual aid, and reciprocal loyalty.[1037] Also, the first chapter of the "Duties" in the edition of 1738 prescribed to the Mason to obey the moral law as "true Noachite" and the French adaptation of the English book that la Tierce had published in 1742 under the title of: *Histoire, Obligations et Statuts de la Très Vénérable Confraterité des Franc-Maçons*, called Noachites the descendants of Noah and made them the ancestors of the Masons.[1038]

The third edition of the Book of Constitutions, drafted in 1756 by the pastor John Entik, who regarded Masonry as founded upon Christianity, and had criticized the innovations of the previous edition, suppressed the passages speaking of the Noachites and of the three articles of Noah, and they were not repeated by the following editions (1767 and 1784)[1039], but the word remained no less in the memory of the French Masons, especially those who read the work of la Tierce; and the proof of the prestige that it preserved in their eyes is found in the fact that one of the Scottish degrees, likely written around 1756, that were published in 1774 under the title: *Les plus secrets Mystères des Hauts Grades de la Franc-Maçonnerie dévoilés*, bore the name of Noachite.

Pasqually seized the word readily as the Talmudists held up the "commandments of Noah."[1040] Applying one of their processes of exegesis, temurah or anagram, he transformed Noachite, or rather following the French style: Noechite, into Chinois [Chinese].[1041] This turn of linguistic sleight of hand had two advantages: it allowed it to represent the Chinese, whose ancient civilization, beliefs, and calendar had been recently brought to public attention by the accounts of missionaries, among the peoples who had clumsily deduced their calculations of time from the sacred computation, and it proved at the same time that the symbolic Masons, who were called the true Noachites or Noechites, were the descendants of people forgetful of the true divine cult. "The Chinese," said the Reintegration, "have introduced into their temporal daily calculations the spiritual calculations of the operations of the divine cult (portioning of the days of 24 hours into four parts of 6 hours each),"[1042] but then "they have made four months for one of those that we employ today to form one year, and they have included in their annual calculation thirty years for one of our ordinary years."[1043] Then, "only celebrating the cult once every seven years, they had years of seven weeks, calculation that they followed for a century and a half of our ordinary time."[1044] The descendants of Ham, Japhet, and Shem, who, as we have seen above, "inhabited the three corners of this region of China," have, it is true, bequeathed "to all the peoples of the world the knowledge of astronomy and of the faculties of power of the planetary stars over the general and particular creation,"[1045] but they composed calendars whose diversity showed that they did not understand the "mysterious" year: the first were one year per season, the second one year from the equinox of March to the following March, the third counted two equinoxes as two years. These different calculations, used also in their civil history, persisted until after Nimrod and until the dispersion of these peoples.[1046] Pasqually saw in all these divisions how the Noachites have made their days, their months, and their years" the reason for which "they call themselves more ancient than Adam by 15 or 20 thousand years."[1047] These errors showed the forgetfulness into which the divine cult had fallen among them. Indeed, Shem, Ham, and Japhet, "being occupied only with establishing and cultivating the portion of the earth which was due them in order to provide for their needs and those of their family present and to come, remained consequently a rather long space of time without meditating on the spiritual instructions that Noah had given them. Their whole cult was limited to the knowledge that there existed an all-powerful being above every created thing and that they called Abavin, which means in Noachite language, doubly strong Spirit by which the Creator has operated everything. This is what we call philosophically (esoterically): the divine action of the Creator. This word, although Noachite or Chinese, is the same as the one that the Jews uttered long ago and that they knew most perfectly came from their language."[1048] But some Jews have preserved the memory of the ceremonies of the cult that the Eternal asks for, whereas the Noachites or Chinese have definitively remained with an incomplete notion of the divinity. On the other hand, the weakness of the three younger brothers of the second posterity of Noah, who have neglected to instruct the peoples, their disciples, on the mystical significance of the deluge, "manifestation of divine justice," "made to feel[1049] in their Noachite of Chinese descendants who live in terrible fear of hideous beings, who perform a cult to animals to which they give the most superstitious care in the idea of power to turn away the evils that they believe are able to be done by these monsters and which they regard as gods or demons."[1050] Thus, whereas the Noachites of China practice the most abject zoolatry, the Noachites of Europe, otherwise called the Masons, see only in God the Great Architect of the Universe, that is to say, only know the creative action of the Eternal, and are unaware of the means to re-enter into communication with him by Reconciliation.

∴

The general organization of the Order was inspired ostensibly by that of the Masonic rites, but it is quite imperfectly known to us. The documents published or described unto this day furnish only incomplete and sometimes contradictory indications on the degrees of which was comprised the Rite of the Élus Coëns.

It seems that this organization, at first rudimentary, was recast and completed from the end of 1768 to 1771, but had not yet received definitive form when Pasqually left France to no longer return and abandoned the effective direction of the association.

The Correspondence shows that Pasqually had drafted, and distributed, in 1767 and in the beginning of 1768, degrees which were modified later on, at least for the titles. It is thus that he cites in a letter sent on June 19, 1767, to Willermoz a "Maître Élu [Master Elect] with the fifth receptacle" and a "Petit Élu [Lesser Elect] with a sole receptacle," that he said to have conferred to four Masons of Rochelle[1051], and that he mentions on May 2, 1768, a "Commander of the Orient" whose papers had to be completely drawn up, since he orders Bacon to extract a conjuration therefrom.[1052]

But there was no longer, eventually, a question of these degrees, and during the autumn of 1768, Pasqually set himself to the duty of raising a complete and coherent Masonic System. In September he was actively employed at drafting "all our degrees, as well as all the ceremonies and catechisms."[1053] Eighteen months later the list of degrees had ended: Pasqually cited, regarding the revenues of the Order, the fees required for the conferring of eight degrees: Apprentice, Companion, Particular

Master, Grand Master Élu, Apprentice (Coën), Companion (Coën), Master Coën, Grand Master Architect.[1054] In 1771, the work of writing, which had probably experienced long interruptions in those three years, had resumed with ardor. In May, Willermoz had already received "the invocations of some degrees," "the ceremonial of the assemblies," "the Duties" of the degree that he possessed, and Saint-Martin copied for himself the Grand Architect.[1055] On May 20, Saint-Martin sent him "the grand ceremonial of the Grand Architect, the table of the degree, the (pass) words of the degree." He announced to him, for the next mailing, the sending of the "ceremonial of the simple ordination of the G.A.[1056], and for soon after, for "there was nothing left but to copy them," "the greater and lesser ceremonial[1057] of the three blue degrees of the Élu, and of the three Coëns." In July, he sent to Lyon "the ceremonial for the holding of assemblies: opening, closing, illuminations, passwords, etc., followed by the three blue degrees, the degrees of the Élu, and the three Coëns, and a catechism of the three blue degrees with an explanation begun on the different questions of this catechism."[1058]

But it was for the Masonic degrees as in the ritual of the Operations. Pasqually embarked for America without having completed his task. On October 12, 1773, he announced from Port-au-Prince that he had "made here all the instructions of the different degrees of L. (Lodges), from the Class of the Porch to that of Réau-Croix, then the general index of names, numbers, in conjunction with the characters and hieroglyphs, the different diagrams of Operations, and the different Invocations that are to follow the diagrams."[1059] Now, in this period the Society began already to dissolve. It had therefore never known but a temporary organization[1060] and Pasqually succeeded no better at giving to his Masonic System a definitive form than to codify therein the theurgical practices in a complete fashion.

We are not even decided on the number, distribution, and current designation of the degrees that were effectively practiced by the Élus Coëns. The Masonic writings do not agree on any of these points:

Thory[1061] gives the following list:

First class: Apprentice, Companion, Master, Grand Élu.

Second class: Apprentice Coën, Companion Coën, Master Coën, Grand Architect, Knight Commander, for nine degrees.

Ragon[1062] reproduces the same list but ranks the Apprentice Coën in the first class.

Bord[1063] follows Ragon, but adds a third class, "secret class," composed of the Réau-Croix, an addition justified by a letter from Pasqually which cites this class as the most elevated of the Order.[1064] It would thus be comprised of ten degrees. Bord notes moreover, rightly so it seems, that the Grand Architect and the Knight Commander formed the Élus Coëns proper. These two degrees would have therefore been the novitiate of the Réau-Croix.

Papus has reproduced the catechisms of six degrees, entitled: Apprentice Élu Coën, Companion Élu Coën, Particular Master, Master Élu, Grand Masters called Grand Architects, Grand Elect of Zorobabel, so-called Knights of the Orient.[1065] If one takes into account the three blue degrees which would precede them and the Réau-Croix which followed them, we find ten degrees.

The documentation of Papus is by far the most reliable, for, rather than presenting lacunas and reproducing only the dogmatic part of the degrees cited, it at least relies on the texts. It has furnished the elements of the following outline, completed with the information given by Thory and Bord.

∴

BLUE DEGREES

The papers of the blue degrees, that is to say symbolic Apprentice, Companion, and Master, imitative of the three degrees comprising original Masonry, have not reached us. This lacuna is of little importance, for the Masonic Systems, which all placed their foundations upon this common base, could not profoundly modify degrees whose main lines were consecrated by a long tradition and known to all Masons. All that Pasqually had been able to do was to slip in some vague allusions to the theories that would be exposed in the superior degrees.[1066] The proof of their insignificance from the dogmatic point of view is found in the open disdain with which they are treated. On July 7, 1771, Saint-Martin, in sending them to Willermoz, reminded him that he had the order to confer them in one sole session[1067] and, as Willermoz asked the following month for instructions on the manner of proceeding with this massive initiation, Saint-Martin responded to him that he could, from the start, make the battery of the Master[1068] and preserve only what he found essential, lest the ceremonial appear too long. But he saw to note that this expeditive procedure was no longer appropriate when it was a matter of the three Coën degrees for the conferment of which one even left rather long intervals between them, "always according to the disposition of the subject."[1069] The blue degrees were therefore conferred only by virtue of information for the neophytes who had not yet been in the Lodge and a reminder for those among them who were already Masons.

∴

CLASS OF THE PORCH

The first three superior degrees practiced by the Order of Élus Coëns, that is to say the Apprentice Élu Coën, Companion Élu Coën, and Particular Master, were called the "three Porches of the Temple" and constituted the Class of the Porch."[1010]

APPRENTICE ÉLU COËN

This degree is, of all the Coën high degrees, the one on which we possess the most complete information given: Papus has published the catechism[1071] and Thory the ritual[1072] according to manuscripts that seem authentic.[1073]

The one who desired to be received had to be a full 21 years old or only 16 or 17 if he was the son of a Master, "having right to 5 years grace in his capacity of louveteau."[1074] He was obliged to present himself in person in order to solicit admission. Introduced in the vestibule called Parvis, he announced himself at the door of the first room called Porch. A Vicar, accompanied by Tuileurs [Tilers][1075], had him enter into the Porch and informed them of his name, his country, and his religious opinions. If the candidate responded in a satisfactory fashion, he was invited to kneel and to take an oath: 1st of discretion; 2nd to flee debauchery and public places; 3rd to not frequent women of bad livelihood and not to commit adultery; 4th to remain faithfully attached to the statutes of the Order. These preliminaries accomplished, the candidate received the order to retire, the reception having to take place only several days later.

This ceremony, divided into two acts called First and Second Point, took place in a locale including four rooms: the Parvis, Porch, Temple or Tribunal, and Chamber of Retreat, where the candidate was "delivered to his reflections."

The "carpet" spread out in the middle of the Temple represented, in addition to the traditional Masonic emblems: (compass, perpendicular, square, tracing board, sun, and moon) six circumferences around which were arranged thirty candles in candlesticks. Each Lodge of Coëns was furthermore provided with the following instruments: a machine suitable for imitating thunder, three others to throw lightning, an earthenware vessel with lit coals, a vase full of water, a vase containing molded clay, a red cloth, a black cloth, a white cloth, a lead pencil, a spiral staircase divided into three landings of three, five, and seven steps, of which the last was perforated by a trap door and triangular holes, a branch of palm, one of cedar, one of olive, one of willow, a rod of holly, one of ash, one of hazel, a censer, and perfumes.

The opening of the works took place, for a reception as well as for an ordinary meeting, according to a complicated ritual: ceremonies of entrance into the Temple; prayers to the Eternal; solemn introduction of the Brothers of the high degrees; exhortations addressed by the president of the Temple, called Très Puissant Maître [Very Powerful Master], with the two Surveillants [Overseers/Wardens], his subordinates; ceremony of the daggers[1076]; call for the passwords and instructions concerning the formulas of opening and closing of the works, as well as on the manner to give the password to the Réau-Croix and to the Grand Officers.

The Lodge duly opened; one approaches the First Point of the reception. The neophyte, received in the Parvis by the Very Venerable Master, who ruled in this part of the Lodge, was immediately enclosed in the Chamber of Retreat. While he remained there, delivered to his reflections, the Brothers proceeded to the final preparations: the branches of palm, cedar, willow, and olive, the vases containing the fire, the water, and the molded clay were arranged around the circumferences. Those who had to throw the thunder and lightning took their place, as well as the Conductor-in-Chief[1077] and the Vicar.

All being in order, the Very Venerable Master, accompanied by the Tilers, crossed the Parvis and penetrated into the Chamber of Retreat. He interrogated the candidate on the motives of his procedures and asked him if he had decided to enter into a society "that held only to virtue and that was the enemy of the vanities of this perishable world." Upon his affirmative response, the Very Venerable Master said to the Tilers: "Prepare this man to retrace to the eyes of the Brothers who are in the Tribunal the spectacle of what has passed in the beginning of time at the center of the universe." At these words the Tilers stripped him of all metals and undressed him in a way that he remained only in his shirt and white flannel under-pants. They blindfolded him and laid him down upon the three superimposed cloths, the white being on top and the black on the bottom. they carefully wrapped him in these cloths, carried him into the Tribunal and there laid him on his back in the center of the circumferences, head to the Occident, feet to the Orient, the two knees in the air and fists over the eyes. They rested his head upon a triangular stone. The vase of fire was placed beside his head, the vase containing the molded clay near the heart, and the vase full of water on the opposite side.

After some minutes of a profound silence, four blows of thunder were made to be heard. Then the Very Respectable Master, president of the room of the Porch, and the Very Venerable Master circulate six times around the circumferences, the one going from East to West by the South and the other from West to East by the North. They stop before the Very Powerful Master "who gives them the blessing of Israel, if their advancement in the Order permitted them to receive it[1078] or only layed hands on them." "During these circuits the lightning flashed, the thunder rumbled, and the circles were censed." Some moments of lull, then the thunder and lightning were unleashed anew, and "the Very Powerful Master, accompanied by his sacred acolytes, operated the miracle of creation."

The Very Respectable Master touched with his hazel rod the knees of the candidate who stretches them out at once. The Very Venerable Master touched with his ash rod the heart of the candidate, then his right side and had him extend the two arms successively. The two officiants removed by turns the black cloth and the red cloth, The candidate, arms extended, and legs separated, was no longer covered except by a white cloth. The Very Venerable Master placed himself at his feet, the Very Respectable Master at his head, and the latter said in a loud voice: "Great Architect of the Universe, you who has indeed wished to make man in your image and your resemblance in order to subdue to him the greater world (macrocosm), of which he will be the victim if you do not fill him with your grace, do not allow the work of your hands to perish. See, on the contrary, that his enemies redden with shame at the uselessness of their efforts to win victories over him. Nevertheless, let your holy will be done." The Very Venerable Master responds: "Amen." The candidate was then completely uncovered; the thunder rolled without stop; "the place of the assembly represented the image of chaos." Little by little the calm was re-established. The candidate was invited to raise himself and he was made to undergo the "travels" by conducting him "from the West to the East and from the North to the South." He was finally placed at the center of the carpet, facing the Very Powerful Master, his bandage was removed, and he saw the Brothers "sword (dagger) in hand."

The Very Powerful Master gave him "the ordination by pronouncing mysterious words" and by pressing the thumb, index, and medius of the right hand, "which offered the image of a triangle, the other fingers being folded into the hand," successively upon the forehead, the heart, the right side, and the head. The Very Venerable Master then conducted the candidate "to the center of the circumferences," showing him the signs of recognition and telling him: "These four branches which are offered to your eyes will be of a great usefulness if you observe the commandments of the one who has given you being. But you will be prey to misfortune and subject to death if you transgress. You may enjoy all that you see; but keep yourself from touching these four branches." (Showing with his rod the palm branch) "Here is the symbol of the universal wisdom of the vivifying God." (Showing the cedar branch) "Here is the emblem of the universal power of the living God." (Showing the olive branch) "Here is the emblem of the power of the God of life." (Showing the willow branch) "Here, finally, is the symbol of eternal death." "Then he had him throw his eyes upon the molded clay, the water, and the fire, and said: See, man, what you are. I have drawn you from this. If you do not wish to return into the abyss of the land of Egypt, observe faithfully the prohibitions that have been made to you and never forget the promises that you will contract with the Order."

They left the candidate alone in the middle of the circumferences, then an Élu Coën, "who represented an evil genius, crossing the circles," approached him and "sought to demonstrate to him the absurdity of the prohibitions that they had made against him." "He engaged him to approach the branches, to examine them, to trace characters around, promising him that it would result in precious knowledge, from which would derive a power superior to the power of the one who created him." "Attach yourself," he told him, "to perfect knowledge which the living tree contains, since it is all knowledge and all power.[1079] You will subdue all to your dominion and you will command all the animals (beings), as much the visible as the invisible."

The neophyte, allowing himself to be tempted, "was overwhelmed with reproaches and driven from the Temple." In the Parvis he fell into the hands of three Tilers, who represented the evil geniuses; "they fastened his arms with strong bonds, loaded him with an enormous burden, and had him make nine circuits of the room while covering him with water and mud; the lightning flashed, the thunder exploded." The first act had ended.

In order to be able to pass to the Second Point, they profited from the absence of the candidate in order to change the decoration of the Temple and set up the spiral staircase "in the middle of the six mysterious circumferences."

The first Tiler came to give an account to the Very Powerful Master of the repentance and humiliation of the candidate and to implore his forgiveness. "Go," he had responded to him, "let the man be presented before me." They tear the candidate away, with difficulty, from the hands of the evil geniuses who do their best to retain him. "Leave this man in peace," said to them the first Tiler, who represented a good genius, "withdraw yourselves and henceforth let none of you surround him. "The Very Powerful Master has granted him grace. Withdraw yourselves, each into your region; obey the one who commands you in the name of the Master."

The candidate was conducted, laden with chains, to the feet of the Very Powerful Master and implored his grace. "There you are, then returned into the land of Egypt,"[1080] "the Very Powerful Master said to him. "How have you been able to forget the prohibitions that have been made against you? How unfortunate! Your crime has rendered you a slave to death, which will exercise its dominion over you and your posterity. Raise yourself, man, your sin is remitted. It is to you to now work to gain eternal life."

Delivered from his bonds, the candidate was conducted by the Very Respectable Master to the entrance of the spiral staircase. His guide explained to him that the three landings, to which one had access by three, five, and seven steps, were the symbol of the three sufferings, "sufferings of the body, soul, and spirit" that he would experience "in the reintegration of his person with his principle," then he made him ascend the staircase backwards. The candidate stopped on the first landing in order to take the first third of his "obligation" (to keep secret the mysteries of the Élus Coëns); on the second he took the second third (to be faithful to the Catholic, Apostolic, and Roman religion, to aid his Brothers by his counsel and his purse); on the third he took the final third (to never frequent those meetings which are held by the type of Masons without knowledge). All these oaths were taken while kneeling. Once raised, the candidate was placed on the trap-door of the third landing. "They told him that the first-born of men had made to God, after his sin, promises equivalent to those that he had just made a moment ago, but that, the malign Spirit having seized him, he had again been seduced, and that he had drawn upon himself the fire from heaven by his conduct, and finally, that he had been hurled into the abyss of the earth in order to be delivered to the eternal fire." "In this instant the trap-door opened under the feet of the candidate who disappeared and fell, in the midst of the flames" (shooting from the triangular holes perforated in the third landing) to the foot of the spiral staircase.

This trial ended the initiation of the Apprentice Élu Coën. He is shown the sign of the degree: "the right hand resting squared over the heart and the left hand squared edgewise over (toward?) the earth," and seven other signs "imitative of the figures of the seven planets." Finally, they proclaimed him member of the Order, and the Very Powerful Master sent him to take his place "in the North" among the Brothers of his degree, after having made him recite the catechism.

This catechism was copied from that of the Symbolic Apprentice paper for the account made by the reciting of the circumstances of his reception, of what he had seen when they removed his blindfold, by the symbolic hours of the opening and closing of the works ("full midday" and "full midnight"), by the moralizing tendency ("to observe perseverance, temperance, and charity towards all his Brothers, to flee calumny, laziness, and slander"), by the name of the Great Architect of the Universe given to God to the exclusion of every other denomination. Certain passages of the model were integrally reproduced:

Q. How were you placed when you were received?

A. I was neither nude nor vested[1081], divested of all metals.

Q. What have you seen and what have you learned?

A. Nothing that the human spirit may comprehend.

Q. Why is that?

A. Because I was deprived of the use of my senses...

Q. What are the conditions of your reception?

A. An authentic promise and inviolable engagements...

Q. What is their kind of work [of the Apprentices]?

A. To raise spiritual edifices upon their base, according to the plan that they have received from their Master...

Q. Of what use is the square in the Temple?

A. To perfect the works of the Apprentices (particulars).[1082]

Q. To what serves the compass?

A. To direct and limit those of the Companions.

Q. To what serves the tracing board?

A. It serves to decorate the Masters (particular) and to designate the superiority of their works.

Q. What are the instruments that the G.A.O.T.U. has used for the construction of the (great universal) Temple?

A. A triangle, a perpendicular, and a perfect square.

Q. What form has your (general) Temple?

A. A perfect equilateral triangle, just as it is represented to us from North to South and from South to West.[1083]

Q. What is its height?

A. Cubits without number.

Q. What is its depth?

A. From the surface to the center.

Q. What is its length?

A. From North to South.[1084]

Q. What covers this edifice?

A. A canopy strewn with stars...

Q. What is their height [the columns]?

A. Eighteen cubits.

Q. What covers their head?

A. A double capital adorned with pomegranates.

Q. What is their circumference?

A. Twelve cubits...

Q. How old are you?

A. Three years...

Q. Have you jewels in your Temple?

A. Yes, (Very Powerful Master) there are three, which are the square, the compass, and the tracing board...

Q. What is the quality of an Apprentice?

A. To be free men, equal to kings and to every man, when he is virtuous.

But, under the cover of this formal similarity, the catechism of the Apprentice Élu Coën emphasizes the particular theories of the Order in interpreting in his way the Masonic symbols that he preserves, and in adding other emblems.

He mentions, like Andersons's Book of Constitutions, the five orders of architecture, but he calls them mystically: the simple, the perfect, the symbolic, the just, and the apocryphal; and they signify for him: the body of man, the universal body, the general terrestrial body, the inferior material body, and finally the apocryphal Temple, that is to say, "the conventional that men strive to establish with impunity in error" (false divine cult). If he asks the Apprentice, as did the English catechism reproduced in Masonry Dissected by Prichard: "Have you seen your Master today, how was he dressed?" instead of having him respond: "In yellow, with blue stockings" (allusion to the compass), he dictates to him: "White, red, and black," while specifying that these three colors symbolize the beauty of the work of the Creator, the virtue, and the wisdom that the candidate must practice. If they have removed from the candidate all the metal objects that he might have upon himself before introducing him to the Lodge, it was not, as said the blue catechism, to teach him the contempt for the riches that create an artificial inequality between men, it was in order "to make allusion to the formation of all the bodies that the G.A.O.T.U. saw to construct in the Universal Temple without the relief of material operations."

The triangle figured on the columns of the Lodge represents "the three different spiritous essences which compose the general, terrestrial, celestial, and particular body." The battery of the Apprentice, which is "three slow knocks" alludes to the three principles which compose his temporal Temple (body), "that is to say Mercury, Sulphur, and Salt," the first principle applying to "the osseous part," the second to "the fluid part," the third to "the pellicular part" (flesh and skin). The solid part corresponds in its turn to the general terrestrial body, the fluid to "the solar part" (heavens of the planets), the pellicular part to "the northern part" (fixed heavens). The attribute of the Apprentice, that is to say the perpendicular, indicates that "all the actions and operations of the Apprentices ought to be directed by the principle of their spiritual emanation." The sun and the moon of the carpet represented: the first, "the faculty of the elementary fire," the second "the influence upon conception and vegetation."[1085]

On the other hand, the Order replaces in the Lodge the two columns Jachin and Boaz, that Freemasonry had borrowed from the biblical description of the Temple of Solomon, with the three symbolic columns of which, it is true, French Masonry spoke under the name of Wisdom, Strength, and Beauty, and that the catechism calls by its example: Wisdom, Virtue, Beauty, but it represented to them, instead of abstract ideas, the three substances composing the material world, for it calls them allegorically spaces "to enclose the powerful instruments (the 'spiritous' substances) of which the G.A.O.T.U. has used for the construction of his Universal

Temple." Upon the carpet of the Coën Lodge are drawn the signs of Saturn, Venus, Jupiter, Mars, and Mercury, abode of the Septenary Spirits, the chalk, the earthenware vessel and the charcoal employed in the Operations and which are, provisionally, given as emblems of zeal, fervor, and constancy, and finally the six circumferences of which the treatise of Pasqually has taught us the mystical significance, and that the head of the Élus Coëns traced in his confidential letters in order to symbolically represent his Order.

The direct allusions to the theories and practices of the Society could not strike the neophyte, but they would serve him as landmarks and sign-posts on the day that his instruction would be complete. The catechisms teach him that the origin of the Order "comes from the Creator and began since the first time under Adam and from then until our day," that is has been able to be perpetuated unto us "by the pure mercy of the G.A. who has, by his Spirit, given rise to proper and suitable subjects to manifest this Order among men for his greater glory and justice," and he reduces to eight emissaries: Adam, Noah, Melchizedek, Abraham, Moses, Solomon, Zorobabel, and Christ, that is to say to the principal Elect of whom speaks the Reintegration, the long list of historical or mythic personages that the Masonic legend relates in the Book of Constitutions and by the Histoire of la Tierce represented as the successive repositories of the secrets of the Royal Art. It is assured to the candidate that the Order will make him "know perfectly the existence of the G.A.O.T.U., the principle of the spiritual emanation of man, and his correspondence with his master." They advise him, as "the most useful numbers that the Apprentice Élu must use in the Order, the 3, the 2, the 5, the 6, and the 7." They indicate to him, in intentionally veiled terms, the final goal of the teaching of which he has received the first principle, that is to say the theurgical practices, in telling him that "the first elements of the Order" are "the tracing, the operation, and the word." The catechism has him give to the question posed by the Very Powerful Master: "Of what use was this Order to the men of the first time?" the significant response, if not to him, at least to the readers of the Reintegration: "It served as the spiritual basis and foundation in order to operate the ceremonial of the cult of the Eternal, and to preserve by it in the regularity of their first principles, divine virtues and spiritual powers." There is nothing as far as the sympathetic cooperation found mentioned but in a roundabout way when the candidate, while reading the catechism declares: "I will attract to myself the beneficence of the chiefs who will unite their works with mine in order to make me succeed in the perfect enjoyment of the rights, fruits, and prerogatives of the Order of the legitimate spiritual Élus Coëns."

In presenting to the new Apprentice Coën these enigmatic remarks, full of promises still obscure to him, the Order aims to transport him into a world of ideas, to open to him horizons unknown in the blue degrees and scarcely suspected by some Scottish degrees. It presented at the same time these ideas, vaguely outlined, but upon which a progressive initiation would throw a brilliant light, as the essence of the Masonic secret. It gave the Coën System as the sole representative of the "true Masonry."

It developed the gloomy ceremony from the reception to the degree of symbolic Master. It borrowed from the high degrees the search of nervous shock, the theatrical apparatus, the series of "Apartments," the richness of a general staff with imposing titles, from the Rose-Croix the "points" of reception, from the Grand Architect and from the Knight of the East or Sword the changing of decorations, from the degrees of the Élus their dagger, but he denied his models after having pillaged them; he treated the Brothers of all Systems and of all degrees as "false Masons," as "apocryphal Élus Masons." Finding too material for a "spiritual" society the symbol of the Temple of Solomon, that French Masonry had put in the foreground as the image of the social edifice successful in its perfection by the triumph of altruistic sentiments, he reproached the members of Symbolic Lodges for "have formed a Masonic Order by the example of the construction of the Temple of Solomon in which they have found some of our emblems of whose virtue, propriety, and perfection they are unaware." The whole purpose of the catechism was dedicated to recalling, or revealing, to the candidate the passwords, signs, and touches of the "apocryphal Élus Masons: Apprentice, Companion, Master," and the passwords of the six high degrees: Master Élu, Scottish Master, Master Architect, Knight of the East, Knight of the Sun or Commander, Rose-Croix.[1086] It was declared that "all these signs, touches, words, and figures of the apocryphal Élus Masons" had "no connection with those of the Élus Coëns," and, in order to explain the conformity of certain emblems, the catechism accused the Masons of having stolen them from the Order, "as having (because they had) penetrated a little into the science and into the mysteries of the Élus Coëns."

COMPANION ÉLU COËN

The information given by Thory on the two other degrees of the Porch is quite succinct. He is content to say that, the Apprentice having already suffered the pains of the body, those of the soul and spirit were the object of the doctrine of the initiations into the degrees of Companion and Master Coëns and he adds: "We will not enter into the detail of these. The trials of the initiate are of the same sort and, as in the first degree, the staircase in the form of a spiral plays a main role there. We are even able to say, and the Élus Coëns will agree, that the two final acts of reception are rather inferior to the first, in which the inventors seem to have exhausted all their resources."[1087]

The little importance attached by Thory to the two superior degrees of the Class of the Porch seems completely justified by the documents published by Papus. The catechism of Companion[1088] is as empty as was its homonym in Blue Masonry, where the Companion was a degree deliberately sacrificed.

The president of the Lodge of Companion Élu Coën was called Very Venerable or Very Respectable Master. The candidate traveled from the West to the North and from the North to the South where was his prescribed place. He had as jewel the triangle, and being promoted to Companion was called: "to pass from the perpendicular to the triangle." His sign consisted in "placing the right had squared, raised over the heart." His steps were "by three triangular steps." His battery was 5 knocks: 3 quick and 2 slow.

The catechism was made, in appearance, the interpreter of the specifically Christian mysticism proper to the family of Scottish degrees, of which that of the Rose-Croix with its Mystical Supper and its emblems: pelican feeding its young from its entrails, cross crowned with roses, was the most emphasized type. It declares to the Companion that the "prevarication," of which the present state of man is the consequence and punishment, is none other than "the crime upon the person of the innocent which yet requires vengeance to the Eternal of the effusion of his blood" which is "a blood superior to all that of human nature."

But, after this profession of faith, which recalls the ambiguous Christology of the Reintegration by the connection established between the Passion and the murder of Hiram, the catechism is devoted to developing, in a most vague and fragmentary fashion, the esoteric knowledge of the candidate by furnishing him some glimpses on the mysticism of numbers and on the nature and consequences of the error of Adam.

It teaches to the new Companion that Two, "number of confusion," is represented by the two columns arranged in the Porch and which signify "the action by that of the North and the contraction (contrary action) by that of the South"; that the Quinary "explains (signifies) the degradation of the First Elect Man by the demonic power"; that the Senary "explains the emancipation" of the candidate, that is to say "the origin of his corporeal emanation, represented by the six circumferences of his admission into the Order" (sic); that the Septenary "explains his reconciliation" and that, consequently, the Companions work to acquire "the age of perfection, which is since (starting from) the number 5, from (passing through) 6 (material world) unto that of 7 (reconciliation) by the intervention of a Septenary Spirit."

On the other hand, the Companion has foreseen that his work "will be limited to knowing the virtue (power) of the First Elect Man, his ambition, his fall, and his punishment" and that above all he will have to acquire "the perfect knowledge of temporal matter," which task is already indicated to him by the allegorical formula, according to which, "he journeys upon the material triangle (world composed of the three fundamental substances) until the perfect expiation of his prevarication," and by the insignia of his grade, the triangle, "for it has no other attribute in the Order than that which his prevarication has procured for him." The heinous crime of which the Companion bears the suffering is recognized "by his spiritual privation represented by his corporeal prison"; therefore, his place in the Lodge is in the South "because it is the place that the G.A.O.T.U. has destined to the Companions of prevarication who have had the misfortune to fall prey to the iniquitous instructions and operations of the demon" and "the frightful dwelling of the first prevaricators against the cult of the Creator."

Nevertheless, the catechism makes to shine a glimmer of hope in the darkness where the Companion is presently plunged. If the candidate must acknowledge "that he has not seen his master"[1089] because he is not "reconciled," and because he is not "permitted (is not able) to name him until his perfect reconciliation," he is made to catch a glimpse of the moment when, having "acquired the promised age,"[1090] he will be allowed to see him and to know his name.

PARTICULAR MASTER

The indigence of this degree, whose catechism, reproduced by Papus[1091], indicates summarily the ritual of reception, is particularly striking, when one compares it to the richness of the papers on the Symbolic Master, whose ceremony of initiation, very dramatic, was of a nature to make a profound impression upon the candidate. The Particular Master evidently figures in the list of the Coën grades only to give the Class of the Porch the trinary organization whose model blue Masonry has furnished.

The officers of the Lodge of Particular Master were a Venerable Master of the Occident and two Surveillants. The Temple was illumined by three three-branched candelabras. The carpet depicted the three columns, the six circles, the branches of palm, cedar, olive, and willow from the carpet of the Apprentice to which was added a "bowl of earth" (terrestrial globe), a "brazen sea," a "flaming urn," "figures and characters," and "innumerable lights."

The candidate was introduced by a Particular Master. He was, following a staging utilized in several Scottish degrees, "as a villain that they led to torture, sorrowfully vested, the cord around the neck, the feet bare." His introducer had him "from the west to the North, to the South and from there to the Orient by trembling steps." The touch of recognition that he was taught was "the circle between the square and the compass."[1092]

A part of the instruction was of a rare insignificance from the intellectual and moral point of view where was repeated what had already been told to the Apprentice. The candidate learned, for example, that the Particular Masters travel by "trembling steps" in order to "make allusion to the fact that every man here below is in error and darkness"; that the attributes of the Particular Master: circle, square, and compass, designate: "firstly, the limits of the operations of the Particular Masters in the Order, secondly, the perfection of their operations, third, the route and conduct that they have to hold in all their temporal and spiritual actions"; that the duties specially imposed by the degree were to practice charity, to be an example to the inferior Brothers by a conduct perfectly conformed to the principles of the Order, to avoid the study of the sciences prohibited by the divine[1093] to flee "the crass ignorance," and finally to not abuse the authority conferred by the title of Master.

Returning without apparent motive to the symbolic interpretation of the Tree of Life, the catechism repeated to the Master what had been revealed previously to the Apprentice, which is, to wit, that the palm branch designated "the power of the living God," that of cedar "the power of the God of life," that of olive "the power of the Spirit," that of willow "the power of death or privation."

Some questions and responses referred nevertheless, in a more or less veiled manner, to the cosmological, anthropological, and penumatological doctrines of the Order. The Venerable Master "designated the thought of the Creator," the First Surveillant "his action," the Second Surveillant "his operation," The candidate passed from the triangle (terrestrial world) to the circles (whole of creation) and was notified that the "three degrees of the Class of the Porch represented the general terrestrial Temple." The Particular Master worked "with the knowledge of the subdivision of the temporal terrestrial matter," that is to say with the "knowledge of the three spiritous principles which compose the general terrestrial body, the celestial, and those of the particular bodies (organisms) permanent on the surface of the earth." The six "circles of expiation" recalled "the six powerful thoughts that the G.A.O.T.U. had employed for the construction of his universal Temple." The "bowl of earth" designated "the origin of the corporeal form of man"; the water (represented by the Brazen Sea) and the fire (represented by the flaming urn) were reminders of the "two elements that sustained it in its whole individual"; the figures and characters symbolized "the superior virtue of the different bodies (stars) superior to that of man," and the number of lights designated "the infinite number of spiritual agents which operate in the universal Temple," The Nonary, "essential number of the Particular Master represented three things: "the subjection of the Particular Master to the work of matter as imperfect being in the Order, the uncertainness of his temporal spiritual operations (because he was not yet completely initiated) and the reintegration of the principles of his corporeal individual." The three columns of the Temple designated "three different kinds of mysterious branches of acacia[1094]: French acacia, representing the Spiritual Elect; grafted acacia, representing his disciples; wild acacia, representing the unclean (uncultivated), errant, and vagabond (prey to error) profanes, scandalous among humans of equity (raising by their false opinions the indignation of the initiates)," Finally, the three-branched candlesticks, which lighted the Temple, represented "the three different classes of Spirits which direct and set in motion the general terrestrial Temple," The Companion and Master Coëns aimed, like the Apprentice, to awaken, by these sparse scraps of a theosophical system, the curiosity of the neophytes, but the final goal of the Order, that is to say the theurgical practices, was carefully left in the shadows. The Class of the Porch constituted a novitiate. The more or less quick taste that its members would bear witness to for mystical speculation would allow them to distinguish those who would be disposed to admitting the consequences that the Order derived therefrom, in other words the Spiritual Minors apt to practice the true divine cult by consecrating themselves to the Operations. This is what was expressed, in carefully weighed terms, by the conclusion of the catechism of the Particular Master in saying: "The Porch serves to rough out and perfect the workers of the Order in order to employ them for the rebuilding of the cult of the Creator, just as it was represented by that of the Temple of Solomon." These final words summed up the particular meaning given by the Order of Élus Coëns to the fundamental symbol of the whole of French Masonry.

CHAPTER II
The Masonic Rite: the High Coën Degrees

Above the Class of the Porch were four High Degrees which were entitled: Master Élu Coën, Grand Master Coën, Zorobabel, and Réau-Croix.

MASTER ÉLU COËN

In the first of the High Coën Degrees, of which we know only the catechism[1095], the Masonic staging became the accessory; it is no longer but a slight veil under which show through the theories of the Reintegration.

The emblems are, in part, borrowed from the degrees of Élu: black cord, death's head surmounted by three daggers; the nine-branched candlestick which lights the Lodge recalls the degree of Élu of Nine, first of the degrees of this family. The carpet depicts, like that of the Scottish Master or Master Architect, reproduced in 1746 by the Francs-Maçons Ecrasée, the two columns of the Temple broken with their capitals overturned. To these figures are added a compass and a square bound together, two triangles likewise bound, a "crossed globe," five "receptacles" (equilateral rectangles) drawn in a straight line, a globe surmounted by three tree branches, the chemical symbols of lead, gold, iron, and copper.

The two broken columns, which, in the Scottish Lodges, made allegorical allusion to the decline of Masonry, represented here the sin of the First Minor and its deadly consequences, that is to say, "the degradation of the power of the two corporeal beings represented by the two columns of the Porch of the Temple, of which the one in the North represents the masculine body and the other in the South represents the feminine body." The capitals detached from the columns "made allusion to the abandon and detachment that the good conductor Spirit (which guided the Minor in the good path) has made from man because of his prevarication and allows him to operate indifferently in error and darkness upon the surface of the earth."

The square and compass bound together "designated the intimate connection of the soul with the Spirit," the two triangles united designated the origin of the human body intimately tied to that of the general terrestrial, as having, the one and the other, the triangular form" (identical composition of the microcosm and the macrocosm form, the one and the other, from the three elements).

The four metals whose symbols were seen on the carpet represented: lead, "the condensation and gravity (weight) of matter," gold, "the sublimity of the spiritous essences," iron, "the solidity of its virtue" (density and impenetrability), copper, "the reversible curse that the Creator has placed upon it (of which it has been stricken for all its duration) after the prevarication of the First Elect Man."

The nine-branched candlestick represents: "the nine different spiritual agents which operate and enlighten in the three temporal material regions represented by the three different universal elements."

"The globe surmounted by three branches represents the satisfaction felt by the three different nations of the earth[1096] after their reconciliation, just as had been represented to us by Abraham, Isaac, and Jacob."

The ceremony of initiation, called "ordination," took place "in a Temple regularly assembled by the divine spiritual thought, action, and operation." It borrowed from the reception of the Symbolic Master the ritual act which spread the candidate upon the carpet of the Lodge, but this remembrance of a traditional custom was accompanied by details whose commentary given by the catechism made the mystical significance to stand out. The candidate, "placed in a decent fashion, but the whole time the soul seized with fear,"[1097] was, "laid down in three circumferences forming a perfect receptacle, resting upon a double equilateral triangle and seconded (flanked) by four circles of correspondence of operation." He received six "marks": on the head, the two hands, the two feet and "towards the heart."[1098] Standing again, he feigns, on the order of his instructor, to be given three dagger strikes: one at the throat, one at the site of the heart, one at the lower abdomen, and he throws a fourth strike towards the earth. He then traveled "in circumference formed by 9 or 27," that is to say he described a circle by making 9 or 27 steps "in the form of a perfect square and the sword (dagger) in his hand."

The catechism taught him the symbolic meaning of the marks and strikes of the dagger: the mark upon the head "designated to heaven (indicated to the Spirits) that his tribute had satisfied (that he had payed tribute to) the divine justice of the Creator for his reconciliation"; that upon the left hand "designated the tribute that the inhabitants of the South (the demons) pay still to the divine justice"; the one upon the right hand "designated the tribute that the inhabitants of the northern terrestrial region (fallen Minors) have payed for their spiritual affiliation"; that upon the feet "designated the seals that the Creator caused to be placed upon matter at the time of its undifferentiated state in order to render it susceptible to retaining an impression on behalf of the different bodies which would come out of it according to the will of the Creator"[1099] the one upon "the heart designated the power of the different spiritual agents that the Creator had marked by his invisible seal in order to cooperated with the spiritous essences of the first matter[1100] from where all the material and temporal bodies are emanated." The four strikes of the dagger "signify the reconciliation that he (the candidate) made from every species of knowledge and other matter contrary to the divine law and to the permanent order (sorcery and alchemy) for the Orient, the South, the North, and the West."

If the papers of the Master Élu Coën had held to these dispersed and fragmentary notions on the cosmogony and pneumatology, the catechumen would not have had the impression of having crossed the Porch, but they were only asides, and the catechism made him take a step towards the sanctuary by revealing to him two essential doctrines of the Order, which is, namely, its concept of esoteric Christianity that it gave as the true interpretation of the murder of Hiram, fundamental theme of the degree of Symbolic Master, and its theory on the faculty granted to the Spiritual Minor to succeed in identifying himself with the Spiritual Elect or Reconciler.

With even greater prudence than the Reintegration, but in terms that would leave no doubt in the candidates capable of some reflection, the Instruction assimilated under the name of Perfect Elect Master[1101], the prophet Elijah and Jesus Christ, all while carefully avoiding to name once this latter. If it declared that the name of the Perfect Elect Master was "Hrlij in Hebrew or Heli in the common tongue, that is to say: Receptacle of the divinity or dedication of his own works," all that it said on the Jewish prophet was applied to the historic Christ. The death's head surmounted by three daggers[1102] "represents the thought, action, and operation of the enemies of the Élus chosen by the divine power, just as it is properly represented by the three nations which have delivered their blows upon the Perfect Master, that is to say the

Hebrew, the Galilean, I will say nothing about the third."[1103] The Lodge of Master Élus Coëns is opened "at the ninth hour of the three final days when the Reconciler finished all his temporal spiritual operations on behalf of the men of the earth." It is closed at the third hour of the day "in order to allude to the withdrawal that the disciples of the Perfect Elect Master made before the consummation of his operations" (the three days separating the Crucifixion and the Ascension).

The black band, upon which are depicted the receptacles, signifies "the frightful dwelling of the men of matter, in which the Perfect Elect Master has operated the reconciliation of the profane mortals." The five receptacles represent "the four operations that the divine Elect has made in the four principal regions (the four cardinal points embracing the universe) and the fifth, that which he has operated on behalf of his disciples to the shame of the demons" (Transfiguration). The "crossed globe" symbolizes "the sensible pain endured by all nature by the (as a result of) blows that were delivered upon the person of the Elect cherished by the Creator." The square represents "the sublime perfection of his virtue (strength) and his powerful words (miracles accomplished by Christ) with which he has reconciled (by manifesting the divine power in a sensible fashion) the earth with man and all with the G.A.O.T.U. The Temple (the Coën Lodge) "represents the place consecrated to the operations[1104] of the Master Élus, just as the Perfect Master has designated it himself to his disciples by his operations made upon the general terrestrial Temple" (the earth). The three circles of the carpet "represent the three gifts that the Perfect Master had given to his first disciples, which are admiration (vision of Christ), understanding (intelligence of the evangelical parables) and contemplation" (vision of the Transfiguration). The receptacle in which are inscribed the three concentric circumferences "designate the place destined (predestined) on which is operated all things on behalf of humanity and the universality (universe), just as every divine spiritual thing was operated on the body of the Perfect Master before his death."

If the Master Élu claims to be 3, 5, 6, 7, 4, and 8 years old, it is first to "recall the different divine spiritual operations that the Perfect Elect Master has operated towards the Creator on behalf of the universal nature,"[1105] then "to allude to the number of times that he has set to fulfill all his duties of Man-God and divine among humans."[1106]

Finally, the catechism teaches the candidate under what form men know the "four powerful words" that the Perfect Elect Master or Reconciler "had received from the G.A.O.T.U. to his destiny" (when he had received from him his mission) and that he "rendered after having consecrated them (having made use thereof) for the manifestation of the divine glory and justice"; they are pronounced, in human language, "Heli, Lama, Saba, Tanie."

That the Master Élu Coën may hope to be raised, by a persevering work, into the hierarchy of beings to the top where soars the Perfect Elect Master, that the catechism called Elijah, but whose terrestrial life, death, and mystical acts recall so clearly those of Jesus Christ, is what resulted from the secret name that he bore and from the numbers that were "essential" to him. "He learned indeed that he was called mystically "Roux" in the common language and "Réau" in Hebrew, that is to say: "Man-God of the earth, elevated above all temporal spiritual sense on which the glory and justice of the Creator are operated." The numbers of his degree being 4, 7, and 8 because "the Quaternary makes allusion to the origin and the power of the Élu, the Septenary to the powerful spiritual faculties that he has received from the Creator since his emancipation, and the Octonary to the double power of the Elect cherished by the Most High when he lives operated (came to operate?) the reconciliation of humans"; now "every Master Élu may procure for himself a similar property and virtue"; therefore, admission to the degree was qualified "by entry into the circle of reconciliation."

The adept to whom is made so important a revelation is henceforth an active member of the mystical society. He must, more than ever, "remove himself (keep himself far from) every clandestine (Masonic) society, giving apocryphal instructions," "to avoid every place of profanation and prostitution of spiritual things and of himself," in order to "never remove himself from (show himself unworthy of) the ordination that he has received," and his first duty is "a perfect and humble obedience towards the principles of the Order." He also knows "the system of living in the Order according to what he has been ordered by the Perfect Master" (alimentary prohibitions) and he must "observe it scrupulously."

However, if the final goal was indicated to him, the path leading there, that is to say the means to obtain the "reconciliation," remained unknown to him. He knew that the First Elect Man (Adam) had lost "the august name of Réau because the determined ambition to elevate himself above the one who had constituted him in virtue and authority over every creature has put him in the case of deviating from (losing) his power, and by these means (consequently) he was rendered an ordinary man from the invisible (immaterial) man that he would have been." But the Master Élu Coën was unaware of the means to recover this inheritance, so that the name of Réau which had been granted him was yet only a promise whose realization he could not foresee. He had to acknowledge that he was unaware of the true pronunciation of the "four powerful words" of the Perfect Elect Master, and the catechism revealed to him neither the nature nor the effect of the Operations. If it was said to him on the subject of the four Circles of Correspondence surrounding the three circumferences where he had received his ordination, that they "represented the spiritual inhabitants of the four different celestial regions which have assisted spiritually in all the temporal spiritual operations that the Master has made in order to remind man of his first principle of virtue, authority, and temporal spiritual power," it was not indicated to him what manner these Spirits, in being manifested to the operant by the Passes, announced to him his reconciliation. Moreover, the catechism recalled to him that he was yet but a "Temporal Master Élu" that is to say ever a prisoner of matter.

GRAND MASTER COËNS
called GRAND ARCHITECTS[1107]

The importance that the adept attached to this degree is shown by the frequent mentions made to it in their correspondence. It results, it is true, from a letter of Pasqually[1108] that those to whom it was conferred were still only "simple emulators," but the word itself designated the disciples destined to receive a complete initiation, therefore the holders of the degree were called in the Order "apprentice Réau-Croix."[1109] The teaching that they were given, the ceremonial of their meetings, the devotions and the mystical exercises which were prescribed to them constituted a theoretical and practical training in the Operations proper.

Of the Masonic forms there no longer existed but a remembrance. This is already indicated in the title of the degree which considers the name of Grand Architect only as a simple "nickname" given to the Grand Master Coën in order to attach it outwardly to the hierarchy of Scottish degrees among which the title of

Architect had been quite popular[1110] and enjoyed still in 1772 a great prestige. The catechism mentioned neither solemn and dramatic entrance, nor terrifying oath, nor complicated travels. The Masonic "reception" is replaced by a veritable "ordination"; the candidate is not admitted into a meeting, formed of Brothers, by the dignitaries of a Lodge, he is "ordained and operated on by the thought and will of the Eternal, and by the power, word, and intention of his deputies." These representatives of God are five in number: a "Grand Master" assisted by four "Surveillants," but, in a difference from Masonic receptions where the president is content to have the officers placed under his orders to act, "the Grand Master," said Pasqually's secretary, "alone makes the openings, instructions, gives the words and the batteries in the Lodge" and the other officers "are only figures of the spiritual subjects (representatives of the Spirits) that the Grand Master makes to act according to his will."[1111] Furthermore, the candidate could, as we shall soon see, be ordained face to face by the Grand Master.

The catechism does not speak of the carpet, but, if it existed, it would only represent the objects of which the Instruction gives a mystical interpretation: ark, tabernacle, cisterns, seven-branched candlestick, tablets of the Law, to the exclusion of emblems properly Masonic, on which it observes the most profound silence.

The reminder of the sign of recognition, which belongs obligatorily to all Masonic catechisms, is considered negligible; the catechism of the degree says only of this sign: "One gives it if he is ordained."[1112]

The reception to the degree of Grand Architect was performed, in principle, in "entire ceremonial," that is to say in the presence of the holders of this degree, but, when the Lodge was not disposed of a sufficient personnel, it was a "pure and simple ordination" of which the sole actors and spectators were the officiant and candidate.[1113]

The "simple ordination"[1114] was given in a sole circle illumined by one candle placed "between the two words that were traced there." This candle had been lit with "new fire." The candidate was kept in the circle, facing East, head lowered, kneeling on both knees, and the hands crossed over the chest. The officiant depicted on the head, two times, that is to say successively with each hand, the triangle "designated (shown on the carpet) in the grand ceremonial." He then depicted on his forehead, by drawing another triangle, the triangular plaque worn by the High Priest of Israel. Then he laid his squared right hand on the forehead while pronouncing the prayers and the consecrated words. The candidate was then raised, taken out of the circle, washed his hands and perfumed the four corners of the room by beginning at the prescribed side. During this time the officiant made a prayer in the East corner, in a low voice and prostrated. The text of this prayer, called "surety," was left to the choice of the officiant: "he would produce it according to his desires and his needs, or those of his fellow-men, and this was the true moment to request graces"[1115]: The candidate, having re-entered the circle, resumed his previous posture, and the officiant pronounced the formula of ordination: "I ordain you and institute you Grand Architect of the Order," while joining there "the words and prayers which are therein attached." He communicated, finally, to the newly received the "signs, grips, and steps," and passed to him the cord distinctive of the degree. As regards the "words and phrases," they were: "Iain, Iva, Moseph, Aaron, Ur, Betsaleel, Heibli, Laugai, Harmon, Zezbaoth, Abigai[1116] the officiant was not obliged to communicate them all and the Superiors left it to his prudence to choose those that he judged suitable to make known to the one that he had just ordained.[1117] The Grand Architect recently received was presented and recognized as such at the first meeting following his ordination.[1118]

The "grand ceremonial of the Grand Architect" is known to us, and very imperfectly, only by some sparse information in the letters where Saint-Martin transmitted to Willermoz the instructions of Pasqually.[1119]

The Grand Master opened the Lodge by the battery of the degree, which was in principle 101 knocks, but he was allowed to abridge it "by describing a square and one knock at the center."[1120] He "consecrated" the ceremonies by reciting entirely the Psalm Quam dilecta. Placing himself then standing at the center of the room, he exorcized the four circles drawn in the corners and called "angles," by "conjuring and quickly molesting the Evil and thereby containing it by some powerful words that he attached to each angle." This molestation was "arbitrary," that is to say that the text thereof was left to the inspiration of the officiant and drew from his great strength of intention "which gave virtue to the words pronounced."[1121]

The candidate was censed having "dedicated eight years in expiation in order to merit his ordination" and had, consequently, the mystical age of eighty years, that is to say the Octonary multiplied by the Denary, "mysterious number" of which Pasqually often signals the virtue. He was received "at the center of a shining light," that is to say that the Lodge was illumined by numerous "stars" (candles) of which we know neither the number nor the arrangement, because the "table" of the Lodge of Grand Architect, drawn by Pasqually in May 1771 and sent to Lyon the same month[1122] has not reached us. The candidate was "assisted by four Grand Surveillants placed at the center of the four circles of correspondence of the Particular Temple" (Lodge) and which, representing "the four celestial regionary chiefs," served during the ordination "to avert and dissipate by their spiritual fires (perfumes) every kind of imperfect beings (demons) who would have been able to pollute him."[1123]

The ritual acts were likely the same as those constituting the simple ordination. The catechism is mute in this regard and is content to indicate that the candidate was "consecrated by names and words of power which made allusion to those that the Creator gave to Moses, his Grand Master Coën, in order to make them reversible and to consecrate his fellow-man to the divine spiritual operations." Among these "words of power" figured the mystical numbers 3, 4, 6, 7, and 8, the Denary being reserved to the Powerful Master.

The patron of the degree was Moses, considered as Spiritual Elect and organizer of the true divine cult among the Hebrews, and the Instruction was devoted above all to revealing the esoteric meaning of the sacred furniture that he had consecrated to the service of the Eternal. The ark, that Moses, whose name signifies: "Issued from the waters," had constructed, was represented as a repetition of that of Noah, or "Saved from the waters," in which "there were only material tabernacles (Minors) to be witness to the divine justice that was exercised upon the Children of God become Children of Men by the covenant that they had made with the daughters of Cain." The ark of Noah prophesied the one that Moses had constructed in order for Israel to come out from the justice (domination) of the demons, to submit to the conduct and justice of the Eternal, "which is represented to us by the different animals placed in the ark and confirmed by the different nations that the ark of Moses has saved from the anger of the Creator, that one may consider (which is represented to us) by the brute animals making (which made) allusion to the idolaters and the reasonable animals to the Children of God.

"The ark being the true figure of the general terrestrial body, by the same reason the Tabernacle is that which designates the particular place where the Creator communicated with his first creature without being confused with the earth."[1124] "This has been confirmed by Moses when he entered into the Tabernacle in order to communicate with the Eternal, to receive his orders, and to manifest them for the greater glory of the divinity." "Moses always kept himself in front of the Tabernacle when he spoke to Israel, in order to receive all the necessary intelligence to make Israel retain the impression of what he wished to communicate to them by order of the Eternal," for "the Tabernacle was the place consecrated to be the deposit of all the divine, spiritual, temporal, material, and corporeal virtues and powers." This Tabernacle had four doors "which alluded to the quadruple divine essence, to the four powers given to man, and to the four celestial regionary powers or four principal grand chiefs operating the universe." "The Tabernacle of Moses being a true representation of our material Tabernacle (our body), the figure of these four doors is found: at the head, archetype of the thought, which corresponds to the door of the East; the power of understanding given to the sense of hearing corresponds to the door of the North; the contemplation given to the sense of sight corresponds to the door of the South; the word given to the strength of the operation (word operating with a sovereign strength) corresponding to the door of the West."

There are four sorts of tabernacles in the grand universal temple: two material ones which are "the particular body of man and woman," the third is the one that Moses constructed temporarily, the fourth "is the temporal spiritual one called the Sun, that the G.A.O.T.U. has destined to contain in himself the sacred names and words of temporal and spiritual reaction, distinguished by Wisdom (star whose role is well known by the initiates), torch of temporal universal life."

The "seven-branched candlestick of Moses makes allusion to the seven celestial powers[1125], to the seven spiritual gifts (sacraments) and to the seven operations that the Eternal manifested for the creation of this universe, which has been represented by the seven-branched candlestick that was placed in the temple of Solomon and perpetuated unto our day by that which exists among the Romans."

The four great cisterns placed "at the four corners of the Temple of Solomon" alludes "to the four principal grand chiefs operating the universe, and also to the four temporal high priests who have operated the divine cult among the humans, represented by the four Evangelists who have carried the different spiritual operations to the four parts of the world." The four principal chiefs were: "Rhéty under Adam, Enoch under the posterity of Seth, Melchizedek under the posterity Abraham, and Christ on behalf of every created being." The four high priests "who have operated the divine cult among the humans are Zalmun among the Ishmaelites, Rharamoz[1126] among the Egyptians, Aaron among the Israelites, and Paul among the Christians.[1127]

The duties and functions of the Grand Architects, styled "Conductors of the Holy Ark and Guardians of the doors of the Tabernacle," were to "work on the purification of the material senses in order to render them susceptible to participating in the different operations of the Spirit (to observe rigorously the ascetic system of the Élus Coëns), to construct new tabernacles and to rebuild the old ones (to show the route to the Spiritual Minors or restore them on the good path), at the example of the ancient Grand Masters, in order to dispose them and render them fit to receive among them the different words of power which govern and set into motion the different actions of every created being (to put them in a state to command the Spirits in order to obtain Passes), to paint and trace all the emblems of the Order, when it will be ordered to offer perfumes (to draw the circles and the figures on the floor of the Lodge before the meetings and ordinations), to consecrate their fellow-men into the circles of Master Coëns (contribute to the reception of candidates to the inferior degree), to apply the powerful word to the four celestial and three terrestrial regions, and to keep careful watch over the ceremonial of the temporal spiritual operations" (fulfill the office of Grand Surveillants during the ordinations of their degree and to assure the regularity of the ritual acts.

Instructors of the Master Coëns and acolytes of the head of the Lodge during the solemn meetings, the Grand Architects exercise their function of exorcist at fixed dates. "They operate their virtue and power (in order to repel the demons) on Wednesday and Saturday each week, every month of the year and in all perilous circumstances where the case requires them to carry out their works and to impose their squared hands upon all the things that are suitable to their operations (exorcism of objects and beings by the laying on of hands). They may be summoned to extraordinary meetings, for, "though time, days, months, and the year are limited, one opens the doors of the Universal Temple (Lodge of Grand Architect) in all perilous circumstances in this valley of tears." Finally, they "serve their Powerful Master" in a most special manner "six days for the two equinoxes, twelve days for the two solstices, fourteen days for the perfect operation of the two equinoxes, fourteen days for that of the two solstices."

But, if the Grand Architect has, like the Levites, access into the Temple, he is not admitted into the sanctuary. He knows how to drive out the perverse Spirits, but he is unaware of the art of summoning the good Spirits. The work to which he is delivered at the equinoxes and solstices is a preparation to the Operations proper. He is still, as said by Pasqually[1126], only an "apprentice Réau-Croix." If he has the right to "knock on all four doors of the Tabernacle," he does not have the power to open them all as Moses did whenever he wanted; he may only open that of the North (to receive the secret and oral teachings), and close that of the South (to defend the beings and things against the demons) "because," the Instruction said to him, "the Grand Master Coëns of our Order are still only temporal beings (prisoners of matter) and they will be able to have a similar power only when they will become, at the example of the first Sages, spiritual men," so this transformation requires a course of seven years[1129], necessary "for the perfect operation of reconciliation."

GRAND ELECT OF ZOROBABEL
so-called KNIGHTS OF THE EAST[1130]

This degree has a rather disconcerting physiognomy: instead of bringing to the candidate new revelations on the doctrines of the Order, it outlines a return backwards in reviving one of the themes of that same Masonry that the previous degree had nearly completely abandoned, and, if it interprets mystically the legend of the Knight of the East, it no longer speaks of the theurgical practices which were the principal occupation of the Grand Architects. The newly received had to have the sensation of walking in place, instead of making steps forward, as he could legitimately hope.

This sudden stop upon the path leading to the final goal may be explained by three kinds of considerations. After having borrowed from the Masonic Élus and Architects degrees their titles and some of their emblems, Pasqually could not, under pain of appearing incomplete, seem to ignore a degree so known and so popular that all the Systems of High Grades regularly had it represented in their hierarchy. In the second place, the role that Zorobabel, principal personage of the Scottish degree, played in the biblical narrative's fit in so well with the character of the Spiritual Elect that the Reintegration attributed to the Jewish heroes, the liberation of the Hebrews captive at Babylon, their return to Jerusalem, the reconstruction of the Temple, and the restoration of a canvas so rich for the esoteric commentaries, that Pasqually has not been able to resist the temptation to embroider there some of these arabesque allegories for which he had a determined penchant. Finally, it is possible that the head of the Order had judged it prudent to have a respite for some time from the practical exercises, and to return to the fundamental theories before proceeding to the definitive admission to the supreme degree of Réau-Croix. The wait imposed on the disciples was a final trial that allowed him to choose the subjects before whom he would be permitted to raise all the veils.

The degree of Knight of the East was supposed to be so perfectly known to the candidate, that the catechism of the Grand Elect made general allusion to its legend without any more explanation than if it were a question of the Illiad or the Odyssey. As the erudition of the present readers would probably be found wanting on so particular a question, it is perhaps not useless to give an idea of the legend and distinctive characteristics of this chivalric degree.

The first edition of the Book of Constitutions (1723) named Serubabel, called by the French Jerobabel or Zorobabel, "Grand Master of the Masons who had reconstructed the second Temple upon the ruins of the first." In the second edition (1738) the head of the Return became "Provincial Grand Master" of the "Grand Master" Cyrus who had him appoint a "Deputy Grand Master" in the person of the High Priest Joshua.[1131] Scottish Masonry had seized on this information to construct a degree which became the prototype for the degrees called chivalric, because they made of the Masonic society an Order of military and medieval origin conferring nobility on its members, whatever were their rank in profane society. The ceremony of reception of the Knight of the Sword or East simulated the combat that the candidate, representing Zorobabel, had had to endure on the bridge crossing the river Starburzarnai in order to clear by force a passage for the Jews returning to Jerusalem after the end of the Captivity. In recompense for this exploit, the candidate was dubbed a knight in all its forms; he was then proclaimed Knight Mason in memory of the role that the members of the degree had ostensibly played in protecting against the enemies of the elect people, the workers occupied with the reconstruction of the Temple. If he carried the trowel in his left hand, while his right was armed with the sword, it was, said the Instruction, in order to recall that he had in passing worked with his hands "to maintain the equality with the Brothers." Ennobled by his promotion, he left the green, ordinary color of the anterior High Grades, for the Red, "true Scottish color" and took his place in the "Tribunal of the Sovereigns of the Lodges" in order to "rule over the workers like Solomon, Hiram, and Moabon."

Of these two word-types of the Masonic degree: Zorobabel and Knight of the East, the papers of the Grand Elect were devoted only to the first and, to better mark that he rejected the chivalric character so marked in the original, he was not content to suppress every war-like staging, he had it say expressly in its title that the Grand Elect of Zorobabel were "so-called," that is to say only for the non-initiated Masons, Knights of the East. Whereas in the Scottish degree the chief of the Return, represented by the candidate, was uniquely a warrior who had conducted his troops to victory, in the Coën degree, Zorobabel, manifestation of the Spiritual Elect, is personified by the president of the assembly and he proceeds with the reception. The two Surveillants, who over there represented the generals Nabuzardin and Mithridate, are called here Zoroal and Zoroael, names whose mystical meaning, for not being very clear, is no less certain.

The catechism first brings to light the secret significance of the legend of the Knight of the East. Prompted, the candidate declared that "the intimate alliance with Assyria with the unfortunate remains of Israel was not ignored by him," that this alliance consisted in the liberty that Assyria had given to the tribes of Israel after the expiration of their captivity, and that the king had lent every sort of relief to the Hebrews whom he had just granted liberty in spite of all those who were opposed to them. He claimed to be informed of the circumstances of the passage over the bridge of the river Starburzarnai, but he added that he knew the symbolic meaning of the expedition of Zorobabel "by the intimate relation and intimate connection of correspondence that he has there of all the spiritual and temporal operations of Zorobabel with ours." He layed out that the alliance of the king of Assyria[1132] with Zorobabel was, in the common sense, "the liberty that Assyria has given to the tribes of Israel after the expiration of their captivity," but that, in the esoteric sense, it made "allusion to that which the Eternal will make with every created being after the expiration of time and their perfect reconciliation." This is what represents allegorically "the agreement that Zorobabel (Spiritual Elect) made with Cyrus (the Creator) and the fruit of their operations which induced the king to lend every sort of relief to the tribes of Israel to whom he had just given liberty (reconciliation), in spite of all those who were opposed to them" (the demons).

The Masonic legend furnished to Pasqually a pretext to return to two themes already exploited in the preceding degrees: the manifestations of the metaphysical Christ and the spiritualization of the Masonic motif of the construction of the Temple. He adds to this one of the fundamental theories of his mystical system, that is to say the thesis according to which the knowledge and practice of the true divine cult have been removed from the Hebrews and perpetuated by a secret tradition of which the Order was the unique repository.

Zorobabel is "the type of Christ" and his operations are "the type of every redemption." To say that "the wise and pacific Zorobabel has fought and conquered at the passage of the redoubtable bridge of the river Starburzarnai" is to say that Christ has vanquished the demons, for the name of the river signifies "passage of confusion," since it is equivalent to the demonic number 5 "just as the counting of this name represents to us: s=1, tar-2, bu=3, zar=4, nai=5."[1133] On the other hand, if the tradition relates that Zorobabel has destroyed the arches of the bridge without the aid of tools composed of metals and left intact the seventh[1134] we must understand that it is a question of six creative thoughts whose work will disappear at the moment of the reintegration of all the beings and of all things into their first principle, which constitutes the redemption, and that the seventh arch left intact symbolizes the absolute existence of the Spirit, without which nothing in the entire universe can be born or exist, so that all the sensible phenomena are only appearances born from his imagination and which will be dissipated as promptly as they have been conceived.[1135]

Just as Zorobabel "had in his power the purely spiritual means of material destruction," so was the Temple of Solomon constructed without "the use of metal tools by the unknown workers who cut the stones in the quarries,"[1136] therefore the candidate declares that he has labored, neither materially, nor mystically, at the reconstruction of this edifice, because "the rebuilding of this temple was only the figure of that of our material temple (Spiritual Minor) that the Spirit must rebuild, not being within the power of man to make a similar re-edification."

The thesis according to which Moses had not been authorized to make known to the Hebrews the true Law is connected in an artificial way to the history of Zorobabel, It had been announced at the end of the Instruction of the previous degree which asked of the candidate: "To what alludes the broken tablets of Moses and those that he brought down to the Israelites?" To which the new Grand Master Élu Coën responded: "I am unaware of it, remaining in the power of (for reason unknown except to) the one who is before me (the one who possesses a degree superior to mine)." The catechism of the Grand Elect gave the key to the problem.

The candidate declares that "although child of the Hebrews and under the election of Zorobabel" (chosen by Zorobabel), he is called mystically Israel in remembering the struggle that Jacob sustained against the Spirit, and when he was conquered. Marked on the left leg after his defeat, he had his name of Jacob changed into that of Israel "which means strong against God, having sinned against the Spirit." "The change of name prophesied the change of the divine Law that the Eternal caused to come out of the Hebrews in order to pass to the enemies of Israel, among whom it resides still. This event had been predicted by Moses when he broke the first tablets of the divine Law that he had received from the Creator on behalf of the Hebrews." Moses has indeed made known a divine Law, "but it was not completely like the first that he would have given them." One recognizes the inferiority of the one in that "the thought and hand of man had not been exercised (had not manifested in the redaction of the dogmas and practices of the cult) in the first as he had made in the second." The breaking of the first tablets of the Law indicated "that Israel remained purely (solely) under the ceremonial and conventional law (Jewish cult celebrated in the Temple of Solomon) without power to operate the divine cult, the true Law being taken out of their hands." Likewise, if "the veil that Moses placed over his face when he gave the second law to Israel made allusion to the veil that the Spirit takes when it wishes to communicate with the one who calls for it under the corporeal veil (glorious form of the Spirit manifesting itself to the Spiritual Minor)," it equally signifies "that Israel has received from Moses only a veiled law, because the Hebrew people doubted the power of the Eternal and that of its conductor," and "the errant Hebrews are the type of the error of the men of the world deprived of the divine cult and of the divinity, and who are spiritual errants like Israel is (since the dispersion of the Jews) in the temporal"; therefore the candidate declares not to belong "to the tribes of Judah and Benjamin or to that of Levi who were captives in Babylon, belonging (because they belong) to a tribe that always enjoyed its liberty, that of Ephraim, the last of the Hebrews and the first of the Elect.[1137]

The duties of the Grand Elect were indicated in a manner much more vague than had been those of the Grand Master Coëns. They had "to combat their material passions in order to render them spiritual and vanquish the enemies of truth and those of liberty by the example of Zorobabel who has fought and conquered." The genre of their works was symbolized rather enigmatically by "the water, the earth, and the fire," which seems to allude to the operations of exorcism consisting in tracing geometric figures, in lustrations, and in censings. The period of those works were "the whole seven months on the seventh day of the first quarter of the moon, which is from the seventh day of the first quarter of the moon of March until the seventh day of the first quarter of the moon of October, time when Israel had received the second law and came out of the towns of Egypt."

The initiation granted to the Grand Elect does not seem to have been much superior to the one that they had received as Grand Architects. Their "numbers of power" are those of the previous degree: "three, seven, and eight, which make allusion to the terrestrial spiritual power, to the temporal spiritual one, and to that of the double divine spiritual power." It is true that the mystical age of seventy-seven years, which is attributed to them in the Temple (Lodge), recalls that of Zorobabel when he brought the Jews back to Jerusalem, for he "was seven years old when he was subjected to the captivity which lasted seventy years," and these seventy-seven years "make allusion to the doubly powerful Spirit ruling in the lower world, represented by the double character of septenary power, and represented by the perfect age of Zorobabel and by his spiritual reign." It is by virtue of this double power that the holders of the degree have been consecrated by Zorobabel (the officiant) "that is to say, enemy of confusion,"[1138] with the assistance of Zoroal (First Surveillant) or "enemy of matter," and Zoroael (Second Surveillant) or "protector of the Minors as friend of Wisdom." But this double power is not that of the Reconciler, that is to say the Octonary, it is only an iteration of the Septenary, number of the sidereal Spirits. The aid of these Spirits, for as powerful as they are, does not suffice to shelter the Spiritual Minors from the demonic attacks. Therefore, the Grand Elect must recognize that they have not yet "reconstructed their material temple" (recovered the mystical purity allowing them to communicate with the divine) "by the force of the opponents set against this rebuilding, (force) prophesied by the multitude of those who were opposed to our passage of the river and to our freedom."[1139]

Their "rank," scarcely more elevated than that of the Grand Architects, making them simply "friends of God, protectors of virtue, and professors of truth," did not render them yet worthy to engage in the Operations proper. This is what the catechism obliges them to confess, in terms whose exact meaning would otherwise escape them. It made them admit that they did not know what instruments Zorobabel had used to break the first arches of the bridge (ceremonies of the Operations that put the man of matter in communication with the Spirits) "since the delivered have not had any knowledge" (the Spiritual Minors, even freed from the domination of the demons, do not know by themselves the true divine cult), learned that "their material Temple was not rebuilt" (their body was not purified by the "regimen of life") and that they "had not yet offered burnt offerings to the Lord" (received the ordination of the Réau-Croix).

∴

RÉAU-CROIX

It does not seem that the degree of Réau-Croix, which constituted a secret and supreme degree of initiation, had been organized on the Masonic model. Before the adept, admitted finally into the sanctuary, the mysterious Isis is stripped completely of the borrowed ornaments which had masked her up until then. He now knew how to pronounce that "Lost Word" that the children of Hiram strove to retrieve. The emblems of Symbolic Masonry, the legends of the Scottish degrees, all these symbols, of which he now knew the mystical meaning, no longer had interest for him. The fact that the ordination of Réau-Croix was only able to take place at the equinox distinguished it essentially from the Masonic receptions which, even in the high grades, had no fixed date.

The circular sent on April 30, 1772, by Pasqually to announce the reception of the "Emulators" Saint-Martin and de Sère to the supreme degree is conceived in purely mystical terms. It said, without employing any of the formulas utilized by the Masons, that after having "been passed and passed again by our ordinary and extraordinary scrutiny, and consequently by the orders that we have been given,"[1139] the candidates have been "received and ordained R.R.++, admitted into our virtuous[1140] circumferences (here two concentric circles) of the Réau++++" and that they have been "delivered four circles (here four concentric circles) in order to make use thereof as will be suitable to him." The "ordinary characters" that authenticate the circular recall nothing of the Masonic emblems; they have an air of family with the mysterious designs that one sees on the pentacles and amulets of the Kabbalists and occultists of the Renaissance.[1141]

CHAPTER III
Mystical Masonry and the Masonry of Adoption

Though the Order of Élus Coëns be the completed type of the occultist Masonic Rite, it does not constitute a unique phenomenon, for numerous were the Degrees of mystical tendency and, as original as had been the Society founded by Pasqually by its theurgical practices, it presented no fewer traits of resemblance, secondary but rather striking, with some Scottish degrees of this category.

The most well-known and widespread of these degrees is the one that was entitled "Chevalier de Rose-Croix" [Knight of the Rose-Croix]. The name of Rose-Croix, which over-excited the curiosity of the public, cultivated during the first third of the 17th century, and which preserves still today prestige among the Masons who are lovers of secret traditions[1142] is an excellent example of the prodigious vitality of the enigmatic works that are lent to all the interpretations, able to symbolize all the tendencies, bright and empty mirrors which reflect with an equal complacency the images created by the plays of the imagination.

According to two little works appearing in Paris in 1614 and 1615, the *Réforme Générale du Monde Entier* and the *Fama Fraternitatis Rosae Crucis*, the Rose-Croix formed a sort of confraternity whose principal occupation was to freely attend to the sick. But, as it was asserted at the same time that these charitable men possessed secret knowledge of the most sublime kind, they soon had a reputation of knowing how to make gold and the panacea, and of being astrologers, Kabbalists, and theurgists. The character and aims of the Society of the Rose-Croix, whose existence was generally held as real, would raise noisy controversies. Defended by avowed occultists like the English physician, chemist, and theosopher Robert Fludd, the Society was attacked violently, in the name of religion, by the Catholic theologians, who treated its members as heretics, magicians, and Kabbalists, and by the Protestant theologians, who suspected them of having parted ways with the Jesuits. In the polemic, which ranged from 1615 to 1623, notably taking part in France, the Jesuits Garasse, Gautia and Robert, Gabriel Naudé, physician of Louis XIII, Fr. Mersenne, the Abbé Gassendi; in Germany the pastor Daniel Kramer, the physician and chemist Libau, the illustrious astronomy Kepler. Descartes, desirous to make a personal opinion on the matter, sought, during the stay he made in Germany from 1619 to 1623, to enter into relations with the Rose-Croix which were said to exist beyond the Rhine. He declared, upon his return to France, that he had learned nothing for certain concerning them, but his researches had already earned him the reputation of belonging to the Rosicrucian confraternity and, forty-two years after his death, his fierce detractor Huet, bishop of Avranches, accused him in his *Memoires nouveaux pour servir à l'histoire du Cartésianisme* (1692) of having been received into the Rose-Croix in Sweden and of having, at the instigation of his Brothers, abandoned geometry in order to devote himself exclusively to chemistry, medicine, and the Kabbalah.

In the 18th century the name of Rose-Croix was currently employed in England to designate the hermetisists, and, when Freemasonry began to speak of it, all those who were intrigued by the Masonic secret and who suspected the Masons of cultivating the occult sciences, turned the members of Lodges into disciples or successors of the Brethren of the Rose-Croix. An alchemist, author of a treatise on the panacea, the *Long Livers* (1722), that he dedicated to the Freemasons, recalled, in signing his dedication by the fictive name of Eugène Philalète Jr., the pseudonym adopted by the adept Thomas Vaughan when he had published in 1652 an English translation of the *Fama*, and the booklet borrowed from the same work a citation from the celebrated alchemical album known under the name of *Liber Mutus*. In 1724, *The Secret History of the Freemasons*, reprinted in 1725, represented the Rose-Croix and the Freemasons as members of the same confraternity or of the same Order. An article in the *Daily Journal* from September 5, 1730, reproduced by the Daily News on September 24th of the same year, claimed that the Freemasons sought to persuade the public that they descended from the Rose-Croix, though they had only borrowed their signs of recognition and their emblems.

In France, Scottish Masonry had taken possession of this prestigious name, but it had given it another significance. The degree of Knight Rose-Croix had quite an emphasized religious character and claimed to represent a sort of cult of primitive Christianity preserved by secret tradition. All the elements of the ritual, of the décor, and of the catechism recalled Christ, the Last Supper, the Passion, and the Resurrection.

Above a triangular altar, placed at the Orient, a transparency depicted the three crosses of Calvary: the two side crosses were bare, the one in the middle bore a rose, a drapery hanging and the placard with INRI. Below the Calvary was a tomb whose displaced cover let a shroud come out. Three columns, arranged in the South, the Occident, and the Orient of the Lodge, bore, in transparency, the names of the three theological virtues: Faith, Hope, Charity. The word of the degree was Inri, represented as the Lost Word, and the conventional age of the candidate was thirty-three years. The catechism declared that the pelican feeding its young with its entrails, of which the jewel of the degree bore the image, was for the Rose-Croix the symbol of the Savior who had poured out his blood in order to redeem the human race. At the end of the works all the Brothers kneeled before the transparency representing Calvary.

The closing of the Chapter was followed by the Third Point of the Rose-Croix or Mystical Supper, during which the Brothers, standing around a table covered by a cloth, and holding in the hand a long rod, shared a piece of bread and passed a cup full of wine while saying "Emmanuel" and by responding "Pax vobis." When the cup was empty, the president of the Chapter deposited there a paper bearing INRI, lit it, and, when there no longer remained but ashes, said: "Et consommatum est," during which the Brothers, crossing the arms, bowed while bending the knee.

It is possible that it is the redactors of the Knight of the Rose-Croix who, of all the solutions proposed for more than one hundred fifty years to elucidate the enigma, had found the most consonance with the anonymous author of the *Réforme Générale* and the *Fama*. The modern critic is indeed led to see in these two little books a masked attack against the Roman Church and an attempt at propaganda in favor of a purely evangelical religion, extricated from dogmas considered as adventitious and attaching themselves above all to the practices of Christian charity extended to all men, whatever be their credo.

Whatever it is, the confessional character of the Knight of the Rose-Croix flattered the secret inclinations of numerous Brothers whose latent religiosity could not be contained by a purely philosophical humanitarianism. It had earned the degree such a success in the Lodges and Chapters that in the 18th century there was no important Masonic System that did not have it represented on their list.

Its popularity, and also its implicit claim to represent the tradition of an esoteric Christianity, recommended it to the attention of the Master of the Élus

Coëns; and so Pasqually has made two manifest borrowings from it: the name that he has given to the supreme degree of his System and the ritual act that closed the ceremony of reception to this degree.

If the Reintegration strove to justify the denomination of Réau-Croix by insisting on the mystical significance of the first term, it never attempted to explain the addition of the second. Its silence on this point is quite understandable, for the whole thing is obviously a counterfeiting of the name of Rose-Croix. Pasqually has speculated on the prestige of which this latter enjoyed among Brothers of every obedience and has wished for the Élus Coëns to believe that they knew, thanks to him, the true form and the secret meaning of a title that the "apocryphal" Masons had adulterated through ignorance of the "true Masonry." This unacknowledged design is betrayed by the care with which the Master employs in his correspondence, in order to designate the holders of the highest degree of his Order, the conventional sign, R.+, which had currently among the Masons the meaning of Rose-Croix.[1143]

As regards the ceremony in the course of which the officiant had the new Réau-Croix drink "the chalice ceremonially" and gave him to eat "the mystical or cementary bread," it is, it is true, a direct imitation of the Eucharistic communion, but it is doubtful that Pasqually had dared, by his authority, to introduce into his degree of Réau-Croix a ceremony that risked scandalizing certain of his adepts as a sacrilegious parody, if he had not been encouraged by the example that the Third Point of the Rose-Croix gave him.[1144]

∴

The degrees of "Mystical Apprentice, Companion, and Master," which formed an embryonic but coherent system, presents some curious concordance with the tables and ceremonies of the Coën degrees.[1145]

These three degrees had taken for their basis the legend of the Sacred Vault, contained in the English degree of Royal Arch and to which the catechisms of some French High Grades make passing allusion. The legend related that, at the time of the reconstruction of the Temple of Jerusalem by the Jews returned from the Captivity, some workers had discovered under the foundations of the first edifice a vault or cellar in which they had found, in addition to some tablets upon which were described divine laws, an altar bearing an unknown engraved word which was manifestly the ineffable name of God and in which they recognized the Word that was believed lost. This mysterious name, communicated to Zorobabel and to the Ancients, had since been transmitted by oral tradition and constituted the true Masonic secret.

Putting the magical and Kabbalistic concept of the Schem-ha-mephorasch and the secret names of the divinity and of his agents in connection with the role of magician attributed to Solomon, the Instruction of the Mystical Apprentice spoke of the "seven vaults or arches that served as the foundation of the Temple where Solomon made his operations."[1146] The Instruction of the Mystical Master related that the Great Architect of the Universe seeing, after the sin of Adam, that the men walked in the paths of iniquity, had, four hundred years before the Flood, given them "agreements" by the intermediary of the Patriarch Enoch. The mysterious seal of this covenant had been the knowledge of his name which was given to the elect alone. Enoch had engraved the ineffable name on two columns, the one of stone and the other of brick, which had been on his order hidden in the subterranean arches excavated at the summit of the mountain upon which was then constructed the

Temple of Solomon.[1147] The Master Masons who worked at the foundations of the Temple freed the stone column into which was embedded a triangular golden teardrop[1148] where was read the secret name. Solomon had ordered this column to be placed in a sacred vault cut into the basements of the Temple. He knew all the properties of a word that he considered as the support of his Temple, also was it the sole power which guided him in his operations. The Masons delivered from the Captivity had at their arrival at Jerusalem, dug in the ruins of the Temple, discovered the pedestal remaining intact under the Sacred Vault, erased the word inscribed upon the golden teardrop, and have since communicated it to the ear.

On the other hand, Mystical Masonry made of Hiram a supernatural being, closely related to the Spirits of the Supercelestial of which the Reintegration spoke. They represented him as "a superior power" that God had sent to Solomon "by way of the king of Tyre." It is under the leadership of this celestial guide that Solomon had, in making successively "the opening of the first four circles," learned, with "the art of purifying the metals in order to enrich his temple," the "relationship of man with the Creator" and the means to "converse with him and taste the sweet satisfaction of enjoying his power." When Solomon, "allowing himself to be persuaded by the pleasure of having opened the circle to women," had "invoked the queen of Saba and seven hundred concubines who would go to his operations," Hiram abandoned him and "deprived of this power that the Lord had granted him," Solomon had not been able to penetrate into the sixth and seventh circles of the supreme power.

The carpet for the first two degrees depicted "four Quarter Circles traced with the chalk," two of which were in the South and two in the North, and in the middle of which was a candlestick with three lights. For the reception of the Apprentice there was in the Occident "a flowering bough in an urn." Upon the carpet of the Companion a triangle, in which was "written in Hebrew the name of the Grand Architect," was drawn in the center of the Quarter Circles. For the Degree of Master, the carpet bore a circle; the Southern part was traced with the "earth" (red ochre), that of the North with charcoal, that of the Orient with the chalk.[1149] In the Orient of the circle was a triangle with the Tetragrammaton and in front of the triangle is found an earthenware vessel filled with water. In the Occident of the circle was set up a staircase whose steps "were arranged in the form of a spiral by three, five, and seven."[1150] At the foot of the steps there was a burner and fire. The catechism taught that "the Masters work with the chalk, the charcoal, and the earthenware vessel."

The head of the Lodge, called "Master of the Orient," opened the works of the Apprentice by pronouncing a prayer by which he asked, "the Supreme Architect" to grant him "like another Moses" the power necessary "in order to announce to the other men that You have chosen the truth of Your agreements," in order to "enjoy the reward that You have promised to the men who will not deviate from Your precepts." He then pronounced a second prayer soliciting communication of the wisdom of Solomon "as being the most precious gift of Your omnipotence": Then he requested "the relief of the Spirits, who preside in the four Quarter Circles, by striking three raps of the mallet on the top of the edge [angle] of each of them while pronouncing aloud the names of the Spirits."

The catechism taught the new Apprentice that "Masonry is the knowledge of the pacts of God with men," that these agreements had been communicated to Enoch and Moses, and that the seal of these agreements was "the proper name of the divinity." It also professed that the columns of Jachin and Boaz were "the figures of the two Spirits that preside in the southern and northern parts," or even of Cain and Abel, and that the four Spirits commanding in the Quarter Circles "represent to us that without the help of the guardian angels we would not know success in any operation."

The Master of the Orient "invoked the four Quarter Circles by the names of the Grand Architect which are assigned to each of them." He said: "Let us pray the Grand Architect of the Universe by the names that he himself gave to Moses in the Burning Bush, in ordering him to pronounce them when he wanted to operate some wonder," and, before closing the Lodge, he proceeded to the lustration of the Quarter Circles.

In order to be received to the degree of Master, the candidate "crossed the burner of fire, ascended the steps, entered into the circle, and prostrated himself at the foot of the triangle, kneeling on the right knee." Coming out of the circle, he crossed the earthenware vessel full of water.

Finally, and here, perhaps, is the clearest characteristic resemblance, Mystical Masonry held, like the Reintegration and by the same processes, to reconcile the Christian concepts with the penumatological doctrines. The catechism of the Companion taught that the Spirits presiding in the Quarter Circles were "the four angels that have accompanied Christ in his passion"; that of the Master professed that the world had seen several incarnations of Christ, who is manifested "under the form" of Enoch, Melchizedek, Aaron, Hiram, Zorobabel, the Messiah, and who will appear one last time to judge the universe.

∴

On an extremely delicate point and which preoccupied lively the Lodges in the times around 1770, on the problem of the admission of women, the Order of Élus Coëns was, just like the secret society from which it copied its organization, obliged to take a position, and at the example of its model, it adopted a bastard solution.

The question was not posed to [English] Freemasonry, narrowly bound by the traditions of professional Masonry and faithful observer of Anglo-Saxon customs. The "Duties" of the ancient corporations of stonecutters forbade women from entering the Lodge, that is to say the covered worksite where labored the companions, lest their presence bring trouble to the concord and discipline, or their curiosity and natural indiscretion end up discovering and divulging the jealously guarded trade secrets. Speculative Masonry had had even less difficulty respecting this custom since the same ostracism was the rule in the numerous English associations of which the clubs are the most known form. The Book of Constitutions brutally ranked women among the profanes excluded from initiation. It put them on the same footing as the slaves, the debauched, and the idolaters, and a formula current in the catechisms designated the Lodge a place of peace where "never shall cock crow (allusion to the denial of Saint Peter) nor woman cackle."

The measure could be most wise, at least in the eyes of the convinced misogynists, but, since Masonry had crossed the English Channel, an aim so insulting as non-reception was not admitted by the interested since the reigning morals in France in the 18th century had become accustomed to playing a principal role in social relations, and to exercising over private affairs, and even public ones, an uncontested influence. The theater plays and contemporary factums show that French women strove to pierce the mystery with which are enveloped the Masonic meetings and that, annoyed at not being able to penetrate therein, they suspected the Brethren of engaging in the worst excesses. This accusation, besides being absolutely gratuitous and unjust, furnished the adversaries of Masonry with one of their better weapons, and the Brethren could not hide the damage that it did to their association already suspected by the royal authority and stricken with anathema by the papal bulls. Nevertheless, they attempted at first to remain faithful to the English tradition and strove to destroy the prejudices that the exclusion of women stirred up against them, by solemnly protesting of the purity of their relations in the Lodge, and in justifying the measure for reasons presented, whether in verse or in prose, with the gallant courtesy then used in our land, but identical to those that the professional or speculative [English] Masons invoked.

The piece of poetry entitled "Les Francs-Maçons, songe" [The Freemasons, dream], which figures in all the collections of Masonic songs published since 1737, said to the ladies:

> Beautiful sex, we have for you
> All esteem and respect.
> But all you do we fear too,
> And our fear is legitimate.
> If the sex is outlawed, let there be no alarm,
> It is not an insult to his fidelity.
> But one fears love entering with its charms
> Producing forgetfulness of fraternity.
> Names of brother and friend would be weak arms,
> To protect the heart from rivalry.

The apocryphal "Discours d'un Grand Maître," written in 1737 by the Chevalier Ramsay and reproduced in numerous Masonic or profane works, made the excesses and debaucheries, which had slid little by little into the pagan Mysteries, come from the admission of women into the nocturnal assemblies, and it concluded: "It is in order to prevent similar abuses that women are excluded from our Order. It is not that we are so unjust as to regard the sex as incapable of secret, but it is because her presence could alter insensibly the purity of our maxims and our hearts."

But it finally happened that Brothers, animated by a less austere zeal or more confident in the solidity of their fraternal principles, found exclusively masculine assemblies distasteful. They were accused "of having been rather unjust for having long believed that the pleasures founded on all the virtues were above the faculties of the souls of the ladies and could not fail to displease a sex that they supposed to have only frivolity as their lot. But, enlightened and too often punished by the isolation and tediousness that the absence of ladies had made them experience, they were convinced that the aim of their existence was to live with them, and that they were unable to be separated without becoming stupid or unhappy."[1151]

These two orders of convergent causes: curiosity and suspicion of the women, regret and remorse of the Brethren in their sensible heart, led to the creation of androgynous societies: Order of Mopses, of Felicity, of the Knights [Chevaliers et Chevalières] of the Anchor, or the Knights and Nymphs of the Rose, of the Woodcutters [Fendeurs et Fendeuses], of the Companions of Penelope. These associations had degrees and ceremonies imitating the Masonic grades and rituals, and furnished the Brothers come from the Lodges the occasion to engage, along with the

Sisters belonging to the aristocratic circles, in banter mixing elegant and egalitarian sentiment with sentimental humanitarianism.

But these societies, the majority of which had only an ephemeral existence, were only pale copies of Masonry and did not have, until around 1760, any direct connection with it. The curiosity of the Sisters, at first amused by this diversion, refused in the end to be thrown off course. The feminine offensive, diverted for a moment by simulated objectives, returned to the attack of the principal position and the Freemasonry of Adoption came into the world. The author of *Essai sur les mystères et le veritable objet de la Confrérie des Francs-Macons* (1771) established the act of birth in writing: "One has for some time initiated by adoption the women into the mysteries of Freemasonry, but they are different from those of the men."

Masonry of Adoption was developed considerably starting from 1772, that is to say at the very period when Pasqually elaborated his system. The doctrine taught by the new Rite professed that the woman had been created to be the auxiliary of man in the conquest of happiness by the practice of social virtues, but that, her curiosity and the amorous weakness of her companion having caused the fall of the first couple and the unhappiness of humanity, the Freemasons would, by their moral strength, restore joy upon the earth. After a first degree familiarizing the Apprentice with the language of the emblems and symbols, the second represented the Edenic life and the original sin, the third the tower of Babel and the dispersion of the peoples; the fourth, where represented, as dignitaries of the Lodge, Moses, Aaron, their wives, and the daughters of Aaron, staged the migrations of the Israelites as a symbol of the time that man and woman pass in this world in order to be prepared to be admitted into a superior world; in the fifth, the curiosity of the candidate was put to the test; in the seventh [the sixth is not mentioned here] Noah, the ark, and the dove furnished the theme of an allegorical teaching; in the eighth degree, which had a very pronounced religious and Catholic character, the décor represented a chapel; the candidate to the ninth degree played the role of Judith in three rooms which were supposed to represent the town of Bethulie, the valley of the same name, and the camp of the Assyrians; finally the candidate to the tenth degree personified the Queen of Sheba and was received by Solomon into the council of the Wise King.

Modeled on the Masonic Systems, the Rite of Adoption claimed to give a moral teaching in the inferior degrees, and in the high degrees, flattered the vanity of the Sisters and their taste for the Romanesque. The titles were pompous and picturesque: Elect Mistress, Perfect Mistress, Scottish Sublime, Sovereign Illustrious Mason, Princess of the Crown, English Amazon, Knight of the Dove, Knight of Beneficence.

Feminine Masonry did not rest until it had been recognized and legalized by the Grand Orient of France and it knew how to find eloquent advocates and even in the court. The Grand Orator of the Grand Orient wrote, in 1773, in addressing the Grand Master: "The priests of Isis and Osiris admitted their wives and their daughters into the impenetrable and terrible mysteries of initiation. The Greeks had their Sibylls, the Romans their Vestals, in all the orders of civil life the whole of Europe has produced heroines. Ah! Why have the Masons of France, who are fathers, husbands, sons, and brothers, not admitted them among them?" Dazzled by such erudition and yielding to the authority of illustrious Sisters supported by influential Brothers, the Grand Orient recognized, by deliberation on June 10, 1774, the Lodges of Adoption.

Three androgynous Lodges of Paris shone with a brilliant light until the approach of the Revolution. La Candeur, founded by the Marquis de Saisseval, the

Marquise de Courtebonne, the Comtess de Polignac, and de Choiseul-Gouffier, counted in 1775 fifty-one Brothers and thirty-one Sisters; it celebrated the same year a Feast of Adoption in which assisted the Grand Master Due de Chartres, the Duchess de Bourbon, and the Princess de Lamballe. The list of its members, published in 1778, bore the names of nearly all the ladies of the court and of all the illustrious military men of the period. Les Neuf Sœurs and the Contrat Social were also well-frequented. The Duchess de Chartres was Grand Mistress of the latter and Madame Helvetius held the first gavel in the former. The Grand Mistresses of the Masonry of Adoption were successively the Duchess de Bourbon and the Princess de Lamballe. In the provinces, notably at Bordeaux, Annonay, Dieppe, Besançon, Rennes, Rochefort, Toulouse, Lodges of Adoption were headed under the masculine Lodges.

But this feminist victory was more apparent than real. The Brothers had opened beside their "workshops" salons where they received in great pomp beautiful visitors. They play acted with them there time and again scenes that mimicked the Masonic ceremonies. The Sister Masons heard excellent music, edifying homilies, dined, danced, appeared in multi-colored ribbons and emblems delicately worked. They made collections for the relief of the needy, to endow the poor women, to raise orphans, and to free prisoners of debt, rewarded by medals the acts of devotion and awarded prizes of virtue, but they did not cross the threshold of the masculine Lodge, and were in no part treated on equal footing.[1152]

The Grand Orient had only recognized the Lodges of Adoption under conditions: each of them had to be attached to a regular Lodge that administrated it and was responsible guardian; every meeting of Adoption was obligatorily presided over by the Venerable or his lawful replacement, and the "officers" could only second the masculine dignitaries; the Sisters would be without exception, wives, widows, or close relatives of Masons. The female Masons [Maçonnes] did not have the power of veto on the admission of new members, whatever their sex. La Candeur had indeed decided, on January 19, 1776, "that no profane Brother or Sister would be admitted without the unanimous consent of the Sisters, who would have been previously consulted," but, if the Grand Orient dared not contradict a Lodge so well frequented, it maintained vigorously the masculine prerogatives in comparison with the androgynous Lodges of the province, and when the Aimable Concorde of Rochefort expressed the claim to have the candidates pass the scrutiny of the Sisters before having them submit to that of the Brothers, it quashed the rebel Lodge which had to revoke its decision before being reintegrated.

The concessions made by Masonry to the ambitions of women had been imposed on it by the rank and influence of the applicants, but the hostility of the Brothers faithful to the Masonic tradition had not been disarmed. In his *Recherches sur les initiations anciennes et modernes*, the Abbé Robin took up again in 1779 the arguments already produced forty years earlier: "the French politeness," he said, "will accustom the Masons little by little to deviate from the rigorous laws of their Order and, too occupied with the care of amusing this sex by brilliant feasts, they will lose sight of their true goal..., the secret that the ones and the others are held to observe make seen the difference which characterizes the two sexes; it is almost without precedent that the ones violate it and it is rather rare that the others guard it scrupulously."[1153]

Pasqually was as opposed as the Masons to the admission of women, although for other reasons. He did not fear their frivolity, their indiscretion, and the amorous rivalries that their presence in the "Temple" could provoke, for the small number of adepts and the period of probation that was imposed upon them allowed a prudent selection to be carried out, while the fervor of their zeal protected them against the seductions of the flesh. The motives for his repugnance were of a metaphysical order: he considered women as inferior beings from the mystical point of view, because he denied their power to command the Spirits, whether to summon the good ones or to repel the evil ones. The Reintegration taught[1154] that "the female posterity of Adam could not assist in the cult of a divine operation because of the few divine virtues and powers innate in the females and their little strength and firmness to sustain such operations."[1155] On the other hand, in admitting women to their theurgical works, the Élus Coëns risked compromising the success thereof, for the daughters of Eve represented the specifically impure part of humanity. Their mother, Houwa, had been the bitter fruit of the first error of the Man-God. He had committed his second fault, punished by the procreation of Cain the Damned, in yielding with and by her to "the furious passion of the senses of matter." The approach of the woman, instrument of pleasure whose dissolving action altered the spiritual virtue of the Minors, was forbidden to the Réau-Croix during the quarantine preceding the Operations. The demonic character of the feminine sex was indicated by the catechism of the Master Élus Coëns: with respect to the two broken columns, drawn upon the carpet, it had noted that, if the one representing fallen man was in the North, region where the heat of divine irradiation did not penetrate, the one that represented his companion was found in the South, abode of the demons.

But in every human work the a priori principles and philosophical concepts must be accommodated to practical necessities. In spite of his most clearly asserted theories, and certainly against his intimate convictions, Pasqually was forced to yield to the entreaties of adepts who had interest to hold on to. An article of the Statutes of the Order permitted the reception of women on the condition that a "direct and physical proof of la Chose itself," that is to say a Pass observed in the course of an Operation made with this intention, justified their initiation.[1156]

Pasqually did not put, moreover, any promptness to drafting the ritual of these extraordinary receptions. To Willermoz, who, most desirous to initiate his sister, demanded in June 1771, the necessary instructions, Saint-Martin instructed on July 17: "I have informed the Master how much you would desire the Instruction for women; he prays you to not be impatient on this point, he will keep his word to you, but he is so little disposed to these sorts of workings that he does not yet believe it necessary to undertake it."[1157] Upon a new demand from Willermoz the intimate secretary of the Master responded on January 18, 1772: "He can hardly send you even now the instruction that X... has promised you for the reception of women. He has just returned to his treatise which occupies him entirely."[1158] In August 1773, Saint-Martin was finally able to "congratulate with all his heart" the sister of Willermoz "on her admission into the Order,"[1159] but, if the profound respect that the disciples professed for the authority of their chief let them suppose that they could count on his tacit authorization, the correspondence proves that Pasqually had affected to disinterest himself from this feminine initiation. Not always receiving the instructions so often promised, Willermoz had had recourse in May to the knowledge of Saint-Martin. The latter approved in principle the initiative of Willermoz since "the feminine soul comes from the same source as that which is clothed in a masculine body, and having the same work to do, the same enemy to combat, and the same fruits to hope for, ought then consequently to have the same weapons." But, if this proposition appeared to him defendable from a religious point of view, he singularly restricted the capacity thereof from the theurgical point of view in adding some lines further down: "As there is a difference in the privileges which are accorded to men, in that they are the elders, I would, in your place, employ for all the women only words of simple quaternary power, in order to constitute their inferiority in regards to the man to whom the double power is reserved."[1160] Therefore, all while acknowledging "to have never seen any piece relative to this object," he counseled as his chief but likely as official informer, to proceed nearly as for the reception of men to the grade of Master Élu Coën. Consequently he "saw no inconvenience" that Willermoz lighted the "new fire" and depicted on the different parts of the body of the candidate "the emblems of power, namely the triangle, the receptacle, and the circumference." As regards the tracing on the ground, the ordinary interpreter of the thought of the Master left the consulter free to draw either a simple circle or a circle bearing the triangle, whether single or double, "in consideration of what he wanted to figure in her reception." Such a latitude showed the little importance attributed by the direction of the Order to the ceremony. Furthermore, Saint-Martin, under the pretext of anticipating the eventual scruples of Willermoz on the validity of the projected ordination, noted that the initiation granted to the sister of the adept was only partial, and he let it be known that she would remain so for a long time. "Moreover," he concluded, "it may not be, in the first steps that one takes in the Order, that the extensions (irregularities) of every kind are to be so feared; it will be some time, without doubt, before final precautions are taken with Madame your sister, and that the errors that she or you could commit upon her be dangerous."[1161]

It does not seem that one has ever been in necessity to take these final precautions, for nothing, at least in the documents presently known, indicates that the sister of Willermoz had, any more than the two other women who were admitted into the Order as long as Pasqually assured the direction[1162], passed at any moment beyond the degree of initiation corresponding to the degree of Master Élu Coën.

CHAPTER IV
Martinès de Pasqually and la Française Élue Écossaise
(1760-1765)

The mystical doctrine that endowed all bodies, celestial and terrestrial, with a soul to which they owed not only their activity, but their very existence, would define most exactly the relationships of cause and effect that have united Pasqually to the Society of which he was the head. Never, perhaps, has the work of one man been undertaken so exclusively. The Grand Sovereign of the Élus Coëns has been the unique mover of the organization that he created. He was at the same time the brain that thinks and sends orders to the nerve centers, and the heart whose pulsations shoot into the arteries the vivifying blood. The Society has really only lived during those years when he was at the helm. From the time that he moved away, it fell into languor, soon to be extinguished.

The history of the Order is therefore inseparable from that of its founder. Unfortunately, it has been found that Pasqually has been, as were Saint-Germain and Cagliostro in France, Rosa, Johnson a Fuelen, Gugomos in Germany, and so many other adventurers of the 18th century, one of those enigmatic personages who appeared then unexpectedly upon the world stage, then promptly disappeared, without one having every known exactly where he came from and what had been or what was their career before and after the short period during which they had attracted upon themselves the public attention.

The greatest uncertainty has long reigned over the very orthography of the name of our hero. Willermoz, one of his lieutenants, sometimes called him Pascualy, sometimes Pasqualy; another disciple, the Abbé Fournié, named him Dom Martinets de Pasquallys; the baron de Gleichen, who had gained the confidence of his intimate secretary, wrote Pasqualis; Joseph de Maistre, who had known of the Élus Coëns having approached the Master, speaks, in his *Soirées de Saint-Pétersbourg*, of Martino Pasquali; the baron de Turckheim wavered between Don Pascuali and Pascualis; the State of the Grand Orient bore Martinez de Pasqualli; Matter opts for Martinez de Pasquallis, Franck for Martinès Pasqualis, Daruty for Dom Martinez Paschalis.

His nationality has remained undecided. According to the *Biographie Michaud*, his most intimate disciples have not known his country, and it is according to his language that one has been able to presume that he was Portuguese and Jewish. For Gleichen he was "originally Spanish, perhaps of the Jewish race." J. de Maistre called him Italian or Spanish. Matter supposes him "Portuguese, of oriental origin and of Israelite race, but become Christian as became the Gnostics of the first centuries." Franck believes to be able to assert that, born at Grenoble in 1715, he was the son of a Portuguese Israelite come, unaware of what date and for what reason, to establish himself in Dauphine, and he supposes that the immigrant, remaining as a number of his Portuguese coreligionists, faithful to his national faith of Catholicism, had raised his son in a jealous isolation that did not permit him to learn the language of his new country except at a rather advanced age, which explains the jargon in which he writes his letters and his treatise. The masked author of *Introduction aux Enseignements secrets de Martinès de Pasqually* claims that the theurgist was born at Grenoble, parish of Notre-Dame (Saint-Hugues). G. Bord has examined the registers of the Saint-Hugues, Saint-Laurent, and Saint-Joseph parishes of Grenoble without finding a trace of our man but has nevertheless "every reason to believe" that he was born in 1715 in the environs of this town, to Jean-Pierre Pascalis, master writer and professor of the Latin language, and Madeleine d'Alençon, and that he was called simply Martin Pascalis.

All that may be established by the documents published by Papus, is that the founder of the Élus Coëns signed his letters sometimes as Don Martinez de Pasqually, sometimes Depasqually de la Tour, and that he was given upon the act of baptism of his son, preserved in the archives of the town of Bordeaux, the name of Don Martinets de Pasqually. As to his race, although Willermoz had assured Turckheim that Pasqually was not Jewish, it is difficult to be content with this assertion. Without putting into doubt the good faith of the adept of Lyon, one may wonder whether his protestation against the "prejudices" that had been given to his correspondent were not aimed rather at the religion than the race of his old Master, and whether he did not seek above all, at the same time as he reassured Turckheim, to be reassured himself on the orthodoxy of the doctrines set forth in the treatise on the Reintegration. On the other hand, the Jewish origin and education of Pasqually seem peremptorily proven by his profound knowledge of the tradition of Israel and the theories of the mystical rabbis[1163] and this is why the thesis of Franck appears extremely likely. One could find again a confirmation in the pride of race that pushes the author of the treatise to exalt the eminent dignity of the "true Jews." Obliged to recognize that the descendants of Abraham have been "replaced by those that they call: children of the divine grace," he adds thereupon a tone full of rancor and menace: "But these new children would do well to take care against falling asleep on the grace that they possess to the prejudice of the Hebrew people."[1164] The memory of past grandeur and the hope in a final triumph vibrates in the prophetic words that Moses addresses to his people: "Be that as it may, Israel never loses hope in the mercy of the Eternal; remember always that you were the immense theater of the first manifestation of the glory and divine justice (theophany and government exercised directly by Jehovah), that it is among you that every spiritual thing has originated, and that a day will come when the posterity of Abraham, heir to the work of the Eternal, will be restored to his first state of splendor, and will be reintegrated with magnificence into his chief place."[1165]

This passage, where resonates a sincere enthusiasm, does not, it is true, allude to the long hopes of the Jews in a political resurrection, nor even to the millennium during which the elect race would dominate the earth before the annihilation of the universe. The apotheosis that Moses predicts will only take place at the moment of the Final Judgment, when, after "having entered a second time into slavery and servitude in the land of Egypt, to come out therefrom only at the end of time."[1166] Israel will see "the manifestation of the glory and justice of the Most High take place for the satisfaction of the Just, to the shame of the criminal demons and the Minors guilty and not reconciled."[1167] Pasqually is not, therefore, a precursor of Zionism, nor a millenialist in the strict sense of the word, but the pride and the invincible hope that breathes these lines, shows the son of a people whose ancestral pride and faith in the greatness of their destinies have never been felled by the most severe trials.

Finally, the language of his letters, of his treatise, and of his degree papers is that of a foreigner having practiced French rather late, and who continued to think in his mother-tongue. This latter is probably a southern language, perhaps Spanish, as well as seeming to indicate barbarisms like "espécial, escrutin, espermatique"; in any case, nothing betrays the influence of a Germanic dialect, which excludes the hypothesis of Mackenzie who, in the *Masonic Cyclopedia* of 1877, made of Pasqually a

German Jew.

Silent on the origin of our hero, the documents that we possess reveal at least some traits of his moral character. The character of Pasqually appears to have been a rather savory mixture of sincere mysticism and charlatanism. He happened to boast with a tranquil impudence. When, for example, he asserts "to have seen and to know by himself" what was related by the travelers on the fear that the demons inspired in the Chinese, and on the cult rendered by the Celestials to the animals, it is prudent to receive his declarations only with a certain skepticism. The tone that he takes in order to gain the confidence of his readers rings false, when he protests in these terms of his sincerity: "You will judge whether I tell the truth or whether I use subterfuges and sophisms in order to abuse the good faith of the men of desire. This is neither my state nor my taste. I have held in horror since my childhood falsehood and pride; I have abjured them in order to make only a profession of the truth of divine spiritual and temporal spiritual things."[1168]

An anecdote reported innocently by Willermoz shows how Pasqually knew how to impose on ingenuous enthusiasts who took him for their guide. "Being in Paris," recounts the old head of the Élus Coëns of Lyon to his friend Turckheim, "on the day that he had chosen to confer upon me my final degrees, he summoned me to receive them one day following at Versailles; he summoned there at the same time some other Brothers of inferior degrees and placed them in the corners of the room where they remained until the end in silence. He stood in the center, and I kneeled before him, no other being able to hear anything that passed between him and me. Before the end of the ceremonial, he fell on me quite suddenly, his arms upon my shoulders, his face stuck against mine, he inundated me with his tears, being able only to push out heavy sighs. Most astonished, I raised my eyes upon him, and I made out there all the signs with a great joy. I wished to question him; he gave me a sign to keep silent. The operation having ended, I wished to thank him for what he had just done for me, and I was completely moved by it. 'It is I,' he said to me, 'who owe much more to you than you think. You have been for me the occasion for the happiness that I experience. I had for a certain time fallen into the disgrace of my God for certain faults that the world counts little, and I have just received the proof, the certain sign of my reconciliation. I owe it to you, because you are the cause and the occasion. I was unhappy; I am now very happy. Think sometimes of me, I shall never forget you.' And, indeed, since that time I have received from him many proofs of friendship and great confidence."[1169]

Such a scene smacks of artifice, but perhaps it would do wrong to the author to see therein but a pure comedy. As theatrical as the gesture was, the sentiment that it expressed with a manifest exaggeration could be sincere. It is quite possible that Pasqually had been sort of delusional, living in a state of perpetual over-excitement, passing without transition from dejection to exaltation, projecting by the unconscious effort of his will, which held always to the same object, sparkling and fleeting images upon the screen of sensible reality, interpreting at the will of his desires or fears the most vague sensations, surrounded by phantoms that provoked his enfevered imagination in the course of the nocturnal Invocations and Operations, preceded by abstinence and accompanied by fumigations and magical ceremonies.

Only, if he was sincerely convinced of the reality of the doctrines that he professed, if he truly believed to have by his personal experiment, verified the exactitude of his postulates, the powerful will and the spirit of proselytism, which make the heads of sects, pushed him to exaggerate the importance of the results obtained and the extent of the supernatural faculties which were attributed to him. In order to assure his dominion over his disciples and to stir up their zeal, he did not disdain to have recourse to these pious ruses which were believed justified by the purity of intentions and the greatness of the aim pursued. When he persuaded his "emulators" that he followed from Bordeaux the works in which they were engaged at Lyon or Paris, that he had healed his wife by his exorcisms, and that he was frequently favored by manifestations and illuminations, he tended to realize in their eyes the ideal type of the Spiritual Minor, or even of the Spiritual Elect, for which he gave himself and that he believed to be in part. The image that he created only had a fictive existence, but it was the reproduction of a model of which he imagined himself to be an imperfect copy. This class of mythomaniacs and half-conscious illusionists, who are neither simple impostors nor professional scammers, is abundantly represented among the occultists. Their unshakable faith in an irrational principle renders them indulgent to the processes aiming to demonstrate victoriously the existence thereof, and their spirit always tends towards the unknowable, ending up no longer being able to clearly distinguish illusion from reality.

The touchstone that allows one to trace, in this domain, a demarcation between vulgar charlatan and sincere adept, between a Cagliostro or a Saint-Germain and a Pasqually, is the result that each of them await from the push that he gives surreptitiously to the scales. The first gives chase to the high-placed dupes, opulent and generous; he seeks pomp, resounding success, the admiration of the gapers; impresario shrewd as well as greedy, he sets the scene of the room which will surely attract a numerous public; he addresses the simple curiosity, the cupidity of men, the coquettery of women, the passions of all; he invents Egyptian Masonry, works Lodges of Adoption, predicts the future, "regenerates" diamonds and sells the water of Youth. The second pursues less dazzling success and feeds higher ambitions. Pasqually, as Matter most justly notes, was "satisfied with the sole success of being head of the school and master of the great mysteries" and "none may reproach him for having sought under the mask of his secret science either renown or fortune."[1170] He has, indeed, never trafficked in his occult knowledge. In his correspondence with his disciples the question of money is never of primary importance, and if, as we will see further on, it gave way from time to time to some rather bitter controversies, it must be recognized that the expectations of Pasqually were quite reasonable. Moreover, the little fortune and rather modest social rank of the majority of the adepts, the financial straits against which the head of the Order ceaselessly struggled during the whole period that the documents permit us to live with him, the respect that a spirit as noble as that of Saint-Martin constantly showed to him proves the real unselfishness of Pasqually. His ability as hierophant and chief of the sect was often less scrupulous than one would wish, but he did not place it at the service of sordid calculations. If he had a hazy mind, a too self-satisfied imagination, and an immoderate taste for fiction, his hands at least remained pure of the contact with gold.

∴

The information that the more recent historians give on Pasqually's entrance onto the scene are rather subject to caution. Matter claims that "Dom Martinez initiated adepts since 1754 in several towns of France, especially at Paris, Bordeaux, Lyon, and elsewhere."[1171] The *Nouvelle Notice Historique* asserts that he has established the same year at Montpellier the Chapter of Scottish Judges.[1172] Bord advances that he composed his Rite at the same date and affiliated a great number of adherents in the South, in particular at Avignon, Marseille, Toulouse, and Bordeaux.[1173] The concordance of these indications is not a sufficient proof of their exactitude, for it seems that they have been drawn, at least in what concerns the date, from a very suspect source: the *Table Chronologique de l'Histoire de la Franche-Maçonnerie* by Thory, where it may be read, in the year 1754: "Martinez Paschalis composes the Rite of Élus Coëns and introduces it into some Lodges at Marseille, Toulouse, and Bordeaux."[1174] But Thory was very badly informed on all that touched the history of the Order. He is mistaken when he places the introduction of the Rite at Paris in 1768[1175] since the Sovereign Tribunal had been installed there since 1767, as the correspondence of the adepts proves. He contradicts himself moreover in the same paragraph when he asserts that "this Régime was only organized in 1775" and he commits an even greater error in having Pasqually die at San Domingo in 1779 after "some years stay at Paris."[1176]

It is only in 1760 that the authentic documents mention for the first time the Masonic activity of Pasqually.[1177] He presented himself to the "Loges de Saint-Jean Réunies" of Toulouse in giving himself the title of Esquire[1178] and in calling himself Inspector General of the Lodge of the Stuwards.[1179] The Toulousian Brothers received his declarations with some skepticism. It appeared strange to them that a man of such modest dress and common look could occupy high functions in the Royal Art, and had earned the marks of esteem and confidence that the Pretender would have given him. They had already been victims of the falsehoods sold by adventurers who, taking advantage of the fact that the Toulousian Lodge "Les Fidèles Écossais" had received in 1747 a constitution from a pretended Sir Samuel Lockhart, calling himself lieutenant of Charles Stuart, had presented themselves as the delegates of a Jacobite power and, under the pretext of completing the instruction of the Brothers of Toulouse, had sold them at a high price charters and titles of fantasy.[1180] The references that Pasqually produced: a hieroglyphic charter, that is to say indecipherable, and some letters seemed insufficient. Nevertheless, he was allowed to set forth his theories in the Blue Lodge.[1181] He summarized a sort of ideal plan of Masonry[1182] in which figured "the mysterious construction of the ancient and the new Temple, the Levite Knights, the Cohenim-Levyim, and the Élus Coëns." This mystical conference left the hearers indifferent, but their attention was roused when Pasqually offered to make, in the presence of a delegation, practical demonstrations. The Lodge designated three Masters, indicated by lots, to follow the experiment. Pasqually, not having success in furnishing in a first session the tangible proofs that he had promised, obtained permission to renew the test, but the result was again "deplorable, Martinès was covered by confusion," and the witnesses made so crushing a report in Lodge that the immediate expulsion of the unfortunate thaumaturge was decided by a strong majority.[1183] He left Toulouse in a hurry while leaving some outstanding notes, a voluntary forgetfulness which was the definitive ruin of him in the minds of the members of the Loges de Saint- Jean Réunies.[1184]

Another attempt, that he made at Foix sometime after, had a better success. He was received with honor by the Lodge "Joshué," where he recruited disciples, among others the chevalier de Grainville, lieutenant-colonel, and Mr. de Champoléon, captain of grenadiers, which made both part of the garrisoned regiment in this little town. Whether Pasqually had had more luck in the course of his demonstrations, or that his proselytes took him at his word, he succeeded in founding a Chapter whose

Lodge adopted the title, in exchanging its old name for that of "Temple des Élus Écossais."[1185] But Pasqually wanted it to occur on a more vast scene; through the intervention of the Masons of Foix he entered, in 1761, into relations with the Brothers of Bordeaux.[1186]

.'.

The capital of Guyenne counted then two important Lodges in activity: the "Française" founded in 1740, and "l'Amitié," six years younger.[1187] Pasqually had addressed the first, much more frequented and which counted among its members several councilors in Parliament. Supported by the recommendation of the Count de Maillal d'Abzac, Chevelier de Saint-Louis, of the Marquis de Lescourt, captain at the Regiment du Roi, and of two commissioners of the Navy, he presented a request of affiliation conceived in these terms:

"The undersigned beseeches most humbly the Very Respectable Lodge to be willing to do him the honor of affiliating him and he will make in recognition vows to the Great Architect of the Universe for the prosperity of the Masons spread upon the surface of the earth and of this Respectable Lodge. Martinès, Esquire."[1188]

The request was accepted and Pasqually, who had come to lodge in the environs of Bordeaux, formed at once in the bosom of the Lodge his "Particular Temple," comprised of disciples among whom were found, in addition to his sponsor, the two brothers from Aubenton, of which the one was pay commissioner general of the Navy and the other "captain of the high board" and Chevalier de Saint-Louis, de Gaze, "gentleman," de Bobie commissioner of the Navy and "gentleman," de Jull Tafar, old major of the Royal Grenadiers and Chevalier de Saint-Louis, the "Messers." Morin and Lexcombart."[1189]

The protection of this little army was soon necessary to him. The Loges de Saint-Jean Réunies of Toulouse, having learned that he had been admitted to the Française, believed it necessary to put the Brothers of Bordeaux on guard against the man who they considered as an imposter and a crook. An official letter, dated August 26, 1762, related the unfruitful experiments of Pasqually and counselled the Française to examine carefully the very suspect titles of a man who, simple worker in carriages in the profane world[1190], called himself Grand Inspector in Masonry. The denunciation finally struck Pasqually a final blow in informing the Masons of Bordeaux that he had left some debts in Toulouse.

The attack had no success. The adepts recruited by the charged defended their "Powerful Master." Moreover, the Parthian arrow, let loose by the denunciation, missed its aim. Informed by the Master himself of the painful conditions in which he had had to leave Toulouse, the disciples had acquitted the arrears in the first months of 1762. At their instigation, the Française took great offense at its Toulousian sister. It responded immediately that the titles of "Puissant Maître Martinez" were perfectly regular, having been attested to in the most detailed manner by several Brothers of Avignon, notably by the Very Illustrious Brother Roubaux[1191], that he had given "marked evidence of his powers" (theurgical), that finally the Française had settled over six months ago, as was easy to prove, the last of the creditors of which there was a question, and that the delay brought to the settlement of these debts was not imputable to unwillingness, but to the poor state of temporal affairs of the Brother Martinez.[1192]

After this alarm Pasqually was able, for eighteen months, to continue his propaganda in all tranquility and, as the majority of his "emulators" were his neighbors[1193], he had the occasion to see them outside of the meetings and in particular to instruct them. His audience was increased during the off-season by Messrs. de Grainville and de Champoléon "who were going to pass all their winter's quarter close to him and boarded with him for six months in order to work under him."[1194]

But the influence that Pasqually had taken over the Française ended by raising a lively opposition in the Masonic world of Bordeaux where the resolution with which the Lodge had taken up his defense in August 1762, had already given rise to unfriendly suppositions for this workshop.[1195] The hostility of the rationalist Masons manifested itself, beginning in 1764, in a noisy manner, some weeks after the reinstallation of the Lodge "l'Anglaise" in Bordeaux.

This Lodge was one of the oldest in France; its foundation dated back to 1732. It had had difficulties from the beginning and had fallen into slumber on two occasions: from September 30, 1733, to June 29, 1735, then from September 27 of the same year to February 26, 1737. Starting from this last date it had traversed a brilliant career. The intendant of Guyenne, Boucher, having given it, on August 29, 1742, the order to be dissolved, it had protested publicly, was content to be installed in another location and had no longer been disturbed. From 1740 to 1760 it had constituted seven daughter-Lodges, of which one was at Bordeaux itself, two at Brest, one at Limoges, one at Pons, one at Cognac, and one at Cayenne.

Founded by a group of English merchants in residence at Bordeaux and having worked in English until 1743[1196], it had remained faithful to its origins and maintained jealously the traditions of [English] Freemasonry in holding itself strictly to the symbolic degrees and by respecting the principles by which were inspired the founders of the English secret society. It is thus that it had, in 1749, indicated to a Lodge of Toulouse that it would no longer receive its visitors if the Toulousian Brethren persisted in dispensing with having their candidates take the oath on the Gospel. Very puritanical, it had, in 1745, pronounced the Masonic intolerance against all candidates belonging near and far to the theater, even against musicians of the orchestra[1197] and it had proposed in 1748 to the other Lodges of Bordeaux to no longer admit henceforth "any comedian, cord-dancer, or charlatan."[1198]

L'Anglaise had, for an unknown cause, suspended its meetings starting from January 13, 1761, but it took them up again on January 31, 1764. Perhaps its awakening was provoked by the indignation caused to its members by the tendencies of its daughter la Française, which had owed it the day in 1740, and also the complacence with which it let itself be controlled by a Jew, or at least by a man reputed as such. Indeed, l'Anglaise, as, moreover, all the English and German Lodges without exception, admitted into its meetings only Christians, not only by confession, but more by origin. It had proclaimed in 1746 this exclusion in express terms, and in 1747 refused to admit to its labors an Israelite from Amsterdam warmly recommended by a Lodge of Holland. In any case, it was eager, scarcely having been reinstalled, to declare war on la Française, which it put on the index from the month of February.[1199]

La Française endured the excommunication intrepidly; it remained faithful to its Powerful Master and, completely won over to his doctrines, or, to speak as a mystical historian, "his Temple being perfected," it hoisted the colors of its chief by taking, at the end of 1764, the title of "Française Élue Écossaise,"[1200] to mark that it possessed a secret Chapter practicing the High Grades. Finally, in order to flaunt its complete independence in the face of its Mother-Lodge, it sought its inscription on the registers of the Grand Lodge of France, a request which it was granted on February 1, 1765.[1201]

The official dedication that it had been able to obtain on the part of the supreme authority of Masonry did not discourage its adversaries of Bordeaux. They received reinforcements in the appearance of Masons that the Chapter of Coëns had refused to admit to its mysteries. These malcontents associated themselves with members of l'Anglaise in order to address to the Grand Lodge of France a memorandum in which they made the case of the accusative letter from the Brothers of Toulouse and requested the annulment of the decision which recognized the Française Élue Écossaise. But the Grand Lodge refused to accede to the complaint, first because it had only admitted la Française in the capacity of Blue Lodge and without taking into account the High Grades that it could cultivate in a Chapter, then because the petitioners were wrong to come and invoke an authority that they themselves refused to recognize, since l'Anglaise claimed to rise directly and exclusively from the Grand Lodge of London, which, indeed, would the following year grant confirmation to its constistutions.[1202] The supreme attack had therefore completely run aground, and la Française could claim all the prerogatives of a regular Lodge.

After having founded, in one of the large towns of the kingdom, a solid establishment, and inscribed, at least as Blue Lodge, upon the official rolls, which allowed him to correspond with all the groups relevant to the central authority, Pasqually was able to dream of extending his action in founding a Rite capable of taking rank among the other Scottish Systems. In order to understand the tactic that he adopted, or rather which was imposed upon him by circumstances, and to appreciate the chance of success that the undertaking presented, it is necessary to know the state in which French Masonry found itself at this moment.

CHAPTER V
The Sovereign Tribunal and the recruitment from 1766 to 1770

The history of Masonry in France is dominated from 1740 to 1766 by the struggle that the central direction had to sustain against the claims of the Chapters and Scottish Systems.

The organization of French Freemasonry, copied on that of [English] Freemasonry, placed over the Lodges, each of which formed a cell having an independent existence, a supreme authority called a Grand Lodge, and presided over by a Grand Master assisted by Grand Officers. The Grand Master was elected by the members of the Grand Lodge, itself comprised of the Parisian Masters of Lodges or Venerables. In principle and by right, each Lodge existing in the kingdom had, in order to be considered as regular, to have obtained constitutions from the Grand Lodge, recognize its jurisdiction, and be inscribed upon its rolls.

The exclusive sovereignty of the Grand Lodge saw itself suddenly threatened by the Chapters, which were first constituted by the Scottish Masters, and which then swelled when the High Grades were multiplied. In wishing to exercise over the regularity of the works, the decency of the meetings, and the recruitment of the Brethren, a supervision that the complacent weakness of the Grand Lodge rendered necessary, the first Scottish Chapters, composed of well-intentioned reformers, interposed resolutely between the supreme direction and the Lodges. The Chapters of the High Grades, whose members were considered as superior to the Symbolic Masons, had the same pretentions.

The Grand Lodge strove to react against this spirit of insubordination when it began to manifest. It declared war on the Scottish Masters whose activity had been felt in the Lodges around 1740, that is to say scarcely two years after the election of the Duc d'Antin as first Grand Master ad vitam of the French Freemasons. When after his death, occurring in 1742, the Grand Lodge named in his place, by the unanimous vote of sixteen Parisian Venerables, on December 11th of the same year, the Comte de Clermont, it took the title of English Grand Lodge of France, to mark well that it refused to recognize the Scottish Rite, and the General Ordinances that it approved on this occasion and which were, within a trifle, a reproduction of the first nineteen articles of the English Constitutions of 1723 and 1738, contained a twentieth and final article saying: "Having learned of late that some Brothers are presented under the title of Scottish Masters and lay claim in certain Lodges to the rights and privileges of which there exists not a trace in the archives and customs of all the Lodges established upon the surface of the globe, the Grand Lodge, in order to maintain the unity and harmony which ought to reign among all Freemasons, has decided that all these Scottish Masters, unless they be Officers of the Grand Lodge or of any other particular Lodge, ought to be considered by the Brethren as equal to the other Apprentices or Companions, of which they must wear the costume without any sign of distinction."[1203]

The authority of the Grand Lodge was threatened again more directly when the "Régimes" were formed, that is to say particular organizations conferring a series of High Grades already existing but slightly modified to form a superficially homogenous "System." These "Rites" constituted in the midst of the Society castes aiming for hegemony. Some of these clans founded schismatic Masonic powers, such as the "Mère-Loge Écossaise du Rite Philosophique" at Paris, and the "Mère-Loge

Écossaise" of Marseille, which proclaimed themselves autonomous and attributed to themselves the right to constitute Blue Lodges. But the majority adopted an even more dangerous tactic, though less brutal in appearance. Their heads, pretending to play the role of secret Superiors of the entirety of Masonry, left to the Grand Lodge the care of constituting and directing the Blue Lodges; they sought not to officially enroll any of these latter into their System, but they did their best to recruit from their numerous adherents in a manner to constitute a rather powerful party in order to exercise a decisive influence over the central government. If the "Souverain Conseil, Sublime Mère-Loge Écossaise du Grand Globe Française," founded at Paris in 1752, seems to have had but an ephemeral existence, the "Chapter of Clermont" which, by its title, set itself of its own authority under the patronage of the Grand Master, began in 1754 to confer High Degrees and to recruit its members from the elite of profane society.

The Grand Lodge, into the bosom of which the Scottish Masters had penetrated by infiltration, had to strike its flag. On July 4, 1755, it renounced its English predicate, probably in response to the desires of those of its members of whom several belonged to the Chapter of Clermont and all of whom possessed some of the different Scottish degrees[1204] and recognized important privileges to the Scottish Masters. The new statutes sanctioned by it conveyed at article 23 that the Scottish Masters had, like the Venerables, and to the exclusion of the Symbolic Masters, the right to remain covered and armed during the meetings and, at article 42, it granted them high supervision over the works: they alone had the right to signal the irregularities committed, to take the word without being invited by the Venerable or his replacement, and to render account only to their equals in degree of their personal faults. These statutes, which had strength of law for all regular French Masons and were signed by sixty Masters and Surveillants of the Parisian Lodges, bore the "secret seal" of the Écossais.[1205]

The Grand Lodge did not grant, it is true, legal existence to the High Degrees and by its ruling of 1756, which referred manifestly to the Scottish Chapters, it decided to only recognize the three degrees of the Masonry of Saint John, and to be comprised exclusively of irremovable Venerables of the Lodges of Paris, presided over by the Grand Master and the Officers at his nomination[1206], but, in granting to the holders of the Scottish degrees particular rights and privileges, it sanctioned their claims. Rival Systems or Régimes argued over the direction of this supreme authority which showed itself so little capable of resisting the ambitions of "Écossisme." In 1756, the "College de Valois," directing committee of the "Knights of the East," which had recruited in the middle classes, constituted at Paris a new Masonic power: the "Souveraine Grande Loge des Chevaliers très libres de l'Orient, Princes et Souverains de la Maçonnerie" [Sovereign Grand Lodge of the very free Knights of the East, Princes, and Sovereigns of Masonry], whose statutes said at article 7 that "just as the Scottish masters are the Grand Sovereigns of the Order, so are the Knights of the East the Sovereigns and Princes born from every Order." This power entered immediately into rivalry with the Chapter of Clermont and each of the Systems sought to get the upper hand at the time of the triennial election of the Grand Officers of the Grand Lodge. The aristocracy of birth and money retorted in 1758 by organizing a "Sovereign Council of Emperors of the East and West," which was a development of the College of Clermont. The Sovereign Council could look forward to exercising a preponderant influence over the Grand Lodge through the intervention of two of its members, one of which was at the same time Substitute

General of the Grand Master and the other his Substitute Particular.

In 1761 the Grand Lodge was divided into two camps by the competition between the Knights of the East and the Emperors of the East and West, each of the two parties striving to occupy with its partisans the posts of the Grand Officers and to dispose of the majority in the Councils of the Grand Lodge. There was a truce in 1762: an accord passed between the two factions permitting each of them to be represented among the Grand Officers elected on July 4th. But, the System of the Knights of the East, finding itself momentarily weakened by internal dissentions which had led to the dissolution of the College of Valois, replaced by a "Sovereign Council," the Emperors of the East and West resumed the fight with an ardor that rewarded a brilliant success: at the triennial renewal of the general staff of the Grand Lodge, on June 24, 1765, they triumphed over their adversaries and took away nearly all the places with an imposing majority. The conquered did not accept their defeat in silence. They made violent protests to be heard, and even published injurious pamphlets to which responded expulsions.

A coalition of the moderates of both parties ended up being formed within the Grand Lodge. Tired of these quarrels, which caused too many Masons to forget the fraternity preached by their statutes, they sought the means to put an end to it. Realizing that "Écossism" was the true reason for these fratricidal struggles, they thought to make the effect disappear by suppressing the cause, and induced the Grand Lodge to make a decree, on August 14, 1766, to prohibit the Lodges of its obedience from cultivating any High Grade whatever it was.

∴

This decision was without practical consequences, for the High Grades found among the Masons too eager a clientele to fear seeing itself abandoned by it, and the official reprobation did not prevent the Chapters from continuing their assemblies outside of the ordinary meetings of the Lodges. But the prestige enjoyed by all that came from the capital of the kingdom in the opinion of the provincials, led the Brothers of Bordeaux to exaggerate the importance of the prohibition decreed by the Grand Lodge. The members of la Française, object of the animosity of l'Anglaise hostile by principle to all the degrees superior to the three symbolic degrees, felt particularly the danger that consisted for them of the disobedience to the orders received from Paris. They were afraid to see their Lodge scratched from the register of regular workshops, where it came to be inscribed in spite of the efforts of its rival. Its chiefs decided, therefore, to submit, at least provisionally, to the decree of the Grand Lodge and the Temple (Coën) was closed.[1207]

So, the Order of Élus Coëns found itself henceforth without a base. In order to give it a prestige permitting it to live an independent existence, it was necessary to constitute in the capital a Masonic authority being able to claim the same privileges as those enjoyed by the Sovereign Council of the Knights of the East or that of the Emperors of the East and West. Pasqually then departed for Paris at the end of 1766 in order to establish there a sort of superior Council, which would have in appearance the direction of the System, but of which he would remain the inspirer and secret chief. He also wished to explore the Parisian Lodges and to try to make some recruits there or to find there some influential protectors. Finally, he had in his head a "mechanical affair," of which we know nothing precise, except that it would not succeed.[1208]

Success crowned his efforts only in part. If he had the satisfaction of learning that the Grand Lodge had recalled on October 2, the decree of August 14[1209], his propaganda was soon known and provoked a violent reaction. The Grand Lodge "repelled his opinions" and "dismissed this secretary from the bosom of the Lodges of his constitution."[1210] This formal excommunication removed from Pasqually all hope of exercising any influence whatever in the Masonic world. It did not, however, have any grave consequence because of the disappearance of the Grand Lodge in February 1767, while Pasqually was still at Paris. The event was brought about by a recrudescence of the hostilities between the Knights and the Emperors. The latter, after having obtained by their pressing steps the tacit recognition of the High Grades, had led the Grand Lodge to submit to the Lodges of its obedience a project of fusion with their Council. This proposition had immediately raised the vehement protestations of the Knights, the noisiest of whom had been expelled from the Grand Lodge. On December 27, 1766, the solemn feast of Saint John of Winter was not able to be celebrated because of these dissentions. On February 4, 1767, the expelled Brothers presented themselves at the doors of the hall where sat the Grand Lodge. They knocked over the guards, burst into the Lodge room, but were expelled therefrom after a lively pugilism, the authors of which were publicly blamed by the Grand Master, Comte de Clermont, who refused to take part in the debate. The public authority saw itself forced to intervene. After some hints of repression, it was, after some thirty years, resigned to tolerate a secret society which seemed to it, in summary, rather inoffensive and to which belonged so many quality people and men of standing, but the scandal made by the affair of February 4th seemed intolerable. On the very next day the lieutenant of police de Sartines ordered the dissolution of the Grand Lodge and on February 21st a royal edict formally prohibited it from assembling in the future.

The prohibition mentioned neither the Lodges of Paris, nor those of the provinces, and according to the *Almanach des Francs-Maçons* for the year 1768, they "remained as active as formerly."[1211] The measures taken by the royal authority favored therefore, in the final count, the schemings of the particular Systems in suppressing the sole authority which, although weakened, gave to Blue Masonry a sort of cohesion and in preventing the most powerful among them, those of the Emperors, from taking control of the general direction of the Society. On the other hand, the care with which the Lodges would henceforth, after such an uproar, conceal their existence made easier the underground work of the occultist Masons. It is indeed during the period when the gatherings of the Grand Lodge were suspended, from 1767 to 1771, that was founded in Paris the first of those Chapters Rose-Croix whose Rite had very prominent mystical tendencies.

Pasqually drew profit from these favorable circumstances. He put himself in contact with some distinguished Masons, among whom is cited Bacon de la Chevalerie, Willermoz, Fauger d'Igneaucourt, de Luzignan, Henri de Loos, Rozé, enrolled them in his Order and was able thus to establish at Paris at the March equinox, 1767, a Chapter at the head of which would be found a committee composed of Réau-Croix and whose title of Sovereign Tribunal announced rather clearly the role and the intention.[1212]

He had filled his recruits with enthusiasm by performing before them an operation which, to believe him, "had the greatest possible success," and, on their authority, he received to the degree of Réau-Croix three among them: Bacon de la Chevalerie, de Luzignan, and Bonnichon, called du Guers.[1213] Satisfied to have thus found in the capital proselytes who he asserted to have recruited "in the intention of making himself a shield of spiritual children,"[1214] which may be taken as much in the proper sense as in the mystical sense, he made of Bacon, lieutenant-colonel of infantry, old Venerable la Félicité of Rouen, and of the military Lodge Saint-Jean de la Gloire, his Universal Substitute at Paris and conferred the title of Inspector General for the Orient of Lyon to J.B. Willermoz, "fabricator of materials of silk and silver and commissionaire of silk goods," old Venerable of la Parfaite Amitié, and founder in this town of la Sagesse, Lodge not affiliated with the Grand Lodge of France and secret, of which he had presided over the meetings from 1756 to 1761.[1215] Finally he founded at Versailles a group of Élus Coëns, probably placed under the direction of Rozé, from whom he received a visit the following year at Bordeaux with two other Brothers of Versailles.[1216]

∴

Pasqually left Paris sometime after the constitution of the Sovereign Tribunal, promising to return in the month of September. He arrived at Bordeaux at least by June after having visited upon his route Amboise, Blois, Tours, Poitiers, La Rochelle, Rochefort, Saintes, and Blaye, at Lodges that he calls "clandestine," perhaps because they had not affiliated with the defunct Grand Lodge, or else because they sheltered secret Chapters.[1217] But if the stops were numerous, it does not seem that they had been very fruitful. Though he boasted to have received "a multitude of politeness on the part of Masons of good faith" who would have asked him "to put them under the protection of the Sovereign Tribunal of the Élus Coëns of Paris" and would have prayed him to grant them himself some constitutions or have them freed therefrom by the Sovereign Tribunal, he had only made some recruits in the Lodge l'Union Parfaite of La Rochelle which desired to quickly obtain constitutions for the "degrees of perfection" and of which the Venerable, Basset, and three other members received from him some Coën degrees.[1218]

Recently having returned to Bordeaux, Pasqually, reassured by the annulment of the decree of August 14, and confident in the support that he had arranged at Paris, "reopened his Temple" and, consolidating his situation in the profane world as he had done in the Masonic society, he wed in September Marguerite-Angelique de Colas de Saint-Michel, daughter of an old major at the regiment of Foix.[1219] The year 1768 was marked by a happy event: the birth of a son that his father, after having had him baptized, received as Grand Master Coën "at the seventh hour of the last solar horizon, conforming to our laws, assisted by four old simple Coëns,"[1220] and marked also by a misadventure from which Pasqually pulled through without great damage, but which caused him grave concern, Bonnichon, called du Guers, whose acquaintance he had made at Paris the previous year, was a man of a rather doubtful morality and living on ill-defined revenues. Although put on his guard by Bacon and Willermoz, who had had the occasion to judge the person and pointed out "his bad conduct and the great number of excesses to which he was inclined," Pasqually had become infatuated with Bonnichon.[1221] Received as Réau-Croix and named member of the Sovereign Tribunal, this black sheep had immediately larked about. In the course of a trip to Lyon, where he had received to the grade of Very Respectable Masters the Brothers d'Epernon and Sellonf, he had taken such liberties with the ritual that Willermoz, indignant of such profanations, had denounced them to Pasqually. The latter, in acknowledging to the Inspector General of the Orient of Lyon, on June 20, 1768, reception of his report, wrote: "I too am no less with a deeply grieved heart at the horrible irregularities which were held during the course of these various receptions by the Very Powerful Master du Guers, Réau-Croix; I am unaware of the motive that has had him act in this way." He begged Willermoz to compare the degree papers brought by du Guers with the originals delivered by himself to Bacon de la Chevalerie[1222], which appeared to indicate that he was suspicious of the adaptations that du Guers may have made surreptitiously to his work.

Nevertheless, when du Guers arrived in the month of August at Bordeaux, he resumed all his influence upon the Grand Sovereign. Pasqually received him with open arms, made him a secretary and a confidant, and, taken as arbitrator of the disputes that had arisen between the Réau-Croix of Paris and their colleague, decided invariably in favor of the latter.[1223] Profiting from the blindness of the Master, the cheat committed numerous abuses of confidence, selling the degrees for hard cash, proceeding, without being authorized, to receptions for cash, and delivering instructions of his invention, meanwhile seeking to discredit Pasqually among the disciples at Paris.[1224] Deaf to the warnings of the members of the Sovereign Tribunal, Pasqually turned again in September to help from du Guers in the writing of the rituals.[1225]

Finally in November, the eyes of Pasqually had decided to open following, he claimed, a divine intervention, the Operations having clearly manifested the unworthiness of du Guers who "had withdrawn (from the Chamber of Operation) covered by shame and confusion." Pasqually announced consequently to the Élus Coëns that "in order to avoid what du Guers used by his name and his instructions, he had removed him from among them and left him to the mercy of the Great Architect of the Universe." "It is necessary to pray him," he added, "that he has pity on him, but he has been rendered unworthy of the confidence of men."[1226]

Touched very little by this gentleness, which could very well, moreover, have been in part the effect of the fear that an unscrupulous individual inspired, the infernal du Guers got together with a Mr. Blanchet and some Masons expelled from la Franrçaise[1227] to bring complaints to the jurats of Bordeaux. He accused Pasqually of being "a foreigner and an adventurer" and to have defamed him "in all the good houses of the town." Pasqually had to go present his defense before Mr. d'Arche, the jurat charged to investigate the complaint. He was able to prove to the magistrate "proofs in hand," that du Guers was "a swindler under the pretext of Masonry" and made him aware of "all the vileness, acts of baseness, and impieties of this crook." The adepts that du Guers, in order to counteract the defense of Pasqually, had cited as respondents refused to lend him their support. Therefore, the magistrates asked the plaintiff to desist from his action, and went even so far, to which Pasqually assures, as to "scold him cruelly."

Nevertheless, du Guers did not yet consider himself beaten. He went everywhere, saying that he would be the ruin of Pasqually and would bring his complaint to the procurator general and to the marshals of France, since the jurats refused to give him justice. It was not very likely that the royal magistrates would consent to occupying themselves with an affair concerning an illegal association, and the marshals of France, charged with ruling by arbitration the affairs of honor between people of quality, had not known of the defamation complaint of the commoner Bonnichon. Nevertheless, Pasqually judged it prudent to make a new visit to Mr. d'Arche in order to draw for him again the portrait of this "swindler and errant knight." The jurat figured that the dispute would be settled between Masons, since Bonnichon was accused of "sharp prevarications in the Order," and he appointed a representative from the Hotel de Ville to assist in the judgment and to give an account.[1228] The tribunal constituted by la Française held session on January 5, 1769, and condemned du Guers to be expelled from the Order of Élus Coëns. The decree, submitted to Mr. d'Arche, was approved by him and Pasqually was eager to send extracts therefrom to the adepts and to make known the text thereof to the Masons of Bordeaux and to the persons that du Guers had talked to about his pretended grievances.

The exiled saw to make a final appearance: he had found the curé of Pasqually's parish and accused the latter of being an apostate and, under the pretext of Masonry, the founder of a heretical sect. Such an imputation could have formidable consequences. The poor Pasqually was forced to justify himself before the ecclesiastic by producing what he calls "his certificates of Catholicity," that is to say his certificates of baptism and marriage, and his confession notes, by establishing that he fulfilled "the exact and essential duties of a zealous Christian." Rendered enraged by these successive failures, du Guers presented himself to Pasqually one day when the latter was found at the country-home of one of his Emulators, Mr. de Brulle, a king's guard. The Powerful Masters de Grainville and de Balzac, to whom the madman declared that he would kill the Grand Sovereign by a pistol shot when he would happen to encounter him again, attempted in vain to calm him and had, with much difficulty, sent him away. They would have been less disquieted if they had known that "the tutelary angel" of the Master had taken precautions to lay obstacles to the homicidal projects of the miserable "impostor swindler" by "following him so as to piss in the bassinet."[1229] Moreover, the magistrates ended up ordering du Guers to leave Bordeaux. He embarked for Cayenne, and one hears nothing more spoken of him.[1230] He had not remained but four months with Pasqually[1231], but they had certainly been full.

∴

Meanwhile the Order had made some progress. The Very Powerful Masters de Grainville and de Champoléon, officers of the regiment of Foix, had presented to Pasqually one of their young comrades that they were able in all conscience to recommend to him as a "man of desire" par excellence. Claude de Saint-Martin, then twenty-five years of age, furnished with a commission of lieutenant after having been for six months king's counsel at the presidential seat of Tours, arrived from Lorient where he had entered into the service. His determined penchant for mysticism had attracted the attention of the two Élus Coëns and they led him to the Master whose doctrines would leave in his spirit and in the works that he wrote later so profound a trace. In order not to lose anything of the teaching that revealed to him his true vocation, Saint-Martin "habitually kept the same gait" as his comrades by "establishing himself as Pasqually's boarder during the whole season of winter that he did not give to his father."[1232]

On August 13, 1768, Pasqually waited for de Grainville and de Balzac, the latter coming from La Rochelle, who would spend some days with him "for their instruction and in order to receive their constitutive patents to raise Temples in the lands where they were going to pass at the end of September or the beginning of October."[1233]

In April 1769, Pasqually would announce to Willermoz the complete ruin of "Blanquet," the old accomplice of du Guers. "I told you," he wrote to his lieutenant of Lyon, "that Mr. Blanquet has lifted foot from Bordeaux with the great talent that I know of him to not reimburse anyone. He is saved with his harlot, they say, in Paris. The truth is one, it is long to broach, but it is demonstrated always such as it is."[1234] The flight of his enemy had at this point set him so at ease that he spoke thereof again four months later to another correspondent: "I inform you that Mr. Blanquet and other chiefs of the bull (the complaint addressed in 1765 to the Grand Lodge) against me and the Order come to be lacking (become bankrupt) and have lifted foot from this Orient (Bordeaux). Blanquet ought to be under less exhaustion at Paris with his concubine the Gauntemps woman. And truth is avenged."[1235] The satisfaction that he experienced was not only caused by resentment; the overthrow of his old adversaries had brought about, in the judgments borne upon him and upon his association by the Masons of Bordeaux, a sudden change that the rest were soon made to feel. He could announce that "this conduct has taken out of our apocryphal Lodges (Blue Lodges, or those not having a Coën Temple) the error," and, if he took on airs a little too presumptuous in adding: "The Lodges henceforth make movement to seek entrance among us, but this takes place only with great circumspection and difficulty,"[1236] it remains no less that a certain number of Brothers until then hostile to la Française Élue Écossaise requested to be received. In November, these old "antagonists of the Order,"[1237] among whom a note of Willermoz cites Duroy d'Hauterive, de Calvimont, du Saingnant de Serre, de Pitrail-Puysegur, Carracioli, Isnard, were inscribed upon the rolls of the Élus Coëns.[1238]

Starting from 1770[1239], the work of Pasqually had no longer to suffer exterior attacks. He wrote on April 7th to the Sovereign Tribunal: "The Order takes on here a brilliant color... Last Thursday, was proposed the entry into the Temple (to receive into the Lodge) some Brothers that Mr. du Guers had suborned from (made come out of) my Temple. They have declared verbally to the Brother de la Dorie and other emulators of my Temple the horrors that Mr. Guers had told them of me, and the errors where they had plunged, just as the evil traits that he had shown them, and that they see today clearly that he has astonished and deceived them cruelly, and that this is unfortunate. I have ordered (indicated) to my Council that it was not in my power to grant them their pardon, and that it was useless to think so. Let them follow their judgment for a time immemorial."[1240]

In this period, the Order would have had, according to one of the official chronicalers, at Bordeaux a rather large number of adherents and counted affiliated Lodges at Montpellier, Avignon, Foix, Libourne, La Rochelle, Eu, Paris, Lyon, Versailles, Metz, etc.[1241]

CHAPTER VI
Paris and Lyon against Bordeaux

If the recruitment marched forth rather satisfactorily, the success of the undertaking was compromised by the inertia of the groups at Paris and Lyon, whose heads assailed the Grand Sovereign with objections and complaints.

The disagreement between Pasqually and the Réau-Croix comprising the Sovereign Tribunal was born scarcely some months after the constitution of the latter. The cause of the dispute was not a conflict of duties; Pasqually had left to the Tribunal the power to issue the constitutions of every kind and had promised to never give them himself "having always been the dupe of his good heart and of his too great readiness."[1242] Therefore, after having conferred two degrees on the Brothers of l'Union Parfaite of La Rochelle, he had referred to the Sovereign Tribunal the new initiates who would return to Paris to obtain the constitutions of their Temple.[1243] In February 1769, the Brothers of Bordeaux received from Paris the letters patent of constitution of the Temple of Libourne and transmitted them to the interested parties while inviting them to officially notify the Sovereign Tribunal of the regular opening of their Temple.[1244]

But these administrative and honorific functions did not suffice to content the zeal of the Parisian adepts. They reproached the Master for being too slow to complete their instruction, more from the point of view of their mystical works than in what concerned the organization of the Order: rituals and degree papers. They found an ally and an interpreter of their grievances in Willermoz whose Masonic dignities and the esteem he enjoyed among the Brothers of Lyon gave him the right to speak out.

Pasqually had always taken care to treat this important adept with respect. He had conferred upon him verbally, at the time of their interview at Paris in 1767, the title of "Grand Master of the Grand Temple of France,"[1245] a denomination that granted to the Lodge of Élus Coëns that Willermoz wished to found at Lyon a sort of supremacy over the other Lodges of the same System. On June 19, 1767, barely having returned to Bordeaux, he sent to Willermoz, whom he called: "Our Very Respectable and Very High Master, Our Knight Inspector General, Conductor and Commander-in-chief of the columns of the Orient and Occident of Our Sublime Orders," a long letter, written in order to comply "with the public and secret conventions taken with its Sovereign Tribunal," where he recounted in detail his Masonic journey from Paris to Bordeaux[1246], and the correspondence had continued in a very regular fashion.

In April 1768, Bacon having requested the authorization to receive Willermoz to the degree of Réau-Croix, Pasqually responded to him the following month: "I would never object to the Respectable Master being rewarded in every respect and even with satisfaction, no one more than he deserves it more." Therefore, all while reproaching Bacon for being engaged by a promise that was difficult for him to keep because, "the operation being outside of time," one was hardly able "to promise some subject (effect) on behalf of the candidate," Pasqually gave him the necessary instructions and was engaged "to make every effort to abandon his domestic affairs in order to dispose himself to strengthen Bacon in his operation to reward the zeal and the laborious works of the Respectable Master." He said again: "I believe him to be worthy of the success that I desire for him in this operation; it will not depend on me for him to be satisfied."[1247] Willermoz was then ordained Réau-Croix at Paris by Bacon on May 13, 1768, and so the letter sent to Lyon by Pasqually on the following June 20 was addressed: "To our Very High, Very Respectable, and Very Powerful Master de Willermoz, Inspector General born of the Universal Order of Knight Masons Élus Coëns of the Universe, Sovereign Judge of the seven powerful Tribunals of justice of the low and high classes of Our Orders, Commander and Conductor in chief of the columns of the Orient and Occident of Our Grand Mother Lodge of France, of the suffragan Lodges and particular Lodges which will be raised by him to the glory of the Eternal under the very powerful constitutions of Our seven Temples, Respectable and Very Powerful Chief of the entire Order over his Grand Orient of Lyon and over all his oriental department."[1248]

Willermoz had to feel quite flattered to bear such imposing titles, but precise instructions would have made his affair much better. The members of the Sovereign Tribunal, who received neither degree papers nor theurgical teachings, shared his discontent. Pasqually had committed the error of recruiting adepts and founding a Masonic Rite before having fixed his ritual. His impudent haste put him, with respect to his immediate collaborators, in a most difficult situation, for his wrong move, of which he could not confess to them under pain of loss of all his prestige, could only be repaired at the price of an intense work and after rather long delays.

The Réau-Croix of Paris, irritated by a delay that they attributed to the negligence or unwillingness of their Master, withdrew into an obstinate silence and showed little zeal for recruitment. In May, Pasqually declared, in a letter to Bacon, to not "count much on the propagation of the Order by the slowness that he saw" with the Universal Substitute.[1249] Bacon no longer responded to the letters coming from Bordeaux, and had not even acknowledged reception in September of the first degrees and general regulations for the ceremonies that had been sent to him the previous month, so Pasqually threatened him to no longer make new mailings so long as Bacon gave no sign of life, and declared himself determined to no longer write him, since it seemed that the occupations and health of the Substitute did not permit him to maintain a regular correspondence. Left without news from Paris, Pasqually was reduced to entreating Willermoz to instruct him on what Bacon was doing and on his present disposition towards the Order and towards its members.[1250]

But Willermoz also had grievances to present. He complained in September 1768 of not receiving instruction allowing him to organize his "Grand Temple of France."[1251] In order to appease him, Pasqually instructed him immediately that he would work with all his might to "finish all our degrees, as well as all the ceremonies and catechisms, in order to have them sent off to Paris, so that the Sovereign Tribunal be filled (furnished) with all the objects that it comprises (of which it has need) in order to satisfy its Grand Temples (Coën Chapters), its Lodges, as well as all its members."[1252]

In the spring of 1769, the situation remained as tense, and for the same reasons. Pasqually continued to make grand promises without keeping any of them. He declared himself on April 29 "all ready to found every kind of establishments, all ceremonies thereof, laws, instructions, and secret explanations, for the general and particular instruction of the Brothers, as well as for the particular discourses of the receptions of Apprentices, Companions, and Particular Masters," which signified that he had simply adapted the symbolic degrees. On the other hand, he admitted that he was only engaged in writing "the instructions of the Apprentice, Companion, and Master Coëns, and other degrees," and, in order to excuse his delay, he accused Bacon of keeping in his own possession the "orders of operation" confided to him at the time of his passage to Bordeaux; he had not kept his promise to send them back immediately after having copied them and, lacking these important documents, Pasqually had been forced to suspend his Equinox Working.[1253] The Grand Sovereign even added in order to make felt at the Tribunal of Paris that it could not do without him, that he "would work to found the establishment of Bordeaux with some presidents and councilors of our Court of Parliament,"[1254] but these illustrious conquests, which existed, moreover, only in design, did not impress the Élus Coëns at Paris. On the other hand, Willermoz, visibly little flattered by the role of informer that Pasqually wished to have him play, aligned himself openly on the side of the Sovereign Tribunal.

An excess of zeal by a faithful Réau-Croix, or perhaps too clever a maneuver by Pasqually, put the fire to the powder. The members of the Tribunal had, several times over, asked their master to come complete the instruction of the Élus Coëns of Paris and Versailles, and even desired to see him definitively settled in among them.[1255] But the pecuniary situation of Pasqually did not permit him to proceed with so seductive a project in so many respects. Already he had had to give up, in 1767, returning for the end of the year to Paris as he had manifested the intention of taking leave of his new disciples. De Grainville, writing in February 1769 to Willermoz, on behalf of Pasqually, to instruct him on what he had to do at the next March equinox, added in post-scriptum: "However zealous each of us in particular may be for the good of the Order, I doubt that any of us are able to instruct anyone. It is therefore absolutely necessary that D.M. (dom Martinès) go to Paris and that there, under the eyes of the S.T. (Sovereign Tribunal) he works in symbolic bonds such as is necessary for the satisfaction of everyone, and that, this work finished, he thinks about the instruction of the new and old Réau-Croix. This transplanting of D.M. and his wife cannot be done without advances on the part of the S.T. Dom M. owes here around 1,200 pounds that must be payed before leaving, otherwise his creditors would make a stir and he would remain, to the detriment of the Order."[1256]

This proposal, that the malcontent Very Powerful Master believed, and not without some apparent reason, to be suggested by Pasqually himself, gave them advantage over their Master. On March 16th, Bacon responded that he was ready to contribute on his part, but that the S.T. had waited for two years in vain for the fulfilling of formal promises, that the Brothers of Paris complained rightfully of being neglected, and that some among them had been up to then manifesting doubts on the loyalty or knowledge of their instructor. Bacon, who had several times over vouched for the good faith of Pasqually, estimated it little advisable to ceaselessly disappoint adepts who could not be reproached for their zeal to be instructed and from whom "some sacrifices were expected."[1257]

Willermoz, who had to return to Paris in April for his affairs, wished to work together with Bacon and de Luzignan before taking position. After having conferred with them[1258] he wrote on April 29, a response which laid out without consideration the grievances of the Réau-Croix of Paris and Lyon. He was certainly not very satisfied, he wrote, to have received prohibition form doing any Equinox Working, nevertheless, "as the reasons to have them suspended by Pasqually himself were beyond his comprehension," he had conformed to the orders of the Master. But upon another subject, "on the necessity to make arrangements so that the Order provides for Pasqually in the future" and "on his difficulties for the acquittal of his debts," it was lawful for him to speak, and he profited greatly from this faculty. "I have found," he said directly to Pasqually, "the Powerful Masters de la Chevalerie and de Luzignan very little disposed towards doing what the Master de Grainville requests in your name and dissatisfied with the excess of your behavior towards them and towards the Order. To get to the point, they have communicated to me all the correspondence held between the Orients of Bordeaux and Paris since my journey last year. I acknowledge frankly, Powerful Master, that it cannot be read with composure. It seems that you have sought every means possible to mortify the Substitute Powerful Master that you yourself have specially charged with the affairs of the Order."

Willermoz then recalled to Pasqually how he had let himself be duped by du Guers and ridiculed relentlessly the blindness which had made him prefer that imposter to Bacon. "When you have no other means to know men than those which are general to the human race, can you only equate the conduct and sentiments of the Substitute P.M. with that of Mr. Duguers? The one enjoys the most entire and best deserved reputation and the other already merited your resentment by a great number of excesses to which he was prone and of which you were instructed, whether by the Substitute M. or by myself... It has been necessary for you to become the victim of Mr. Duguers in order to open your eyes to his nature. I acknowledge frankly that this has been a great embarrassment for me. You have assured me so often that your knowledge gives you the infallible means to know the heart of men that, seeing to what point you yourself have fallen on this occasion, I am reduced to doubt more strongly than ever a knowledge which is so sublime that an intelligent man may add there a full and entire faith upon any other witnesses than that of his own." Indeed, Willermoz was always disposed to follow the career that he had entered on the assurances of Pasqually, de Grainville, and Bacon on "the truth of la Chose," and, although he had followed exactly and in good faith all that had been prescribed to him "without being any happier thereby" (without having obtained any manifestations), he did not want, by too much haste, to lose the success that he had been promised, but his confidence was shaken by the remarks of Pasqually himself. Had the latter not written one day that Duguers had convinced him "to give things in truth." "If we are not entered into the truth therefore," wrote Willermoz," are we then abused? Judge for yourself where these reflections ought to lead us!"

So Willermoz and his colleagues posed their conditions. "In the perplexity where your letters have thrown us, we are in the position to request of you some unequivocal proofs of the truth of la Chose, which put us in a state to judge for ourselves. Show us sincerely the true path, prescribe the means; the most exact without doubt will be best and the Order will be engaged to show you its recognition and to make fixed appointments for the future. What the Messers de la Chevalerie and de Luzignan have done in the past guarantees you the continuation of their good will.[1259] I will contribute to it voluntarily as much as my means will permit as soon as I know to what I am held...we are, at Lyon, five initiates to whom for over a year I have promised instructions without having received any. I have there a number of very suitable subjects and all ready at the first sign, but to whom I would have a scruple to have make the least expense without being sure myself of the truth of the aim to which they aspire. The Temple of Lyon may, in very little time, take a real consistency; it is upon you to throw up the foundations, you will find therein your advantage and to us the satisfaction that we desire...I want to be able to announce at Lyon an objective true and worthy of honest folks and not to play the charlatan. You will not reprimand, I think, my fastidiousness, the sentiments of Messrs. de la Chevalerie and de Luzignan are the same; thereupon we have explained ourselves, they are repulsed by your conduct... The Order demands the carrying out of your promises, nothing is more just."

Nevertheless, after having so clearly established the respective position of the Master to his principal disciples, Willermoz, who, fundamentally, only asked to be convinced, set aside his natural courtesy and gentleness to take up the above, and all while soliciting a prompt response that found him again at Paris where he gave his address: "chez Glavot, wig-maker, Golet-des-Bourdonnois street," he concluded: "I would be charmed, before leaving this town, to see the taking up of a definitive arrangement and confidence re-established."[1260]

The documents published at this time do not make known to us the very text of the response that Pasqually made to being put in his place. According to the *Nouvelle Notice Historique*, he let pass the thick of the storm and responded that he was most disposed to communicate the general and particular ceremonies and instructions, but that he feared that they would not study them any better than those that he had given them previously, because it seemed to him that the Brothers were more desirous to advance in the Order than determined to work on their instruction. However, he sent a certain number of papers.[1261] Three months later, at the beginning of August, the question was always to the same point: Pasqually said he was most desirous to fulfill the vows of the members of the Sovereign Tribunal, but he announced that he was still kept for some time at Bordeaux by the present situation, his domestic affairs and the recovery of a small inheritance that one of his relatives, deceased in the Antilles, had left him in this town.[1262] In October or November, he attempted to revive the zeal of Willermoz by announcing the reception of numerous Brothers at Bordeaux and the "great success" (theurgic) of Mr. de Balzac.[1263]

It seems that the calm opposed by Pasqually to the reproaches, insinuations, and demands of the Réau-Croix in revolt had made an impression on the latter. Furthermore, they had conceived since their encounter with him hopes too vast to abandon them without going back. This obstinate expectation convinced them to open a new moral credit account to their Master. A letter that Pasqually addressed to Willermoz on January 20, 1770, mentions a recent agreement passed between Bordeaux and Paris and which restrained the prerogatives of the "Substitute Very Powerful Master." Under the pretext that "his great domestic affairs" took up too much of Bacon's time for him to be able to "attend to all that was suitable to the Order and for the satisfaction of its members," it had been agreed that the constitutions issued by the Sovereign Tribunal would henceforth bear the signature of Pasqually who, in return, made the promise to "issue all the ceremonies of reception of the different degrees of the Order, as well as the different catechisms and the secret explanations of the questions and responses which are contained in said catechisms." "Finally," promised the Grand Sovereign, "I will give from A to Z and everybody will be content."[1264] As to what personally concerned his correspondent, Pasqually asserted to him that, as soon as he would have received some funds from the Antilles from where would return to him "a considerable inheritance that he had had in these lands,"[1265] he would not hesitate to go and install himself at Lyon "to have him work vigorously."[1266] But, his financial difficulties nailing him down to Bordeaux, he enlisted Willermoz, "if he truly had the intention to raise his Grand Temple,"[1267] to have him issue by the Sovereign Tribunal, at the time of his next trip to Paris, a constitution for his Temple of Lyon, and promised for his part to have copies made for him of all the papers by the secretary general and particular that he had had for a year, the Brother Fournier, "good citizen of Bordeaux, very intelligent and very instructed," nephew of the prior of the Grand Augustines of Paris, who had "abandoned all to follow la Chose in all circumstances." But Willermoz was given notice that this copy work would take a good two months.[1268]

Pasqually had manifested the sentiment of having retaken his people in hand and, in order to keep a tight rein, he alternated the curb with encouragement.

In the letter of January 10, Pasqually encouraged Willermoz to be patient in the most cordial terms and affected to treat him even better than the other Réau-Croix. "I exhort you," he told him, "to allow yourself to be led by that which is truly attached to you, just as you must judge it by the things enclosed herein that I send you in order to prepare you for la Chose that you would know. The favor that I ask of you is to not speak thereof to a living soul, seeing that I have not yet transmitted it to anyone, not even to none (any) of my Réau-Croix... If truly la Chose was not such as I have asserted, and that it had not manifested as it has done so before me, and before such persons who have wished to know it, not only would I have abandoned it myself, I would have removed therefrom conscientiously all those who would have wished to approach it in good faith."[1269]

On February 16, he roughly reminded of his modesty the Grand Master of the Grand Temple of France who had probably alleged his title of Réau-Croix in order to demand more light. "You have," he told him, "been received by a man who had neither right nor power in this regard; the Universal Substitute Master not having himself the right and ability to transmit the power to make any Réau-Croix, nor to give any supreme degree, except to transmit his power for the degrees of Apprentice through Master Coën and no more."[1270] By contrast, Willermoz having announced in March, 1770, that he would go the following month to Paris, where de Grainville would likewise go, "in order to make definitive arrangements for the general good of the Order," Pasqually affirmed to desire ardently this encounter and wrote him: "And may the Eternal bless your undertaking to all for this subject. I will contribute no less by my next Working so that he deigns to favor you as much spiritually as temporally and your own for a time immemorial to follow."[1271] But he reminded him some weeks later, in the middle of April, that, according to the agreement passed with Bacon, the Sovereign Tribunal was only able to issue constitutions and that he, Pasqually, would give directly to the interested parties the ceremonies of the different degrees, "the Sovereign Tribunal having neither the time nor the health suitable to be given entirely to this."[1272] Finally, as Willermoz had dared to complain of the raised prices of the patents of constitution, degree papers, jewels, and accessories, he was ashamed of Pasqually's stinginess when such spiritual interests were at play. "All the Brothers that I have here paid, as well as all the Brothers of your Orient, for their degrees. They do not object to the money which must be given for their constitutions and for their furnishings. They need not fear placing their money to things so useful and advantageous to the man of desire."

It must be noted that, the Brother secretary "not being extremely rich," it was natural that in exchange for a considerable work: "extracted from all the ceremonies of reception of the different degrees, as well as from the catechisms and different general and secret explanations," "he was presented with some honoriaries," so that he "did not lose his time absolutely." On the other hand, the indemnity which was due him for the writings of the Grand Temple had been fixed at the rather elevated number of 86 pounds. "This was in order to not multiply the establishments because of the difficulty of finding proper subjects to be admitted into the Order." Furthermore, Pasqually, appealing to the commercial spirit of the merchant of Lyon, showed him that his own interests would be on par with those of the Order, since he would have the right to confer up to the degree of Grand Architect, which would return to him sixteen gold louis, the fee being two gold louis per degree.[1273] For the push to continue the Operations, he let him know that Brother Barbarin "saw and heard much" and that this adept so well-endowed was going to be promoted to the degree of Grand Architect. He finally prayed Willermoz to inform him of the intentions of the Sovereign Tribunal, if he wished "to go forward" or "to retire within his state of Réau-Croix,"[1274] a task that he estimated more to the ability of Bacon and de Luzignan, because of the bad health of the one and the occupation of the other, than that of carrying out la Chose."[1275]

Pasqually was soon set on this last point; he received this same month of April some firm propositions on the part of the Sovereign Tribunal. We do not possess the text thereof, but, from the summary of the response that Pasqually made[1276], it stands out that the Réau-Croix had decided, following the small conference in which Willermoz and de Grainville had taken part, "to procure for him a temporal well-being, whether directly for him or for his wife and children, relative to his works." They demanded in exchange that Pasqually come to live at Paris "to perfectly instruct and found the Réau-Croix," that he show himself "entirely of good faith" towards them in bringing with him "the secret papers and instructions concerning the Order," and in furnishing them the papers allowing the opening of the Lodges of the System. Finally, they posed various questions that Pasqually did not address in his response, but which seem to have been directed towards the Operations and the effect that one should expect therefrom.

Pasqually took his time responding to the offer that he had had called into action a year prior, but his message of July 11, 1770, was copious.

The Master remarked that it is by pure goodness and condescension that he responds, for, as "the Réau-Croix have not accompanied their requests by a sign at the bottom, characteristic of their names, with their grades and dignities in la Chose, the Master could very well ignore such representations and requests and was in the right not to respond, the stamp not being sufficient to obtain it, (and) those who have conducted similar things have been negligent of the laws of the Order."

After having excused himself for the delay caused by the illness of his mother-in-law, which had forced him to suspend all communication, he thanked the Réau-Croix for a proposal "which proves their true zeal for la Chose." He protests "that he wanted to find a physical means to open his heart to his Réau-Croix, so that they are able to read therein his sincere affection for them and his recognition." He nevertheless had to refuse "such advantageous temporal offers," because he does not believe to have yet merited them and because additionally "he cannot and must not hope for any temporal and spiritual goods in this lower world that has not come directly from the Eternal to whom it has devolved entirely feeling rather sufficiently payed and satisfied by his subjects when he is happy enough to restore a man into his first principle of spiritual virtue from which he had had the misfortune to be separated." Finally, "he does not wish to be a burden upon the Réau-Croix." He formally disavowed de Grainville who had let himself be carried away by his zeal and, not only had not consulted him before writing to the Sovereign Tribunal, but even had acted contrary to his counsels of prudence and his recommendations to "procure la Chose as much towards its heads as towards its members." De Grainville had had, additionally, the error of wishing to act upon Pasqually himself by the intermediary of his wife in writing to the latter in order to "engage her to convince her husband to accept the offers of the Sovereign Tribunal." De Grainville would have done better to know the disposition of Madame de Pasqually "who is strongly opposed to what her husband professes as la Chose[1277] having seen the great worries that it has had from the bad subjects who had been admitted therein." Having received this awkward letter in the absence of her husband, Madame de Pasqually had unsealed and read it aloud in the presence of her relatives, "who gave their support and counsel," and some strangers. She burned this letter in rage and she very nearly secretly burned "the things most essential to the Order, which are at their country-house." This letter had caused a serious quarrel between the husband and wife; they were reconciled on the mediation of a third party, but Pasqually had had to promise to no longer correspond with de Grainville. In short, if the latter had not awkwardly meddled in this affair, if he had limited himself to writing directly to Pasqually, as had done the Sovereign Tribunal, Pasqually would now be en route to Paris, whereas he "had been forced by his condition of husband and father of his family to deprive himself yet some time from seeing in person his faithful subjects, which will be as soon as possible, his only consolation while awaiting this time is to see them in spirit."

Moreover, the pecuniary situation of Pasqually was not as critical as de Grainville depicted it. He owed around 3,000 pounds; he had acquitted the majority of it and owed no more than 1,000 pounds that he hoped to be able to pay by constraining himself yet some time. Then, he would be able to leave Bordeaux without fearing any affront to his creditors. If he rejoined his Réau-Croix, he wanted to do it at his expense. He asked no more than to go to Paris; "he would have even gone on foot rather than horse for the sole satisfaction of the Sovereign Tribunal." He is most disposed not only to staying in the capital, but even to transporting himself elsewhere in order to instruct more particularly his disciples, but what benefit would those latter draw from his presence if they did not place themselves, through personal efforts, in a condition to draw profit from his teachings?

The Réau-Croix had believed that "la Chose coming immediately from him," they had therefore only to "entreat him, frighten him, or offer him a concession of gold in order to have his secret"; but they were in error. "its knowledge is not a particular secret, but rather the fruit of a long and laborious work of the spirit, and of total renouncement of every impure thing. All that the Master may do and say for the advantage of his Réau-Croix do not come directly from him, it is the fruit of the constancy of his works. La Chose comes from above and not from the Master. He is only an agent of la Chose." But he had to remind the adepts that "the one who is elected first among them is not elected by them and by their will, but it is by his laborious works, and his election is his reward." If an Operation has succeeded before them at Paris it is "because it had been guided in this by the principal chief of la Chose." Without its relief, Pasqually "would have fallen to the center of his assembly all covered with shame and confusion" and this aid was all the more necessary to him that he had business with subjects so poorly prepared to "attain to (succeed in) a similar physical operation." But one cannot count on the uncondional repetition of an intervention which has been able to manifest one time exceptionally "for the triumph of the truth." Therefore, having "seen all the difficulties and cruel fatigues that he has felt and feels still for the works that he had done on behalf of some subjects before time, he no longer wishes to henceforth take on absolutely anything, and he will undertake nothing with this subject that has not been given and taught to him by someone stronger than him and "for this effect he falls back upon what he may know to be produced by some particular working."[1278]

It depends therefore on the Réau-Croix, and them alone, to obtain these proofs of their vocation. It is necessary that they have more fervor in the future, "that they walk exactly in the path that has been prescribed to them by his instructions." "Before testifying such ambition under the pretext of seeking to be instructed," let them study "the few ceremonies that he has given them." "Let them observe with precision all that he will prescribe to them for spiritual and temporal conduct, in the different prayers of the days of the year, the equinoxes, the solstices, and the abstinences that they must observe during their life and in the course of a working." In order to procure the perfect condition, they must put therein much of their own, "la Chose being more towards them than towards the Master," to fulfill exactly the promises that they have contracted with the Great Architect of the Universe, that is to say to receive with resignation and indifferently the good and the difficult that pleases the Eternal to send them for the expiation of their sins, and to renounce totally the goods of this world.

For the moment, there is not among all the Réau-Croix a single subject to whom the Master may "give all in good faith" (without fear or reserve) without "profaning la Chose," none of them having yet accomplished "the work of seven years, made consecutively in the circles of the Master and within his person," novitiate which is "of all necessity," as well as "the regiment of temporal and spiritual life," that Pasqually would communicate to the Sovereign Tribunal only after having received the assurance that all the Réau-Croix will follow it point for point.

Additionally, Pasqually does not have the right to let go of the secret instructions that the Réau-Croix demand so presumptuously; "it has never transported to the right and to the left similar effects, unless it leaves the kingdom it inhabits." These papers are only confided to him as a deposit that he must remit to his successor; he is content to extract from his originals the things that he believes necessary for the subject who has earned them. In insisting to receive communication of the originals, the Réau-Croix would wound their Master, for "a similar request made him see the little confidence that the Sovereign Tribunal has in him on what he may know and say concerning la Chose."

As for the Lodges that the Sovereign Tribunal is pressed to found, Pasqually dissuades all haste. "It is not prudent to make many establishments, having seen the great difficulty in finding good subjects disposed to fulfilling all the duties demanded by la Chose." If the Sovereign Tribunal persists in its intention, all that Pasqually will be able to do, will be to furnish ceremonies of reception, catechisms, and allegorical and symbolic instructions, for, to suppose that one finds among the holders of the blue degrees one or two subjects capable of being "disposed to the true aim of la Chose," this advantage would be counter balanced by the curiosity of the other Brothers "who would want to be instructed in the truth," which could be done neither by the Sovereign Tribunal nor the Master. It is necessary, therefore, following the advice of Pasqually, to be content "to have go forward" the Sovereign Tribunal and the Temple of Versailles.

After these explanations the Réau-Croix would understand that they wrongly accuse their Master of lacking good faith in their regard, "since he would not be able to veil himself with impunity before his disciples without seeking to veil himself before the Eternal," which is impossible for him. All that for which he may blame himself is, to the contrary, "to have made too good use of them in taking it upon himself to advance them before the fixed time; the little success that they have withdrawn therefrom proving that little usage and knowledge they have of la Chose."

It is therefore no surprise "if they have not preserved that firmness that he expected of them when he left them alone at Paris."

If he may count on their docility, he will surrender to them one day and "sacrifice himself entirely to all that will be suitable for their advantage and their success." While waiting he promises to write before long, despite the promise made to his wife, to de Grainville, "his chief G.V. (Grand Vicar?) always returning to his zeal for the Order and to the friendship and affection that he knows for the Master, of which he is entirely convinced," and, in order to prove to the Sovereign Tribunal that he is far from "wishing to abandon the Order and its members," he informs him "that he is working on the instructions by writing more than ever and is presently occupied with a work which will satisfy not only the righteous men, but will be most suitable for removing the great scoundrels from their errors and lead them to the fullness of joy." He did not write this work (the treatise on the Reintegration) in an egotistical aim, "the things that he knows sufficing for himself," but in thinking of his faithful subjects that he will not abandon from his life provided that they wish to persevere in la Chose and to follow him blindly," also, considering them as his children, he asked them to pray for the rest of the soul of his mother-in-law, "just as she had asked before her death."

The published documents have not preserved any echo of the impression that this memorandum, at the time a defense and reprimand, made upon its readers. It shows in any case that Pasqually, husband without authority and without voice but imperious chief of the sect, learned not to yield an inch of ground to his disciples and it must be recognized that repelling their offers of subsidy and their demands in the tone of a regent who scolds an undisciplined and lazy class, he extricated himself rather cleverly from the delicate position where his diverted request for subsidies had placed him. He had all the more reason to call for a "blind" confidence and to refuse to communicate his "originals" since he had just, as we have seen above[1279], conceived a new plan of organization for the Order from the point of view of the name and character of the degrees and since it was necessary at the time in order to execute it, as well as to write his treatise. He was therefore only able to satisfy his disciples with promises to revive their hopes, while his admonishments and his rigors curbed their impatience and whims of revolt.

We see him use again the same tactic on December 16, 1770, in a letter addressed directly to Willermoz. He speaks again of the Reintegration, "this immense work made for the general good of la Chsoe and of its members," and he decreed that no (collective) Operation will take place so long as the members of the Order in general "are not in order." The decree of prohibition, already communicated by the Master to the adepts of Bordeaux, forming "his circle," to the Very Powerful Masters of Foix, and to any other members of the Order living far away, would be immediately sent off to Lyon.[1280]

In summary, after three years of quarrels, demands, and promises never or imperfectly kept, the Order of Élus Coëns had not yet a complete set of rituals of Operation, nor degree papers, nor book of doctrine. Pasqually had a good hand at pretending that the adepts did not have the necessary disposition of spirit to profit from his teaching; in reality, it was admirable that they had not yet left discouraged by his slowness and procrastination, and the impartial spectator does not know at what he ought to be more astonished: the lack of foresight of a host who, without having prepared any meal, invites to his table famished travelers, or the patience of guests that the reader of an alluring menu retains so long before empty plates.

CHAPTER VII
The End of the Reign of the Grand Sovereign
(1771 - May 5, 1772)

Pasqually ended by understanding that his disciples were about to rally to the conclusion of the sonnet of Oronte; he made, during the year 1771, a desperate effort to furnish them a theoretical teaching and theurgical rituals incorporated into a Masonic System. He tackled the drawing up of his dogmatic treatise, the preparation of degree papers, and made, meanwhile, some apostolic rounds to revive the sacred fire among the Emulators.

The principal object to which he devoted his cares first was the degree of Grand Architect which, as we have already been able to see, was the first degree of true initiation, since it familiarized the Élus Coëns with the practices of the Order, conferred ordination on him, and made of him an exorcist, an acolyte, and a catechist. The "works" could not dispense with these mystical auxiliaries.

The papers were already drafted in part at the end of 1770, and in December, Pasqually had authorized Willermoz to have a copy drawn up of the outline that he had sent to him and to send it along to Bacon. He promised to eventually supply what still lacked, so that Willermoz was soon in a position to complete the instruction of the adepts promised to this degree. Willermoz had not delayed in asking for complementary information. In February 1771, he demanded them for the second time, as well as instructions for the Equinox Working which had been planned for the following month.[1281] On March 15, he complained for a long time of the "languors experienced by his Orient" and which arose from the impotence found in his chief's "rewarding of the zeal of his Emulators"; he insisted on obtaining necessary clarifications "as much for his particular instruction as for the advancements of his children." He had some doubts and scruples on the nature of the ceremonies which were prescribed to him, on the suitable tracings and hieroglyphs. He was above all tormented and disquieted "to have not yet had any sensible effects" and attributed the lack of manifestations to either a lack of virtuality on his part, or rather to "the invalidity of the ceremonies."[1282]

In the absence of the Master, departed for Paris in the month of February, his grievances were received by a new intimate secretary. Claude de Saint-Martin had recently renounced his commission of officer and grade of captain, that he had just obtained by the protection of the Duc de Choiseul[1283] in order to be able to dedicate himself entirely to the school of Pasqually. "I have just," he wrote to Willermoz on March 4, 1771, in entering into epistolaries with him as mandated by the Master, "abandoned the service in order to be able to better follow the career that you travel."[1284] Saint-Martin was all the more at a loss to give satisfaction to the demands of the adept of Lyon, since the archives were in such great disorder and since Pasqually had not left him any note on the number of papers already sent to Willermoz, on their titles, and on the subjects which were found treated therein. Saint-Martin supposed that Willermoz should have received, by the intermediary de Grainville, the Duties of the degree of Grand Architect and, directly from the Master, the Instructions, but he was unaware whether the Temple of Lyon possessed anything on the "Work of the Assemblies", and he found himself reduced to praying his correspondent to forward the exact list of the Invocations received by him and to indicate carefully to what degree each of them is related. Finally, he promised

Willermoz to go find the Master at Paris, "a conversation with him would be more advantageous than a long correspondence," and he assured him of the zeal of the copyists of Bordeaux: "We are working hard for you, T.C.M. (Très Cher Maître [Very Beloved Master]), we are all engaged in sending you the necessary materials for the advancement and instruction of your limits...I have just copied for you the degree of Grand Architect. The Master is going to make the tracing of the reception, or the tableau, and on a separate sheet will be put all the words that you will have to employ in this Operation, all with references as exact as we are able. I hope that this matter will be enough in order so as to satisfy all the questions that you have had for the Master previously; we will take the same care in drafting the other materials. We carry ourselves with all the more zeal, as our Master assures us every day that we can never do too much for you. I desire with all my heart that you take therefrom the success that you deserve."[1285]

On May 20, Saint-Martin sent to Lyon five sheets containing the Grand Ceremonial of the Grand Architect and a sheet bearing a prayer or invocation for the Daily Work, a table indicating exactly the placement of the candles, a list of words having to be used for the reception and ordination, with the corresponding references, an index of words utilized in the Daily Invocation, and various information on the ceremonial and the tracing of this Invocation. He promised to send by the next mailing the simple Ordination of Grand Architect, the French translation of the Invocations in Latin, language that Willermoz seems to have been unaware of, a particular instruction of Pasqually on the manner to proceed with the Invocations and announced that these documents would be soon followed by the Greater and Lesser Ceremonial of the Blue Degrees, papers of the Élu and the three Coëns, that he only had left to copy. He promised finally to remind the Master not to forget Willermoz.[1286]

All these papers were mailed out four days later. The letter accompanying them gave numerous clarifications on the obscure passages of the papers, "a more exact Instruction on the Daily Work," the ritual of simple Ordination of Grand Architect, and the text of the conjuration of the South for the equinoxes. The Master had him tell Willermoz that he continued to work on what he had promised, and that the first degrees were well advanced.[1287]

But Willermoz, as soon as the package was received, raised objections, for the new instructions were, on certain points, in contradiction with those that Pasqually had given him verbally at Paris. The Master, to whom Saint-Martin had referred, was obliged to recognize "that he had made errors in the Instruction of the various workings compared to what had just been transmitted" to Willermoz. He sent, consequently, some modified instructions which "agreed enough with the remarks of Willermoz: The Daily Work was no longer made but one per twenty-four hours and at the moment which best suited the majority of the adepts; it was additionally relieved of the Invocation and Excommunication which became the essential part of the Working of Three Days, reserved to the equinox. Before forwarding to Willermoz the Grand Invocation of precise Midnight and the lesser particular Invocations that he demanded, he was counseled to be content for his Equinox Working with the instructions received, and Saint-Martin hurried to "forward the new resolution of the Master, lest, the moon soon becoming new," he make ill-timed usage of the Grand Invocations whose text he had and "which were not made for the present time." Bordeaux promised, on the other hand, to "forward rather considerable packages when they have finished copying the relative catechisms and instructions" that

Willermoz required with reason, for "without them the degrees would be useless to him." To excuse these delays, Saint-Martin informed his correspondent that "the Master was a little side-tracked as much by his personal affairs as by the assiduity that he had to have in the service of the Prince de Rohan, our archbishop, who filled him with blessings."[1288]

The last mailings from Bordeaux provoked again some observations on the part of the conscientious Willermoz. He noted that on June 18, he had received at Paris, from the hands of de Grainville, for the Working of the Three Days, an Exconjuration and some Invocations that had been recommended to him to employ in preference to all others, and the ones that he just received had only very slight resemblance to them. Pasqually had completely forgotten this old shipment, but, in order not to have to flatly contradict himself, he had Willermoz told that he was not yet advanced enough to make use this year of the work transmitted by de Grainville and that he ought to reserve it for later.[1289]

On July 7, Saint-Martin sent word to Willermoz that a merchant from Bordeaux, who would depart for Lyon from the 18th to the 23rd of the present month, was charged with a "considerable package," that had been confided to him under the mention of "business and family papers" and which contained the ceremonial for the holding of Assemblies: "opening, closing, illuminations, passwords, etc." the three blue degrees, the Élu and three Coëns, and, furthermore, a catechism of the blue degrees "with an explanation begun on the various questions of this catechism." Willermoz was advised that this commentary would be quite long when the Master will have had time to give it the anticipated development. In the same package was also found the alphabetical collection of names that he had requested, and hieroglyphs of the Prophets and Apostles that he had to set aside for the day when he was told to use them.[1290] There were, it is true, some lacunas in the index of names and Pasqually did not know when he would have the leisure to fill them; but it was noted to Willermoz that what he received was more than sufficient for what he had to do and that the copyists of Bordeaux also had to work "for the other heads."[1291]

This afflux of documents of all kinds did not succeed, however, to satisfy the insatiable curiosity of Willermoz and to lift his final scruples. He had indeed received the large package sent from Bordeaux by Mr. David, but he continued no less to assail Pasqually with questions. On the date of August 1st, he requested an instructional supplement for the work that he had to execute at the equinox, and desired to know the advice of the Master on what he had to do following the withdrawal of a member of the Temple of Lyon, Brother Sellonf. On August 3, he requested clarifications on eight points which troubled him for the conferring of the three symbolic degrees, the three Coën degrees, and the Grand Architect.[1292] The approach of the September equinox particularly tormented him. Questioned by him, Saint-Martin admitted, on August 12, 1771, to knowing nothing of this important work. He informed Willermoz, moreover, that the Master "completely occupied with temporal affairs," had left him to understand that there would be no Equinox Working this time. Also, he added: "I fear that for this year it will not yet be going according to your desires." As for the tables, of which Willermoz demanded a copy for each degree, Saint-Martin did not possess any of them and had only ever seen them in the hands of the Universal Substitute.[1293]

The fears that the prognostics of Saint-Martin had been able to inspire in the ardent Willermoz were confirmed by Pasqually himself. Having received at Paris, where he was then found making a brief stay, the letter from Willermoz, he was called to the despair of not being able to assist him in his next working; he counseled him therefore to suspend it presently and announced to him, in the guise of consolation, that Mr. and Mrs. Luzignan "would not be working this time any more than him."[1294] To make amends for his deception, and to show him that he was not forgotten, Pasqually wrote him personally on November 1st, to inform him that "the M. (Master) de Saint-Martin worked (copied) always for him."[1295]

∴

If the willingness that set Pasqually to respond, whether directly or by the intermediary of Saint-Martin, to the incessant questions of Willermoz, did not always elucidate the points so troubling to the timorous conscience of the adept of Lyon, it proves at least the good will of the Master, and Willermoz had to recognize that the Brothers of Bordeaux spared neither their late nights nor their ink in order to provide him copies of the secret documents. He seems to have appreciated this earnestness, for his letters no longer contained the bitter reproaches and wounding allusions that had escaped him two years prior, and the correspondence revealed the cordiality of the relations existing in 1771 between the Grand Sovereign and the head of the Élus Coëns of Lyon. It was announced to him from Bordeaux, on June 8, that Madame de Pasqually had just "increased her family with a large boy to the general satisfaction of all those who occupy the house and that she was in marvelous health, as well as the newborn."[1296] Pasqually sent him from Paris some news of "Mademoiselle"(sister of Willermoz) to whom he had paid a visit and who had him tell her brother "that she had not yet received the sausages."[1297] In May, Willermoz was honored by a mission of confidence and for which his professional competence suited him most particularly: he had been charged to fabricate for the wife of the Master a large brocaded Tours gown; Madame de Pasqually had left to the choice of the agent "the color, the design, and the taste of material," and the fashion. Willermoz was only advised that she was "light brown."[1298] A post-scriptum, added to a long letter concerning the works of the degree of Grand Architect, informed Willermoz on August 12, by the pen of Saint-Martin, that Madame de Pasqually was most satisfied with the silk sample received from Lyon, and entreated him to send the piece by the most favorable and least expensive means, with indication of the price.[1299] The husband wrote for his part to Willermoz: "As to the look of Madame's gown, send it to her at your liking with the usual pieces; mark for me the cost of the gown and what I must remit at Bordeaux."[1300]

Zealous disciple but informed merchant, Willermoz estimated that, Pasqually being then found at Paris, the most expedient mode of settlement was to draw upon his Master and debtor a bill that this latter would pay to the hands of the correspondent that the manufacturer of Lyon had in the capital. He sent, on September 20, 1771, to Mr. Clairjon de Cramail a piece of brocaded taffeta, white base stained rose, at the price of 13 pounds an ell, and whose workmanship amounting to 214 pounds 10 sou had to be payed to the Messrs. Razurel, uncle and nephew, at Paris.[1301] Unfortunately, the bill did not meet with the drawee, having set out meanwhile for Bordeaux, and Pasqually, "being a little deprived of money for the arrangement of his temporal affairs," had to ask on November 1st, for a delay "until the next fair at Bordeaux."[1302] The moratorium had to be prolonged beyond this term and it seems indeed, as we shall soon see, that Willermoz had to pass the operation to profit and loss.

Pasqually made two trips to Paris in the course of a year. Departing the first time in February, he had gone down to the Grand Augustines, quay of la Vallée, and had his letters addressed there under the cover of Fr. Fournier. The adepts of Bordeaux thought that he left Paris around April 15, "the affairs that he was called there for taking a favorable turn," and they hoped to see him again sooner than they had thought.[1303] The precise date of his return is not indicated by the correspondence; in any case, he had returned to Bordeaux by May 5, 1771, day when he changed dwellings and went to live at rue Judaïque[1304] in that long thoroughfare through which penetrates into the town the travelers arriving form the South and where lived the descendants of the Jews driven from Spain, Portugal, and Navarre at the end of the 15th century.

We are very poorly informed on the Masonic activity of Pasqually during this first stay. The correspondence cites only a new recruit, the Abbé Rozier, canon-count of Lyon, of whom Pasqually said on April 27, in a letter addressed to Willermoz: "The Abbé Rozier has had to write you in order to be admitted among you (in the Temple of Lyon) and with me (into the Order). Respond to him accordingly. This is a man full of desire. He does not leave my sight when he is able to join me; he remains with me until midnight. He begins to be persuaded that it is here that he will find what he has sought for so long. I am doing a little to act on his behalf for his admission; in the meantime, I would abbreviate his anxiety according to what you will write me and that I would find him capable."[1305]

The second stay of Pasqually at Paris was around two months. Departing from Bordeaux on August 5[1306], he had returned in October. He was accompanied by the Brother de la Borie[1307] whom he called: "my second myself."[1308] His address this time was: "Master de Pasqually de la Tour, at the Trois Rois, Montorgueil street, next to the Comédie Italienne,"[1309] If he is to be believed, "some affairs of the utmost temporal importance," which had to keep him the whole month of September in the capital, were the principal cause of this trip.[1310] It is no longer a question, like in 1766, of a "mechanical project," but of a plan of a whole other scope, for it ought to be "advantageous to the public, to the State, and to the most oppressed nation." As Pasqually was held to this sibylline, "not being able to write of this undertaking, in order not to divulge the secret which is the soul of the affairs," it is impossible to divine whether he had conceived a project to re-establish the kingdom of Jerusalem or to come to the aid of the English colonies in the New World whose protestations against the taxes levied by the mother country began to move the public opinion in France, still embittered by the treaty of Paris and very hostile to England. Pasqually assured, in any case, but we are not forced to take his word for it, that his presence at Paris was indispensible "to have his project with the ministers end," that "all his memoranda were returned into the desks" and "that he had been made to hope in the success thereof." He wrote to Willermoz that he had the intention, in case of success, to go to Lyon to confer with him, for, "the undertaking was advantageous for the contractors and for the public," he counted on his correspondence contributing "some part in this affair, as there were placed some of his best friends."[1311]

As Pasqually returned directly to Bordeaux, it must be supposed that the mysterious and grandiose project issued from his fertile imagination remained definitively buried in the administrative boxes, supposing that they had consented to opening themselves to him.

Pasqually did not frequent only the ministers; he saw the Abbé Rozier again, who he recommended anew to Willermoz, and was the object of "many blessings" on the part of the Chevalier d'Arc, who he considered as "a gentleman of a very great credit by all fashions, being the uncle of our King after the manner of Brittany."[1312] He did not see in August the Réau-Croix and member of the Sovereign Tribunal de Luzignan, who had set off with Mrs. de Luzignan to "their country-home," but he gave meetings to the noble couples for the month of September.[1313] He "completed the instruction of the old and new Réau-Croix of this Orient (Paris) and installed definitively the Temple of Versailles."[1314]

He had also seen at Paris his cousin Caignet[1315] with whom he had ascertained "an astonishing zeal." Also, upon his return to Bordeaux, he issued Caignet patents of constitution which permitted him to open a Temple at Port-au-Prince, where he was returning in the capacity of commissioner general of the Navy.[1316]

But, at the very moment when the Grand Sovereign could rejoice of the victories that his Order was going to make over-seas, the Temple of Lyon caused him concern. The Abbé Rozier, become the subordinate of Willermoz, complained of not being promoted according to his merits and remarked acrimoniously that the Order had been much more obliging in regards to an adept, Miss Chevrier, who had been admitted to a degree superior to his own. Willermoz had for his part exceeded the exorbitant pretentions of the occultist canon. The instructor and the neophyte concurrently acquainted Pasqually with their respective grievances. He intervened in person in order to lead Rozier to a more exact conception of his rights, all while encouraging him to persevere in his studies. He reminded him that the promotion of Miss Chevrier to the degree of Master Coën was the reward "for an assiduous work in this part for long years"; he persuaded him to be content for the moment with that of the Companion Élu Coën, assuring him that, "if he did not allow himself to persevere in confidence, the light could withdraw from him."[1317]

∴

In January, Pasqually was given again to the writing of the Reintegration which "occupied him entirely."[1318] He was resolved to finish this capital work, which he had in hand for close to a year[1319] and which was only outlined. The "Réau-Croix of the Regiment of Foix," that is to say the Chevalier de Grainville and the Marquis de Champoléon, who continued to pass their winter close to their master, would aid him as well as they could in "correcting his errors of style and orthography on each sheet as he had written them," collaboration of which the author certainly had great need, and which would have had only to be more active for the relief of the reader. It nevertheless weighed heavily on the pride of Pasqually; "he often quibbled over certain words that they judged more French, and he struck them out under their eyes as contrary to the sense that he wished to express."[1320]

The two officers "then took the trouble to copy for Willermoz some little pamphlets that they sent him, after Pasqually had approved them,"[1321] so Saint-Martin, from July 1771, made allusion to the "some knowledge" that the adept of Lyon had already of the treatise.[1322] Pasqually had decided moreover that copies of the manuscript would be issued to the adepts who would pay an annual contribution of fifty crowns, as much for the salary of the labors of the Master as for the maintenance of a secretary charged with making all the copies." Nevertheless, "not intending to impose what be an onerous tax," he "left each his own judge in this affair" and "ask of each only what he could give,"[1323] But these copies would only be communicated to disciples proven by a long probation; so Pasqually had it told to the presumptuous Abbé Rozier, demanding in October of 1771 the right to become aware of the little pamphlets already received by Willermoz, that "concerning the treatise, he is yet too newly admitted to our mysteries for it to be confided in him."[1324]

Willermoz had read the little pamphlets with great attention, but he regretted that he had not found therein any indications on the manner in which he ought to comport himself "with respect to the subjects that he desired to lead into the Order." On this point Pasqually refrained on January 13, 1772, from giving him any rules of conduct, because they "could be disturbed by the slightest circumstance." He counseled him to rely, in the difficult cases, on divine inspiration, which can make no error, and he reminded him that "this is why Christ refrained with such care with his disciples from ever preparing on what they would have to say and this because they had to have the confidence that he will be always with them and that they would have need of nothing."[1325]

In return, the documents which were sent to him on January 18 and 27 were numerous and varied: text on the lesser Invocation which he yet lacked, table, which originally had to be of four circles, but, "the Master had judged it appropriate to put only three in order to not too much overcharge his disciple,"[1326] and which relieved his final doubts on the tracing, abundant commentaries of Saint-Martin on the choice of names to inscribe or pronounce during the Invocations. Finally, he had given him advice on the day (March 5th) when he would begin the preparatory ceremonies for the Equinox Working. Provided with these various instructions, Willermoz was finally going to be able to work in regularity, and Saint-Martin expressed the hope that "the Eternal would answer the perseverance of his desires and that he would enjoy the convictions (manifestations) that he deserved at least by his confidence." A complete success was so anticipated, at least officially, that Willermoz was invited to observe with the greatest care if "any of the figures" (characters or hieroglyphs of the Patriarchs, Prophets, or Apostles), or "anything else," was "rendered" to him and to send it to the Master who made use thereof that he judged fitting for the advantage and instruction of the operant.[1327]

Nevertheless, Willermoz was not yet satisfied. From February 5, he posed again four questions relating to the place of prostrations, to the manner of the consecration of the four corners, to the position of the candles, and to the corner where the Passes ought to be contemplated. Additionally, he prayed Pasqually to postpone until March 9 the beginning of the works, set on the 5th, because of "inconveniences of the carnival," because he was unable "to give himself to the customary enjoyments of the family without doing harm to his preparation." Pasqually saw to respond to the questions concerning the ritual, but refused to move back the workings, arguing that, all the orders being given, and all its arrangements made for the 5th, it was not possible to modify them without considerable difficulty and without exposing the distant Réau-Croix, who would not be able to be notified in time, to miss the period fixed for operations which had to be made in concert. As for the scruples expressed by Willermoz, the Master thought to dissipate them in revealing to him that the work prescribed for that year, "not yet being of the first strength,"[1328] did not require a preparation any more rigorous. He counseled him then to engage in all tranquility of conscience the familial joys of the carnival since "this would be better in order to keep up appearances." Furthermore, if the mundane diversions of Shrovetide were of a nature to trouble his collectedness, Willermoz would always have the resource of "feigning some indisposition in order to color his withdrawal or his fast" and all while exhorting "to observe exactly what has been taught him," he was reminded of "his prudence to reconcile his duties with the mundane obligations of which he was absolutely not able to dispense."[1329]

All the cares taken by the unfortunate Willermoz were in pure loss; he had not yet this time any "reward for his works" and Pasqually had to send him on March 24, consolations and encouragement "following the failure of his experiments."[1330] Saint-Martin and de Serre, who had been more successful[1331], or that the Spirit designated at the choice of Pasqually, were ordained Réau-Croix on April 17th by the Master.[1332]

∴

This reception was the final notable act of the Grand Sovereign. On April 30, he dictated to Saint-Martin a letter by which he announced to Willermoz his impending departure for San Domingo, where he had, he said, two "powerfully rich brothers-in-law," from whom he had good reason to expect "considerable relief," He wished therefore "to withdraw from the hands of a man who withheld unjustly a donation of a great blessing that this land had given him." He counted on not being absent for more than a year, and "upon his return to be able to dedicate himself entirely to la Chose for his own satisfaction and that of his Emulators, after having definitively put in solid order his temporal affairs and assured a fortune for his family."[1333] A post-scriptum, for which Pasqually himself had taken the pen, probably in order to add it without the knowledge of his secretary, strove to reassure Willermoz on the subject of payment of the famous silk gown, which could appear to him as a compromise for the departure of his debtor for lands so far away: "Do not be troubled about your due of the two hundred forty pounds that I owe you for the gown that you have had the goodness to send to Madame. You will be the first payee on my return, my letter will serve you as security or guarantee. De Pasqually de la Tour."[1334] On May 5, 1772, Pasqually embarked from Bordeaux for Port-au-Prince, from where he would never return.[1335]

CHAPTER VIII
The agony and death of the Order

The departure of the Grand Sovereign tolled the knell of the Order of Élus Coëns. His presence was indispensable for the enlivening of his work. It was in vain that he did his best through his letters and the sending of new instructions to keep his disciples going. The body deprived of its soul fell into a mortal languor.

Pasqually had not left any lieutenant capable of replacing him. He had dismissed Bacon de la Chevalerie from his functions as Universal Substitute, who had given him serious grounds for discontent, and replaced him some weeks before his departure by the Very Powerful Master de Serre[1336], who does not seem to have exercised his proconsulate with much energy and authority.

Nevertheless, the Master was resolved to maintain contact with his disciples and to write new papers. He sent from San Domingo to de Serre a file of papers containing all the instructions of the different degrees of the Lodge, from the class of the Porch to that of the Réau-Croix, the different tables (tracings) of Operation and the Invocations relating to these tables, the general index of names and numbers in conjunction with the characters and hieroglyphs. On October 12, 1773, he wrote to Willermoz a long letter where he asserted that the Order prospered at San Domingo and counted "great subjects" among the members of the Sovereign Tribunal that Caignet had established, for the colony, at Port-au-Prince. Pasqually protested that, although his temporal affairs had forced him to cross the sea, he "had never lost sight of la Chose" and he was pleased that the Eternal, "which knew his views in the temporal and the spiritual, protected his person and preserved him in his most perfect health." He hoped to be finished at the end of 1774 with his affair of inheritance, although it advanced very slowly "despite the force of great protections," and to return then to France, "in order to live in the midst of his spiritual children and to compensate them with interest for lost time." While waiting, and on the report that the Universal Substitute had made to him "on the exactitude of Willermoz to fulfill scrupulously all his duties in la Chose and towards those who followed him," he had decided "to leave him nothing to desire in order to put him in a position to go all alone to the aim that he desired of la Chose that had troubled him" Thus he announced to have ordered de Serre to forward as soon as possible to Lyon all the instructions received from San Domingo, so that Willermoz may take cognizance thereof and communicate them to those of the faithful of his Grand Temple that he found most worthy. Pasqually noted that "the general index interpreted the fruit issued from the Operation" and that, consequently, "with all these pieces the Réau-Croix would be able to interpret without his aid the fruit of their works."[1337] He promised, finally, to send Willermoz an instruction that he had just written for the reception of a lady from San Domingo and which could also serve for the initiation of Miss Willermoz, "of whom praise had been spoken on the desire that she had to succeed in the aim of la Chose."

But, if Pasqually made some concessions to the desires of his disciples in renouncing one of his principle prerogatives and in finally being occupied with the initiation of women, he kept no less the tone of the chief who congratulates, encourages, or punishes, and confides the key of the sanctuary only to the elect of his choice. He had Brother Orcel embraced, "of whom he was assured would made a great subject for la Chose, which pleased him beforehand of the success he would have in Lyon," but he ordered to "suspend until new orders the recognition of the Very Powerful Master de Cressac, last Réau-Croix (received), for reasons known to the Sovereign Tribunal of San Domingo," and he informed the Élus Coëns of France, "for reasons powerful to his knowledge," that he had the intention to leave in deposit "all his originals" in the hands of Caignet with whom Willermoz would have to be put into contact.[1338]

On August 3, 1774, Pasqually announced the departure of Brother Timbale who brought to the Réau-Croix of France, on behalf of the Sovereign Tribunal of Port-au-Prince, the new General Statute, the catechism of Commander of the Orient[1339], the statutes for the reception of women, and the tables relating to the reception to the first three degrees. These papers would be sent off to Willermoz by Duroy d'Hauterive who found himself then at Bordeaux. He had planned for a subsequent date to send the Secret Statutes. Pasqually sent notice of the nomination of the Very Powerful Master Caignet de Lester to the functions of Grand Master Réau-Croix with "right of custom" and having at San Domingo "the absence and presence" of the Grand Sovereign. Pasqually recommended to Willermoz to read with care the General Statute, certified and sealed with the great crest of the Order, to follow it exactly, to have it observed "by all his disciples in all its contents" after which all the Brothers of his Grand Lodge would have affixed their signature "to the sheets which are remaining with the present Statute."[1340]

∴

The activity displayed by Pasqually did not succeed in surmounting the obstacles that the distance and the slowness of postal communications[1341] opposed to his activity upon the spirit of his disciples. The dominion that he had exercised until his departure depended less perhaps upon the hopes that his mystical doctrines aroused than upon a sort of personal magnetism which no longer acted at a distance. Since they no longer felt placed upon them the vigilant gaze of the shepherd, the flock began to scatter. The relaxing of the discipline manifested itself by two manners equally disquieting for the vitality of the Order: by heterodox innovations, and by schismatic tendencies.

Willermoz did not await, for the initiation of his sister, the special ritual that Pasqually had finally resigned himself to compose overseas. The superior of the Grand Temple of Lyon was not, as believed the Master, content to give Miss Willermoz "some instructions relative to la Chose while waiting for what may be sent that is necessary for her reception, and the order to receive her."[1342] He had ordered it entirely by his privileged authority, and with ceremonies whose details he himself had drawn up, on August 16, 1773[1343], that is to say a year before the paper written to this effect by Pasqually had set off from Port-au-Prince in the luggage of Brother Timbale.

At the same moment, in autumn 1773, the Brother Duroy d'Hauterive, recently ordained Réau-Croix by correspondence, "pretended to consider the ceremonial of the various degrees as a most accessory thing, and very probably sought to have his opinion shared with some members of the Order.[1344] Informed of this campaign, Pasqually was eager to raise an indignant protestation against the disdain that was flaunted by the new Réau-Croix with regard to the sacramental character of the Coën rituals. "As to what the Very Powerful Master Duroy would have been able to say," he wrote on November 16, 1773, to Brother de Gaicheux[1345], "I instruct you to the contrary. It does not suffice to think as us (to believe in the supernatural manifestations) in order to be a Free and Legitimate Mason and a Perfect Knight of the Particular and General Temples, for, then, whoever wanted would be Élu or Grand Architect, if they had had in hand the secret instructions or explanations of these degrees... Instruct me on his manner of acting among our members, and I exhort you to keep watch that all our postulants have well received their instructions in the symbolic or that they receive it as Emulators, according to what I have sent to my Sovereign Tribunal of Paris. For the rest, make thereof the conferring (confer it) according to my own instructions (and not according to the principles of Duroy) and with the ceremonial that you will have from the powerful Substitute Master (de Serre). Lacking this you will make members without any of the powers of their degree and who will not be of any use to the Order, then advancing them after similar profanations, and thus you will have harmed not only the Order, but more gravely the subjects desirous to be instructed and to progress in the good."[1346]

While the liberties taken by Willermoz and d'Hauterive with the ritual, and the campaign made by the second against the ceremonial, attacked the theurgical doctrines by which was inspired the "divine cult" practiced by the Élus Coëns, other plots threatened the independence of the autonomous Masonic System that the Order claimed to constitute. In deciding that his disciples would be at the same time Emulators and Masons, Pasqually had simply envisioned the advantages, from the point of view of recruitment, that this double character would have. But the medal had its reverse, as he was soon obliged to ascertain. Certain adepts, more ambitious than mystical, were tempted to sacrifice the spiritual to the temporal, and to be preoccupied less by entering into communication with the beyond than playing a role with a view to the Masonic world by engaging their Order in the struggles that the various Régimes engage in in order to achieve hegemony.

From 1770, Bacon de la Chevalerie had been engaged in this dangerous path. He had entered into relations with some emissaries of the German Rite of Strict Observance and, considering that the Order, of which he was at Paris the representative most qualified as Universal Substitute of the Grand Sovereign, found in this association, which began to make recruits in the French Lodges, a precious aid permitting him to enter into competition with other Masonic Systems; he had imagined to conclude from his chief a treaty of alliance between the two Régimes and to show Pasqually the truth of the fact. The Master had caught wind of the intentions of his Parisian lieutenant and repudiated it in time in a letter addressed on July 11 to the Sovereign Tribunal. He let it be understood that he was aware of certain errors and declared to be content for the time to pity those who fail thus in the duties of their charge, but all while proceeding by allusion, he expressed himself in rather clear terms in order to be understood by the interested party. "It is," he said, "of the Réau-Croix who seek to veil themselves before the Master and serve him in appearance, he nevertheless is aware of the prevarications which are committed thereby; they must be determined of good faith to serve only a single and legitimate Master, their state of Réau-Croix cannot suffer any fractioning."[1347] Bacon had at first learned his lesson, but two years later, he had been convinced of new schemes, and Pasqually, in order to put an end to it, had resigned himself, at the moment when he prepared to leave France, to remove him from office and replace him with de Serre.

His absence left the field free to the "fusionist intrigues." The Élus Coëns of Lyon had taken up again the negotiations begun by Bacon and led them to a good end. They had constituted in 1773, under the presidency of Willermoz, a Provincial Grand Chapter relating to the Strict Observance. The following year this Grand

Chapter was transformed into the Directory of the 2nd Templar Province, Auvergne[1348], which was officially installed by a delegate of the German Rite, the Baron de Weiler, and this Directory, of which Willermoz was the head under the title of Cancellarius Provincialis, made in March 1774, an act of obedience to the authority of the Duc Ferdinand de Brunswick, "Magnus Superior Ordinis Strictae Observantiae." On August 2, the Élus Coëns of Lyon confirmed their schism in constituting under the name of Chevaliers Bienfaisant de la Cite Saint [Knights Beneficent of the Holy City][1349], a French branch of the German Templar Masonry. So Willermoz kept himself from responding to the letters from the Grand Sovereign[1350], but a Masonic document that had arrived at Port-au-Prince had revealed in part to Pasqually the betrayal of his old Emulators. At the beginning of 1774, the Universal Substitute Caignet, who, from a Masonic point of view, was Venerable of a Lodge of San Domingo, had received a circular from the National Grand Lodge of France, or Grand Orient[1351], which solicited voluntary contributions on the part of Masons to the effect of raising a Temple where it could solemnly install the Most Serene Grand Master, Philippe Duc de Chartres.[1352] Among the signatures figured Willermoz, Bacon, Grand Orator of the national Grand Lodge, the Abbé Rozier, President of the Chamber of Provinces, as well as deputies of Lyon, Strasbourg, and Bordeaux.[1353] If Pasqually knew nothing yet of the collusion of his old disciples with the German Templars, he was disquieted by the prominent role they played in the new central organism of French Masonry. He wrote on April 24th to Willermoz in order to make known the astonishment that this circular had caused "to the Grand Sovereign, the Universal Substitute, and to all the members of the Grand Sovereign Tribunal of his Grand Orient." He affected to suppose, with this "mendacity" to the profit of "persons of so high esteem, whose personal state announces an infinite wealth and opulence," the most vile motives: "someone in the know" and "a financial gain that they wished to make." He suspect Bacon "of being at the head of this new establishment" and the Abbé Rozier of playing much more active a role in this undertaking than he claimed. "The Order," added Pasqually, "retains none of its subjects by force; on the contrary, it leaves them as they are taken; they always have their liberty." And, in order to drive Willermoz into a corner, he entreated him to explain how his name was found at the bottom of a circular that the Élus Coëns of San Domingo had refused to grant the least attention.[1354]

The letter from Pasqually betrayed a certain discouragement. Giving pause for once to his optimism of command, he claimed that the majority of the Lodges of San Domingo had "entirely fallen" and that, in that of Port-au-Prince, there no longer remained but "some subjects that the general and secret statutes exclude in perpetuity from la Chose, being overall marked by the letter B from birth (having some congenital or mental deformity) and, among others, the bastards and mixed-bloods."[1355]

Pasqually felt that the evil was without remedy when he had been informed precisely by de Serre. He wrote, on July 23, to Brother Mallet, of Verailles: "I know sufficiently thereof now, so that my fever leaves me little rest, sick that I am from the certitude of (of the little confidence that may be had in) their spirit and that they do not see what they are doing." So, he had no illusions as to the value of the promise that apostate Emulators made in affixing, as he asked them, their signatures to the end of the General Statutes sent by Brother Timbale, but it seems that he had experienced a bitter satisfaction in forcing these deserters to perjure themselves: "This did not pledge them too much," he said, "but I wish them all to sign it."[1356]

This letter, dated August 3, 1774, did not reach its address, as well as the package that accompanied it, until November 5, that is to say six weeks after the death of Pasqually. He was in very bad shape when he wrote these final lines: "I am," said a post-scriptum, "with fever at the moment that I write you this letter of advice, occasioned by two large sores, one in my left arm and the other in my right leg. I write to no one, being absolutely unable."[1357] He died on Tuesday, September 20, at Port-au-Prince, after having named the Very Powerful Master Caignet de Lestère his successor.[1358]

∴

After the death of Pasqually, the Order entered into its death pangs. If on July 30, 1775, the Universal Substitute de Serre, on the request of the Master Corby, invited Saint-Martin to return to Meaux in order to constitute there a Coën Temple[1359] the Brothers of the Temple of La Rochelle abandoned the Order the following year in order to place themselves again under their old obedience, that is to say under the authority of the Grand Lodge of Paris, and their example was soon followed by the Emulators of Libourne and Marseille.[1360] The most ancient Lodge of the System, the Françoise Élue Écossaise of Bordeaux, forgetful of the repugnance that its founder had always testified to towards the initiation of women, was annexed as a Lodge of Adoption, which mingling the mundane diversions with the political, gave on March 5, a great feast followed by a ball in order to celebrate the return of the members of the Parliament of Guyenne re-established to their seats after the disgrace of chancellor Maupeou. In 1776, the Duc de Chartres, in the course of his triumphal return in the Lodges of the South, placed, in the presence of 136 Masons, the first stone of its new location, a favor that it owed to the old Élus Coëns become chiefs of the Templar Directories.[1361]

In 1777, the ceremonial and the theurgical formulas taught by Pasqually were no longer in use except in some Coën Temples to the north of the Loire that remained under the administration of the Sovereign Tribunal of Paris and under the direction of Caignet de Lestère.[1362]

Not all relations, it is true, were broken between the old groups. In March 1777 or 1778[1363], the Brothers of Bordeaux sent to those at Paris some new documents arriving from San Domingo: "Three drawings relating to the instruction contained in the secret statutes, one relating to Moses, another to Joseph, the other to Zorobabel" and they were told to engage in copying a fourth one. Saint-Martin re-copied the three drawings for Willermoz, while d'Hauterive did the same for de Grainville.[1364] On August 24, 1778, the Brothers of Paris again received a package containing "an instruction in the form of statutes on the ceremonial of the work and on the preparation, invocations, conjurations on the names of the planets and the corresponding days, etc." that d'Hauterive copied for Willermoz and Saint-Martin for de Grainville.[1365]

But it seems that this legacy of their late Master no longer had for them but a retrospective and sentimental interest, like those old love letters that one finds at the bottom of a drawer, and which evoke the memory of forgotten times and extinguished enthusiasms. Saint-Martin, who had already spoken rather slightly on the three drawings, which to him "appeared beautiful, if it suffices for the frame to be most abundant in embellishments," said of the last mailing, where he recognized "the ordinary style of our Master": "I do not wish to diminish your pleasures, if you yourselves promised much of this work, but I would not want to abuse your hopes too much; it contains several things that we know already and little of that of which we are unaware." All that he found that was truly new were "some transpositions of numbers in the articles" and some "repetitions"; he supposed, moreover, that Caignet had intentionally left some lacunas, in order to gather them perhaps into another mailing. He concluded from the polite, but a little cold, tone of an enthusiast receiving for his collection an object without great value: "It cannot be denied that this is an excellent thing to have, especially if we have one day some need for it."[1366]

The detachment to which these lines addressed to Willermoz bore witness was indicative of the change that had been carried out in the dispositions of Saint-Martin. The old intimate secretary of Pasqually was perhaps further removed from the school of his first master than the superior of the Grand Temple of Lyon. Willermoz, head of a schismatic party, from the Masonic point of view, continued to practice the operations taught by Pasqually and always awaited a success which was for him nevertheless mercilessly refused by la Chose. Saint-Martin, remaining a stranger to the scission, prepared himself to take up again the campaign begun four years earlier by d'Hauterive, and to secretly undermine the doctrines which formed the most solid bond between the members remaining faithful to the Order of Élus Coëns.

After having, at the age of twenty-eight, left the service abruptly despite the exhortations of his family, his friends, and his protector, the Duc de Richelieu, and being on bad terms with his father for "devoting himself to the works of his mystical science and to poverty,"[1367] Saint-Martin had been, from 1771 to 1774, an enthusiastic and submissive disciple to Pasqually. The impression that he received from his lessons was so profound that it left in his imagination and in his works indelible traces, but the exclusive dominion that the teachings of Pasqually had exercised upon his spirit was weakened since, in the absence of the instructor and his helpful maturity, the disciple paid closer attention to his personal conceptions on the nature of the relationships that man may have with the divinity. To the extent that Saint-Martin disengaged from the influence, at first absolute, of his initiator, he turned away more and more from theurgy, or, to employ his own expressions, from the "exterior way," in order to follow in preference the "inner way," in other words, in order to seek to enter into direct communication with what he called "the Center," that is to say God himself, "profound center which does not produce itself any physical form."[1368] He now placed above the supernatural phenomena striking the ear or vision what he later defined as "delicious interior movements" and "very sweet understandings" and which constitute for the intuitive mystics, "the intimate experience." He felt at the present that "his understandings were a little removed" from his Brothers, whom he reproached for being "initiated by the forms," that is to say by the theurgical rites, whereas contemplation, prayer, and meditation had become for him the true means to reach the Center by solitary and individual illumination.

The change that was produced in the mystical concepts of Saint-Martin did not, however, take the form of a radical conversion, nor even that of a definitive evolution. It manifested itself rather by a perpetual oscillation of his spirit between two opposite poles: need of material proof on one hand, and, on the other, fear and disdain of the sensible phenomena of supernatural origin. The first tendency, common to all the mystics of the 18th century, was satisfied by the Passes; the second, granting value only to the spiritual relationships of man with God, rejected the magic practiced by the Élus Coëns. Saint-Martin has never been able to definitively claim a side between these two antagonistic principles. He has never formally repudiated the doctrines which had opened to him the path of mysticism, nor placed in doubt the reality and the value of the results obtained by the Operations, or the permanent character of the "seal" that he had received by the ordination of Réau-Croix.

His correspondence with Willermoz proves that, from 1773 to 1778, he had never completely abandoned the theurgic practices. When he is, in August 1773, about to depart for Lyon, where he had the intention of establishing residence, he wrote to Willermoz: "I would be charmed to be able to join you before the next equinox, in order to join my works with yours and to be able to mutually support ourselves."[1369] In announcing his arrival for September 10, he remarked: "thus we will have the time to prepare ourselves for the work,"[1370] that is to say to observe the preparatory quarantine for the Equinox Working.

From 1774 to 1776 he engaged at Lyon, in the company of d'Hauterive, in a series of experiments whose official reports, which Mr. Matter has had before him, reveals, on the word of this particularly competent witness, the research of "the highest pneumatological discoveries."[1371] The successes obtained by his associate filled him with admiration. He wrote to Willermoz from Paris on July 30, 1775: "I am not at all surprised, Very Beloved Master, that you find in d'Hauterive all that you expect; I am, in comparison with him, only as the shadow of a tablet to bring the light into better relief thereupon. This is, incontestably, the strongest subject of the Order and with whom there is the most to gain. I know for myself how useful he will be to me and how much I am punished for my escapade at paris, since I have deprived myself of an occasion favorable to being encouraged by the example of a man that I love and enlightened by his instructions."[1372] If he raised objections to inaugurating a Coën Temple at Meaux, it is because he thought that "this function would be much better in the hands of d'Hauterive,"[1373] During the same stay, he complained to be unable to engage in the ritual invocations and prescribed secrets, his room at Paris being "turned in a manner that he was thus hardly able to do anything, being everywhere in the open."[1374] The following year, when he had learned from the mouth of the Abbé Fournié the details of the manifestations by which the latter had been favored, he was moved by enthusiasm. "Our Abbé," he wrote, "is an elect for the intelligence.[1375] As to the physical favors, I do not know whether our late Master has ever had them in so great a number and so direct. I see him as being on the verge of elevation into what all the Réau-Croix of France, and perhaps the Sovereign at their head, would not expect."[1376] Nevertheless, he estimates that the exceptional gifts of the Abbé could be more developed by a more complete initiation into the Operations of the Order; so he wrote to Caignet in order to point him out as "a subject more worthy than any other admitted to the work," because his mystical vocation is proven by "a multitude of attractions and physical deeds," perceived outside of "his quarantine" and obtained, not by an anticipated working, but by simple prayers and "the ardent desire for any blemishes to come out from over him"; that is why Saint-Martin beseeched the successor of Pasqually to do for the Abbé "all that he believed suitable and all that he was able."[1377]

On March 23, 1777, he calls the statutes of the Order "our statutes" and praises the wisdom thereof. He recounts to his correspondent that he has asked "in his last working for proofs for Madame de la Croix," that is to say a sign indicating that the candidature of the Marquess, who begged admission into the Order, was agreeable to la Chose. Not having obtained it, he declared: "I am determined to do nothing for her, since la Chose has not spoken affirmatively, either to me, or to those of my Brothers who have more power than me."[1378] The following year, being at Paris in July, he promised Willermoz to "assist him surely on the 6th, 7th, and 8th" for the Work of the Three Days in which his friend was going to engage at Lyon.[1379] In 1790, he invoked again the mystical relationship which united him always to the old members of the Order and declared that, if he gave his resignation as Mason, he remained no less "bound to his Brothers as Cohen and by the initiation."[1380]

But, if the persistent research of supernatural fact, associated indissolubly in the spirit of Saint-Martin with the memories of his first school, has never ceased to haunt the imagination of the theosopher, the "delicious movements" and the "sweet understandings," effect of the intimate experience and reward of fervent meditation, demanded no less their part, and with so much more persistence since Saint-Martin, declaring that he had less virtuality than d'Hauterive and Fournié, an inferiority that he attributed to having "little of the astral," had felt, perhaps without acknowledging it, a little humility in his showy conceit. In order to reconcile the two contrary tendencies which partitioned his soul and to rehabilitate himself in his own eyes, he came to consider especially the dangers that pursuing the external path make to the man of desire in exposing them to the attacks of the perverse Spirits and the ruses that they set in motion to abuse him on the origin of the manifestations of which he may be witness, the judgment on the nature of the Passes perceived by the operant remaining essentially to an ever-necessary interpretation. Now, the rules of this interpretation appeared to Saint-Martin less sure than the infallible indications given directly to the consciousness by the inner way.[1381]

The writing, then the publication in 1775, of his first work, the treatise *Des Erreurs et la Vérité*, gave Saint-Martin awareness of his value as theosopher and enough assurance and confidence in himself to play in his turn the role of master. He then cherished the project to recruit among the members of the Order, as well as outside of the association, a superior class of intuitive mystics who saw no more in the theurgy practiced by the Élus Coëns but an inferior method of communicating with God, or a sort of noviciate preparing one for the true mystical life. This is the mission to which he dedicated, from 1776 to 1778, the better part of his efforts.

In June 1776, he returned to Bordeaux, where he is the host of the widow of Pasqually, "Saintonge street, near the Sainte-Eulalie port."[1382] The task that he is given frightens him as much as it tempts him. He wrote to Willermoz on June 9 that he plans on staying at Bordeaux only two or three weeks: "I believe," he said, "this time sufficing for what I am in a state to do, for, in truth, I am going there less by confidence in my credit than by scruples inseparable from charity." In other words, the affection that he bore for his Brothers of the Order oblige him to convert them to the true mystical doctrine, whatever difficulty the undertaking presents, thus he addresses this pressing prayer: "Above all things that they (the Brethren of Lyon) support me by their prayers in the immense task that I undertake in which all possible aids would not be too much."[1383] Ever faithful to the formulas of his school, he prays the Eternal to watch over Willermoz "for a time immemorial." One month later he said to him again: "I commend myself to your remembrance and your prayers for the new career that I am going to pursue; ask also the aid of all yours for me, one cannot have too much to be supported in such undertakings. - A.A.A.A."[1384]

He was associated at this time with the visionary and exorcist Madame de la Croix, "who had been very far though alone" (without having passed through Pasqually's school) and with d'Hauterive, "still in his first fire" (still also a supporter of the liturgical simplifications that he had recommended in 1773) to lead his campaign. The three conspired to set upon the same "subjects" and, if Saint-Martin recognized that d'Hauterive and Madame de la Croix had, for having "pushed" too much, repulsed a certain general of whom Willermoz would "make the acquisition," it is on a "warm invitation" from the same d'Hauterive that he returns to Toulouse with Brother Percin, to whom he recommends not to breathe a word of his arrival to Brother Marie or to "several aspirants of whom he has spoken, before they have conferred together."[1385]

In 1777 he made, during his stay at Versailles, some propaganda among the Élus Coëns of this town where the Order counted its most faithful disciples.[1386]

In 1778, it is at Eu that he describes to the Élus Coëns of Normandy that all the sciences taught by Pasqually were full of uncertainty and dangers because they led to operations requiring spiritual dispositions that the Emulators did not always possess, so that "what the Élus Coëns had was too complicated and could only be useless and dangerous, since only the simple is sure and indispensible.[1387] This campaign, that the Powerful Master Salzac, from the Temple of Versailles, denounced with indignation on February 3, 1779, to the chief of the Order, does not seem to have had great success. If Saint-Martin was able to note with satisfaction that the Brother Fremicourt, from the Temple of Eu, "had withdrawn from the operative order by the power of a beneficent action that had enlightened him," a modest but most clear formula[1388] he had by his suggestions provoked at Versaille the "not very friendly remarks" of Brothers Salzac and Mallet. Some other Élus Coëns, who, at his instigation, had renounced their works, had not obtained any results by the inner way; when, out of despair, they had resumed their theurgical operations, they had no longer drawn "any of the fruits that formerly gave them joy"; they had concluded from this failure that "their conduct had irritated the Majors" and broken the bonds that formerly united them to the Spirits. They now repented of the confidence granted too lightly to "a Brother whose virtue was praised by all, but whose great advantages of spirit prevailed too much upon a just estimation of their needs (of sensible proofs) and upon a natural equity," and they suspected "the seductive propositions of this Very Powerful Master to be but a new machination of their enemy (the demon)."[1389]

Nevertheless, the preaching of a Brother holding the supreme degree of the Order, old confidant of the Master, well known in the most distinguished society, famed author, endowed with an eloquence at once warm and insinuating, was naturally to bring doubt and discouragement into the hearts of the disciples remaining attached to the teachings of Pasqually. The dissolving action of his propaganda was reinforced by the plans of reform that de Grainville and Champoléon laid out at the same moment. If the correspondence did not furnish any light on the economy of the respective projects of the two oldest Réau-Croix in the degree, it reveals to us at least that the first, who, since 1772, informed Saint-Martin of "his afflictions,"[1390] that is to say likely of the little success in the theurgical works, had made, at an indeterminate date, a first attempt at reform which had not found supporters, but that he presented in 1778 to the votes of his Brothers a new mystical system whose "principles he invited them to examine."[1391]

∴

On December 19, 1778, Caignet de Lestère died at San Domingo, after having transmitted his title and his powers to the Very Powerful Master Sebastien de Las Casas.[1392] The third Grand Sovereign would be the last and reign only two years.

The success obtained on the Masonic terrain by the schismatic System of the Chevaliers Bienfaisants ended up delivering the Order of Élus Coëns the fatal blow. On April 13, 1776, the Directory of Lyon, associated with the two Templar Directories of Strasbourg and Bordeaux, had signed a treaty of union with the Grand Orient, then constituted, in August 1777, a commission charged with preparing the gathering at Lyon of a congress of Masons affiliated with the System of the French Strict Observance. This assembly, after having been seated from November 25 to December 27, 1778, under the significant name of Convent National des Gaules, had organized a Templar Rite, if not original, at least clearly distinct from the Rite from beyond the Rhine, and which was estimated to act on equal terms with the German Strict Observance.

The importance taken by this Rite, or Reform, of Lyon as it was currently called, placed the Élus Coëns in a very spurious situation from the Masonic point of view. All official relations had indeed ceased since 1774 between the heads of the Order and the Brothers of Lyon, and Las Casas, in taking possession of his functions, had not judged it necessary to renew them.[1393] Nevertheless, the rupture had never been manifest, by affectation of scorn on the part of the Order, for reasons, on the part of Willermoz and his friends, of rather complex motives, where sentiment, conviction, and interest played equally their role.

As mystics, the Chevaliers Bienfaisants respected the memory of their first instructor. They were proud to have been elevated by him. They had preserved intact the faith in the power given to man by the divinity over the Spirits, in the possibility of communication with the beyond.[1394] On the other hand, the prestige that the knowledge of the secret sciences conferred upon them in the eyes of the Brothers belonging to other Systems, knowledge which was commonly attributed to them and that they owed to their initiation in the capacity of Coëns, served as a stepping-stone to their ambitions of Masons desirous to excel in the Lodges and to walk on par with the holders of the highest degrees.

But this confusion, so favorable to the aims of the Brothers of Lyon, ended up appearing intolerable to the true Élus Coëns. These latter were before all occultists, indifferent to the competitions of the various Systems, all busy as they were with their pneumatological experiments, but who, as Masons, claimed to constitute an aristocracy and remained independent of Régimes whose principals were unknown or antipathetic to them, and of a central authority born from the suffrages of the Masonic commoners. They sighed to see the oldest and most intimate confidants of the Master, Réau-Croix such as Willermoz, Saint-Martin, d'Hauterive, de Grainville and Champoléon, undermine with impunity his mystical and Masonic work without the chief responsible thinking to put an end to their schemings by severe sanctions, or at least by an official blame.

They finally decided to address the Grand Sovereign for remonstrance, to the effect of provoking an intervention. On August 16, 1780, de Lsa Casas received a request signed by eight Orients (Lodges) that the Order still counted in the kingdom, and which alluded to, without naming them, Saint-Martin and Willermoz. The Grand Sovereign was respectfully, but earnestly, beseeched to take measures to safeguard "the peace and the dignity" of the Élus Coëns remaining faithful to the Order, "since certain Brothers, abusing the considerations that had always been shown to them, sought to have their particular views prevail in the works of the Temples, and did not fear to introduce other (Masonic) powers into the affairs of the Order." The petitioners insisted particularly on the necessity where they were placed to take a position in the Masonic politic as a result of the false position where the intrigues of the Brothers of Lyon had placed them.[1395]

In order to save the disabled boat from shipwreck, it had been necessary for an experienced and resolved pilot to steer it. But de Las Casas had neither the energy nor the spirit for the necessary decisions. Summoned by the crew in disarray to act as chief, he lost courage before even having attempted the least maneuver to avoid the reefs that they had pointed out to him. He was traveling in Italy when the supplication of his subjects reached him. He took advantage of his distance to wait a rather long time to respond. When he decided to give a sign of life, it was to announce that he was abandoning the struggle on all points. He refused to throw the anathema against the undisciplined Brothers or the deserters, and, taking up the formula employed already by Pasqually in 1774, he was content to declare that the subjects of the Order were free, and remarked that they would be punished enough by their defection, "since they could only work upon their own foundations and at their own risk and peril without great chance of obtaining any truth that does not hide some atrocious trap." As regards the Order itself, he gave up on maintaining it as a Masonic Régime and, so that the abdication was complete and without return, he ordered his subordinates to divest themselves of their archives, palladium of every Lodge and particularly precious treasure for the occultist circles. In the case where the Coëns Orients wanted to attach themselves separately to Masonry, he authorized them, "if they judge it useful to their tranquility," to "place themselves in correspondence," that is to say to affiliate themselves in order to form another Régime, "provided that these arrangements bring along nothing composite," in other words: to not bring about any real fusion having for conditions and effects the divulging, to the profit of Masons not regularly initiated, any of the secret theories and practices received from Pasqually.[1396]

A sole point of final instruction from the Grand Sovereign ready to abdicate, the name of the System designated to become the beneficiary of trust of the expiring order, betrayed the rancor inspired in the Élus Coëns by the victorious rivalry made to their association by the Chevaliers Bienfaisants. Savalette de Langes, into whose hands de Las Casas invited his subordinates to deposit the sealed packets containing their papers, was President and Conservator of the Archives of the Régime of the Philalethes, a Masonic association with occultist tendencies, founded in 1773 on the Parisian Lodge Les Amis Réunis, which came to lead against the Reform of Lyon a violent campaign. The negotiations of Willermoz with the Strict Observance of Germany, had provoked a lively movement of protestation on the part of numerous French Masons who, despite their theoretical cosmopolitanism, felt speak within them the national conscience, whose disillusionment, very sensible following the setbacks and humiliations of the Seven Years' War, had manifested, among other symptoms, by the success of the patriotic pieces of Belloy.[1397] The Philalethes, though counting in their ranks several occultist and mystical Masons of foreign nationality, were made the noisy interpreters of this opposition, perhaps by conviction, in any case to be made a weapon against the Chevaliers Bienfaisants that disputed their supremacy in the various Councils of the Grand Orient. They had loudly reproached their rivals to recognize the suzerainty of a German prince and to be enfeoffed to an association from beyond the Rhine. They had allowed in irreconcilable enemies of the French Templars. In their confiding of the archives of the Order, the Élus Coëns inflicted upon their old Brothers in occultism the bloodiest affront.

The instructions of Las Casas were executed in the course of 1781. Savalette de Langes received two distinct files: one containing the correspondence, the monthly plans, the catechisms and ceremonies of the various degrees in sealed packets, each, from their particular Orients; the other, the annual plans, the tables and their invocations, the general and secret explanations in envelopes adorned with the stamp of the Grand Sovereign or that of the Universal Substitute.[1398] The Order of Élus Coëns ceased to exist as a Scottish System or Rite, and those of the adepts who continued to engage in the Operations were no longer honorary Masons.[1399]

CHAPTER IX
Legends and Statistics

The Order of Élus Coëns which, by the acknowledgment of the Grand Orient, was, of all the Masonic Rites, the one "which has preserved with the greatest care the secrets of its mysterious works,"[1400] has very much caused the imagination to work in the Masons and the profanes. It has woven around the name of the Master and of the denomination under which its disciples were known a fabric of fables and hypotheses, vestiges of which are found in the works, writings, and critical spirit, of the Masonic historians of the 19th century.

The legends spread with regard to Pasqually himself have, moreover, nothing original. They are summarized in the notice, full of invented facts and inexact dates, that Daruty has devoted to it[1401] after having consulted the works of Thory, Clavel, Jouaust, Bezuchet, Ragon, and the State of the Grand Orient. The most remarkable passage is the one which has Pasqually travel for some years in the Levant, in order to visit Egypt, Arabia, and Palestine before coming to open his school in the South of France. The author of this fable is not set to the strong winds of invention. The same peregrinations had been, at the beginning of the 17th century, attributed by the presumed author of the Fama Fraternitatis Rosae Crucis, Valentin Andreae, to the mysterious Christian Rosenkreutz, founder of the Confraternity of the Rose-Croix[1402] who, if his biography is to be believed, had traversed the Holy Land, Cyprus, Damascus, Egypt, and Morocco in order to receive the lessons of the Sages living in these faraway lands.

These journeys of learning had become in the 18th century the principal theme of the story sold by the impostors who pretended unanimously to have been instructed in the Orient, particularly by the Greeks and Arabs, in the secret sciences of which they made trade and merchandise. The mysterious Lascaris, who traversed central Europe from 1701 to 1717, making brief appearances in various places in order to operate transmutations and distribute pieces of the Philosopher's Stone, was said to be archimandrite of a monastery of the isle of Mitylene, and assured to have been raised at Constantinople. Another alchemist, Michael Sendivogius, sent into the Orient by emperor Rudolph, claimed to have received there from a Greek patriarch the revelation of the Great Work. Cagliostro recounted again in 1786 to the barrister Thilorier, who has related the declarations of his client in the *Memoire pour le Comte de Cagliostro*, that he had spent his early childhood at Median close to a mufti, received his lessons from the wise Althotas, learned oriental languages and visited Mecca as well as Egypt, where he had been initiated into the Mysteries of the Pyramids.

The name of Coëns, of which the Masons, little familiar with Hebrew, did not know exactly the etymological significance, has exercised the sagacity and erudition of Alexandre Lenoir. This ingenious architect has attempted in his large work, *la Franche-Maçonnerie rendue à son véritable origine* (1814), to find an explanation for each of the different manners by which one could correctly spell the word. Not content to have Coën come from the name given to the priests of the Hebrews, he derives Choen from Choes, formed from the root of the Greek verb cheo, a word which designated the priest making the libations, and Koen from the verb choeo (to hear), term indicating the priest who received the confession of the initiates and revealed to them their faults. As this latter name was borne by the hierophant who presided over the Mysteries of the Cabiric gods at Samothrace, Lenoir, who claimed "to prove the antiquity of Freemasonry by the explanation of the ancient and modern Mysteries," advanced that "the Order of Élus Coëns or Koëns could be considered as a tribunal in which the initiates are supposed to make public admission of their faults or their weaknesses to the modern Koes or other persons fulfilling nearly similar roles, in order to obtain forgiveness therefrom and to merit, by a conduct exempt of reproaches, their reintegration into their primitive innocence."

The final words of this passage show that the essential doctrine and certain terms familiar to Pasqually had been divulged within the Masonic milieus by indiscreet disciples. Thory, although only knowing the theories and history of the Order by the degree papers of which he had had communication asserts intrepidly that the Society "had been formerly widespread in Germany" and that "in nearly all the large towns were found societies that were designated under the name of Lodges of Coëns"[1403] He summarized exactly enough the doctrines of the Order in the following terms: "The creation of man, his disobedience, his punishment, the pains of the body, soul, and spirit that he experiences, form the whole of the doctrine of initiation into the Rite of the Élus Coëns. His regeneration and reintegration into his primitive innocence, as well as into the rights that he has lost through the original sin are the aim that they have in view."[1404] Only, in attributing to these mystics the study and knowledge of all the secret sciences, he confuses them with the occultists of all shades. According to him, the Élus Coëns taught that "man, having recovered his primitive rights, and having been reproached by his creator by his speculative life, is animated with the divine breath. It becomes proper to know the most hidden secrets of nature; high chemistry (alchemy), cabala, divination, the ontological sciences are for him only common knowledge in which he may be easily instructed." These privileged beings form the second class of the Order in which "they teach to the initiates, according to their tastes and their genius, the cabala and the occult sciences in all their parts."[1405]

Stricken by the likeness that the candidate to the degree of Apprentice Coën, at the moment when he was stretched out on his back, arms and legs spread, offered with the figure of the Microcosm, such as is represented in the *Carte philosophique et mathématique* copied by Duchanteau on the charts designed by the occultists of the 16th and 17th centuries, Thory added: "The instructed Freemasons will see at first glance that in these initiations the authors have put into action the systems developed in the chart of Tycho Brahe[1406], in that of the R.F. Sabatier[1407], and in that of Duchanteau. This last especially, which is only an amplified copy of the first two, contains in its entirety the great mysteries of the Élus Coëns, of which the cabala is one of the principal studies. Following this plan, it is seen that the Order of Élus Coëns has had to unite not only all persons who had a taste for the supernatural sciences, but yet all those who have called attention by their singular opinions, to matters of mystical theology, such as the followers of Martinès Paschalis, of Swedenborg, etc."[1408]

In order to put a final touch on this portrait of fantasy, Thory confused the disciples of Pasqually with the benevolent medical orderlies and the mysterious adepts whose virtue the Fama has vaunted, which allowed him to issue them a certificate of loyalism and philanthropy: "The Élus Coëns," concluded his notice, "are often noted by their therapeutic manners. Counted formerly among them, in France and in foreign lands, were many modest scholars whose lessons tended to inspire the love of prince, country, justice, and humanity."[1409]

Although better informed, the Baron de Gleichen gives in his Memoires only a very incomplete idea of the doctrines of the Order. Very connected with Bacon de la Chevalerie, eventually becoming friend and disciple of Saint-Martin, he had elicited and received from these two adepts confidences that had given him some knowledge of the Operations. Bacon, whom he knew to have been "favorite aide-de-camp" of Pasqually, had shown him some "carpets of the magical Operations." Saint-Martin had allowed him to see some drawings representing luminous figures appearing in the course of the Passes. Gleichen knew that the carpets bore circles by which, according to the doctrine of the Order, "the chief, though absent, sees all the operations of his disciples, when they work alone, and supports them," and that "the ceremonies were done particularly at the equinoxes." But, confusing the Operations proper with the ordination of the Grand Architect, he believes that the works were generally practiced in the presence of the "Grand Master," to whom was reserved a great circle represented at the center of the carpet, while the assistants were kept in two or three small circles; finally, the true aim of what he calls "the magical works" of the Élus Coëns has escaped him; he imagines indeed that they have "for their object overall to combat the demons and their satellites, ceaselessly occupied with spreading physical and spiritual evils over all nature by their black magic," and that they are essentially in "combat" against the demons. He has seen in the Operations only acts of anti-demonic magic and has not suspected their theurgical aims.[1410]

∴

The errors which have had a long course on the mystical theories and the numeric importance of the Élus Coëns arise especially from the double confusion which was established in the spirit of the contemporaries on the one hand between Pasqually and Saint-Martin, as a result of the resemblance existing between the first name of the master and the family name of his celebrated disciple[1411], and on the other hand between the Masonic activity of Willermoz and the written and oral apostolate of the Philosophe Inconnu [Unknown Philosopher], whose first and brilliant manifestation was the publication of the treatise *Des Erreurs et de la Vérité*.

The enthusiastic readers of this book, that they admired perhaps all the more the less they understood it, were commonly designated under the name of Martinists, and Sebastien Mercier pointed out in his *Tableau de Paris* (1783) this "new sect which has hurled itself into a new world that only it can see." As, in this period, every mystical sect was organized into a secret society affiliated with Masonry, and that in addition the Reform of Lyon (Chevaliers Bienfaisants de la Cité Sainte) staged by Willermoz, whose slight connections with the Élus Coëns were known, had made much commotion, Masons and profanes imagined that Willermoz was only the figure-head of Saint-Martin and that the mystical school of which the latter had been constituted the chief had taken the form of a Martinist System, Rite or Order. One Masonic work, appearing in 1796, was entitled *Chevaliers Bienfaisants ou Martinistes*; another, formed from extracts of the treatise that Saint-Martin had published under the title of *l'Homme de Désire*, claimed that the Martinists had entered onto the scene towards 1775 and were united, in 1778, at the Convent de Lyon, with the French Strict Observance.[1412]

The erroneous concept that united under the name of Martinists as much the adepts recruited and instructed by Pasqually as the isolated disciples of Saint-Martin was also found in the Memoires of Gleichen. While recognizing that the science of Pasqually was "much less theoretical than that of his apostles," since he "practiced magic quite freely, while they themselves were hidden from it and carefully prohibited from it," he said nevertheless: "Martinez Pasqualis has been the founder of the mystical Order of the Martinists, named thus because of the consideration that Saint-Martin, one of the seven masters[1413] that their chief had designated to protect his doctrine after him, had obtained over his colleagues by his personal merit and by his famous book *Des Erreurs et de la Vérité*."[1414]

The legend which saw in Saint-Martin the creator, or at least the former of a secret society was established so solidly that it is found among all the Masonic writings-of the 19th century.

Thory, making manifest allusion to the mystical treatises of Saint-Martin, supposes that it is from "this school (of Pasqually and Swedenborg) that have come many philosophical works, often more ingenious than solid." He has even found, in his imagination or in some apocryphal documents, the organization of this phantom society; he knew that "the degrees of instruction of its reform (of Saint-Martin) were at the number of ten, divided into two parties or Temples, of which the first included the three symbolic degrees, those of Ancient Master, Élu, Grand Architect, and Master of the Secret, and the second the superior degrees of Prince of Jerusalem, Knight of Palestine, and Kadosch or Holy Man."[1415]

Ragon attributes to the theosopher the founding of "l'Écossais Rectifié de Saint-Martin" [Scottish Rectified (Rite) of Saint-Martin], a rite composed of seven degrees and practiced in Germany, which had taken as its eponymous hero the charitable Roman soldier, who became bishop of Tours in the 4th century.[1416] Daruty, referring to Findel, Clavel, Bezuchet, to the State of the Grand Orient, and to the *Documents Maçonnique of François Fabre* (1866), relates the following history: "It is above all to Saint-Martin that is owed the introduction into the Lodges of France the doctrine of Martinism. After his initiation by Pasqually in 1769 he travels at first for some years, going to England, Germany, Switzerland, and Italy[1417], where he preaches the doctrine of his master, then, preferring the intimate and secret paths to the violent works of theurgy preconized by Pasqually, he settles at Lyon; there, completely with his new ideas, he stuck to propagating them and to organizing the regime. He soon separated from his master and instituted a new rite whose central principal is established at Lyon in the Lodge of the Chevaliers Bienfaisants, and which soon acquires a great influence in France and Germany. To the cabalistic absurdities of Martinism[1418] he adds the reveries of illuminism, the first notions of which he has drawn from the Swede, Swedenborg, and from the German Boehme of whom he has translated several works."[1419]

J. de Maistre, who was, of all the Masons not regularly initiated into the doctrines of the sect, the one who has best known and judged them, has also been deceived by the name Martinist. Placed in touch with Willermoz, of whom he was the colleague in the Templar Strict Observance, he had assiduously frequented some of the Élus Coëns of Lyon who had attempted to affiliate him with their society and had instructed him of its aim and its credo. "Their fundamental dogma," said in the XIth Discourse of the *Soirées de Saint-Pétersbourg*, the Count, interpreter of the author, "is that Christianity, such as we know it today, is in truth only a blue Lodge made for the vulgar, but that it depends on the man of desire to raise himself degree by degree unto the sublime knowledge"… "Supernatural knowledge is the great aim of their hopes; they do not doubt it possible for man to be placed in communication with the spiritual world, to have commerce with the Spirits, and to discover thus the rarest mysteries. Their invariable custom is to give extraordinary names to the most known things under consecrated names; thus, a man for them is a *minor*, and his birth *emancipation*. The original sin is called the *primitive crime*[1420]; the acts of divine power or of its agents are called *benedictions*, and pains inflicted on the guilty, *sufferings*... I have had the occasion to convince myself for over thirty years[1421] in a large town of France[1422] that a certain class of these illuminati had superior degrees unknown to the initiates admitted to their ordinary assemblies[1423], that they even had a cult and priests that they called by the Hebrew name Cohen" ... "These men, among whom I have had some friends, have often edified me, often too have they amused me, and often too...but I do not want to recall certain things. I seek on the contrary, to see only the favorable sides."[1424]

However, the reason he praises them and that for which he criticizes them concerns much less the true Élus Coëns than those who follow "the most instructed and the most elegant of the modern theosophers, whose works were the code of the Martinists."[1425] J. de Maistre gives credit to the partisans of this "seductive error," which was "in all that they said in truth only the catechism covered by strange words," for an influence more useful than they have exercised in the schismatic lands, and even in the Catholic countries, in an era when irreligion triumphed, because "this system is opposed to the general incredulity and is Christian in its sciences[1426]; it accustoms men to the dogmas and spiritual ideas; it preserves them from "protestant nothingism" and "maintains the religious fiber of man in all its vivacity." This judgment, which justifies and confirms numerous contemporary witnesses[1427], concerns much more the results of the mystical teaching dispensed by Saint-Martin than the rather restrained action exercised directly by Pasqually in the Masonic milieus. On the other hand, when de Maistre reproaches the Martinists for making of the priest a thaumaturge and Kabbalist, he aims well at the disciples of the Grand Sovereign, but when he accuses them of considering the Catholic priests "as officers who have lost the password," the inculpation attacked Saint-Martin directly. Like many educated mystics and Catholics by faith, Saint-Martin was very anticlerical in the proper sense of the term. Questioned on the value of the Abbé de Crillon by Willermoz who thought about recruiting him, Saint-Martin responded: "The gown of said Lord will always be a fright to me, and I believe that we would have to treat the priests like the women."[1428] In his *Lettre sur la Révolution* he rejoiced at the "overturn of the former Church," at the disappearance of this clergy "which has only sought to establish its own reign in speaking of this God whose existence it often does not even know how to defend," which has "covered the earth with material temples of which it has made everywhere the principal idol," and whose representatives are "monopolizers of the subsistence of the soul." His *Ecce Homo* reproached the Catholic priests for having lost "the power to know the mysteries of the kingdom of God and that of healing the sick" and for no longer possessing the powers "to operate the Supper of the Lord or to remit sins." He declared in a passage of his *œuvres Posthumes* (I, 307): "These are the priests who have engendered the philosophies and the philosophers that engender nothingness and death."

If it is indeed the disciples of his own school that Saint-Martin indicates when he relates in a note from his *Portrait*, with an air of detachment that hides poorly a pleasantly tickled vanity: "The Empress Catherine II has saw fit to compose two comedies against the Martinists, with whom she had taken umbrage,"[1429] it is by contrast the Élus Coëns, the Chevaliers Bienfaisants, and the passionate readers of *Des Erreurs et de la Vérité* and *Tableau Naturel*, arranged pell-mell under the banner of Martinist, that the *Memoires pour servir à l'histoire du Jacobinsime* (1796-1799) by the Abbé Baruel qualified as descendants of the Albigensian Manicheans and revolutionaries, and that J.-J. Mounier defended in his work: *De l'influence attribuée aux Philosophes, aux Francs-Maçons et aux Illuminés sur la Révolution de France* (1801), in citing among the adepts that he had personally known: Amar, "one of the most enthusiastic Martinists who followed with much assiduity the practices of the Roman Church"; Milanes of Lyon "member of the National Assembly, fallen victim to the siege of Lyon," and Prunelle de Lière, member of the Convention.

This denomination, become the generic name of all the lovers of mysticism and the marvelous, whose number was considerable in the cultured class of all the lands of Europe at the end of the 18th century, has permitted to the historians of Masonry to count among the disciples of Pasqually any number of Brothers who were suspected of occultist tendencies. It is thus that Thory writes in a peremptory tone: "Everyone knows that Saint-Martin, the Baron d'Holbach[1430], Duchanteau, and many others were members of this Order,"[1431] and Daruty cites "among the most fervent disciples of Pasqually," and on the same rank as Saint-Martin, Bacon, d'Hauterive, de Grainville, and the Abbé Journie, "the celebrated painter Van Loo, d'Holbach, Duchanteau, the Comte de Lerney, and Saint-Amand."[1432]

∴

The reader who is not content with assertions that do not support any material or intellectual proof has the right to show himself skeptical with regard to gratuitous assimilations which tend to arbitrarily grow the ranks of the Élus Coëns, but it is presently impossible to oppose to these hypotheses a seriously conducted inquiry.

The insurmountable obstacle is the insufficiency of the documentation. It is not that the written testimonies have disappeared. Some private archives have preserved the official reports of the Sovereign Tribunal, the degree papers, the administrative registers, the correspondence, the archives of all the Coën Temples of France and San Domingo, save two; except, these materials have not up to the present bee rendered public, and the author of the *Nouvelle Notice Historique* has been able to make only too discreet borrowings.[1433]

On the other hand, the correspondence of Pasqually, Saint-Martin, and Willermoz, drawn from the archives of the Temple of Lyon, fallen into the hands of Papus and that he has published in part, gives on the point which occupies us only slightly clear indications. It is often difficult indeed to decide, according to the context, if certain names cited designate effective members of the Order, postulants, eventual recruits, or simply Masons with whom the signatories had only some relations as mystics. Doubt is particularly imposed when Saint-Martin speaks, in the letters that he addressed to Willermoz after 1781, of Brothers that he appears to have known for the most part through the intermediary of his correspondent and who have been able to figure on the rolls of the Chevaliers Bienfaisants without having ever been inscribed on those of the Élus Coëns.[1434]

Finally, if the names, unknown to the documents of Lyon published by Papus but cited by the Nouvelle Notice Historique, seem, in the majority, to show sure sources, certain ones among them, for whom he has given no references, may appear suspect with good reason.[1435]

We must therefore, for the moment, be content to note that the number of probable Élus Coëns, indicated by the documents known at this time, amounts to about a hundred, including three Sisters[1436], the number of Réau-Croix promoted while Pasqually was alive had been a dozen[1437], and the Order, which counted in 1770 Lodges affiliated to Avignon, Bordeaux, Eu, Foix, La Rochelle, Lobourne, Lyon, Metz, Montpellier, and Versailles[1438], that is to say, including the Sovereign Tribunal at Paris, eleven Temples in France, had no more than eight at the moment of its disappearance as a Masonic Rite.[1439]

These given are obviously not very precise, especially as concerns the number of adepts, but we need not exaggerate the seriousness of the lacunas presented by the documentation that we presently have at our disposal. On the essentials, that is to say on the doctrines, the theurgical practices, and the principal ceremonies of the Élus Coëns, the treatise on the Reintegration and the letters addressed by Pasqually and Saint-Martin to Willermoz have given us sufficient light. The integral knowledge of the archives remaining unto the present inaccessible would permit perhaps to elucidate certain small problems: economy of the Mystical Supper which terminated the ordination of the Réau-Croix, ritual of reception to the various degrees[1440]; it would put us in a position to cast a glance on the intimate life of the Temples and to prepare a list of their ministers and their faithful, but these are questions of secondary interest, and it is, in short, rather immaterial to know by how many tens the effective total has been able to surpass the number indicated above.[1441]

The importance of the Order from the point of view of the history of morals at the end of the 18th century, the action that it has exercised over the contemporary mystics is not measured only by the number and the extent of its conquests; they are manifested also by the reactions that have been provoked among its disciples by its doctrinal teachings and the exercises that it prescribed to them. On this point, which remains for us to treat in order to achieve our task, the published documents furnish some precious information.

CHAPTER X
Profiles of Emulators

Those members of the Order, or candidates to affiliation, who, outside of Saint-Martin and Willermoz, are known to us otherwise than by their name, represent the most diverse types of mystics and illuminati: visionary priest, ecclesiastic seeking in the high Masonic degrees a new revelation, mystic practicing ecstasy, career Mason converted passingly to theurgy from which he hopes to draw honor and profit in the great secret association where he wished to play a prominent role, titled exorcist exercising the antidemonic magic in his parlor, successful man of letters seduced by the pneumatological doctrines of Pasqually.

∴

The Abbé Fournié is, of all these personages, the one who has received the most profound and most durable impression. "Whether I consider his life," wrote Matter, "or I examine his theories, I find him, after Saint-Martin, of whom he has not the genius, the most considerable man of the school, and he merits incontestably, not the first place in the annals of a work which until here have scarcely mentioned him[1442], but the top half of the first. Without him is understood neither the school, nor its founder."[1443] Saint-Martin was indeed the disciple with the original and vigorous spirit who recast, and definitively distorted by putting his mark thereupon, the doctrine of the Master, like Plato made use of the philosophy of Socrates, and we would know very poorly the principles of Pasqually, if, deprived of the Reintegration, we were reduced to going to seek in the works of the Unknown Philosopher. Fournié on the contrary is the catechumen with the simple soul and the docile spirit who admits without reserve and without change the postulates of his instructor, and who is not limited to making of it an object of speculation, but who lives them and verifies them by his personal experience. It is by this qualification that he merits this half of the first place that Matter accords him; he is the most pure product of the mystical institution founded by Pasqually.

In a treatise, mixed with personal confessions, that he published in 1801 at London, where he had taken shelter during the Revolution, and that he entitled: *Ce que nous avons été, ce que nous somme et ce que nous deviendrons*, he recognized with a touching sincerity and modesty that his intellectual culture was rudimentary, and he lays out the doubts for which his want of faith suffered. He had "never read any other books than the Holy Scriptures, the Imitation of Our Divine Master Jesus Christ, and the little book of prayers in use among the Catholics under the title of Petit Paroissien."[1444] Saint-Martin, in whom "our beloved Abbé" inspired a tender and slightly mocking sympathy, and who said of him: "This is an angel for the purity of the heart and for charity,"[1445] reveals to us that, candidate with a benefit, Fournié, in August 1771, "sweat blood and water after his Latin," of which "he knew not a word," and strove desperately to take on a sufficient smattering thereof "in order not to do harm to the honor of his robe."[1446]

This humble priest had submitted to the contagion of skepticism reigning in this century. After having "passed his youth in a manner tranquil and obscure according to the world," he had been taken by the "ardent desire that the future life were a reality, and that all that he heard said concerning God, Jesus, Christ, and his

Apostles were also realities."[1447] In other words, his faith demanded tangible proofs to support what the Church taught him, and as he did not personally discover these proofs, "he heard as inner response only these distressing ideas: there is no God, there is no other life, there is only death and nothingness."[1448] He underwent this torture for eighteen months, then he encountered Pasqually who told him: You ought to come see us, we are honest people. You will open a book[1449], you will look at the first page, at the center, and at the end, reading only some words, and you will know all that it contains. You see walking all sorts of people in the street; ah well! these people do not know why they walk, but you, you know."[1450]

This good man and his promises at first appeared suspect to the excellent Abbé. He asked himself if he had not had business with a "sorcerer or with the devil in person." But this latter supposition had the effect of tranquilizing him, which would appear strange unless we know what Fournié sought before all was a material proof of the reality of the dogmas professed by his catechism. He told himself that "if this man (whom he had seen with his eyes) was the devil, it was therefore that there is a real God (since the antithesis implied the thesis) and that, "as he desired only to go to God, he" "would make as much a path towards God as the Devil would believe to have him make towards himself."[1451] Reassured by the idea that the purity of intention would frustrate the ruses of the demon, if Pasqually was truly his emissary or his incarnation, Fournié was going to find the Master "who admitted him to the number of those who followed him."

His noviciate was painful. Although the moral teaching given by Pasqually seemed to him to conform exactly to that "which appears in the Gospel that Jesus Christ gave to those who walked after him,"[1452] he sometimes asked himself if his instructor was "true or false, good or evil, angel of light or demon." Tortured by new crises of faith, "he cried out again more ardently to God and without interruption, no longer sleeping almost at all, and reading the Scriptures with a great attention, without ever seeking to learn them by himself."[1453] It happened even that he would receive from time to time "from on high some light and rays of intelligence, but it would all disappear in a flash." He also had, but rarely, some visions, without finding himself any more satisfied, for, "although they were realized a few days after such as he had seen them," he suspected Pasqually "of having some secret for causing to pass before him" these premonitions.[1454]

Finally, after five years of "fatiguing incertitudes mixed with great agitations," he received in 1776 the reward ardently desired, and it was proportionate to the length and sincerity of his efforts towards la Chose. This extraordinary favor was, moreover, purchased at the price of a "traction" superior in violence to all that of which the teachings of Pasqually could give an idea. Fournié was "slightly (rapidly) stricken by a hand which struck him across his body." This trial was so terrible that the Abbé, writing twenty-eight years later the account of his visions, declared: "I would give heartily the whole universe, all its pleasures, and all its glories, along with the assurance of enjoying it for a life of millions of years, in order to avoid being thus stricken anew only once."[1455] This "blow" so painful, which announced the presence of la Chose, was followed by a series of manifestations of which the seer gave account in these terms: "One day that I was prostrated in my chamber, crying to God to succor me, I heard all of a sudden the voice of Mr. de Pasqually, my director, who was corporally dead for more than two years and who spoke distinctly outside my chamber, the door of which was closed as well as the window and the shutters. I looked to the side from where came the voice, that is to say from the side of a large garden next to the house, and forthwith I saw with my eyes Mr. de Pasquallys, who set about to speak to me, and with him my father and my mother who were also both corporally dead... I saw in my chamber Mr. de Pasquallys with my father and my mother speaking to me and I speaking to them, as men ordinarily speak to each other. There was also one of my sisters, who was also corporally dead for twenty years, and finally another being who is not of the species of men... I add to what I have already said concerning the first vision that I had of Mr. de Pasquallys, my director, of my father and my mother, that I have not seen them only once in the manner that I have reported, or only a week, or a month or a year; but that, since that first moment, I have seen them for entire years and constantly, going and coming together with them, in the house, outside, at night, during the day, alone and in company, as well as with another being who is not of the species of men, all of us speaking mutually and as men speaking among themselves."

"A few days after this first vision, I distinctly saw passing before me and close to me our divine Master Jesus Christ, crucified upon the tree of the cross. Then, after some days, this divine Master appeared to me anew and came to me in the state he was in when he came out of the tomb quite alive, where they had buried his dead body. Finally, after an interval of some days, our divine Master Jesus Christ appeared to me for the third time all glorious and triumphant over the world of Satan and its pomp, marching before me with the blessed Virgin Mary, his mother, and followed by various persons."[1456]

Fournié declared in his treatise that he neither could nor should confide anything of the impression of what was done, said, or passed in these visions, and Matter reports, according to the information given by the friend of one of the dearest correspondents of Saint-Martin[1457] that the Abbé gave up on having a second part of his work appear because it "contained some things that could not be published."[1458] But he had told his Brothers some secrets that Saint-Martin relates in a letter addressed to Willermoz. "His death has been shown to him in all its courses; those (of the Spirits) who have not left him for several weeks have prepared him for it. All the funeral ceremonies were carried out before him, so well that he has believed for twenty-four hours to be actually in the other world, and never, he has said, has he known such bliss. He has been ordered for seven straight hours by a number of spiritual agents, several of which had had some very powerful bonds with him during their corporeal life, such as the master, his father and mother, etc. After having submitted to several other trials of every kind and that one letter could not contain, they sentenced him to every observance of the Church without exception; they even prescribed to him to hear the mass every day at six o'clock in the morning and additionally not to drink wine; so much that he was scolded handsomely the other day for having eaten a salad, where he had not paid attention that there was vinegar that came from wine...Although he is much more tranquil today, there is not a day that they do not lead him like a child in all his actions. The prescription for mass at six o'clock in the morning is what prevents him from leaving the area[1459] because, not having a vehicle for himself, he could not arrange his time along the routes in a manner to execute the orders that he has received. Finally, it would require books to contain all that he has seen, heard, and felt in the last six weeks."[1460]

These extraordinary favors of la Chose gave to Fournié the necessary assurance to write an apocalyptic work calculated on the model furnished by the Reintegration. It was immediately after "having been favored with these visions or apparitions of Our divine Master Jesus Christ in his three different states" that he wrote his treatise "with an extraordinary quickness." This work contained some long discourses on Adam, Lucifer, angels, and calculations and combinations of mystical numbers. The arithmosophy is all the Fournié had retained from the Kabbalah of which the treatise of Pasqually reproduced so many weakened echoes. What had stricken him above all in the theories of his Master, upon which he insists predilection, is the identity of the man of desire and of Jesus Christ, and the assurance that the initiate, witness to manifestations, will enjoy an eternal beatitude. "Since," he said, "this Man, Jesus Christ, is born of God Man-God, in order to have done the will of God, we must conclude that if we do the will of God, we will likewise be born of God"... "If we persevere in doing the will of God, receiving from that time insensibly the whole portion of his infinite Spirit that he gave to us originally to receive in order to be one as he is one, we will empty ourselves of the totality of the spirit of Satan, we will become one as God is one, and we will be consummated in the eternal unity of God the Father, of God the Son, and of God the Holy Spirit, consequently consummated in the bliss of the eternal and divine delights."[1461]

∴

The Réau-Croix Duroy d'Hauterive was a disciple less submissive to the teachings of the Master, but he was not less favored with "communications" quite superior in clarity and evidence to those that the emulators sought to obtain by the Operations.

We have seen that he had, in 1773, attempted to lead the members of the Order to modify the ritual of the Coën degrees. It seems that the reform that he preconized would above all consist in eliminating all that Pasqually had borrowed from the Masonic emblems and legends, for it came to him one day to declare to Saint-Martin that he "could not regard as being his Brothers all those who held to Masonry."[1462] Time had not extinguished his reformative ardor, and nine years after having raised for the first time the standard of revolt, he strove again to found an association of theurgists applying his own method.[1463]

We do not know exactly of what nature were the Operations recommended by him, but it is sure that they had a great analogy with those practiced by the faithful disciples at the instruction of Pasqually, since Saint-Martin, who in this period (1782) was more and more carried towards the inner path, assured that he did not allow himself to be "governed" by d'Hauterive, "knowing," he said, "by experience that the aim towards which he directs the ship is mixed (ceremonial magic) whereas mine is as simple as the truth (inner illumination)."[1464] Saint-Martin was then very poorly disposed towards his old confrere, whom he blamed for indiscreet proselytism, reproaching him for "talking shop on the sciences with all who came"[1465]; but, at the time when the spirit of the future Philosophe Inconnu submitted to the rising dominion of the Master, Saint-Martin had been seduced by the virtuality of which d'Hauterive gave proof in the theurgical operations. It was in great part in order to work with him that the theosopher had returned to Lyon in 1773[1466], and the two adepts were dedicated there to some experiments that had lasted three years, from 1774 to 1776, except for some sensible interruptions noted in the official reports remaining thereof. Drawn up by Saint-Martin in a very laconic form, these minutes threw an extremely vague light on the works of the two theurgists and on the results obtained[1467], but two letters exchanged in 1792 by Kirchberger and Saint-Martin make known to us at least what d'Hauterive said of it and the very high opinion, though expressed with reserve, that his collaborator had conceived thereof. "The school through which you passed during your youth," wrote Kirchberger, "reminds me of a conversation I had two years ago with a person who came from England and who had some relations with a Frenchman living in that land, Mr. d'Hauterive. This Mr. d'Hauterive, according to what I was told, enjoyed the physical knowledge of the active and intelligent Cause.[1468] He succeeded therein following several preparatory operations and during the equinoxes, by means of a sort of disorganization[1469], in which he saw his own body without movement, as detached from its soul, but that this disorganization was dangerous, because the visions then have more power over the soul separated from its envelope which served as shield against their action." Kirchberger showed himself curious to know whether the operations of d'Hauterive conformed to the teachings of Pasqually.[1470]

"Your question on Mr. Hauterive," replied Saint-Martin, "forces me to tell you that there is something exaggerated in the accounts that have been given to you. He was not stripped of his corporeal envelope; all those who, like him, have more or less enjoyed the favors that have been reported to you of him, no longer emerge therefrom. It is no less true thereof that, if the facts of Mr. d'Hauterive are of secondary order[1471], they are only figurative relative to the great inner work of which we speak, and if they are of the superior class[1472], they are the great work itself."[1473]

∴

Besides these two disciples remaining attached, the first integrally, the second for the essentials, to the school of Pasqually, Bacon de la Chevalerie, Universal Substitute, represents the type of the ambitious and intriguing Mason, entering into the Élus Coëns through curiosity, but less anxious to exercise the quaternary power over the Spirits than to acquire authority over the Brethren of the other Systems and to play a prominent role in the Masonic world.

Bacon was a career officer: black musketeer for fifteen years. he had been lieutenant to the regiment of Gustine-Infanterie, captain of the dragoons, lieutenant-colonel of the infantry at San Domingo. He was pensioned as colonel, when he made the acquaintance of Pasqually in 1767. He then resumed his service, for we find him corporal of infantry in 1780, and in 1789 he was elected captain general of the patriotic troops of San Domingo with the grade of lieutenant-general. His service record makes mention of several splendid achievements during the Seven Years War of which it had related three wounds.[1474]

His Masonic career had brilliant beginnings. He was, at thirty-one years old, Venerable of la Félicité of Rouen, constituted on his behalf by an unknown power.[1475] At thirty-two, he presided over the military Lodge Saint-Jean de la Gloire, sitting at this period at Lyon. It was these titles, proof of his Masonic experience, which merited him being chosen by Pasqually to preside over the Sovereign Tribunal.

Bacon appeared at first to be conscientiously delivered to the works of the Élus Coëns. But he quickly took a dislike to them, either because he had had less perseverance than his compatriot, Willermoz of Lyon, or that the sorely tried anguishes in the course of the Operations had inspired in him the fear of the dangers presented by theurgy. Willermoz, alluding in a letter addressed in 1780 to the Duc Ferdinand of Brunswick to the relations that Bacon had formerly maintained with the Order of Élus Coëns, said of the old Universal Substitute "that he had received for a long time some distinguished knowledge, but that it was all erased for having neglected it, although he does not admit it."[1476] His dismissal in 1772, as deserved as it was, had excited among him a profound resentment, of which Gleichen has gathered the echoes. Questioned on the value of the Élus Coëns, Bacon made a sound, possibly in order to turn his interlocutor away from this doctrine that he asserted to have made him most unhappy. "They had excommunicated him for ever for a sin without remission, and he never ceased to slander Pasqually and his successors. He depicted the first as a man full of vices and virtues, who was permitted all, despite his severity for the others, who took the money of his disciples, cheated them at the game, and then gave their money to the first come, sometimes to a passer-by that he didn't know; he said to those who witnessed this of him to their astonishment: "I act as Providence, ask me no more about it."[1477]

Not having found in the Order of Élus Coëns what he sought above all therein, that is to say a means to satisfy his Masonic ambitions, he aimed his batteries otherwise. He collaborated actively in the foundation of the Grand Orient in 1773 and intervened the same year to re-establish the peace between two Lodges at war, the Lodge Saint-Alexandre and that of the Amis Réunis. Member of the latter, which was the citadel of the Régime of the Philalethes, affiliated at the same time with the Strict Observance, where he attained to the superior degree of Grand Profés under the characteristic of Eques ab Apro, he cleverly maneuvered between the two rival systems, and in the end worked with the Philalethes. From 1773 to 1782, he is one of the most active members of the Grand Orient. He was, on March 8, 1773, one of three deputies sent to the Duc de Chartres and the Duc de Luxembourg to inform them officially that their election as Grand Master and Substitute Grand Master of the Grand Lodge of France, with which the Parisian Venerables had proceeded, had been ratified by the delegates of the provincial Lodges. It is upon this proposition that the Grand Orient decided on October 27, 1773, that artisans and servants were unable to be received as Brother Servants and that the terms: "minutes and minute-books" would be replaced by the Masonic expressions: "tracing-boards and sketches [esquisses]." On December 27, 1773, he is designated to take part in the three-member committee charged with fixing the list of the High Grades. On January 26, 1774, he is president of the Chamber of Paris and deputy of the Provincial Grand Lodge of Lyon, of the Lodges Parfaite Amitié, Vrais Amis Réunis, Sagesse, and Parfaite Union. On April 2, he contributed to the foundation of the military Lodge la Candeur, of which he is Grand Orator, then Grand Almoner. In 1776, he is deputy to the Grand Orient of the Amitié and the Française of Bordeaux, of the Concorde of Colmar, of the Provincial Grand Lodge of Lyon, of the Auguste Félicité of Nancy, and of the Directoire Écossais of Strasbourg. Grand Orator of the Grand Orient, he proposes on March 31, by virtue of the powers that the Templar Masons of Lyon and Bordeaux have conferred on him, conjointly with Willermoz, a treaty of union with the Directories of Lyon, Bordeaux, and Strasbourg, treaty ratified by the Grand Orient on April 13. On January 6, he provokes the same union with the Directory of Septimanie seated at Montpellier. From 1777 to 1782, he wrote the annual States of the Grand Orient and represents without interruption the Bienfaisance of Lyon.[1478]

Not content with the charges and honors with which he was vested, Bacon signaled himself as a spirited partisan of the Masonry of Adoption which would earn him other titles and dignities. The Grand Orator of the Grand Orient, whose learned argumentation on behalf of the Sisters who wished to continue the tradition of the priestesses of Isis and Osiris, of the Sibyls and Vestals we have cited above[1479], was none other than the ex-Universal Substitute. Once Adoption was recognized by the

Grand Orient, he took part in these androgynous diversions; at the time of the inauguration of the Lodge of Adoption annexed at la Candeur, the couplets sung by the count and countess de Bethisy during the reception of the countess de Rochechouart had been written by Bacon.

A passing quarrel with the Grand Orient kept him away from 1782 to 1784, but he reappeared there the following year and represented until the Revolution the Bienfaisance of Grenoble, the Urbanité of Montpellier, the Lodge of Saint- Jean de Saint-Quentin, the Braves Maçons de Saarbruck, the Parfaite Union, and the Bonne Amitié of Martinique. He was finally invited, in his capacity as representative of the Strict Observance, to the two Convents convoked in 1785 and 1787, by the Régime of the Philalethes.

The passage of Bacon de la Chevalerie into the Order of the Élus Coëns was only one episode of his long and brilliant Masonic career. By an unfortunate encounter Pasqually had at first taken as his second the man least suitable to become a true Emulator.

∴

The Abbé Rozier, canon-count of Lyon, holds to the mean between the pure mystics, like Fournié and d'Hauterive, and the ambitious Masons, in the genre of Bacon. He did, like the latter, chase honors and was mixed up in the intrigues and negotiations of the rival Masonic authorities, but he was at the same time a convinced and zealous occultist.

Old Venerable of the Parfaite Amitié of Lyon over whose meetings he presided from 1744 to 1753, then during the year 1761[1480], he was of the number of enterprising and diplomatic Brothers who contributed to the foundation of the Grand Orient[1481], and having become President of the Provincial Chamber, he drew up and presented to the Grand Lodge in 1773, a project to establish Provincial Grand Lodges in the principal regions of the kingdom.[1482] But his Masonic occupations did not prevent him from studying with ardor the secret sciences. He associated himself with the arithmosophical speculations in which Saint-Martin engaged in 1775 at Luxembourg with the duchess of Bourbon and composed with her a magical square[1483] establishing "the number of the elements, their relationship[1484] with the perverse beings, and those of the divine and spiritual powers with the universal circle,"[1485]

The confreres of this ardent mystic were not far from considering the circumstances of his death as a proof of the communications that he maintained with the supernatural world and as the effect of a supernatural intervention. "I informed you," wrote Saint-Martin to Kirchberger, "that the Abbé Rozier was lost in the last siege of Lyon. One evening, he offered himself to God in sacrifice, resigning himself to remain alone upon the earth if it was necessary but asking that he be withdrawn therefrom if it could be useful for anything. At night, during his sleep, a bomb fell upon his bed and cut his body in half."[1486]

∴

The Marchioness de la Croix had probably never been inscribed on the rolls of the Order, since the Grand Sovereign Caignet refused in March 1777, to admit her to initiation.[1487] But Matter notes that she was a part of the disciples that Pasqually had recruited at the time of his stay at Paris.[1488] Saint-Martin found that she "had been very distant though alone,"[1489] that she had a soul "permeated by a true desire,"[1490] and he assures that she had "sensible manifestations."[1491] Finally, what Gleichen reports on the subject shows that she shared the beliefs of the Élus Coëns in pneumatology. It is therefore likely that the goal of not receiving her candidature was uniquely motivated by the repugnance that, for mystical reasons, the feminine sex inspired in the occultists with whom she was, on the other hand, so well suited to understand one another. Her portrait may figure in our gallery, like those pictures that the museum displays in the room dedicated to a celebrated painter, because, although not being by his hand, they belong to his school.

The Marchioness had not had a very edifying youth. Born de Jarente, niece of the prelate of the same name who was bishop of Orléans and withheld the list of benefits at the time of the Pompadour, she was wed to the Marquis de la Croix, general officer in the service of the king of Spain. Soon, weary of living beyond the mountains and with her husband, she had resided for some years at Avignon where the vice-legate, the cardinal Aquaviva, madly enamored of her and quite lazy by nature, left her to govern the Comtat. At the death of the cardinal, she resigned herself to rejoin the marquis, then viceroy in Galice, then, this latter having died on his tour, she had returned to France in the greatest destitution. A serious illness which surprised her while passing through Lyon, and the reading of the book *Des Erreurs et de la Vérité* had caused her to pass from absolute incredulity to the most fervent mysticism, and she had begun to have visions.[1492] As she attributed to the treatise of Saint-Martin the principal merit of her conversion, she assiduously frequented its author, and it was in part with her that the theosopher composed his *Tableau Naturel*.

Madame de la Croix showed great dispositions towards the mystical speculations; she applied, for example, to the divinity the notion of the Quaternary, that she had found in Saint-Martin's book, and professed that the Father had first engendered the Son, and the Son the Holy Spirit, and that this latter had finally engendered Melchizedek, thesis combining the emanationist doctrine of the Gnostics with the 3rd century heresy that saw in Melchizedek the true Messiah, superior even to Jesus Christ. But her great affair was the practice of antidemonic magic. She believed, like a German exorcist, Fr. Gassner, whose cures made great noise in this period, that the devil was the author of nearly all illnesses, because the latter had in general their source in some sin that had submitted the affected organism to the injurious influences of the demon. She operated by prayers and the laying on of hands moistened with holy water and anointed by holy chrism.[1493]

The most diverse illnesses were amenable to this magical treatment. Gleichen claims to have been witness to several healings of headaches and toothaches, of colic, and of "rheumatic pains."[1494] But the method was particularly efficacious for relieving the obsessed, that is to say the sick who, "by some practices of false magic, had the devil upon them and around them," and the possessed, whose case was much more serious, because the demon had penetrated into their body and had installed itself there to remain. As this amiable therapeut was well known in better society and placed her talents at the service of all those who entreated her, she had a numerous and distinguished clientele: the obsessed such as the Comte de Schomberg, atheist and friend of d'Holbach, "who saw nearly every week the figure of three old women rise from the foot of his bed and bend themselves backward toward him while making frightful grimaces," or like Tiemann, occultist strongly tied to Saint-Martin, who saw at each place that he looked at steadily for some minutes a head whose features and eyes were so animated that it appeared living to him"; the possessed, victims of a "diabolical incarnation," like the Duc de Richelieu, the Marquis de Montbarrey, the Marquis, the Marchioness, and the Chevalier de Cossé, a consul of France to Salé, "who frequented the Encylopedists."[1495] The marchioness was also mingled, magically, with politics. As a good royalist, she opposed herself with all her power to the antidynastic campaign that the Orleanist party led. "A prowess of which she particularly boasted was to have destroyed a lapis-lazuli talisman the Duc d'Orléans had received in England from the celebrated Falk Scheck, first rabbi of the Jews." This talisman, which would lead the prince to the throne, was broken upon his chest, by the virtue of the prayers of the marchioness, "in this memorable moment when he was taken by a fainting fit in the middle of the National Assembly."[1496]

The demons that pursued Madame de la Croix were avenged sometimes cruelly. "Often entire processions of penitents in large rose-colored robes or the most stinking Capuchin friars, vested in celestial blue, or other ridiculously jumbled together ecclesiastical personages arrived with her at night and crossed her bed; the Capuchins offered to kiss her, and the penitents flagellated her bed." It happened, nevertheless, that the apparitions were most agreeable to contemplate: "Sometimes they gave her a ball where she saw the most curious apparel and the fashions of all the ages; another time it were a magnificent artificial fire, of diamond pyramids and jewelry, of superb illuminations or enchanted palaces that they showed her."[1497] An imp, from which she had freed a possessed, presented itself to her in the most gracious manner. "When the evil Spirit had come out of the body that it occupied," recounted Gleichen, "I ordered it to appear under the form of a little Chinese pagoda. It gave us the courtesy of taking a truly delicious form; it was dressed in colors of fire and gold; its visage was quite pleasing; it moved little hands with much grace and was hidden under this curtain of green taffeta that you saw there, of which it was enveloped and from where it made all sorts of grimaces at its old host. But this latter, having without doubt committed new sins, remained obsessed, for, returning one day to the house, he found the little pagoda on his bureau, and I was obliged to take myself to him in order to drive it from his bedroom"[1498]

∴

Jacques Cazotte, known as author of an elegant and fantastic tale, the *Diable Amoureux*, was one of the Emulators of whom we could not decide if they had belonged to the Order itself or if they had only been part of the schismatic group of the adepts of Lyon. Matter cites him among the Parisian disciples of Pasqually.[1499] A work of Boehme, which was sent to him by Saint-Martin, with this inscription: "Pour Monsieur Cazotte, à Versailles,"[1500] could have us suppose that the recipient was affiliated with the most fervent Temple of the Brothers of Versailles. Daruty claims, on the other hand, that Cazotte had been initiated at Lyon[1501] and it is to "the school of Lyon" that Gerard de Nerval attaches him.[1502] Cazotte himself has declared, at the time of his court appearance at the Revolutionary Tribunal, that the sect into which he had entered was that of the Martinists.[1503] This term, of which we know the equivocal meaning, does not resolve the problem; it is possible, moreover, that Cazotte had employed a denomination well known by the public in order to keep secret the actual name of the Rite to which he belonged, which was that of the Élus Coëns or that of the Chevaliers Bienfaisants. He had certainly kept himself from saying anything that might denounce his old confrères, of whom he courageously acknowledged to have remained a friend, although, according to his own declaration, various causes had led him to give his resignation after he had remained three years a member of the association. It is to this concern for discretion that must be attributed another of his responses, manifestly false, according to which his initiators were no longer found in France, "being continually traveling in order to make receptions." Whatever the case, the circumstances which led to his initiation would be rather curious, if we are to believe the memoires of the time.

Cazotte, pensioned as old controller of the Leeward Islands, enjoying an honest affluence after having received the inheritance of an elder brother, had been able to engage in his taste for letters. Desirous to give to his productions the allurement of the fantastic, he had first imitated the old popular ballads and the Italian chivalrous poems. In a song entitled: *La Veilée de la Bonne Femme*, he had the phantoms of two damned return at night into a castle in ruins: an adulterous lady of the manor and the monk who seduced her. The *Prouesses inimitables d'Ollivier, Marquis d'Edesse*, first appeared as a song then under the form of a long poem in prose, recounting the marvelous adventures of a page pursued by the vengeance of the lord whose daughter he had dishonored and gone off to make war in the Holy Land. Encouraged by the favorable welcome that these two works had received, Cazotte had sought a new source of inspiration in the *Démonomanie* of Bodin, in the *Monde Enchanté* of Bekker and probably also in one of the numerous treatises on sorcery published in the 18th century.[1504] He had drawn therefrom a delicious tale, this *Diable Amoureux*, which has saved his name from forgetfulness.

It is an elegant subject whose charm is enhanced by diabolical condiments. A young Spanish officer, Alvare, evokes Beelzebub in the ruins of Portici. The demon appears under the form of a camel, then of a white spaniel, finally of a charming girl who becomes the companion of the dilettante sorcerer. All the interest of the narrative centers around the struggle that is engage in the spirit of Alvare between the love at once sentimental and sensual inspired in him by the one whom he has called Biondetta, and his scruples or doubts on the nature of this mysterious being of whom he knows not whether it is an elementary Spirit, a sylph, or a fiend of Hell. Finally, the diabolical apparition vanishes, and the adventure is ended as well as it can be.[1505]

This novel would have, according to a tradition related by Gerard de Nerval, attracted to Cazotte the attention of the "Illuminati" (Élus Coëns or Chevaliers Bienfaisants), who took seriously what was only a play of imagination. A short time after the publication of the *Diable Amoureux* (appearing in 1772), he received a visit from a "mysterious personage with a grave demeanor, with features emaciated by study and whose imposing stature was draped by a brown cloak." As the unknown, without saying a word, drew "bizarre signs, such as the initiates employ in order to be recognized between themselves," Cazotte had to admit to him that he did not understand this pantomime in the least, and he was not even a Freemason. The visitor then declared to him that after having read "these invocation in the ruins, these mysteries of the cabala, this occult power of a man over the Spirits of the air, these theories so striking on the power of numbers[1506] over the will[1507], over the fatalities of existence," he believed the author one "of our own and in the highest degrees" and that he was presenting himself to him with the intention of reproaching him for having betrayed the secrets of the sect. Since he found in Cazotte a profane who had discovered by intuition a part of the occult doctrines, the unknown proposed to the author to instruct him completely, to demonstrate to him notably that the science of the adepts has not any connection with sorcery and "to penetrate deeper into the mysteries of the world of the Spirits which press us from all sides." Cazotte accepted this offer and was received into the secret society to which belonged his recruiter.[1508]

G. de Nerval notes that all the biographers of Cazotte concur to indicate the subtle evolution which then occurred in his ideas[1509], but "that he did not appear to have taken part in the collective works of the Martinist Illuminati and had only made for himself according to their ideas a particular and personal rule of conduct."[1510] "Cazotte," states Matter for his part, "becomes a sincere Christian under the direction of Pasqually and even remains there, the Gospel suffices him. Cazotte, it is true, is not characterized as Martinezist in his publications, but he is always spiritualist there and this is thanks to his master, whose teachings he spreads from his point of view in the *Contes Arabes.*"[1511] What must be retained from these two concordant judgments, is that Cazotte has been led back to the spiritualism and religion of his childhood by the Martinist doctrine, and that he was not a practicing Élu Coën, but it is an exaggeration to say that he held on to the dogmas of the Church. Under the influence of the pneumatological concepts that were taught to him by his initiators he became and remained all his life, in theory and in action, a true theurgist.

Two of the fundamental postulates of the Martinist theosophy had particularly stricken him: the primordial distinction that must be established between the perverse Spirits and the divine Spirits, and the power given to men over the two classes of Spirits.

The heroin of the *Diable Amoureux* was, as notes very justly G. de Nerval, none other than one of those goblins that one may see in the article "Incubi and Succubi" from the *Monde Enchanté* of Bekker and "the not-very-dark role that the author had the charming Biondetta play in the end would suffice to indicate that he was not yet initiated in this period to the mysteries of the cabalists or the illuminati, who had always carefully distinguished the elementary Spirits: sylphs, gnomes, undines, and salamanders, from the black fiends of Beelzebub[1512] or, to employ the terms of the Reintegration, the ternary Spirits from the prevaricating Spirits. By contrast, in his novel of the "Chevalier," which was part of the *Contes Arabes*, written after his initiation[1514] the luminous genii (Spirits of the Supercelestial and the Celestial), submissive to Solomon, delivered a strong fight to those following Eblis (Iblis) and in this struggle the conjurations and the talismans played a large role[1514], as in the Operations of the Élus Coëns.

On the other hand, Cazotte is profoundly permeated with the fundamental idea of the Reintegration, that is to wit the eminent role of man here below and the struggle that he must lead against the demons. "Good and evil upon the earth," he wrote to a confidant, "have always been the work of man, to whom this world had been abandoned by the eternal laws. God does nothing without us, we are the kings of the earth; it is to us to bring about the moment prescribed by his decrees. We will not suffer our enemy, who can do nothing without us, to continue to do all and through us."[1515]

It rather seems, moreover, that Cazotte has carefully studied the dogmatic writings of the Élus Coëns, for he employs the favorite expressions of Pasqually when he writes: "I would bind upon the earth what seems suitable to me to bind for the greater glory of God and the need of his creatures."[1516] But nothing indicates that he has participated in the practices proper to the Order, nor sought the same manifestations. The operations in which he engaged were before all exorcisms. Their nature and the results that he thought to obtain are indicated by the notes where he had lengthily recorded all the details of a dream that he had had in 1791 "in the night from Saturday to Sunday before the Saint-Jean." Having penetrated into a "capharnaum" [place of confusion], he found then in an isolated room a young lady who "is in a vision with a Spirit." He ordered, while making the sign of the cross upon the forehead of the young lady, the Spirit to make itself seen. He then saw "a figure of fourteen to fifteen years old, not at all ugly, but in the attire, the appearance, and the attitude of a naughty child." He bound her and the figure protested against this ligature. Another woman appeared, similarly obsessed and to whom he rendered the same service. The two Spirits "left their effects, faced him and were rude" when a man dressed as a turnkey presented himself and passed them two little manacles. Cazotte put the two prisoners "under the power of Jesus Christ." Attacked by a large man at the moment when, having perceived that his two shoes were slipshod, he prepared himself to lift the quarter of his footwear, he placed his hand upon the forehead of his aggressor and bound him in the name of the Holy Trinity and "by that of Jesus Christ under the support of whom" he had placed him.[1517]

The clairvoyance that had developed within Cazotte the initiation into the pneumatological doctrines did not only allow him to track down the malign Spirits, it also revealed to him the constant presence of spiritual beings that a mind of our days, who would have read the Reintegration, would call disincarnate Minors. "We live always," he wrote to his friend Ponteau, "among the spirits of our fathers; the invisible world presses us from all sides... there are there ceaselessly friends of our thought who are approached familiarly by us... Each of our ideas, good or evil, as each of the movements of our bodies shake the column of air that would support us. All is full, all is living in this world where, since sin, veils obscure matter... And I have raised them, as the wind lifts a dense fog... sometimes the confusion of the beings is so much in my eyes that I do not always know how to distinguish immediately those who live in the flesh from those who have stripped the coarse appearances... There are some souls who have remained so material, their form has remained so well, so adherent, that they have carried off into the other world a sort of opacity. They long resemble those living... This morning, during prayer, the room was so full of the living and the dead that I was unable to distinguish between life and death; it was a strange confusion, but nevertheless a magnificent spectacle."[1518]

This hallucinatory state was sometimes painful for him; thus, it came to him to complain of a faculty that had given him "an initiation that he had not sought and that he often deplored."[1519] He considered in addition, as a faithful disciple of Pasqually, that the communication with the beyond exposed one to the danger of being duped by malign Spirits. After having recorded in his intimate notes a prophetic dream, he added: "Holding myself in defiance of this dream, as against so many others by which I may suspect Satan of wishing to fill me with pride, I will continue my prayers to God by the intercession of the Holy Virgin and without rest, in order to obtain the knowledge of his will over me."[1520] He wrote again to Ponteau: "You are not an initiate; commend yourself for that. Remember these words: *Et scientia eorum perdet eos.* The knowledge of occult things is a stormy sea from where you cannot see the shore."[1521]

When the political events took a turn in 1791, becoming threatening for the royal authority, Cazotte, ardent legitimist, entered into the struggle by using, to the profit of Louis XVI, the supernatural power that was attributed to him. He deplored the revolutionary spirit that had seized several of his old Brothers. "I received," he wrote to his usual confidant, "two letters from intimate acquaintances that I had among my confrères the Martinists; they are demagogues like Bret[1522], people of name, honorable people up until now; the demon is master of them."[1523] "If I am not without danger, I that divine grace has withdrawn from the trap, judge for yourself the risk of those who remain."[1524] He believed that the ever- growing hostility witnessed by public opinion in regards to the traditional monarchy had for its hidden cause the magical operations of the prophetess Broussole, who had obtained some communications from the Rebel Powers on behalf of the Jacobins, and the marchioness of Urfé, "the eldest of the French Medeans, whose parlor overflowed with empirics and people who rushed after the occult sciences," and who he accused particularly of having raised and disposed towards evil the minister Duchatelet.[1525] To these diabolical intrigues he opposed his mystical action. "I have informed you," he said to Ponteau, "that we were eight in all in France, absolutely unknown to one another, who would lift, but ceaselessly, as Moses, eyes, voice, and arms towards heaven, for the decision of a battle in which the elements themselves are put into play."[1526] "Fear nothing from La Fayette; he is bound (magically) as his accomplices. He is, as his cabal, raised to the Spirits of terror and confusion. Let us not, however, discontinue raising our arms to heaven; let us think in the attitude of the prophet during which Israel battled."[1527]

The house where Cazotte and his family lived at Pierry, in the environs of Epernay, was a small fortress from where set out counter-attacks aiming at the enemies of the kingdom, supernatural or corporeal. The Marchioness de la Croix had come to live near her confrère in secret sciences. "She was part of the family and exercised there an influence due to the relationship of her ideas and convictions with those of Cazotte to which were united those intellectual bonds that the doctrine regarded as a sort of anticipation of the future life." The "mystical marriage" that the two adepts had contracted vexed a little bit the legitimate spouse, but the three children, a daughter and two sons, sincerely shared the ideas of their father and of his old friend.[1528] When, after the turning of Varennes, the royal family appeared directly threatened, Cazotte sent to Paris his son Scévole to be part of the corps of volunteers who replaced the Constitutional Guard, dissolved since May 31, 1792, and participated in the defense of the Tuileries on the day of August 10th. But the young man would also employ for the security of the sovereign and his own other arms than the sword. When it was time for his departure, Madame de la Croix joined Cazotte in giving him what they called their "mystical powers." She made upon the forehead, the lips, and the heart of the young man three mysterious signs, accompanied by a secret invocation, and thus consecrated the one that she named the "son of her intelligence."[1529]

After the anniversary celebration of the Federation, Scévole gave an account to his father of the manner by which he had executed his orders: "My dear papa, July 14 is passed, the king is returned safe and sound. I have performed to my best the mission with which you have charged me… on Friday I approached the holy table, and while coming out of the church, I delivered myself to the altar of the fatherland where I made, at the four sides, the necessary commands in order to place the entire Champ-de-Mars under the protection of the angels of the Lord. I have gained the cart against which I was supported when the king reascended… The Champ-de-Mars was covered with men. If I was deserving that my commands and my prayers were carried out, the perverse were furiously bound. On the return all cried: Vive le Roi! [Long live the King] along the passage."[1530]

Unfortunately for him, Cazotte had not limited himself to hurling commands or having commands hurled against the evil Spirits and to bind the enemies of the King. According to his principle that "man must act here below, since it is the place of action, and that good and evil can only be done by him,"[1531] he had, in a memoire, counseled Louis XVI to show more decision and energy, notably "to go rapidly with twenty-five guards, by horse like himself, to the place of the fermentation." He had, after August 10, traced a plan in order to have the king escape, and offered his house as a halting place on his flight in the direction of Metz. Finally, he had drawn up for his father-in-law, registrar of the Council of Martinique, some instructions on the means to resist six thousand republicans sent to seize the colony. These compromising writings, addressed to Ponteau, who was secretary of the civil list, were discovered in the papers of Laporte, intendant of this service, and seized at the Tuileries. Cazotte, arrested at the end of August 1792, found himself at the Abbey at the time of the September massacres. The supplications of his daughter, imprisoned with him, would soften the assassins; he was set at liberty. But, having refused to hide, he was arrested anew on September 11, and condemned to death by the Revolutionary Tribunal. He was guillotined on September 25 at 7 o'clock in the evening after having said in a loud voice, at the moment when the executioners took hold of him: "I die as I have lived, faithful to God and my King,"

His quality of Illuminati was recalled, during the proclamation of the verdict, in terms which, according to a witness, "struck the hearer with stupor by their strange, mysterious, and antiquated character." The president of the tribunal, named Lavau, was "initiated, like Cazotte, into the works and doctrines of Martinism." When he would announce to his Brother the sentence that sent him to the scaffold, he addressed to him a small discourse, full of sensibility and emphasis, in the style of the day, and which ended by this phrase, rather remarkable indeed if it was truly pronounced exactly as reported: "You were man, Christian, philosopher, initiate; you know how to die as a Christian; this is all that your land can expect of you."[1532]

ENDNOTES

1. This new edition, conceived in a more scientific spirit than its predecessor, would not be able to replace it, for it has, through concern for brevity and objectivity, regrettably sacrificed the abundant documentation which made the edition of 1863-1867 a collection, a little chaotic, but precious, of text and citations particularly instructive.

2. III, 84.

3. III, 85 & 111.

4. J.B. Willermoz, who had been one of the principal disciples of Pasqually, affirmed, in a letter addressed in 1821 to the Baron de Turkheim (VI, 144), that the treatise "goes only up to Saul." It is likewise at the first king of the Hebrews that the edition of the Bibliothèque Rosicrucienne stops, from which are borrowed the citations that one will find in this chapter and in the following chapters. Turkheim had in his hands another manuscript, brought to Alsatia by a Strasbourgian who had lived at Bordeaux, at the period that Pasqually taught there; the initial and final phrases, which he cites fully (VI, 142), correspond, save an insignificant variation, to those of the Rosicrucian edition, but he indicates a division in 732 paragraphs that seem to have ignored the manuscript of Mr. Matter. This latter, who has had beneath his eyes two copies of the treatise, notes that in each of them the work remains unfinished (VIII, 13).

5. I, 247.

6. I, 30-31.

7. I, 312. Following the excellent formula of Mr. Matter, Pasqually is only the "recorder of Moses" (VIII, 17).

8. I, 17.

9. I, 8.

10. I, 176-177.

11. I, 21-22.

12. I, 49.

13. I, 11.

14. I, 12.

15. I, 12. The sense of the word "emancipated" is not always indicated in so clear a fashion. Pasqually seems to have distinguished in principle: 1. The emancipation, state of the Spirits existing in the circle of the divinity and destined to act in accordance with its views; 2. The emancipation, which is the state of the Spirits sent by the Creator into the outer circles, where they enjoy, at their risk and peril, a complete liberty to act. It is in this way that he defines (p. 293) present man: "a being emancipated from the circle of divinity." But it occurs to him often also to use the word "emancipated" in the sense of "emanated," as for example p. 299 where "divine emancipation" signifies exactly "emanation." The uncertain terminology of the treatise contributes to

much of his obscurity.

16. I, 32; 223.
17. I, 13.
18. I, 19.
19. I, 313.
20. The adjective "glorious" is, in the vocabulary of Pasqually, the equivalent of "luminous." He has probably given it this sense by analogy with the Shekinah, the glowing cloud by which Jehovah revealed his presence in the midst of the Burning Bush and upon the Propitiatory in the Holy of Holies. The luminous manifestation by which the divinity became known to the gross senses of humans had, according to the Jewish conception, nothing of the material. This idea has inspired the scene of the Transfiguration of Christ. We will see later that the Élus Coëns considered this glimmer, even weak and fleeting, as one of the modes of manifestation of the Spirits, and thought to have obtained a satisfying result from their theurgical ceremonies when they believed to have perceived it, if only for an instant. In regards to the etymology, it is perhaps necessary to seek it in the "glory," name under which is designated the triangle bearing the Tetragrammaton and surrounded by rays, which figures upon the altars of Jesuit style, and which was represented in the Lodges under the form of a transparency placed above the chair of the Venerable.
21. I, 12. - The "active and passive forms" signify the living organisms and inanimate bodies.
22. I, 25.
23. Pasqually remains, as a rule, faithful to these definitions; he only varies in one passage where he says expressly: "Here the word 'general' is attached to the irrational animals and the word 'particular' to those which are animated by a divine spiritual being, whether celestial or supercelestial," (I, 287).
24. I, 13; 14; 50; 320.
25. I, 347.
26. I, 312-313.
27. I, 319-320.
28. I, 331.
29. I, 309.
30. That is to say pure elements, constitutive of the material bodies. The adjective "spiritous" is derived by Pasqually from the word "spirit" following the sense that the usage in the 18th century gave it in the expressions: spirit of wine, spirit of salt, etc.
31. Substances composed of spirit and matter and which, in being combined, have given birth to the living organisms (among which figure the stars). "Temporal" always signifies "material" in the special terminology of Pasqually.
32. In other words: the inferior Spirits have created the celestial bodies or

stars, the minor Spirits the terrestrial bodies, that is to say, in total, the two material worlds.

33. I, 332-334.
34. I, 321.
35. I, 321.
36. I, 331.
37. I, 331.
38. I, 330.
39. I, 15-16.
40. I, 27.
41. I, 316.
42. I, 26.
43. I, 28.
44. I, 13.
45. I, 17.
46. I, 21.
47. I, 36.
48. I, 27.
49. I, 53.
50. I, 29.
51. I, 30.
52. I, 28.
53. I, 54.
54. I, 28; 35.
55. I, 315.
56. I, 315.
57. I, 315-316.
58. I, 139.
59. I, 139.
60. I, 162.
61. I, 53.
62. Pasqually seems to have given this particular, and unusual, sense to the adjective "pensive" by analogy with "passive," which, for him, just as we have seen, signifies: subject to suffering.
63. I, 34-36; 75-76.
64. I, 36.
65. I, 314.
66. I, 313.
67. I, 24.
68. I, 50.
69. I, 317.
70. I, 348.
71. I, 334.
72. I, 319.
73. That is to say: had been forced to leave the celestial world, where the

beings would not be able to remain, having become in part material.

74. I, 61-62.
75. I, 63-64.
76. I,101.
77. I, 67.
78. I, 65.
79. I, 71.
80. I, 73.
81. I, 73.
82. I, 118.
83. I, 119
84. I, 90-91
85. I, 129.
86. I, 130.
87. I, 162.
88. I, 32.
89. I, 34.
90. I, 386.
91. I, 290.
92. I, 20.
93. I, 129; 40; 43.
94. I, 43.
95. I, 40; 42; 45; 48; 49.
96. I, 37.
97. I, 37-38.
98. I, 372.
99. I, 372.
100. I, 129-130.
101. I, 125.
102. I, 164.
103. I, 171.
104. I, 174.
105. I, 174-175.
106. I, 281.
107. I, 259.
108. I, 255-256.
109. I, 272.
110. I, 263.
111. I, 125.
112. I, 350.
113. The Bible gives to the Tabernacle only one door, turned toward the Orient.
114. I, 351.
115. I, 353.
116. I, 353.

117. I, 356.
118. I, 358.
119. I, 356.
120. I, 353.
121. I, 153.
122. I, 158.
123. I, 215.
124. I, 80.
125. I, 354.
126. Allusion to Genesis I, 2: "And the spirit of God rested upon the waters."
127. I, 240.
128. I, 354.
129. I, 80.
130. I, 81.
131. I, 81-82.
132. I, 275.
133. I, 214.
134. I, 213-214.
135. I, 214.
136. I, 215-216.
137. I, 223-224.
138. I, 43.
139. I, 235.
140. I, 324.
141. I, 253.
142. There is frequent confusion in the Reintegration between the Elect Minor and the divine envoy who transmits to him the divine inspiration. For example, it declares (I, 44) that the seal placed by the Creator upon the Patriarchs Abraham, Isaac, and Jacob was "a spiritual major being, more powerful than the glorious Minors, and that they were only able to distinguish by the different spiritual operations what this being operated himself." This major spiritual being is called once Heli, when it serves as intermediary between the Eternal and Seth (I, 119). Elsewhere Noah, Abraham, and Moses communicate directly with the Eternal.
143. I, 110.
144. I, 82.
145. I, 102.
146. I, 74.
147. I, 48.
148. I, 38.
149. I, 291-292.
150. I, 290.
151. The role of spokesman of Moses, assigned by the Lord to Aaron, conforms with the indications given by Exodus (IV, 14-16; 27-30). Ur

figures also in the same book (XVII, 10; 12) where he helps Aaron, during the battle against the Amalecites, to keep the arms of Moses raised.

152. I, 270.

153. I, 119.

154. I, 78.

155. I, 119.

156. In this connection Pasqually makes allusion, in order to contradict it, to a tradition of medieval origin and according to which Seth had inscribed upon two columns, the one of bricks, the other of stone, the elements of the "divine sciences" that Adam had transmitted to him, and which he had thus saved from the Flood. Pasqually asserts that the "natural spiritual sciences" (in the species of arithmosophy) were not able "as they have told it," to be communicated to Seth by his father, "since Adam, by his prevarication, was stripped of all spiritual power and that he did not even obtain, after his reconciliation, anything but a sole minor power, which he was not yet able to transmit on his own authority, but only by the supreme authority of the divinity," (I, 127).

157. I, 78.

158. I, 75.

159. I, 78.

160. I, 77.

161. I, 355.

162. I, 160.

163. I, 99-100.

164. I, 323.

165. I, 309.

166. I, 58.

167. I, 78.

168. I, 309.

169. I, 124.

170. I, 306.

171. I, 310.

172. I, 320.

173. I, 322.

174. I, 325.

175. This phrase, that the jargon of Pasqually renders nearly incomprehensible, probably signifies that life may not exist in any organism unless there is found there a fragment of the central fire (animal heat), by which the inferior Spirits, who preside at the axis, animate the bodies.

176. I, 84-86-87; 100; 122; 283; 306.

177. I, 24.

178. I, 76.

179. I, 77.

180. I, 124-125.
181. I, 78.
182. I, 323-324.
183. I, 78.
184. I, 123-124.
185. I, 303.
186. I, 303.
187. I, 122.
188. I, 123.
189. This expression probably designates the vital energy emanated from the divine center. Concerning the "central axis fire" mentioned previously, is it a material manifestation, like the ordinary mercury was, for the alchemists, the crude form of the "mercury of the philosophers"? The supposition seems logical; but, in fact, Pasqually employs indifferently the two expressions without appearing to establish differences between them.
190. I, 122-123.
191. I, 203. In other words, the vital energy, which has organized, and which animates matter, only acts upon the organisms under the influence of the planets which regulate the rhythm of the universal life; and over each of the seven planets presides a Major Spirit, which serves as intermediary between the First Cause and material creation.
192. I, 78.
193. I, 203.
194. I, 303.
195. I, 82.
196. I, 254.
197. I, 303.
198. I, 204.
199. I, 291.
200. I, 324-225-335.
201. I, 78.
202. I, 88.
203. I, 78-89.
204. I, 78.
205. I, 323.
206. I, 326.
207. I, 309.
208. I, 364.
209. I, 110.
210. The text reads "opposed," a printing error that renders the phrase unintelligible.
211. I, 174.
212. I, 307.
213. I, 323.

214. I, 120; 306.
215. I, 121.
216. I, 326.
217. I, 120.
218. I, 322.
219. I, 325.
220. I, 120; 325.
221. I, 120; 325.
222. I, 363.
223. I, 364.
224. I, 325-326.
225. I, 325.
226. I, 307.
227. I, 136.
228. I, 174.
229. I, 310.
230. I, 326-327.
231. I, 321.
232. It seems then, without Pasqually saying it explicitly, that the circle of the Ternary had been the second emanation, which has taken place after the revolt of the perverse Spirits, and which has preceded that of the Minor or Man-God.
233. In other words, the earth, created to be the prison of the perverse Spirits, receives the vital energy emitted by the major and inferior circles, conservators of time and matter, between which it is found placed, and which acts upon it "in latitude."
234. I, 296-297; 300; 314; 321; 329-330. The situation of the First Man before the fall, "the spiritual stratum in which the Creator placed his first Minor," is also represented by seven concentric circumferences. "By the 6 circles, the Creator represented to the First Man the 6 immense thoughts that he had employed for the creation of his universal and particular temple (universe and beings). The 7th, joined to the 6 others, indicates to man the junction that the Spirit of the Creator made with him in order to be his strength and support," (I, 26).
235. I, 332.
236. I, 299.
237. I, 46-47.
238. I, 286.
239. This very obscure passage seems to signify that the Minor comes out of the sensible circle by corporeal death and passes then into the visual circle for a space of time superior to that of his terrestrial life; Pasqually indeed advances (I, 47) that, "the expanse of this second circle is infinitely more considerable than that of the first, in which the Minors have finished the course of the natural operation of their being."
240. I, 47; 171.

241. I, 286. In another place (I, 294), Pasqually speaks of 4 supercelestial circles: "These 4 supercelestial circles are also called divine spirituals, because they adhere to the circle of the Divinity and contain only spiritual beings, deprived of bodies of matter. These Spirits are not all denaries, but each spiritual being inhabiting these circles has received, at the instant of its emancipation, the particular divine laws by which they must operate their power. Thus, no being inhabiting one of these circles operates the same actions nor the same powers, as the inhabitants of the other circles."

242. I, 126.

243. I, 304.

244. I, 82.

245. The liberties taken by Pasqually with the cosmographic terms manifest, in another place, by the particular meaning that he gives to the words "latitude," "longitude," and "horizon." "The space," he says, "which is found between the extremity of the material world and the extremity of the celestial world forms the longitude of the limits fixed to the prevaricating Spirits. The expanse of these same limits in latitude is the whole horizontal surface of the material world, and the celestial world is the envelope of the material world. You must understand that the longitude which goes from one of these two worlds to the other is greater and more considerable than upon the horizontal face of the material world, seeing that this world of matter has only three remarkable (sensible?) horizons: North, South, and West, and that the celestial world has four regions without horizons, because indeed the horizons belong only to the material world, whose inhabitants are subject to being fed and substantiated by the material elements and are exposed to the change of the season," (I, 333).

246. I, 132-133.

247. I, 82.

248. I, 126. The Reintegration gives the sketch.

249. I, 323.

250. I, 129. Pasqually forgets in this moment that he attributes in general the role of catalyzer to "the central axis fire," but it is not nearly an inconsistency.

251. I, 287.

252. I, 232.

253. I, 67; 81; 124; 223.

254. I, 13.

255. I, 13; 25.

256. I, 13.

257. I, 255.

258. I, 299.

259. The letters addressed by Pasqually and Saint-Martin to Willermoz "in order to complete his instruction," shows that the ritual of the

Invocations has varied often from 1768 to 1771.

260. Willermoz, stricken by the differences that he noticed between what was prescribed to him in 1771 and what Pasqually had communicated verbally to him at Paris in 1767, asked, in May 1771, for clarifications on several flagrant contradictions; Saint-Martin responded to him that Pasqually recognized having forgotten what he had previously taught to the adept of Lyon, and this confession was accompanied by a new instruction which takes into account the objections of Willermoz (III, 98-99).

261. II, 106.

262. III, 102; 103; 108.

263. III, 110.

264. II, 105.

265. III, 112.

266. II, 195.

267. III, 149; 153.

268. III, 95; 99; 103.

269. This invocation, which was probably a development of that of which it has already been spoken, has kept from time to time in the correspondence of the adepts the name of Daily Invocation, a meaningless expression which may only be explained by its origin.

270. II, 86 and III, 92; 94-95. The letter of May 24 was accompanied by 3 sheets of 6 pages containing the French text of the instruction on the invocation called daily. This instruction, which indicated "the words and all the other parts, as much of the operation as the ceremonial" has not been published by Papus. A letter from Pasqually to Willermoz, from February 16, 1770, (III, 92) also alluded to "another work, which may be done, after the Working of the 3 days, every week, every month, or two or three times per year," following which Willermoz will find himself disposed to the undertaking. This operation could be made "in all places," without tracing the circle and "without other form of process." As the letter of February 16 was written in the era when Willermoz demanded insistently instructions, it is possible that Pasqually wished to calm his impatience by vague promises.

271. II, 83-84.

272. The explanation of this term, as well as that of the "passes," which will be found further on, will be given in the following chapter.

273. III, 109.

274. II, 84-89.

275. The first Equinox Working executed in these forms was the one of March 1772, (III, 115).

276. This is probably the "great invocation of exact midnight" of which Saint- Martin speaks in a letter to Willermoz on June 8, 1771, (III, 109).

277. Belzebuth and Leviathan had been strongly feared during the whole Middle Ages; they had even played a role of primary importance in the

possessions of Loudun under the reign of Louis XIII; the name of another demon, Balam, which was equally distinguished on this occasion, recalls that of the demon exorcized third in line by the operant.

278. Upon the significance of the numbers, see what has been said in the preceding chapter on the arithmosophy of Pasqually. Likewise, the names of Satan, Belzebuth, and Baran are, at the beginning of the exconjuration, subscribed by the number 5 and that of Leviathan by the number 11.

279. It seems that there is a lacuna here in the text.

280. III, 96-98.

281. III, 100.

282. That is to say, probably, the Working of the Three Days; it is said, in any case, expressly in a letter from Saint-Martin to Willermoz that the Invocation of the Three Days was transferred to the Equinox Working (III, 102).

283. II, 94-98.

284. II, 90.

285. The two indications given by the letter from Pasqually on the position of these two circles are particularly obscure; the interpretation adopted here has seemed most likely.

286. By mystical addition, $28=2+8=10$.

287. St.-M. to Will., January 27, 1772; letter accompanying a drawing of three circles, that we know only by the commentaries of St.-M. (III, 111-114). St.-M. to Will., February 14, 1772; response to four questions posed by Willermoz on the subject of the ritual (III, 115).

288. St.-Martin had sent, on July 7, 1771, to Willermoz an alphabetical collection of mystical names and hieroglyphs of Prophets and apostles, "so that he knew where to find them when he was told to use it," (III, 102).

289. It is represented by 5 on our draft, because the Equinox Working of March 1772 was practiced by six adepts, (III, 115).

290. The prescriptions for the censing are likely all that was written of this ritual of the Work of the Four Circles which does not seem to have ever been finished or put into practice in entirety.

291. V, 229.

292. II, 76-77.

293. II, 105.

294. II, 77-78.

295. II, 77-79.

296. On March 4, 1771, Saint-Martin doubts that Pasqually, then at Paris, can carry out the Equinox Working, "the circumstances not permitting him to make all the necessary preparations on the subject," (III, 85). It is possible that the term "quarantine," employed by Saint-Martin in order to designate the retreat observed by an adept, the Abbé Fournié, (III,

144), had not indicated a period of exactly forty days; the word may be used as a synonym for a time of meditation, without having preserved its etymological significance, as in the case of a sanitary quarantine.

297. III, 93.

298. III, 152.

299. This orientation was, moreover, fictive, for the burner "representing the North," and upon which consumed the major portion of the burnt offering, was, in order to facilitate combustion, and, probably also in order to save the sense of smell of the persons present, placed upon the fireplace of the room, whatever its relation was to the cardinal points.

300. V, 229. The instruction recommends to have within reach the water "as it is fitting," without the context indicating whether it is a matter of a lustral water, specially consecrated, or a provision of ordinary water destined to extinguish the fire after the combustion of the flesh.

301. Titles indicated in the documents by R.M. and T.P.M.

302. V, 229-230.

303. Pasqually promised to Bacon to abandon his domestic affairs "in order to prepare to strengthen him in his ordination at the moment when the Universal Substitute would proceed to the ordination of Willermoz and he notified the recipient at the same time to be at "his East corner on the 27, 28, and 29th of September 1768, in order to receive there his sympathetic ordination of virtue and power relative to his dignity and quality as Réau-Croix," (V, 228; II, 82).

304. II, 117.

305. V, 230.

306. II, 79.

307. III, 114.

308. V, 229.

309. V, 229. The mystical role of numbers was equally emphasized by that of the operations and ceremonies: "The different ceremonial acts of our Operations are 4 in number, to which (by which) it is given to us one sole power with each (Operation), which makes (so that the four Operations form) 4 powers, which complete, with the four ceremonies, the infinite number of 8," (V, 229).

310. III, 88.

311. V, 228.

312. III, 88.

313. II, 92.

314. II, 92.

315. II, 92.

316. III, 90.

317. II, 109.

318. III, 90.

319. II, 87.

320. III, 90.

321. IX, 18.
322. II, 92.
323. II, 94.
324. II, 93.
325. Pasqually sent to Willermoz, on May 9, 1772, a design representing a luminous rod surmounted by a triple tuft of fire and considered this manifestation as particularly significant, (II, 109).
326. II, 110.
327. I, 33.
328. I, 292.
329. I, 257.
330. I, 209.
331. III, 99.
332. I, 15; 139.
333. I, 271.
334. I, 57-58.
335. I, 55.
336. I, 283-284.
337. I, 307.
338. I, 357.
339. I, 181.
340. I, 308.
341. I, 364.
342. III, 113.
343. I, 286.
344. Franck (IX, 15), has believed that by reintegration Pasqually meant "the annihilation of the limits which determine our being, the destruction of our consciousness and our individual will, the return of our soul into the bosom of the universal spirit." This is to attribute to the treatise a gnostic concept which is foreign to it. Pasqually did not teach, as believes Franck, "that every emanation is a downfall, that is to say a lessening of the infinite substance." If his doctrine has had, just as we will see later, points of contact with Gnosticism, it nevertheless left man in possession of his individual existence following his reintegration into the supercelestial. The Minor would only lose it at "the end of time," when every emanation, every creation, and, consequently, all distinct existence returned to lose itself in the first source. It is therefore wrong to say, as does Franck (p. 13), that all the beings, those who surround the throne of the Eternal and people the heavens, as those who are in exile upon this earth, "all feel with suffering the evil that keeps them removed from their divine source and await with impatience the day of reintegration."
345. I, 171-172.
346. I, 171.
347. 47; 171; 220; 286.

348. It is important to note the essential difference existing between two revolutions that Pasqually has mistakenly designated by the same term. The error committed by Franck shows in large part the confusion created by the blunder of Pasqually.

349. This is what is indicated in the words expressed by the original title of the treatise, that Pasqually had at first entitled: "The Reintegration of every spiritual created being to its first Virtue, Force, and Power in the personal enjoyment of which every being will enjoy distinctly in the presence of the Creator," (II, 191).

350. I, 44.

351. Idea inspired by the angelic vision with which, according to the Bible, the three Patriarchs were favored.

352. I, 324.

353. I, 342.

354. I, 41.

355. I, 171.

356. I, 40; 49.

357. I, 214.

358. I, 325.

359. I, 214.

360. I, 38.

361. I, 47; 171.

362. It is possible that the supreme aim of an Operation had been to obtain a true apparition, that is to say a vision accompanied by auditory phenomena. This is, as we have seen above, what the Abbé Fournié asserted. His testimony seems confirmed by a passage of the Reintegration (p. 271) where Pasqually, presenting the epiphany of which was favored Jacob as a model of "perfect reconciliation," teaches that the Spirit shows itself as "a natural vision which is offered to him under a human form," so that "by these means Jacob was restored in divine spiritual power." But the Élus Coëns could not, as a general rule, aspire to so exceptional a favor, reserved in principle to the Spiritual Elect.

363. I, 332.

364. I, 120.

365. I, 248. He gives elsewhere a very un-mystical definition of ecstasy: "When the contemplation is strong enough to lively affect the soul, the body falls into a kind of inaction, it is not susceptible to any impression by reason that the soul bears itself entirely towards to object of its spiritual contemplation. One must not believe by this that the soul is detached from the body. It is only separated in spiritual action and not in nature," (p. 249-250).

366. I, 285.

367. I, 338.

368. I, 332.

369. I, 356; 358-359.
370. I, 249.
371. I, 66.
372. I, 185.
373. I, 195.
374. I, 207.
375. I, 69; 351.
376. I, 359.
377. I, 60.
378. I, 24; 50.
379. I, 19.
380. II, 110.
381. I, 219.
382. I, 127.
383. I, 200.
384. The word "prevarication" that the text of Charcornac presents here is manifestly a copyist error.
385. I, 220.
386. I, 257.
387. I, 328.
388. I, 31.
389. I, 66.
390. A passage of the treatise (p. 204), which considers the "divine spiritual operations," as the means "to maintain in the disciples the divine spirit," seems to indicate that the spiritual cult consisted in prayers and invocations; in this case the temporal cult would have especially designated the operations, which used figures, perfumes, and candles, and brought about sensible phenomena.
391. I, 69.
392. I, 219.
393. I, 103; 105; 131. This "rule of life" is the type of that which Pasqually prescribed to his disciples.
394. I, 187.
395. I, 185-186.
396. I, 194.
397. I, 196.
398. I, 185.
399. I, 196.
400. I, 197.
401. I, 198.
402. I, 206.
403. I, 207.
404. I, 207.
405. I, 207.
406. I, 228-230. Pasqually often used the words "blessing" and "benediction"

in the sense of re-establishing communications with the divinity. It is in this sense that it is necessary to understand expressions like "God blessed Adam," "God blessed creation." The relationship existing between the "benediction" understood as supernatural manifestation and the "divine cult" assimilated in the Operations, is clearly established by Pasqually himself in the following passage: "Under the name of benediction, Esau wanted to try to obtain from his father some power or some spiritual gift (faculty to provoke manifestations) seeing himself outside of a state to operate any divine cult for the glory of the Creator," (p. 225).

407. I, 271. The vision of Jacob is thus represented as the type of the operation crowned by a full success and this success is the proof and the seal of reconciliation.

408. I, 246-248, 250.

409. I, 251.

410. This act of Moses is, to employ the language of Pasqually, the "type" of the power that the Operant possesses to force the wicked Spirits to strip off the fallacious form that they would have taken in order to dupe him. The gesture indicated, which resembles the defensive sign employed against the evil eye, probably figured in the ritual at the moment of the exconjurations.

411. I, 269. That is to say that he re-established the ten ritual ceremonies indicated above.

412. I, 220.

413. I, 191.

414. I, 70.

415. I, 102-105.

416. I, 187.

417. I, 199.

418. I, 378-387.

419. I, 246-248.

420. I, 248.

421. I, 253.

422. I, 69.

423. I, 105.

424. I, 195.

425. I, 258.

426. I, 74.

427. I, 90.

428. I, 93.

429. I, 218.

430. I, 228-229; 232.

431. I, 387.

432. I, 197.

433. I, 198.

434. I, 186. This passage is a dogmatic justification of the ritual which placed during the night the Invocations and Operations of the Élus Coëns.
435. I, 200.
436. I, 199.
437. I, 200.
438. I, 187.
439. I, 200.
440. I, 200.
441. I, 211.
442. I, 205.
443. I, 207. This is at least what must be supposed from a text particularly obscure, and which has manifestly undergone alterations.
444. I, 205.
445. I, 209.
446. I, 201.
447. These are, under another name, the invocations of the Élus Coëns.
448. I, 233.
449. I, 269.
450. I, 334.
451. I, 136.
452. I, 135.
453. I, 137.
454. I, 282.
455. I, 203.
456. I, 286.
457. I, 285.
458. I, 285.
459. I, 301.
460. I, 330.
461. I, 331.
462. I, 301.
463. I, 302.
464. I, 302.
465. I, 305.
466. I, 302.
467. I, 305.
468. I, 135. A drawing, reproduced on this same page, represents an igneous globe bearing the Pentagram, or Pentalpha, and emitting two currents of effluvium, of which one reached the sun and the other turned into a comet.
469. I, 275.
470. I, 334.
471. I, 138.
472. I, 145-147.
473. I, 209.

474. I, 208. Justification of the importance attached by Pasqually to the Operation of the Spring Equinox. The preponderance of this equinox is underscored by the Reintegration which has it coincide with remarkable events in the history of Israel. Moses is come into the world on the 14th of the moon of Nisan or of March (p. 238). The Israelites have come out of Egypt at midnight from the 14th to the 15th of the month of the moon of Nisan or of March (p. 252) "It was in the night from the 14th to the 15th day of Nisan or March, that Moses arrived with all his army on the bank of the Red Sea"(p. 265). When, having reached the other end, the Israelites finished giving thanks to the Eternal, "the break of the 15th day of the moon began to appear. It is in this moment that the manna fell for the first time," (p. 266).

475. I, 209.

476. I, 209; 212.

477. I, 205.

478. I, 206.

479. I, 206.

480. I, 205.

481. I, 205. Pasqually asserts moreover that this year, so brief, was then introduced into the calendar year, just as, later, the descendants of Ham counted four profane years, those of Shem two years, and those of Japhet only one for one solar year.

482. I, 208.

483. I, 220.

484. I, 184.

485. I, 183.

486. II, 77.

487. II, 107.

488. II, 107.

489. II, 78.

490. II, 100.

491. V, 229.

492. I, 120.

493. I, 48.

494. I, 35.

495. I, 25.

496. Philosophie der Geschichte, 1824, chap. VI, parag. 487.

497. VI, 144.

498. It is particularly necessary to eliminate Swedenborg, who, according to Papus, had "initiated" Pasqually in the case of a journey made by the latter to London, so that the Rite of Élus Coëns would only be a "Swedenborgian adaptation." This comparison, inspired by the superficial resemblance existing between the visions of the Swede and the pneumatology of Pasqually, had already led Reghellini de Schio (La Maçonnerie considérée comme résultat des religions égyptienne, juive et

chrétienne, Brussels, 1829, II, p. 434) to establish a filiation between the doctrine and rite of Swedenborg and those of the Élus Coëns. It is possible that, as supposes the pseudonymous author of the Introduction aux Enseignements Secrets de M. de Pasqually (IV, 17), Reghellini had confused the Illuminé d'Avignon [Illuminati of Avignon], members of the Mother Lodge of the Rite of Swedenborg, with the Élus Coëns of the same town. This erroneous indication, already reproduced by Ragon (Orthodoxie Maçonnique, 1853, p. 149), has been received by Papus who has enriched it with details drawn from his imagination, for Pasqually had never been to London.

499. Cf. Vuilliaud: La Kabbale juive, II, p. 192.

500. Bischoff: Kabbalah, p. 61.

501. Bischoff: Gnosis, p. 4.

502. The principal ones are: Apocalypse of Baruch, Assumption of Moses, Testament of Adam, Apocalypse of Elijah, Apocalypse of Esdras, Testament of the Twelve Patriarchs, Apocalypse of Abraham, Testament of Abraham, Apocalypse of Salathiel, Book of Jubliees, Book of Enoch, Ascension of Isaiah, Sibylline Oracles, (Kreglinger: Religion d'Israel, p. 349).

503. Kreglinger: op. cit., p. 253; 274-275.

504. Ledrain: Histoire d'Israel, p. 117.

505. Bischoff: Kabbalah, p. 38.

506. The Targum (Interpretation), attributed to Onkelos, also called Targum of Jerusalem, is a commentary on the Pentateuch written in Aramaic. It was begun in the 2nd century of our era in Palestine and finished in Babylonia towards the end of the 2nd century. Another Targum, told by Jonathan Ben Uzziel, written in approximately the same period, comments on the Prophets.

507. "And he heard the Word of the Lord when he passed in the garden," (III, 8); "And the Word of the Lord closed the door of the ark," (VIII, 17); "And the Word of the Lord made it rain upon Sodom," (XIX, 24).

508. Already the syllable "el," which signifies: divine power, figures in most of the names of the angels cited by the Bible.

509. This name was inspired by: Ecclesiasticus XLIX, 10: "Ezekiel saw the glory of the Lord upon the chariot of the Kerobim," Psalms XVIII, 11: "He was carried by the Kerobim," I Chronicles XXVIII, 18: "He (David) gave pure gold...for the Kerobim who formed the resemblance of a chariot."

510. Bischoff: Gnosis, p. 10; 14, and Thalmud, p. 76.

511. This process seems to have been known since the 2nd century of our era. We know that the Hebraic letters have a numerical value.

512. The Book of Jeremiah had already used this mode of cryptography to designate secretly Babylon and the Babylonians, if one judges it by the translation that the Targum and the Septuagint have given of the conventional terms employed by the prophet.

513. These two types of Zeruph rest on a mystical principle of Chaldean origin according to which "the things which are on high are similar to those which are below."

514. They sometimes attribute to the Essenes the invention of the symbolic interpretation of Scripture.

515. They have been able to compare in the lessons of Gamaliel I the processes employed by Saint Paul in the Fourth Epistle to the Galatians to make a comparison between Agar and Sinai, between Sarah and the Celestial Jerusalem.

516. The theme of the Microcosm and the Macrocosm may have been borrowed by Philo from the Platonic doctrine, but, even in this case, he still drew from the sources of the ancient Orient, from where Plato had likely drawn himself the foundation of his philosophical system. Several centuries before Plato, Chaldea had imagined that the sensible is only an imitation of the intelligible, and that the world where we are corresponds down to the least detail to the superior world. We have seen likewise that the notion of the primitive androgynous man expressed by the Talmud comes, not from the Banquet of Plato, but from the two hermaphrodites of Chaldea.

517. Vulliaud: Kabbale Juive, p. 135; 137.

518. Vulliaud: op. cit., p. 139-140.

519. They are: the Book of Splendor, which has given its name to the collection, the Book of the Secret, the Great Assembly, the Lesser Assembly, the Faithful Shepherd (mystical name of Moses), the Additions to the Zohar, the New Zohar.

520. I, 194.

521. I, 367.

522. I, 217.

523. I, 225.

524. I, 209. Pasqually seems to lose sight here that he has previously protested against "the convention of man," who "without divine participation, has distinguished Ishmael, Israel, the Christians, and the Idolaters," that he has declared that the posterity of Cain, that of Seth, and the female posterity of Adam had first formed "the three nations inhabiting the surface of the earth" and finally that he had affirmed that, in accord with the Bible, the earth "was after the Deluge, on the order of the Eternal, portioned among the three children of Noah," so that "there can only be upon the earth three principal nations, from which every composite and conventional nation of name is emanated," (p. 132-133). Perhaps he meant that the descendants of Shem, Ham, and Japhet have forgotten, in proportion as they multiplied and as they succeed themselves, the teaching which had been given to them by the Spiritual Elect of the second posterity of Noah and to explain thus the birth of the polytheist religions among the people of antiquity.

525. I, 156.

526. I, 156.
527. I, 194.
528. I, 194.
529. Pasqually gives to this last word a more mystical sense than historic. He remarks, indeed, after having called the seven Spiritual Minors, disciples of the three last born of the second posterity of Noah, "true Israelites": "I use here the word Israelite although the name of Israel was not yet known in the time of which I speak (it was indeed, according to the Bible, given to Jacob after his struggle with the angel). Israel signifies: strong against God, but Israelites signifies: strong in God; that is why I give this name to the Noachite sages of the posterity of Noah," (p. 204). It is true that some pages further he declares, as we come to see, that one of the two servants of Abraham remaining at the foot of Moriah symbolizes the abandon "that Israel will make in the future of the divine cult," (p. 217). There are, therefore, for Pasqually, elect and damned among the Israelites as among the Jews of nationality.
530. I, 194.
531. I, 259-262.
532. In the 2nd Chapter of Genesis, Adam calls Eve ischschah, artificial feminine form of the word signifying man, and which corresponds exactly to the word "hommesse" forged by Pasqually.
533. In Genesis (XVII) Jehovah, after having promised a son to the Patriarch, tells him: "They will no longer call you Abram, but Abraham, for you will be father of a multitude of nations." Following the Hebraists Ab-ram signifies: Raised Father, First Ancestor, and Ab-raham: Father of the Multitude. Pasqually develops: Abram, "carnal and terrestrial father, raised above ordinary fathers of material terrestrial posterities"; Abraham, "father raised in multitude of posterity in God," (p. 212). Nevertheless, in another place (p. 114), he is content to call Abraham "father of the multitude," as done in the Bible.
534. I, 193.
535. There is no agreement on the date of the introduction of the vowel-points attributed to the Masoretic who first separated the text, up till then continuous, into chapters and verses. The reform, which had for its aim to make the reading easier, dates back, according to the different linguists, to 570 at the earliest, 800 at the latest AD. Until the 16th century, the antiquity of the vowel-points was universally accepted by the Jewish Hebraists, and when Elias Levita put forth that they were relatively modern, his opinion created a scandal. The problem took on a confessional appearance with Mathias Flacius, and in the 17th century provoked a celebrated polemic between Capelle and the Buxtorf father and son Hebraists. It must be noted that the question had been brought up again in France in 1743 by the Abbé Michel Fourmont, Syriac interpreter at the Bibliothèque de Roi [Library of the King] (Cf. Vulliaud: Kabbale Juive, II, p. 156-268).

536. I, 193.
537. I, 193.
538. I, 193.
539. I, 192.
540. The Talmud notably has two principal types of writing: one for the text, which is squared Hebrew, and one for the commentaries; the notes placed in the margin or at the bottom of the pages are sometimes printed in several other types. The abbreviations, quite numerous, are of different forms according to the editions, above all in the commentaries and notes. The language is a mixture of new Hebrew and Aramaic with numerous particular dialects. The text presents neither paragraphs nor chapters. Certain passages are only intelligible through comparison with other passages dispersed in different treatises; even an extensive knowledge of the mystical literature still leaves many obscure points for the reader if he is not aided by an experienced Talmudist and knowledgeable in the tradition of the teaching. (Cf. Bischoff: Thalmud, VII-VIII.)
541. Latin translations of the Talmud had appeared in Amsterdam at the end of the 17th century, and Knorr von Rosenroth had translated into Latin numerous passages of the Zohar in his Kabbala Denudata (1677 and 1684).
542. Cf. Dreglinger: Religion d'Israel, 69-71.
543. III, 93.
544. Kreglinger, op. cit. p. 187; 199; 243.
545. I, 127; 129.
546. The Bible also put the patriarchs like Abraham, Isaac, Jacob, and Tobias in communication with the Lord by the mediation of the angels.
547. I, 95,
548. I, 357. It says also (Ibid. p. 46): "No matter may see and understand the Spirit without dying or without the Spirit dissolving and annihilating every form of matter."
549. The modern critic designates under this name the most recent of four documents founded in the Pentateuch and which had been written after the capture of Jerusalem by Nebuchadnezzar in 586 BC.
550. Frazer: Folklore dans l'A.T., note 210.
551. I, 331.
552. I, 30.
553. It is curious to note that in giving this double translation of Zebaoth, Pasqually preceded the modern exegesis which believes that the term designated the host of stars before being interpreted as signifying the Israelites under arms.
554. Ledrain: Hist. d'Israel, I, p. 137-139.
555. V, 229.
556. Ledrain: op. cit. I, p. 149.
557. I, 227-228.

558. I, 164.
559. I, 165.
560. I, 166.
561. I, 231.
562. I, 246.
563. I, 278.
564. I, 253.
565. "The life of the flesh is in the blood; that is why I have given it to you so that it be spread upon the altar for the expiation of your sins, for it is by the blood that the soul will be purified," XVII, II.
566. I, 114.
567. I, 221.
568. I, 363.
569. I, 171.
570. I, 120.
571. I, 377.
572. IX, 11.
573. I, 360.
574. Benjamin signifies "vulgarly": "Son of my days."
575. Exodus (XXXVI) calls him Bezalel: "in the shadow of God."
576. Cain: "rejection."
577. Scheth: "steady."
578. Jered: "descent." It is possible that Pasqually had interpreted the original meaning from the mystical point of view as: descent of the divine Spirit. He has elsewhere from time to time followed the etymology rather closely; he translates Noah (Noha: "repose") as "repose or relief," (p. 172), Enos (Enosch: "man") as "weak mortal," (p. 130). His translation of Enoch (Hanock: "tried, initiate") which he renders as "dedication" (who has been dedicated) has a mystical significance pertaining to the true meaning (p. 104), but the reason for which we wants the word to begin with an E and not by an H remains mysterious (p. 131).
579. I, 237.
580. I, 238.
581. I, 277.
582. I, 94.
583. I, 263.
584. I, 135.
585. I, 104.
586. I, 73.
587. I, 64.
588. I, 91.
589. I, 67.
590. I, 67.
591. It is possible that Pasqually had known directly the works of the Alexandrian mystic of which there had appeared several Latin

translations in the 17th century and one quite recent (1742). It is remarkable that he agrees with him to assume in principle that the phenomenal world has time as a necessary condition, in order to make of man the crown and conclusion of creation, a copy of the ideal model of the transcendent First Adam, and for him to recognize a free will by virtue of which he is completely responsible for his actions.

592. I, 24.

593. I, 64.

594. I, 163.

595. That is to say that the demons obscure the intelligence of the Minors who listen to them.

596. I, 117.

597. I, 236.

598. I, 179.

599. I, 252.

600. I, 277.

601. I, 199-200.

602. I, 13.

603. I, 14.

604. I, 379-388.

605. I, 159.

606. I, 90-91.

607. I, 91-94.

608. I, 237.

609. I, 266.

610. I, 237-238.

611. I, 242-245. This anecdote is found in part in the Jewish Antiquities (book II, chap. IX, parag. 7) which are, in the first half, only a summary of the Bible in use by the pagans, but where the author has inserted legendary features foreign to the Scripture and showing oral traditions. According to Josephus the daughter of the Pharaoh, who had adopted Moses because she had no progeny, presented him to her father when the child had reached his third year, in order to persuade him to take Moses as his presumptive heir. The Pharaoh, as a game, placed his diadem upon the head of the child, but he threw the diadem to the ground and trampled it under foot. As a hierogrammat sought to persuade the king to have him kill Moses, the princess quickly removed him in this way. This legend is found under the same form in the Midrash Tanhuma. The trial by burning coal, of which neither Josephus nor the Midrash speaks, had to have been borrowed by Pasqually from a Haggadah seeking to explain the stammering of Moses indicated by the Bible (Exodus IV, 10). The work of Josephus being well known in France by the translations of Arnauld d'Andilly (1676, reprinted several times) and of P. Gillet (1756), one could be tempted to seek there one of Pasqually's sources, but the most indisputable concordances are not

decisive proofs. For example, the appellation of "roux" that he gives to Adam is indicated in terms expressed by Josephus who said (J. Ant. book I, chap. I, parag. 2): "This man was called Adamos, which in Hebrew signifies roux [red, ruddy], because it is from the diluted red earth that he was formed." The commentators have observed that Josephus has combined the two interpretations that the consonants expressed in the Hebrew name of the First Man can receive, and it is true that the meaning of "earth" is the only one which is indicated by the Bible. But the meaning of red, unknown to rabbinical literature, is read in the Pirke (Chapters) of Rabbi Eliezer, work attributed to Elieser Ben Hyrkan (2nd century AD), but dating in reality to the 8th century, which is a paraphrase of the first two books of the Pentateuch and contain a great quantity of mystical elements of which many of the most ancient sources are no longer able to be identified (Bischoff: Kabbalah, p. 53). Likewise, if the J. Ant. give to Adam and Eve daughters and a great number of other children after Cain and Abel, one of the Tannaim of the 2nd century AD, reports the same tradition and the Book of Jubilees, written in the same period, calls one of the sisters of Abel: "Avan," which name strangely resembles that given by the treatise of Pasqually (p. 67) to Abel himself. The tradition noted by Josephus (L. I, ch. III, parag. 1) and according to which the descendants of Seth remain for seven generations faithful to the cult of the true God and practiced virtue is also reported by the Pirke of the Rabbi Eliezer who says: "From Seth descends the race of virtuous men." The sign that, according to Josephus, God placed on Cain in order to protect him from the ferocious animals, whose attacks the assassin feared in the place of exile where he was relegated by divine justice, and the inurement of his posterity to the crime are indicated by the Kabbalists of the Middle Ages, heirs of the Talmudists.

612. Bischoff: Kabbalah, p. 54-55.
613. I, 174.
614. Daanson: Mythes et légendes, p. 146-149.
615. IX, 206.
616. I, 8.
617. I, 176-177.
618. I, 309.
619. I, 78.
620. I, 326.
621. I, 8.
622. I, 364.
623. I, 8.
624. I, 359.
625. I, 97.
626. I, 56.
627. I, 353.

628. I, 98-99.
629. I, 99-120.
630. Idea that the Kabbalah had perhaps received from Plato by the intermediary of the Neoplatonists, but that Plato may have borrowed from the ancient Chaldean doctrines which considered the stars as beings of colossal stature being moved in the sky.
631. I, 287.
632. I, 161.
633. I, 33.
634. I, 334.
635. I, 161.
636. Vulliaud: op. cit. II, p. 127.
637. Vulliaud, p. 83-85.
638. Ibid. p. 93.
639. Ibid. II, p. 110.
640. Ibid. II, p. 126.
641. I, 301.
642. The Kabbalistic Tree is reproduced in Bischoff: Kabbalah, p. 101.
643. Vulliaud: op. cit. I, p. 464. One may also note in this connection that when Pasqually calls creation "the realization of the six thoughts of God," he employs an image familiar to the Kabbalists who often call the world: "Sepher," in comparing it to a book where God has inscribed his thoughts.
644. I, 136.
645. I, 123.
646. I, 202.
647. I, 203.
648. I, 122.
649. I, 334.
650. I, 120; 325.
651. I, 364.
652. I, 333.
653. I, 275.
654. I, 138.
655. I, 134-135.
656. I, 136.
657. Bischoff: Kabbalah, p. 40.
658. I, 171.
659. Bischoff: Kabbalah, p. 4. The situation culminating with the heaven of Saturn is likewise specified by the Book of the angel Raziel (7th century AD) and by the Kabbalists who placed it at the limit of the sensible universe.
660. I, 253.
661. I, 351.
662. Vulliaud: op. cit. II, p. 48.

663. I, 189.
664. I, 147-148.
665. I, 113.
666. I, 111.
667. I, 98.
668. I, 148.
669. I, 85.
670. I, 85. This is why "the place of the South is the type of the universal part (of the universe) where the Creator will manifest his justice and his glory at the end of time," (p. 86).
671. I, 173.
672. I, 237.
673. I, 214.
674. Chaignet: Pythagore, II, p. 54; 75; 85; 140.
675. Cf. Zielinski: La Sibylle.
676. I, 166.
677. I, 256.
678. I, 82.
679. I, 254.
680. I, 291.
681. See above, Book I, chap. 2.
682. It is again from Plato, who, in the Laws distinguishes the "first cause movements" which are "the divine kind of cause" and the "secondary cause movements" which hold their activity as something other than from the divine thought, that seems to have been borrowed the idea of the discrimination established by Pasqually between first causes, expressions of divine will, and the secondary causes which respect the free will of the creatures and particularly of man. But it must be remarked that with Plato the secondary causes are by order of necessity, "separated from thoughts," and operate "by chance and without plan," whereas Pasqually considers them, no longer as physical laws established by the divine intelligence and will, as the structure of a finalist physics, but in fact manifestations of the human intelligence and will, in order to save the free will of man and to exempt the Creator from the responsibility of evil. Moreover, Pasqually may have found these ideas scattered in the Jewish mystical works which have drawn much from the Neoplatonists.
683. I, 171.
684. V. Henry: Parisme, p. 201.
685. Franck: Kabbalah, p. 216-217; 379.
686. I, 141.
687. I, 136.
688. Because 4+9=13 and 1+3=4.
689. This hypothesis is confirmed by a declaration of Saint-Martin. In a letter addressed to Kirchberger (Unpublished Correspondence, pub. Sauer

and Chuguet, p. 272), he asserts that Pasqually believed in the "repentance of the perverse being" and even taught that "man was charged to labor there." If the memories of Saint-Martin have remained exact after twenty-five years (the letter is from July 11, 1796) this last idea to which there is made no allusion in the Reintegration, proves that the oral teaching of the master was an indispensible complement to his dogmatic treatise.

690. One could even pick up in the Reintegration, and without appealing to the texts too much, traces of Hindu concepts. Does not Pasqually seem to have been with the school of the gymnosophists when he declares that the creation is come out of "the imagination" of the Creator who has "operated six divine thoughts by the universal creation," (I, 24) and that the end of the world will arrive "at the moment when nature will fade from the eyes of the one who has made it come into being by his divine imagination," (I, 119)? He says again: "General matter will be entirely eclipsed at the end of time and will fade away from the presence of man like a picture fades from the imagination of the painter. By this last comparison you may learn that the principle of the matter of the general body is nothing more for the Creator than a spiritual painting conceived in his imagination," (I, 115-116).

691. Chaignet: op. cit. II, p. 3; 4; 8.

692. Ancient authors have maintained that Pythagoras had been of the school of the Bramans and Burnouf, following them, made of him a Buddhist missionary whose name is a transcription of Buddhagura (initiate of Buddha). For other historians, Pythagoras would be of Semitic race, and they identify him with Ezekiel. An English writing claims that the sole authentic fragments of Philolaus which have appeared to us are those that contain the Sepher Yetzirah, and he supposes that the Pythagoreans were Jewish sectarians who were called in Palestine Essenes, term derived from Yeoschouah, Hebrew name of Pythagoras, (Vulliaud: op. cit. I, p. 202).

693. It has been often claimed that the numbers would have not only served in the architecture of the Middle Ages to express the proportions and the symmetry, but that they would have also had a mystical meaning which made of the architecture an esoteric language.

694. Op. cit. II, p. 327.

695. Chaignet: op. cit. II, p. 330.

696. Ibid. p. 330-331.

697. Ingeniously reconciling the Christian Trinity and the Kabbalistic Sephiroth, Agrippa imagines that God, first monad, issues forth first by emanation in the number 3, then in the number 10 which represents the forms of everything and the measures of all the numbers.

698. Chaignet: op. cit. II, p. 338.

699. Nevertheless, Pasqually seems to once rather clearly allude to the bisexual Adam - unless he had copied without understanding well one

of his anonymous authors-: he says on page 82 of his treatise that Adam had a "power of corporeal vegetation" (faculty of reproduction) and that he has "vegetated two sorts of vegetation: the masculine and the feminine."

700. Four is a most important number among the Egyptians and among the Hindus. The first distinguished the 4 bases or elements, the 4 zones, the 4 funerary divinities which were also the 4 cardinal points, and the 4 winds. For the second, there were 4 luminous powers subordinate to Vayu (wind or respiration, that is to say vital energy): fire, sun, moon, and lightning, and 4 psychic forces corresponding to them respectively: speech, sight, hearing, and thought (Oltramare: Hist. des idées théos dans l'Inde, p. 91). The Manichaeans counted 4 magnificent essences, 4 attributes of the Father of Light, 4 luminous seals.

701. In the primitive religions of the Near East the Dyad, which represented the union of the male principle and the female principle, was the sign of fertility and, consequently, the good.

702. Vulliaud: op. cit. I, p. 388-389. The Zohar finds again moreover the number six in the plan of the universe constituted by the six directions in space: north, south, east, west, above, and below (Ibid. I, p.7).

703. I, 303; 304.

704. Vulliaud: op. cit. II, p. 89; 90; 215.

705. I, 303.

706. Chaignet: op. cit. II, p. 118; 121-122.

707. It is curious to note in the 5th century, in the doctrine of a Father of the Church, the presence of an idea, repeated, as we have seen, by the Jewish Kabbalah, and which attributed to the number 7 the mystical faculty to put an end to the 6 periods of all existence.

708. On these demonstrations, for which we cannot find room here, consult Chaignet: op. cit. II, p. 62-66.

709. On the fundamental characteristics of magic, its origins, and the secret paths that it had followed in order to traverse the centuries and reach the Occident, see from the same author: L'Occultisme et la Franc-Maçonnerie Écossaise, 1st part, chap. I, II, III, IV.

710. F. Lenormand: Magie chez les Chaldéens, p. 93.

711. Kreglinger: op. cit. p. 156-157. It seems, nevertheless, according to the same Talmud, that the High Priest was thought to know how to spell the secret syllables.

712. Vulliaud: op. cit. II, p. 133.

713. The conjurations by the Schem-ha-mephorash were still utilized in the 17th and 18th centuries. A manual of Practical Kabbalah, entitled "Kabbalah of the Psalms," circulated in manuscript form among occultist circles. In the middle of the 17th century the Hermeticist physician Lazare Meysonier, of Lyon, author of "Philosophie des Anges," made use of it and claimed to have discovered by this means a pentagon permitting miracles to be performed. A copy of this

manuscript issued in the 18th century under the title of: "Cabale sacrée et divine des soixante-et-douze noms des anges qui portent le nom de Dieu, qui furent révélés par le saint ange Metatron à notre père Moise, par moyen desquels on obtiendra des anges, comme lui, tout ce qu'on leur demander de licite et permis, lorsqu'on sera en état de grace" [Sacred and divine Cabala of the seventy-two names of the angels who bear the name of God, which were revealed by the holy angel Metatron to our father Moses, by licit and permitted means, when one is in a state of grace], and bearing the magical signs or characters of the angels to invoke them, has recently been put up for sale by a Parisian bookseller (Catalogue de Nourry, July, 1925). It must be left to the notice accompanying the announcement of this document, the responsibility of its assertion when it adds "that the illuminated lodges of Martinez de Pasqualis used it for the accomplishment of their marvels, and one will find thereof an exemplar in the papers of Cagliostro seized by the Holy Office."

714. I, 192-193.

715. I, 192.

716. I, 361.

717. I, 362.

718. I, 364.

719. These four letters also represent, as it has been said previously, the four classes among which were distributed the first emanated Spirits.

720. I, 105-106.

721. I, 8.

722. I, 361.

723. I, 361.

724. I, 362. Pasqually attempts to give a mystical basis to this idea of magical origin by saying that "the spiritual name given to the impassive soul announces the junction of a distinct and spiritual being or of a particular septenary Spirit that the Creator has subjected to the powerful virtue of the quaternary minor Spirit, as it learns that it is joined to his first Man-God after his reconciliation," (p. 364). This Spirit, servant and auxiliary of the Minor, is for another and better self: "Here is the true neighbor that you must cherish and love as yourself," (I, 365).

725. I, 233.

726. I, 35-36.

727. I, 56.

728. I, 358.

729. I, 57.

730. I, 55.

731. I, 17.

732. I, 349.

733. I, 297.

734. IV, p. xxxvii.

735. Talismans existed through all antiquity: the Persians called them Hamaletes, the Romans Amuleta, the Mesopotamians Teraphim, the Basilideans Abraxas, the Greeks Phylacteries or Stoikeia, the Egyptians and the ancient Hebrews Totaphoth, the Chaldeans Tebhulim. It is possible that the earrings, adornments of the arms and the chest, rings of the fingers, the brow, the nose, had been firstly talismans. The objects sometimes bear figures of stars, especially the moon, or the names of protective divinities. A writer of the last century, Brière, in a work in part out of fashion (Essai sur le symbolisme antique de l'Orient, 1847), has put in relief quite well the nature of the talisman: "In the Orient, the religious symbol was not only the expression of an idea, it was moreover an active cause which, according to the intention of the one who put it to use, effected or destroyed the thing that it represented in the present time or in a distant time... There existed a bond of correspondence between the world and the earth, and the figures that one supposed in the archetypal world were obliged to operate in the terrestrial world by the strength of the imitation and by the power of the words. Behind the symbol there was the name of the object... This name, written or pronounced with intention, was an injunction to the supernatural powers charged with the administration of the world to accomplish the will of the one who had represented it," (cited by Vulliaud: op. cit. p. 33). The talismans nearly always displayed points, like that of the Élus Coëns.

736. Bischoff: Kabbalah, p. 141-142.

737. Bila: Croyance à la magie au XVIIIieme siècle, p. 132-133.

738. Ibid., p. 29.

739. M. Prost, who has devoted to C. Agrippa an important monograph in 2 volumes, assesses that nothing proves that the 4th Book is from Agrippa, but that neither is there any proof to the contrary. One may add that this book is conceived in the same spirit as that of the first three volumes of the Occult Philosophy which are certainly from Agrippa. The thesis is the same: the efficacy of the incantations arises from the words pronounced in the magical ceremonies, from the use of numbers, from the figures, and from the names of the Spirits. The 4th Book was published for the first time at Bale in 1565 following the first three books. It had not been translated from the Latin, at least into French, before the end of the 19th century, whether out of respect for the law of silence imposed at the beginning of the work, or as supposes with some likelihood its translator, Mr. Jules Bois, "because the occultists have preferred to keep it secret, in order to be able to make borrowings from it without being accused of plagiarism by the mass of readers, ignorant of an abstract and scientific Latin," (Haute Science, 1893, I, p. 657). Pasqually was able to plagiarize without fear, since he was obliged to have his instructions translated into French, first drafted in Latin, in order to render them intelligible to some of his adepts, (III,

92; II, 108).

740. This citation is, as well as the following, borrowed from the translation published by J. Bois in the review La Haute Science, I, p. 658; 33.

741. Pasqually was content with a piece of chalk; he took great care to avoid any collusion with the Christian cult.

742. "These are kinds of seals upon which are engraved lines, markings, unknown characters," says, in the Pentacules article, the Dictionnarie Mytho-Hermétiques of Pernety, 1787. The pentacle proper, also called pentalpha or pentagram, represented a star with five branches, but the name was given to every magical figure displaying angles. Agrippa fabricated more complicated pentacles bearing "the image of the serpent suspended from the cross and still others that we find in great number in the visions of the prophets Isaiah, Daniel, Esdras, in the revelations of the Apocalypse." The Quarter Circle of the Chamber of Operation and the "shield" of the operant, less picturesque, were essentially pentacles. Gleichen states it in his Memoires (VII, 157) when he remarks that the figures employed by the Élus Coëns were "none other than what one calls the seals of the Spirits that one sees upon the talismans, on the pentacles, and around magical circles."

743. Frazer: Rameau d'Or, French edition, p. 557.

744. Kerglinger: op. cit. p. 75.

745. That is to say: "Holy."

746. Kreglinger: Ibid., p. 99.

747. III, 93.

748. Réville: Religions du Mexique, p. 142-145.

749. Saintyves: Essai de Floklore biblique, p. 24-25.

750. Ibid. p. 18.

751. Frazer: Rameau d'Or, p. 575.

752. Ibid. p. 19; 18; 40.

753. Ibid. p. 577-578; 580-587; 595-597.

754. I, 226.

755. The Hebrew term designating the priest, kohen, derives from the same root as the Arabic kahin, divination, and brings to mind that the prediction of the future was at first the domain where the authority of the priest was exercised (Kreglinger: op. cit. p. 300).

756. Kreglinger: op. cit. p. 95. Pasqually insists on the mystical virtue of the unction of holy oil which had, according to Leviticus (VIII), figured in the consecration of Aaron and his sons as priests of the Most High. The Reintegration relates that when the "seven principal universal Spirits" appeared to Noah under the form of the rainbow, to announce the rebirth of the life of the world and the re-establishment of the cosmic order, the patriarch was not at first able to understand the meaning of this manifestation. It was necessary, in order for him to understand that "his deliverance was near," that the dove flies to Mount Ararat and let fall from its feet the olive branch that it brought back: "This olive

branch, taken by the dove in preference to any other wood, pointed out to men the fruit of which they would use for the unction and the mark of the powerful outstanding ones (elect), appointed by the Creator for the manifestation of his cult, just as they practiced it among Israel and among all the Sages," (I, 175).

757. I, 119-120.
758. I, 206; 207.
759. II, 90-91; 96-97.
760. I, 325.
761. II, 100.
762. II, 89.
763. IV, p. xxxvii.
764. I, 190.
765. I, 190-191.
766. I, 82-84.
767. I, 127.
768. I, 187.
769. II, 110.
770. He sent them from Port-au-Prince on October 12, 1773, "a general index of names and numbers in conjunction with the characters and hieroglyphs interpreting the fruit arising from the Operation," assuring that these pieces would allow the Réau-Croix "to interpret the fruit of their labors without any help," (II, 195-196). But this concession imposed by the distance and the desire to prevent defections was more apparent than real, for Saint-Martin declared, after having learned of the papers sent by Pasqually, that these documents contained few things unknown by Élus Coëns (III, 153).
771. III, 113. Saint-Martin, pressed with questions by the Baron de Gleichen, to whom he had made known the first grades of the Élus Coëns, (Fiches de Savalette de Langes, reproduced by Fabre in: Eques a Capite Gabato, p. 88), ended up showing him "hieroglyphic figures written in markings of fire, which would appear to him in his workings and of which he was ordered to preserve the designs," (VII, 152).
772. II, 99.
773. II, 109.
774. I, 188.
775. II, 99.
776. I, 188.
777. II, 77.
778. II, 81.
779. II, 77.
780. II, 107.
781. II, 107.
782. I, 188.
783. I, 239. Recourse "to the first divine spiritual principle," that is to say to

a divine intervention healing magically, had found a certain popularity in England, America, and Germany at the end of the last century; heritage of the ancient anti-demonic magic, it may, for the Christian Pietists, appeal to the Epistle of St. James (V. 14-15): "The prayer made with faith will save the sick and the Lord will relieve him."

784. II, 89.

785. II, 98-99.

786. II, 101-102.

787. VI, 142-143. Despite the disdain that he affected for the remedies borrowed from the pharmacopoeia, Pasqually sometimes deigned to have recourse to it. Consulted by Willermoz on an illness of the womb with which suffered the sister of the adept of Lyon, the head of the Order, who seems to have been an all-around expert in gynecology, prescribed after having discoursed on the cause of this illness, the following treatment: "Take the four milks that you call the four reliefs, which are cow's milk, goat's milk, ass' milk, and sheep's milk, about half a cup of each in which you will dissolve a quarter ounce of pure spermaceti: put it all into a bottle of white glass and no other; you will heat it all for a good quarter hour in a double boiler which will be in a new pot of spring water, you will attach there the aforesaid bottle where will be the spermaceti and the different milks, so that the bottle does not touch in any manner the pot, and that it is well suspended in the air in the water. One sets the whole thing cold, leaves the bottle uncorked, and when the bottle is rather hot, the aforesaid time, you take it all off the fire, you let it lose the great heat all together, then take the bottle of milk out of said pot, and when it is lukewarm, you put it in a little syringe that you give to the sick in order to be squirted into the womb; she will take these little anodynes, such as she sees fit; she may take two in the morning, two in the afternoon, and even one at night and even more if she feels, which does not cause any pain to use this remedy. Tell her that I assure her of a perfect success," (II, 29-30). One will notice that this treatment does not consist of any magical or mystical adjuvant.

788. Pasqually probably means: "What one presently knows thereof."

789. I, 383-385.

790. I, 316.

791. In reality, B. Valentine only discovered these 3 elements in metals alone, where they represented, according to him, indifferent proportions according to the metal considered. Most of the other bodies only consisted, according to his theory, of two of these elements.

792. The virgin earth, or materia prima, was considered by the alchemists as the mysterious body from where must be drawn the philosopher's stone. In their symbolic language this earth lost its virginity in order to give birth to the pure gold, or philosopher's gold. Pasqually seems not to have understood the meaning of the allegory and to have given it either a naturalist signification, which would be rather coarse, or a

symbolic interpretation whose meaning remains quite obscure.

793. I, 27.

794. I, 373.

795. I, 325. The "demonic spiritual power" signifies the commandment exercised over the perverse Spirits.

796. I, 128.

797. I, 260.

798. I, 128.

799. It is in this sense that Pasqually calls the operant: "Head which draws the circles of intellectual adoption," (V, 229), that is to say, during the Operation, the Élu Coën commands in the domain (delimited by the circles and the Quarter Circle) where the major Spirits, bearers of the good intellect (divine energy and intelligence), manifest in order to announce to him that he is "adopted" by God (reconciled). But the Spirits only obey the orders of the operant if the divinity consents to the reconciliation.

800. VI, 144; VII, 13.

801. I, 105; 141; 166; 227. We note moreover that the expressions employed by Pasqually were sometimes able to allude, not to another part of the treatise, but to the confidential instructions given orally to the disciples more advanced in initiation. One passage of the Reintegration refers very clearly to this secret teaching: having spoken, regarding the institution of the divine cult by Enoch, of "his listed Catholic works," that is to say of the general index of hieroglyphs that the operant was able to trace in the Chamber of Operation, Pasqually adds in parentheses: "one will give in its place (probably at the time of the ordination of Réau-Croix) the precise interpretation of these two words which belong to the divine spiritual sciences," (I, 105).

802. I, 92-93.

803. I, 118.

804. I, 166.

805. I, 215.

806. I, 248.

807. I, 161.

808. I, 138.

809. I, 141.

810. I, 304.

811. This is likewise the opinion of Mr. Matter who remarks: "In my opinion, Martinez would add nothing to his teaching by finishing his work and he would perhaps lose several of his adepts. Indeed, his Christian listeners would not have accepted discourses attributed to Jesus-Christ, St. John, or St. Paul," (VIII, 14).

812. I, 117.

813. I, 241.

814. I, 254.

815. I, 241.
816. I, 365.
817. I, 52.
818. I, 112.
819. I, 241.
820. I, 235.
821. I, 48.
822. I, 322.
823. I, 40.
824. One may note on this topic that the allegorical exegesis systematically employed by Pasqually was able to appeal to the example given by the Christian doctors. St. Paul (Galatians IV) declares that certain passages of the Scripture, for example the one where it speaks of the two wives of Abraham, have a symbolic meaning. St. Augustine (de Genesi; against the Manicaeans I, 2) recognizes that one cannot take literally the text of the first three chapters of Genesis without attributing to God thoughts and actions unworthy of him, and that it is necessary to interpret it allegorically.
825. I, 225.
826. I, 234.
827. I, 66.
828. I, 132-133.
829. I, 112.
830. I, 67.
831. I, 110.
832. I, 219.
833. I, 113-114.
834. I, 114.
835. I, 80.
836. I, 74.
837. I, 134.
838. I, 141.
839. I, 43.
840. I, 172.
841. I, 170.
842. I, 222.
843. I, 221.
844. I, 236.
845. I, 245.
846. I, 252.
847. I, 241.
848. I, 211.
849. Baumann: Saint Paul, p. 17.
850. I, 158.
851. I, 375.

852. I, 338.
853. The confusion that Pasqually constantly makes between the reconciler Spirit and the intermediary (Prophet, patriarch, Minor Elect) that he takes as interpreter is found in seed form in the passages of the Bible where, in order to conceal the primitive anthropomorphism, Jehovah has been replaced by his angel of the Lord, but recognizes in its voice that of God (Genesis XVI, 7; 9; 10; 13) or even the angel appearing in the Burning Bush, but it is Jehovah himself who from the midst of the Bush addressed Moses (Exodus III, 2; 4). The confusion is greater still, when, as it happens from time to time, Pasqually against places a Spirit between Christ and the Minor interpreter, as in the following passage: "The number Four is given to the Minor, the number Seven is given to the Spirit, and the number Eight to the double Spirit which is the Christ. Christ presides over the Spirit, the Spirit presides over the Minor, and the Minor (his soul) presides over the terrestrial form," (I, 47-48).
854. That is to say: Abel and Seth; I, 38-39.
855. I, 43.
856. I, 38.
857. I, 79.
858. I, 44.
859. I, 43.
860. I, 45.
861. I, 110.
862. I, 235.
863. I, 48-49.
864. I, 129.
865. I, 125.
866. I, 38. It is to note that Heli does not figure on the list of the ten Elect Minors cited above, although Pasqually ordinarily accorded him an eminent role among the instruments of reconciliation, but such oversights are frequent in the Reintegration. As regards the interest that the treatise shows for Heli, it is explained by the Jewish tradition that represented Heli as the privileged being who would reappear before the advent of the Messiah and reveal the secrets that had remained until then impenetrable to the human spirit. We recall also that the mystical Jewish literature attributed to Enoch, as well as to Noah and to Melchizedek, various apocalypses and that Melchizedek was cited in the apostolic writings as an annunciating figure of Jesus Christ and his supreme priesthood.
867. I, 48.
868. I, 38.
869. I, 38.
870. I, 102-103.
871. I, 108-109.

872. I, 235-236.

873. I, 191. In only one place, Pasqually seems to set Jesus apart among the Elect Minors, but it is in order to associate him with Moses when he says that the present posterity will be more severely punished for its perversion than the preceding, because it has "seen and heard speak directly the one who has operated every spiritual reconciliation (divine law retrieved from Sinai) and the one through whom the Creator has manifested all his works to the eyes of his creature (miracles of Jesus)," (I, 154). It is evident that Pasqually has never had for the historical Christ the exclusive and profound veneration that he inspired in the true Christians. Another proof of the radical, and perhaps hereditary, incapacity of Pasqually to show the sentiments which, from the religious point of view, animate his disciples, is found in the passage where, speaking on the types that the Pharaoh's daughter represented, he puts on the same line the "mother of Christ and that beautiful virgin girl of whom it is said: I am black, I am beautiful," (I, 245), that is to say the Virgin Mary and the lover from the Song of Songs. This comparison, which would have never come to the spirit of a Catholic, recalls the comparison established by Heine in his Histoire de l'Ecole Romantique between the Virgin, whose cult the Middle Ages would have instituted in order to attract the sentimental hearts, and the "beautiful counter lady," who sat enthroned in his period in the Parisian cafés.

874. I, 66.

875. I, 112.

876. I, 32.

877. I, 315.

878. I, 320.

879. I, 180.

880. I, 375.

881. I, 322. The identification of Jesus Christ with the First Man in his state of innocence is established clearly in a letter from Pasqually where, addressing his most intimate disciples, he speaks of the "different operations of Christ who has actually operated in two substances, the one as Man-God in the quality of true Adam operating on the earth among material men, the other as divine man operating by the resurrecting operant among all the spiritual men," (II, 185).

882. I, 373. 374.

883. I, 172.

884. I, 60.

885. I, 322.

886. I, 234. Pasqually admits, moreover, only in appearance the dogma of the Trinity. When he is unfaithful to Jewish monotheism, he adopts the Kabbalistic concept of the quadruple, or to employ his vocabulary, "quadruple essence of the divinity." "These three persons," he notes after the phrase that we just cited, "are only in God relatively to their

divine actions and one cannot conceive of them otherwise without degrading the divinity which is indivisible and cannot be susceptible in any fashion to having in its different personalities distinct from one another. If it was possible to admit in the Creator three distinct persons, it would then be necessary to admit four instead of three relative to (by reason of) the quadruple essence which ought to be known to you (which it is necessary that I make known to you), to wit: the Divine Spirit 10, the Major Spirit 7, the Inferior Spirit 3, and the Minor Spirit 4. It is here that we conceive of the impossibility that the Creator is divided into three personal natures. Let those who wish to divide the Creator into his essence observe at least to divide him in the contents of his immensity," (I, 234-235). In another place Pasqually composes "the quadruple divine power," that is to say the four unfoldings of God, with "10, first divine power (immanent God or sum of the Sephiroth), 7, second divine power (planetary Spirits and astral forces), 6, third divine power (material universe and physical forces), 4, fourth divine power of the Creator (man-god of the earth and of the universe)," (I, 122-124). The repugnance with which Pasqually is inspired by the trinary conception of the divinity is so strong that he refuses to the triangle the mystical significance adopted yet by the Jews from the most remote times and taken in by the Christians. "One cannot conceive," he said, "that the triangle is the figure of the Trinity, although they give to the angles of an equilateral triangle the names of Father, Son, and Holy Spirit, because in the end the Trinity cannot be represented by any form sensible to the eyes of matter," and in order to give to the traditional figure an interpretation conforming more to his private opinion, it must be noted that the center of the triangle, from where emanates the three angular points, is composed of four letters, that is to say the Tetragrammaton (I, 126).

887. I, 53.
888. I, 219.
889. I, 217.
890. I, 112-113.
891. I, 112.
892. I, 43.
893. I, 335.
894. It is to note that in this phrase the word "Christ" designates, not the Jesus of the Gospel, but the Reconciler who has manifested periodically by means of the Elect Minors and for which Jesus of Nazareth has been the organ.
895. I, 115.
896. I, 116.
897. I, 87.
898. I, 113.
899. I, 230.

900. I, 211.
901. I, 212. Moreover, Pasqually notes in another place, little esteem for the Gregorian calendar. After having declared, as we have seen above, that the lunar calculation had always been the true sacred calculation, he adds disdainfully: "The solar calculation is almost solely adopted by the Christians," (I, 206).
902. I, 42-48.
903. I, 65.
904. I, 114.
905. I, 222.
906. I, 135.
907. I, 131.
908. Remembrance of a legend very popular in the 2nd and 3rd centuries of our era and according to which Christ would have, either at the Mount of Olives, or in the course of an appearance posterior to the crucifixion, revealed to the disciples remaining faithful the true path of salvation. It is to this disciplina arcani, replica of the secret teaching given by Jehovah to Moses on Sinai, that the Gnostics appealed.
909. I, 103-107.
910. I, 140.
911. Ascension of Elijah and despair of his disciples (IV Kings, II, 11-17); Assumption of Enoch (Genesis V, 24).
912. I, 211.
913. I, 201.
914. I, 212.
915. I, 195.
916. De Faye: *Gnostiques et Gnosticisme*, p. 433. It is remarkable that the attitude adopted by Pasqually with respect to Christianity is much clearer than that taken by the Talmud itself. The latter, all while condemning the dogma of the Trinity and that of the divinity of Jesus, is often left seduced by the Christian images and dogmas. It borrows from the Gospels the apologues of the beam and of the straw, of the workers of the vineyard, of the healing of the centurion's son. It believes in the guardian angels and admits a sort of Purgatory where the venial sinners are purified by their sufferings and by which they are able to be redeemed by the alms and the prayers of the faithful (Bischoff: *Thalmud*, passim); Pasqually, on the contrary, does not annex the dogmas having a specifically Christian character, except to adapt them to his doctrines. The Holy Spirit, whose office he had his adepts read in a Catholic breviary, is none other than the Ruach, the spiritual emanation of Jehovah which inspired the prophets and is materialized, or rather individualized, by the Spirits of the Supercelestial. The role that he attributes in the Reintegration to this "God the Son in whose presence all creation has been operated by the Creator" and who "said to each divine operation: all is good," corresponds to the one that plays

in the Proverbs (VIII, 22) and in the Targum of Jerusalem the divine Wisdom assisting in the creation of the world (Bischoff: *Kabbalah*, p. 9-11).

917. De Faye, op. cit., p. 42.
918. I, 176.
919. I, 177.
920. I, 309.
921. I, 15.
922. I, 300.
923. I, 313.
924. I, 259.
925. I, 259.
926. I, 186.
927. I, 299.
928. I, 365-366.
929. I, 130.
930. I, 115.
931. I, 173.
932. I, 48.
933. I, 42.
934. I, 45.
935. I, 40. The seal that those who will be saved receive is probably an imitation of the Tau that the Book of Ezekiel (IX, 4-6) put on the forehead of the Jews of Jerusalem who had not sacrificed to the idols, but it had become for the Gnostics a magical means to assure the salvation of the Psychics.
936. Alfaric: *Ecritures manichéennes*, I, 1-2.
937. Alfaric: op. cit. II, 213. Pasqually seems to have copied a Gnostic text when he defines Christ: "Divine Son, type of the divine action in the great posterity of God who arises from him, in whom the election and manifestation of God has operated," (I, 234).
938. I, 116.
939. Alfaric: op. cit., I, 2-8; de Faye: op. cit., p. 333-335.
940. Alfaric: op. cit. II, 153-154.
941. Alfaric: op. cit., II, 156.
942. Ibid., II, 158.
943. De Faye: op. cit., p. 313-325.
944. In one sole place, the Reintegration betrays a borrowing made directly from the Gnostic doctrines. In the course of the mystical addition producing the Denary is thus posed:

$$10+2+3+4+5+6=30$$
$$30+7+8+9+1=55=5+5=10$$

Pasqually stops at the number 30, which is that of the Aeons composing the Pleroma. One may not see for what other reason he would place in relief this number of which he no longer ever speaks, and which does not play any role in his arithmetical exegesis.

945. VIII, 11.

946. Vuliaud: op. cit. II, 134.

947. Franc,: Kabbalah, p. 13.

948. Saint-Martin, to whom Kirchberger had indicated the Gnostic characteristics revealed by him in the Reintegration, assured to his correspondent that Pasqually had never spoken to his disciples of Sophia nor of the King of the World, but was satisfied with Mary and the Demon. Mr. Matter, quite the expert in the matter and who has carefully studied the treatise, notes that his author had manifestly not read the Gnostic texts (VIII, 12).

949. I, 149. In an isolated passage Pasqually lays out a rather curious cosmogonic theory, which constitutes a middle term between the Jewish concept and the dualist thesis of the Gnostics. The birth of the material world would be due to "the explosion of the chaos," that is to say "at the moment of creation, the major or doubly strong Spirit (transcendent Christ, but considered here as Word of God and no longer as Reconciler) had left the chaotic envelope in order to go to be reunited with his Father, so that starting from this moment everything was presented in passive (material) and active (spiritual) nature to the eyes of the Creator, conforming to the image that he had formed therefrom." Herein is the secret meaning of the words of Scripture: "The light was in the darkness and the darkness had not comprehended it," (I, 162). In other words, the primitive substance, or chaos, was composed of spirit and matter, the latter only beginning to exist in an independent state when the spirit was withdrawn from it. Inert and amorphous, it then gave way to all the combinations and has taken all the forms that the imagination of the Creator begat, and each of these forms received the life of a particular Spirit which animated it.

950. I, 176.

951. I, 373.

952. Pasqually does not always hold to such a rigorous distinction between emanation as he teaches it and creation proper. The confusion in the terms reveals the uncertainty of his thought. It is thus that he speaks of the return of matter to its "principle of emanation," (I, 291) and that he declares "uncreated" the central axis fire, "principle of the material life and organ of the inferior Spirits which inhabit it and operate within it on the principle of the apparent corporeal matter, (I, 306). Supposing that in the latter case he wishes to present the central axis fire as an intermediary between spirit and matter, an idea found among some Ionian naturalist philosophers, there remains therein nothing but to imagine a third sort of formation which is neither spiritual emanation nor material creation.

953. I, 357.

954. I, 373.

955. I, 167.
956. I, 164.
957. I, 176.
958. I, 124.
959. I, 149-150.
960. I, 150.
961. I, 291.
962. I, 176.
963. I, 140.
964. I, 250.
965. I, 306.
966. I, 176.
967. I, 311.
968. VIII, 355-356.
969. Complete title of the treatise and faithful summary of its contents.
970. I, 145.
971. I, 167.
972. Appelle, disciple of Marcion, professed that the God of Israel was an angel that he named Igneus, because he was revealed to Moses on Sinai in the Burning Bush. It is to this thesis that our passage seems to clearly allude.
973. See what has been said in Book I, chap. IV, on the false "glorious forms."
974. I, 145.
975. The Talmudists notably drew from the theory of reminiscence, which had probably been transmitted to them by the Neoplatonist Philo, an argument in favor of the moral conscience from where follows the full responsibility of man. According to the treatise Niddah, the souls have had, during their preexistence and before their incorporation, knowledge of the Torah. An angel continues to instruct the embryo in the course of gestation, then gives it, at the moment of childbirth, a strike on the mouth so that all that has been taught to the newborn remains in the subconscious, but the diffused memory survives nevertheless as moral conscience. Thus, man is always able to follow his good instincts and to resist the evil (Bischoff: *Kabbalah*, p. 42). Philo and the Talmudists following him insist on the absolute liberty of determination of which the normal man enjoys and on the entire responsibility which results therefrom.
976. I, 341.
977. I, 7; 33.
978. I, 21.
979. I, 10.
980. I, 9.
981. I, 33.
982. I, 22.

983. I, 15.
984. I, 32.
985. I, 18.
986. I, 359.
987. I, 358.
988. I, 343.
989. I, 21.
990. I, 15.
991. I, 344.
992. I, 345. Curious justification of Christian charity treated as "weakness" by the Jews remaining faithful to the law of retaliation.
993. I, 385-386.
994. In a passage where he treats the mystical action of the "seal," he admits that the principle of the moral liberty and absolute responsibility of man may suffer one exception. The seal, he said, made of the Minor who received it "the trustee of the spiritual good and the door-keeper (jailer) of the prevaricating Spirits," therefore "all the Minors who have been restored into their first virtues and divine spiritual powers and have found grace before the Eternal, such as Adam, Abraham, Isaac, Jacob, and several others, have no longer prevaricated after their reconciliation, although they were yet always in corporeal forms. Since the Minors were sanctified and reconciled, they have delivered their liberty to the power of the one from whom they have received it," so that "this liberty has no longer given birth to wills except those pure, and the will of these reconciled Minors has no longer adopted thoughts except those wholly spiritual. These Minors thus reconciled have no longer been susceptible to succumbing to the snares of the demon, nor to adopting its intellect of abomination," (I, 343-344). It is evident that this state of grace, where the faithful no longer have any other will than that of the Father, and which recalls the abdication in God of the mystical doctors, is considered by Pasqually as a privilege specially accorded to the Patriarchs and announced by an extraordinary manifestation, that is to say by a complete theophany, and like the ordinary Minors, even the most favored cannot expect therefrom similar results from their Operations. Pasqually forgets moreover that he has, at the start of his treatise, shown Adam to fall again several times into sin after his first reconciliation, and that it has been necessary to sacrifice Abel so that this latter was complete.
995. I, 249. It is true that he explains this state of insensibility by an ecstasy which transported the spirit of Christ near to God and thus suspended the organic consciousness. He extends this privilege to several martyrs who, "having been at the example of Christ exposed to frightful tortures, enjoyed the same grace as him. Christ was in contemplation of the spirit of the Father, and the fortunate mortals who have imitated him were in contemplation of the divine Son," (I, 249-250).

996. Frazer: *Rameau d'Or*, French Edition, p. 95.

997. Ibid. p. 57.

998. We have already sufficiently seen how Pasqually knew how to juggle with the words: Christ and Man-God, in giving to them alternately their traditional meaning or a significance responding to his secret theories. Here is another example of his dexterity in this genre of evasion: when he speaks "of the men come since the last period of Christ," (I, 151), he means: "Since the most recent manifestation of the reconciler," but a reader was able, and ought, without suspicion, to understand: "Since the period when Jesus had come and taught."

999. VIII, 64-65.

1000.   VIII, 374.

1001.   I, 66.

1002.   The Lyonnais advocate Milanois, very mixed into the occult movement, wrote to Willermoz on the subject of Bacon: "Although you have drawn from the same sources (the Order of Élus Coëns), you think rather differently; you believe in Jesus Christ and believe yourself similar to him. This is what I have not been able to understand without astonishment and without scandal," (V, 336).

1003.   VIII, 36-37.

1004.   In every case, Pasqually did not hesitate to compare himself to Christ, considered as Spiritual Elect. In the course of a mercurial address to insubordinate disciples, he engaged them to meditate on the Gospel which taught them "to submit their will to the one to whom the gift is granted in order to make la Chose act (obtain manifestation) and to serve as an example to his disciples," (II, 188).

1005.   I, 142.

1006.   I, 129.

1007.   The particular meaning given here to the word "works" is a novel example of the ability with which Pasqually re-purposes common phrases. The term, which currently designates virtuous or charitable acts by which the faithful proved the sincerity of his faith, is applied to the supernatural manifestations.

1008.   I, 152.

1009.   I, 151.

1010.   I, 51-52.

1011.   I, 359.

1012.   I, 152.

1013.   I, 152.

1014.   I, 41.

1015.   I, 44.

1016.   I, 226-227.

1017.   IX, 18.

1018.   The mistrust that inspires in Pasqually the intuition proving the ecstasy is characteristic in this regard. The ecstasy is rather, he says, the effect of a "violent trouble" caused by the presence of a Spirit, but this may be a demon. When the perverse Spirit, appearing to Adam under a glorious form, suggested to him to exercise his creative power, the First Man "fell into ecstasy." It is in this state that the malign Spirit inserted into him his demonic power, and Adam, "returned from his animal spiritual ecstasy, but having retained an evil impression of the demon, resolved to operate the demonic science in preference to the divine science," (I, 16). The mystic may therefore be deceived on the value of the revelations that the intimate experience has brought him, whereas the head of the Élus Coëns reserving the right to interpret the Passes, the danger of error is reduced to a minimum for the adepts who are witnesses.

1019.   I, 170.

1020.   For more details on the probable origin, character, and grades of the two kinds of Masonry, see, by the same author, *L'Occultisme et la Franc-Maçonnerie Écossaise*, 2nd part.

1021.   In a letter addressed to the head of the Élus Coëns of Lyon, Pasqually counsels to only admit to the mysteries of the Order the candidates showing a true zeal, because "it is the sole means of sheltering the sublime knowledge, which is contained within our Order, hidden under the veil of Masonry," (II, 161).

1022.   II, 90. The Masons simply said: By the numbers which are known to you. The addition of the word "all" alludes to the arithmosophical doctrines of the Order.

1023.   II, 158-159. The Masons were arranged in the Lodge in two "columns," designated by terms borrowed from the cardinal points. As concerns the lunation, the prescribed formula was: "From the last to the first quarter of the moon," when it was in its last quarter, and: "from the first and second quarter," when the first quarter had commenced (II, 162).

1024.   III, 83.

1025.   II, 162-163. Pasqually recommends to inscribe the formula: "Very High, Very Respectable," etc., only two lines distance from the address: "To the Grand Orient," etc., and to have the text of the request begin only at "four fingers distance" from the first formula.

1026.   In the Masonic vocabulary "Élu" signifies simply "chosen" The term constituted a distinction for the Mason who bore it, but it did not have the mystical sense that Pasqually attached to it in his treatise.

1027.   I, 106-107.

1028.   The grades of Élu had for their principal theme the punishment of the murderers of Hiram, pursued and put to death by zealous Masons. The candidate was supposed to have "avenged" the architect of the Temple of Solomon. The password was Nekom [Nekam] which was considered to signify: Vengeance.

1029.   The distinctive attribute of the grades of Élu was a dagger suspended from a black cord that the bearers wore on a bandolier passed over the right shoulder, so that the dagger hung on their left thigh. They put the dagger in hand in the course of the ceremonies of reception as well as at the opening and at the closing of the Lodge. The flat blade of which the Reintegration speaks, and which, according to it, "is rested on the left thigh" of the Israelites, designated most clearly the weapon that the Élus brandished in the Lodge.

1030.   I, 279-280.

1031.   XXXII, 26-28. The Bible said only that Moses having called to himself those who were for the Lord, all the children of Levi were gathered around the prophet and, on his order, were passed and passed again across the camp, in going and returning from one door to the other, killing all the idolaters that they found on their route. All the other details given by Pasqually are drawn from the ceremonial of the grades of the Élu.

1032.   I, 73.

1033.   II, 83.

1034.   II, 84.

1035.   I, 199.

1036.   Begemann: *Vorgeschichte und Angange der Freimaurerei in England*, II, 174.

1037.   Begemann: op. cit., II, 215-220.

1038.   *Allgemeines Handbuch der Freimaurerei*, 1901, art. Noah und Noachiden.

1039.   Begemann: II, 222.

1040.   Anderson, author of the first two editions of the Book of Constitutions, has been able to understand this tradition through an English translation of the Tagums, appearing in London at the start of the 18th century, and which seem to have inspired certain details of the degree of Master. But, if he takes from the Talmudists the idea of the commandments of Noah, he modifies their nature and number. The Talmud indeed knows seven, which are: prohibition against profaning the name of God, practicing idolatry, shedding blood, contracting illegitimate unions, eating the flesh cut from a living animal, committing larceny; order to keep the path of the Lord and to perform justice and judgment (Vulliaud: *Kabbale*, I, p. 100).

1041.   This inversion appeared less likely in an era when "oi" was pronounced "wè."

1042.   I, 201.

1043.   I, 205. In reality, the missionaries reported that the Chinese counted 13 lunar months in a year.

1044.   I, 207.

1045.   Idea inspired at the time by the instruments of astronomy whose presence at Peking was indicated by the Jesuits, and by the antiquity to which the Chinese chronology dates back, an antiquity of which the

18th century knew no other example. Pasqually involuntarily alluded to the accounts of the missionaries in saying (p. 210): "This is what teaches us all these accounts."

1046.   I, 209.

1047.   I, 209.

1048.   I, 192.

1049.   "sentir" supplied for a lacuna in the text.

1050.   I, 210.

1051.   II, 160.

1052.   V. 229.

1053.   II, 32-33.

1054.   II, 178. In another place of the same work, Papus gives an identical list that he claims to draw from a letter dated June 16, 1760. The date must be attributed to a printing error, for all the letters reproduced or cited by him go back to 1767 at the earliest.

1055.   III, 91.

1056.   That is to say: Grand Architect; the reading of the book of Papus: G.R. is certainly a printing error. The simple ordination likely signifies: reception in particular.

1057.   Ceremonies of reception and ordinary meetings.

1058.   III, 101.

1059.   II, 195.

1060.   Even the titles of the grades were never invariably fixed: on March 4, 1771, Saint-Martin saw to follow his signature by the qualification of Commander of the Orient (III, 83), whereas this designation does not figure in any list subsequent to 1768.

1061.   XI, 245.

1062.   *Orthodoxie Maçonnique*, p. 149.

1063.   V, 245.

1064.   II, 195.

1065.   II, 215-283.

1066.   A passage from a letter of Saint-Martin shows that the catechisms of the three blue degrees indeed contained allusions to the secret doctrines of the Order, but presented under a form so veiled that Willermoz did not know how to explain them to the candidates. Saint-Martin promised to send him next a complementary instruction, but he noted that this commentary would be completely superfluous when Willermoz had in his hands the complete text of the Reintegration, and he referred his correspondent, while waiting, to "some understandings" that he already had of the treatise (III, 101-102).

1067.   III, 101.

1068.   The number of knocks stricken at the door of the Lodge by the introducer of the candidate and repeated by the mallet of the Venerable were different in each of the three symbolic blue degrees. This usage had been adopted by Scottish Masonry, of which each degree, or at least each family of degrees, had its particular battery.

1069.   III, 109.

1070.   II, 195; 218; 246.

1071.   II, 215-229.

1072.   XI, 244-252.

1073.   The document published by Thory may, at first approach, raise some doubts in this regard. Thory said, it is true, (p. 247, note) to have had under his eyes a manuscript of the degree having belonged to Savalette de Langes, and he claimed to fear no contradiction on the part of the Élus Coëns still living in the period when this work appeared. But, if it is true that the Régime des Philalèthes, of which Savalette was the founder, the head, and the residuary legatee, received by virtue of deposit in 1781 the archives of the Order of the Élus Coëns, which came to be dissolved, they were confided painstakingly sealed, to the good care of the Philalethes, and Savalette has never, whatever Thory says thereon, took part in the Order. On the other hand, the catechisms published by Papus make allusion to a ceremony of reception much more simple than that of which Thory's work gives an account. Nevertheless, these objections, as strong as they appear, are not decisive. The secret that protected the Coën degrees against the curiosity of the other Masons was violated more than once. They figured in the papers left by Saint-Martin, who died in 1803, and several Brothers then lifted them from the copies. It is likely, moreover, that Savaletted did not make scruples, after the disappearance of his Régime, to take cognizance of documents henceforth without legitimate owners, and they have had, in any case, to be included in the auction sale which was made of the Masonic papers of Savalette at the moment of the Revolution. It is therefore quite possible that Thory had had in his hands an authentic paper. What confirms this thesis is that the spirit and style of the numerous passages that he reproduces textually nears well the mark of Pasqually. As to the divergences that one notices between the two documents, catechism and ritual, they may arise from a development given to the original ritual by Pasqually himself, or by the Parisian Élus Coëns and with which they would have neglected to make fit in the catechism.

1074.   (The quotation marks indicate the passages that Thory said to have copied textually from the manuscripts of Savalette). Blue Masonry granted the same privilege to the "wolf-cub." This term, written in French as "louveteau" or "louveton," appears to have been borrowed from the stonecutters, among whom it designated the corner serving to set into its layer the "louve" [she-wolf], or double iron hook in the middle of which one raised the dressed stone in order to hoist it into its place. The son of a Mason was thus elevated by the paternal influence to the dignity of member of the Lodge before having reached legal age. The term "lufton," used with the same meaning by the English Masons, probably came from the French. The two terms, English and French, are only presented in Masonic documents starting from 1738.

1075. The Vicar was a replica of the "Brother Terrible" who, in the French Lodges, introduced the candidate. The Tuileurs prevented the profane from entering into the Lodge; their name came from the Tyler or Tiler which, in the English Lodges, fulfilled the same office.

1076. Thory does not tell in what consisted of this ceremony, but the dagger was a borrowing made from the degrees of the Élu, the "benediction" was likely an adaptation of one of the ritual acts common to these degrees. The papers of the Parfait Maçon Élu [Perfect Elect Mason] describes it in these terms: "When the Lodge is assembled, the Très Sage [Very/Most Wise] sets himself at the foot of the altar and passes the black cord (from which hangs the dagger) to all the Brothers, one after the other, observing that all the Brothers have kissed it, each particularly, before passing it around the neck," (*Les plus secrets Mystères des Hauts Grades de la Franc-Maçonnerie dévoiléi*, 1774).

1077. This one played the role reserved to the "Master of Ceremonies" in the ordinary Lodges.

1078. That is to say, probably, if they were Réau-Croix.

1079. The Reintegration saw in the "tree of life" (Kabbalistic interpretation of "the tree of good and evil," cited by Genesis) the type of "the Spirit of the Creator that the Minor attacked unjustly with his allies (the demons)," (I, 24).

1080. This expression, already encountered above, indicates in the metaphorical language of the Talmudists, the state of Israel, object of the anger of the Eternal and abandoned by him; the paper uses it to indicate what the Reintegration called "state of privation."

1081. In the catechism of the Blue Apprentice this expression alludes to the dress of the candidate who was introduced into the Lodge with the shirt open, the right knee uncovered, and the shoes slipshod.

1082. The words between parentheses have been added by Pasqually to the original text.

1083. Here Pasqually modifies the traditional text which gave to the allegorical Temple (the universe) a squared form (because the universe is limited by the four cardinal points), but the occasion was too tempting to make allusion to the mystical concept of the triangular form of the earth (cf. Book I, chap. II).

1084. Pasqually forgets, in following blindly his model, that he has, eight lines above, omitted one of the cardinal points.

1085. It is curious to find in the catechism an echo of very ancient oriental concepts on the fecundating action of the moon, echo which the Reintegration has neglected.

1086. The chart of specimens of Scottish degrees was rather judiciously composed. It included the most current types, which, consequently, the

Apprentice had the greatest chance to hear spoken about.

1087.   XI, 252.

1088.   II, 233-237.

1089.   Mystical adaptation of a question posed by the catechism of the Apprentice: "Have you seen your master today?" (that is to say the compass).

1090.   This expression signified in the Masonic style the degree of initiation attained by a Brother; it made allusion here to the degree allowing the adept to engage in the Operations and to obtain Passes.

1091.   II, 241-246.

1092.   This sibylline formula meant perhaps that the Master, after having traced the sign of the Companion (the square), had a circle described in the hand of the Brother that he put to the test, and represented at the same time a compass with the legs separated, or with his feet joined by the heels.

1093.   Probably allusion to sorcery.

1094.   We know the important role played in the symbolism of the French Lodges of the acacia, come, by a false translation, from the branch of cassia planted, according to the English legend of the degree of Master, upon the tomb of Hiram.

1095.   II, 249-259.

1096.   One is reminded that, according to the Reintegration, all the peoples of the earth were issued from three original nations.

1097.   Probable allusion to a trial upon which the catechism gives no information.

1098.   Judging by a passage from a letter of Saint-Martin which seems to be related to this ceremony, the officiant affixes these "marks" or "emblems of power" by drawing in the placed indicated the image of a triangle, of a receptacle, and of a circumference (III, 117).

1099.   This phrase, borrowed almost word-for-word from the Reintegration, signifies that the divine action has rendered amorphous matter, or chaos, capable of receiving the imprint of ideas conceived by the divine "intention" or "thought," in order to make possible "the temporal material operation" (creation).

1100.   This is the Materia Prima of the Hermeticists. Pasqually faithfully follows the occultist tradition, in considering the constitutive elements of this substance as "essences," that is to say as the modes of a sublimated matter whose properties draw their origin from the action of determined Spirits. These essences are to the physical bodies and to the material phenomenon what "the gold and mercury of the philosophers" were, according to the alchemists, to ordinary gold and mercury.

1101.   "Perfect" had been one of the titles given in the first degrees of the Scottish Rite which were originally called: Masonry of Perfection.

1102.   In the legend of the Symbolic Master, Hiram is assassinated by three rebel Companions.

1103.   It is probably a matter of the Roman (represented by Pontius Pilate and his soldiers) for it is further said that "the other nation lives to the North." It is likely that the catechism feared, in designating nominally the third executioner of Christ, to appear to be attacking the Catholic, Apostolic, and *Roman* religion. It takes, in another place, the precaution to explain that, if the Master Élus Coëns perform their journey sword in hand, it is "in order to be always ready to fight against the enemies of the Christian religion, those of the King, and those of the Order." This affirmation of loyalty and of the orthodoxy of the Élus Coëns, occurring so unexpectedly in the middle of mystical commentaries, addressed the scruples that the esoteric teachings of the Order could awaken among certain adepts.

1104.   Here "operation" signifies simply: ritual ceremonies, mystical works.

1105.   3 = action upon matter; 5 = upon the demons; 6 = upon creation; 7 = upon the heaven of the stars; 4 = restitution to the Minor of the quaternary power; 8 = reconciliation.

1106.   3+5+6+7+4+8=33, number of years that Jesus Christ spent on earth.

1107.   This is the very title of the catechism published by Papus, II, 263-271.

1108.   II, 93.

1109.   II, 77.

1110.   The word expressed quite adequately the goal and pretensions of the first Scottish Masters who seem to have been well-intentioned reformers. In qualifying themselves as Architects, they attributed to themselves the role of guides and chiefs of the Symbolic Masons, if they were abandoned to their knowledge alone, to construct the ideal temple of human society. The term, soon eclipsed by more ambitious titles, had not, however, fallen completely into forgetfulness and numerous Scottish degrees carried it unto the Revolution.

1111.   St.-M. to Will. Aug. 12, 1771; III, 107.

1112.   This apparent indifference could, moreover, be dictated by the fear that the papers could come to fall into the hands of the profane or of "apocryphal" Masons. The same reserve is observed in regards to the ritual: to the question: "What are the circumstances of the reception of a Grand Master Coën?" the catechism is content to respond: "One gives them if the Grand Master requires it." All that concerns the ritual of the degree must be transmitted orally, therefore the ceremonial of the ordination is only known to us by the confidential correspondence of the adepts.

1113.   St.-M. to Will. III, 017.

1114.   The ritual of the simple ordination had been definitively drawn up by Pasqually in the first half of 1771. Saint-Martin announced on May 20th from Bordeaux to Willermoz that he would forward "very soon" to Lyon "the ceremonial of the simple ordination of Grand Architect," (III, 92).

1115. St.-M. to Will. III, 95-96; 107-108.

1116. The particular orthography of Pasqually and the possible errors of the copyists and typographers make it difficult to identify these Hebrew names. One can, however, recognize Sabaoth, as well as Moses, Aaron, Ur, and Betsaleel of which the Reintegration speaks at length. Abigai, Iain, and Iwa are perhaps Abigail ("whose father is exultation"), the column of the Temple: Iakin ("consolidate"), and Hava ("the living") or Eve.

1117. This authorization is significant. It shows: 1st, that these terms were not simple signs of recognition, but "words of power"; 2nd, that all the Grand Architects were not admitted to the same degree of initiation. The complete list of words of power were probably only revealed to those among them who were shown worthy to be promoted to a superior degree. The others did not go beyond this degree and knew only a part of its mystical arsenal.

1118. St.-M. to Will. III, 95-96; 108.

1119. These complementary instructions, addressed to an adept who had before his eyes the papers of the degree, are extremely vague. The loss of this document is all the more regrettable as the ritual seems to have been very developed. Its description covered five large sheets, and the "words of the degree" filled a sixth sheet (III, 91-92).

1120. III, 108. Saint-Martin speaks in the same letter of a battery of 81 knocks "which ought not suffer any change because it contains a double power which is not at the disposition of man," but nothing in the context indicated to what grade it was connected.

1121. III, 107.

1122. III, 111.

1123. When the assembly was less numerous, he was allowed to trace only three circles (St.-M. to Will.; III, 112).

1124. That is to say without having taken material form, but in manifesting itself by its "glory" or Shekinah.

1125. The modern exegesis agrees completely on this point with Pasqually. It admits that the apparatus bearing seven lamps represented the seven planets worshipped from the most ancient times by the Chaldeans.

1126. As it has been said above, and for the same reasons, it is impossible to guess what historical or mythical personages are represented here under the names of Rhéty, Zalmun, and Rharamoz.

1127. One will notice that the mention of Christ, of the Evangelists, and Saint Paul tends to give a Christian hue to the commentaries of this Judaizing degree.

1128. II, 77.

1129. This number is certainly meant mystically, but taken in its ordinary sense, it furnishes to the Superiors an excellent argument for calming the impatience of the Grand Architects demanding a more complete initiation, if one judges them as yet, or forever, unworthy to receive it.

1130. Catechism published by Papus: II, 175-283.

1131. Begemann: *Vorgeschichte und Anfange der Freimaurerei in England.* II, 181.

1132. The strange confusion that Pasqually makes between Mesopotamia and Assyria, between the Assyrian and Persian dynasties, is found already in the Instruction of the degree of the Knight of the East which calls Cyrus "king of the Assyrians."

1133. Pasqually certainly would have been put in an awkward position if it had been necessary for him to justify this "numbering." It would in any case be useless to seek the key in the numeric value of the Hebraic letters, for the French S can only be rendered as the letter Shin, which is worth 21, or as Samech, which is worth 14.

1134. These details are given neither by the Bible nor by the legend of the Scottish degree. Pasqually has perhaps borrowed them from a Taludic Haggadah.

1135. This is at least what the passage referred to seems to signify, once put into French, which furnishes a characteristic example of the jargon in which these catechisms are written. Here is the text: "The seventh arch left in all perfection alludes to that of the perfect existence of the Spirit that nothing in the entire universe exists or subsists but by him and that every being of form in this universe are (sic) only apparent beings which must be dissipated as promptly as they have been conceived in the imagination of the Spirit whose abandoned arch is the image of the perfect existence."

1136. The stonecutters, of whom the English Masons are called the successors, are presented then by this catechism as the "types" of the Spirits who move the spiritous essences.

1137. This declaration is in absolute contradiction with the symbolic interpretation given elsewhere, as we have seen, to the liberation of the captive Jews at Babylon. As regards the mystical significance of the name of Ephraim, of which mention is not made in the Reintegration, there is no plausible explanation asserted. Another particularly obscure passage is the following: "What are the different operations that Zorobabel has carried out on behalf of Israel at the time of its captivity?" Response: "Seven particulars and sixty-six annuals; the annual ones consisted of reminding the slaves of their first crime with their just punishment, their expiation, and their perfect reconciliation, and the seven particulars informed the slaves of their future liberty, or the different eras that had occurred in the past with Israel, those present, and all those which must occur in the future." To attempt to find a meaning acceptable to such topics would be, it seems, to fall into the trap laid by Pasqually; having no important and decisive meaning to the candidate, he gathers the clouds to mask the indigence of the degree.

1138.   The Hebrew name Zorobabel actually signifies: "Dispersed to Babel." 1139. Here again Pasqually makes use of these prudent subterfuges that we have already seen employed several times over in order to take precautions against an eventual accusation of heresy. The catechism adds that "the opponents of Assyria against the liberty of Israel are the type of the iniquitous operations of the Hebrews when they were opposed by those of the Redeemer," alluding most clearly to the accusations leveled by the priests and scribes against Jesus Christ.

1139.   (2). It is not a question of a prerequisite vote of the members of the Order already holding the degree, as was practiced in the Lodges, but of a mystical proof, the ordination being considered valid only if the officiant had been witness to a Pass in the course of the ceremony. This is what the formula clearly indicates: "consequently by the orders that we have been given." The Grand Sovereign can only receive orders from la Chose and by the intermediary of a Spirit manifesting itself under a glorious form. For want of having read attentively the documents that he has reproduced, Papus has estimated falsely that the adepts could only obtain the degree of Réau-Croix "after having had several appearances of Spirits duly certified at the time of the great magical operations in which engaged several times a year the members of the Order," (II, 157). This is clearly putting the cart before the horse, for the ordination had precisely for its aim to make of the adept a Very Powerful Master, that is to say to confer on him the mystical force that allows him to more easily induce supernatural manifestations.

1140.   "Virtuous" has here the sense of "powerful," just as the substantive "virtue," from which the adjective is derived, is always employed by Pasqually in its Latin etymological sense (virtus).

1141.   II, 57.

1142.   See namely the recent work of Wittemans: *Histoire des Rose-Croix*, 1925.

1143.   Papus has fallen innocently into the trap in translating, in his commentaries, as Rose-Croix the usual abbreviation that he has found in many places in this documents published by him.

1144.   A ceremony of like character figured also in the ritual of the degrees of Little Architect or Scottish Apprentice and Scottish Companion.

1145.   The papers of these degrees are reproduced in whole in their French text on pages 383-393, volume II, of the *Allgemenes Handbuch der Freimarurerei* (edition of 1865) according to a private edition that the German Mason Bode had made for his collection which played an important role in the Templar Strict Observance and in the Order of the Illuminati of Bavaria. Bode, sensitive rationalist and uncompromising Protestant, accused the Jesuits of having introduced into the Lodges the High Grandes, and especially the degrees with occult tendencies, in order to incline the Brothers toward Catholicism. He printed with the help of a hand press all the degrees that appeared to him of a nature to complete the dossier that he established to support his thesis. Those that he had gathered under the title of "Mystical Masonry" seem authentic. Unfortunately, the clandestine edition does not bear a date; it is therefore impossible to know whether the Order of Élus Coëns has imitated the Mystical Masonry or inversely. The first hypothesis is the more likely given the care with which the disciples of Pasqually held secret their rituals.

1146.   We have seen in the previous chapter that the degree of Grand Elect of Zorobabel discourses on the mystical significance of the seven arches of the bridge thrown over the river Starburzarnai.

1147.   The legend of these two columns dated back to the *Jewish Antiquities* of Flavius Josephus, according to which the sons of Seth had inscribed there "omnem disciplinam rerum coelestium" in order to save it from the destruction which, according to a prediction of Adam, would, first by water, then by fire, annihilate the perverted human race. This tradition, widespread in the Middle Ages, which called the two monuments: "columns of Seth," had been enriched with new elements by the *Historia Scholastica* of Petrus Comestor (12th century). It reappeared in the manuscripts containing the legendary history of Masonry that clerics had composed from the 13th to the 14th centuries in order to confer more prestige to the "Duties" or regulations imposed on the professional Masons. The columns of Seth were considered by the occultist Masons as the prototypes of the two columns Jachin and Boaz which figured in the symbolism of the Blue Lodges.

1148.   The Hebrew High Priest applied a similar teardrop to the forehead when he solemnly officiated.

1149.   It is remarkable that the catechism of the Master says expressly that these three materials represent respectively the red, the black, and the white, colors which are cited in the first degree of the Porch among the Élus Coëns.

1150.   This is exactly the arrangement of the staircase that the candidate climbs in the degree of Apprentice Élu Coën.

1151.   *Recueil Précieux de la Franc-Maçonnerie*: III, p. 6.

1152.   Here, by virtue of example, is what was the program of the meeting of the Neuf Sœurs Lodge, March 9, 1779, in the hall of the Cirque Royal, Mont-Parnasse boulevard, to celebrate the birth of Madame Reale:

1st, Lodge at precisely 3 o'clock (purely Masonic meeting in which only the Brothers assisted).

2nd, at 5:30, introduction of the ladies for a meeting of Adoption;

reception of a Sister; reading of various pieces of eloquence and poetry.

3rd, concert performed by the most celebrated virtuosos.

4th, banquet with military music.

5th, ball.

1153.   The same year an incident, which had caused a scandal at the time of the reception of a girl to the Neuf Sœurs, had forced the Grand Orient to take sanctions against the organizer of the ceremony. A resounding polemic provoked by this affair had attracted the attention of the profanes and of the Brothers on the inconveniences that these mixed assemblies presented. (Cf. on the nature and the results of the incident the monograph by L. Amiable: *La Loge des Neuf Sœurs*, p. 102-128).

1154.   I, 69.

1155.   The inferiority of the woman from the theurgical point of view is moreover a biblical tradition. In Numbers (XII) one sees Mary, sister of Moses, stricken with leprosy for having claimed to receive directly the communication of Jehovah, whereas Aaron, who was associated with his complaint, remained unpunished, although rebuffed like her. Mary is only healed on the intercession of Moses and after having been excluded from the camp for seven days.

1156.   III, 147.

1157.   III, 103.

1158.   III, 110-111.

1159.   III, 120.

1160.   Saint-M. to Will. May 15, 1773, III, 117.

1161.   III, 118.

1162.   One of them was the wife of Prince de Luzignan, whose recruitment inspired in Pasqually a great pride, and there is no doubt that the initiation of the princess had been a politeness made to the noble Emulator.

1163.   It is this character, quite prominent, as we have seen in the whole treatise of the Reintegration, that has made Gleichen to believe that "his disciples had inherited from him a great number of Judaic manuscripts." (VII, 150).

1164.   I, 118.

1165.   I, 367-368. "Chief-place" signifies: privileged situation.

1166.   I, 369.

1167.   I, 210.

1168.   I, 236.

1169.   VI, 159-160.

1170.   VIII, 9; 132.

1171.   VIII, 9.

1172.   IV, p. XII.

1173.   V, 244.

1174.   X, vol. 1, 68.

1175.   X. vol. 1, 93.

1176.   X, vol 1, 94.

1177.   If we accept an expression employed by Pasqually at the foot of the letter, we would be obliged to have the beginnings of his propaganda at Bordeaux go back to 1758. He writes on September 2, 1768, to Willermoz (II, 169) that the two from Aubenton have been his disciples for ten years; but as he cites them in relation to their impending promotion to the degree of Réau-Croix, that Willermoz does not yet possess, it is likely that the Master exaggerated the duration of the training period imposed on the initiates, in order to calm the impatience of his Lyonnais disciple.

1178.   The pseudonymous author of IV (p. XVII) believes that the term designated one of the degrees, called Templar, that served as noviciate to the degree of Knight of the Temple, or Levite Knight of the Interior. It is more likely that in qualifying himself thus Pasqually simply claimed to belong to the intermediate social class between nobility and commoner.

1179.   "Stuwards" is put probably for "Stewards"; thus, were named among the English Brethren those specially charged to organize the solemn feasts of the Grand Lodge of London. They ended up obtaining, because of the importance of their functions, the right to wear a special insignia and to constitute a particular Lodge which was considered superior to the ordinary Lodges.

1180.   The fable of a Rite of High Degrees, organized and directed by the exiled Stuarts in order to dominate Masonry entirely and to put it into the service of their dynastic interests, was born from the name that was given to Scottish Masonry. This legend has made a fortune especially in the last quarter of the 18th century, among Protestant Masons of Germany, who accused the Jesuits, partisans of the Stuarts, of having fabricated the High Grades in a political aim, but the pretended Jacobite Masonry had, since the beginning, seduced in France, and also in Germany, the imagination and sensibility of Romanesque spirits and numerous imposters while being used to strike currency. It is moreover possible that a linguistic error, similar to that which had given birth in our land to the symbol of the acacia and to the title of gentleman conferred to Masons, had contributed to accrediting the Jacobite legend, the name of the Stuarts having been confused with that of the Stewards of which we just spoke. The same confusion would have made the Toulousian Brethren believe that Pasqually presented himself as an emissary of the Stuarts.

1181.   IV blames (p. XIX) the imprudence of Pasqually who should have had to proceed to an individual recruitment before addressing the assembly of the Lodge. The true blunder was to promise manifestations. Instructed by experience, Pasqually reserved them, when he organized his Rite, to the supreme degree.

1182. "A little in the manner of Ramsay," says IV. We do not see, according to the summary it gives, in what way the exposé of Pasqually resembles the famous Discourse of Ramsay. One recognizes there, on the contrary, under a covered form and with other names, the features of the Reintegration.

1183. IV, p. XVI-XX.

1184. IV. p. XX.

1185. IV, p. XX. VI, 157-158.

1186. IV, p. XXI.

1187. V, 409.

1188. IV, p. XXI-XXII.

1189. IV, p. XXII.

1190. It is impossible to know whether this allegation, which had not been raised by any of the biographers of Pasqually, rested only upon rumors without foundation, or if, on the contrary, the founder of the Order of Élus Coëns has, to subsist in the course of his journeys of propaganda, exercised the trade of cartwright, following the example of Saint Paul making tents.

1191. It would seem according to this passage that Pasqually had passed through Avignon before presenting himself at Toulouse. Avignon was indeed found along his route, if he came from Grenoble. He would have therefore frequented one of the Lodges of the town of the Popes and would have encountered there Brothers less suspicious than those of Toulouse, without, nevertheless, having been able to form an establishment, since he had not set himself up there. As regards Brother Roubaux, he is, despite his Masonic title of "Very Illustrious," completely unknown to the Masonic encyclopedias and biographies.

1192. IV, p. XXII.

1193. II, 166.

1194. VI, 157.

1195. IV, p. XXIII.

1196. In 1742, Desaguliers, born a La Rochelle, emigrated to England after the revocation of the Edict of Nantes, become Magister Artium of the University of Oxford, Grand Master, in 1719, and Deputy Grand Master, from 1722 to 1726, of the Grand Lodge of London, had made a rather long stay at Bordeaux where he had engaged in active propaganda on behalf of Masonry.

1197. French Masonry has, during the whole of the 18th century, forbidden entry into the Lodges by comedians. A circular from the Grand Orient justified, in 1777, this ostracism in arguing that "the state of the people destined to the public theaters puts them in the dependence of the caprices of the public" and that the Order would not be able to come to their relief if they were "unjustly humiliated." But exception was made on behalf of musicians and singers, whose talent was put to contribution on the solemn occasions.

1198. V, 407-408; Gould: *History of Freemasonry*, III, 98; Daruty: Recherches, 233.

1199. *A Histoire de la Loge Anglaise n° 204* (this number recalls the roll under which the Lodge was inscribed in 1792 on the registers of the Grand Lodge of London) by the Brother Renou, who has communicated his manuscripts to Mr. A. Lantoine, relates that on February 28, 1764, the head of the Élus Coëns, Martinez Pasqualis, having wished, sword raised in hand, to penetrate by force into the locale of the Française Élue Écossaise during a meeting, this Lodge had borne a grudge against its Mother, l'Anglaise of Bordeaux, which had stricken to suspend the "Lodge of Mr. Pasqualis," (Lantoine: *La Franc-Maçonnerie chez elle*, p. 212). It suffices, in order to establish the absurdity of this anecdote, to note that "the Lodge of Mr. Pasqually" is precisely the one that had borne a grudge against it, and that la Française had only taken the qualification of Élue Écossaise at the end of 1764.

1200. IV, p. XXIV.

1201. V, 409.

1202. The account that we just read on the petition of the Masons of Bordeaux, on its cause and its negative result, is the rational interpretation of the following version given of the episode by IV, p. XXIV and which seems, to judge it by certain expressions, to have been borrowed from a letter of Pasqually: "Some bad fellows, that Martinès had believed ought to be expelled from the Temple des Francs-Élus-Écossais, furious to not have been initiated into the mysteries that had been revealed to them by the untoward letter of the Freemasons of Toulouse...plotted with the bastard Lodges of Bordeaux...and succeeded in producing against Martinès a bull in which they supported themselves on the old complaints of the Loges Saint-Jean-Réunies and upon the pretended injustice of which they themselves had been victims for requesting from the Grand Lodge of France the closing of the Française-Élue-Écossaise. They were strangely mistaken, for although the Française-Élue-Écossaise worked in its capacity of symbolic workshop under the obedience of the Grand Lodge of France, it was evident that his Grand Lodge would not accept the complaints of people who no longer accepted its authority. Their petition remained, therefore, without result. The term "bull" is currently employed by Pasqually to designated an official writing; "bad fellows" also seems rather to be of his style.

1203. V, 174-175.

1204. Gould: History, III, 144.

1205. Kloss: *Geschichte des Freimaurerei in Frankreich*, I, 82-83.

1206. V, 177.

1207. IV, p. XXV.

1208. IV, p. XXVI.

1209. X, I, 88.

1210. It is certainly by error that Thory (X, II, 362) dates this decree from December 12, 1765, for he cites as reference the register manuscripts of the deliberations of the Grand Lodge containing the proceedings of the session of November 16, 1766.

1211. Kloss: op. cit. I, 105.

1212. IV. p. XXVII. The same Notice claims that Pasqually profited also from his stay at Paris "in order to create numerous relations in the Lodges of the provinces thanks to the deputies that these Lodges had sent to Paris following the decree of August 14," (p. XXVI). Perhaps Pasqually did indeed make the acquaintance of some agents of the Lodges that he visited in returning to Bordeaux, but it is doubtful that these relations had been numerous and important.

1213. V, 227-231; II, 187. That the Parisian neophytes had been persuaded by the success of the Operation, whether visually, or as is more likely, on the faith of the declarations of their instructor, that is what follows from the letter reproduced by II, 187, in which Pasqually makes, three years later, appeal to their memory in order to prove to them the reality of his theurgical doctrines.

1214. II, 187.

1215. IV, p. XXVIII.

1216. II, 169.

1217. II, 160.

1218. II, 160-161; IV, p. XXVIII.

1219. II, 24; IV, p. XXVIII; V, 247.

1220. II, 27.

1221. IV, p. XXVII. If the pretended du Guers was, as it seems, the same man as Bonnichon who had been Orator in 1758, then, in 1765, Venerable of the Lodge l'Amitié of Lyon, disappeared the same year (V, 441), Willermoz had been able to provide Pasqually inside information on the account of a Brother having been part of the Masonry of Lyon.

1222. II, 165; 167.

1223. II, 44.

1224. II, 35; IV, p. XXIX.

1225. II, 32.

1226. II, 34-35.

1227. IV, p. XXIX.

1228. This is at least what Pasqually relates: he even adds that Mr. d'Arche "intimated to du Guers that he had sent him back to be judged by our secret tribunal," because it "was not advisable to make a conflict of jurisprudence." In short, the jurats dismissed the parties back to back, not wishing to meddle in this affair, and delegated only one informer to learn the result that the interested parties had given him.

1229. II, 34-40.

1230. IV, p. XXIX.

1231. II, 36.

1232. VI, 158.
1233. II, 31.
1234. II, 174.
1235. II, 174-175.
1236. II, 174.
1237. IV, p. XXX.
1238. IV, p. XXX; II, 174-175.
1239. Pasqually lived then "with Carvalho, converted Jew, Poiraud house, near the port of la Monnaie," (V, 244).
1240. Pasqually claims that "the Lodges of Bordeaux" had "sent to seek constitutions at Dublin," because they "had not been able to obtain it from him for their constitution," (II, 179-180) and IV, p. XXV adds that he had not been able to fulfill their request because "his own bull" did not authorize him to found two establishments in the same town. It is possible that some bastard Lodge of Bordeaux had attempted to affiliate with the Order of Élus Coëns, then addressed itself, not to Dublin, but to some Chapter practicing the degrees called Irish, which competed momentarily with the Scottish degrees. But it is certain that no regular Lodge of Bordeaux has asked to be incorporated as a body into the Order founded by Pasqually. As regards the "bull" whose dispositions the Grand Sovereign invoked, there is every reason to believe that he himself was its author.
1241. It is necessary to leave the responsibility of this enumeration to IV, p. XXX, which does not give justification thereof. Outside of the groups of Paris, Lyon, Versailles, Foix, and La Rochelle, the correspondence mentions, in this period, only that of Libourne to which constitutions had been sent in February 1769; it was then composed of 6 Brothers, 5 of which were part of the Order (II, 172; 176).
1242. II, 160.
1243. II, 161.
1244. II, 172.
1245. II, 178.
1246. II, 158-160.
1247. V, 227-230. The objections raised by Pasqually were justified by his astrological doctrines, since the equinox had passed; but the unfavorable astral conjunctions were likely only a pretext; in reality Pasqually would have wished to reserve to himself the monopoly of the ordination to the supreme degree; perhaps he also foresaw the alliance that Willermoz was going to contract with the Parisian Réau-Croix; but he yielded so as not to dissatisfy him.
1248. II, 164. The text has been greatly altered by the negligence and incomprehension of the copyist; it has been necessary to correct some of the grosser errors of orthography and punctuation, and to fill some obvious lacunas.

1249. V, 230.
1250. II, 170-171.
1251. II, 169.
1252. II, 32-33.
1253. II, 173-174.
1254. II, 274.
1255. IV, p. XXXII.
1256. II, 172-173.
1257. IV, p. XXXII,
1258. II, 43.
1259. The general sense of the phrase indicates that "good will" was not limited to the scrupulous observation of the instructions but was already expressed in a tangible way by the money sent to Bordeaux.
1260. II, 42-47.
1261. IV, p. XXXIII.
1262. II, 41. It is probably a question of a relative of his wife, deceased in the Antilles.
1263. II, 174-175.
1264. II, 175.
1265. We see that this inheritance, qualified by "small" in August 1769, had grown much in some months. The question is often posed as to whether at that time Pasqually sought to mislead or was misled himself.
1266. II, 48.
1267. At the beginning of 1770, there were yet in Lyon only six Élus Coëns including Willermoz (IV, p. XXXIII); the group had therefore not made any recruits since 1769.
1268. II, 176.
1269. II, 104.
1270. II, 177.
1271. II, 100.
1272. II, 177.
1273. II, 170; 177-178.
1274. That is to say to engage in the Operations without being mixed with the direction of the Order. Papus has falsely rendered the conventional sign "R. +" as "Rose-Croix."
1275. II, 179.
1276. II, 180-191. IV says (p. XXXIV): "This summary is presented in such a manner that one cannot know whether it is a question of a rough draft of Martinès, or a summary taken by Willermoz on the original document. We are inclined towards this last hypothesis, because the document of Papus does not mention a number of important facts. It is probable that Willermoz would be content with a trip to Paris to depend on the document from the archives of the Sovereign Tribunal the collection of the responses of Martinès relative to the propositions made by the Réau-Croix." The supposition is justified by the form, and

especially by the style which, although presenting turns of phrase and expressions familiar to Pasqually, is much less incorrect than that used by the head of the Élus Coëns in his letters and in his treatise.

1277.   One will note that Pasqually employs this term indifferently to designate the Order of Elus Coëns, its theurgical doctrines, and the supernatural power to which the Operations were addressed.

1278.   This phrase, which is found full of the difficult style of Pasqually, signifies that the Master will no longer occupy himself with the Réau-Croix who will have been designated by la Chose, that is to say will have been witness to manifestations in the course of their ritual works.

1279.   Cf. Book III, chap. 1.

1280.   II, 192.

1281.   III, 84.

1282.   III, 86-89.

1283.   VII, 154.

1284.   III, 86.

1285.   St. -M. to W. March 25 and May 5, 1771; III, 87-91.

1286.   III, 92-93.

1287.   St.-M. to W. May 24, 1771. III, 94-98.

1288.   St.-M. to W. June 8, 1771; III, 98-101.

1289.   III, 102-103.

1290.   III, 101-103.

1291.   III, 105.

1292.   Note from w. III, 105.

1293.   III, 107.

1294.   II, 52.

1295.   II, 94.

1296.   III, 100-101.

1297.   II, 54.

1298.   III, 98.

1299.   III, 110.

1300.   II, 53.

1301.   Note from the hand of Willermoz, written by him on the back of the letter from Pasqually, II, 53.

1302.   II, 55.

1303.   II, 87.

1304.   II, 91.

1305.   II, 193.

1306.   II, 106.

1307.   This is the orthography adopted by IV; Papus called (II & II) this Brother: de la Boris.

1308.   II, 53.

1309.   II, 51.

1310.   II, 51.

1311.   II, 51-52.

1312. II, 55.

1313. II, 52.

1314. IV, p. XXXVII.

1315. Caignet de Lestère could only be the "cousin" of Pasqually by marriage. He was probably the nephew of the major of the regiment of Foix, father of Mrs. de Pasqually. A brother of this Caignet had been, by the testimony of Saint-Martin, an officer of the same regiment.

1316. II, 193.

1317. II, 194.

1318. III, 111.

1319. III, 84.

1320. VI, 157.

1321. VI, 157.

1322. III, 101.

1323. III, 85.

1324. II, 194.

1325. II, 194-195.

1326. This was only a pretext, for Saint-Martin said expressly that this table was simply drawn from the Grand Architect communicated the previous year.

1327. III, 110-114.

1328. If this assertion is not a simple excuse destined to calm the anguishes of Willermoz, it would confirm the thesis of Matter, laid out earlier, and according to which the ultimate aim of the Operations was to obtain a manifestation of the Christ or Reconciler.

1329. III, 114-115.

1330. II, 109.

1331. The fact is proven for Saint-Martin. He later shows to the Baron de Gleichen "some hieroglyphic figures, written in flashes of fire, which appeared to him in his workings," (VII, 157).

1332. II, 57.

1333. II, 58.

1334. II, 59.

1335. II, 63.

1336. IV, p. XXXVII. The date of this nomination is not indicated by the *Nouvelle Notice Historique*, but it was unable, logically, to have taken place before the ordination of de Serre as Réau-Croix, that is to say before April 1772.

1337. This "general index" therefore probably contained some designs representing the different forms that may be taken by the luminous manifestations and indicated at the same time to what class of Spirits each of these form corresponded. Furnished with this occultist lexicon, the adepts, to whom it had been communicated, were able to proceed in all competence with the interpretation of the Passes, operation of the ultimate importance, and of which Pasqually had until then reserved the monopoly.

1338. II, 59-61; 195-197.

1339. The designation of this degree is, if not new, at least unexpected. We have seen (Bk. III, ch. I) that Saint-Martin had followed his signature with this title in 1771, but that it did not figure in the list of degrees cited or published. Perhaps Pasqually had resumed an older denomination attributed originally to the paper later entitled: Grand Elect of Zorobabel.

1340. II, 200-201.

1341. The letter written on October 12, 1773, arrived at Lyon the following January 29; the one of August 3, 1774, was not delivered to Willermoz until November 5 (II, 61; 63).

1342. II, 196.

1343. II, 120.

1344. II, 196; IV, p. XLI.

1345. Cited by IV, p. XXXIX-XL according to the Anciennes Archives Villareal, D, IX. This Brother de Gaicheux seems to have been, to judge by the recommendations that Pasqually made, the Superior of the Temple of Versailles.

1346. IV, p. XXXIX-XL.

1347. IV, p. XXXIV-XXXV; II, 121; 184.

1348. The Strict Observance, which claimed to revive, at least symbolically, the Order of the Temple, were given to the task of "restoring" the old provinces of this religious and military Order with their administrative divisions: dioces, baillages, and prefectures, submissive to the authority of a Provincial Directory. The Provinces were: I, Aragon; II, Auvergne; III, Occitane (Languedoc); IV, Lyon; V, Bourgogne (including Lorraine and Alcace); VI, Great Britain; VII, Lower Germany (including Poland, Livonia, and Courlande); VII, Upper Germany (including Italy and Sicily); IX, Greece and Archipelago. The Ist, VIth, and IXth Provinces were never "peopled." The IInd and IVth had been united to the advantage of the Brother of Lyon.

1349. Date borne upon some diplomas issued by the Chevaliers Bienfaisants of Lyon and cited in the catalog of the Chacornac bookshop, October 1921.

1350. IV, p. LVI.

1351. The new Grand Lodge of France, which was entitled Grand Orient beginning from June 26, 1773, had been constituted in 1771, after having brought some rather important modifications to the general statutes of French Masonry. It had notably suppressed the immovability of the Parisian Venerables, submitted henceforth to election by the members of their Lodge, as were for a long time their colleagues in the Lodges of the provinces, and granted to these latter a regular representation in the bosom of the central organism. It had elected *ad vitam* the Duc de Chartres, the future Philippe-Egalité, which likewise recognized the old Grand Lodge of France. The struggle between the two rival authorities endured until the Revolution; it resumed at the time of the reopening of the Lodges in 1796, to end up in 1799 by the fusion of the two Grand Lodges.

1352.   This circular dated from several months back, for the Duc de Chartres had been installed on October 28, 1773.

1353.   That is to say as representatives of the IInd, Vth, and IIIrd French Templar Provinces, whose Directories were seated respectively at Lyon, Strasbourg, and Bordeaux.

1354.   II, 198-199.

1355.   II, 199.

1356.   IV, p. LVI, cited according to the Anciennes Archives Villareal, D. XVII.

1357.   II, 62.

1358.   Note from Willermoz, II, 63. One of Pasqually's sons, Jean-Anselme, was raised in 1779 to the college of Lescar, near de Pau. His widow remarried the same year with a Mr. d'Olabarat (Note from Willermoz, II, 64).

1359.   II, 135. Perhaps this establishment is the origin of the error committed by Thory (X, volume I, 93) who believes that "the Régime of the Élus Coëns was not organized into any Lodges" until 1775.

1360.   IV, p. LXVI.

1361.   IV, p. LXVI-LXVII; V, 409.

1362.   IV, p. LXV-LXVI.

1363.   The date is uncertain, the letter alluded to bearing only: "This Sunday, March 28"; it follows a letter of March 23, 1777, and precedes one from April 11, 1778.

1364.   III, 148.

1365.   III, 153.

1366.   III, 153.

1367.   VII, 155.

1368.   Letter from Saint-Martin to Kirchberger, April 24, 1793.

1369.   III, 120-121.

1370.   III, 122.

1371.   VIII, 61; 63; 85.

1372.   III, 133-134.

1373.   III, 135.

1374.   III, 134.

1375.   Word taken here in the mystical sense, for Saint-Martin recognized elsewhere that the intellectual faculties of the Abbé were very little developed, to the point that "in his letters one does not know three-fourths of the time what he means," (III, 143).

1376.   III, 143.

1377.   III, 144.

1378.   III, 147.

1379.   III, 151.

1380.   III, 107-108.

1381.   He had, some years later, to find an explanation of the Passes which rendered them independent of all ceremonial magic and all theurgical appearance in attributing them to the action of what he called the "intimate Word," that is to say by a Mediator sent to the man of desire by the First Cause. "This intimate Word," he wrote to Kirchberger on April 24, 1793, "influences and sets into motion all the second, third, fourth powers, etc., and makes them produce their forms according to the plans that it has in our regard; that is the sole source of the manifestations." But this divine intermediary itself does not merit an absolute confidence, especially if it begins to speak: "If the evil power may imitate all, the intermediary power very often speaks like the supreme power itself. This is what one has seen at Sinai where the simple Elohim have spoken to the people as being the sole God, the jealous God," (*Correspondance inédite*, Edition Schaver et Chuquet, p. 118.)

1382.   III, 138.

1383.   III, 137-138.

1384.   The final capital letters represent Amen four times; III, 145.

1385.   III, 141.

1386.   IV, p. XCVI.

1387.   IV, p. LXXXVIII-XCII.

1388.   IV, p. LXXXVIII.

1389.   IV, p. XCI; XCV

1390.   III, 116.

1391.   III, 151.

1392.   IV, p. LXXXVI.

1393.   IV, p. LXXXVII.

1394.   Willermoz in particular testified of the attachment that he had, even after his schism, kept for his old Master, while looking after his widow. Having learned that she found herself in financial difficulties, he sent her, in July 1776, a draft of 216 pounds, payable at Bordeaux and of which he prayed her to receive the sum total.

1395.   IV, p. CV.

1396.   IV, p. CVI-CVII.

1397.   "Siège de Calais" (1765); "Gaston et Bayard" (1771).

1398.   IV, p. CVII.

1399.   Some groups of Élus Coëns likely existed, at least for some years, in different places, but the known documents are silent in regards to them. The *Nouvelle Notice Historique* indicates only in 1783 at Avignon the existence of a Coën Temple, which, on February 23, admitted five Chevaliers Bienfaisants of Montpellier to their old school (IV, p. CXXII), and in 1784 a correspondence of Brother Astier with the Élus Coëns Labory and de la Martinière of Avignon (IV, p. CXLII). If d'Ossun was, the same year, invited by the Philalethes, in his capacity of Substitute of Las Casas, "Grand Sovereign of the Élus Coëns," to assist with the preparatory assembly of their Convent de Paris (IV, p. CXL), this was probably in the hope of obtaining some information on the secret knowledge that the defunct Masonic Rite was reputed to have possessed.

1400.   V, 246.

1401.   *Recherches sur le Rite Écossais*, 227-228.

1402.   Valentine Andreae had, for his part, drawn from the other ancients. One tradition received by Diodorus of Sicily, Pliny the Elder, Diogenes Laertes, and Clement of Alexandria mentioned the secret teachings that had been received from the Egyptian, Chaldean, and Persian priests, during the course of his travels in Egypt, Babylonia, and Iran, by the famous Dioscuri, that the Hermeticists considered as one of their learned masters and to whom they attributed the paternity of the treatise entitled *Physica et Mystica*, which contained, in addition to alchemical recipes, a magical part whose principal elements were of very ancient origin.

1403.   XI, 239.

1404.   XI, 242.

1405.   XI, 143.

1406.   *Calendarium naturale magicum*, 1582.

1407.   *Idealis Umbra Sapientiae generalis*, Parisiis, A.D. 1679.

1408.   XI, 243.

1409.   XI, 243-244.

1410.   VII, 151-152.

1411.   When the public papers announced in 1803 the death of Saint-Martin, they confused him with Pasqually, deceased thirty years earlier (IV, p. CLXXXI).

1412.   Wolfsteig: *Bibliographie der freimaurerischen Literatur*, no. 33.593 and no. 43.099. This Bibliography, appearing in 1912, arranges in its Index, under the rubric of Martinists, all the documents concerning the Chevaliers Bienfaisants.

1413.   Gleichen probably alluded to the principal Réau-Croix, of whom Bacon had been able to speak to him, that is to say Willermoz, Saint-Martin, Luzignan, Champoléon, de Grainville, d'Hauterive, and de Serre.

1414.   VII, 151-152.

1415.   XI, 244.

1416.   *Orthodoxie Maçonnique*, p. 168.

1417.   It is actually a question, in the correspondence of Saint-Martin, of an excursion to Turin in 1774, of another to Rome in 1787, and of a short stay at London the same year, but one finds there no trace of travels in Switzerland and Germany, and the letters written from Italy and England prove that Saint-Martin was occupied there with an entirely other thing than propaganda for his theories or for those of his old master. (III, 123- 127; 196; 201.)

1418. Here the word designates the body of doctrines which was the gospel of the Élus Coëns proper.

1419. Daruty, op. cit., 229-230.

1420. This term is found neither in the Reintegration nor in the correspondence of the adepts, but it characterizes quite will the crime or "prevarication" of Adam who has had as consequence the formation of the material envelope of the Minor. It is therefore possible that it had been employed by the Élus Coëns from whom J. de Maistre had received his information.

1421. That is to say before 1776, for the *Soirées*, appearing in 1821, were written in 1806.

1422. Lyon.

1423. Meetings of the blue degrees and of the Class of the Porch.

1424. We see already in the Vth Discourse a very clear echo of the Reintegration when de Maistre uttered the idea that it is a question in this life of recovering the rights lost since the fall, that these gifts of grace are the enjoyment of the divine presence (ecstatic vision), the commerce with the superior Spirits (supernatural manifestations), or even the dominion over matter (alchemy and action over natural phenomena), and especially when he asserts that "the law which wants the human will to only be able to act materially in an immediate manner upon the body that it animates is purely accidental and relative to our state of ignorance and corruption."

1425. It proceeds from this passage that the Élus Coëns, whose confidences de Maistre has received, had not revealed to him the existence of the treatise written by Pasqually.

1426. This phrase shows that de Maistre knew in particular the Martinism after the manner of the Philosophe Inconnu and was completely unaware of the ritual magic of the Operations and the astrological theories of Pasqually.

1427. Gleichen wrote in his Memoires: "Plenty of folks have believed that this work *Des Erreurs et de la Vérité* had only been composed in order to restore the world to religious ideas with the lure of the marvelous. It is certain that he has produced this effect upon several persons and upon myself," (VII, 156). The German rationalists, like Nicolai and Bode, accused Saint-Martin of being an emissary of the Jesuits and an agent of Rome, and discovered in the treatise *Des Erreurs et de la Vérité* an allegorical history of the Order founded by Ignatius of Loyola.

1428. III, 147. We have seen that the Order admitted women only with much difficulty and did not allow them to pass beyond the inferior degrees.

1429. VIII, 137.

1430.   D'Holbach was a practicing Hermeticist.

1431.   XI, 243.

1432.   Op. ct., 228. It is from this list that Bord has drawn in order to cite a certain number of "disciples of Pasqually." He is content to replace the painter Van Loo with the Hermeticist Henri de Loos (V, 248-249). He supposes that Saint-Amand is the same personage as Boudon de Saint-Amand (1748-1831), naturalist, archaeologist, literary man, and agriculturist. He points out the different names under which is known the Mason that Daruty calls comte de Lerney: Gabriel de Bernege, Berney, Lernay. Bord notes that he was a major in the service of the king of Sardinia and introduced in 1758 into the Lodge Aux Trois Globes of Berlin the high degrees of the Council of Emperors of the East and West (statement confirmed by the *Handbuch der Freimaurerei* which added that Gabriel, Marquis de Lernais, had arrived in 1757 at Berlin as a French prisoner of war), but he confused him with the comte de Bernez, Eques a Turri Aurea in the German Strict Observance, who was Banneret of the Grand Priory of Italy, and not, as believed Bord, Provincial Grand Master of the VIIIth Templar Province. This latter had been able to be part of the Chevaliers Bienfaisants.

1433.   IV gives on the history of this deposit the following information: With the death of Savalette de Langes, arriving unexpectedly during the revolutionary period, the archives of the Philalethes, which, as we have seen, preserved the papers of the Order, were sold by auction and were acquired jointly be two Philalethes, Astier and Tassin, and two Élus Coëns, Fourcault and de Pontcarré. These latter took for their part the documents arising from their Order and delivered them in 1809 to the Very Powerful Master Destigny, having returned from San Domingo after the loss of the island by France. The new trustee enriched the material with the archives of the Temple of Port-au-Prince, those of the Temple of Léogane having been destroyed by a fire. In 1812, the Very Powerful Master d'Ossun, on his return from Italy, returned the papers of the Temple of Avignon, that he had, with the help of the Brother de Bonnefoy, put in safe-keeping at the time of the troubles of 1793. Destigny preserved these archives until 1868, the date at which he confided them to Brother Villaréal, in whose hands they were still in 1900 (IV, p. CLXIX-CLXXII).

1434.   This is notably the case for the Brothers de Barbarin (III, 188), Court de Geblin (III, 156; 157; 160), Juliénas (III, 187; 193), Le Doyen (III, 190), de Monspey (III, 160), O'Brenau (III, 190), Pagamini (III, 176), de Ribas (III, 166; 171), de Tiemann (III, 157-158), de Virieu (III, 159).

1435.   For example, those of Amar and of Prunelle de Lière, who seem to have been taken from the work of J.-J. Mounier, and that of d'Espréménil for which he has furnished no explanation.

1436.   The contribution of II and III is of 54 names, plus five anonymous Brothers of the Temple of Libourne; IV furnished 35; the Sisters were: Mrs. de Luzignan, Miss de Chevrier, and Miss Willermoz.

1437.   The first by date were the "Réau-Croix " of Foix: de Grainville and de Champoléon; Bacon, de Luzignan, and de Guers were ordained in March 1767; Willermoz in May or June 1768, de Balzac in October or November 1769. Saint-Martin was promoted to Réau-Croix on April 17, 1773, at the same time as Saignant de Serre, Sub-commander of the artillery of the castle of Bordeaux, named the preceding year Universal Substitute in place of Bacon, revoked of these functions. Caignet de Lestère, that Pasqually calls Very Powerful Master in October 1773 (II, 60) and who received his succession, had to have been ordained at San Domingo. In the same period was the ordination in France of de Cressac, whose "recognition" (inscription upon the official control) was moreover suspended on the order of Pasqually (II, 197) and Duroy d'Hauterive "ordained by correspondence" (II, 196). The two brothers of Aubenton, who, according to a letter from Pasqually, were prepared in September 1768 "to be admitted into the degree of Réau-Croix this present equinox" (II, 169), were probably not accepted by la Chose, for there are no mentions among the Réau-Croix taking part in the Equinox Working of March 1772, and who were only six: Pasqually, Willermoz, de Luzignan, de Grainville, de Champoléon, and de Balzac (III, 115). The only Réau-Croix who, to our knowledge, were ordained after the death of Pasqually are: de Las Casas, third Grand Sovereign, Caignet, brother of the second Grand Sovereign, old comrade of Saint-Martin in the Regiment of Foix, who, according to the latter, were Réau-Croix in 1778 (III, 148), Destigny and d'Ossun (IV, p. CLXXI).

1438.   Those of Versailles and Eu seem, to judge from certain citations of IV, to have sheltered some very zealous adepts.

1439.   According to IV (p. CLXXII) the Order had not counted, in the times of its greatest prosperity, more than thirteen Temples, of which eleven were in France and two at San Domingo.

1440.   A reproduction of the "tables" or tracings employed for the Operations and in the meetings of the various degrees would facilitate notably the intelligence on several details remaining obscure, and on some passages of the correspondence.

1441.   It does not seem in any case that the deviation could have been very considerable. It would be necessary, in order to go from single to double, that the average number of affiliates of each of the 13 Temples had been 15, a likely exaggerated estimation.

1442.   Matter only knew that there was often a question of Fournié in the correspondence of Saint-Martin and Willermoz. It teaches us that Fournié brought to Bordeaux in May 1771, the instructions written in Latin of which Willermoz required a translation (III, 93); the messenger came probably from Lyon that Matter supposes to have been his diocese. The following month the Abbé collaborated on the work of copying with which the adepts of Bordeaux engaged; in return they gave him some help in "his affair of tonsure," where there had been "slight difficulties," (III, 100). Finally tonsured in July, he was, in August, charged by Saint-Martin to give to Willermoz the address of Pasqually at Paris, commission which would provide Fournié the occasion to thank Willermoz for the interest that he took in his affairs, that is to say in the benefit which he still lacked "to be entirely tranquil," (III, 190-210).

1443. VIII, 49.
1444. VIII, 40.
1445. III, 143.
1446. III, 110.
1447. VIII, 40-41.
1448. VIII, 42.
1449. It is probably a matter of one of those pamphlets, the collection of which would form the Reintegration.
1450. VIII, 41.
1451. VIII, 41.
1452. The expression "appears" [Fr. paraît] does not indicate that Fournié had ever put in doubt the authenticity of the evangelical accounts. The habitual awkwardness of his style betrays his thought here; he means to say: "that Jesus Christ, just as it proceeds from the Gospel, gave," etc.
1453. That is to say without making use of reason in order to find an interpretation that the reader expected from a supernatural revelation.
1454. VIII, 41-43.
1455. VIII, 44.
1456. VIII, 43-45.
1457. Matter calls this correspondence Mr. de V.: it is a question perhaps of the colonel Comte de Virieu, member of the Strict Observance in the Province of Auvergne, which was strongly tied to Willermoz.
1458. VIII, 47-48.
1459. The Abbé had been announced and expected at Toulouse for a long time.
1460. III, 143-145.
1461. VIII, 37.
1462. III, 196.
1463. III, 159.
1464. III, 160.
1465. VIII, 158.
1466. III, 119.
1467. VIII, 61; 85. The notes of Saint-Martin are so enigmatic that Matter asks himself whether it is not a question of Mesmerian experiments. The hypothesis goes too far. Matter himself recognizes that in this era mesmerism "was still concerned with therapeutic fluids and animal

magnetism." He claims indeed that the doctrine of Mesmer began then to be transformed and that they laid on hands since 1773, but he acknowledges that, if clairvoyance was researched already, it limited its pretensions to the view of the physical state of the sick. We add that it is difficult to admit that Saint-Martin, despite all the enthusiasm that the manifestations verified by d'Hauterive inspired in him in 1775 (III, 135), would have consented to practicing magnetism, in regards to which he had always shown the most vivid repugnance.

1468.   The metaphysical Christ or Word.

1469.   The word had been put in fashion by mesmerism; it designated a sort of cataleptic state.

1470.   *Correspondance inédite*, Schauer & Chuquet edition, 5th letter, p. 19.

1471.   Luminous manifestations.

1472.   Vision of Christ.

1473.   *Correspondance inédite*, 10th letter, p. 37.

1474.   Bord has dedicated to him (V, 328-337) a very detailed note, but containing some irreconcilable data on occasion.

1475.   V, 471.

1476.   V, 336.

1477.   VII, 153. There is no room to linger over these charges.

1478.   X, V.I, 107, 108, 110; V. II, 93, 207, 208, 212, 214.

1479.   Bk. III, ch. III.

1480.   V, 437.

1481.   X, V. II, 373.

1482.   X, V. II, 107.

1483.   Thus, were called tables of numbers, combinations invented, or at least brought to the Occident, by the Kabbalists. The numbers, arranged in symmetrical columns and rows, were chosen so that their sum, made according to the vertical, the horizontal, or even the diagonal, always gave the same number.

1484.   That is to say the mystical number which is the reason for the relationships existing between the elements and the perverse beings.

1485.   *De nombres, par L.-C. de Saint-Martin*, reprinted from the edition of 1861, Paris, 1913, p. 56.

1486.   VIII, 378.

1487.   III, 146.

1488.   VIII, 34.

1489.   III, 142.

1490.   III, 139.

1491.   VIII, 60.

1492.   VIII, 166.

1493.   VII, 167.

1494.   VII, 172.

1495.   VII, 169.

1496.   VII, 176.
1497.   VII, 173.
1498.   VII, 168.
1499.   VIII, 34.
1500.   Vulliaud: *Kabbale*, II, 273.
1501.   Op. cit. 228.
1502.   Note on Cazotte placed at the front of a reprint of *Diable Amoureux*, with illustrations by Ed. de Beaumont, Paris, 1845. It is this note that had inspired Daruty, and in part, Matter. It contains, in what concerns the occultist Masons, that it calls Illuminati, much of fables. It asserts, for example, that "Martinez had covered France with Masonic lodges of his rite" and that, for the school of Lyon (Chevaliers Bienfaisants), "the secret of the domination of the Spirits was contained in the Triple Contrainte de l'Enfer [Triple Constraint of Hell], very powerful conjuration in use by the cabalists of the Middle Ages."
1503.   *Procès de Jacques Cazotte*, anonymous brochure appearing at Hedde, palace of the Tribunal, passage of Perron, analyzed in Fabre: *Documents Maçonnique*, Paris, 1866 (p. 50-56).
1504.   The works of Bodin and Bekker are cited by Cazotte at the end of his novel. The first had had five editions from 1580 to 1604. The second, published in 1684, treated "on the effects that men are capable of producing by their communication and their virtue." As to the contemporary treatise, Cazotte had made a discreet allusion in a note where he says: "This little work was inspired by the reading of a passage of an author infinitely respectable, in which it is spoken of the ruses that the demon may employ when it wishes to please and seduce." This "author infinitely respectable" may be the Dominican Costadeau, the Abbé Jean Pierquin, the medical doctor Saint-André, Pierre le Lorrain, Abbé de Valmont, or even the councilor to the Parlement Legendre, Marquis de Saint-Aubin, who, from 1717 to 1752, had kept the public from all possible sorts of demonic sorcery, obsessions, or possessions.
1505.   In the first edition of this novel, Alvare overcame his passion, saw that he is "obsessed," and by an energetic order, forces the devil to disappear. In a second version, the young man succumbs to the temptation and becomes "possessed." But he only expiates his fall by a night of nightmares and rediscovers close to his mother the peace of the heart and the forgiveness of his sin.
1506.   Biondetta spoke indeed to Alvare "of the secret science of numbers which governs the universe," but in order to teach him an infallible combination that would make him win at games of chance.
1507.   The initiator of Alvare told him indeed: "In reality we are born to command them" (the Spirits), and to bid them to come out of the circle only "when all will be submitted to him."
1508.   G. de Nerval, op. cit. p. XX-XXIV.
1509.   Ibid., p. XXII.

1510.   Ibid., p. LII.

1511.   VIII, 58-59.

1512.   G. de Nerval, op. cit. p. XIX-XX.

1513.   These stories, composed with the help of don Chavis, Arab monk, form four volumes of the *Cabinet des Fées* and constitute a continuation of the *Mille et une Nuits.* "This is not only a clever pastiche, but an original and serious work, written by a man entirely permeated with the spirit and beliefs of the Orient," (Ibid., p. 11).

1514.   Ibid., p. XXVIII.

1515.   G. de Nerval, op. cit., p. LXII; LXIV.

1516.   Ibid., p. LXXII.

1517.   G. de Nerval, op. cit., p. LXIX, LXX.

1518.   Ibid., p. LVI-LVII.

1519.   G. de Nerval, op. cit., pl LVI.

1520.   Ibid., p. LXXIII. The recourse to the intercession of the Virgin is, in all the disclosures of Cazotte, the sole manifestation of his Catholic orthodoxy. This characteristic is, it is true, all the more striking since Pasqually never names, either in the Reintegration or in his mystical correspondence, the mother of Christ.

1521.   Ibid., p. LXIV.

1522.   It is probably a question of Antoine Bret, writer and dramaturge (1717-1792) who had cultivated one of Cazotte's favorite genres in publishing in 1772 the *Fables Orientales.*

1523.   G. de Nerval, op. cit. p. LXIII.

1524.   Ibid., p. LXVI.

1525.   G. de Nerval, op. cit., p. LXVII.

1526.   Ibid., p. LXIII.

1527.   Ibid., p. LXIV-LXV.

1528.   Ibid., p. LIV.

1529.   Ibid., p. LVII-LVIII.

1530.   Ibid., p. LVIII-LIX.

1531.   Ibid., p. LXV.

1532.   We only related this anecdote by virtue of curiosity. It seems indeed as little authentic as the famous prophecy of Cazotte, invented after the fact by La Harpé, for she expressed some facts and dates of a manifest falsity: the Revolutionary Tribunal had held its first session on April 6, 1793; Cazotte could only, therefore, have been able to appear in September 1792 before the *Criminal Tribunal* instituted the previous August 17 by the Legislature, which pronounced in only eight hours three condemnations to death and whose indulgence seems derisive. In order for him to have been condemned by the Revolutionary Tribunal we would have to read September 25, 1793, that is to say he would have lived at Paris for a year undisturbed whereas the account represents his second arrest as following some days after coming out of the Abbey. This strongly suspect anecdote has given space to some very hazarded conjectures; it has been inferred from this that the Martinist Illuminati have played a role, secret but decisive, in the preparation and explosion of the Revolution. G. de Nerval makes himself the defender of this thesis on page LX of his note on Cazotte. The author of this present study cannot treat here the very controversial question of the influence attributed to Freemasonry, taken as a whole, on the revolutionary events; he must refer the reader to a previous work where he concludes for the negative, and to indicate a recent book (*la Franc-Maçonnerie Française et la préparation de la Révolution* by G. Martin) which supports the contrary opinion. In any case, the participation of the occultist Masons, notably the Élus Coëns and the Chevaliers Bienfaisants, in the over-throw of the old régime still remains to be demonstrated; some among them may have become ardent revolutionaries, such as those cited above by J.-J. Mounier, but the spirit which animated the two associations was entirely indifferent to political or social questions.

www.ingramcontent.com/pod-product-compliance
Lightning Source LLC
Chambersburg PA
CBHW030812100426
42814CB00002B/87